New Encyclopedia of Philosophy

NEW ENCYCLOPEDIA OF PHILOSOPHY

J. Grooten & G. Jo Steenbergen

with the cooperation of

Prof. Dr. K. L. BELLON — Dr. F. BENDER — Prof. Dr. I. J. M. VAN DEN BERG — Prof. Dr. E. W. BETH — Dr. M. A. BRUNA — Prof. Dr. E. DE BRUYNE — Prof. Dr. A. M. J. CHORUS — Dr. B. DELFGAAUW — Prof. Dr. R. FEYS — Prof. Dr. J. GONDA — Prof. Dr. L. VANDER KERKEN, S. J. — Dr. A.P.M. KIEVITS — Prof. Dr. J.P.A. MEKKES — Prof. Dr. A. G. M. VAN MELSEN — Mevr. C. J. M. VAN MELSEN-BERNSEN, Arts — Prof. Dr. J. H. NOTA, S. J. — Prof. Dr. J. A. J. PETERS, C.ss.R. — Dr. J. J. POORTMAN — Prof. F. DE RAEDE-MAEKER, S. J. — Prof. Dr. L. DE RAEYMAEKER — Prof. Dr. H. ROBBERS, S. J. — Prof. Dr. F. L. R. SASSEN — Prof. Dr. F. VAN STEENBERGHEN — Prof. Dr. TH. C. VAN STOCKUM — Drs. P. STOLKER — Dr. C. F. P. STUTTERHEIM — Dr. J. VANSTEENKISTE, O. P. — Prof. Dr. G. VERBEKE — Prof. Dr. C. J. DE VOGEL — Dr. A. WYLLEMAN — Drs. E. ZÜRCHER

Translated from the Dutch,
Edited & Revised by Edmond van den Bossche

PHILOSOPHICAL LIBRARY
NEW YORK

Library of Congress Catalog Card No. 62-15052 SBN 8022-1634-X

A

A

In logic: symbol for a universal affirmative proposition (e.g., every whale is a mammal).

A=A

Formula for the *law of identity. A is A and has always to be considered A. A thing is and remains what it is.

A—Not-A

Formula for the *law of contradiction. A is not not-A and can never be considered not-A. At the same time and in the same respect, a thing cannot be and not-be what it is.

ABDUCTION (Greek: *apagogè*)

An indirect proof, of a proposition, by pointing out the absurdity of the conclusions of the contradictory proposition.

ABELARD, PETER

Born near Nantes 1079, died at Cluny 1142. As university professor in Paris, he taught logic and later theology, and met with unequaled approval. His illicit relations with Héloise, niece of his colleague, forced him to leave Paris (*ca.* 1115), but he resumed his teaching in 1136. Because of his rationalistic tendencies, Abelard's theories were condemned at Soissons in 1121 and at Sens in 1141. He had a very rich personality and a passionate and combative temperament, and was also a first-class logician. His achievement in this field was the most important philosophic event of the 12th century. He insured the triumph of Aristotle in epistemology (modified realism) and logic, and thus prepared for Aristotle's authority in the 13th century; he gave the scholastic method its definitive structure (e.g., in his *Sic et non,* a collection of 150 model discussions on theological questions).

Modified realism admits (as does *nominalism) that universals exist only in the mind, but affirms (as does *ultra-realism) that universals have a real objective meaning. According to Abelard, the universals are mere names (*nomen*), i.e., words with meanings that express ideas, and that an idea represents a real nature composed of different individuals. To know a concrete reality through an universal idea is to know it really but inadequately. The method of human knowledge is such that it sees common natures (genera and species) through abstraction in single objects, which are perceived by the senses. These natures are multiplied and individualized by matter. F.V.S.

ABSOLUTE

Opposed to relative. That which is not related to anything else and independent of all conditions. In itself it is total, complete; it is self-sufficient, unconditioned. This basic meaning of absolute has many different applications.

In grammar, an absolute term (e.g., man) has a meaning of its own, whereas a relative term refers to another term (e.g., father is

1

relative to child). All terms can be used absolutely, that is, without condition. They are used relatively when dependent on certain conditions and with due regard to circumstances.

In the order of knowledge all ideas are, according to their nature, related to other ideas and can therefore never be absolute, but are always relative. Considered as a whole, the order of knowledge can, by definition, not be relative to extraneous ideas and presents itself, in this particular case, as absolute. Realism accepts that we teach reality through knowledge. This reality is, in its existence, independent of our knowledge, and sometimes we call this reality absolute, inasmuch as we consider it in relation to our knowing.

All that exists independently is really absolute and free from any ties. Dependence appears under different forms; thus it calls for many distinctions and more limited considerations, which are always susceptible of broadening, and which at the same time shift the contrast between absolute and relative. In this sense we call quantity and quality absolute *accidents as compared with the accident *ad aliquid* or the relation. The *substance is called absolute as compared with all accidental categories. He who holds that all finite beings, through their *contingency, are dependent upon a Divine Creator, considers them relative to this Cause; at the same time he must eventually call God, the total and in all respects independent cause, the Absolute Being, the Absolute.

ABSOLUTENESS

That which characterizes the absolute as such. The *absoluteness of ethics* means the absolute character of ethics, considered as the totality of moral prescriptions. Against this conception of the absoluteness of ethics, some philosophers contend that good and evil differ according to different countries, eras, civilizations. However, very different precepts can embody the same—absolute—value.

ABSORPTION (laws of)

Specific formal principles in regard to the relation between concepts of classes or between propositions, inasmuch as they include or presuppose each other: e.g. the A's of the class A and the A's of the class B fall all under class A; the A's, falling under one class, which contains as well the A's as the B's, fall all under the class A.

ABSTRACTION

Operation of the active intellect through which a distinct characteristic of a being is brought out, overlooking the other aspects. The *partial* or *isolating* abstraction has to be distinguished from the *generalizing* abstraction. The first one brings out part of a being without considering the rest (e.g., the human intellect); this is the root of all intellectual *analysis. The generalizing abstraction forms general concepts from individual beings. This form of abstraction is *total* or *extensive,* insofar as the characteristics which constitute the concept are still considered as borne by a (indeterminate) bearer: e.g., "man," "reason" (*see* concrete concept); it is *formal* or *intensive* insofar as the characteristics are considered in themselves, separated from their bearer: e.g., "humanity", "rationality" (formula abstract concept).

Scholasticism distinguishes three degrees in formal abstraction, from which three degrees of science arise. In the first degree, abstraction is made from the individual matter, but sensory matter is kept in the definition of the concept: *physics (experimental sciences of sensory nature). In the second degree, abstraction is made from sensory matter; intelligible matter only (i.e., spatial and numerical relations which can be conceived without sensory qualities) is kept in the definition of the concept: *mathematics. In the third degree, abstraction is made of all matter, and this is *metaphysics. J.P.

ABSTRACTIONISM

Way of thought which is interested in only those concepts which are obtained by *abstraction from the concrete, in the conviction that we reach through these concepts concrete reality itself.

ABSURD

That what is not only senseless or meaningless, but also excludes all sense, since it is intrinsically contradictory. In existentialism the absurdity of human existence, which wants to be infinite, although it is finite, is strongly emphasized. *Reductio ad absurdum seu per impossibile* is the indirect refutation of a proposition by showing that it leads to absurd and impossible conclusions. *See* abduction.

ABU-BAKR . . . ibn Tufail

Born in Guadix (Granada) *ca.* 1110, died at Marrakus 1185. Typical representative of the western branch of the liberal *Arabian philosophers, who were under influence of Greek philosophy. In a famous novel, *Haj bin Yakzan,* Abu-Bakr preaches a natural religion in which no revelation or obligations imposed from outside are necessary for those who are able to discern and reason intelligently. According to Al-Gazzadi, Abu-Bakr

followed his predecessors. Avienna defended a similar theory, and Averroes, Abu-Bakr's disciple, expressed the same ideas in a more theoretical form.

ACADEMY

School founded by Plato in a country seat and gymnasium in the suburbs of Athens, dedicated to the hero Academus. It was organized as a society of scientific scholars, under the inspiration of Plato's philosophy. In the Academy, Plato and his immediate successors (Speusippus and Xenocrates) were very much concerned with mathematics and astronomy (*see*: Theaetetus, Eudoxus and Heraclides Ponticus). The main objective of Plato in organizing the Academy was the formation of political leaders and legislators, and the Academy played a very successful role in this field. After Polemo and Crates, who still belonged to the Old Academy, *Arcesilaus introduced skeptical ideas in the Academy (the Middle Academy). *Carnedes was the main representative of the Third or New Academy. After his death Antiochus of Ascalon brought the Academy back to dogmatis. We do not know what happened during the following centuries, until Proclus directed the school (5th century) and Justinianus closed it in 529. Damascius and Simplicius were the best-known representatives of the Academy during the last period of its existence.

ACCIDENT

In general, that which is part of something without being an *essential factor of it. One can find applications of this in the domain of knowledge as well as in reality.

In logic: in the broad meaning of the term, accident is a nonessential predicate that is not found in the definition of the subject. If this attribute is necessarily connected with the subject, we call it an essential quality, *proprium* (e.g., man is free); if, on the other hand, the connection is not necessary but *contingent, then we call it, in the narrower sense of the word, an accident. The sense of the term is further narrowed when people use it, as in daily conversation, to express the fortuitous and at the same time the unfortunate.

In metaphysics: accidents are the nonsubstantial principles which belong to the real structure of a being: they are not data of experience which we establish, but ontological grounds for anything which appears in this being except the substantial identity itself. That their reality has to be distinguished from the substance requires a proof. How can we formulate their relation to the *substance? What accidental *categories must be distinguished and what is their mutual relation? What is the part played by accidents in the activity and development of every finite being? Inquiry into these questions takes up a large part of metaphysics.

ACKNOWLEDGE

In a philsophical sense: to gain an insight into the truth, not only personally, but also with all one's feelings and entire personality.

ACOSMISM

(Greek: *a-kosmos,* denial of the world) Used by Hegel and others to characterize the system of Spinoza, in which the world is absorbed into God rather than God disappearing in the world. The latter would be *atheism.

ACQUIRED

A quality which appears during the course of life through *interaction with the milieu. Opposed to *innate.

ACROAMATIC (or esoteric)

Applied especially to those writings of Aristotle which contain his lectures for more advanced students. The term "acroamatic" applies, strictly to the method of teaching by which the student only listens and is not interrogated. Contrary of *erotematic.

ACT

Is related to activity: act means thus, in general, action or even conduct. In a stricter sense, act means the moment, limited in time and qualitatively determined, in which an activity is exercised, especially by consciousness. We speak of an act of consciousness, act of the will, etc. In the act psychology of Brentano and others, the only object of psychology is the study of acts, rather than of the content to which they are directed (*See:* *intentionality).

In metaphysics, act is opposed to *potency, as definiteness is to definableness. Aristotle exposed this opposition in his analysis of motion. What comes into motion goes from potency to act, or is "activated"; it changes because it reaches another definiteness and gains actual possession of it. Potency and act are therefore correlative terms: *potentia est ordo ad actum; actus ordo ad potentiam.* The meaning of these terms determined, we can say that it is self-evident that the act has priority over potency. Act is also the act principle, or, in a composed being, the structural principle, which is the real reason of definiteness. The correlation of potency and act was applied, in scholasticism, to all oppositions of definableness and definiteness, even outside of motion. Thomas Aquinas even conceives all structural connections modeled on the relation between potency and act. There are thus different kinds of acts: the notion act is characterized by *analogy. The substantial form is an act principle, cause of specific definiteness (the corresponding potency is the so-called first matter). The principle of essence, the reason for the *"actus essendi"* in a being is called the first, i.e., fundamental, act (the corresponding potency is the total essence, in matter hylomorphically constituted); accidental principles, reasons of secondary definiteness, are called second acts (the corresponding potency is then the substance). God, subsistent Being, therefore simple Being without potency, is considered the Pure Act, *actus purus*. L.D.R.

ACT (verb)

To be active, pose actions. All existence is connected with acting (*operari sequitur esse*), because by acting that which exists persists and develops. On the other hand, acting belongs to the suppositum (*actiones sunt suppositorum*). One acts therefore according to his nature, as one exists according to his nature or substance: a bird is known by its note. The kind of acting differs according to ways of being; and one deducts the nature of beings from their acting. Action in the Cosmos is a continuous interaction between beings and their environment and contains implicitly change of accidental nature, in which substantial identity is retained. This change happens through borrowing from other beings, in the process of appropriating them in a physical (nourishment) or a mental (knowledge) way. Only by acting on others can a being develop himself in the cosmos. Through acting a being penetrates deeper into the order of the beings and is there more strongly established.

Acting, in the narrow sense of the word, implies consciousness of oneself. Only persons act, therefore, because only they can consciously pronounce judgment and make free and autonomous decisions. Their action is connected with initiative, has some creative power, offers essential contributions to the development of the world. Man creates culture on the grounds of existing nature; in himself he realizes cultural values, does the same in his environment, and the one is a function of the other. This acting happens on different levels (biological, ethical, religious, etc.), becomes the object of scientific investigation and creates major philosophical problems.

ACTIO IN DISTANS

Literally: acting from a distance, action of a force upon a body with which it is not in contact, even through a medium. The possibility of such an action has been, from the earliest times, a problem. Some philosophers believed they could prove that the *actio in distans* is impossible. In physics this problem became more acute after Newton's studies on *gravity. Newton, himself, was interested only in the description of this force, not in formulating an hypothesis about the way gravity works. As soon as Faraday, Maxwell and Hertz proved the existence of a *field for magnetic and electric forces, which work according to analogous laws, hypotheses of an *actio in distans* were abandoned in physics; especially after Einstein presupposed a field for gravity.

ACTION

The sum of the operations which are performed by man in order to bring about a well-defined change of the reality. In a narrower sense, that complete moment in which this change is accomplished; this operation does not so much "happen" as it does rise from the profound spontaneity of his free will. It is performed at the same time with spiritual consciousness, so that there is insight into the structure of the action as regards means and ends, realization and effects, as well as its implications in the total striving of man. Action consists, in fact, of a whole of physical operations, which eventually is animated by a value. It therefore always represents a double aspect, a physical aspect and a value. It can be even better defined as the realization of a content in which a value is embodied. And this occurs through the concatenation of different moments as the result of an *intention or the pursuit of a well-defined value, the *presentation of the content in which the pursued value is embodied, the *resolution to perform this particular action, the *decision and *execution, by means of all kinds of physical motions, etc. The question arises, whether all these moments are determining for the *moral value which every action, as purely human action, necessarily possesses. This is much debated. According to Kant, the moral value is determined only, and completely, by the intention (so that the content and everything which produces the results of the action are arbitrary). Thomas Aquinas teaches that the intention is determining, but not the intention alone; to be morally good an action should be good in all its moments. J. Gr.

ACTIVISM

The theory which emphasizes the active character of the mind. This theory is essentially directed to intervening in real life. Knowledge seems then to serve action; even if science has value in itself, it is valuable only when it contributes to the successful expansion of the individual and the social life of man. Marx and Lenin explicitly recognize activism, since they consider philosophy no longer as the contemplation of the truth but as the alteration of reality. Kant, Fichte, Nietzsche and others also recognize activism, insofar as they affirm the primacy of practical reason. In Eucken's philosophy activism is close to *pragmatism. Eucken believes that truth is a matter of life, not of pure intellect, although he rejects the idea that truth is a pure human decision. Truth, he says, is not *made* arbitrarily by man, but is intuitively *discovered* through a life of activity.

ACTIVITY

That what is characteristic of a reality which acts, i.e., brings something about, or in a narrower sense does it repeatedly. * *Immanent activity* or self-determination, autodetermination, proper to life, is different from *transitive* activity, in which the product is found outside the agent. In a narrower sense, one uses the term "transitive activity" for *physical activity, i.e., activity in space, when the product is found spatially outside the agent. Physical activity is naturally correlative to *passivity and therefore always a reaction. In psychology activity is considered as the activity of man's strivings, and in this case opposed to knowledge.

ACTUAL

In philosophy: that which is in *act, not in *potency.

ACTUALISM

The theory according to which reality is a ceaseless process of becoming and changing. In metaphysics actualism is the position that °substance, existing in itself and based on itself, is not the final reality, but only the manner in which reality, which is in itself pure and independent action, imposes itself on the mind and is accepted by the mind. Being would be only a particular form of becoming. Actualism is found in the works of Heraclitus, Fichte, Hegel, and Bergson, insofar as the latter considers reality as creating evolution. Actualism applies especially to the theory defended by Gentile (*idealismo attuale*), the process of the mind through which it becomes self-conscious, in which, for the neo-Hegelian °Gentile, reality consists, never attaining its end but always advancing. In psychology actualism denies the existence of the soul as a substance which supports physical activities. The soul is nothing else than unceasing psychic activity itself.

ACTUALITY

That which characterizes actual things as such.

ACTUS PURUS

The divine Act: not an °act which forms, together with a correlative °potency, a structured being, but an act which is in itself and in its absolute simplicity, transcends all structure.

ADAEQUATIO REI ET INTELLECTUS

Latin: (agreement between object or being and intellect) Albert the Great and Thomas Aquinas adopted this term from Isaac Ben Salomon (± 900) as a definition of the °truth. (Logical) truth is then the faculty of the intellectual judgment insofar as "it says that is which is, and that is not which is not" (Aristotle).

ADAPTATION

Fitting of the qualities of a plant or animal to its environment. One should distinguish individual adaptation over a long period of time, i.e., evolution. There are many different opinions as to the causes of adaptation, but, in any case, adaptation cannot be explained by external causes only.

ADEQUATE

That which reaches the level of something, attains complete equality with it, harmonizes entirely with it, expresses it completely. An adequate presentation, °idea, judgment, expresses completely that which it intends. A perfect definition has to be adequate with what it defines.

ADLER, Alfred 1870-1937

Austrian psychologist, founder of *Individual psychologie,* in which the problems of power and impotency, of superiority and inferiority is central.

AENESIDEMUS OF CNOSSUS

Second part of the 1st century B.C. Representative of skepticism in Alexandria, together with Agrippa and °Sextus Empiricus. Taught that truth cannot be known through the senses, through the intellect or through both together, because of the multiplicity of knowing subjects and conditions. He is famous for the "Ten Tropes," arguments to prove that it is necessary to suspend all judgment.

AESTHETICS

The doctrine of the aesthetic, as it is experienced or realized in art or in nature. Aesthetics was practiced in empirical psychology as well as in philosophy. In philosophy it tries primarily to reveal, by way of phenomenological description, the meaning of the aesthetic.

AESTHETICS, TRANSCENDENTAL

Term used by °Kant to imply the study of °forms a priori to sensible experience (time and space).

AETHER

(Literally: thin air above the atmosphere) Of old, people admitted the existence, next to simple matter, of another kind of matter, and its characteristics have been described in different ways by philosophers of different periods, e.g., °quintessence.

When the theory of the waves of light was introduced, ether was considered as the medium of the wave motions. When electromagnetic phenomena were connected with those of light, the ether was considered as the medium that penetrates everything and fills the complete universe, in which all phenomena of light and electromagnetics occur. The Dutch physicist Lorentz (1853-1928) especially tried hard to form a satisfactory theory about the ether. In the field of philosophy the existence of the ether would simplify many problems about °space and °place.

In the 20th century many physicists doubt the existence of the ether because of the negative results of particular experiments. Some conclude from these experiments that ether would always be in rest, others that ether is dragged along with the moving bodies in the universe (theory of °relativity). Many other phenomena have been discovered which tend to break down the absolute opposition of ponderable matter on the one hand and the phenomena of light on the other. Ponderable matter seems to have qualities which up till now have been ascribed only to light and other electromagnetic phenomena (waves), while light seems to show a corpuscular character also. Following this discovery physicists now believe that all space has some physical properties, and no longer accept the idea that there is a basic difference between space filled with ponderable matter and space not filled with it. One can therefore still speak of ether, but not as a separate kind of physical extensiveness, different from ordinary matter.

AFFECT

A sudden, strong emotion which collides with discernment and self-control. Is much used in psychiatry, especially in psychoanalysis.

AFFECTION

Inclination, positive or negative, regarding a person or a thing.

AFFINITY

The tendency of chemicals to react upon each other. Sodium has, for instance, a strong affinity to chlorine, from which NaCl is formed.

AFFIRMATION

In general: an assertion, to maintain something, or to declare that something is certain. Opposite of doubt, hesitation, being uncertain. In a narrower sense: an affirmative assertion; opposite of denial or °negation. The basis for every negation is inevitably an affirmation. With reference to this, every philosophical system has to answer a question which conditions all other questions: Does man attain completely founded certainty, or truthful assertions, and can he thus justify his fundamental affirmations? Or are his assertions founded on postulates which are, at best, only probable since they have a practical value for life?

AFFIRMATIVE

See judgment.

AGENT

That which is in the process of acting. Very often used as opposed to patient, i.e., that which undergoes an action. *Intellectus agens*: *see* intellect.

AGGREGATE

A collection of bodies of the same or mutually different species, forming a certain totality, but whose parts keep their own independence; e.g., a heap of bricks, a machine. *Atomism and *mechanism consider all composed bodies as aggregates. Aristotle, however, and with him the scholastics, made an essential distinction between aggregates and real compounds, in which the composing parts lose their own character and become a new body.

AGNOSTICISM

(Greek: *a-gnostos,* unknown) Doctrines of an attitude of mind which does not admit htat man can have a theoretical or rational knowledge of a reality beyond (sensual) experience; it expresses no opinion in regard to the existence of such a reality. The agnostic denies the possibility of metaphysics or of any knowledge about God. Was first used in this sense by Thomas *Huxley. *See* criticism, positivism.

ALAIN

Pseudonym of Emile Chartier, French philosopher, 1868-1951, disciple of *Lagneau.

ALANUS AB INSULIS
(or Alain de Lille)

Born at Lille(?) *ca.* 1128, and died in 1202 at Citeaux. Taught in Paris and became a Cistercian.

Doctor universalis. Eclectic thinker, was especially influenced by the School of *Chartres. Renowned for his allegorical works: *Anticlaudianus* or *Antirufinus,* in which he opposes the pessimistic world view of the pagan poet Claudianus (died 408?), author of a satiric poem *In Rufinum.* He wrote also *De planctu naturae,* an imitation of the *De Consolatione* of Boethius.

ALBERT OF COLOGNE
(Albertus Magnus)

Born in Lauingen (Swabia) in 1206 or early 1207, died in Cologne, 1280. Joined the Dominican Order in 1223, taught theology in Germany from 1228 to 1240; in Paris 1240-1248; in Cologne 1248-1254 and 1257-1260; bishop in 1260. *Doctor Universalis.* His works in the Parisian edition (Borgnet) are divided into 38 volumes; a critical edition is in preparation in Cologne (*Editio Coloniensis*). His great philosophical work consists of a commentary on the writings of Aristotle, probably begun after 1256. Conscious of the dangers for Christianity, of the pagan sciences, Greek as well as Arabic, Albert conceived the idea of composing an encyclopedia which would make available to the Western world the entire Greek and Arabic sciences. These sciences were enriched with his own research and he left out everything that contradicted Christian orthodoxy. The method of his commentary was taken, principally, from Avicenna. In this ambitious enterprise Albert definitively integrated the profane sciences with Christian wisdom; in a remarkable way, he made a distinction between the respective methods of theology, philosophy and the positive sciences. As philosopher he is not only a compilator, but also an authentic thinker; however, his philosophy did not achieve the solidity which one finds in the works of his disciple, Thomas Aquinas, and shows many other influences beside that of Aristotle, although the latter dominates.

ALBERTISM

Philosophy of the Albertists, in 15th-century Paris and later at Cologne. The founder of this school was Joannes de Novo Domo, professor of the liberal arts in Paris between 1400 and 1415. In his *Tractatus de esse et essentia* he contrasts the doctrine of Albertus Magnus and that of Thomas Aquinas, in favor of Albertus. Especially in Cologne, where Albert died, his doctrine was revised in the 15th century. In the early years of the century, the "realists" of Cologne, in their reaction against °nominalism or the °*via moderna,* referred to Albertus as much as to Thomas. But a division soon occurred among the realists and Heymeric van de Velde became the leader of the Albertists. Violent controversies erupted between 1423 and 1460, because Heymeric emphasized the doctrinal differences between Albertus and Thomas; he protested strongly against the Thomists, who tried to minimize these differences. The controversy was based especially on metaphysical problems concerning the nature of created (spiritual or material) being; and the problem of intellectual knowledge. Heymeric had several disciples, and arguments between Thomists and Albertists continued through the 16th century.

ALCHER OF CLAIRVAUX

12th-century Cistercian of Clairvaux, probably the author of the *Liber de spiritu et anima,* long ascribed to Augustine. This compilation, inspired by Augustine, is probably in answer to the *Epistola de Anima* of Isaac de Stella.

ALCUIN

Born in England *ca.* 730, died in Tours 804. Was at first head of the School of York. In 781 entered the service of Charlemagne, taught during eight years at the Palatine School in Aachen, directed and reorganized the abbatial school at St. Martin of Tours. His philosophical works are useful compilations, but lack originality.

ALEMBERT, Jean le Rond d'

Born in Paris 1717, died there 1783. French Encyclopedist. Philosophy has, according to d'Alembert, nothing to do with metaphysical hypotheses, not even with naturalistic and materialistic impressions. Although we cannot know the essence of things, and have to profess skepticism in this field, we still cannot question that we know through experience, which receives its best explanation by accepting the existence of the outside world. We are not sure of having ethical freedom, but it suffices us to act as if we were free. Later positivism is based on such grounds.

ALEXANDER, Samuel 1859-1938

English neo-realistic metaphysician. Most important work, *Space, Time and Deity,* 1920, teaches pantheistic metaphysics. Philosophy is the science of being. Being appears in the world, which is constituted of space and time, yet it appears, not in one way, but in different forms which cannot be reduced to one. It appears as motion, as matter, as life and as mind. No succeeding step can be deducted from the previous one, but is an entirely original form of being. Knowledge is knowledge of beings; the object is not terminated in knowledge, but is as real as knowledge itself. Knowledge is a being-together of subject and object. The subject also has an attitude of appreciation. In this attitude also there is a being-together of subject and object. From this being-together, the subject gets his value, which is always reducible to truth, goodness or beauty. In the motion of the world from the lower to the higher level of being, the life of the deity emerges. Man, in his knowledge and appreciation, takes part in this divine world life.

ALEXANDER OF APHRODISIAS

Latter part of 2nd century and early 3rd century A.D. Especially known as commentator of Aristotle. Also wrote personal treatises: *De anima*, the *Aporiae* (there is a doubt whether they come directly from Alexander), *De mixtione* and *De fato*; in the latter he denies the existence of Providence and teaches a universal determinism.

ALEXANDER OF HALES

Born in England between 1170-80, died in Paris 1245. Appointed to the chair of theology in Paris at 1226(?). Became a Franciscan in 1236, but, lectured at the university till 1238 or 1240, when he resigned in favor of his colleague Joannes of Rupella. He was the first Franciscan *magister regens*, and the founder of the Franciscan School in Paris. Recently his *In Sententiis* has been discovered, and his doctrine can only be defined when this work has been studied. *The Summa universae theologiae* or the *Summa Fratris Alexandri* (critical edition at Quaracchi near Florence, 4 vols., 1924-48) is a compilation, which uses his works but is not composed by him; the real author is Joannes of Rupella. Alexander belongs to the first generation of theologians who, under the influence of the new philoso-phical movement, accentuated, from around 1220 on, the part of the speculative method in theology, and more and more used the new philosophy i.e., Aristotelianism, in theological expositions. This Aristotelianism, affected by several neo-Platonic influences, was mixed with Augustinian doctrines, which had long since been introduced into the Western world. The philosophy used by Alexander (as by all the theologians of his time) is thus an eclectic Aristotelianism, with a neo-platonic tone, especially Augustinian neo-Platonism. F.V.S.

ALEXANDRIAN SCHOOL

Christian school, founded by Panthenus (converted Stoic, died 200) and known mostly thanks to *Clement of Alexandria and *Origenes. They found their inspiration in Philo, in Christian sources (N.T., the apologists) and in pagan sources. They contributed greatly to bringing Hellenistic and Christian ideas closer together. They created a generally orthodox Christian *gnosis, notwithstanding a few partial errors, especially in Origenes' works.

Alexandria was also the seat of a pagan school, which flourished from the first half of the 5th century A.D. to the first half of the 7th century; its principal representatives: H e r m i a s, Ammonius, Joannes Philoponus, Asclepius, Elias David, Stephanus of Alexandria (all commentators of Aristotelian and Platonic works), Hypatia, Synesius of Cyrene, and Hierocles. The general tendency was Platonic, but with less metaphysical contemplations and a heavy use of mathematics and natural sciences.

AL-FARABI, Alfarabi, Abu Nasr al-Farabi

Born in Turkestan, died in Syria

950. One of the four great, more Aristotelian, Greek-oriented philosophers of Islam. With Alkindi and *Avicenna he belongs to the Eastern branch (he was not a true-born Arab). Commentator of Aristotle and Plato, fusing them somewhat together, (as A.M.S. *Boethius did in the West); he knows the Greek commentators of Aristotle, and deals with all branches of philosophy (according to the scholastic view). He contains, in undeveloped form, almost the entire system of Avicenna: emanation, eternity of the world, difference between essence and existence in created being, *intellectus agens* as *dator formarum*, rationalistic religion, etc. Was known in the medieval West through translations.

ALFREDUS ANGLICUS (Alfred of Sareshel)

Born in England 12th century, died 13th century. One of the translators of Toledo. Author of Arabic-Latin translations and of the first Aristotelian commentaries in the Middle Ages; wrote *ca.* 1210 his famous treatise *De motu cordis*, of very eclectic inspiration.

AL-GAZZALI, Algazel, Abu Hamid . . . al-Gazzali

Born in Tos in Chorasan 1059, died there 1111. He tried to purify Greek-oriented *Arabic philosophy and subject it to the orthodoxy of Islam. He adopted also a purified mysticism (as did some of his predecessors). He united the three great currents of Arabic philosophy. The spirit of his work is very close to medieval Latin scholasticism. Only the introduction to his philosophical criticism was known in the West. He attacked especially the rationalism of *Avicenna, *Al-Farabi and the Brothers of the Purity. Later Averroes disputed his criticism.

ALGEBRA

LOGICAL, is in the contemporary sense, a form of abstract algebra or of a deductive system with "free" and without "bound" variables, of which an interpretation is given, which agrees with the simple logic.

The first systems of the formal *logic, from Boole (1847 and 1853) to Schroeder (1890) are systems of logical algebra, resting on an analogy between logic and simple algebra. In these systems is the notation of the simple algebra used: the symbols have about the same meaning as in the modern theory of the system of numbers. So is expressed in "$\underline{a} = \underline{b}$" the *assertion: the collection of the $\underline{a}$'s is the same as the collection of the $\underline{b}$'s; in $\underline{a} < \underline{b}$, or similar notations: all $\underline{a}$'s are $\underline{b}$'s; in $\underline{ab}$: the collection of the $\underline{a}$ and $\underline{b}$; in $\underline{a} + \underline{b}$: the collection of the $\underline{a}$ or $\underline{b}$. Class of the not-$\underline{a}$'s are noted as $\underline{a}'$ or $\underline{a}$. In that time existed already many similar forms of logical algebra, logic of the propositions and of the relations. With the development of the modern abstract algebra came also more interest for the logical algebra.—R.F.

ALGEDONIC

Term applied to feelings of pleasure and pain. Algedonic aesthetica is the theory of beauty which uses as criteria the pleasure or pain produced by a work of art (Marshall).

ALGORITHM

(LOGICAL) is a synonym of logical *calculus, if one understands calculus as being: deduction by means of a technical symbolism.

AL-KINDI, Abu Yusuf . . . al-Kindi

Born at Kufa, died shortly after 870, first of the great Arabic Greek-oriented philosophers who were more aristocratic. Fairly eclectic and neo-Platonic, showing a close relation between Islamic and Mu'tazila philosophy. He wrote above all on natural philosophy. He is an early precursor of *Avicenna; some of his rationalistic theses are very close to the latter's, e.g., his determinism. Was partly known in the Latin Middle Ages.

ALLEGORY

A symbolic form of presentation in which more general and abstract realities, qualities or relations, such as love, justice, peace, fatherland, the seasons, etc., are represented in a concrete, often personal way. In wordcraft the allegory is initially a *metaphor, which develops into a series of different, but representatively and figuratively related figures. This development can become a complete work of art (story, poem, play). In the plastic arts the allegory develops generally a variety of attributes, e.g., the blind and the balance in allegoric presentations of justice.

ALLEN, Ethan 1738-89

American philosopher. One of the first who defended and diffused the ideas of the Enlightenment.

AL MUKAMMAS, David Ibn Merwan

Died c. 937. Born in Babylonia, author of the earliest known Jewish philosophical work of the Middle Ages: a commentary to the *Sefer Yetzirah (Book of Formation)*.

ALOGICAL (Greek: a-logos)

Unreasonable, unwise. According to Schopenhauer, the world foundation has to be sought in the alogical world will, a blind and senseless striving.

ALS-OB PHILOSOPHY

See Vaihinger.

ALTERNATION

of *classes* is an operation which forms from the classes (concepts) a and b the class: a or also b.

An alternation of *propositions* is an operation which forms from the propositions p and q the proposition: p or also q.

ALTERNATIVE

Generally a difficult choice between two possibilities. In logic it is, more distinctly, an incomplete or not exclusive *disjunction of two notions or propositions. *See also* judgment, syllogism.

ALTRUISM

A conscious devotion to the good of others, even at the expense of one's own profit. Opposite of egoism. Although not all moral systems claim that altruism is part of human nature, several of them believe in it. *Comte especially considers it as the highest moral principle: *"Vis pour autrui"*. But others are human beings, so that altruism becomes a way of life for humanity. This principle is in fact connected with the entire social thinking of Comte. He not only believes, in contrast with his English contemporaries (*see* Bentham), that egoistic inclinations are not inherent, but he thinks also that human happiness is more in harmony with the happiness of others, as it is guaranteed in an organized society. J. Gr.

AMALRIC OF BENA

Born in the 12th century, died in Paris (?) 1206 or 1207. He taught logic and later theology at Paris. Taught a form of pantheism, which considers God the form of all things (formal pantheism). He founded a school (*Amauriciani*). The Council of Paris condemned his doctrine and that of his disciples. His principal sources were Scottus Erigena and the School of Chartres.

13

AMELIUS

Born in Etruria. One of the oldest and most important disciples of Plotinus, whose lessons he attended from 246; he was secretary of his master. Wrote a treatise to defend the originality of Plotinus; he distinguishes three more hypostases in the Noûs and defends the unity of all souls with the world soul.

AMES, Edward

Born 1870, North American pragmatic philosopher of religion.

AMMONIUS SACCAS

Ca. 175 to 242 A.D. Christian converted to paganism. Was teacher of Plotinus, Origenes, Longinus and Herennius; no works. Nemesius gives us the most important elements of his philosophy; is considered the founder of neo-Platonism.

AMORAL

That which is not so much against morality (*immoral) as indifferent to morality or outside the moral realm.

AMORALISM

Amoral attitude or conception.

AMOR DEI INTELLECTUALIS

Intellectual love of God. The more we purify our ideas through conforming them with the idea of God, the higher we reach in the moral order, and then happiness will come to us, created by everything accompanying the idea of God, says *Spinoza.

AMPERE, Andre Marie

Born at Lyon 1775, died in Paris 1836. Physicist and philosopher, under the influence of *Maine de Biran. Because of the constant relations between phenomena, he is certain of the existence of an outer world. With Kant he calls it nou-mena; they form the object of intellectual knowledge; physics converts their relations into mathematical formulas.

AMPHIBOLY

Ambiguity of a syllogism. *Transcendental Amphiboly* is called by Kant the ambiguity arising when predicates which apply to the relations between intellectual categories are applied to sensual phenomena.

ANAGOGE

(Greek: anagogè, a leading up)
Reduction of something to its principles or of a phenomenon to its causes.

ANALOGIA ENTIS

There are analogous words, analogous concepts and an analogy in "esse"; this is the basis for analogous words and concepts. There is an analogia entis when the "esse" of the one is related to the "esse" of the other, as the creature is related to the Creator as caused to cause. This does not mean that the relation is mutual: the infinite has no relation to the finite, and can not be measured or defined by it. This does however involve that one can situate God in a way, by going out from the creatures, because that what is in the effect also is, in more intense manner, in the cause. Analogia entis expresses therefore conformity and difference. Analogous concepts have therefore, because of the conformity, a positive moment (God is good), and, because of the difference, a negative moment, which both united, express the eminence of good and "esse" in God.

Often is a distinction made between the analogy of attribution and the analogy of proportionality. In the former we confer the analogically conformed to the creature, as dependent from the creator; in the latter we see an analogous identity between two relations namely between essence and existence ("esse") in the creature and in God: the creature being has "esse" (existence), while God's essence is "esse" (existence).–H.R.

ANALOGICAL

By relation, by comparison; with great differences, indicating many similarities. *See* term.

ANALOGY (Greek: ana-logon, proportionate)

Originally a mathematical relation (a:b) and comparison of proportions (a:b=c:d). Now applicability of terms and ideas in a different, but partly similar, sense, to which things correspond which, although different, have some relations to each other. Analogy indicates primarily very great differences and secondarily some conformity notwithstanding these differences. (*See* equivocity, univocity). The things to which these analogue terms or ideas are attributed, are called *analogata*.

Analogy of attribution or *external analogy* occurs when the same term or notion is used for different things, by reason of a relation to the same thing; a healthy stroll, for instance, gives health, a healthy color shows health, a healthy body is healthy.

Analogy of proportion or *internal analogy* occurs when the same term or notion is proportionally applied to different things; e.g., light of the sun, light of the eyes, light of faith, light of reason. We use the term "light" as a necessary expedient in our knowledge, in which the difference is proportionate with the nature of knowledge: what sunlight is for seeing colors, reason is for seeing conclusions from given premises. This latter analogy is considered a real analogy; it is, for instance, the foundation of all strict metaphysical and t h e o l o g i c a l sciences. The concept of being (*See* analogy of being), as well as all notion of God, is an analogical notion.

ANALOGY REASONING

Reasoning through which we conclude from an analogy in a specific point between two things, to an analogy in another connected point; e.g., John and Peter have the same handwriting, they have therefore the same character. It is founded on the relation between the first and the second, and the reasoning will be more certain when the relation, the so-called third point of the comparison (*tertium quid*) is more incontestable. It is of great importance in the evolution of the natural sciences. Many discoveries are the result of implicit or explicit analogy reasoning, in which we can distinguish the proof "*a pari*" (on the grounds of a corresponding reason), "*a fortiori*" (on the grounds of more convincing reasons), and "*a contrario*" (on the grounds of contrary reasons). I v.d.B.

ANALYSIS (Greek: ana-lyein, solve)

Solution, refutation, reduction of something to its elements and principles; opposite of *synthesis. The analysis of a thing into its components is naturally the best way to know it better; pushed by an urge to know, a little child will analyze his toys. We analyze a machine for the same reason. Next to this *real analysis* there is a *logical analysis*, in which the parts of a totality are not separated but only distinguished from each other. We speak of analytically explained notions, when they are analyzed into their characteristics (*see* definition); of analytic °judgments, whose predicate is included in the notion of the subject. *Critical analysis*, as Kant and his followers use it, inquires under what conditions the affirmation of a fact is possible, i.e., not contradictory. (*See* criticism.) I.v.d.B.

ANALYTIC, Transcendental

The analysis of intellectual understanding in order to find in it a priori notions and principles, without which no knowledge of objects is possible.

ANALYTICAL, analyzing

Analytical is the method which reduces the specific to the general, facts to rules, what is dependent to what is independent; this method has to be completed with a synthetic consideration. Basically every judgment is a synthesis of analytically obtained notions of the same object. (*See judgment.*)

ANAMNESIS (Greek: calling to mind)

Knowledge of general notions is considered by Plato as the awakening of the recollection of ideas, which were immediately perceived by the soul in a previous life.

ANARCHISM

Social doctrine which admits only the will of the individual, and rejects all state authority. Such doctrines can be found in antiquity and in early Christian times, but were especially developed in modern times. (*See* Proudhon.)

ANAXAGORAS OF CLAZOMENE
499-428 B.C.

One of the most important pre-Socratic philosophers, friend of Pericles. He had to leave Athens because he was accused of atheism. He tried to reconcile °Heraclitus' theory of eternal motion with Parmenides' theory of the invariable

esse. According to Aristotle he invented the theory of the *"homoiomeriae"* (identical little particles). In every body are little particles of all other possible bodies. Things are defined by the predominant number of such "seeds." In blood, for instance, are little particles of bone, iron, etc., but the blood globules are in greater number. Everything comes into being and changes through different doses of "seeds," everything is composed except the mind (*nous*).

Anaxagoras seems to have been the first to reach a notion of something spiritual. The spirit is entirely pure, not composed, autonomous and not mixed with anything. It is intelligent and governs matter. It directs matter, but is not contaminated by it. The *"nous"* of Anaxagoras seems to point toward a certain transcendency of God. F.D.R.

ANAXIMANDER OF MILETE
610/9 - 546/5 B.C.

One of the older °cosmological philosophers. The world, he teaches, comes forth from a first element, which he calls the indefinite or the infinite (*apeiron*). From that the *"kosmos"* developed, through the contrast of warmth and cold. In the same way earth, water and air came into existence. The earth is posed like a drum in the middle of the universe, which is composed of air and belts of fire. The apertures in these belts are the celestial bodies.

ANAXIMENES OF MILETE
585-528 B.C.

One of the older °cosmological philosophers. He teaches that the first principle is the air, from which everything proceeds, through dilution (fire) or through condensation (water and earth). He was the first to connect the first principle of the universe and the soul of man. As our soul exists of air and governs our entire being, so the entire *"kosmos"* embraces breath and air. His cosmology is, however, very rudimentary.

ANDRONICUS OF RHODES
Ca. 70 B.C. Tenth scholar of the Peripatetical School, after Aristotle; best known for his edition of the works of Aristotle. Considers logic as an instrument of philosophy. We know now that the esoteric treatises of Aristotle were not unknown in antiquity between Theophrast and the edition of Andronicus.

ANGEL
A being which belongs to an order higher than the spatial order, and therefore is considered an immaterial, purely spiritual entity.

ANGELUS SILESIUS (real name Johann Scheffler) 1624-1677
German mystical poet, converted to Catholicism in 1653, best known for his *Geistreiche Sinn- und Schlussreime* (1657), in which his mystical experience of God is expressed in a beautiful aesthetic form.

ANIMA, ANIMUS
Antithesis, which, since Paul Claudel and Henri Bremond, is often used in connection with the aesthetic experience to express the opposition between a more discerning and understanding experience and a more subjective and mindful one.

ANIMISM
Belief in spirits, that has been developed especially in primitive cultures. According to Tylor, animism came from a belief in the existence of the soul, which itself originated in the wrong explanation of the phenomena of dreams and death. It is the source of all religions. This purely positivistic ex-planation of the origin and essence of religion is no longer accepted. The idea of God has another source than the belief in spirits, and this belief itself cannot be explained by animism alone. This does, however, not mean that some of the theories of Tylor have no value for the theological sciences.

ANNAEUS SENECA
See Seneca.

ANONYMUS IAMBLICHI
The *Protrepticus* of *Jamblicus contains a small politico-aesthetic treatise of an unknown author, who belonged to the circle of the older Sophists. He teaches how always to act according to the norms of the good and the lawful.

ANSELM OF CANTERBURY
Born in Aosta (Piemont) 1033, died at Canterbury 1109. Educated by Lanfranc in the Benedictine monastery of Le Bec (Normandy), became prior in 1063, abbot in 1078, Archbishop of Canterbury in 1093. As a disciple of Augustine, Anselm has many characteristics in common with his master, such as his preference for contemplation and for the study of God and the soul. He is more theologian than philosopher and his general method is characterized by the well-known formulae, *Fides quaerens intellectum* (originally the title of the *Proslogion*) and *Credo ut intelligam* (in the *Proslogion*) and belongs to more speculative theology. In general his doctrine is not very original, except for his well-known proof of the existence of *God, which was explained in his *Proslogion* and is often called the ontological proof of the existence of *God. It is an argument a priori, i.e., constructed from the idea of God (and not from the works of God, as are the arguments a pos-

teriori). Anselm considers it an argument against the fool who negates God (allusion to Psalm 13: "*Dixit insipiens in corde suo: non est Deus*"). His reasoning is: one calls God a being so great that nothing greater can be conceived; this definition is accepted by the atheist, that God exists at least in the mind. But that which is so great that one cannot think of anything greater cannot exist only in the mind, since under this supposition one could think of something greater, i.e., the same being existing in reality. Thus God exists both in mind and in reality. Gaunilon, monk of Marmoutier (Tours) thought that this proof was insufficient, and he wrote a criticism on the *Proslogion*: *Liber pro insipiente*. One cannot, he says infer the existence of a reality which departs from the idea one has of it; it is not enough to have the idea of a beautiful island to conclude that it also exists. Anselm gave his answer to Gaunilon in the *Liber apologeticus ad insipientem*: the remark of Gaunilon is exact for all ideas except the idea of God, because only this idea indicates the most perfect being; therefore real existence is an essential quality of this being. Discussions about this argument have been going on ever since. F.V.S.

AN SICH

(Literally: in or by self) Without relation to anything else, especially to a knowing subject. The *"Ding an sich"* for Kant is thing as it is in itself and not only as it appears to the conscience (*°phenomenon*). The *"an sich sein"* of the idea is, for Hegel, the idea inasmuch it has not yet opposed itself (*see Für sich*) in order to be eventually by itself in the *an-und-für sich-sein*.

ANTECEDENT

Is in an *°assertion of deductibility* p q the *°proposition* p, in the assertion p, p' ...+ q. q the series of propositions p, p' ... *Antecedents* of a *relation* r are the things x which are opposite to others in the relation r.

Previous, already present, knowledge, inasmuch as it is used to deduce, through reasoning, the new knowledge contained therein (*°consequent*). (*See* appendix.)

ANTHROPOCENTRIC

The conception that man and human experience are the center of the universe. One can, to a certain extent, apply it to the world vision of the Christian Middle Ages. °Copernicus was the first to decisively abandon this view.

ANTHROPOLOGISM

Philosophical school, considering man as the measure of all things (Protagoras) and so deducing all knowledge and moral values from the study of man. In its most extreme form, anthropologism was defended by Feuerbach, who opposed anthropology to theology as Hegel considered it. Sometimes anthropologism is considered as the conception that the determining factor in history has to be sought in the differences between races (de Gobineau, H. S. Chamberlain, Gunther).

ANTHROPOLOGY

Literally, the science of man. Empirical or positive anthropology is concerned with man on the grounds of experimental data of biologico - genetic, psychological, ethnic, linguistic and historical nature. Philosophical anthropology gives us a philosophical interpretation of these data, in which man as such is the object. In this the other philosophical sciences have an important part. There certainly are many different philosophical conceptions about man. When these reflections are part of a theological system, we speak of anthroposophy. One starts not from reasoning or perception, but from intuition and the extrasensory. The doctrine of reincarnation, the spiritualization of matter, pantheistic theories and astrological speculations have their part in this. In Christianity theological anthropology, on the grounds of experience and revelation, is very important. P.S.

ANTHROPOMORPHISM

Humanization of the divine; means that one not only represents the divine in human form, but also attributes to it many human qualities. Generally the idea that the divine is greater, more powerful, and wiser than man is accepted. The human qualities are then enlarged to gigantic proportions and idealized in different ways (Greece, India). Anthropomorphism is in certain ways an inevitable consequence of the imperfect knowledge man has of God, since we try to know God through the created world. The doctrine of analogy (see analogy of being) is an effort to purify the idea of God from anthropomorphism. But it must also be accepted that man cannot have a purely abstract notion of God, but has to use sensory images. Christianity, in the same way, represents God the Father as an old man with a gray beard. K.L.B.

ANTILOGISM

Such a connection of three incompatible theses with not more than three different terms, so that from every pair follows the negation of the third. So $\underline{a}=\underline{b}$, $\underline{b}=\underline{c}$, $\underline{a}\neq\underline{c}$.

ANTILOGY

Logical contradiction and incompatibility of two or more propositions. Antilogical: logically contradictory and incompatible.

ANTIMORALISM

Theory which rejects the absolute value of morality and thinks that one can transcend morality in some specific cases (e.g., in art).

ANTINOMY

Apparent contradiction which exists when two contradictory principles seem to apply to the same premise, or when from the same premise two contradictory conclusions seem to be deducible. In *Kant antinomy means contradictions, in which the mind is necessarily entangled, when it thinks it can reach the unconditional in the phenomenon and acts as if it could know the *Ding an sich. In the Kritik der reinen Vernunft he indicates four pairs of antinomies: it is possible to prove that the world (1) is limited and that it is indefinite in space and time; (2) that its substances are simple or composed of simple parts and that nothing of what exists is simple; (3) that all causality according to the laws of nature presupposes liberty, and that there is no liberty in the world; (4) that anything belongs to it as part or as cause, and that an absolutely necessary being exists, in or outside the world, as its cause. In the Kritik der praktischen Vernunft he speaks of the antinomy of virtue and happiness. The Kritik der Urteilskraft considers the antinomy of mechanical and final causality. J.P.

ANTIOCHUS OF ASCALON

Disciple and successor of Philo of Larisa as director of the *Academy. Abandoned the skeptical viewpoint, and came back to the doctrine of the *"veteres"*: Plato, Aristotle and the Stoics. He does not see any difference between these three.

ANTISTHENES

Ca. 444-368 B.C. Founder of the old *Cynic School of Athens. Disciple of the Sophist *Gorgias, later of *Socrates. We find in his works the intellectualism of Socrates, because of his high esteem for definition, and because of the doctrine according to which virtue is the fruit of the moral sense, so that it can be taught and becomes an inalienable possession. Virtue is the highest purpose of man; it presupposes the greatest possible detachment from all human needs. Pushed to the extreme, this cynicism will lead to an absolute condemnation of all human institutions, such as the state, social conventions, civilization. The modern meaning of cynicism comes from the extreme form of ethics taught by Antisthenes; one can find it also in *Diogenes (Cynicism=of the dog). From the intellectualism of Aristotle, Antisthenes concluded also two logical propositions: (1) All contradiction is impossible, be cause if we speak of the same thing how can we contradict each other? If we speak of different things, then contradiction is certainly not possible. (2) Only identical judgments are possible: e.g., man is man. It is impossible to add to a subject a predicate which is not the subject itself; otherwise the proposition would be false. This doctrine was attacked by *Plato. F.D.R.

ANTITHESIS

Opposite to assertion. In the Hegelian dialectics the opposition of thesis and antithesis emerges in a higher *synthesis.

ANTITHETIC

A term used by Kant: the methodical antinomy of two apparently established theses (thesis and antithesis), which, although contradictory, can both rightly be defended.

APAGOGE

(Greek *apagogè*, deduction from) *See* *abduction.

APATHIA

The insensibility with which, according to the Stoics, the wise man looks at events. He finds this equanimity of mind in the certitude that everything which happens is determined by a reasonable determinism.

APEIRON

Literally, the indefinite, the unlimited; according to *Anaximander, the primal matter, "the principle of what exists." All things would come from this, it would be present in all things, but imperceptibly, it could be defined only negatively.

APODICTIC

Expressing absolute and necessary truth (*see* judgment).

APOLLONIAN

Kind of artistic feeling, in which objective contemplation is more important than subjective feelings. The Apollonian artistic feeling is characterized by a certain preference for vivid forms, a greater clearness of intuition and conscience and an open sense of the ideal. The Dionysian type, on the contrary, puts the accent more on the feeling. While the Apollonian type dissociates itself more contemplatively from the object, the Dionysian type experiences his relation to the object as a blending unity, in which affectivity and emotion have a greater part. It experiences its object more as a living reality than as an appearing ideal, more in the form of a subject-obsessing and emotional grip than by way of a calm and controlled vision. The Apollonian type prefers plastic and classical form; the Dionysian prefers the museful and romantic form. L.V.K.

APOLOGETICS
(literally, art of defending)

Autonomous section of Catholic theology, generally called *fundamental theology*, because it defines and proves the foundations on which theology is built. They are: the fact of divine revelation, the fulfillment of revelation by Jesus Christ, the infallible and unadulterated preaching of the content of this revelation by the Catholic Church, which was founded by Jesus Christ. Sometimes also considered as part of the apologetics: the argument of the existence of a supernatural personal God and of the natural obligation of man, His creature, to adore and venerate Him. This argument does not really belong to the apologetics, but rather to natural theology and the philosophy of religion. Apologetics have the task of making credible, on purely reasonable grounds, that Christianity is the absolute divine revelation and that the Catholic Church is its only mediator. The reasonable grounds are called the *motiva credibilitatis*, grounds of credibility, to be distinguished as external grounds (miracles, prophecies) or internal grounds (psychological or moral). The first have an absolute objective value as proof, the latter a more subjective value. K.L.B.

APOLOGISTS
Fathers of the Church of the 2nd and 3rd century, who defended Christianity against paganism and Judaism. They used Greek philosophy, although not all to the same degree. They are divided into the Greek apologists (Marcianus Aristides, Justinus, Athenagoras of Athens, Tatianus, Theophilus of Antioch) and the Latin apologists, who are generally freer of pagan influences. (Minucius Felix, Tertullianus, Arnobius, Lactantius).

APORIA
(Greek, *a-poros*, no exit)

A difficulty which embarrasses us so that we cannot find the issue. Aristotle is known for his methods of *aporiae*, in which he introduces beforehand a number of difficulties against the thesis he has to prove, difficulties which are or could be brought against it.

A POSTERIORI
Based on experience, opposite to a priori (*see* a priori).

APPERCEPTION
Term used since Leibniz, to indicate a more active attitude of the knowing subject toward his known objects, in opposition to perception, which is more passive. Leibniz considers it as a reflexive knowledge or consciousness of simple perception. *Pure or transcendental perception* is called by Kant the identity of the ego, which is given in the original consciousness of "I think" which should accompany all our knowledge, insofar as this identity is the a priori condition for the unity of our several representations (and also for their remembrance). This identity is not considered an autonomous being but only a formal principle (*see* formalism).

In psychology since Wundt, apperception is the process, directed by the will, by which we apprehend attentively and order (°analysis, °synthesis) the perception

21

given objects of our consciousness. In pedagogy since °Herbart: the assimilating reception of new experiences into the totality of previous ones.

APPLICATION

of a symbol, indicates that both symbols (usually between parentheses) follow each other. In the simple logic the application of the sign of a class *a* to the sign *x,* indicates the proposition: *x* is an *a.* In the combinatory logic the application indicates the determination of an object of thought by another. A °*theory* is then applied on specific (constant) objects of thought, so that through the constant symbols for these objects of thought the variables in theses of the system are replaced.

APPLY (To be valid to)

Special way of being which characterizes ideas, truths and values. These have no existence in time and space, but they still press themselves upon he who thinks and acts. °Lotze was the first to emphasize this way of being. But, on the one hand, the question arises: on what do the contents which apply rest? Do they form a world, related to the world of ideas of Plato? On the other hand, it should be precisely determined how they impose upon the subject. A distinction is probably necessary according to the object. *Ideas* have a specific content, which is not created by the subject, but only discovered by him; they therefore apply insofar as the thinking subject cannot withdraw from this specific meaning. Thus "two" has a meaning which must be accepted by all those who think this idea. *Truths* apply inasmuch as they are in force in several fields. They therefore impose themselves on the thinking subject not only in their specific meanings, but also as being applicable in different fields. That bodies fall, taught Kant, is absolutely applicable, i.e., everywhere and always in force in the world of experience.

Values, finally, impose themselves on the subject in still another way. For if values are not realized, as such their attractive character is not necessarily felt. In *conscious application,* the °consciousness of a value is reduced to a purely rational knowledge of the propriety of the value. It is expressed in a so-called ideal *judgment of application,* as, e.g., "There has to be justice in the world." A relation is here corroborated which is not but should be, and of which we say that it should be because we have established that it is not. This opposition between "have to" *sollen* and "be" can only be lifted through the intervention of a subject which realizes the proper value. The ideal judgment of value appears, therefore, more clearly in practical norms, which present the realization of the value as a duty which has to be performed.

A PRIORI

Literally previous, the earlier element (*prius*) in regard to a later element (*posterius*); opposite to a posteriori. The earlier element can be earlier in the chronological, logical or ontological sense.

An argument is a priori when it reasons from a cause, whether adequate or not, to an effect. The cause, as fundamental of being, is the ontological *prius*; the reasoning, which concludes from this fundament of being, is logically a priori. The reasoning from effect to cause (from the ontological *posterius* to the ontological *prius*) is logically a posteriori.

The first judgments in regard to

being are called a priori, since they are not dependent on a specific situation of beings, but are applied to all beings, even in the hypothesis that no being was empirically given. They express relations (part is smaller than totality) or are founded in the identity of the being with itself (*principle of identity, *principle of contradiction, *principle of the excluded third).

*Kant says that a priority, which is proper to judgments inasmuch as they are general and necessary, is exclusively formal and subjective. One could object to this that first principles of being are a priori in regard to all particular judgments, not only in their form but also in their content: because all more particular judgments are in their content explanations of the first principles of being. Universality and necessity, revealed in the knowledge of the actual and contingent, are never exclusively a subjective a priori, because they proceed from a discernment of the cohesion of beings. A priori is, in this connection, opposite to the individual and the contingent as a posteriori.

APULEIUS OF MADAUROS
Madauros (Numidia)

Born ca. 125 A.D. Was interested in philosophy, especially Plato, in oratory and literature. Most important work: *De Platone et eius dogmate* (in two books, the first treating physics, the second ethics); *De Deo Socratis*, which considers demons as the link between ticular judgments are in their condivinity and man.

ARABIC PHILOSOPHY

In a narrower sense means Islamic philosophy. Has two different currents: the one oriented more to Islam and the second attracted more to Greece.

1. Islamic Arabic philosophy developed from the study of the more obscure texts of the Koran. The central point of the religious development was naturally the main dogma of Islam: the absolute eternity and sovereignty of God. This dogma gave rise to such problems as: what are God's qualities, what is His relation to man, can we know Him, what about His justice, man's free will, predestination, the revelation (whether the Koran was created or not). The reasoning about these questions is the *kalām*. The more traditional current is called the *orthodox kalām*, and the more progressive, also influenced by Greek and Christian philosophy, is the *mu'tazila*. Both currents were for a long time rivals, also in political affairs, but an attempt to form a synthesis of both currents diminished the conflict. In the al-Asa-rī (873-935) school atomism was made subservient to the doctrine of the absolute sovereignty of God. "The mediating theology of Asjari or of his school, stayed in principle the theology of orthodox Islam." (De Boer, 1921, Pg 59)

Another attempt at unification was made by al-Māturidī (born 944) and eventually perfected by *Algazel (born 1111), who knew Greek Arabic philosophy as well as the mystics. Later theology is not very original except the contemporary reformation.

2. Greek Arabic philosophy, which began earlier in eastern Islam, is founded upon translations from Greek or Syriac of the works of Greek philosophy or sciences. The most important philosophers in eastern Islam are: *Alkindī (born ca. 870); al-Rāzi (born ca. 925), defender of philosophical religion, with as a center an eclectic neo-Platonic atomism; *Alfarabi

23

(born 950); the *ihwan al-safā* or the pure companions, who in the second half of the 10th century published a philosophical encyclopedia, in which the neo-Platonic doctrine of emanation is accentuated; Ibn Miskawayh (born 1030), also a neo-Platonist; especially °Avicenna (born 1037). Later the philosophy loses its independence, and especially under the influence of °Algazel philosophical questions will be studied in the light of Islamic theology, so that from *kalam* and Greek-oriented philosophy a synthesis is built, which had nothing original any more and stayed inside Islam.

Western Islam gave Greek-oriented philosophy perhaps a still more rationalistic aspect. The most important names are: Ibn Masarra (born 931) who probably introduced the philosophy in Spain and taught a curious doctrine of emanation; Ibn Bagga, or °Avempace for the Latins (born 1138); Ibn Tufayl (born 1185); and especially °Averroes (born 1189); also Ibn Sab'in (1270), who contacted Frederick II. After the decline of Islam in the West, nothing important was done in the field of philosophy. One can also name here Ibn Haldun, "father of the philosophy of history," who was of Spanish-Arabic descent. J.V.

ARCESILAUS

Head of the °Academy after Crates (mid-3rd century B.C.), inaugurates the skeptic period in this school (the so-called Middle-Academy). He attacks the stoic criterion of truth with the argument that representations which do not come from a real object can have the same evidence as real ones. The wise man will therefore abstain from all judgment. For his acts he will, however, find a direc-

tive in what is reasonable (the *eulogon*). This principle, defined by the Stoics as a practical equivalent for truth, is different from the later principle of probability (*see* Carneades) in that the latter is an empirical principle, whereas the *eulogon* depends only on reason.

ARCHETYPE

Literally, first form, in which one sees the prefiguration of a specific kind of beings, which are considered their images. Such are the ideas of °Plato and of °Malebranche and °Berkeley. For °C. G. Jung archetypes are the original forms in the "collective unconscious" which determine a priori the experience of the individual.

ARCHEUS

Called by °Paracelsus and Van °Helmont, the principle of life in seed.

ARCHITECTONICS

The art of bringing unity to the multiplicity of our knowledge. According to Kant, it is the essence of all science and scientific knowledge.

ARDIGO, Roberto

1828-1920. Most important representative of the positivistic way of thought in Italian philosophy.

ARISTIDES, Marcianus

2nd century, Greek apologist, author of an apology (*ca.* 140) of Christian monotheism against polytheism.

ARISTIPPUS OF CYRENE

Ca. 435-355 2.3. Founder of the Cyrenaic or °hedonistic school. Knew the doctrine of the °Sophists, belonged to the circle of °Socrates, lived often at the court of Syracuse where he met °Plato. Aristippus taught a completely sensualistic and relativistic epistemology, in which one can find some influence of *Protagoras. We know only the experiences of each moment, he says; we do not know anything about an objective world. Upon this simplistic epistemology he built ethical hedonism. Man has to strive for the highest immediate pleasure. The feeling of pleasure justifies the act producing this pleasure, whatever be the judgment of the general opinion. This theory of Aristippus brings him close to *cynicism. His ethics are, however, not those of gross pleasure. Inconsequently, he ennobled his doctrine with the Socratic theory of rational discernment, which compels us to evade a pleasure in order to avoid the bad consequences and makes us accept a difficulty or burden in order to obtain a consequent pleasure. He also is close to Socrates' attitude of life: the self-sufficiency of the wise man. F.D.R.

ARISTOBULUS

Ca. 150 B.C. Wrote a commentary on the Pentateuch and is one of the first representatives of Jewish-Hellenic syncretism. Uses the allegoric explanation for the Bible and tries to prove that Greek philosophy derives from the Old Testament.

ARISTON OF CHIOS

Early 3rd century B.C. disciple of *Zeno of Citium, took the direction of a dissident school. Wanted to reduce all philosophy to ethics, which itself had to part with all parenetics and casuistics; he kept only the general or fundamental ethics.

ARISTOTLE

Born in Stagira (Chalcedice) 384-322 B.C., son of a Greek physician, who came to live in Pella and was personal physician of Amyntas II, King of Macedon. At seventeen Aristotle went to Athens where he was for nineteen years the disciple of Plato in the Academy. After Plato's death (348-7), he left the Academy with Xenocrates and lived for three years in Assos, Asia Minor, where he opened his first school. He married Pythias, niece and adopted daughter of Hermias, tyrant of Aterneus. He went then to Mytilene, where he lived for two years and was especially interested in the study of nature. In 343-2 he returned to Pella in Macedon, and was in charge of the education of King Philippus' son Alexander, for seven years. When Alexander came to the throne in 335-4 Aristotle returned to Athens and opened there his own school in the Lyceum, a gymnasium dedicated to Apollo. He had many important disciples: Eudemus of Rhodes, Theophrastus, Callisthenes and Meno. After Alexander's death (323-2) he felt menaced at Athens; he was accused of atheism, fled to Chalcis in Euboa, and died there in 322-1.

Although the *Corpus Aristotelicum,* as it was transmitted, contains principally didactic works, Aristotle also wrote works in other fields. First, *philosophical dialogues,* addressed to the general public, polished in style and form. Should be mentioned: *Eudemus (On the Soul); Protrepticus* and *De philosophia;* in the latter dialogue we can already discover criticism of Plato's doctrine of ideas. Then his *hypomnematic works:* a series of documentary works which he wrote with the assistance of his disciples. Finally didactic works: related to logic (Organon), to the first philosophy or metaphysics, to natural philosophy (*Physics, Treatise on the Soul,* some elaborate studies of animals), to ethics (*Ni-*

comachean *E t h i c s, Eudemian Ethics, Magna Moralia*), to politics and rhetoric.

The form of these works seems to be influenced by their source and their destination; they are not complete treatises, written to be published, but are personal notes of the author, especially prepared for his teaching at Athens. The different works have therefore a very difficult structure, which has been more and more clarified by continuous studies. The treatises do not present a logical exposition, but a totality in which different pieces, sometimes from different periods, have been put together. There is much work to be done in order to study the literary structure of the different treatises. This study is also connected with the evolution of the philosophical ideas of Aristotle. This evolution was especially classified by Werner Jaeger, who tried to determine a separate criterion, for every one of the great parts of philosophy, so that he could fix in each domain the sequence of the different treatises. F. Nuyens resumed that inquiry with the help of one criterion (relation of soul and body) for the entire work of Aristotle; in this respect also many questions remain unanswered. Philosophy comprises for Aristotle also the domain of the positive sciences. Logic, however, is excluded, and the later peripatetics considered it as an instrument (*organon*) to philosophy. Scientific knowledge becomes then a search of the "why" of things or of the causes (physical, formal, efficient and final cause); when one goes back to the last cause of a datum, one arrives at the first philosophy.

Aristotle played an important role in the development of logic. He considers it a scientific doctrine or a study of scientific argumentation. He criticizes the diaretical method of Plato, and discovers the syllogism, in which the relation between two terms is determined by a third, which has the function of intermedium and tie between the two extreme terms. The Platonic influence is, however, still strong, since science is limited to the universal, the necessary and the invariable, so that concrete existence is only included in an implicit, universal and abstract way.

In metaphysics Aristotle rejects also Plato's theory of ideas as independent s u b s t a n c e s, distinguished from the sensory perceptible; the term idea is used by him to indicate the immanent essence of things. This is understood by intellectual knowledge, which is characterized by an abstractive process, in which here-and-now definitenesses are abandoned in order to arrive at a universal comprehensible view. The formal object of metaphysics is now being as such. This notion is, however, analogical: its different meanings refer to the first fundamental meaning, that of substance, and among substances the immaterial one will have the first place in the analogy of being. Eventually Aristotle has to accept the existence of a pure act, which has to be the principle of eternal cosmic motion. This First Principle moves the world as final cause, i.e., it directly moves the first heaven only and determines, in this way, the entire cosmic evolution. It is not considered as the creator of the universe; it does not know the world, since its knowledge is directed only toward the most perfect object. i.e., itself.

Opposite to Eleatism, which considers all change impossible, Aristotle was looking, in his doctrine of act and potency, for an explanation of the evolution of the physical world; it is then reconstructed according to the doctrine of matter and form. Matter is a composing principle of everything which is physical, it is the principle of determinability, as much as possible potential or undefinite; next to it exists the principle of form, which is identical for Aristotle, with the essence of the thing. This principle gives a being its specific perfection amidst other beings. Since the form gives beings their own perfection, it is also the principle of order and suitability in cosmic events.

This doctrine of matter and form is also applied to living beings, so that the soul is considered to be the form of being of the living being: There is only one soul for every living being, and it determines directly matter; it cannot be considered a being, but is an element of being and is therefore as transitory as the compound. An exception, however, is to be made for the intellect. Aristotle makes a distinction between the passive intellect, which is potent in regard to the object of thinking, and the active intellect, which makes images intelligible, so that they can actualize the passive intellect. The status of the intellect is, however, not very clear in Aristotle's work: the passive intellect seems to be transitory whereas the active intellect is eternal and imperishable; the latter seems also to exist separately, the same for all human beings, although there is a special connection between this intellect and the human soul.

In the *Nicomachean Ethics* Aristotle searches for the highest human perfection and concludes that it is found in the activity most distinctive of man, namely, thought. This ideal is, however, so sublime that Aristotle also outlines a more generally realizable way of life, which is not separate from the first, but is dependent on it: it exists in the harmonic efficacy of all faculties, for the rational virtues as well as for the ethical ones. To achieve the *eudemonia* some other conditions have to be fulfilled: an inner factor, pleasure (which is the natural effect of efficacy), and the presence of some external goods.

The state is considered by Aristotle as being a natural community, essential for the happiness of the individual; the state seems to be subordinate to the individual, the individual on the other hand is subordinate to the state as part of a totality; the power of the state is far-reaching and comprises even the education of the children. Aristotle studies in a deductive way the different political systems and concludes that the best system is the kingdom; after that comes the aristocratic system, and lastly the system in which the power is in the hands of many. He also speaks of a mixed system, where the power is in the hands of many, with a preponderance of aristocracy.

One should also indicate that Aristotle studied rhetoric in a scientific way and appreciates poetry more than Plato does. G.V.

ARISTOTELIANISM

(Christian) Philosophical school, developed in the Middle Ages as a result of the diffusion of the works of Aristotle. In the West, Aristotle's logic had already been introduced by *Boethius in the 6th century, general diffusion of his works came only in the middle of the 12th century through Arabic-Latin and Greek-Latin translations, which became more and more numerous till the end of the 13th century. Under the influence of the new philosophical literature, which made a deep impression, the curriculum of the schools of liberal arts was constantly enlarged, so that around the middle of the 13th century they became practically schools of philosophy. At the beginning of the 13th century, a philosophical current was introduced into the schools of liberal arts of Paris and Oxford. This current was deeply influenced by Aristotle and, in spite of the opposition of the Church, gained more and more importance. In the second quarter of this century it was introduced into the theological schools. It remained till the end of the Middle Ages, and in some institutions even later, the predominant factor in scholasticism. This Latin or Christian Aristotelianism has never been a pure aristotelianism, i.e., a complete and exclusive adoption of the philosophy of Aristotle; the latter was too incomplete and imperfect, especially in its metaphysics, to satisfy monotheistic thinkers. (Jews, Christians or Moslems). Under all its different forms, Aristotelianism was always, in the Middle Ages, completed and perfected by religious or philosophical, especially neo-Platonic, influences. In the Latin world Aristotelianism before 1250 was very eclectic and sometimes in the spirit of Avicenna (i.e., Aristotle is interpreted as *Avicenna interpreted him). With Bonaventura Aristotelianism is more in the spirit of Augustine (i.e., it is mixed with Augustinian doctrines). Thomas remodeled it so much that we can no longer speak of Aristotelianism any more, but of Thomism. With Siger of Brabant it becomes heterodox or radical. In the 14th century Joannes de Janduno (Paris), Taddei da Parma and Angelo d'Arezzo (in Italy) defended Aristotelianism in the spirit of Averroes (or Latin *Averroism), which was confined to Padua until after the Renaissance. During the Renaissance Averroistic Aristotelianism came in conflict with an Alexandristic Aristotelianism (which interpreted the psychology of Aristotle according to *Alexander of Aphrodisias) and Platonism. F.V.S.

ARNOBIUS

Teacher of rhetoric in Sicca (Numidia), Latin apologetist, author of *Adversus Gentes* or *Adversus Nationes* (after 303), in which we find empiristic and materialistic leanings, reminding us of Tertullianus and the Stoics.

ART

The expression in matter of an esthetical intuition by means of a sensible form created by man. The relation between intuition and expression is however not such that a preexisting intuition is exteriorized, but this intuition comes into being only in its gradual artistic finding of a form. The more general tendencies in art are:

a) A *representative art* which is limited to a certain fidelity to nature and an *abstract* or *formal* art, which expresses its intuition and feeling in artistic forms and shapes, which are not found as such in nature and which do not immediately remind us of nature. Opposed to the extreme form of representative art, namely the *imitative* art, which is the as faithful as possible reproduction of the natural forms, is the *absolute* art, purely personal and independent. Representative art can decline and perish in the excess of servile copying and abstract art can become artless, when it becomes, free from all sense or value of living, a pure content-less construction.

b) *Authentic art,* based only on contemplative-disinterested satisfaction, is opposed to *functional art,* in which human useful and practical forms are realized in matter in such a way that they are also in a certain measure object of an esthetical pleasure and they make a contemplation of the form as form possible. The useful use of these forms (as in buildings, furniture, tools etc.) is then integrated in a higher human intuitive pleasure, without harming the usefulness.

c) the *physioplastic art,* which finds inspiration and artistic origin in images of experience and remembrance and therefore has a certain tendency towards fidelity to nature and the *ideoplastic art* in which inspiration and origin are mostly found in inner and spiritual experience of values; they are often characterized by a certain schematism in form.

d) A *typical art* is opposed to a *characteristic art.* In the former the form of representation goes back to a certain generality, which is a medium for the individual diversity, in the latter the unique characteristics of the individual are more underlined.

e) *Realistic art* is opposed to *idealistic art:* the former wants to represent the reality of life as it is —this is however not as such identical to faithful rendering of nature—; the latter tries to purify the reality into an ideal representation.

f) *Impressionistic art* builds its forms on the immediate feelings produced by an object (in painting for instance the ephemeral perceptions of light spots and colour points). In *Expressionistic art* is the form first of all the expression of a human interpretation and feeling and the reproduction of a personal thinking and feeling.—L.V.K.

ARTISTIC CREATION

The process in which the artist raises his work from its only possible existence in the inspiration to a completely real and independent form. It depends then from the nature of the art if this independence includes a real separation with the artist. There is in this respect, for instance, a difference between a sculpture and an executed dance-form. The first very undetailed form finds a work of art in the artistic vision, in which the unity of form and sense is first experienced in a vague but strong totality. The vision evaluates further to real creation by which, in an interplay of totality and itself revealing diversity, the work of art grows into a more clear shape. As external action, is the creation the execution in the matter. Inner and external creation come however together in the real artistic creation, as an indivisible occurrence. L.V.K.

ASCETICISM

Literally, exercise connected with effort; namely, to observe the moral law. This law can be observed by man, a composed being, only at the cost of a struggle against other leanings. Asceticism is then considered an often painful exercise in the control of the bodily and other leanings. Also, the view that morality necessarily includes or is even limited to the painful control of the leanings of the body.

ASEITAS

(Literally, to exist by itself) Quality of God, opposing Him to everything which is not divine and which receives its existence from Him, while He exists by Himself and did not become.

ASOMATIC

Not pertaining to the soma, unbodily. Contrary of somatic (*see* soma).

ASPELIN, Gunnar
Born 1898. Swedish philosopher and historian of philosophy.

ASSERTION
Is not what is asserted but the contention in its whole, thus which is translated in the sentence: this is true.

In the methods of natural deduction is an *initial* assertion an assertion which applies as axiom. An assertion of *deductibility* ("Sequenz" of Gentzen) is an assertion: From $\underline{p}$ we can deduce $\underline{q}$, rendered here by $\underline{p}$ $\underline{q}$. A conditional assertion (in the N-methods of Gentzen) can be translated as follows: Under this or that condition is this valid. $\underline{p}$, $\underline{p}'$, $\underline{p}''$ . . . $\underline{q}$, $\underline{q}'$, $\underline{q}''$ can be translated by: if one has $\underline{p}$ and $\underline{p}'$ and $\underline{p}''$ . . ., then one has $\underline{q}$ or $\underline{q}'$ or $\underline{q}''$ . . . . or $\underline{q}'$ . . .

ASSERTORIC
Simply enunciating (*see* judgement).

ASSOCIATION
The spontaneous connection of two or more elements in the psychic life. Aristotle stated that association follows four laws: on the grounds of conformity (equivalence), opposition (contrast), simultaneity (coexistence), and succession.

There is a distinction between *progressive association* (when an idea evokes the next one) and *retrogressive association* (when an association evokes a previous idea). *Logical association* is an intellectual connection, *mechanical association* when the connection is obtained by mechanical means. The opposite of association is dissociation. Free association has been experimented in by Jung. One gives a person certain words to which he has to react with the first word occurring to his mind. From the differences in the time of reaction and the words the person chooses, Jung thinks it is possible to determine certain complexes. Freud calls association, in the analysis of dreams, the involuntary thoughts of the dreamer, which have no relation to the dream. Jung speaks of directed association: the involuntary thoughts of the dreamer, which have a connection with the dream-content. P.S.

ASSOCIATIONISM
The theory which physical psychology had to defend to reconstruct the unity of psychic life, after it separated it into elements (sensations, representations, reflexes, instincts, etc.). The elements would be reunited by association in a more or less mechanical way. This theory of association has only a limited value. Wundt opposed the idea of psychic synthesis to the idea of association. The mechanical character is thus taken from the association, because one accepts a final aim in which the will also has his part. Gestalt psychology also rejects the theory of association because it accepts the priority of the totality above the elements.

ASSOCIATIVE
Is an operation Ω if $(\underline{x} \, \Omega \, \underline{x})$ $\Omega \, \underline{z}$ is equivalent to $\underline{x} \, \Omega \, (\underline{y} \, \Omega \, \underline{z})$. In the simple algebra is the formation associative, because $(\underline{x} + \underline{y}) + \underline{z} = \underline{x} + (\underline{y} + \underline{z})$

ATARAXIA
Impassivity, which for the epicurean is the highest bliss. The highest bliss is obtained when one feels completely free even from his own pleasures.

ATHEISM
Negation of the existence of God, either in life by living as if no God

existed, or on a theoretical level by defending a system that denies the existence of God. One can further distinguish between the negation of a personal God (the God of the religions), while still calling divine an unpersonal principle, and the exclusion of all governing principle over nature and man. Pantheists are among those who subject themselves to an absolute moral order, still keeping a germ of the divine.

ATHENAGORAS OF ATHENS

Greek apologist, well versed in Greek philosophy, especially in Platonism. Wrote *ca.* 177 *Supplicatio pro christianis*, in which he defends Christian monotheism against the accusation of the pagans that Christianity is atheism.

ATMAN

See Upanishad.

ATOMIC PROPOSITION

Is an individual *proposition without operation sign. a̲x̲, r̲ x̲ y̲ (x̲ is an a̲, x̲ and y̲ are in the relation r̲) are atomic propositions, but not Na̲x̲ (x̲ is not a̲), a̲x̲ V b̲x̲ (x̲ is either an a̲ or a b̲).

ATOMISM

Doctrine proposed by Leucippus and Democritus, according to which everything consists of unvariable and indivisible atoms (literally: indivisibles). Atomism was an attempt to reconcile the idea of unique and immutable being (Parmenides) with the multiplicity and mutability which we experience. These can be explained through differences in configuration in the composing atoms. Atoms are only different from each other in their quantitative properties, size and shape.

Through Gassendi, Boyle and others, atomism became the background of the natural sciences in the seventeenth century. This remained through the 19th century, although Dalton attributed qualitative properties to the atoms. Every atom of an element had, according to Dalton, specific qualities in accordance with the chemical properties of this element. Since those properties were different, the atoms must also have different qualities. He kept, however, the idea that atoms are immutable. They mixed only by juxtaposition with each other. It was only in the 20th century that the idea of mutable atoms was accepted. *See also* theory of *atoms. A.G.M. v. M.

ATOMISTS

The pre-Socratic philosophers who accepted as final elements of being small material particles, or atoms. *Leucippus and *Democritus are the most important atomists. Also *Epicurus and *Lucretius.

ATOMS, THEORY OF

In contemporary physics atoms are defined as the smallest possible quantity of weight of a chemical element in a compound. Chemical reactions act always so that the weight-quantity of the reacting chemicals is always a multiple of the weight-quantity of the atoms concerned. In chemistry atomic weight is thus the most important characteristic quality of the atom. Initially the atoms were considered indivisible, because in chemical reactions, the most operative reactions which were known, no particles smaller than the atom played a role. In the structure theory of matter, atoms were thus considered the initial unities, out of which all matter is constituted. According to the periodic system of the elements, composed by Mendelejew and Lothar Meijer (1871) on the grounds of the qualities of matter,

31

there exist ± 90 different sorts of atoms.

The physical sciences have since discovered many things from which it can be concluded that atoms are composed of a nucleus, which is positively electrically loaded, and a number of electrons, as many as the loading of the nucleus has. This number is characteristic for a specific sort of atom. Initially one considered the atom as a planetary constellation, in which the electrons moved around the nucleus: the atom model of Rutherford-Bohr (1913). Later it was found, however, that this idea brought up insurmountable difficulties, so that while this model is kept as a graphic model, it is recognized that the atom is certainly not such a simple mechanical planetary constellation as the model presents. Difficulties arose when scientists discovered that the particles in the atom—which have to be considered elementary particles—rather than the atom itself are not really particles, i.e., *corpuscula.* They present themselves in different ways as *corpuscula,* i.e., strictly limited unities, but in other ways they have the characteristics of waves. Waves have as their characteristic quality that they are not strictly limited, but spread themselves continuously in space.

In recent years the theory of atoms has concentrated especially on the study of the nucleus. This also does not seem to be immutable. When radioactivity was first discovered (1895), which was explained by the fact that the nucleus spreads particles of matter (electrons and helium nuclei) and waves, scientists succeeded in provoking the nuclei reactions artificially. In such a reaction, the weight and load of the nucleus

change, which means that one sort of atom is changed into another sort. All this tended to the opinion that all nuclei are composed of the same elementary particles: positrons and neutrons, which can also react mutually and so produce electrons, which are separated by radioactivity. For philosophy, the important thing is that not much of the ultimate atom or *atomism is left. One has the impression that matter even in its most elementary elements, is always subject to change, which is more in conformity with the ideas of Aristotle (*hyleformism) than with those of Democritus. A.G.M.v.M.

ATTENTION

The personal turning of the mind to something; actively (voluntary attention) or passively (involuntary attention). Attention or attentiveness is closely related to personal disposition and interest. One can distinguish concentrative attention or concentration (application of the mind, during a long period, to one single thing) from distributive attention (turning of the mind to more than one object). The attention is subject to fluctuations or pulsations, which vary according to the different senses and to the personal interest.

ATTRACTION

Mutual attraction exists between all bodies, even the smallest. This attraction is directly proportionate to the *mass of the bodies and inversely proportionate to the square of their distance from each other. It was Newton who, for the first time, clearly formulated this law. With it he explained gravity as well as planetary motion. There exists also attraction (or repulsion) between magnetic and electric charges, and this attraction can be described with analogical laws.

ATTRIBUTE

What is ascribed to a subject. Descartes and Spinoza especially consider it as that which the intellect conceives as being the essence of substance. Thus extension is the attribute of a physical object, and thinking the attribute of a spiritual reality.

ATTRIBUTE, DIVINE

In general, everything we attribute to God. In scholastic philosophy: pure absolute perfection, which is formally in God, and proceeds, according to our human way of thinking, from the divine being. Although we speak of a number of attributes of God (omniscience, omnipotence, goodness, etc.) proceeding from His essence, they are in reality the same as God's essence. The infinite perfection of God, which is all perfection in simplicity together, can only be conceived by our limited knowledge as different analogic ideas of many perfections, and so we acknowledge the existence in God of the perfection of all creatures, but deny them the specific characteristic of being created, which indicates an all-surmounting or eminent form of being. Since wrath, contrition, hearing are not formal, but only *eminent in God, i.e., without the essential imperfection, they are not divine attributes. Mercy, justice, providence are not absolute perfections, but point out the relation between creatures and God; therefore they are not divine attributes in the strict, but only in a larger sense. H.R.

ATTRIBUTION

(Latin: *ad-tribuere*) Ascribing a quality to a subject.

ATTRIBUTIVE ANALOGY

See analogy.

AUGUSTINE, Aurelius

Born in Tagaste (North Africa) 354, died in Hippo Regius 430. His mother Monica was Christian, while his father was heathen; was well educated and taught rhetoric at Tagaste, Carthage, Rome and Milan (384-386). Was attracted to Manichaeism, in which he found a satisfying solution to the problem of evil. Turned later to the skepticism of the new academy and finally to neo-Platonism; some works of Plotinus converted him to spiritualism and prepared the road to his conversion to Catholicism (387); this conversion was made under the influence of Abrosius, who was not a stranger in neo-Platonic thought. In 388 he returned to Africa, was ordained priest in 391 and elected Bishop of Hippo Regius in 395. He remained there and was active till his death.

In philosophy Augustine was especially under the influence of Plotinus, Plato and the Stoics. He knew Aristotle only superficially and indirectly. The Church writer who influenced him most was Origenes.

Augustine does not make a real distinction between revealed truth and natural knowledge; both form one wisdom which contains all truth. His guiding principle for this unique wisdom is *"Intellige ut credas, crede ut intelligas"*; which means that a thorough natural knowledge will bring man to the acceptance of religious truth, and in the same way brings him to accept religious truth, a more profound knowledge of God and His creation. In attacking skepticism, Augustine emphasized that man is able to reach the truth; one can doubt everything, but not his own doubt; so one knows that he lives and judges. On the other hand, consciousness gives us knowledge of certain truths which are immediately clear, such as the first logical principles, the mathematical axioms, moral and aesthetic norms.

Augustine makes a distinction between intellectual and sensual knowledge. The former is conceived as a pure psychic act, which brings us a certain message which is in itself neither false nor true; it has to be seen in the light of the eternal truth, which is contemplated in the soul, and then only we have truth or falseness. This view in the eternal truth can, however, be obscured by human passion, so that error has to be considered a fault, guilt, at least in principle. In his first philosophical works Augustine admits the doctrine of reminiscence of Plato; later he rejected it, though its influence was maintained in his work.

Augustine repeatedly proves the existence of God through the grades of perfection in the real world which does not exist eternal-the contingency and appropriateness of the world, the testimony of consciousness, the existence of the moral law. These different data are not, however, constructed as a systematic proof. He underlines very strongly divine transcendency: God treated the world freely and because of his goodness, according to the ideas present in Him. In the world which does not exist eternally there is an evolution through the *rationes seminales* which are connected with matter. Man's soul is apprehended by immediate intuition as immaterial; it is not considered as the form of being of matter, as with Aristotle, since it is dedicated to governing the body. Augustine first accepted the pre-existence of the soul, but in his *De Trinitate* he rejects it as being untenable. The immortality of the soul is proved in the *Soliloquia* and *De quantitate animae.* Augustine does not admit a difference between the soul and its abilities: he sees in the soul with its memory, intelligence and will a symbol of the Trinity.

In the psychic world Augustine admits the priority of the over intelligence: the will orders intelligence and the purity of the will is a necessary condition to obtaining wisdom. In the final instance all moral norms are based on God; He is for man the highest good, that can be pursued only for itself. Evil in the world cannot be considered real: it is an absence of good, which, considered in the whole, contributes to the harmonic structure of the cosmos. G.V.

AUGUSTINIANISM

Philosophical and theological school of the Middle Ages, inspired by the doctrine of °Augustine. There certainly was a theological Augustinianism: the entire Latin theology, Thomism included, is highly Augustinian. Was there in the Middle Ages also a philosophical Augustinianism? Was the entire period drenched in it, as Mandonnet thought? To a greater or lesser degree one can find the influence of Augustine in Anselm, the Victorians, P. Lombardus and Bonaventura, but Augustinianism became a school after 1270, when Joannes °Peckham became the leader of the conservative theologians in Paris and later at Oxford, and appealed to Augustine in his attacks against Thomism. The new school is better called neo-Augustinianism, because of the many differences between this school and Augustine. Neo-Augustinianism has never been a coherent system, and did not survive the birth of the philosophy of °Joannes Duns Scotus. F.V.S.

AURIOL, Pierre
   See Petrus Aureoli.

AUROBINDO, Sri 1872-1950
   British-educated Indian philosopher and forerunner of Gandhi in organizing passive resistance as a political weapon. Author of *The Life Divine* and *The Synthesis of Yoga* and editor of the philosophical journal *ARYA*.

AUTARCHY
   The self-indulgence which according to the cynics, characterizes virtue. It consists in this, that someone who has renounced everything, probably with much pain, retreats completely into himself.

AUTHORITY
   Quality of a person or group of persons because of which other people know that they are their subjects. The kind of subservience and the way in which the authority is used depend upon the field in which the authority is valid (authority of the state, religious authority, etc.).

AUTONOMY (Literally: self law-giving)
   Considered by Kant not only as a quality of the moral subject but also a necessary condition for morality. The moral subject is thus autonomous: he does not receive the moral law from outside but generates it himself insofar as it is reasonable. (*See* factum rationis.) The moral law thus has a general and necessary character: the lawmaker is not so much the individual as well the rational subject or the subject that takes part in the reasoning. The individual subject is not only rational but also sensual, so that he does not simply obey morality. The self-imposed moral law is thus always a strict commandment. In a universal moral law, the dignity of the moral subject will be saved only when this subject himself freely creates the law or proclaims it himself. In the latter instance autonomy is nothing else than liberty in its positive appearance. If the subject is submitted to rules which he does not create himself (*see* heteronomy), then he is only a means and not a goal in himself. This seems to be the case when God is the author of the moral order. For Kant God cannot be the source of the moral law, although the moral law can be in accordance with His rational will. Outside Kantianism autonomy can also be considered as the real quality of morality. Then it is, as it is for M. Scheler, the autonomy of the notion of moral value (in the sense that moral action presupposes a personal notion of moral value) more than the creation of the value itself. J. Gr.

AUTOTELIC
   That which contributes to self-realization, which man makes his object (Stern). In American literature it has a less favorable meaning; it is a more egoistic characteristic (self-defense, self-development, domination).

AVEMPACE, Abu Bakr . . . ibn Bagga
   Born in Saragossa, died in Fez 1138. Belongs to the Western branch of Greek °Arabic philosophy and through his rationalism is the companion of °Aboe Bacer and °Averroes. He is very interested in natural philosophy (the so-called exact sciences, also musical theory). Less known in the Latin Middle Ages.

AVENARIUS, Richard
   1843-1896. Swiss philosopher, of empirio-criticism. Most important work: *Kritik der reinen Erfahrung*, 1888-90. Avenarius wants, like ancient philosophy, to give

equal certitude to philosophy and mathematics. In order to achieve that, philosophy has to use the same method and expression as mathematics, so one comes to the *"reine Erfahrung."* From here on it is now possible to get a pure notion of the world. Then it is clear that there are no absolute laws of nature. A law of nature is only a certain way to bring facts in connection with each other. The question of truth cannot be asked here. It is only a question of putting facts together, in the simplest way. Possibly this manageability of actuality could be called truth. Avenarius can be considered the precursor of neo-positivism. B.D.

AVENCEBROL, Avicebron (Solomon ibn Gabirol)

Born in Malaga *ca.* 1020, died at Valencia *ca.* 1058. Jewish philosopher writing in Arabic. In his major work, *The Source of Life,* he seems to be a typical representative of neo-Platonism with Aristotelian elements. Tries to combine all creatures by finding everywhere a compound of matter and form. His doctrine of immaterial matter, of the multiplicity of forms of being, the argument for the proof of the existence of the angels, the mystical contemplation of the One and of the light, influenced the Latin scholastics, especially the so-called Augustinianism of the Franciscans.

AVERROES (Abu'l Walid, C. Rusd)

Born in Cordova 1126, died in Morocco 1198. He is the most Aristotelian representative of Greek *Arabic philosophy in the Western branch. He has no counterpart in the Eastern branch. He was rather young when he was already known as a jurist, medicus and philosopher, because Ibn Tufayl had presented him to the court of the Almohades and he was judge in Se-

ville and Cordova. Orthodox Islamic jurists could later use the political situation to ban him because of his rationalistic views which were considered heretical, and his works were burned. By the end of his life he was readmitted to the favor of the sovereigns.

Besides his medical works, he wrote especially commentaries on the writings of Aristotle, in three series, which titles are not always easy to distinguish. They are: little commentaries or paraphrases, which do not follow literally the aristotelian text, but condense it and even change it sometimes, since some are not made directly upon the text. The medium commentaries accurately follow the text, and the great commentaries contain many questions and digressions. There are also a few treatises which discuss specific points of Aristotle's doctrine, logical questions, about the soul (unity of intellect and man), about the celestial bodies and their movers about the connection between philosophy and religion. Finally, there is also the great polemic work, the so-called *Destructio destructionum,* a defense of Aristotelian philosophy, directly against the attacks of *Algazel and indirectly against the presentation of this philosophy by *Avicenna. The complete corpus of the three commentaries was not known in the Latin West. What came to us in the Arabic text or Hebrew translations is incomplete. Wolfson (1931) gives us a tentative list.

The goal of Averroes was certainly to give a faithful account of the doctrine of Aristotle. For certain incomplete or much discussed points he tries to give an authentic complement based on the spirit of Aristotle. These complements are, along with the theories of the relation between religion and philosophy, the original part of Averroes' work and are especially related to the methodology, the *substantiae separatae*. A complete and systematic exposition of this doctrine is still missing.

Especially important are: the partial rejection of God's providence and the exclusion of the *particularia* from His knowledge, the eternity of the *substantiae intellectuales* and the limitation of their power, the separation of the intellect from man. J.V.

AVERROISM

Latin philosophical school which was created in the Middle Ages and the Renaissance in the Latin world under the influence of Arabic philosophy (*see* Averroes). E. Renan thought that there were already some signs of Latin Averroism at the beginning of the 13th century, a few years after the death of Averroes (1198). P. Mandonnet thinks that Latin Averroism began *ca.* 1250 and that *Siger of Brabant was the leader of this school in the 13th century. It is clear now that there was no Latin Averroism before 1265, and that even the philosophy of Siger cannot be considered as Averroism. In the 13th century the defenders of the monopsychism of Averroes were called Averroistae—i.e., his pernicious idea about the "one intellect" for all man; this is certainly an important doctrine but too specific to characterize an entire philosophical system. Real Latin Averroism begins in the 14th century, with *Joannes de Janduno (in Paris), Taddeo da Parma and Angelo d'Arezzo (in Italy). These scholastics accept the Averroistic interpretation of Aristotle, as the only authentic one. When their ideas are in opposition with Catholic dogma, they declare that their conclusions are "necessary" in philosophy, but that the contrary is "true" according to faith (theory of the double *truth). They never admit, in a strict sense, the existence of two contradictory truths: they maintain that philosophical conclusions are "necessary," and that religious truth is "true." If we could accept these assertions, they would involve the bankruptcy of philosophical reason in some domains, since reason comes to certain conclusions which we know through religion are false, and religion would inform us of a supernatural order which would invalidate some laws of nature, discovered by philosophy. Historians do not believe in the sincerity of the Averroists of the 14th century; they think that the formulas of "double truth" were only a means to conceal their rationalism, in order to avoid difficulties with the Inquisition. In both cases we see that the doctrine of the double truth never has been taught in its extreme consequences. F.V.S.

AVERSA, Raphael 1589-1657.

Italian philosopher from the Clerici Regul. Min. In his *Philosophia metaphysicam physicamque complectens* (1650) he constructs his own system, supplementing Aristotle with his own erudition.

AVICEBRON

See Avencebrol.

AVICENNA (Abu'Ali . . . abn Sina)

Born in Efsana (near Bukkara) 980, died near Hamadan 1037. The greatest Greek-oriented philosopher in Eastern Islam. Besides philosophy he also studied medicine, among others with a Christian medicus. His renown as a scientist brought him constantly in contact with the dynasties of the smaller Eastern states, and he became therefore a victim of politics. The works of Avicenna, for a small part written in Persian, contain, according to the latest bibliography of Anawati, 276 items, which deal with almost the entire realm of human life. His most important works are: *Book of Theoremata, Book of Definitions*, the so-called *Eastern Philosophy*, the two encyclopedias, *Sifa* and *Nagat,* and the *Compendium de Anima*. His *Canon* of the medical sciences is his most-read work. In order to know the real Avicenna one has to read his mystic treatises.

No adequate study has been made of Avicenna's doctrine. Avicenna did not write, as *Averroes did, a systematic commentary on the works of Aristotle, but he interpreted the doctrine of Aristotle in a syncretistic neo-Platonic way, especially with due regard to the doctrine of emanation. In religion he was closer to Islam than Averroes, who accused him of being too much under the influence of the Kalam scholars, the so-called *Loquentes in lege Maurorum.* *Algazel gave a good synthesis of the doctrine of Avicenna, and he was known in the Latin Middle Ages. But Algazel wrote a criticism on Avicenna's works, the *Destructio*, to which Averroes answered with his *Destructio destructionum* in which he attacked Algazel and Avicenna.

A short and good summary of the most important theses of Avicenna is given by *Aegidius of Rome in his *De erroribus philosophorum* under the articles: Avicenna and Algazel. He mentions the doctrine of the eternal emanation with which is connected the determination of God to one effect, the creative power of the intermediate *substantiae separatae*, the depen-

dence of the soul in existence and beatitude, from the final *intelligentia*, the limited knowledge and providence of God; the doctrine of the *unitas formae in composito*, and the naturalistic explanation of prophecies, answers to prayer, etc. J.V.

AVICENNISM
De Vaux tried to find some traces of Latin Avicennism in the late 12th and early 13th centuries: Christian philosophers would have taken the essentials of the doctrine of *Avicenna, even those principles which are not reconcilable with Christian doctrine. In fact, there does not seem to be in the Christian world a philosophical school which was primarily inspired by Avicenna; but before the commentaries of Averroes were translated (*ca.* 1230), Aristotle was principally studied via the paraphrases of Avicenna, so that Latin Aristotelianism was imprinted with a certain Avicennism. Some Documents also identify Averroes with the source of Latin neo-Platonism, together with other sources, such as the *Liber de Causis* and Joannes Scottus Eriugena among others. F.V.S.

AXELROD, Pavel Borissovich 1850-1928
Disciple of Bakunin and friend of Plekhanov, Alexrod was one of the founders of the Russian Social Democratic Party. Taking a leading role in formulating the policies of the Menshevist party, he was a member of the executive committee of the Second Internationale and a foe of Lenin and the Bolshevists.

AXIOLOGY
Deals with the nature, properties and mutual connection between values. Has very recently taken the place of traditional eth-

ics and aesthetics, or lays the foundation of both: ethics, which has as object the realization of value, and aesthetics, which is the representation of these values.

AXIOM

Was in the older deductive systems, e.g. in the geometry of the Greek mathematicians, a not proved, but evident assertion; postulates, on the contrary, were not proved assertions which were asked to be accepted. In the contemporary purely deductive systems does the difference between axioms and postulates not exist any more; both are not proved assertions, to whose terms, at least for the time being, no meaning is given. The axiom can therefore not claim any evidence.

Among the axioms in the above mentioned broader sense we distinguish: 1) real axioms or assertions which, expressed in the language of the deductive systems, are accepted as valid without proof. 2) primitive rules: they are not completely expressed in the language of the deductive system, because they are the rules itself of this language. They determine on what symbols can be reasoned (rules of structure) and how from valid assertions another valid assertion can be deduced (rules of deduction). Rules of substitution and definitions can be reduced to rules of deduction.

Real axioms have in general the form of assertions concerning variables. One can for instance in the theory of the algebra agree to the axiom $ab = ba$. Axioms of this kind are completed by rules of substitution. In some contemporary systems are the real axioms renamely to the infinite number of placed by schemes of axioms, namely through rules which can be translated as follows: all assertions of the form $ab = ba$ are valid. Such rules are deductively equal to an infinite number of axioms, assertions of the above mentioned form.

A system forms an *axiomatica* (undergoes an *axiomatisation*) if in it all assertions are deduced from axioms according to rules. We consider axiomatica and *formalism* as synonymous. R.F.

B

Capital B: symbol indicating the possibility of a direct reduction of the syllogistic mood in *Bamalip, and of indirect reduction of the moods in *Baroco and *Bocardo to the mood in *Barbara of the first syllogistic figure.

BAADER, Franz von

Born at Munich 1765, died there in 1841. One of the leaders of the Catholic renaissance in the romantic period. He thought that with the help of idealistic philosophy the notion of Catholic faith could be transposed and rationally justified. He attacked capitalism and free trade and defended a corporate society.

BAAL SHEM-TOV 1700-1760

Israel ben Eliezer began, in 1740, to teach the mysticism that later became known as Hasidism and earned him the name of Baal Shem-Tov (Master of the Good Name). His teachings gained a large following among the Jews of Eastern Europe.

BACHOFEN, Johann Jakob 1815-1878.

Swiss scholar in the philosophy of religion and history.

BACON, Francis, Baron of Verulam

Born in London 1561, died there in 1626. Made a career as barrister and politicus, became Lord Chancelor under James I. As did Descartes, Bacon tries in his *Instauratio magna*, of which he completed only a part (1620-1623), to renovate entirely the theoretical and applied sciences. Center of his interest is inductive logic, which he opposes to the inductive method of traditional metaphysics. To attain real science we have to eliminate at first four groups of prejudices, originating in human nature; they are individual disposition, language and public opinion, and invented philosophical systems (*see* idols). He elaborates a doctrine of induction (*Novum Organum*) differing from Aristotle and the scholastics.

To discover the cause of a phenomenon one has to compose four tables: (1) in which the phenomenon appears; (2) with the previous similar cases, in which it is absent; (3) in which it varies in degree; and (4) in which there is no connection to be found. It is a method of discovering the reality of laws in the positive sciences, although one acquires only a provisional knowledge.

His orientation toward the positive sciences inaugurated *empiricism. Natural law expresses itself in man by instinct and a natural light, in the world by the general agreement of men. H. R.

BACON, Roger

Born in Ilchester (England) *ca.* 1210-14, died at Paris 1292 or shortly thereafter. Studied in Paris and was later *magister artium* there; in 1247 returned to England and devoted himself under the direction of Robert Grosseteste to experimental study. Became a

Franciscan *ca.* 1250 and returned to Paris *ca.* 1257, but because of his original thinking and aggressive character he came into conflict with his superiors, who denied him the right to teach and publish. When his patron became Pope (Clement IV, 1265-1268), Bacon composed, at his request, his major work, *Opus maius*, completed by the *opus minus* and the *opus tertium* (in the same period). He continued his work after the death of Clement IV. In 1277 his astrological theories were condemned, together with the general condemnation of pagan philosophy. *Doctor mirabilis*, Bacon belongs among the most original and strongest personalities of his century. Because of his admiration of Robert Grosseteste, Adam of Marsh and other English masters, he counted himself as a member of the School of Oxford; his first education was, however, received in Paris, where he taught and spent the major part of his life. He belongs to the conservative group because of his ideas about Christianity and theology, as well as his traditional conception about the origin of knowledge, but he was also an innovator through his enthusiasm for experimental methods and through the view he held of the role of observation and mathematics in the progress of science. The *Quaestiones*, rendering his teaching in Paris as *magister artium ca.* 1245, show him as an ardent aristotelian, but very eclectic; he was then under the strong influence of Avicenna, Avencebrol and Averroes; in this period he had not yet felt the influence of Augustine. F.V.S.

BADEN SCHOOL (Southwestern German School)

One of the two schools (*see* Marburg School) in which, by the end of the 19th century, the phil-osophy of Kant was revived in °neo-Kantianism. The name comes from the fact that two of its most representative members, °Windelband and °Rickert, taught at southwestern German universities. It is very much influenced by °Lotze. The thinkers of this school made a distinction between the realm of perceptible reality, also called the *esse*, and thought and values. In principle there is unity between reality and thought, but in fact thought always has to absorb reality. This happens in the natural sciences, but there is also a kind of thinking that influences reality itself: the cultural sciences. Thought has this influence because it realizes values. Values have an absolute definite meaning. Cultural sciences are appraising (*wertende*) sciences. In this way the Basel School escapes the domination of the natural sciences and at the same time the domination of mere logic. In epistemology the Basel School is idealistic, but so prudent and moderate that it prepares, with other systems, for the breakthrough of neo-realism. *See* Münsterberg, Lask, Bauch. B.D.

BAHYA IBN PAKUDA c. 1050

A judge in the rabbinical court in Saragossa toward the end of the eleventh century whose *Hobot ha-Lebatot* (*Duties of the Heart*) is notable for its simple faith in the Bible and the Talmud.

BAKUNIN, Michael

Born in Pyamouchino (Russia) 1814, died in Bern (Switzerland) 1876. Revolutionary socialist, in philosophy he belongs to left-wing °Hegelianism.

BAMALIP

Artificial word to indicate the first mood of the fourth syllogistic °figure, in which major and minor

41

are a-propositions; the conclusion, however, is i. E.g.: Every square is a rectangle; every rectangle is a parallelogram; therefore one or another parallelogram is a square.

P a M
M a S
———
S i P

BANEZ, Dominicus, O.P.
Born in Medina del Campo 1528, died there 1604. Spanish theologian and philosopher, commentator on Thomas Aquinas, especially in the conflict of the *futura contingentia* and *predestination. Adversary of *Molinism. He explains the *concursus divinus* as if God *determined* physically the free act of creatures; this word combination was invented by Banez.

BARBARA
Artificial word to indicate the first mood of the first syllogistic *figure, in which major, minor and conclusion are a-propositions. E.g.: Everything which has intellect has free will; every human being has intellect; therefore every human being has free will.

M a P
S a M
———
S a P

BARDILI, Christoph Gottfried
Born in Blaubeuren (Würt.) 1761, died in Mergelstetten 1808. Prepared the transition from the idealism of *Kant to that of *Schelling and *Hegel.

BAROCO
Artificial word to indicate the second mood of the second syllogistic *figure, in which the major is an a-proposition, minor and conclusion are however o-propositions. E.g.: Valid banknotes have a wa-termark; one or another banknote has no watermark; therefor one or another banknote is not valid.

P a M
S o M
———
S o P

BARTH, Heinrich
Born 1890. Swiss philosopher, professor in Basel, brother of Karl Barth.

BARTH, Karl
Born 1886. Swiss theologian, professor in Basel, founder of dialectical theology.

BARTHOLOMEUS ANGELICUS
13th century. English Franciscan, taught in the monastery in Paris, and then later on in Magdeburg. Author of a compilative work, *De proprietatibus rerum* (*ca.* 1230-40).

BARTHOLOMEUS DE SPINA, O.P.
Also called Bartholomeus of Pisa. Born in Pisa ± 1480, died in Rome 1547. Theologian and philosopher. Attacked Cajetanus and *Pomponatius; defended the processes of witches.

BARUZI, Jean, 1881-1953.
French spiritualistic philosopher, professor at the Collège de France, was especially interested in the philosophy of religion.

BASCOM, John 1827-1911.
Many-sided American philosopher.

BASILIUS
Born in Caesarea (Cappadocia) *ca.* 330, died there 379 as bishop, older brother of *Gregory of Nyssa and friend of *Gregory of Nazianzus. Important theologian, knew and used Greek philosophy, especially neo-Platonism and stoicism.

BASSO, Sebastian
French scholar of natural philosophy, early 17th century, defended the atomism of Democritus on physical grounds. The space between atoms is filled with world ether, comparable to the vacuum in Democritus' works.

BASSOLES, Joannes of
See Johannes of Bassoles.

BAUCH, Bruno 1877-1942.
German neo-Kantian. Most important work: *Wahrheit, Wert und Wirklichkeit*, 1923. He tried to make a synthesis of the ground ideas of the schools of *Marburg and *Baden.

BAUMGARTEN, Alexander Gottlieb 1714-1762.
German philosopher, professor in Frankfurt an der Oder, with his *Aesthetica* (1750-1758) the founder of aesthetics as an independent science.

BAUMKER, Clemens 1853-1924.
German neo-Thomist, editor of the *Beitrage zur Geschichte der mittelalterlichen Philosophie*.

BAUTAIN, Eugene Marie
Born in Paris 1796, died there 1867. After his return to the Catholic faith, he was ordained priest, professor in Strassbourg and Paris. Fideist: considers that the only basis of certitude for the principles of reason and for all philosophy is the divine revelation in the Scriptures, as the Catholic Church teaches and explains it.

BAYER, Raymond
Born 1898. French philosopher, specialist in aesthetics, professor at the Sorbonne.

BAYLE, Pierre
Born in Carlat 1647, died in Rotterdam 1706. Son of a minister, converted to Catholicism and returned later to Calvinism. Between faith and knowledge he finds an unbridgeable gap; belief is meritorious because it goes against reason. He is against all dogmatism. He follows Descartes in many points but criticizes him in others. He is against Leibniz and Spinoza. The principal character of human intellect is not in finding the truth but in criticism. Especially in his *Dictionnaire historique et critique* (2 vols.) he criticizes scientific philosophy and religion and had much influence with this work. In the field of ethics he overcomes his critical skepticism: the moral law is innate to man and can be clearly understood. Conscience is the highest norm of our acting, and its morality is only determined by our inner disposition. The moral attitude of man is independent of Christian revelation. He taught at Sedan, and later in the illustrial school at Rotterdam (1681-1693), from which he was expelled because of heterodoxy.

BEATITUDE
Complete happiness, happiness which not only satisfies completely, but also exhausts all the possibilities of a being. At the same time, the perfection of the human being is presupposed, which, according to the scholastics, cannot exist without union with God. Beatitude can therefore better be defined as the joy which comes from the contemplation of God. In any case, happiness and beatitude are the final *ends for which man strives, or, in Kantian perspective, the highest *good. See also eudemonism.

BEATTIE, James 1735-1803.
British philosopher and poet, belonging to the Scottish school. In his *Essay on the Nature and Immutability of Truth* he explains

that what our human nature impels us to believe, the convictions in which all men agree, has to be true.

BEAUTY

The aesthetical category, in which the aesthetic experience reaches its purest form. Beauty presupposes a sound melting of matter and spirit, of sensory form and ideal sense. This melting reflects in the sensory form itself by means of undisturbed, serene and perfect harmony of all the elements, which compose this form. Without gliding to the sublime or the gracious or other categories, beauty can reveal a series of nuances, which already begin to enlarge its olympic serenity with gentle eagerness: a certain waiting for the still more beautiful, a desire for clearer intuition of the eternal, a certain nostalgia for the finite—or a kind of impotence, produced by the overwhelming of the experience, a feeling of the fragility and momentary of the more beautiful appearance, an inchoative striving to the ideal, etc. L.V.K.

BEAUVOIR, Simone de

Born 1908. French existentialist philosopher and author, disciple of Sartre.

BECHER, Erich 1882-1929.

German critical realist, professor at Munich. Continues the ideas of Külpe in methaphysics, and begins with the problems of biology.

BECK, Jakob Sigismund

Born in Marienburg 1761, died in Rostock 1842. German philosopher, disciple of *Kant, but rejected, however, the realistic elements in his thought.

BECOME

To become is to change, to go from one definiteness to another. On the substantial level this means that a being becomes another being; in the line of the quantitative and qualitative, that a same being is defined otherwise. The nature of becoming is directly seized in the experience of our conscious activity. Becoming appears there always as "one" becoming, which namely, as such, happens in a same subject as progressing: synthesis therefore of identity and "otherness". The metaphysical structure is therefore considered by scholasticism as a correlation of *potency and *act namely as the actuation of a being in the line of his potentiality.

Becoming is sometimes opposed to *being. It is however nothing else than becoming being, a being in the process of becoming. But the question is now important if all being is integrally becoming being, so that being and becoming could be interchangable. This can have a double interpretation: every being is, in every aspect, becoming; or, every being is always in a certain (but not in every) respect, becoming. In the first interpretation is hardly a place for the identity-moment, required in every becoming; in the second we should further investigate in the line of the *causality. If one accepts the priority, in the theory of potency and act, of the act, then one must accept that all that moves is moved by a *cause and then follows the question if this eventually contains implicitly the existence of an unmoved mover. L.D.R.

BEDA VENERABILIS

Born in Durham *ca.* 674; died in the monastery of Jarrow (England) 735, Benedictine. Was an important help in the spreading of ancient culture through his writings about the liberal arts and other profane sciences.

BEECHER, Henry Ward 1813-1887

A leading minister and public figure of the American nineteenth century who strongly advocated social reform, especially the abolition of slavery.

BEHAVIORISM

Method of experimental psychology which is limited to the observation and description of the behavior of man and animal, and which abandons all °introspection. Especially represented by °Thorndike and °Watson.

BEING

What is being is not the same as °"esse": it °participates on the "esse" according to its °essence: because a being not only is, but it is at the same time this, defined in itself and also limited, this means distinguished from others, so that it, together with these, forms the °order of beings. An investigation must determine if this distinction is fundamental, in other words, if a being is a substantial whole (not only a part of a whole), a °suppositum, that itself is and acts. Metaphysical questions about the beings go generally in these three directions: what is, logically and ontologically, the inner structure of a being, taking into account its existence and substantial definiteness, also the different lines of evolution of its activity? What is the place of this being in the order of the beings and its relation to the others? What is finally the relation of this being, in existence and activity, to the absolute Source of "esse"?

BEING-SUCH

Answer to the question: how is it? mostly in the sense of: what is it? Being-such means therefore in what manner something is, the way of being, °essence.

BELIEF

In the broad sense, acceptance of something as true because of somebody else's testimony, or thinking or supposing that something could be true. In the primary sense, however, belief is the strong agreement of the intellect, without fear of error, because of the testimony of somebody else whose authority one accepts, because one sees that he is competent and trustworthy. Since such an agreement of the intellect is not founded on inner evidence of the truth, the intervention of the will is always required, to bring the intellect to agreeing. This intervention of the will is not arbitrary, however, but is motivated by knowledge of the credibility or authority of the witness. To this kind of belief belongs the supernatural belief in divine revelation. Here also the authority of the witness is essential, not the least in Protestantism. Although the different sects have different opinions of belief, it is, according to Luther, the only sanctifier (*fides fiducialis*); the certitude of our justification through Christ is always considered as a necessary quality. The certitude of salvation, which Luther considered as created in man by God alone, received in liberal Protestant theology, especially under the influence of °Schleiermacher, a more subjective psychological character, and was described as an "experience" and psychologically analyzed. This conception also had influence on modernism.

BELLADONNA

See Adam pulchra mulier.

BELLARMINUS, Robertus, S. J.

Born in Montepulciano 1542, died in Rome 1621. Cardinal, celebrated theologian, apologist and controversialist. Canonized (1930).

Mixed in polemics over the oath formula of James I of England and the demands of the Gallicans. He defends the indirect power of the Pope over kings. From the role of the Church he deducts that the Pope can depose apostate princes and exempt their subjects from their oath. Bellarminus is one of the most important writers on the rights of church and state.

BELLE AME

Name given to the human being by Rousseau and by Schiller (*schöne Seele*), in which the ethical and aesthetic, or duty and inclination, are harmoniously united.

BELLUTIUS, Bonaventura

Born in Catana 1598, died there 1676, Conventual, defended the philosophy of Scotus.

BENDA, Julien 1867-

ᵼA philosophical writer and novelist who fought the cults of romanticism, mystic nationalism and the blending of the arts, and defended science and political justice. Works: *La Trahison des Clercs* (*The Treason of the Intellectuals*) (1927) and *Uriel's Report* (1926).

BENEKE, Friedrich Eduard 1798-1854.

German empirical philosopher, finds in psychology the basis of philosophy.

BENEVOLENCE

The will or at least the tendency to do something about the well-being of the others. It is different from the love which is directly directed towards the person of the other. One speaks sometimes of the °love of benevolence.

BENNETT, John Coleman

Born 1902. American theologian and philosopher.

BENTHAM, Jeremy

Born in London 1748, died there 1832. English positivist and utilitarian; he tried to apply the theories of °Hobbes and °Locke to the practice of ethical and juridical life. The determining principle of good and evil is the utility of the action; experience only can determine if an action is useful; i.e., brings us happiness or preserves us from evil: in one word serves our interest. Self-interest orders us to overlook the interest of our fellow-man and brings this also into harmony with our own interest. His principle of ethics was later formulated as "the greatest happiness of the greatest number." In politics Bentham defended radical democratic theories, with which he influenced the evolution of constitutional institutions in England. F.S.

BERACHYAH c. 12th or 13th Century

An itinerant teacher, scholar and writer whose personal life is solely conjectural; remembered for his *Mishle Shualim* (*Fox Fables*), adapted from many sources, and his encyclopedic philosophy, *Sefer Hahibbur* (*The Book of Compilation*).

BERDIAIEV, Nikolai Alexandrovitch 1874-1948.

Russian philosopher. After 1922 he lived outside Russia, a long time in Paris, where he died. His basic ideas are best expressed in the works which were published in French during the last years of his life: *Cinq méditations sur l'existence,* 1936; *Esprit et Réalité,* 1943; *Essai de métaphysique eschatologique,* 1946; *Dialectique existentielle du Divin et de l'Humain,* 1947. The thought of Berdiaiev can be characterized as a philosophy of the person. As such, the person is free and directed toward God. But for this reason the human person is caught between the organized world, which limits his freedom, and the divine, only in which can he be himself. Evil ties the person to the world, deprives him of his freedom and removes him from the divine. This does not lead to the conclusion that the world is bad in itself, but is rather the arena of the struggle between good and evil. The person is responsible for his own freedom, but also for social freedom in the world. Freedom is, however, only possible where the divine as such is experienced. There should therefore not be a separation, in the person, between philosophical thought and religious faith and experience. B.D.

BERGSON, Henri 1859-1941.

French spiritualistic philosopher, professor at the Collège de France. Principal works: *Essai sur les données immédiates de la conscience*, 1889; *Matière et mémoire*, 1896; *L'Évolution créatrice*, 1907; *Les Deux sources de la morale et de la religion*, 1932. Bergson is the philosopher of freedom. He shows how on the one hand human action has the character of spontaneity, never can be reduced to what precedes; but on the other hand how it is rooted in the life force (*élan vital*), in which all action originates.

Bergson's work consists in this, that he tries to understand both these aspects of the human essence. He knows that they are two entirely different aspects. The material-vital aspect is descendant and is also found in animal instinctivity, in the life motion of plants and is finally stilled in dead matter. The spiritual-vital aspect is ascendant and shows itself in the higher expressions of humanity: science, art, ethics, religion. Man thus comes to the recognition of a personal God. The unity of both aspects has to be kept. The simple intellect cannot achieve that, because it necessarily decomposes everything in accordance with the physical principle of time, which is proper to the intellect. Intuition, however, surpasses the intellect, because it is able to catch the duration (*la durée*) of reality. Reality does not come about through impulses, as our intellect necessarily represents it, but it evolves with a spontaneous smoothness, in which there are no transitions between phases, but in which everything is always in transition.

Bergson's effort to conceive spiritual and material vitality as a unity has often led to the interpretation that he defended a certain vitalism which reduces all reality, even man, to the purely biological level. But in his first *Essai* he already emphasizes clearly that freedom transcends this level, and in the following works he emphasizes more and more the spiritual character of freedom. Intuition cannot be seen as a biological-vital force, but as spiritual intuition. Putting intuition above intellect does not mean then that he puts the biological-vital above rational spirituality. Bergson's philosophy can, however, be considered a philosophy of life, because his idea of the spontaneity of life, as unity of material and spiritual vitality, is central.

Outside France, Bergson is practically always understood in terms of a biological vitalism. His last work can, however, not be understood in this way and the more profound meaning of his other works becomes then understandable, because vitalism is as spiritual as it is biological. In France itself this misinterpretation was not common, for Bergson was understood to be in the spiritualistic tradition of *Malebranche, *Maine de Biran and *Lachelier. His influence on the renovation of spiritualistic thinking (Charles Péguy) was important. Most discussions have been related to the problem how both aspects of vitality were united in one intuition. Bergson never formed a real school, even in France, but his influence outside France was equally great. His system gradually penetrated all Western thought. Specific ideas of Bergson influenced philosophers of different schools, partially because his ideas were connected with the evolution of the positive sciences, e.g., the dynamic character of reality, the intuition of duration as opposed to time, the emphasis put on the innate character of spontaneous life and the thesis on character and meaning of human freedom. It is his analysis of a few ideas, which at first seem to have no connection with each other, but whose unity has been developed by Bergson, which made him have such a profound influence on philosophy. B.D.

BERKELEY, George

Born in Kilkenny 1685, died in Oxford 1753. British philosopher. Studied at Trinity College (Dublin) where he later became lecturer in Greek and Hebrew and was librarian. He was ordained deacon in 1709 (Anglican Church). He lived in England from 1713 to 1721, where he became the friend of Swift, Steele, Pope and Addison, and visited France and Italy. In 1728 he came to America to found a seminary for missionaries, but he had to return to England in 1731 because the money promised by the English Government for his work, did not reach him. In 1734 he was named bishop of the Irish diocese Cloyne where he was occupied by his professional work, charities, and improving the education in this poor country. He lived for one year in Oxford and died there. He is buried in the chapel of Christ Church College.

Berkeley continues the teaching of English empiricism, developed by Bacon, Hobbes and Locke. The problem of human knowledge is also central for Berkeley, as the title of his genial work, edited in Dublin in 1710, indicates: *A Treatise Concerning the Principles of Human Knowledge*. Objects of knowledge are the "ideas of sensation," also called "perceptions" (sensual presentations), "ideas of reflections" and "imaginations." Berkeley is against the concept of material substance, which was still defended by Locke to guarantee the connection between representations of things. Locke admitted that these substances, although existing, could not be known. Berkeley denies their existence, and believes that only ideas of things and the observing of them, representing spirit in which these "ideas" are present, exist. In this way he is considered a disciple of idealism, and in his denial of matter an immaterialist, while this theory is connected with a metaphysical and strongly religious-oriented spiritualism.

This conception does not prevent Berkeley from believing, with the man not philosophically trained in the existence and durability of sensory objects, in our world, in form and color. The orderly connection of objects is not guaranteed by their unknown physical substance, but by their continued presence in the divine spirit, which also guarantees the continuity of nature. Following the theory of Malebranche and the Augustinians, Berkeley distinguishes between an absolute existence (also called archetypal or eternal) in the eternal Spirit, and relative existence (also called ectypical or natural) in the human spirit. This latter existence is actually relative when objects are perceived by human beings, potentially relative when there is only a possibility of perceiving. This conception is clearly expressed in another work of the philosopher, *Three Dialogues between Hylas and Philonous* (published in 1713 in London): "When things are said to begin or to end their existence we do not mean this with regard to God, but His creatures. All objects are eternally known by God or what is the same thing, have an eternal existence in His Mind; but when things imperceptible by creatures are by decree of God perceptible by them, then they are said to begin a relative existence with regard to created minds."

Historically the conceptions of Berkeley are important because they paved the way for Hume and Kant in the direction of a radically changed view in epistemology. Because of his theistic spiritualism, his acceptance of the priority of the mind and the spiritual nature of all that exists, he is one of the great Christian philosophical thinkers of all times. F.B.

BERNARD OF CHARTRES

Born in the 11th century, died between 1124-30. Elder brother of Thierry of Chartres, professor and later chancellor of the School of Chartres, best known through *John of Salisbury, who called him the *perfectissimus inter platonicos saeculi nostri*. He was clearly a Platonist in his natural philosophy, but under Aristotelian influence in epistemology, as John of Salisbury himself points out.

BERNARD OF CLAIRVAUX

Born near Dijon 1091, died at Clairvaux 1153. The most impressive figure of the 12th century. *Doctor Mellifluus*. Entered the monastery of Cîteaux (center of the reformed Cistercians) and founded the Abbey of Clairvaux. Favored the reformation of religious life by founding 68 monasteries and by indefatigable activities in order to impose monastic discipline. He preached the Second Crusade and had, as papal and princely adviser, much influence. He fought against heresy and against Abaelard because of his rationalistic views in theology and got him condemned by the Council of Sens. The reformation of Cîteaux was the cause of the flourishing of religious life, which favored theological studies for monks. The religious literature which followed these studies gave the world a series of philosophical concepts and themes with regard to God, the nature of man, the activity of the soul and the virtues. The Cistercian authors contributed to the evolution of natural philosophy, psychology and ethics. Bernard was the dominating figure of the Cistercian school. His work is of more importance to the history of theology (especially spiritual and mystic) than to the history of philosophy. He took part, however, in the evolution of important doctrines, especially in the field of psychology and ethics: man as creature, humility toward God, freedom, conversion, love of God, contemplation. Bernard of Clairvaux has no system and does not belong to a particular school. This great mystic and extraordinarily active man was not a speculative thinker; he mistrusted reason, which he considered as the source of pride and a danger to the simplicity of the faith. His most important theological source, outside the Bible, is Augustine. F.V.S.

BERNARD SILVESTRIS (or of Tours)

Ca. 1100-1167. Friend of Thierry of Chartres, to whom he dedicated his *De mundi universitate* (between 1145 and 1153), an allegorical and pantheistic cosmology, inspired by Plato's *Timaeus.*

BERTHOLD VON MOSBURG

Dominican, early 14th century, disciple of Dietrich of Freyburg, author of an important commentary on Proclus' *Elementatio theologica.*

BHAGAVAD GITA (Literally: Song of the Blessed One).

Famous Sanskrit text of the Mahābhārata, probably ± 2,000 years old and up till now of great importance for Indian spiritual life. In the form of a revealed doctrine, orally taught by Krsna (Krishna) who was later identified with the god Vishnu and who calls himself the Blessed (Bhagavat) or God, this rather short text explains that the highest principle, which is and out of which everything is, is a *Brahman, a personal God (Highest Soul). This doctrine is connected with the older Upanishads. God, who cannot be defined, is in everything, soul and matter, and everything is in Him. He is the essential and fundamental element in everything. He is the formal cause of all being, spiritual fundament and physical substratum of the universe. The phenomenal world is a manifestation of His essence. He creates it out of itself by His creative power. He is ele-

vated above the *karman and acts without interest: so this activity does not touch Him and does not tie Him in the *samsāra. For man also disinterested devotion to duty and methodically disciplined efforts are the most appropriate way to attain his liberation, i.e., to reach God. He has also to try to discern the essence of the very root of his personality and realize its identity with Brahman, i.e., with God. The third way to redemption is explained in the second part of the work, and this revealed way is called the *bhakti. By underlining that the best way to receive salvation is to direct oneself psychically and spiritually to God, and try to become united with Him, the Bhagavadgita became a great authority in the later theistic schools. J.G.

BHAKTI

Important Indian spiritual school first found in the *Bhagavadgītā, where it occupied a central place. The term means: share, belong to, love, venerate, and it expresses the idea that the worshiper is deeply imbued with the notion that he is a part of the essence of God, that he concentrates his strength and being on Him and loves and serves Him completely. Through Bhakti one learns how to know God and participate in salvation. Because of the Bhakti schools the veneration of the god Vishnu (Visnuism) has had more and more importance in the last 2,000 years. Many poets and religious leaders have been inspired by it.

BIELINSKI, Vissarion Gregorevitch

Born in Tchmenbarsk 1810, died in St. Petersburg 1848. Russian philosopher, disciple of conservative Hegelianism, later defender of left-radical *Hegelianism.

BIOGENETIC LAW of °Haeckel

States that the development of a young organism from germ to adult recapitulates the °phylogeny. This would give us the opportunity to learn what stadia were completed during the °evolution. This biogenetic law has been abandoned, the arguments do not hold and it can not provide a further explanation.

BIOLOGY, DIALECTICAL

Covers a theory of organic life according to the philosophy of K. Marx. Dialectical biology acknowledges that there are biological laws, that the organism is a °totality, but eventually it reduces everything to pure laws of matter. The theory of evolution is central, and is explained according to the dialectic outline of synthesis from antitheses. Dialectical biology is the official doctrine in the Soviet Union, the only one in accordance with Marx and Lenin. An important aspect is dialectical genetics, also considered the official doctrine, so that the laws of Mendel are contraband (Lysenko). In Western Europe M. Prenant and J. Haldane are its representatives. The latter is more moderate. Dialectical biology is an improvement over the theory of °mechanism, because living beings are considered real unities. But because of its materialism it fails to explain order and finality in nature. M.B.

BION OF BORYSTHENES

Early third century B.C. Born in Borysthenes. Wandering philosopher who lived, among other places, in Pella and Athens. Influenced by Crates, the cynical school, Theodorus the atheist, and the Lyceum. He did not leave a systematic philosophy but a number of fragments. His doctrine is founded on experience and has a special interest in poverty.

BLINDNESS FOR VALUES

Is had when an individual or even a group do not seem to be able to feel certain °values. This incapacity can be explained by the fact that the striving is not necessarily differentiated when several values exist. This blindness for values does certainly not prove that specific values would not exist. Values are indeed a priori.

BLONDEL, Maurice 1861-1949.

French spiritualistic philosopher, professor in Aix-en-Provence. Most important work: L'Action, 1893. Blondel investigates the meaning of human action. In action is an inner finality: everybody poses a specific action with a specific goal in mind. Thus one action is posed because of another action. Action is not defined, only the definiteness of actions. Action itself as the total activity of man, in which thought and volition are included, requires a meaning. This means that the question of the significance of a specific action brings us to the question of action itself, or in other words to the question of the meaning of life. It is impossible to evade this question, because implicit in all action is thought. Man is only a man of full value, when he makes this implicit thought explicit in conscious action. From its nature it is impossible that all action be completely conscious, but the ideal is to reach this consciousness as much as possible, without killing the spontaneity of action. Conscious action means that one accepts the responsibility of his action and this brings us again to the question of the meaning of all that we do, in other words the question: why do we live.

51

Is our life senseful or senseless? In life a specific action can be senseless, but the total solution of the sense of our life has to be looked for outside of our life; it has to surpass our life. Life is directed toward a personal God, near whom we try to get; then life is senseful. If life were not directed toward God it would be senseless, in the last instance. But if we are directed toward a personal God, then this relation cannot be broken by death; thus there has to exist a form of survival for the human being who strives for a contact with God and the perfection which is connected with it, otherwise it would be senseless. All religious and moral, even intellectual, actions require survival, if they are not to be entirely senseless.

This question is never asked *in abstracto*, but always from a concrete situation in a specific human being, who himself lives in a world limited by space and time. In this world religion gives an answer to the question of the meaning of life. Philosophical thought brings us thus to the religious question and shows us that human responsibility requires from us that we investigate religion, especially the message of the Christian religion. We can accept or refuse it, but this is not a philosophical question any more.

The main ideas of his book of 1893 were repeated, after a long silence, in several important publications, especially in the trilogy: *La pensée* (2 vol., 1934), *L'Etre et les êtres* (1935), and *L'action* (2 vol., 1936-37; this is not a new edition of the book of 1893. The latter was re-edited in 1950). These works are very often prolix, since Blondel had to defend his thought against many false interpretations (positivism, pragmatism, vitalism, idealism, Thomism). The two volumes of his *La Philosophie et l'esprit chrétien* (1944-46) are interesting for philosophy as well as for theology, since they are a philosophical contemplation of the contents of the Christian religion. The influence of Blondel is very important, especially on spiritualism and the progressive school of neo-Thomism. He did not found his own school (see *Paliard).

BOCARDO

Artificial word indicating the fifth mood of the third syllogistic *figure, in which major and conclusion are O propositions, the minor is a; e.g.: Some birds cannot fly; all birds have wings; thus some animals with wings cannot fly.

$$M \ o \ P$$
$$M \ a \ S$$
$$\overline{}$$
$$S \ o \ P$$

BODIN, Jean

Born in Angers 1530, died in Leon 1596. Laid the foundations of politics as a science; clearly anti-Christian. He influenced the *L'Esprit des Lois* of Montesquieu. First one to compose the rules for a philosophy of history. His *Demonomanie* is a mixture of superstition and atheism.

BODY

And soul would be the two distinct, component principles of man. The physical aspect of the body is then opposed to the spiritual frame of the soul, as systematic point of departure of further philosophical observations. This way for Plato and Descartes. There are also several theories about the ontological connection between the two (as in *monism and *dualism).

The body is considered in Aristotelic-Thomism as the individuation principle of the soul, so that this individual man exists. The soul realizes its activities through the body and it is determined by it in its concrete phenomenal form. The soul, on the other hand, incarnates itself in the body. Descartes on the contrary posits the body as the "res extensa," which cannot be reduced to the soul, which latter is characterized as the "res cognitans." The corporeity became then object of physics. The evolution of philosophical and empirical psychology has found only disadvantage in this distinction and objectivation. The validity of the distinction between body and soul has long been contested, because of the determination of the subject of psychology. It is only in the modern anthropology that the body (and soul) were considered in another function than *object* (res). The ideas of philosophy of life defended by °Maine de Biran and Bergson inaugurated this new phase in the conception of the body. It is only the newest form of phenomenology and psychology which posed and tried to give a solution to the problem of corporeity (Marcel, Sartre, Merleau-Ponty, Buytendijk). Not only the corporeity but also the psychical activity (observation, motor etc. . . .) is withdrawn from the pure objectivation.

Corporeity is never given to us as object only. We experience our body from inside, not in the separation object-subject, but always as a quasi-object (Strasser). Man is a body and has a body (Marcel). The analyses of Sartre are very important for the modern anthropology. Sartre distinguishes three dimensions of corporeity. (1) In the normal, irreflexive conduct, man surpasses his body according to the world, i.e. I am not conscious when I act of my body, but I experience the world to which my activities are oriented. (2) For the eye of the spectator is my body only the relation-point of my intentional conduct. The spectator can not see *in* me, but experiences my activity as involved with me through the body. So he knows my innerness. (3) If I realize the other, my body will be the medium of the meeting. In my corporeity I appear before the look of the other. Many strong criticisms have been brought against these fundamental views. P.S.

BOEHME, Jakob 1575-1624.

German philosopher and mystic, for a long time shoemaker in Görlitz. In his mystical writing he shows affinity with and the influence of the great medieval mystics, also of Luther and Schwenckfeld. Paracelsus influenced him in his system of concepts and terminology. He starts from a "groundless" divinity, which is neither good or bad, but pure will from nothing to something. To satisfy this will a splitting has to take place inside the divinity, and thus is created the example of our world of experience, which now is divided between good and evil, and becomes reality because of God's "wrath." Man is also part of this nature; in him also are good and evil, and as an image and part of God he possesses the freedom to choose one or another: i.e., choose between being one's self, the Ego, the world, or a return to and unification with the divinity. The most original part of Böhme's work is found in the doctrine of self-division, the self-realization of the One, which did not become, and its connection with the inevitable genesis of evil. Th. C.v.St.

BOETHIUS, Anicius Manlius Severinus

Born in Rome *ca.* 480, died in

Pavia 524 or 525. Studied Greek philosophy in Athens, and became in 510 minister of Theodoric, king of the Ostrogoths, fell into disgrace, was jailed and later died by order of the king, probably because of his Catholic faith, which was attacked by Theodoric, who was Arian. Boethius discovered the cultural value of the philosophers and wanted to reconcile the treasures of Greek science with the Italo-Gothic civilization. In this he played an important role as educator of the West, especially through his translation of and commentary on the logic of Aristotle and the *Eisagoge* of Porphyrius. He also brought to the attention of the Latin world many Platonic, Aristotelian, Stoic, neo-Platonic and Augustinian ideas in the domain of psychology, metaphysics and ethics. He admired both Plato and Aristotle, and thought that both doctrines could be brought together. He also wrote personal works on logic, mathematics, music, theology (*Opuscula sacra*) and especially the famous *De consolatione philosophiae,* which was composed during his imprisonment. Philosophy appears before him under the shape of a majestic woman, who comforts him and teaches him that real happiness is found in the love of the highest Good and abandonment to divine providence. His role was very important. His works were an example followed in the commentaries and translations of pagan works; he gave fame to the literary genre of the "works of consolation"; he introduced into the West the technical terms used by Aristotle, including a series of important definitions. His commentary of Porphyrius' *Eisagoge* brought about the famous dispute over *universals. The intellectual life of the Middle Ages would have been en-

tirely different if the logic of Aristotle had not been introduced in the West before the 13th century, as was the case with his *Politica.* F.V.S.

BOETHIUS OF DACIA

Born in Sweden, before 1250, died after 1285. *Magister artium* in Paris *ca.* 1270-1277, condemned together with *Siger of Brabant in 1277, was in the papal curia in Oviedo in 1283, possibly became a Dominican. Wrote many commentaries on Aristotle, a small work *De summo bono,* and *De mundi aeternitate.* Like Siger, he taught a heterodox *Aristotelianism.

BOLINGBROKE, Henry St. John Viscount

Born in Battersea 1678, died there 1751. Politician, defends the theory of knowledge of Locke, accepts the existence of God because of the order in the universe, deist. His writings were considered dangerous in England for state and religion. Voltaire admired him very much.

BOLSHEVISM

Extremist political philosophy introduced in Russia, based on the radical interpretation by *Lenin of *Marx's historical *materialism.

BOLZANO, Bernard

Born in Prague 1781, died there 1848. Czech priest, theologian, philosopher, mathematician, long unknown precursor of *phenomenology. Accepts the existence of truth, as having absolute value, independent of any thought, including divine thinking. To this truth belongs also the highest ethical law, which imposes the obligation to promote the happiness of mankind. His metaphysics are related to the monadology of *Leibniz. In politics he defends utopian socialism.

BONAVENTURA

Surname given by St. Francis of Assisi to Joannes Fidenza, born in Balneoregio (near Viterbo) 1221, died in Lyon 1274. After his studies of the liberal arts (probably in Paris) Bonaventura became a Franciscan in Paris, around 1243. He taught at the theological school from 1248 to 1257, became general of the Franciscans in 1257, cardinal in 1273, participated in the ecumenical council at Lyon in 1274 and died there after the council closed. *Doctor Seraphicus.* Bonaventura was aware of the danger of pagan philosophy for Christianity; his entire life was devoted to defending and promoting unity of Christian knowledge. He strongly emphasized this truth, accepted by all orthodox thinkers: for a Christian thinker, philosophy is only a means, a step to acquiring complete wisdom. He condemned more and more strongly such Christian thinkers as *Siger of Brabant and *Boethius of Dacia, who tried to establish philosophy as a definitive and complete wisdom.

The scientific works of Bonaventura belong to theology; the method is primarily theological and the most important sources are the Scriptures and the Fathers of the Church. His theology, however, constantly uses the speculative method and in this sense is based on philosophy which is not definitely established. Many historians, following Gilson, think that Bonaventura taught an Augustinian philosophy, but they acknowledge the fact that in many instances he was influenced by Aristotelianism. We think, however, that the philosophy which Bonaventura received from his Parisian masters was neo-Platonic and an eclectic Aristotelianism, which was generally accepted in Paris before 1250. This Aristotelianism was, however, mixed with Augustinian theologian doctrines, and became an Augustinian aristotelianism. Research in the most important philosophical writings of Bonaventura (theory of knowledge, metaphysics, conception of the material world, psychology) corroborates this opinion. One cannot speak of a philosophical system in Bonaventura's works: he constructed a wonderful theological synthesis, which shows his rich personal talents; the philosophy used in this synthesis is, however, unstable and eclectic: Aristotelianism is worked out in different ways or perfected, and the choice of additional elements is often determined by theological reasons, without taking into full account the rational connection on the philosophical level. The Augustinian "spirit," which is often underlined by historians as the main inspiration of Bonaventura's works, can be found in the synthesis of Christian wisdom but not in his philosophy as such (*see* Aristotelianism, Platonism). F.V.S.

BONNETTY, Augustin

Born in Entrevaux 1798, died in Paris 1879. French priest, philosopher, moderate traditionalist, founder of the *Annales de philosophie chrétienne* (1830). Bonnetty concedes that man can reach truth and certitude about the things he experiences by his own power, but for the knowledge of the existence of God, of the moral law, and immortality, he is dependent upon revelation, which reaches him through tradition.

BOODIN, John Elof 1869-1950.

American idealistic philosopher, professor in Los Angeles.

BOOLE, George 1815-64.
Mathematician and logician, became in 1849 professor at Queen's College in Coek and laid the foundation for mathematical logic in his work: *The Mathematical Analysis of Logic* (1847).

BORDAS-DEMOULIN, Jean-Baptiste
Born in La Bertinie 1798, died in Paris 1859. French mathematician and philosopher, spiritualist, neo-Cartesian. Tries to detach Catholic philosophy from *traditionalism and fideism and reconcile the Church with the principles of the Revolution. Like *Malebranche, he teaches that man by reflection on his own ideas, begins to know, through the divine ideas, the reality of things and so remains the master of his thinking without losing its objective foundation.

BOSANQUET, Bernard 1848-1923.
English neo-Hegelian philosopher. Most important works: *The Principle of Individuality and Value*, 1912; *The Value and Destiny of the Individual*, 1913. Bosanquet teaches that only the Absolute is real in the strict sense. The Absolute is therefore the only real individual. Man has reality only insofar as he participates in this Absolute. Man must therefore strive to transcend himself and lose himself in the Absolute. The Absolute is consequently the ideal of moral striving. This ideal is always partially realized in the state; man therefore must obey the laws of the state. Since state and individual are directed toward the Absolute, the state is not an impediment to the individual's reaching the Absolute; it is a road to the Absolute. The individual, however, is not absorbed in the efforts of the state, for in religion the individual surpasses all laws of the state and believes in the actual existence of the Absolute. B.D.

BOURKE, Vernon J.
Born in 1907. American neo-Thomist, professor at the St. Louis University.

BOUTROUX, Emile 1845-1921.
French spiritualistic philosopher, professor at the Sorbonne. His main work consists of research in the domain of the foundations of the exact sciences. In 1874 his pioneering work *De la contingence des lois de la nature* was published. Boutroux wonders if the deterministic world image, formed by the exact sciences, is defendable. The first thing which imposes itself upon our consciousness is freedom. He inquires then if the exact sciences rightly chose determinism rather than freedom. It appears that in none of the sciences does an absolute necessity prevail. A margin is always left for the contingency, the spontaneous, in other words for freedom itself and for what prepares it. Science does not reveal the essence of nature, but shows us the means by which we can influence nature. A complete explanation of reality is not possible without an appeal to freedom, i.e., the freedom of the knowing man and the freedom of the creating God. B.D.

BOWNE, Border Parker 1847-1910.
American idealistic philosopher, very much influenced by *Lotze.

BRADLEY, Francis Herbert 1846-1924.
English neo-Hegelian, professor at Oxford. Most important work: *Appearance and reality*. 1893. He was the leading figure of the neo-Hegelian school by the end of the century. Relation is the central concept in his thought. Every being is

identical with the totality of relations, which it does not have, but which it *is*. This idea brings him to the concept of the inseparable connection, i.e., the unity, of reality. There is only one reality, which shows itself in different complex structures of relations. This unique reality is the absolute idea, which manifests itself in the subject as interior and in the object as exterior. There is therefore no essential difference between subject and object. This does not mean that the object aspect of reality does not show many inner contradictions. These indicate to us that exterior reality is only semblance, because through the subject the contradictions are abolished in the unity of the idea. This again does not mean that the reality of the idea is a pure abstraction; it is, on the contrary, the only concrete thing, but it is at the same time general. It is general because everything is idea, but for the same reason it is concrete, because it comprises everything. B.D.

BRAHMAN

Central "concept" in Indian thought. The least improbable hypothesis about the original meaning of the term corresponds with what it expressed actually for the Indians for centuries: the firm ground, the last, only solid basis, on which all phenomenal and temporal things rest, from which they come and to which they return. Brahman is that with which all things, including living beings, are united, although it is not realized and experienced because of blindness (unacquaintance with this truth).

BRANDEIS, Louis Dembitz 1856-1961

U.S. Supreme Court Justice whose once seemingly radical views have become orthodox. Greatly influenced by Oliver Wendell Holmes, Jr., in stressing the historical development of law, the necessity of adapting legislation to economic and social change, and the broad social responsibilities of jurists.

BRENTANO, Franz 1838-1917.

German philosopher, professor in Vienna. The center of his thought is the idea of intentionality. The phenomena of consciousness are not absorbed by their content, but point at an object, toward which consciousness is directed. In knowledge we can distinguish three aspects: the psychical aspect, in which knowledge is experienced; the logical aspect, for which knowledge has value; and the intentional aspect, which comprises the relationship between knowledge and its object. Evidence is the criterion of the truth of our knowledge, which is on the one hand logical exactitude and on the other hand intentional reality. Logical exactitude is evident in itself; this is also true of intentional reality, inasmuch as it has a relation to inner experience. Logical exactitude and intentional reality of inner experience are in themselves immediately evident; this evidence applies also to the intentional reality of exterior experiences, but not immediately: only the existence of an outer world can make understandable the intentional reality of the experience. He influenced the °Polish School, and °Husserl and °Meinong. B.D.

BRIDGMAN, P. W. 1882-

Professor of mathematics and natural philosophy at Harvard University; also an authority on thermodynamics, electricity and other physical sciences. Works: *The Logic of Modern Physics* (1927), *The Nature of Physical Theory*

(1936) and *The Intelligent Individual and Society* (1938).

BRIGHTMAN, Edgar Sheffield 1884-1953.
American philosopher, personalistic idealist, professor in Boston.

BROAD, Charlie Dunbar
Born 1887. English neo-realistic philosopher, professor at Cambridge. Most important work: *The Mind and Its Place in Nature*, 1925. Broad is pre-eminently analytic. He is not interested in constructing a philosophical system, but in the exact analysis of fundamental concepts used in daily life and in science. Experience is achieved by the cooperation of object and subject. The content of experience is different from the object, to which observation is directed. The object is never completely known in observation, our knowledge is always fragmentary. The object exists not only in space but also in time. Our knowledge of things is thus never completed, because the thing is identical with its own history. Since every thing is composed of elements, it cannot be known completely from these elements; a new combination of elements can show qualities which cannot be deducted from the elements as such (emergency). We have to explain the origin of life in the same way. B.D.

BROWN, Thomas
Born in Kilmabreck (Scotland) 1778, died in Brompton 1820. Scottish philosopher, united common-sense philosophy with °Hume's empiricism and prepared in this manner English °positivism.

BRUNO, Giordano
Born in Nola 1548, died in Rome 1600 at the stake after eight years' incarceration. From 1563 to 1576 he was a Dominican. He later went through most of the important cities of Europe to teach his philosophy, which attacked the Aristotelian concept of nature and Christian doctrine. The world, he said, is eternal and there are many world systems. This was not the reason for his condemnation by the Inquisition, nor was it his admiration for the theories of Copernicus, but his theological opinions. He defends a pantheistic neo-Platonism. All hypostases: God, intellect, world, soul, matter, can be reduced to one, which is the one and at the same time manifold life of the universe. God is the substance of all composition; the substance of bodies is as indestructible as that of spirits; divine essence is the same thing as matter, which is as eternal as space. The world exists from eternity. The soul can go from one body to another and even be in two bodies at the same time. The Holy Spirit is the soul of the world. Before Adam and Eve, from whom the Hebrews descend, two other beings existed, ancestors of all other people. In the universe there is no place for heaven or hell; there is therefore no eternal punishment. One does not have to believe because of authority but because of evidence. Free choice does not exist. Natural law is clear enough in telling us what is good and wrong. Christ is not God.

In a didactic poem *De triplici minimo* he accepts the existence of the smallest part in metaphysics as well as in mathematics and physics. Thought can divide indefinitely, but one has to accept a first principle in reality. The concept of a continuum is connected with discrete unities.

Like Raymundus Lullus, he considers memory a résumé of thought (*De umbris idearum*). Thought and Nature both originate in the highest, divine unity; but Nature, formed according to divine ideas and carrying their image, is as object principally directed to thought.

In *Eroici furori* he endeavors to reach God in His complete unity and beauty, through the highest unfolding of intellectual consciousness and unlimited love.

Bruno excepts from his system, as did Ficino from his Platonism, true religious unity and he objects therefore to all reformers. Since this feeling of unity is so important in his work, he influenced Spinoza. The disputes with Church authorities and his tragic death gave him a greater reputation than his capricious doctrine. H.R.

BRUNSCHVICG, Leon 1869-1944.

French idealistic philosopher, professor at the Sorbonne. Main work: *Le progrès de la conscience dans la philosophie occidentale*, 1927. Brunschvicg gives an idealistic interpretation of the human mind, as it reveals itself in the construction of the sciences. He holds a special place in French philosophy between the two world wars. He marks a strong approach to positivism. The mind is not directed to objects, but the activity of the mind itself creates those objects. Philosophy is not interested in objects but in their production. This is most accurately experienced in the processes of the exact sciences. Mathematics and physics are the sciences which most reveal the activity of the mind. A concept is not an image of an object, but an activity of the mind by which truth is created. The mind, which is known through its activity, is not transcendent, but is the human mind itself. The humanism which follows from this is a humanism which sees man as absolutely autonomous. Man is only dependent on his own mind and it is his duty to discover it. Although Brunschvicg's thought is strongly directed toward the unity of idealism, it cannot be identified completely with it. In several works, among others those about Montaigne and Pascal, he is interested in the religious problematics of the concrete man and treats them in a way which changes idealistic systematics in the direction of a more existential thought. B.D.

BUBER, Martin

Born 1878. Jewish existential philosopher of religion. Died 1965.

BUCHANAN, George 1506-1583.

British historian and educator of King James I of England. Teaches that God is the creator of worldly states, but that law and justice are fundamental in the constitution of the state. The King will apply laws which are accepted by the people, but he is always responsible before the citizens and can even be brought to court.

BUCHNER, Louis

Born in Darmstadt 1824, died there 1899. German physician and philosopher, he spread the theories of German *materialism through his book: *Kraft und Stoff* (1854).

BUDDHA, Gautama c. 563-483 B.C.

The term "Buddha" means "the enlightened one who enlightens," and Buddhism is understood as the possession of perfect wisdom and supernatural powers. The first of a long line of Buddhas is the one named Siddhartha, or Sakyamuni, of the Gautama family, a warrior caste who wandered through the East as a mendicant, and finally founded an order.

BUDDHISM

Indian doctrine of salvation, developed from the teachings of Gautama ($\pm$ 560-480 B.C.), named Buddha, i.e., the enlightened one. Like many other Indian preachers Buddha directed his doctrine to those who were living outside the normal society, in order to teach them how to be saved (*Yoga). He also indicated to his disciples a "Path," a series of rules, which would enable them to follow him in reaching the redeeming insight. Buddha taught a middle course which avoids sensual activities and attachment to the world (ritualism inclusive, since the Vedic rites pursued worldly profit), as well as a one-sided severe asceticism.

His doctrine consists of the four "noble truths" and the Eightfold Path. The truths are: the existence of suffering or unrest, discomfort in birth, age, sickness, death, etc.; the cause of this suffering is the insatiable but senseless desire for wordly goods; the possibility of release, i.e., the destruction and expulsion of this desire, is the path which leads us to the solution. Only practice, when one personally follows that path, can explain the truth of this doctrine. The Path is eightfold: an introduction, complete confidence in Buddha as the competent leader and in the correctness of the doctrine: 2-7; the so-called ethics (sīla), personal moral attitude (pity, amiability, honesty, generosity, chastity, temperance, avoidance of temptations, etc.), which is not a goal in itself or a divine law (Buddhism is atheistic) but necessary for salvation.

Ignorance of these values for salvation, and the transgression of these ethical rules which necessarily follows this ignorance, lead to the maintenance of the potencies which attach us to our bodily state and reincarnation. These potencies, the so-called dharmas—to which belong in general all elements of being—are the only reality. They form, by combination, forever hanging empirical phenomena; they gather together as in bundles and attach themselves to beings— the existence of the soul and matter as distinguished from the soul is denied—their sum establishes the surplus of karman (*see* karman). In the last part of the Path, the samādhi (the so-called concentration), one reaches the consciousness of teaching and having gone through the four stages, in which one totally dies to the world, loses the notion of outside objects, etc., and reaches the state of arhat, "qualified"; the personality changes and one is out of reach of worldly powers. J.G.

BUFFIER, Claude, S. J.
Born in Warsaw 1661, died in Rouen 1737. French writer of literature, asceticism, history and philosophy. Moderate Cartesian, attacks Descartes with Locke. He had influence on the *Scottish School of Thomas Reid.

BURCKHARDT, Jakob 1818-1897
A historian and teacher of history at Basle, whose *Culture of the Renaissance* (1860) is one of the landmarks of nineteenth-century scholarship.

BURIDAN
See Joannes Buridanus.

BURKE, Edmund 1729-1797
An Irishman who became one of the greatest orators in the history of the British Parliament, he was author of many political pamphlets and essays. Especially fought changes in the British Constitution, King George III's attempts to enslave Parliament, and the French Revolution.

BURNET, John 1863-1928.
English historian of Greek philosophy.

BURROUGHS, John 1837-1921

American naturalist, he was also a scientist, poet and philospher in his descriptions of natural phenomena, and a disciple of Bergson and Emerson. Works: *Birds and Poets* (1877), *Ways of Nature* (1905), *Accepting the Universe* (1920).

BUTLER, Joseph 1692-1752.

British theologian and moralist, at first bishop of Bristol and later of Durham. Sees the world as a harmonic system, in which wisdom, justice and goodness reign. Follower of Shaftesbury's doctrine of the "moral sense," he elaborates it further into an ethical theory. "Moral sense" is autonomous, he says; actions which comply with the criteria of the conscience are good.

He admits, however, a divine providence, which gives man, in an other than worldly life, the possibility of achieving his striving for virtue and happiness.

BUTLER, Samuel 1835-1902

English novelist, essayist, satirist. His *Erewhon* (1872) compared to Swift's *Gulliver's Travels* and Voltaire's *Candide* as a commentary on human existence. His masterpiece was, *The Way of All Flesh* (1903), an ironic dissection of his time and culture.

BUZZETTI, Vincenzo

Born in Piacenzo 1777, died there 1824. Italian priest and philosopher, was the first in Italy, in spite of the various philosophical theories of his time, to return to Thomistic principles.

C

C

As capital, symbol to indicate the possibility of a direct *reduction of the syllogistic moods in *Cesare, *Camestres and *Calemes to the moods in *Celarent of the first figure. As a small letter it is the symbol indicating the possibility of a figurative *conversion; *contraposition.

CABANIS, Pierre Jean George

Born in Roznac 1757, died in Reuil 1808. Professor of hygiene, follower of the sensualism of Condillac, constructs a parallel between physiology, psychology and ethics.

CAIRD, Edward 1835-1908.

English neo-Hegelian, professor at Oxford. He is convinced that critism of Kant necessarily leads to the idealism of Hegel. In Hegel's philosophy a unity is obtained to which Kant already strived. This unity is not, however, an abstraction, but a concrete unity of counterparts; it is the self-realizing Absolute. This Absolute is God. It is the highest knowability. It can, however, reveal itself only gradually to human beings, since man has first to learn how to endure the light of the highest knowability. Caird created, thanks to his clear and vigorous style, a great enthusiasm for the Hegelian philosophy in England.

CAIRD, John 1820-1898.

Elder brother of Edward, introduced neo-Hegelianism into English theology.

CAJETANUS, Thomas de Vio, O.P.

Born in Gaeta 1468, died in Rome 1534. General of the Dominicans, Cardinal and papal delegate in Germany in the beginning of the Reformation (1518-1519). Commentator of the writings of Thomas Aquinas; wrote about philosophy, theology and exegesis. Best known is his *De nominum analogia* (1498). He objects to the Averroistic rationalism of Petrus Pomponazzi, to prove the immortality of the soul. Renovator of Thomism, which he proposes in a strictly systematic form.

CALCULUS, (logical)

Is in broad sense identical with formal logic. Curry proposed to reserve this name for theories with bound variables. This term is however generally used to indicate the parts of logical algebra in which simple methods for decisions and solutions are used.

CALEMES

Artificial word to indicate the second mood of the fourth syllogistic *figure, in which the major is an a-proposition, minor and conclusion however are e-propositions. E.g.: true knowledge is universally prevailing; what universally prevails is not a pure personal opinion; a pure personal opinion is thus not true knowledge.

P a M
M e S
————
S e P

CALLICLES

A possibly fictitious character from Plato's *Gorgias*. He pushes the effects of principleless ethics of the *sophists to the extreme. Plato let him explain the law of the strongest in a way which reminds us of Nietzsche.

CAMBRIDGE

In Cambridge, in the 2nd half of the 17th century, several thinkers, many of them clergymen, opposed *empiricism. Starting from the intuition of Descartes they reached a new Platonism, sometimes mysticism. *Ralph Cudworth* (1617-1688) defended the final causes in physics and explained the organism with a kind of Platonic idea, connected with the Aristotelian entelechy. In psychology he adopted the theory of innate concepts, in ethics innate moral ideas, as being as valid as the mathematics which have their origin in the divine mind. He considered Christianity as the norm of Platonism (not as Plethon). *Henry More* (1614-1687) turned away from Descartes and reached mysticism: all bodies are penetrated by spirits; everything is filled with the world spirit, which is a tool of God; immaterial space does not exist. God is also extensive, otherwise He could not be omniscient and all-moving. *John Smith* (1616-1652) thought that we experience the immortality of the soul in a higher illumination; although we cannot give a logical proof thereof. Also belonging to the Cambridge School: *Whichcote* (1610-1683) and *Nathanael Culverwell* (died 1651?) H.R.

CAMESTRES

Artificial word to indicate the first mood of the second syllogistic *figure, in which the major is an a-proposition, minor and conclusion are e-propositions. Every jealous man is a slanderer; no saint is a slanderer; therefore no saint is jealous.

$$P\ a\ M$$
$$\overline{S\ e\ M}$$
$$S\ e\ P$$

CAMPANELLA, Tommaso, O. P.

Born in Stilo (Calabria) 1568, died in Paris 1639. Defends with Telesio a "sensism": all knowledge is only a change of sensory awareness. He attacks the natural philosophy of Aristotle's works and exalts nature itself. Since he was also involved in political and social reforms in Spain, he lived there for thirty years in captivity. According to Campanella there are no universal ideas; he does not end in pessimism, because the hesitating man is certain that he hesitates and can therefore come to knowledge of himself, from which he can reach certainty about other things, even the higher being. He paves the way for the *"cogito"* of Descartes and his proof of the existence of God. We also experience God in an inner contact. In the process through which creatures come forth from God, the pure essence is mixed more and more with not-being. Everything which is, is animated and possesses perception, even space. Campanella defends a kind of animistic pantheism. In his *Civitatis solis* he plans, as did Plato, an idealistic state, in which homes, land, wives and children are community property and in which eugenics are applied. This communistic state is theocratic; there has to be a supreme perfect high priest, to whom the political powers are also submitted. H.R.

CAMUS, Albert 1913-1960.
French existentialist philosopher and literary writer, considers existence as absurd. God does not exist. We have to live humanly and humanely.

CANDIDUS OF FULDA
Died 845. Successor of °Rhabanus Mauras as head of the School of Fulda, author of *Dicta* in which we can find some theses of Stoicism and Augustinianism.

CANO, Melchior, O.P.
Born in Tarancon 1509, died in Toledo 1560. Theologian. Main work: *De locis theologicis,* treatise on the method of theology as a science.

CANTOR, Georg 1845-1918.
Became professor in Halle (1879) and originated the theory of systems of numbers, which had been discussed for a long time but for modern mathematics is of fundamental importance. For Cantor this theory is based on the comprehension axioms, which can be formulated as follows: (1) Mathematical entities which have a certain property in common compose a system, determined by this property. The entities form the elements of this system. (2) Systems are mathematical entities and can be elements of a system. (3) Systems having the same elements are identical. The unlimited application of these axioms led to the °paradoxes.

CARDANO, Geronimo
Born in Pavia 1501, died in Rome 1576. Italian mathematician, physician and scholar in hylozoistic natural philosophy. A primeval matter fills all space, in which there is no vacuum; in all bodies a soul is the cause of motion. The duty of man is to unite the eternal with the finite. His goal is to harmonize religious certitude with scientific research; God can also be mathematically understood. Spiritual and temporal power should not be separated (contrary to Machiavelli).

CARDOZO, Benjamin Nathan 1870-1938
United States Supreme Court Justice and one of the great American philosophers of law, devoted to the rights of the individual and opponent of vested interests.

CARLYLE, Thomas 1795-1881
English essayist, distinguished from other British philosophers by his penchant for emotional expression, detestation of cold logic and intellectual abstraction, and concern for society as a brotherhood of men. Most famous work: *Heroes and Hero Worship* (1840).

CARNAP, Rudolf
Born 1891. German-American mathematician and philosopher, professor in Prague and Chicago, was one of the few auditors of °Frege and became the most important logician in the °"Wiener Kreis" (Vienna Circle) and leading spokesman of neo-positivism. He is now professor in Los Angeles. Died 1970.

CARNEADES OF CYRENE
The most important representative of the so-called New °Academy (middle of the 2nd century B.C.), very penetrating mind and brilliant orator. Strong opponent of dogmatism, especially of the Stoicism of °Chrysippus. He renews the attack of °Arcesilaus on the Stoic criterion of truth and opposes, with classical arguments, the existence of the gods, indicates inconsistencies in the concept of god and refutes the foundations of the mantics. In ethics he opposes the ground ideas of the three dog-

matic systems (Plato, Aristotle and the Stoics), i.e., natural law, which is rooted in the order of the things. Man is not naturally just and what is virtuous does not lead to happiness.

The *principle of probability* which Carneades opposes to the dogmatic concept of truth is not only a directive for our actions (as is the case for the eulogon of Arcesilaus). It is an empirical principle, which also has meaning on the theoretical level: one has to experience things as much as possible in order to perfect as far as possible one's degree of certitude. C.J.d.V.

CAROLUS, Josephus a S. Floriano, O.F.M.
Tries to unite Scotism with the contemporary natural sciences in: *Johannis Duns Scoti philosophia* (1771).

CARR, Herbert Wildon 1857-1931.
American idealistic philosopher, professor in Los Angeles.

CARREL, Alexis 1873-1944.
French physician and cultural philosopher.

CARTIER, Gallus, O.S.R.
Born in Porrentuy 1693, died 1777. Lawyer and philosopher. In his *Philosophia eclectica* (1756) he unites the innate concept of God and the clear ideas of Descartes with the theses of Locke.

CARUS, Paul 1852-1919
German-born philosopher who emigrated to America; editor of *Open Court,* a forum for the discussion of religious and ethical subjects, and *The Monist.* Calling himself "an atheist who loves God," he was in fact a pantheist, steering a course between idealistic metaphysics and materialism.

CASE, Thomas 1844-1925.
English philosopher, precursor of neo-realism.

CASOTTI, Mario
Born 1896. Italian neo-Thomist.

CASSIODORUS, Aurelius
Born in Squillace (Calabria) *ca.* 487, died in Vivarium *ca.* 565, disciple of *Boethius. At first minister of King Theodoric, then became Benedictine monk in Vivarium, monastery which he had erected on his property; there he taught the liberal arts.

CASSIRER, Ernst 1874-1945.
German neo-Kantian philosopher. Most of his works treat with the history of philosophy. But his own ideas are apparent in these works as they are clearly expressed in his *Philosophie der symbolischen Formen,* 1923-1929. He belongs to the *Marburger School, but he occupies a particular place in its history, since he applies the way of thinking of his school to the structure of the spiritual sciences. Cassirer transcends the pure theory of knowledge in his attempt to describe the concrete motion of the mind. Here he enters the Hegelian way of thought. B.D.

CASUALISM
Theory that all things and events come to be by *chance.

CASUISTRY
Part of *ethics in which universal moral principles are applied to the so-called *casus conscientiae* (cases of conscience). They still have a universal value, although they are in each case particular and originate, in a case of a collision of duties, in one point. Casuistry was used by the Stoics, the Jews and in Christianity by the scholastics. Casuistry is contestable in ethics, if it brings man to give up his own

responsibility for his decisions by appealing to general solutions, which are very often too subtle. This was the reason for the attacks of Pascal upon the Jesuits and their casuistry.

CATALEPSIS
Or cataleptic representation (Greek: katalambano, to seize), in stoic philosophy a representation, by which the intellect, in a way, seizes reality tangibly and is forced to accept it.

CATEGOREME
See predictables.

CATEGORICAL
Unconditional. *See* imperative, judgment, syllogism.

CATEGORICITY
Characterizes a system which determines, as it were, completely its meaning in respect to the deductive theory. It is required that all realizations of the system be °isomorphic.

CATEGORY
(Greek: *kategoria*) or predicate (Latin: *praedicamentum*). A specific, not further reducible and thus highest, group or class under which one can classify things. Aristotle considers it in the first place as an arrangement of concepts, thought as possible predicates. This arrangement is also important in metaphysics in as much as it is based on ontological grounds. There would be ten categories. The first expresses the substance, the other nine express accidental properties: quantity, quality, relation, place, time, action, passion, position and state (*h a b i t u s*). Kant distinguishes twelve categories, which have only a logical meaning. He calls them: "*Stammbegriffe des reinen Verstandes*": the a priori forms of thought under which sensory experiences are ordered. L.D.R.

CATEGORY, Aesthetic
Called the universally distinguishable variations of the aesthetic, as this principally appears as a term of intuition. The principal universal categories are: the °beautiful, the °sublime, the °gracious, the °tragic, the °comic, the °ugly.

CATEGORY, Semantic
By Polish logicians characterized as the collection of all things whose appellations can replace a kind of variable. The so called types are such categories.

CATHARSIS
Initially the beneficial influence of the tragic play on the spectator. The impression of the suprahuman grandiose purifies the affective life, resulting in a strong and renovated psychical harmony. We can also apply this purifying and harmonizing action to every inner artistic experience or aesthetic experience although this action is highest in the contemplation of tragedy. The foundation of the catharsis lies in the fact that man, in intimate aesthetic contact with a sensibly-appearing absolute sense of being, will feel his own relation with the absolute and therefore will be liberated from his own littleness, self-sufficiency and psychic-utilitarian attitudes. L.V.K.

CAUSA SUI
(Latin: Cause of itself) Nothing can be the cause of itself or be under the same aspect both cause and caused. The free will is sometimes called *causa sui* to indicate that it determines itself. Spinoza says of God that He is *causa sui* to express the fact that his essence includes existence and can only be considered as existing.

CAUSALITY

That which is proper to the cause as such; also the real relation of a cause to its effect. Man has a tendency to presuppose a cause as a necessary condition for everything which begins or changes, but can this be justified by philosophy? Those who reject the principle of causality, find psychological, critica-theoretical or pragmatical reasons to explain our spontaneous tendency to accept this principle. Those who accept the principle differ widely in its interpretation. They appeal to empirical data, to analysis of concepts and reduction to a more general concept (e.g., to the principle of *sufficient reason, or of *contradiction), to an immediate view into the truth of the principle, to phenomenological descriptions of typical cases of causality. To be of universal metaphysical value, the principle of causality has to be based formally on the cognition of being: we would assert that it is contained in the participation of being, which characterizes beings in their multiplicity and connects them mutually as well as with the common foundation of being. L.D.R.

CAUSALITY, Principle of

One of the first principles of thought, which indicates in what case causality appears. It is formulated in different ways. The much used formula "Everything which comes into being is caused" is too narrow, because an effect is not only what succeeds something in time, but everything which is dependent. It is therefore better to say, "Everything which is due to something but not by virtue of its essence is due to it by virtue of a cause."

The principle of causality is not created by pure analysis of the concept that appears as subject. In this sense the principle is not analytical. Since it is not, however, a generalization founded only upon experience (which would give only probability), but is necessarily accepted in its universality as evident, we can call it synthetically *a priori. This however, has to be explained in a way other than *Kant did. He attributed a value to the principle only so far as our experiences are condensed in it under the subjective category of causality; it applies only to sensory phenomena in time and space. On the contrary, we must say that the principle of causality is founded on the view that all being as being is intelligible, thus has *reason or ground for being. This ground for being, which has firstly to be considered as an immanent ground, will be looked for, in those beings who have not in themselves sufficient reason for being, (because they are not what they are by virtue of their own being) outside of these beings, in what is in virtue of its essence. Although the principle of causality is valid for all finite beings, it is found more in the natural sciences. It is used here, however, in a narrower sense, because under cause is mostly considered only the work cause. Only a constant relation between two phenomena is often asserted (e.g., between warmth and radiation) so that the nature of the relation is totally left out of consideration. In contemporary physics, and particularly in quantum mechanics (see *quanta), the constant character is even reduced to a statistical average. J.P.

CAUSE

The real principle which plays a role in the existence and the way of being of a reality. Aristotle distinguished two interior and two exterior causes. The interior causes are: the *material* cause and the *formal* cause; which respectively constitute the being as the principle of determinability and the principle of determination. The exterior causes are the *efficient* cause and the *final* cause: i.e. the "from which" and the "why" of this being. Under the influence of Plato a fifth cause has been accepted; the °exemplar, exterior formal cause; this is the image according to which a being got its definiteness. When one speaks of cause one generally wants to indicate the exterior causes and especially the efficient cause.

There are many causes and they form, as the beings do, an ordered whole, their terms are connected by coordination and subordination. The *auxiliary* cause is the tool one uses, it is dependent from the *main* cause (the person who uses the tool), and the means get its attraction as such from the end; but only by collaboration of the one and the other will the effect be realized.

First cause is God; *second* cause is any other cause, if one accepts that all others, as creatures, depend completely in the same way from God, and no place remains for a third or fourth cause. In an analogous sense God can be called the last final cause.

One distinguishes also sometimes the *nearest* and *last* cause, in order to determine, by this distinction, science and philosophy. It is however difficult to see the sense of this distinction. Nearer is the cause which acts immediately on the considered effect but which is itself dependent from another (in this sense farther) cause; last is then the uncaused cause of the prior. It still is an unsolved question how one could distinguish by these means the philosophy from science. One has probably to consider as nearer cause and its effect the empirical antecedents and its consequences; last cause would then indicate the exterior cause in the philosophical and meta-empirical (and not in the empirical) sense of the word: but the choice of these terms, nearer and last can hardly be defended. L.D.R.

CELARENT
Artificial word to indicate the second mood of the first syllogistic °figure, in which major and conclusion are e-propositions, the minor an a-proposition. E-g: Mammals are not fish; whales are mammals; therefore whales are not fish.

M e P
S a M
———
S e P

CERCIDAS OF MEGALOPOLIS
2nd half of the 3rd century B.C. General, politician and legislator in his native city. Wrote poems in which he gave an interpretation of the cynical attitude in life: sublimation of simplicity, criticism of the unjust division of the worldly goods, and liberal attitude toward traditional religion.

CERTITUDE
Being certain, situation of the mind wihch, without fear for contradiction, agrees with a statement. All °doubt is therefore excluded. Opposites: °doubt, °m e a n i n g, °probability. The judgment pronounced with this kind of firmness can be called certain. Although certitude requires a foundation in the object of the knowledge, it is still a quality of the knower and his judgment; that which bases the certitude in an object should not be called certitude (except by at-

tribution-analogy), but *evidence. Certitude indeed, which is more than supposed certitude, originates through the influence of the object which reveals itself directly or indirectly, or also through the mediation of a witness, to whom the object reveals itself directly. One can therefore distinguish (immediate or mediate) certitude of evidence or certitude of faith.

If the evidence which is the basis of the certitude, is absolute then we can call it absolute (often called metaphysical) certitude. If however the connection between mediate and immediate evidence is not absolute, then we call it physical (i.e. based on the experience of our nature) or moral (i.e. based on the experience of our human actions) certitude. Although they do not exclude all possibility of the contrary, they still do exclude all fear for the opposite.

Moral certitude is then true, although imperfect certitude. The human activity is free, but not necessarily unmotivated; the motives of actions are indeed determined by self-determination, but still against the background of the chosen aim of life. The human activity can therefore have a certain regularity, which can be stronger in the measure that man acts more freely, i.e. more from his own essence. Through a participating understanding of the world of motives of the other, it is possible to acquire certitude about his actions. This moral certitude has sometimes relation to the general (a mother will love her child), sometimes to the individual nature of the other. The certitude of faith, which rests on the human credibility of a witness, is such a moral certitude.

One speaks sometimes of moral (or also called practical) certitude,

where it is in fact a more probable meaning, which, although it does not exclude all fear for the contrary, it still is a sufficiently justified basis for responsible action. J.P.

CESARE
Artificial word indicating the third mood of the second syllogistic *figure, in which major and conclusion are e-propositions, the minor an a-proposition. E.g.: No ruminant is carnivore; all beasts of prey are carnivores; therefore beasts of prey are not ruminants.

$$P \ e \ M$$
$$S \ a \ M$$
$$\overline{}$$
$$S \ e \ P$$

CH'AN
See Zen.

CHANCE
In natural processes one speaks of chance when something does not happen according to a specific rule or order. In human activity however chance is that which happens without intention.

In both cases therefore does chance point out the missing cause, not in an absolute but in a relative sense. When an accident happens and a doctor passes by, then we have chance, not however if the doctor was called. In the first case there was a cause for the fact that the doctor was there at that particular moment (he was, for instance, on a sickcall) but this cause was independent from the accident. When a die is thrown and shows "six", then it is a chance, because that "six" is an effect of a series of accidentally converging causes; when the die is however fixed with lead on that side, then the "six" is no chance; because the throw follows necessarily from the structure of the die.

The missing causality in chance

is therefore the lack of a coordinating causality. In an accidental event therefore come two or more causal series in an accidental way together. A.G.M.v.M.

CHANGE

Opposed and to remaining equal, and to creating or annihilating. It is therefore essential in a change, that the changed thing remains in a certain respect, the same, while it does not remain the same in another respect. If the former is lacking then exists annihilation in the strict sense of the word, not change. If the latter is lacking then we have no reason at all to speak of change. The changing of something points to a certain non-simplicity. What is completely simple can not change.

In the experience we speak of substantial and accidental change. In the *accidental change*, as for instance becoming older, the substantial "esse" remains equal to itself during the change. It is the same human being who is now older. What differs is his age, which is not the essence of the man. It should be noted that an accident is always a further determination of the substance. That in an accidental change the substance remains the same, is therefore an abstract way of expressing it, it has only relation to the substantial "esse" when it is considered abstractly as *principle* of substantial being. Seen concretely we can say that this particular man is changed in his substantial being in as much as an accidental definiteness of the substance became another.

Accidental changes are divided into qualitative (related to a quality), quantitative (related to the quantity) changes and changes of place.

The *substantial change* is a change in which the substantial "esse" does not remain the same, e.g. die. The possibility of substantial change points to a non-simplicity in the substance itself. This brought Aristotle to his theory of *hylemorphism, according to which the substantial "esse" itself exists in a potential and an actual principle (primitive matter and form of being). A.G.M.v.M.

CHANNING, W. E. 1780-1843.

American philosopher, developed transcendentalism, which accepts supersensual truth, which is grounded in the soul as such.

CHAOS

(Greek: *chaos*, abyss) The formless, completely lawless and disorderly. Plato, for instance, considered it the orderless condition of matter before the world-former (Demiurge) introduced order and regularity, changing chaos into the cosmos.

CHARACTER

(Greek: stamp, mark), structure of individual properties (especially in relation to feeling and will). The popular language has added a moral meaning; this is not used in psychological sense, except perhaps in so far as a person lives in accordance with the norms he himself accepts. Both popular and scientific psychology are interested in the resistance of man against the human environment (independence as opposed to subject to be influenced) CHARACTEROLOGY (Bahnsen), doctrine of the individual disposition of man.

CHARACTERISTIC, The

Middle form, which connects the beautiful with the onaesthetic plain and unspectacular; while in the beautiful the individual features come together with the general, these particular features assert themselves more as such in the characteristic. Since the pure beautiful is rather unusual, most of the aesthetical forms are somewhat mingled with the characteristic. *See* also characteristic *art.

CHARACTERISTICA Universalis
Name given by Leibniz to the symbolism which would express all scientific concepts.

CHARTIER, Emile
See Alain.

CHARTRES, School of
Founded in 900 by *Fulbert, in the 12th century an important center for the study of the profane sciences, where the limits of the seven liberal arts were often crossed. Ancient culture was highly honored and philosophy was inspired by *Platonism.

CHERBURY, Edward Herbert
English politician, diplomat and philosopher, from 1619 to 1624 English ambassador in Paris, was a friend of Hugo Grotius and in 1640 entered the army of the Prince of Orange. He can be considered one of the first deists, because in his doctrine *revealed* faith is dependent on human reason, which is also the norm for ethics.

CHERNYSHEVSKY, Nicolai Gavrilovich 1828-1889
Russian philosopher who suffered imprisonment for his socialistic views under Czarism. His novel, *What Is To Be Done?*, written in prison, was a source of inspiration to Russian revolutionaries until the Revolution of 1917.

CHINESE PHILOSOPHY
5th century B.C.: *Confucius, moralistic traditionalism. Since the 4th century B.C. different schools developed. *Confucianism is represented by *Mencius and *Hsün

Tzu; *Laoism* by *Lao Tzu and *Chuang Tzu; *legalism* (absolutism, ideal of the legal norm) by *Han Fei Tzu and Shang Yang; mohism (pacifism, humaneness, dialectics) by *Moti. Since the 4th century A.D., Chinese Buddhist *philosophy*, with the most important school of *Zen. After the 10th century, the revival of Confucianism and its definite systematization; *Chu Hsi, Wang Yang-ming.

CHOICE
Decision between several possibilities. The moment of choice is a phase of the process of the will. Here the free act, preceding the action, is actually made. *See* also: Freedom of the will.

CHOICENEGATION
The difference between choicenegation and exclusionnegation is made by the *Significa, which opposes indicative to emotional elements of meaning. The choicenegation has an indicative character; it supposes a disjunction of positive possibilities, e.g. big or small, so that to "not-big" the concept "small" corresponds. The character of an exclusionnegation is on the contrary mostly emotional or purely formal. In "infinite", "empty" one has an exclusionnegation in view, so that, according to Mannoury, they do not have really an indicative meaning. R.F.

CHRISTIAN PHILOSOPHY
The term Christian philosophy is often used to indicate philosophical thought which expresses the Christian convictions of a thinker. But this is a difficult question, which produced in the twenties many discussions in France, by Bréhier, Gilson, Forest, Sertillanges, Blondel, Maritain, Jolivet. Later the same question was discussed in other countries and be-

71

came a real controversy involving non-Christian philosophers, as well as Catholic and Protestant thinkers. In general, all agree that one can speak of philosophy only when the inner construction of thought does not use the data of the revelation as such. Christian thinking that starts from the Bible can only be theology, not philosophy.

The philosophy of the °idea of law takes another point of view: the Christian, because he is a Christian, can only start his thought with the Bible, without being necessarily a theologian. Even if the thought of a Christian is not openly based on the Bible, is it not influenced by revelation? The °neo-Thomists generally make this distinction: from nature, insofar as he is Christian, the Christian thinker will be impregnated by Christianity in his whole personality. When this thinker thinks philosophically, however, he makes an abstraction of the truths of revelation and uses only rational conceived truths, for the foundation as well as for the development of his thought. Since faith has no part in the formal development of philosophy, many authors reject the word combination "Christian philosophy" as a contradiction in terms. Thinkers who are oriented toward °existential philosophy, Protestant theologians and defenders of the philosophy of the law-idea contend that philosophy for the Thomist becomes a purely formal question, which does not involve the personality as totality, as has always been the case in the history of philosophy. The neo-Thomist, however, answers to this that the rationality of philosophical thought is only saved when one retains the distinction between faith and purely intellectual knowledge, between theology and philosophy. This

does not exclude the fact that both philosophy and theology reach the complete human being, but approach him in different ways. B.D.

CHRYSIPPUS
Born 277 B.C. in Cyprus, died 204. Third scholarch of the °Stoic School after 232-1, was considered as the second founder of this school. Wrote many works (705 treatises, according to Diogenes Laertius) dealing with the important branches of philosophy. He was for a long time a devoted disciple of °Cleanthes, and he was distinguished for his dialectical abilities. He wanted to teach his disciples a justified view of life and of the world.

CHU HSI 1130-1200.
Chinese philosopher, one of the founders of neo-Confucianism. The material world came into being through the spontaneous differentation of original matter (*ch'i*) and is dominated by primitive, eternal, perfect "principles" (*li*), culminating in the "Great Extreme," origin of all *li*, and at the same time is immanent in each of them. Matter and principles are both eternal. Without *li* no *ch'i*, and without *ch'i* no *li*.

CHUANG TZU
Ca. 370-285 B.C. The greatest philosopher of early Taoism. Every act and every judgment is futile, because of the unity of everything in the "Path" (*see* Tao), in which all differentiation is dissolved. The ideal is an actless and wordless intuitive unification by complete adaptation to eternal transformation, i.e., the totality of the natural processes.

CICERO
102-43 B.C. Received his philosophical education mostly in

72

Athens and on the island of Rhodes, was a disciple of Antiochus of Ascalon, and of Posidonius. His philosophical works were mostly written during the last years of his life. He is not an original thinker; he is an electic writer who takes a skeptical attitude toward philosophical problems and solutions; his work gives us many important data for the history of Greek philosophy. Against skepticism Cicero opposes the immediate certitude of some innate concepts and the agreement of man; he accepts providence and the immortality of the soul, teaches that virtue is sufficient for human happiness and that the ideal of wisdom excludes all passion. G. V.

CIRCUMSTANTIALITY

Is the accidental element in the content of the actually existing action. Circumstantiality can be morally neuter (commit a murder with an axe or a knife) or morally important, either because one gives the action a moral character (sexual relations outside marriage become adultery) or because the action changes within its kind (to steal a big sum makes the theft worse). This last circumstantiality is circumstantiality in its strict sense.

CIVILIZATION

Applied to people it means: (1) in the active sense, a person or a people make progress in the development of their spiritual abilities and in the related refinement of their morals; (2) in the passive sense, the result of such a development in the social life of a people or a group of people, in the sciences and the philosophy, in technical sciences and art, in customs and usages, in moral and religious life. A civilized person or people is one with a great measure of intellectual development and a great refinement and ennoblement in its attitude. By civilization we mean social phenomena as a whole, scientific, technical, aesthetic, moral and religious character as a whole, through which we think that the Western world is elevated above the people who have not yet or only in a small part attained the scientific and intellectual development of the West. O. Spengler opposed civilization (*Zivilisation*) to culture (*Kultur*). See Culture.

CLARENBALD OF ATRECHT

Died after 1170. Disciple of Thierry of Chartres, author of a commentary on Boethius' *De Trinitate*, defender of the *ultra-realism.

CLARKE, Samuel 1675-1729.

British theologian and philosopher. Was a follower of the new physics of Newton and opposed atheism and materialism. His correspondence with Leibniz is famous; in it he defended the freedom of the will against Leibniz's determinism. In the controversy with the deists of his time he was in favor of the theistic concept of God and the immortality of the soul. He thinks that the natural law is founded in the harmonious, God-intended relations of nature, which one has to obey; he who disturbs this harmony by doing evil acts against his own reason and purpose.

CLASS

(Socio-economic), social standing, which is first of all determined by the profession. *Marx reduces the different classes to two: the propertied class or bourgeoisie, and the proletariat or the unpropertied class. History is explained through the rivalry between those two classes: the so called *class struggle*. Dialectically the dictatorship of the proletariat must follow the rule of the propertied class (capitalism), until a classless society is born where everybody will have wages according to the work he produces (communism).

Is synonymous with *concept as well in respect to content as to extent. A *total* class is a class which contains all things or a concept which is applicable to all things. An *empty* class is a class which contains no things or a concept which is applicable to nothing. One speaks of *the* total or *the* empty class, because one can identify classes which are applicable to the same thing.

CLASSIFICATION

To place something in one or another category, series or class. This is, in fact, achieved in every proposition: "Whales are mammals" is identical with "Whales belong to the class of the mammals." Aristotle distinguished ten *categories as primary classification of all things; everything can be placed in one of them. One can also understand the term *classification as the complete systematical division of a categorical concept down to the last unities of individuals, who are its *extension. An example is the famous "*tree of *Porphyry."

CLASSIFICATION OF THE ARTS

The arts are classified according to the nature of the material used (material has however not to be considered as too physical, i.e. too independent from the creative phantasy). We can distinguish in general, apart from the many subdivisions: the *plastic art* (more spatial and objective), namely architecture (creation in the first place of the aesthetic space),

sculpture (wherein the solid form dominates) painting (where colour and two-dimensional space are used); *musical art* (more temporal and subjective) whose most pure form is music; the *verbal arts*, which find their objects in the spoken and written language and in which space and time have already a more spiritual and inner synthesis; the *locomotive arts*, which express themselves directly in the human motions and gestures (the dance is certainly its most original form). Among the most successful combinations, which indeed developed themselves into a real independent artistic class, we have to mention the dramatic art and the cinematographic art. L.V.K.

CLAUDIANUS MAMERTUS

Died *ca.* 474. Priest in Vienne (France), author of *De statu animae* (468 or 469), in which he defends the immateriality of the soul, in the style of Augustinian neo-Platonism.

CLEANTHES

End of 2nd and 3rd century B.C., died 232 or 231. Loyal disciple of Zeno of Citium and his immediate successor as head of the Stoic School. He differed in several points with his master, especially in his psychological dualism, ethical voluntarism and ethical radicalism; also in a stronger accentuation of divine transcendency. He was clearly under the influence of Aristotle and therefore a precursor of Posidonius and Panaetius.

CLEAR

See concept.

CLEMENCEAU, Georges 1841-1929

French statesman; Premier who led France through World War I and headed French delegation at the Peace Conference at Versailles.

Defender of Dreyfus. Author of *Demosthenes* (1926) and *In the Evening of My Thought* (1929).

CLEMENT OF ALEXANDRIA
Born probably in Athens *ca.* 150, died in Cappadocia 215. Convert, disciple of *Panthenus, later headed the Christian school of *Alexandria until 202, when the persecutions forced him to leave Alexandria. With much respect for Greek culture, he wanted to make Greek philosophy the servant of Christianity. His main sources were *Platonism, *Stoicism and *Philo.

CLITOMACHUS
Disciple of Carneades, and following him head of the *Academy. Through him we know the arguments of Carneades.

CODOMAIN
The collection of all the consequences of a relation. E.g. the codomain of "father of" are all the children.

COEFFICIENTS
In formal logic can be compared with those of the traditional algebra; they appear in algebraic developments.

COERCION
A not-free impulse to pose or omit a specific act, which can come from inside or from outside. Neurotic coercion or compulsion is inescapable and often runs counter to the conscious will. The cause can be found in repressed or not manifested experiences. *See* neurosis.

COGITO
(Latin: I think) Part of the expression *"Cogito ergo sum,"* in which *Descartes expressed the unquestionable fundament and the radical starting point of his thought. In the methodical doubt of all objects of thought, clearly appears in the foreground the self-presence of the ego to the ego, which accompanies all thought, even when it doubts, errs, or is false. The fundamental meaning of self-presence in thought was already underlined by Augustine and Thomas Aquinas, among others. While Descartes separates the *cogito* from the material and bodily world, other philosophers consider the *cogito* as essentially directed to the "other." *See* intentionality.

COGNITION
As it is in man, an immanent activity, by which something is made present for the active subject: an activity thus with an objective content which is founded on a relation between the subject and the object.

The problems which are connected with the cognition are of epistemological, psychological or metaphysical nature. Epistemologically we inquire what and how the subject can reach things in himself or in the outer world, if and to what extent this cognition is founded on an absolute or only relative basis. From a philosophic-psychological point of view one tries to discover the meaning of the cognition in the whole of the human behaviour, and also to show the structure of this cognition, by defining the nature of the different functions, sensory and intellectual, and by formulating their correlative relations. These problems lead us finally to the domain of metaphysics, where man is considered in his relation to the whole reality and where, on the grounds of this relativity, an answer is eventually given to the question about the ontological role of the cognition in the existence.

There has always been a double tendency in philosophy: an exaggerated separation in cognition, of intellect and sense and an exaggerated union of both; there were however also constant efforts to find a balanced structure. Cognition has on the other hand, too often been considered outside of the complete situation and behaviour of man; there is in contemporary philosophy a main reaction against this tendency; but in many cases is this reaction also faulty, especially when it overlooks, in one or another way, the relativism. L.D.R.

COHEN, Hermann
1842-1918. German neo-Kantian philosopher, professor in Marburg, founder of the °Marburg School. Main work: *System der Philosophie*, 1902-1912. Cohen tries to dispose of the inconsequences in the philosophy of Kant, and to form a logical idealistic system. Nothing exists outside of thought, which is the only thing that is, in the strictest sense of the word. Reality is only that which is thought. Although there is no other reality, this does not mean that there is not a distance between reality and thought. This distance is occupied by science, but this process is never achieved. It is carried out in the different special sciences, of which mathematics is pre-eminent, the example of all other sciences. Philosophy examines the methods used in science and unifies them. The fundamental question in philosophy is thus the question of method. Therefore the philosophy of Cohen is often called "pan-methodism." B.D.

COHEN, Morris Raphael
1880-1947
Russian-born American philosopher, teacher, logician and mathematician. Works: *Reason and Nature* (1931), *Law and the Social Order* (1933).

COHESION (rule of)
Can not be used in the formal logic as in the not-formal languages, in which one has to be attentive to the cohesion so as to guess the correct meaning of the word. It can however happen that, in order to avoid complicated forms of expression, a rule (rather a rule of abbreviation) is expressly fixed, which determines the exact type of a symbol, the extension of a description etc.

COINCIDENTIA OPPOSITORUM
(Literally: coincidence of all opposites in a fundamental unity) Nicolas of °Cusa applied this term to God, because the oppositions existing between the many finite beings are not present in the unity of the infinite being of God.

COLERIDGE, Samuel Taylor
Born in Ottery St. Mary (Devonshire) 1772, died in Highgate 1834. English poet and philosophical spiritualist; he thinks that all reality is of a spiritual nature and that practical reason, incited by feeling, penetrates it.

COLLINGWOOD, R. G. 1889-1943.
English philosopher, oriented toward history, under the strong influence of °Dilthey.

COLLINS, Anthony 1676-1729.
British philosopher, counted among the deists. Friend and follower of °Locke and critical of the Christian revealed faith. Doubts the historicity of the Biblical stories and defends those religious convictions which can be accepted by human reason. Collins thinks that the atheist, from Socrates to Locke, had on the whole a noble character.

COLLISION

Bound variables, would exist when, in virtue of a rule of substitution, one same bound variable would depend from two different signs of abstraction.

COMBINATION

Is a compound symbol, produced by operations. Is, in a more narrow sense, reserved for that what is produced by purely combinatory operations (writing symbols in all possible orders, repeating symbols, omitting them, placing them between parentheses).

COMBINATOR

Is, in the so called combinatory logic combinatory operations (and mostly purely combinatory operations), which have to be executed on a series of symbols. A combinator indicates, in itself, an empty operation, and cannot be translated by an adjective but by an adverb.

Combinators are either *primitive* or deduced, "e" formed from the primitive combinators by applications to each other. A special kind of combinator is the *numerical* combinator, which corresponds to the whole number.

COMBINATORY MEANING

Combinations are generally conceived as compounds of symbols, produced by operations. *Combinatory qualities* are then qualities, possessed by the symbols, because of the rules of their composition. *Combinatory relations* correspond to combinatory qualities, they are relations between symbols regarding deductions. —A symbolism produces a *combinatory representation* of a system of entities, when to each symbol corresponds at least one object of thought of the system, and to each combinatory relation at least one relation (deduc-tive connection) between the objects of thought. The meaning which rests on a combinatory representation, is then a *combinatory meaning;* it is *purely combinatory* if it rests exclusively on this representation. R.F.

COME INTO BEING

Begin to exist through evolution: as the brook originates from a spring or a being is born from another being. Also, originate from a cause; with or without beginning; so the creature which is created, either eternal or in a moment of time. Finally, be produced by something, even if the latter were not a source of evolution nor a cause; according to the catholic faith the second person of the Trinity is produced eternally, in one and the same nature, by the first and the third persons.

COMENIUS, Johann Amos
1592-1670

Bishop of the Bohemian Brethren and first great democrat among Christian educational philosophers; forced to flee Czechoslovakia, his native country, for political reasons. Works: *The Way of Light* (1642), *Patterns of Universal Knowledge* (1651), *The Great Didactic* (1657).

COMIC (AL), The

Esthetical category, which is based on a conscious and wanted contradiction of the—often expressed in words—representation and the represented content and by which a specific sense or human value is manifested backwards, namely by way of nonsense or invalidity. The structure of the comical is always a suddenly appearing contrast. When the comical loses this play-value and becomes serious, then it becomes the simple and unesthetic ridiculous and painful.

COMMANDMENT

An order which contains a force and is directed toward a being which not only can, but is inclined to resist it. The moral law is therefore a commandment. *See also* imperative.

COMMON SENSE

The totality of the conceptions which are accepted, in a given period and specific community, so spontaneously and by so many, that they are considered commonly human. The *Scottish school, and especially *Reid, consider common sense, which is an innate knowledge given to man as man, identical in all men and spontaneously accepted by them, the final ground of all knowledge of truth.

COMMUNISM

Subsequent form of the historical *materialism of *Marx. *See also* socialism.

COMMUNITY

A group of human beings who are mutually united by a natural or organic bond, such as the same descent or disposition (e.g., family, nation). Since *Tönnies opposed to *society.

COMMUTATIVE

Is an operation Ω, if $a \ \Omega \ b$ is equivalent to b AE α. E.g. the addition in the traditional algebra is commutative, because a $+$ b $=$ b $+$ a.

COMPASSION

To participate in the sufferings of others (see sympathy). Schopenhauer teaches that the ground of the morality lies in the compassion. Indeed, when man takes up the sufferings of others together with his own ones, he comes easily to the negation of life with which it is ultimately concerned.

COMPLETENESS

Of a deductive system can be considered in different ways. 1° a system is complete in regard to a specific collection of *propositions, when it is sufficient to a deduction of these propositions. 2° A system is *satiated or not-completable if a proposition which can not be proved in the system, can not be added as an added *axiom without creating thereby a contradiction. 3° A system is *categorical if all realizations of the system are *isomorph.

COMPLEX

In logic a *term and a concept, composed of parts, which have each meaning and are known. E.g. in a *definition.

Unity consisting of several parts. *See* complex *concepts and *terms.

COMPREHENSION

Or content, of a concept. The sum of the *characteristics which form the content of a concept and into which this concept can be analyzed; e.g., man is a rational, sensual, living, physical, independent being. The smaller the comprehension, the greater the *extension or volume of the concept.

COMTE, Auguste

Born in Montpellier 1798, died in Paris 1857. Founder of *positivism (a term he created). With his teacher, *Saint-Simon he wanted to form a new order in society. The means are: the progress of the human mind in a positive direction and the creation of a science of social phenomena: sociology. The human mind, in history, traversed three stages, which are also reflected in the evolution of the individual: the theological, the metaphysical, and the positive. In the first stage, all natural phenomena were explained by the activity of supernatural personal beings or by the animation of things. In the second stage, phenomena were reduced to the activity of abstract impersonal causes and principles. In the third stage, the philosopher is no longer interested in research of the causes but is only concerned with the observation of the phenomena themselves. Experience is able to find definite relations between them. These relations are indicated by the term "laws." Everything which is outside the phenomena and their laws is imaginary; metaphysics is replaced by positive sciences, which sooner or later will be able to solve all the problems of nature and life, through the application of their empirical and experimental methods. The duty of positive philosophy is, then, to assimilate the data of the positive sciences and unite them in a synthesis, which will bring the human mind and society into order. To improve the evolution of human knowledge in a positivistic direction, Comte proposes a new division of the sciences, founded on the six fundamental ones: mathematics, astronomy, physics, chemistry, biology and sociology. The later comprises also psychology, economy, ethics and the philosophy of history.

Positivism will be the only world view in the society reordered according to positive principles. The direction of minds will be entrusted to scholars, political power to the leaders of industry. No place is left for the concepts of God or religion, as Comte knew them through the teaching of the Catholic Church in France. He is not, however, opposed to every form of religion; he even wants to replace Catholicism with a new religion, which cannot be theism, pantheism, atheism or materialism, because they all belong to earlier stages of evolution. The positivistic religion is the cult of humanity, i.e., of the mass of all men who in the past, the present and the future are living, live or will live. It will put an end to the revolt of the mind against the heart, by putting reason definitely in the service of the heart. Comte created his own sacraments for this religion, with their own ceremonials, his own calendar and priesthood, in which Comte himself would occupy the highest function. Because of the creation of this positive religion, many of his followers, under the influence of *Littré, left him. *Laffitte continued after Comte's death the worship of humanity. His ideas have been principally written down in his *Cours de philosophie positive* (6 vols., 1839-1842). F.S.

CONCEPT
(Latin: *Conceptus*) An intellectual "grasp" of something, under which we can understand as well the simple psychological act of knowing as the result of this act. In the latter case it is an intellectual means of knowing, through which and in which the *abstract universal essence of something is known; it can thus be conceived in two senses: as subjective means of knowledge (subjective concept) and as that which is objectively known (objective concept). In logic we deal with the subjective concept, in other words with the concept as such or as formally taken, which can be divided: (1) according to the *content*: in simple (Latin: *simplex*) concept, rendered by one *term, e.g., man, philosopher; or complex concept, rendered by more than one term: e.g., rational being, somebody who is interested in philosophy; (2) according to the *scope*: transcen-

79

dental concept, embracing all possible things, to which °category they may belong, and thus with many (*see* analogy); or °*abstract universal concept,* embracing a specific category of things and thus with one single meaning. (*See* univocity); the abstract universal concept can be further divided, according to its logical use in a judgment, into *distributive* universal concept, embracing everything in this category; a *particular* universal concept, embracing one or more undetermined things; and an *individual* universal concept, limited to one individual of it; (3) according to the *way of presentation*: a °*concrete* concept or complete concept that renders the known thing in its entirety, e.g., man; an °abstract or incomplete concept, which renders only the formal part of it, through which it is what it is, e.g., humanity; (4) according to the degree of *perfection*: a concept is *clear* or *obscure,* the former if it is a concept of the thing itself, e.g., man, the latter if it is a concept of something which is proper to different sorts of things (common concept), e.g., sensual being; *clear* and *unclear,* the former when it is a concept of essential, the latter when of accidental characteristics of a thing; *adequate* or *inadequate,* the former when it gives us the complete attributes, the latter when it does not give us the complete attributes; (5) according to the *origin*: *intuitive* concept, obtained from directly perceived facts and things, and *abstract* concept, obtained through other concepts and thoughts; Kant distinguishes *a posteriori* concepts (or empirical or experience concepts) from *a priori* concepts which are nothing else than °synthesizing functions of our intellect (*conceptus dati*), the concepts formed by

ourselves (*conceptus facticii*); (6) according to their *mutual relation*: (a) on the grounds of their content: concepts are *identical* when they mean the same thing, or *different* when they do not mean the same thing; *sociable* concepts can be attributed to the same subject and *unsociable* ones cannot; these are called *disparate* when they have nothing in common, e.g., plant and intellect; they are *oppositional* when they have a certain relation to each other; the latter can be distinguished in *relative, constrasting, privative, contradictory* concepts (*see* opposition); inasmuch as pairs of concepts presuppose each other we can call them *correlative;* (b) on the grounds of their extent: *equipollent* concepts having the same extent, *inequipollent* concepts which can be divided in the most general *transcendental,* the general °*generic,* and the less general °*specific* concepts. I.v.d.B.

CONCEPT, (primitive)

Is in a deductive system a concept which is neither defined nor built by means of operations. In the most common form of the propositional logic are the variables $\underline{p}$, $\underline{q}$ . . . and the operations $\underline{v}$ (or), $\underline{N}$ (not) primitive concepts. The concepts $\underline{p} \underline{V} \underline{q}$ or $\underline{np} \underline{v} \underline{q}$ are not primitive concepts, because they were built by means of operations; neither $\underline{p} \rightarrow \underline{q}$ (as $\underline{q}$, then $\underline{q}$), when it is for instance defined equal to $\underline{Np} \underline{V} \underline{q}$.

CONCEPTIONISM

Theory that the qualities which occur in sensory perception are not qualities of the percepted objects, but subjective impressions, which are at most, produced by the objects in the perceiving man. Opposed to °perceptionism: in between: °interpretationism.

CONCEPTUALISM

Theory that man in his thought uses absolute concepts which belong to thought and never grasp the object as it is in reality. In opposition to *nominalism, conceptualism accepts the presence of general concepts in thought, but these concepts are only the symbols of beings in reality (*William of Ockham), or only expedients for the logical classification of thoughts. *Criticism and *Neo-Kantianism are also conceptualistic. They both accept the existence of concepts, underlining their general and necessary character, without considering them as being more than necessary forms in which thinking takes place. J.P.

CONCLUSION

The final proposition of an argument, inasmuch as it follows logically (see consequens) the knowledge which is already present (see antecedens) in two or more previous propositions (see premises). One could distinguish between mediate and immediate conclusion, the latter being the result of only one previous proposition (see consequence).

CONCRETE

Latin: con-cretum, grown together; that which is not considered in one or another respect, but is sufficiently defined, or even completely defined, according to its real way of being. What exists, matter or spirit, is concrete; what is considered possible forms the concrete content of knowledge. Concrete is opposed to *abstract, i.e., a pure aspect of reality which is represented separately by the mind but cannot exist as such: man, humanity, body, corporeality, etc. *Concepts or terms, however, such as man, body, which express directly formal aspects and are thus abstract ideas, are sometimes called concrete, because they also indicate the individual, although in general: with the term "man" we mean the one who possesses (but in general—i.e., an individual, but any individual) human definiteness.

In Hegel's philosophy "concrete" has a different meaning. To be able to think concretely, one has to consider reality in its complete definiteness, with all the relations it contains. The universal content of thought is now an abstract concept, inasmuch as it is thought separately from the individual; but the individual as it is apprehended by the senses, without insight into the universal, is also abstract; in this perspective concrete exists only in the synthesis of the universal and the individual. Such a synthesis is realized on different levels (the collective will, for instance, in a society is a synthesis, and not only the sum of the individual unities of will appearing in the members): but the concrete in its complete reality exists ultimately in the all-synthesizing absolute idea. L.D.R.

CONCUPISCENCE

A permanent inclination and desire to something. Concupiscence lies behind inclination. In empirical psychology the word is not used very much. In philosophical psychology one distinguishes between sensual and rational striving. The first has a relation to that which is pursued by the senses, the second to the intellectual good. In itself concupiscence is morally neutral.

CONCURSUS DIVINUS

The cooperation of God's power with the actions of His creatures. Since creatures do not exist unless God causes their existence, they also are unable to act unless God creates them as acting. The *concursus divinus* of the supernatural order is called "actual grace."

CONDILLAC, Etienne Bonnot de
Born in Grenoble 1715, died near Beaugency 1780. Began his studies for the priesthood, but left the seminary of St. Sulpice. With Condillac France began the period of *Enlightenment. At first he was a follower of Locke, but later he rejected inner observation as the source of knowledge and in his *sensualism impressions of the accepted exterior senses as the only source. He also rejected the possibility of uniting and comparing images, which was accepted by Locke; there is only the simultaneous appearance of two or more sensations, which are or are not similar. To explain how sensations are the source of all psychical activity, Condillac uses the fiction of a marble statue which is able only to smell, with which consciousness is related. Judgment, reflection, thought and love all have their origin in sensory perception and let themselves resolve in it. The subject which has sensation is not physical, however, but a simple immaterial soul. H.R.

CONDITION
Which is required for the reality of a being. In narrower sense which is required next to the inner and exterior *causes, just so that these causes could play their role. In the most narrow sense: the exclusion of what hinders an action; conditio sine qua non, e.g. to see the light of the sun in a room, nothing should hinder the sunrays to enter the room.

CONDITIONAL
Dependent from a condition.

CONFIGURATION
See Gestalt.

CONFLICT
Collision of opposite forces. In the *psychic* domain, conflict occurs when the acting subject is moved in different directions by motives. To be free an action does not necessarily presuppose such a conflict. In *ethics*, a conflict of duties occurs when the same action can be lawful and unlawful at the same time, according to the rule which is applied (*see* casuistics).

CONFORMITY
Specific relation between religion and metaphysics, used by *Scheler in his *"Konformitätssystem"* in opposition to partial and total identification and to the dualistic separations of belief and knowledge: religion and metaphysics have their own unity and independence; religion can therefore not be founded on metaphysical views in the final and highest world foundation. We can, however, establish that metaphysical conclusions are in conformity with the foundations of religion.

CONFUCIANISM
Philosophical, ethical system, based in principle on the teachings of *Confucius and his school, with several changes and additions which occurred later. Since the 2nd century B.C. the official national doctrine. Since the 11th century: *neo-Confucianism*, a reinterpretation of the old Confucianism, with a strong metaphysical impact. Strong influence of Taoism and Zen-Buddhism. Most important schools: the schools of *Chu Hsi and of *Wang Yang-ming.

CONFUCIUS, K'ung Fu Tzu: Master Kung, (real name K'ung Ch'iu)
551-479 B.C. Philosopher and moralist, official career in the state of Lu (South Shantung). After 497

he made peregrinations with his disciples in order to get his doctrine accepted by the feudal sovereigns of the China of that time. He gives a new interpretation of the old Chinese world view. In it he emphasizes the central position of the sacred Ruler, "Son of Heaven," who reigns by magic power (*Tê*), to harmonize the activities of the three dominions: Heaven, Earth, Man. The *tê* became for Confucius and his school a moral principle: (still magically acting) "virtue." This can be self-cultivated, based on the study of the writings of tradition (later called the canonical books). Moral interpretation of these books is used to cultivate the fundamental qualities: the sense of duty, sincerity, love of children and fidelity, each with its own sphere of application; the universal application of the principles of humanity (jên) and decorum (*li*). "Virtuous" government creates in itself universal application, because it conforms to the "Will of Heaven" (*Ming, fatum,* which is for Confucius a moral principle). The doctrine of Confucius is directed toward practical application; the metaphysical element is very small. The ideal is *Chün-tzu,* the noble man, whose life is dedicated to the ennoblement of himself and his environment. E. Z.

CONGRUISM
(Latin: *congruum,* fitting) A form of *Molinism, defended by Suarez and Saint Bellarminus. If God wishes to have mercy on somebody He chooses such naural (and supernatural) help (grace) as prepares that man to achieve the proposed result.

CONJUNCTION
Is an operation which can be translated by "and." There are con-

junction *propositions (p and q), conjunction of concepts or classes (an a and a b are). The *relative conjunction* is the operation which connects the relations r and s to the relation: r of s of . . . If for instance r is brother (of), s friend (of), then is the relative conjunction of r and s: brother of friend (of).

CONJUNCTIVE
See judgment, syllogism.

CONSCIENCE
(Latin: *conscientia,* co-knowledge) The moral consciousness inasmuch as it experiences morality in its practical meaning as being done or not done by the individual. It also has a relation to the concrete actions of a particular person. This definition is connected with the scholastic tradition: Bonaventura underlines the affective character of conscience, so that it co-stirs (*con-scientia*) the will; Thomas Aquinas sees it as the practical reason inasmuch as it opposes the *synderesis, judges the moral value of a concrete (*conscientia*) action. If this judgment is made before the action, we call the conscience *antecedent;* if it follows, we call it *consequent;* if it is made at the same time as the action, it is called *accompanying.*

For the scholastics, the conscience is in fact the immediate standard of morality, even if it is involuntary or erroneous. For conscience can be, insofar as it has to apply general principles to specific cases, either *doubtful* or *certain.* When it is certain, it is either *correct* or *erroneous.* In any case, the ruling of the conscience is binding; it is also the voice of reason (which makes man man), and eventually of God, who created man a reasonable being. Other philosophers see in the conscience the voice of alien forces (social, biological or psychological) which try to dominate us. For Heidegger, however, the voice of conscience originates in the person to whom this voice is directed, from the human being who is concerned about his existence to the man who is lost in the world. In complete silence, conscience summons man to consider himself fundamentally guilty. (*See* guilt.) J. Gr.

CONSCIENTIALISM

The theory that only what is empirically given in the consciousness of the individual is real. By explaining being as the content of consciousness in the unique being, conscientialism (also called empirical or psychological idealism) comes necessarily to °subjectivism, °relativism and eventually to °solipsism.

CONSCIOUS

In the active sense (as usually): knowing with certitude, having the known object present in an immediate emotion. In the passive sense: conscious of what is known with certitude and is present to somebody in immediate knowledge.

CONSCIOUSNESS

Indicates the specific form of being proper to man and in a certain degree also to the animal: man (as man) inasmuch as he is immediately aware of something is such that this awareness of contents (*see* intentionality) is in a certain way co-knowing.

1. With the attention focused on k n o w l e d g e, consciousness means, in the general sense, the totality of the actual and previous experiences which are at the disposition of an individual, in a more restricted sense, only that which is experienced here and now. These contents can be present in greater or lesser quantities (preconscious, subconscious, unconscious). One can also speak of the threshold of consciousness, the height of consciousness, etc. (Wundt). W. James, who speaks of stream of consciousness, thinks that the dynamics of consciousness are primary, not separate representations.

2. Consciousness can also be considered in what it characterizes as such. In *spontaneous* or *direct consciousness* the i n t e n t i o n a l awareness of contents is itself hardly co-known. It is, however, the object of consciousness in *reflexive* or *indirect consciousness*. But in sensual knowledge there is already the lowest degree of reflexive consciousness, although the reflection has to remain incomplete. In intellectual knowledge there is a higher degree of reflection present, inasmuch as the different activities of the consciousness are reduced to the origin from which they proceed. In argumentative thinking, reflection is still more important. In a proposition such as "I know this or that to be so," knowledge (of the content) is known as originating from the root of the independent being which "I" am. Consciousness became here, because of the complete reflection, *self-consciousness,* present from self to self.

Although self-consciousness is not a complete transparency of man to himself, which would include complete independence and freedom, it is the most fundamental certitude man can achieve, since all other certitude (also unconscious) achieves only absolute certitude through its connection with this existential evidence: that I am knowing this or that. Whether experiences express correctly or not the beings to which I am intentionally directed, it is in any case certain that I have consciousness of

84

this relation, and that I *am* in this consciousness. All intentional relations are dependent, in their certitude, upon the, above the intentionality rising self-presence of me in myself as being. Augustine and Thomas Aquinas underlined the importance of reflection. Since Descartes, the theory of knowledge has originated in this *cogito. And this is right if consciousness is seen in its entirety and thus also in its relation to other beings. *Phenomenology also originates rightly in consciousness, which it wants to describe. This theory is only contestable inasmuch as it denies that the phenomenon, as pure phenomenon of consciousness, is not nothing, but already "is" in the absolute and universal meaning of that word. J. P.

CONSCIOUSNESS OF VALUES

The consciousness we have of the *values. It is here for us not a question of intuition of contents sui generis, but the consciousness of values rises from the consciousness of striving. Man indeed, inasmuch as he knows himself as striving, knows also all the conditions to which this striving is subordinated; knows the different qualities through which the reality must satisfy his differently oriented strivings. These qualities appear to him on the one hand as strictly determined (as the nutritive for instance is clearly distinct from the sexual or the moral), on the other hand as vague and undefinite in respect to the concrete goods in which they are actually present. In any case, the value is not abstracted from valuable goods: we can only call a conduct heroic, when we have already seized the value of heroism, or better, when we have felt it. The characteristic of this consciousness is indeed that the value, as opposed to other contents (as for instance the definition of a triangle or even of the value itself), appears with an emotional character and appears as attractive and urging. Even if the value is not directly experienced and if the consciousness of value limits itself to a purely rational "knowing", the consciousness remains that the value has meaning for the acting subject, be it as consciousness of *application or as consciousness of *obligation.

The consciousness of value is therefore primarily affectively tinted and appears as the spiritual experience of the motion which drives man to the value as an objective and real content with attractive character. This feeling of the value does however not include the actual pursuit of it: although the value is not experienced outside of the striving, can the natural striving towards the felt value be assented or not, can it develop or not into pursuit. J. Gr.

CONSENSUS GENTIUM (Literally, agreement of people)

Considered by *deism as a proof of the universal human capacity of reason to discover, on its own, religious and moral truth, by *traditionalism as proof of the existence of a primitive revelation, which tradition has maintained among the different peoples on earth.

CONSEQUENCE

Such a logical connection of the three propositions of reasoning that when the first two (*see* antecedens, premises) are given, the third follows necessarily (*see* consequens, conclusion). Establishing this consequence is called inference. Some distinguish between a *mediate* and *immediate* inference, as in the *conclusion.

Is, in a relation, a thing with

which something has a relation. In an *assertion* of deductibility with the form α, $\underline{P} \pm \underline{Q}$, $\underline{B}$ *or* $\pm \underline{Q}$, $\underline{B}$ ($\underline{P}$ and $\underline{Q}$ *propositions, α and $\underline{B}$ series of $\underline{0}$, $\underline{1}$, $\underline{n}$ propositions) is the consequence the series of propositions.

CONSTANT

Is better defined negatively as a non-variable. Constants are not only symbols for specific things about which one reasons, but also symbols of logical operations. One can distinguish *primitive* (not-defined) and *inferred* constants.

That which continues to exist while it changes. The apparent contradiction between being which goes on existing yet evolves, which stays the same and at the same time becomes something different (*see* become) has always been an important question for philosophers.

CONSTITUTIVE

To an expression are, in broad sense, all parts with which this expression can be built by means of logical operations. In narrow sense are constitutive the forms of the disjunctive evolution.

That of which something is constituted. In *Kant: "constitutive of knowledge" is everything that is required for valid thinking; i.e., phenomena and categories. Is opposed to *regulative.

CONSTRUCTION

The *a priori definition of an object of study; as in mathematics; e.g., by circle "I understand" a line every point of which is equally distant from a point within, called the center (*see* definition). In Kant all objects of knowledge, formally taken, are constructed by our intellectual functions of knowledge (*see* synthesis). See *also* existency (mathematics).

CONTACT THEORY.

A body has only *place and *distance when it is in contact with another body. Place is then an exterior relation with another body. Without this other body, which provides place, a body cannot have a place. If there existed only one body, it would be senseless to speak of place or position. This opposes the *position theory, which considers the position of a body as an inner quality of the body, given with the body itself, independent of the existence of other bodies. The contact theory teaches also that there is no question of distance between two bodies unless both are in contact with each other via a third body. If there existed two bodies without a third one in between, these two could not be at a certain distance from each other. A.G.M.v.M.

CONTEMPLATION

Practice of the aesthetic experience as insight and intuition. Contemplation means the same thing as intuition. However, it puts more accent on restful dwelling upon the object and on the enjoyable and feeling aspects which are inherent in aesthetic inspection. Since every aesthetic object, either in its nature or in art, has a certain structural harmony, contemplation will direct itself freely and alternately to the whole object and to detail, in order to achieve a deeper insight into the whole object through a contemplation of the details. Aesthetic contemplation is distinguished from other forms of contemplation (religious, philosophical, etc.) since in aesthetic contemplation sensibility and mind melt together in a more intimate copenetration.

CONTENT

As an *assertion* is the asserted *proposition. Content of a *concept* is this concept itself. The traditional logic speaks here generally of *comprehension in opposition to the extension, in other words the aggregate which corresponds to the concept.

Content of an action: inner meaning of an action, or the meaning of an action, abstraction made from the *intention of the acting subject, as well in the physical as in the ethical order. In this case the content can still more narrowly be defined than the physical changes (e.g. a robbery) by which a specific value (e.g. the economical value) is to be realized. Seen in this light, the content remains for Kant entirely indifferent for the morality of the action. Content in art, see art.

CONTENTMENT (disinterested)

The specific human satisfaction experienced in the aesthetic and artistic experience. The real aesthetic contentment surpasses the sphere of the practical utility and of the theoretical eagerness for knowledge. It is a purely intuitive pleasure in the aesthetical form as form and in the values of life which are symbolically and graphically connected with this form.

CONTIGUUM

When two bodies are exactly next to each other, but do not compose a unity, they are called contigua: e.g., two cubes adjacent to each other, and forming apparently a parallelepipedon. Contiguum is opposed to *continuum and *discrete.

CONTINGENCY

That which characterizes the not-necessary as such. Necessity can touch different relations: the mutual relations of the different elements of a being, the relation of a being with another being, etc. The term contingency is used more when we explain being as such. The first question, then, is whether the contingency which we affirm really exists and is not merely an image created by our ignorance. If contingency exists, we have to look for a being which explains it. Following this approach, one of the traditional proofs of the existence of God argues from the existence of contingency the necessary existence of God. In existentialism, however, the contingency of man (which, insofar as it is conscious, is called facticity) is naturally inexplicable and gives us rather the proof of the non-existence of a necessary being.

CONTINGENCY OF NATURAL LAWS

The contingent character of natural laws, in spite of the necessity which is generally ascribed to them. On the one hand, natural laws least of all give us firm relations which would be found in nature as such; French *critical science has pointed out that these laws express only the human view of nature. Modern physics, on the other hand, demonstrate that *determinism can no longer be defended, and that one has to limit oneself to relations which indicate only an average.

CONTINGENT

That which is not necessarily, which can be or not be; which therefore is only actual. More particularly, contingent expresses the modality of the *proposition in which the non-necessary way in which a predicate is due to its subject is stressed.

CONTINUUM

Quantity as cohesive extension. A line, a plane and a body are examples of continua. Opposed to continuum are the *contiguum and the *discrete.

In geometry we consider the investigated objects as lines, planes and bodies, which are homogeneous continua. In arithmetic however, objects are considered absolutely discontinua (*see* discrete). It is clear that both views are based on an abstraction, the real physical order contains continuity and discontinuity. Classical natural science considered ponderable matter as discontinuous, composed of atoms situated at a certain distance from each other. It considered light phenomena however as continuous.

Today both views are connected, so that all physical phenomena are considered continuous or discontinuous, depending on the point of view under which we consider them (*see* wave-and quantum mechanics). The combination of continuity and discontinuity brings us to the concept of *heterogeneous continuity*, in which a continuous unity exists, but in such a way that the different parts of it have different qualities. One can thus consider a crystal as a continuous unity, in which, however, we can distinguish the different atoms at the junctions of the crystal structure. If we only pay attention to these junctions, the crystal appears to be discontinuous; if we consider the unity of the whole, the same fundamental qualities as seen in all parts, then the crystal appears to be continuous. In the heterogeneous continuity we can further distinguish between a smooth heterogeneity and an abrupt heterogeneity.

By continuum in a narrower sense we mean a compact and continuous ordered relation M. Such a relation M has to be (1) ordered, i.e., from the two elements of M, x and y, there is always one which precedes the other, so that if x precedes y and y precedes z, x always has to precede z. The order

in M has (2) to be compact, i.e., if x precedes y, there must be an element u, so that x precedes u and u precedes y.

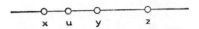

Finally (3) the order has to be continuous, i.e., if we separate M in two not-empty relations P and Q, so that every element in P precedes every element in Q, either P has to contain a last element or Q has to contain a first element. The function of all natural numbers is ordered (if we always give the smaller numbers precedence over the greater ones), but the order is not compact: 3 precedes 4, but there is no natural number u, so that 3 would precede u and u precede 4. The relation of all rational numbers is ordered and the order is compact, but it is not continuous: If Q is the relation of all positive rational numbers of which the square is greater than 2, and P the relation of all other rational numbers, then every element of P precedes every element of Q, but P does not have a last and Q does not have a first element.

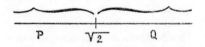

The relation of all real numbers is compactly and continuously ordered, and this relation is an example of a continuum in the narrower sense. Being a compactly and continuously ordered relation, the relation of the real numbers has several specific qualities, of which we will indicate a few.

(1) An ascending series of real

88

numbers, upwards circumscribed, always has a limit. For in a series consisting of the real numbers $a1$ $a2 \ldots$, ak $ak+1$ is always greater than ak, but all numbers ak are smaller than a certain number m. If P consists of all real numbers which are surpassed by at least one number of the series, while Q contains all other numbers, then P contains the number $a1$—because $a1$ is surpassed by $a2$—while Q contains the number m. P and Q are then not-empty relations and every number in P precedes every number in Q.

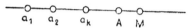

P contains then a last, or Q a first element; and this element is evidently the limit of the series.

(2) If we call this limit A, then we understand easily that A cannot be a part of the relation P, so that A must be the first or smallest element in the relation Q. If we take a (possibly very high) number k: since A belongs to Q, A will always be greater than ak. Since the order is compact, there certainly is a number between ak and A, e.g., B.

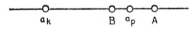

Since A is the smallest number in Q, and B is smaller than A, B will be part of P and will be smaller than a certain element of the series, e.g., ap. We cannot find a number B which will stay between ap and A, however high the number p, even if we can find with every k, however high it may be, a number B between ak and A. This is expressed clearly when we say that the segment between ak and A

with an indefinite ascending k becomes infinitely small, and one calls this indefinitely shrinking segment *infinitesimal*. E.W.B.

Dynamic continuity: Continuity whose parts are not realized simultaneously, but successively, as in time and motion. A.G.M.v.M.

Permanent continuity: Continuity of which the parts are realized simultaneously, e.g., spatial dimensions.

CONTRACT SOCIAL or Social Contract.

In Rousseau's work *Du Contrat Social,* the author says that society, more specifically the state, comes into being through a contract. In this contract the individuals give up their natural freedom in exchange for the "civil liberty." This civil liberty consists in the fact that one does not have to obey another will than the common will (and at the same time one's own will).

CONTRADICTIO IN ADIECTO, or IN TERMINIS

Addition to a concept or term of a definition which is contradictory to that defined, e.g., a round square.

CONTRADICTION

Applied to the contents of thought, the term "contradiction" is used to express that one is the pure negation of the other. E.g., white and non-white. Applied to judgments or propositions, it is the relation between two propositions of which one is the pure negation of the other. Contradiction is also present when a compound content of thought combines contradictorily related contents, or when a proposition has a predicate which is the pure negation (or the contrary) of the subject.

CONTRADICTION, Principle of

Really the principle of non-contradiction or excluded contradiction, as formulated by Aristotle: "It is impossible that a same thing is and is not at the same time in the same respect." This applies primarily to being, concerning which it does not express identity with itself (as does the principle of identity), but contradiction with not-being: to be is not not to be. But not-being "is" not and is only thought by us in the form of a contradiction. The negation therefore can never relate to beings as beings and in their totality: it can only be denied that a particular way of being pertains to a particular being. The principle of contradiction is based on the principle of identity, from which it is distinguished, however. It refers, thus, first of all to finite beings, and distinguishes them from what they are not. Negation, as a distinctive act of the mind, is the effect of the limitation which the "esse" undergoes in beings.

In the second place, the principle of contradiction is logically formulated as follows: "The same thing cannot at the same time and in the same respect be affirmed and denied." Of every proposition it can be said that it cannot be affirmed and denied. Two contradictory propositions are not both true; at least one of them (if not both) is false; if one is true, the other has to be false (according to the principle of the excluded *third).

We have to conceive the principle of contradiction as the principle of the exclusion of contradictory propositions being together true. It is thus one of the most elementary and fundamental principles of thought. J.P.

CONTRADICTIONLESSNESS

Characterizes a system in which it is impossible to infer at the same time a *proposition and its negation. It could be that in a system the principle of contradiction, namely: it is false that p and not-p is not provable; the system is therefore not necessarily contradictory, as long as no contradiction can be inferred. The importance of the contradictionlessness lies in the fact that in most systems everything can be inferred from a contradiction; the system becomes for that reason *not-consistent*. A system can be not-consistent without being contradictory, e.g. when it is a system which is purely positive, without negation.

CONTRADICTORY

Fundamental opposition of *concepts or *judgments, between which there is a contradiction.

CONTRAPOSITION

The figurative *conversion of a proposition, in which the original terms are replaced by *contradictory terms; it can be applied to a and o propositions.

CONTRARY or opposite

Contrasting concepts or propositions. *See* contrast.

CONTRAST

Opposition between two concepts or propositions which cannot go together, so that only one of them can be right or true; but both can be wrong or untrue; e.g., white and black; everything is changeable and nothing is changeable.

CONTRITION

Act of the will through which a person repudiates his free action or attitude, because it is not proper. This preceded and perhaps prepared for by remorse, but is different from it and is more: not a feeling but an act, not a persistence but a conversion or reversion of the will. By removing the contradiction between intellect and will, contrition stops remorse and makes the person free for the future.

CONVENTION
See Postulate.

CONVERSION
An interchange of *subject and *predicate in a proposition so that not only the truth, but also the same proposition is maintained. It can be applied completely and without change (see S) to e and i propositions; e.g., no animal has intellect, and what has an intellect is not an animal; one or another philosopher is a mathematician, and one or another mathematician is philosopher. It can be applied incompletely to e and a propositions, when we use the primitive term of the predicate in a narrow sense (see P). E.g., no man is perfect, and one or another perfect being is not a human being; existentialists are emotional, and some emotional people are existentialist.

By contraposition (see C) or in a figurative sense it also applies to a and o propositions (see A); e.g., all human beings are mortal, and an immortal being is not a human being; some politicians are not prudent, and some imprudent people are not politicians.

CONVERSION
Is used in the *logic of relations as synonym of inversion (for the operation through which a relation is changed into its *inversion). In the modern theory of the lambda-conversion (Church) is the conversion the relation between two expressions which are, as it were, verbally identical. There are three rules of lambda conversion. According to the first rule two expressions can be changed into each other if they only differ in the choice of the bound variables. The second rule is a very general form of the rule of *concretion. The third rule is the inverse of the second one.

CONVICTION
Firm opinion with strong feeling of truth or untruth. It is the psychological finale of the reasoning. In broader sense the acquisition of intellect and mind.

COOK, Josephus Flavius 1838-1901
Popular lecturer on science and religion in nineteenth-century America. Works: Heredity (1878), Socialism (1880), Current Religious Perils (1888).

COPERNICAN REVOLUTION
Is called by Kant the revolution he introduces into criticism. As Copernicus considers the sun and not the earth as centre of the universe, so explains Kant the knowledge not through the object of the knowledge, which is the being, but through the knowing subject itself.

COPULA
The link verb "to be," which has in a proposition a double function: a connecting and a judging function. Although it is itself not a term of judgment, it connects the subject and propositional term and expresses our judgment of this connection.

COPULATIVE
See proposition.

COROLLARY
(Latin: corolla, little wreath). Initially a small wreath given as a reward, therefore in logic the mention of one or another truth added to the proof of a theorem of which it is a direct consequence.

CORPUSCLE

In the 17th and 18th centuries the term "corpuscula" was used to indicate the smallest particles (see minima). The philosophers of that time ascribed to them qualitatively different properties, as opposed to the *atoms of Democritus.

The term "corpuscular" is now used to indicate a certain granulated structure, which means that one represents now the natural processes as evoluting with jumps and not uniformly (see Continuum). See also atoms, quanta.

CORRELATIVE

See concept.

CORRELATOR, Ordinal

Is a relation between the elements of two ordered functions which have the same *structure. So, for instance, the relation which exists between the towns of a region and the points which correspond to it on a correct map.

COSMOLOGICAL PHILOSOPHERS

The presocratic thinkers, who expressed their philosophical reflexions in the form of a cosmology or philosophy of nature. Belong to the older group: the School of Milete (*Thales, *Anaximander, *Anaximenes); *Heraclitus; the *Pythagoreans; the *Eleates (*Parmenides, *Zeno of Elea, *Melissus). They all search for a first principle or "archè," by which they want to explain the origin and changes in the world. They generally accept one element as forming principle: water (Thales), air (Anaximenes), fire (Heraclitus). Anaximander poses as first principle the indefinite (apeiron), the Pythagoreans see in the number the fundamental substance of all things. The Eleates refer all changes to the "unreal," and represent the one "esse" as unchangeable.

The younger cosmological philosophers are *Empedocles, *Anaxagoras and the *atomists: *Leucippus, *Democritus. They try to evade the difficulties of the Eleates by accepting a great number of primary elements. Therefrom comes the theory of the four elements (Empedocles), of the hemeomeries (Anaxagoras), of the atoms (atomists). F.D.R.

COSMOLOGY (literally theory about the cosmos)

Is used for the physical theories of the universe, closely related to astronomy, as well as for the natural philosophy, in the sense of the philosophical studies of matter.

Since the 17th century the physical sciences and the philosophy went each their own way and many doubt the necessity of a natural philosophy. Is the physical science not the only natural philosophy? Compare the titles of the well known classic works in the natural sciences: Newton's *Philosophiae Naturalis Principia Mathematica* and Dalton's *A new system of Chemical Philosophy*. It is however clear that the physical sciences always give occasion to several philosophical questions, which justify the existence of the cosmology as a separate branch of philosophy. The cosmology has a very important role in the study of the presuppositions of the physical sciences. For instance: the experimental induction presupposes the *species-individual structure of matter. Philosophical cosmology can therefore be described as the philosophical doctrine of the general properties of matter, namely those properties which the physical sciences always presuppose and which therefore can not be investigated by them. A.G.M.v.M.

COSMOPOLITANISM

The world-citizenship of man.

92

Diogenes and the cynics were the first to honor it; but the Stoics emphasized it more, while it was especially helped by the universality of the Roman Empire and the Catholic Church. It became again strong in the 17th and 18th centuries, under the influence of the Enlightenment as opposed to the differentiation which originated in the national states and the religious cults.

COSMOS (literally: ornament, ordering)

The *universe, considered as an ordered whole.

COURNOT, Antoine Augustin

Born in Gray 1801, died in Paris 1877. French mathematician and philosopher, founder of French scientific criticism. The application of the scientific method can never give us a complete understanding of the order of phenomena; there are always phenomena which are "accidental" or "contingent" and therefore outside every law and of which only probable knowledge can be acquired. Here theoretical knowledge a l l o w s pragmatical views. F.S.

COUSIN, Victor

Born in Paris 1792, died there in 1867. Founder of spiritualistic eclecticism, which contains related elements of German idealism, the spiritualism of *Maine de Biran a n d *common-sense-philosophy. During the monarchy of July it became the official doctrine of French philosophical education.

In order to give a firm ground to the truth of "general human thought" (i.e., the immateriality of the soul, the liberty of man, divine Providence, the law of duty, the difference between virtue and vice) Cousin seeks the basis of metaphysics in psychology. The immediate datum of consciousness is supra or unpersonal reason, which becomes subjective through reflection only, but produces, in spontaneous situations, the axioms and concepts of the Infinite and Absolute, which, applied to the phenomena of inner and outer perception, lead to knowledge which has a more than subjective value. His most important work: *Cours de l'histoire de la philosophie moderne* (1829-1846, 2 series, 8 volumes, later published under separate titles). F.S.

CRANTOR OF SOLI

Ca. 300-268 B.C. Came to Athens when Xenocrates was head of the *Academy and with Polemo became his disciple. He was the first to write a commentary on Plato's *Timaeus.* His consolatory writing, *Of Sorrow,* was the prototype of a long series of later consolatory writings.

CRATES OF ATHENS

Ca. 300 B.C. Disciple and friend of Polemo, his successor as head of the *Academy.

CRATYLUS OF ATHENS

6th-5th century B.C. Carried the doctrine of *Heraclitus so far that absolutely everything changes, so that one can no longer judge anything.

CREATIO CONTINUA

(Literally: continuous creation) The divine activity which perpetuates the created world. Without this *creatio continua* the created world would fall into not-being. The activities of creation and perpetuation of the world are not distinct in God.

CREATION

The activity of God or the result of this activity. In the first meaning it is the production of something, with its entire substance, from nothing. If one does not consider the act of creation, then nothing is left, not even an uncreated matter or material, from which it would have been made. Even all co-cause is excluded from the act of creation by God, even if God creates the creatures in such a way that they have causal relations with each other and evolution is not excluded. In the second meaning the word creation points to the result of the divine activity, in as much as this result in its entire existence is related to the Creator.

The philosophical concept of creation of thomism does not necessarily mean: began in time. Time is, as duration of the physical world, co-created. Creation can therefore not be compared with a fact which happens in time, but forms the basis on which all the happenings of facts appear in time. In the creation God also put order among the things so that mutual connections are created, also those of the succession of past, present and future. The act of creation of God is entirely free, without inner necessity of the freely chosen order of creation, and is therewith distinguished from any *emanation.

Although many of these elements were present in Aristotle's works, he did however never come to this philosophical concept of creation. It does not exist either in the philosophy of Kant, for whom the concept "cause" only exists within the world of experience. In the idealism of Fichte and Hegel creation exists on the level of the ideal becoming of God in the world. H. R.

CREATIONISM

The doctrine which teaches that the soul of the child is immediately created by God at the moment of the conception; opposed to the doctrine that the souls of both parents each create a proper soul's potentiality which come together when the child is born (generationism).

CREDO QUIA ABSURDUM

(Literally: I believe because it is absurd) Reproachful expression of those who think that in Christianity one has to believe theses which are against reason. Tertullianus gave rise to this expression, because he taught that the death of the God-man is the more credible since reason could not arrive at this fact by itself.

CREDO UT INTELLIGAM

(Literally: I believe in order to understand) Words of *Anselm of Canterbury, meaning that philosophical and theological speculation do not produce faith, but can exist only when faith already exists.

CREIGHTON, James E. 1861-1924.

American idealistic philosopher, professor at Cornell University.

CRESCAS, Hasdai 1340-1410

Medieval Jewish philosopher, authority on Jewish law and ritual. His principal work, *Or Adonai (The Light of God)*, was a refutation of Neo-Platonism and Aristotelianism and criticized Gersonides and Maimonides for attempting to reconcile Judaism with Greek philosophy.

CRITERIOLOGY

See epistemology.

CRITERION

(Greek: *krino*, distinguish) Distinguishing mark, standard: (1) sign indicative of a thing or a concept and distinguishing it from others; (2) standard according to which we judge a thing or a concept. CRITERION OF TRUTH: Criterion which allows us to determine whether a proposition or a judgment is true or untrue; e.g., *evidence.

CRITICISM

Critical idealism or transcendental idealism is the philosophy whose foundations were laid by *Kant and which in a philosophical system, reserves the main place for the criticism of knowledge, or even confines the system entirely to this.

Criticism inquires about the possibility of knowledge, particularly necessary and universally valid judgments, and attributes the most important place in knowledge to the factors which give form, present in the subject a priori, i.e., independent of all experience. (*Anschauungsformen, Kategorien*); no factor outside the subject contributes to the content of the knowledge, even if its existence is accepted by Kant (*Ding an sich*).

Criticism has been carried to its ultimate consequences by the School of *Marburg of Neo-Kantianism (*see* Cohen, Natrop, Ovink, Goedewagen and others) which rejects the *"Ding an sich"* in order to retain only the formal subject as the only function of knowledge; it also teaches as to the origin of the world of being, the "Dingen," that objectivity for the subject is in and with thought.

CRITIQUE, Transcendental

For Kant the philosophy inasmuch as it answers to the question: how is it possible that we have universally-valid knowledge which is not borrowed from experience (what is borrowed from experience can not be universally-valid) but is still valid for the experience.

CROCE, Benedetto 1866-1952

Italian neo-Hegelian. Is close to *Spaventa, but has an original view on Hegel so that the historicism of *Dilthey is introduced into the Hegelian form of thinking. In his main work, *Filosofia dello spiritu*, 1902-1917, Croce considers reality as a spirit, which constantly realizes itself. This realization is accomplished in four different phases. The spirit appears first in aesthetic activity, intuition of the concrete; later, in its logical activity, it is conscious of the unity of the universal and the concrete. These two phases form the theoretical sphere, The spirit first wills the particular, other two phases form the practical sphere, the spirit which wills itself. The spirit first wills the particular, as it appears in the struggle of life; but later it puts the particular under the general, as happens in moral activity. The individual human being is only a transitory phenomenon. This is also true for all human creations: art, science, philosophy, religion, are all transitory moments in the eternal process of the spirit. Only the spirit is eternal, but this eternity is not static, but a continuous, everything-renewing process. Only the spirit is absolute. In his many works Croce is especially interested in the questions of philosophical aesthetics and historical methodology. His influence outside of as well as in Italy was very important. B.D.

CUDWORTH, Ralph 1617-1688.

British philosopher and main representative of the School of the Platonists of *Cambridge. He turned against the materialism of Hobbes in his work *The True Intellectual System of the Universe* (1678). He also opposed materialism and formulated proofs of the existence of God. Ethical principles do not originate in experience, human laws or in the will of God, but are universally valid and necessary principles of divine and human reason. Goodness is an idea, present in eternity in God's mind and it can be communicated to the human mind.

CULTURAL PHILOSOPHY

Has received its own place in philosophy in modern times. It often laid claim to the absolute right to determine the laws and norms of cultural life, proceeding from an idealistic dialectic or a positivistic naturalism. It aimed in this way at deriving a rational psychology as well as general sociology from the evolution of culture. It had necessarily to arrive at a relativistic *historicism, which rejects every absolute norm in the appreciation of cultural life, and accepts only the historical moment as normative. The idea, however, that cultural philosophy is only possible on the grounds of a metaphysics of human nature gradually won ground, more specifically on the grounds of a social anthropology or doctrine of man and his spiritual and social nature. Cultural philosophy should therefore be defined as the critical science which, led by social anthropology and normative ethics, tries to understand the true values of actual cultural life, and to indicate the norms according to which it has to direct itself. K.L.B.

CULTURE

(Latin, *colere*, plow, provide for, inhabit) In opposition to nature, everything man changes in nature in order to make it more suitable to his own purpose. We speak in this sense of agriculture, physical culture, mental culture. Man, however, always lives in communities. They possess a technical and spiritual apparatus for living, through which they not only supply the material necessities of life, but also make their stand in the world. *Subjective culture* can mean here the measure, to which a tribe, a nation or a group of nations have developed their biological and spiritual vitality. *Objective culture* means the totality of common forms of life, economical and spiritual goods proper to a tribe, a nation or a group of nations.

According to how one relates the forms of life and spiritual goods to the human group which carries them, culture will have a different meaning. Spengler considers it the organic totality of the biological and spiritual forces of a nation or a group of nations, with its own style and personality, and its own soul (*Kulturseele*). In the theory of the culture centers, culture means more the total technical and spiritual apparatus of life by which the tribes are indeed distinguished from each other, but which can detach itself from its bearers and move elsewhere. Toynbee's idea is closer to that of Spengler, not only because he does not care to speak of primitive culture, but also because he conceives culture as a closed unity, with its own inner vitality. In imitation of Bergson, however, he conceives the possibility of the evolution of closed communities toward a universal human culture. This is only to be attained by a universal religion, which is Christianity. Culture receives here a normative value. This changes with different views on life and the world. This is why a universally accepted definition of culture is not possible, unless it is limited to a purely formal concept. Then we can say: culture is the totality of forms of life characterizing a nation or a group of nations, or, in a universal sense, culture is the totality of forms of life which humanity creates for itself in and through its history. K.L.B.

CUMBERLAND, Richard 1632-1719.

British philosopher, one of the Platonists of *Cambridge. Criticizes and rejects the materialism of Hobbes and develops an ethic which is based on experience. Good is what promotes the general well-being: *"Commune bonum summa lex,"* and the individual's striving toward happiness should be subordinated to this higher law. The doctrine of Cumberland had much influence in the evolution of later English ethics.

CUSA, Nicholas of
(Real name: Nikolaus Krebs, Kryfts or Chrypps, from Kues on the Moselle) 1400-1464. German philosopher, mathematician, diplomat and theologian; 1448 cardinal; 1451 Bishop of Brixen and papal delegate in charge of the reformation of the monasteries in Germany; 1458-1460 vicar general in Rome. This many-sided intellect, under the strong influence of neo-Platonism, faithful son of the Church and apostle of tolerance, transitional figure from the Middle Ages to the modern way of thought and life, is philosophically a predecessor of Leibniz and Hegel. The first of the philosophical-theological works he wrote in Latin is the genial *De docta ignorantia* (1440). Other works are *Idiotae libri quattuor* (1450), *De visione Dei* 1453) *and De beryllo* (1458).

Centrally located in his doctrine is the theory of conscious not-knowing (ignorance), i.e., of the impossibility of a conceptual, provable, scholastic philosophy, and at the same time of the possibility of another, intuitive-mystic, suprarational knowledge. He is convinced that the divinity cannot be reached with human predicates, that we can know this divinity only in the form of a human-relative concept. But through speculative intuition it offers itself to us as the unity above all plurality, the coincidence of all oppositions (*coincidentia oppositorum*), in a mathematical symbol such as the eternal circle, in which the central point, diameter and circumference are the same; conceptually as the idea of all ideas, out of which came the whole concrete world by unfolding and particularization. In this world, the image of God, man is also indirectly an image of God since he is an image of the world; he is a world in miniature, but also a God in miniature, and every individual human being is a different, equivalent, but not interchangeable image of the universe and of God.

This doctrine leads toward the greatest tolerance in practical religious matters. According to his work *De pace seu concordantia fidei* (1454), there is only one prototype of things, but many mirrors reflect this prototype according to their own curve. In all the diversity of the cults there is also only one universal religion, one religion with only few dogmas, because dogmas, morals and usages have no other than symbolic value.

As astronomer and cosmologist Cusa broke with the medieval view of the world; every element of the cosmos is equivalent and the earth is as noble a star as any of the others, not the center of the infinite universe. God is, metaphysically, that center, and place and motion are only to be defined with the help of imaginary, but not really existing, fixed points. Therefore, the earth cannot be at rest, but has to be moving in one or another way. Thus this intentionally orthodox philosopher is the precursor of the heretics, Copernicus, Bruno, Galilei. Th.C.v.St.

CYNICS
A group of thinkers who deduce from certain assertions of °Socrates a relativistic and hedonistic philosophy, in opposition to °Plato, who deduced from the definition theory of Socrates the idealistic doctrine

of ideas. If it is true, as Socrates taught, that the wise man or the virtuous man suffices unto himself, then the laws of the state, the usages and ethics of the period he lives in, have no longer any meaning for him. Ethics is therefore conceived very individualistically. To this a hedonistic conception of life was easily joined: everything the wise man desires or does is morally justified. *Antisthenes, the founder of this school, developed, however, a moderate system. But his followers, as often happens, made the principles of the founder acceptable by pushing them to an extreme. The cynicism of *Diogenes, for instance, was the first appearance in European thought of an amoral and shameless attitude toward life, which elevates the crude, primitive instincts of man as the ideal motive of human life. F.D.R.

CYRENAICA, School of
*Aristippus of Cyrene and other disciples of *Socrates defended a subjective sensualism and relativism, to which was added a hedonistic morality. This hedonism had different forms.

D

D

As capital: symbol to indicate the possibility of a direct *reduction of the syllogistic mood in *Darapti, *Disamis, *Datisi and *Dimatis to the way of reasoning in *Darii of the first syllogistic *figure.

DALHAM, Florian

Born 1713, died in Salzburg 1795. Austrian Piarist, admired Francis Bacon. Empirical and sensualistic theory of knowledge, in the spirit of Locke and Condillac.

DAMASCUS

First half of the 6th century A.D. Last representative of pagan neo-Platonism, head of the School of Athens, where he taught when the edict of Justinianus closed the school in 529. He emphasized the transcendency of the "One" and the possibility of apprehending its relation to the lower beings; his philosophy shows a strong mystical tendency.

DARAPTI

Artificial word indicating the first mood of the third syllogistic *figure, in which the major and minor are a-propositions, the conclusion an i-proposition. E.g.: All ruminants have a compound stomach; all ruminants are herbivora; therefore some herbivora have a compound stomach.

M a P
M a S
———
S i P

DARII

Artificial word indicating the third mood of the first syllogistic *figure, in which the major is an a-proposition, minor and conclusion are i-propositions. E.g.: All lozenges are symmetrically divided by diagonals; some parallelograms are lozenges; therefore some parallelograms are symmetrically divided by their diagonals

M a P
S i P
———
S i M

DARING

Readiness to run a risk and danger. This is closely related to the personality. When one feels himself strong and safe he will more easily run a risk. The absence of a lively imagination can also lead to daring. In this case it is more short-sightedness, which is often lauded as courage.

DARWIN, Charles

Born in Shrewsbury 1809, died in Down 1882. Founder of the theory of *evolution in biology. All sorts of plants and animals descend from a few simple primitive types. He tries to explain the origin of their differences by accidental, small variations which were continued and accentuated in later generations; in the struggle for life only the most fit individuals remain and only those qualities are conveyed which appear to be useful. Later Darwin included human beings as well in his general theory of evolution.

DARWINISM

Based on the theory of Darwin (1859), looks for the explanation of changes in living nature, especially during *evolution. New species are created, according to Darwinism, as an effect of continuous small variations, of which—via the struggle for life—by natural selection the best remain. Consequently, Darwinism explains everything through chance; positive *adaptation and appropriateness are denied. Criticism of the theory: progress during evolution and the creation of new types cannot be explained by this theory. "One does not build a house by throwing bricks." Darwinism often resulted in atheism and materialism, although Darwin himself was a believer. Biologists are divided into defenders and opponents of Darwinism. M.B.

DATUM

Generally everything which presents itself to the knowing person, independent of the activity of knowledge itself. In this broad sense it is closely related to some meanings of object and phenomenon.

However, something can be, in a specific order, a datum as starting point of further investigation and intellectual development, and also appear to be, in a deeper order, already the result of constructive activity. E.g., the concept is a datum for the intellect, but only for the rationalist (and especially for the inneist) is it an absolute starting point. In the empirical sciences data are the presuppositions which are accepted without challenge: complexes of facts, and (in a less strict sense) also the axiomas.

In a narrower sense, datum is the object as it presents itself, before any formation of concept or judgment, in a fundamental experience, which has the character of a certain *intuition.

While prescientific knowledge and the positive sciences accept data without comment, philosophy cannot fail to investigate in what sense a datum is a datum. Does the datum really exist independently of the subject to which it is given? What are the conditions for something to be a datum? How is it possible that knowing, which is an activity arising in and remaining in the knowing subject, can be created under the influence of something which is outside of knowledge? Philosophy must also inquire into the original unity between subject and (given) object. J.P.

DAVID OF DINANT

Born in Dinant near Namur 12th century, died probably *ca.* 1210. Wrote *De tomis, id est de divisionibus*, probably in 1210, condemned by the Council of Paris. He seems to have taught a materialistic pantheism, with some elements from Aristotle, Alexander of Aphrodisias and Joannes Scottus Eriugena.

DAWES-HICKS, George 1862-1941.

English philosopher, professor in London.

DEATH

The definitive interruption of the process of life, by which the organism dissolves itself into inorganic elements. Much discussed in biology is whether death is inherent in life: in any case it appears in a being as a sudden separation. Death is then considered as purification, or as a transition to a higher life. Existentialism emphasizes the brutal necessity of death; Heidegger calls human existence itself a *"Sein zum Tode,"* in such a way, however, that man acquires the possibility of a real existence.

De BROGLIE, Louis 1892

French recipient of Nobel Prize for physics (1929), best known for his research on the quantum theory and wave mechanics.

DECISION

The moment in which an *action as such is accomplished, after meditation on the ways wherein a specific intention can be realized. It is an internal act of the will, but always implicitly connected with the actualization of the action, which does not have to happen immediately. A decisive proposition is a proposition in which a decision is expressed. It can be elementary or the conclusion of a syllogism. It is always put in the subjunctive mood.

DEDEKIND, Richard 1831-1916

German mathematician who originated a theory of irrational numbers. Works: *Continuity and Irrational Numbers* (1871) and *The Nature and Meaning of Numbers* (1888).

DEDUCTIBLE

Is an *assertion when there exists a deduction for it. In some systems with natural deduction deductible is considered as a primitive concept.

DEDUCTION

Reasoning opposed to induction, in which a general truth is deducted or proved from a previously and better known truth.

In modern logic one can only speak of deduction in relation to a specific deductive system, with a specific deductive theory. In a *real axiomatic deductive theory* the deduction happens from unproved theses (axioms or postulates); by means of deduction theses are inferred (we can neglect the difference between theses, corollaries, scholia etc. . .; they only differ in their importance). Definitions are not real deduction rules, because two objects of thought which can be deduced to each other by definition, have to be considered identical. An example of real axiomatic theory is the Euclidean geometry, which was for centuries the pattern of deduction "more geometrico." In this deduction are used, silently, the rules of the *proposition and *conceptual logic. If we explicitate the use of these rules, we will have made clear all the theses and the rules which are used in our deductive system. We can, in the same way, explain all mathematical theories, e.g. the arithmetics; we can also treat separately the logic of the propositions and concepts. All these theories remain *real*, in as much as the terms have a meaning which we grasp intuitively (intuition of the numbers, of space, also of the logical operations.) If one gives these terms this intuitive meaning, then the axioms and the definitions would be evident.

It has become clear now that such unconditioned evidence for the axioms and definitions does not exist. All deductive theories are therefore enunciated as *pure* theories. The meaning of the terms has therefore no role in the deduction. This however does not mean that the terms should be considered definitely as meaningless but that one can neglect the meaning in the deduction. This is true not only for the mathematics but also for logic.

Such a situation could be reached more or less with a theory using the usual language. One would in this theory use the word "a straight line" without determining if it is used in the euclidean or non-euclidean meaning. Or one could use the "if . . ., then" according to specific rules which would be valid in the intuitionistic logic as well as in the classical logic. It would however be impossible to make such a theory independent from a specific grammar. The modern deductive theories use therefore a *formalism. (This does not only mean an artificial language with symbols, but a language in which abstraction is made of the meaning of the symbols by deduction). R.F.

DEFINITE

A concept is definite when it is so clear that it can be distinguished from every other concept. All being is definite, since the indefinite cannot be conceived and can not exist.

DEFINITION

Elucidation of a simple concept through a complex concept. According to the way it is obtained, a definition can be *analytical* or *synthetic*. An analytical definition analyzes (*see* analysis) a concept into the characteristics which compose its content (e.g., a parallelogram is a quadrangle of which the sides are parallel); a synthetic definition (or genetic definition) is constructed out of already known elements, which determine the being or becoming of something (e.g., by letting two parallel lines intersect two other parallel lines, one constructs a quadrangle, which is called parallelogram.)

The distinction between *nominal* and *real* definition is classical. The prior gives an explanation of a word by which the concept is indicated. It can then be an *etymological* or deductive definition, explaining what the word as such means (e.g., philosophy is the love of wisdom) or a *popular,* i.e., usual, definition, responding to the question in what sense the word is used (e.g., philosophy is the knowledge of all possible things). The latter is an explanation of the known thing itself; it is either a *descriptive* definition, consisting in as complete as possible an enumeration of its characteristics (e.g., philosophy is a certain, thorough, disinterested knowledge of all, even the most difficult, things by which one is able to enlighten and convince others); or an *essential* definition, by which a thing's most fundamental characteristic is indicated, from which its other characteristics naturally proceed (e.g., philosophy is the knowledge of the last grounds of explanation of all things).

The nature of a definition will be determined by the nature of what is defined: in physics we give *a posteriori descriptions; in mathematics *a priori word definitions (*see* construction); in philosophy we proceed by means of etymological, popular and descriptive definitions, to reach an essential definition.

Since a definition is an explanation of a simple concept, it cannot contain that which is defined, or something that only becomes clear through the definition itself, as a defining element (*see* tautology). It cannot be purely negative; it has to be free of *metaphors. It has, finally, to be as short as possible and at the same time complete, so that it is neither too large nor too narrow. One of the characteristics of a good definition is its complete reversibility (*see* conversion) with the defined. Socrates emphasized the great importance of the definition: the delimitation, outline and sharp demarcation of that which is to be further discussed and disputed. A philosophical definition is, as it were, a theory crystallized in a few words. Our knowledge will not be broadened by it, but we will obtain better insight. Not everything can be defined, naturally, e.g., neither the very first simple concepts (*see* transcendentalia) nor the highest-class concepts (*see* categories). I.v.d.B.

In the traditional logic one can distinguish *real* definition (definition of things) and *nominal* definition (definition of symbols). We can consider all definitions in the modern formal logic as nominal definitions: they explain that a not yet introduced symbol, the *definiendum* or *definitum,* can be exchanged with another (compound) symbol, the *definiens.* It is preferable for the *correct* definition that the definitum be a new, not yet used expression, otherwise we could fall into a vicious circle.

A definition, as defined here, is a conventional rule. If we, however, consider a system in which a symbol has already been introduced, and in which we can prove that this symbol is equivalent to another, then the first symbol can give a possible definition for the other. E.g. in the classical logic of propositions we can prove that: if $\underline{p}$, then $\underline{q}$ is equivalent to: not-$\underline{p}$, or $\underline{q}$. This latter (compound) symbol gives a possible definition of: if $\underline{p}$, then $\underline{q}$.

In formal logic a definition is a special exchange- or substitution-rule. Substitution rules are better formulated unconditionally. In some theories the conditional definition is however used: if $\underline{a}$ and $\underline{b}$ are numbers, then is $\underline{a} + \underline{b}$ ....;

It is mostly said that in the deductive theory a symbol is implicitly defined by the axiomata, to which it is subjected. We have then an *improper* definition.—R.F.

DEGENERATION
Is called by the biologist the phenomenon that removes in the reproduction with limited possibility of crossing (or in-breeding), the viability of a race. Such have been the causes, in the course of the *evolution, of the extinction of many forms.

DEISM
Doctrine created in England, (Herbert of Cherbury.)

It accepts a personal God as creator, but denies that this God preoccupies Himself further with the world; supernatural revelation and miracles are rejected. Many philosophers of the French Enlightenment followed this doctrine. Some deists accept the existence of providence but all of them are skeptical in regard to the revelation.

DELIBERATION
That moment in the action when the most suitable means for the realization of a proposed goal are considered.

DELMEDIGO, Joseph Solomon 1591-1655
Physician and teacher who wandered through Europe in the seventeenth century, a disciple of Galileo and critic of the medieval philosophy of nature.

DEMETRIUS
Contemporary of Seneca and *Cynic philosopher of the Roman period, probably author of 51 letters, in which he connects the ethics of the Cynics with that of the *Stoics.

DEMIURGE (Artisan)

Plato uses this term to designate the one who regulates the universe. He has not, however, all the duties of the creating God.

DEMOCRACY

Form of government in which the subjects rule themselves by means of representatives, chosen by them.

DEMOCRITUS OF ABDERA

5th-4th century B.C. With *Leucippus founder of the school of the atomists. Only a few fragments of his extensive works have survived. A hundred ethical proverbs have also reached us under his name. Democritus tried to reconcile the mutability of the universe (see Heraclitus) with the absolute unity of being (see Parmenides). Everything, he said, is composed of an infinite number of small, not further divisible particles or atoms. They do not show any qualitative difference, except their impenetrability or density. They differ in quality: some are big, some small, some circular, square and polygonal, etc. They are also different either in form, as A and Z, or in order, as AZ and ZA, or in their position, as Z and N. These atoms, infinite in number, move in empty space; if there were no empty space, the atoms would be unable to move.

Atoms, emptiness and motion are the three elements of the system of Democritus. Through their motion the particles bumped against each other, and in this way a mechanical sorting came about, i.e., equal particles came together. The result was that the earth came to be in the middle of the universe, while the lightest atoms— those of fire—gathered as illuminating bodies revolving around the earth. Democritus developed his elementary psychology on the same basis. The soul is composed of especially fine, circular atoms of fire, which interpenetrate the atoms of the body. Thus the soul has a temperature halfway between cold and warm, and, thanks to this condition, it can observe and think. It can also intercept the radiations of demons or spirits, who live in the air and who can influence souls to good or evil. We do not have to deduce materialism from this doctrine. The smoothness, the fineness and smallness of the atoms of the soul are probably a first effort to indicate the spirituality of the soul. The ethical proverbs of Democritus deal often with the happiness of man, namely, tranquillity of mind, an intimate and tasteful pleasure to the soul of the wise man. F.D.R.

DEMONAX OF CYPRUS

2nd century A.D. *Cynic, but very eclectic in his thought. Is dissenting and critical of the religious cult and manticism; represents a more humane and mild direction in the Cynical School.

De MORGAN, Augustus 1806-1871

English mathematician and logician, inventor of De Morgan's theorem and developer of a new nomenclature for logical expression. Works: *Formal Logic* (1847), *Essay on Probabilities* (1838).

DEONTOLOGY

Theory of obligation, a part of ethics, in which are discussed obligations versus God, versus oneself, and versus one's fellow man. In this sense deontology was developed by the Stoics and Christianized by Ambrosius. Since Kant placed *duty at the root of all ethics, deontology has tended to mean the often casuistical definition of that which, in a specific domain (e.g., in a specific profession) and in specific cases, is morally allowed.

DEPENDENCE

Form of relation. There is real dependence ($\underline{a}$ cannot exist without $\underline{b}$) and ideal relation ($\underline{a}$ has no sense or value without $\underline{b}$). Considering objects which have a relation to each other, dependence can be: religious (relation of man to God), logical ($\underline{b}$ proceeds from $\underline{a}$), mathematical ($\underline{b}$ is a function of $\underline{a}$), causal ($\underline{a}$ is caused by $\underline{b}$). One can also speak of moral dependence, political dependence, etc.

DEPICTION

Be $\underline{f}$ a *function, whose argument values $\underline{x}$ form the aggregate $\underline{A}$, while the functionvalues $\underline{y} = \underline{f}(\underline{x})$ belong to an aggregate $\underline{B}$. It can then appear in general that one same element $\underline{y}_1$ of $\underline{B}$ belongs as functionvalues to two (or more) argument values $\underline{x}_1$ and $\underline{x}_2$; therefore $\underline{f}(\underline{x}_1) = \underline{f}(\underline{x}_2) = \underline{y}_1$. It is

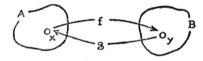

also possible that an element $\underline{y}_0$ of $\underline{B}$ does not at all appear as function value. We accept now however that for the above mentioned function $\underline{f}$, none of these cases appear; every element $\underline{y}$ of $\underline{B}$ corresponds then as function value $\underline{f}(\underline{x})$ to one specific element $\underline{x}$ of $\underline{A}$. There is then in reverse a function $\underline{g}$, which makes correspond this element $\underline{x}$ of $\underline{A}$ with the element $\underline{y}$ of $\underline{B}$, so that we can write instead of $\underline{y} = \underline{f}(\underline{x})$; $\underline{x} = \underline{g}(\underline{y})$. One says that the function $\underline{f}$ produces a *depiction* of the aggregate $\underline{A}$ on the aggregate $\underline{B}$—or a *one-one-relation* between the elements of $\underline{A}$ and the elements of $\underline{B}$. —or that it transforms the aggregate $\underline{A}$ into the aggregate $\underline{B}$. —E.W.B.

DE SANCTIS, Francesco
1817-1883

Italian professor of comparative literature who, after imprisonment for his part in the 1848 revolution in Naples, became a private tutor and free-lance writer, and minister of public education under Victor Emmanuel II. Considered founder of modern literary criticism in Italy.

DESCARTES, Rene (Cartesius)

Born in La Haye (Touraine) 1596, died in Stockholm 1650. From 1604 to 1612 or 1605 to 1614 student at the college of the Jesuits at La Flèche, where he meets Mercenne, who became his friend for life. Studied law in Poitiers, engaged himself in the army of the states of Holland, and later in the imperial armies in Germany. During the winter of 1619, in a camp on the Danube, a light of a miraculous discovery dawned upon him, an inspiration which gave a steady direction to his studies. The following years he traveled through Hungary, Germany, H o ll a n d, Switzerland and Italy. To fulfill a vow he had made. Descartes stopped in 1628 in Loreto, where he thanked the Blessed Virgin for the miraculous inspiration. From 1628 on he lived in Holland (Franeker, Utrecht, Deventer, Amsterdam, Leiden, Santpoort and Egmond). His most important works were written in those cities. Here he found the rest which he could not find in his native country because of social intercourse. He traveled a few times to France, Germany, Denmark and eventually to Sweden on the invitation of Queen Christina. He had relations with the Dutch writers P.C. Hooft and C. Huygens, and with many important personalities around the world, although he was always searching for the solitude of the study. He became involved in disputes with the Protestant theological schools of Leiden and Utrecht, but found followers in other schools.

The most striking element in his system is the place he reserves for the method (*Discours de la méthode*, 1637). To renew the method of science and philosophy he considered a task imposed on him by God which he must fulfill with unwearying diligence. The fruitfulness of his method was evidenced in the scientific domain. With his *Geometrie* (1637) a new era began in mathematics, although mathematicians hesitate to define clearly that newness. It is often said that he invented analytical geometry, but this is not exactly so; he perfected and enlarged it. He revised what already existed and applied modern algebra to the analysis of the ancients. He opened the way for the infinitesimal calculus. By applying the mathematical method to the physical science he completed the rupture with the old physics which were still used. Leonardo da Vinci had possessed mathematical intuition, Galileo made an effort in that direction, but it was Descartes who elaborated the mathematical apparatus with which modern physics works. He enriched the theory of the refraction of light and reworked the theory of the weight of air.

The method seems no less useful in the domain of philosophy. Since nothing is absolutely certain, Descartes begins philosophy with a doubt of everything, until he reaches the unshakable point: *Cogito ergo sum* (I think, therefore I am). This proposition is not an argument, but the immediate intuition of his own existence even when he doubts that existence. Here lies the *primum philosophicum* or the point of departure of Cartesian Philosophy, which includes also the criterion of certitude and truth. Why am I sure that I exist? Because I see it clearly and distinctly. Therefrom comes the general rule that everything which is seen *clairement* and *distinctement* is true.

This philosophy was developed in the *Meditationes de prima philosophia*. (1641, French translation 1647). It is the foundation of mathematics and physics. The centerpiece is the ontological proof of the existence of God which is formulated in this manner: Nothing is as clear and distinct as the thought of the existence of God, i.e., a sovereign and perfect being, in whose idea necessary and eternal existence is already included, and therefore He exists. The existence of God is as certain as any geometrical proof. The existence of God, perfect and therefore not deceitful being, guarantees further the objectivity of our knowledge. In so far as we see matter clearly and distinctly as extensive, we have to accept its existence. Further qualities of matter are divisibility, figurability and mobility; it is motion (in the sense of local motion) that explains the transformations of the physical world. The only causes of this motion we know are the mechanical causes, not the final causes since we do not penetrate the plans of God. In the beginning of the creation God gave the world a quantity of motion, which always remains the same: this is the law of the preservation of energy of modern mechanics. The peripatetic theory of motion is entirely relinquished with this theory.

Dualism of the spirit which is naturally active and of matter which is naturally passive gives Descartes insurmountable difficulties. It brings him to consider animals as *bêtes-machines,* whose actions are only explained by mechanical causes. In man there seems to be an interaction between the soul as spiritual substance and the body as material (physical) substance. How this is possible is still an open question: Descartes thinks that the soul resides in the pineal glands, whence it directs, by way of the *esprits animaux* or animal spirits, the movements of the members of the body. The soul also experiences the repercussion of the body. He compares it with the idea of strength, but we cannot conceive it very clearly.

Descartes does not develop an elaborated ethics. In order to have a calm life, he constructs, in spite of the doubt, a few rules: conformity with the laws and the religion of the country; moderate desire and passion; one must not be dissauded from following reason; not look for anything else than happiness, which is found in the practice of virtue. We can identify here a few of the doctrines of the Stoics.

The influence of Descartes on philosophy is very important. He has been named, and justly, the father of modern philosophy. By elevating the ego to the *primum philosophicum* he introduced *subjectivism,* which is without doubt characteristic of modern thought. The influence of his *rationalism* was also far-reaching. *Malebranche, *Spinoza and *Leibniz continued in this direction. As a reaction to rationalism came empiricism, which considers experience the only source of certitude, as opposed to thinking with innate ideas (inneism). Kant was the first to destroy the naive confidence in the possibilities of knowledge. Descartes still believes in the virtue of our thinking ability; the only

question is its appropriate use. His rationalism, on the other hand, is limited to his defense of the independence of reason in its own domain. He does not reject dogma and tradition, and remained a faithful Catholic. Finally, he made modern psychology possible as a doctrine of consciousness, with his theory of the dualism of spirit and matter. He established mechanism in the physical world. H.R.

DESCRIBED FUNCTION

Is a description which characterizes an individual or in general the object of thought by means of a relation, e.g. the father of John, the sinus of $\underline{x}$.

DESIDERIUM NATURALE

(Latin: natural desire) In scholastic philosophy and theology the natural desire of reasonable creatures to see God. The question is how it can be realized. Thomas Aquinas teaches repeatedly that a natural desire cannot be vain, and that it must be possible for a created intellect, such as the human intellect, to arrive at the contemplation of the divine substance. It does not, however, explain what it learns, through analogical knowledge from the world, of the existence of God and His qualities, and it desires naturally to see the essence of God. But on the other hand it is clear for Thomas that this contemplation of God is only given through supernatural grace, to which human nature can have no claim. With subtle distinctions and divergent explanations the scholastic philosophers and theologians try to give an explanation of the natural human plan of being, which desires things which are more than natural. Human nature is metaphysically most intimately seen when one reaches this stratum, from which it can be elevated to a higher order by means of a gift, coming from God, possible (certainly not necessary) and free; it is humbly searching for more than nature, as well as the final *end. H.R.

DESIRE

Mostly the spiritual form of concupiscence. Desire contains an anticipation of the satisfaction although one can also speak of a vague desire.

DESTINATION

Goal to which any person or thing is naturally and ultimately directed. The different philosophical systems give different views on the destination of man. Fichte thinks that it is the realization of the Divinity. Also final *End.

DESTINY

See fate.

DE STUTT DE TRACY, Antoine Louis Claude

Born in Paris 1754, died in Paray-le-Fresil 1836. Sensualist influenced by Locke and Condillac. The connection between the ego and the outer world is a voluntary and felt action on the ego's part, and resistance on the part of the other.

DETERMINABILITY

Is valid for a system when there is a method to determine in a finite number of steps if an assertion is valid or not. The logic of *proposition and the logic of concept (logic of classes) are determinable. Determinability does not mean that all problems which can be formulated about a system, can be solved by means of mechanical calculations (as this is the case for comparisons of the 1st and 2nd degree in algebra). Determinability means only that one can determine if an assertion which was formulated, is or is not a thesis.

It has long been accepted that all deductive systems would be determinable; Gödel has proved the opposite in his famous incompleteness-theorem.

DETERMINATION

Limitation of the extent of a concept by the addition of further determining characteristics. In this way the *comprehension of the concept is enlarged, while its *extension is narrowed; e.g., Germans, Sudeten-Germans. Is opposed to abstraction.

DETERMINISM

Doctrine that everything that happens is strictly determined. In the first place, natural phenomena. This doctrine was generally accepted in modern natural sciences (and from there applied to other domains), especially under the form of mechaxin, but it has been abandoned in contemporary physics. More and more the *contingent character of natural laws, which have been reduced to pure statistical regularities, cannot describe light, for instance, as particles (see quanta) and at the same time as waves. This led to the so-called uncertain relations of Heisenberg.

Determinism is accepted in psychology insofar as human behavior is strictly determined (opposed to *indeterminism, *freedom). We either simply follow our instincts or experience a conflict and follow the strongest inclination; in both cases we are psychologically, and in the last instance physiologically, determined. It is therefore the task of deterministic psychology to determine the necessary causes of human behavior. Extreme determinism in psychology is not accepted any more, but in many psychological systems there are still deterministic elements; e.g., in

Freud's theory of the genesis of phantasmata. Determinism as a theory does not belong to empirical psychology, but the feeling of freedom which is experienced does. The theories of Lombroso (human action is determined by bodily and spiritual constitution) and Heymans (determinism of motives depends on inclination and character) are therefore not a part of psychology.

A special form of psychological determinism is the *rational determinism* of Leibniz. He does not consider physiological antecedents, but only judgment. But if one judges reasonably, he will choose the best. We are therefore committed by reason to the choice of the best. Freedom lies only in the judgment (*see* liberum arbitrium).

Determinism can also mean that the course of the human life is determined by God. *See also* predestination, fatalism.

DEUSSEN, Paul 1854-1919.
German philosopher, disciple of Schopenhauer, professor in Kiel.

DEVELOPMENT OF A CLASS
Is defined in the same way as *°normal forms* of a *°proposition. Here however are negations, *°alternatives, *°conjunctions of classes and not of propositions. One has therefore disjunctive and conjunctive, special and complete disjunctive and conjunctive developments of a class.

DEWEY, John 1859-1952.
American pragmatical philosopher, professor in New York. Among his works: *Reconstruction in Philosophy*, 1920; *The Quest for Certainty* (G i f f o r d Lectures), 1929. Dewey was very much under the influence of *°James, but has his own view in many instances. In content, his work is inspired by social and pedagogical problems.

In method, Dewey developed his own experimental or instrumental logic. Man moves in an always changing world. When he encounters difficulties he tries by reasoning to find means to overcome these difficulties. Thought is therefore an instrument for action. Every idea is created by experience; its veracity can only be deduced from its success, with which it influences the reality. This reality is first of all the social reality of human society. It is on questions about this society that Dewey concentrates. Therefore social pedagogy lies at the center of his thought. Education is education for society. Here thus also lies morality: All real morality is directed toward society as such. Dewey had especially great influence in the development of pedagogy. B.D.

DIAELUS
See vicious circle.

DIALECTIC
Initially the art of the dialogue. While it had degenerated with the Sophists to the art of contentless discussion, Socrates brought it back to the art of real conversation which, through questions and answers, reaches clearly outlined concepts and orders these according to species and genus. With Plato dialectic is at the same time ontological, since by this means are attained those ideas through which reality in last instance "is." Dialectic is then like philosophy itself: the activity of the mind which, e.g., from the contemplation of beautiful bodies rises to the contemplation of beautiful souls, and so to the contemplation of Beauty itself, or the idea of the beautiful. Aristotle reduced dialectic to the doctrine of those judgments which, while they rest on current opinions and are not found-

ed in the essence of the thing itself, are only apparently true or false. Thus limited to formal logic, dialectic constitutes with rhetoric and grammar the trivium of the Middle Ages.

In modern times Kant reintroduced the term "dialectic" to indicate the motion of thought toward complete unity, or the study of judgments in which this thought, going further than the limits of experience, expresses itself (*transcendental dialectic*). But it was Hegel who reinstated dialectic as the motion which is made by thought, in accordance with the evolution of the essence itself. The Absolute, in fact, goes through an inner evolution: it opposes itself to return to itself, enriched by this opposition, to attain complete possession of itself. In opposition to the dialectic of Plato, which is *dichotomic* and *incomplete*, Hegel's dialectic is *triadic* and therefore *complete*. Every given definition turns to its opposite, which opposition is lifted by a reconciliation. While for Hegel the reconciliation is factual and therefore *closed*, it remains for Kierkegaard an eternal problem, and his dialectic is therefore *open*.

In an inferred and less strict sense, dialectic is every cohesion of thought in which the mind, progressing from point to point, does not rest until it reaches the last one. Also, every totality of judgments which logically follow one from the other. J. Gr.

DIALECTICAL METHOD

The form in which thinking and being developed, according to Hegel; i.e., from affirmation over negation to negation of the negation, or, as it is usually termed, from thesis, over the antithesis to the synthesis. Every given definition removes itself necessarily and goes over to its contrary definition. The mutual struggle brings us to a new definition, which is richer and more concrete insofar as it embraces the original definition, but on a higher level. The reconciliation thus obtained is again the point of departure for a new trial, until complete concreteness is obtained. Although the method cannot be detached from its content, it was valued for itself and received an infinite variety of applications. Marx, particularly, applied it to matter and thus created dialectic *materialism.

DIALECTICAL MOMENT

The second or negative moment in the dialectical triad. It is called dialectical because it makes dialectical progress possible.

DIALLELON

See vicious circle.

DICHOTOMY

The principle of the division of a concept (*see* division), in which only two *contradictory groups are found in every level of division; e.g., living and not living bodies. See Tree of Porphyrius.

DICTIO or REDUCTIO PER IMPOSSIBILE

The indirect argumentation of a thesis by proving that the contrary cannot be true; also the indirect refutation of a thesis by proving that it leads to an absurd and impossible conclusion.

DICTUM DE OMNI ET NULLO

The thesis of everything and nothing, classical fundamental principle of all deductions: what applies or does not apply to a group or class of things applies or does not apply to everything that belongs to that group or class. *See also* Nota notae est nota rei ipsius.

DIDEROT, Denis

Born in Langres 1713, died in Paris 1784. Started with the edition of the French *Encylopédie* (*see* encyclopedists) in which the philosophy of the Enlightenment is expressed. Through deism, skepticism and materialism he arrived at a pantheistic naturalism. Thought is the action of atoms with sensation. He denies personal immortality and freedom of the will; he considers religious faith to be naive. Man must attain a combination of virtue and beauty (*see* Shaftsbury). The beautiful is that which is in accordance with nature.

DIETRICH OF FREIBERG

Probably born in Freiberg (Saxon) *ca.* 1250, died after 1310. Dominican, *magister regens* in Paris probably between 1290 and 1293, author of many works of science, philosophy and mysticism. Most typical philosophical work: *De intellectu et intelligibili.* He was strongly influenced by Proclus, whom he placed at the same level as Aristotle and Augustine; taught a neo-Platonic metaphysics within the limits of orthodoxy, but with very personal ideas.

DIFFERENCE

The *distinction between the one and the other thing. It can be a difference in *degree*, different measures in which things conform to each other: somebody can for instance be more or less strong; this difference in degree is present in things which and inasmuch as they fall under one analogical concept (*analogy). It can also be a *specific* difference or difference in species, which exists in a different element determining the species, in things of a same *category. We could also call it difference *in essence.* We would then call differ-

ence in *nature* the difference in activity, proceeding from their individual or specific nature: a cat for instance differs in nature from a dog.

DIFFERENTIATION

Appearance of a multiplicity of organs in a living being, each with its own form and function. Differentiation is reached in the course of individual development. Differences in human nature are founded on this differentiation, which, compared to the forms, is gradually ordered. "Higher" often means, then, more differentiated.

DILEMMA

Also called "horned syllogism" (Latin: *syllogismus cornutus*). A compound hypothetical syllogism, in which the major is often a dual disjunctive proposition (*see* lemma), the minor two conditional propositions. If, from the affirmation of both members of the disjunction, the affirmation of what is thus conditioned follows, we often call it a *constructive* dilemma. E.g.: You were present or not present when this happened. If you were present, you should have prevented it. If you were not present, you were not at your post. In both cases you did not do your duty. If the negation of both members causes the negation of the condition, we call the dilemma *destructive*. E.g.: On Sunday you take a walk, whether the weather is good or bad. If the weather is good I do not go for a walk, because there is too much traffic on the road. When the weather is bad, I certainly do not go, since it is no pleasure. Thus I never go for a walk on Sunday.

The dilemma can also be formulated as a compound categorical syllogism. E.g.: Plants multiply and so do animals. Bacteria are either plants or animals. Therefore they multiply in any case. A good dilemma requires a complete disjunction, exact partial conclusions and a solely possible final conclusion, so that the dilemma cannot be turned against us (Latin: *retorsio*, turning). Disjunctions which have more members are called trilemma, quadrilemma, polylemma. In a broader sense "dilemma" means a necessary, but difficult choice between two possibilities, both of which have something disagreeable about them. I.v.d.B.

DILTHEY, Wilhelm 1833-1911.
German philosopher, historian. Main work: *Der Aufbau der geschichtlichen Welt in den Geisteswissenschaften*, 1910. Dilthey starts from the idea that everybody has his own view of life and the world, which is determined by his place in historical evolution and by the nature of his own essence. The intellectual man forms for himself a materialistic or positivistic philosophy; the sensible man a pantheistic philosophy, such as German idealism; the willful man finally emphasizes freedom, as did Plato, Christianity and Kant. These three forms of philosophy appear in several variations, depending upon the historical situation. Philosophy is the study of these different forms, in order to clarify their *structure*. Only then can we understand alien forms of life. The humanities consist of the ways in which man understands himself. Dilthey applies himself to an understanding of the humanities and to distinguishing them from the natural sciences. In the humanities it is not a question of understanding man, in the sense of finding causal explanations, but of understanding the way in which man experiences himself. Dilthey therefore makes a distinction between causal-explanatory and "*verstehende*" psychol-

ogy. His method is set forth in *Das Erlebnis und die Dichtung* (1905), in which he examines the fundamental inspiration of Lessing, Goethe, Novalis and Holderlin. B.D.

DIMENSION
A body has three dimensions: length, width and height; a plane has two, and a line only one, while a point has no dimensions at all. The position of a point on a given line can thus be determined for the indication of a number; namely, the distance ($\underline{x}$) from a given point to another point, considered as the origin. In a plane two numbers are required ($\underline{x}$ and $\underline{y}$), in a body three ($\underline{x}$, $\underline{y}$ and $\underline{z}$). A connection is also made between geometry and algebra. Since there is no objection to working with more than three unknowns in algebra, a greater-dimensional geometry has been developed, although graphic space admits only three dimensions.

It is clear, through the natural sciences, that the greater-dimensional consideration is fruitful. It is often very useful to consider time as a fourth dimension. A four-dimensional consideration thus includes space and time.

In physics the term "dimension" is also used in a different sense, namely, to indicate how a specific physical quantity can be reduced to other quantities, e.g., to length, time or mass. Quantity-velocity (distance divided by time) has the dimension l/t, acceleration the dimension $1/t^2$, and force ml/t^2. A.G.M.v.M.

DING AN SICH
For Kant, that which is insofar it exists on its own, outside and independent of human consciousness. It is thus opposed to *phenomenon, which indicates an existing thing

112

insofar it exists, not in itself, but "for us." It is not "known" but only "thought" by man. It can be apprehended only by an intellectual *intuition, and is therefore called *noumenon. Man is not able, however, to achieve such an intuition; he knows only what is given to him through sensual knowledge. Practical reason alone brings us certainty as to the existence of the *Ding an sich*. For to have a sense to freedom, which is a necessary condition to morality, we must accept as a postulate that freedom, which is not due to any man, is a quality of man as noumenon or as *Ding an sich*. J.P.

DIO CHRYSOSTOMUS

Ca. 40 A.D. Native of Prusa (Bithynia), first a rhetor, later a philosopher. Taught the Cynical view of life: sublimation in a simple rural type of life and concern for social problems, especially in regard to impoverished city people. Came under the influence of the Stoics in his doctrine of the harmonic unity of the cosmic *polis*, which embraces man and the gods.

DIODORUS CRONUS

Died 307 B.C. Philosopher of the School of Megara, known because of his assertion that nothing which will not be in reality, is possible. The possible that did not become reality is impossible. He also opposed the possibility of motion.

DIOGENES OF SINOPE

4th century B.C. Disciple of *Antisthenes and the most popular representative of the *Cynics. Like Plato, he defended common possession of women and opposed world citizenship to nationalism. He was, however, better known for his rejection of all traditional ethics and for a few anecdotes. Looking for "the human being," in the middle of the day, with a lamp, he asked Alexander the Great to step aside so that the sun could reach the barrel in which he lived.

DIONYSIAN

See Apollonian.

DIONYSIUS THE CARTHUSIAN

Productive Dutch mystical and philosophical writer. Born in Rijkel near Saint-Trond (Belgium) 1402-03, died in Roermond 1471. *Doctor extaticus.* Was first a Thomist, later more inclined toward *Albertism. Condensed the whole theology and philosophy of the *via antiqua* into a strong synthesis. Rejecting the Thomistic doctrine of the real difference between essence and existence, and the principle of *individuation, he taught that things are individuated by their actual existence, that the intellect can have a direct knowledge of the existence of immaterial things, and is not in every instance dependent on the senses. He was a follower of the *metaphysics of light, but considered that the competence of reason in the metaphysical field was very limited.

DIONYSIUS THE GREAT

Died *ca.* 265. Bishop of Alexandria. Disciple of *Origenes, whom he succeeded as director of the Christian School of *Alexandria. Opposed the materialistic atomism of Democritus and Epicurus.

DIRECTION

In physics there are quantities with and without direction. For a *quantity without direction* (called scalar quantity) a number is enough to indicate the value, e.g. mass and temperature. For a *quantity with direction* (called vector quantity) one has to indicate, next to the number the direction if one wants to determine the quantity, e.g. velocity and force.

DISAPPROVAL

The act by which dislike is manifested for a person's action which is regarded as implicitly bad. It does not matter whether the action was freely made; one disapproves of the action in itself, since it is judged a bad action by the intelligence, or is considered morally wrong. Disapproval is thus an act of the total person as a moral subject.

DISCONTINUOUS

That which is not continuous, °discrete, opposed to °continuous.

DISCRETE

Said of quantities which are separated from each other. It is therefore opposed to continuous and contiguous. It offers the possibility of numbering and is therefore the basis for the theory of natural numbers.

DISCURSIVE

Human thought is called discursive because it has to proceed from concept to concept and from proposition to proposition toward a more complete, expressive and clear knowledge of beings in their totality. This progressive knowing is necessary because man does not have a positive intellectual °intuition of reality. See also reason.

DISINTEGRATION

In biology and physics, the reduction of a higher structure into a lower. Disintegration occurs upon the death of an organism; the activity of life itself is directed more toward the creation of a higher structure or integration. In inanimate nature one can consider, among other things, radioactive fission as disintegration.

DISINTERESTED or UNSELFISH

Without °selfish intentions. Unselfishness or disinterest includes, not necessarily the absence of every practical inclination toward the reality of the object, but the absence of all attitudes which eventually would serve only the subject's own pleasure.

DISJUNCTION

See judgment, syllogism, alternation.

DISLIKE

A negative attitude toward a person or a thing. One can distinguish a dislike on a sensual level (e.g., to loathe a stench) from dislike on a spiritual level (e.g., aversion to a writer).

DISPARATE or disjunct

See concept.

DISTANCE

When two bodies do not border upon each other, there exists between them a certain distance. The question arises whether there can be a distance between two bodies when no other body is found between them. (See °contact-and position-theory.) Apart from philosophical considerations, the contemporary natural sciences no longer speak of "empty °space" in the strict sense, since they have adopted the field theories. They do not accept, therefore, mere distances, but always distances in a particular medium with physical qualities.

DISTINCTION

Firstly, the absence of identity between things and concepts (Lat: distinctio). This can exist objectively before and independently from all intellectual conception (Lat. distinctio realis), as between soul and body; it can also be subjective and as a result of our intellectual conception (Lat: distinctio rationis); in this case we have either a metaphysical or virtual distinction, which is immediately founded on an objective ground as it is between the sensual and the intellectual in man, or a *logical* distinction, which is only based on a distant objective ground, as exists between the essence and nature of things.

Secondly, that in which this distinction exists: the point of difference (Lat: differentia). It can be an *essential* distinction, as life is the essential or specific difference between the organic and inorganic beings; or an *accidental* distinction. The first one is part of a substance, the latter only presupposes a substance as carrier. In this case it can be a property which proceeds from the essence of the thing (Lat. proprium) as for instance the human ability to laugh; or a distinction which is only accidentally connected with the essence of the thing (Lat. accidens) or individual quality. This can again be of a consistent nature (individual *characteristic) as for instance the fact of being white for a swan, or of a temporary nature, as for instance the fact of having a tooth ache for John Johnson.

The making of a right distinction between different things and concepts is of utmost importance for the logical thought and speech. The untruth of many assertions and conclusions rests often on a lack of correct distinctions: the simple way to refute them is then to point out that a distinction should have been made, also a distinction between the different sorts of distinction. (see predicables)

DISTRIBUTIVE
The logical use in a proposition of a *universal concept in its complete extent; e.g.: whales (= all whales) are mammals; opposed to *particular.

DIVERSITY
What is the ground of the *difference between the one and the other. Is therefore opposed to *identity. It is mostly taken in the narrow sense, not pointing to a pure *numerical* difference of individuals of the same species, but to a *qualitative* difference, which concerns the genus.

DIVISIBILITY OF THE CONTINUUM
In a purely mathematical sense, the continuum is infinitely divisible. Every division of a line produces another line, which, as such, is again divisible, etc. In the real physical order, a limit can be set for divisibility. Physics first met such limits in ponderable matter (theory of atoms). Later scientists discovered that the transfer of energy was also limited to specific minima (*see* quanta). A.G.M.v.M.

DIVISION
In the sense of *classification,* putting something in a specific *category; in the sense of *partition* (*lat. Distinctio*), the analysis of a logical unity in its parts according to a specific principle of division. A good division should rest from the beginning to the end on the same principle of division; it has to be done orderly and not progressing abruptly but systematically; it has also to be complete, so that no part is forgotten. As the *tree of Porphyrius.

DOCTA IGNORANTIA
(Latin: learned ignorance) Knowledge conscious of its own insufficiency. Applied by *Nicolas of Cusa to human knowledge of God.

DOGMA
Initially an authoritative decision of a head of state or a specific philosophical doctrine. In theology a truth revealed by God, which the Church proposes as an article of faith.

115

DOGMATISM

Initially the conception that human knowledge is able to attain truth and certitude. This is then opposed to °skepticism. Further, the same conception insofar as it precedes a critical inquiry into the possibilities of human knowledge. It is then opposed to °criticism, and expresses, according to Kant, more exactly the °rationalism of his time, especially that of °Wolff. Finally, every doctrine claiming that its theses contain the irrefutable truth, because they come perhaps from a superrational source.

DOMAIN

Of a relation is the collection of all the antecedents of this relation. So is, for instance, the domain of the relation "father (of)" the collection of all the fathers.

DOMINICANS, SCHOOL OF THE

The order of the Dominicans was founded in 1216, and came to Paris in 1217. Received a chair in theology in 1229 and a second one in 1230. They came to Oxford in 1221 and were accepted into the university when Robert Bacon entered the order as a secular magister, probably in 1227. They also introduced the *studia generalia,* centers of study for one or more provinces of the order (e.g., Cologne 1248, Naples 1272). Finally, they also taught at the *studium* of the papal curia, created in 1234 or 1244. Thanks to the name of Albert the Great and Thomas Aquinas, the school of the Dominicans soon had great authority. By the end of the 13th century the authority of Thomas Aquinas was the strongest in the order, which became the most important branch of the Thomistic school.

DOMINION

Generates wherever protection exists. Protection requires power so that dominion is at the same time a relation of power, although not exclusively.

DOUBT

Means originally a real abstention of agreement with the two possibilities, i.e. with the contradictory positive and negative form of a judgment. The abstention of agreement is based either on the fact that the grounds for the "yes" or "no" keep each other in balance (real or *positive* doubt), or because there are not yet grounds for the "yes" or "no" (*negative doubt*).

Since °Descartes this term is also used for the methodical abstention of agreement. This *methodical* doubt has however several nuances. In Descartes we could name the doubt hyperbolic, in as much as, presented too positively, it also accepts the "extravagant hypotheses of the scepticists". Husserl and the phenomenology, following Kant, see the methodical doubt as a °reduction. In general we can best understand the methodical doubt as a methodical initial abstention or epoché.

The *°sceptic* doubt however is not an initial abstention but a result. It strives to a final (not only methodical) abstention of agreement. If the sceptic doubt wants to be universal, i.e. applied to all certitude, it is contradictory and as cultivated doubt impossible, because the sceptic thinks that he has sufficient reasons to withhold his agreement or thinks that no agreement is wiser than agreement, and therefore implicitly denies what he explicitly affirms.— J.P.

DOXA

(Greek: meaning) Called by °Plato that knowledge which, in opposition to episteme, is concerned with changeable and accidental beings. For *Husserl doxa (especially as passive protodoxa or urdoxa) is the domain of the most primitive and so-called prepredicative evidence; it is nevertheless not inferior to episteme.

DRIESCH, Hans A. 1867-1941.

German realistic philosopher. Proceeds in his biological investigations from the monism of *Haeckel, but in studying the division of the cells, he discovered facts which do not agree with monism. From this initial experience Driesch gradually constructed a philosophy in which justice would be given to the modern data of biology and the other sciences. Materialism, which knows only work-causality, is not able to explain the causes of the world. There seems also to be a finality, which requires a further explanation. First of all, the essential difference between living and not-living matter has to be worked out. There seem, however, to be phenomena which surpass life as such, namely the phenomena of consciousness. I not only know, but I also know that I know. We encounter here the concept of the spiritual. Thought and freedom are the essential moments of the mind. The mind is *Ganzheit,* but it is in reality always connected with the *Nichtganzheit.* Reality has therefore a dialectical structure. This structure brings us to the question of human survival, which we have to accept in one or another way. It raises at the same time the question of the existence of God, whom we also have to accept, without being able to acquire certitude about a theistic or pantheistic conception. Driesch progresses from *Philosophie des Organischen* (1909), through *Ordnungslehre* (1912) and *Wirklichkeitslehre* (1917), to *Metaphysik* (1924) and *Der*

Mensch und die Welt (1928). —B.D.

DUALISM

Doctrine which accepts, in a specific field or in the entirety of philosophy, two distinct principles. Dualism can then be called the doctrine which accepts two irreducible prime principles: a good and a bad god (*Manichaeism). Or also the doctrine which teaches that the finite world is not entirely absorbed into the infinite world, in other words does not identify God and the world (opposed to *monism). Or the doctrine which makes a sharp distinction between matter and spirit, knowledge and essence, will and intellect, senses and reason.

Psychical dualism sees body and soul as two irreducible elements, which are, at most connected in an accidental union (Plato, Descartes). Then we have the question of the interaction of body and mind in man (*see* monism, parallelism). This problem does not exist in the hylomorphism which Aristotle and Thomas Aquinas defend. There cannot be in this case a purely accidental connection: Body and soul are two substances, imperfect in their substantial essence; as matter (body) and form (soul) both together constitute the living being. Hylomorphism can have stricter or less strict forms.

DUEHRING, EUGEN

Born in Berlin 1833, died in Nowawes 1921. Follower of biological materialism and precursor of national socialism. Defended the purity of race and the elimination of the Jews.

DUHEM, Pierre 1861-1916.

French physicist and philosopher, investigated the structure of physics as a science. The laws of

117

physics are never more than an approximation of reality which has to be continuously perfected. They therefore never render reality directly, although they are directed toward metaphysical reality.

DUNS SCOTUS
See Joannes Duns Scotus.

DURAND DE GROS, Joseph Pierre
Born in Gros 1826, died in Arsac (Aveyron) 1900, French philosophical spiritualist. Rejects *positivism, because the positive sciences point toward metaphysics. In all organic life he sees an effort of the soul to adapt itself to the physical environment. The soul is only the synthesis of several physical forces or monads which try to develop their energy freely and to adapt themselves harmoniously to each other.

DURANDUS OF SAINT-POUR-CAIN
Born *ca.* 1275, died in Meaux 1332. Dominican, magister of theology in Paris in 1312, lector at the papal curia at Avignon (1313-17), Bishop of Limoux (1317), Puy (1318) and Meaux (1326). His main work is the commentary on the *sententiae* (three redactions). Because of his criticism of Thomistic doctrine he was in conflict with his order (1309-1317) and was repeatedly condemned. Durandus was an independent thinker, critical of many traditional theses and contributed to the collapse of scholasticism.

DURANT, Will
Born 1885. American popularizing historian of philosophy.

DURATION
The totality of *time between two given moments. In time we have to distinguish between topological and metrical structure, referring respectively to the order of before and after, and to the distance between two moments of time.

We also have to distinguish between *subjective* and *objective* duration. The latter is duration as it is objectively determined, i.e., with the aid of measuring instruments, while subjective duration is related to the way in which we go through a specific period of time. Bergson notes that the subjective experience of duration, what he calls *"durée,"* consists of the way we primitively experience reality. There is a qualitative quantity present, which is not a pure succession of homogeneous moments, but a continual progression of heterogeneous conscious situations into which the previous one intervenes and which carries over into the following.

DURKHEIM, Emile 1858-1917.
French positivistic philosopher and sociologist, who reduces ethics to sociology.

DUTY
Was identified by Kant with the ethical. The ethical coincides with that what the duty prescribes. This opinion cannot be followed, already because all distinction is missing between the content of the duty and the way in which man performs his duty. It is here a specific form of the moral consciousness in which first the conflict between that what is satisfying and that what should be done is experienced, and later, immanent to this consciousness, the feeling of absolute necessitating or *obligation. As for the duty as content, it is the minimum morality which has to be absolutely honored if one does not want to deny the essence of morality. Indeed, also on the moral level the distinction between the essential and the accidental is valid, so that at least the essential of the

ethical, as well in connection with the content as with the intention, should be realized. This essential is the duty, inasmuch as we see it as that what has not as much to be realized as that what can not be denied. Therefore we often formulate the duty in a negative way in a prohibition which cannot be transgressed. E.g.; "Thou shall not kill." J. Gr.

DUTY (ETHICS OF)

Are the ethics which reduce the moral life to the performance of the duty because of the duty. The most purely can this doctrine be found in the Stoic philosophy on the one hand and in Kant on the other hand. In both cases it has a rationalistic and rigoristic character.

DYAD

Duality considered as the principle of being. Used by the Pythagoreans.

DYNAMIC THEORY

Theological theory, which sees in an impersonal suprasensual force, if not the source of all religious life, at least one of its roots. It is distinguished from magical theory through the importance it places on the sentiments of dependence and respectful diffidence, which go along with the belief one has in this force. It is also to be distinguished from the primitive monotheistic theory, by placing belief in the force as an independent root of religion next to belief in God.

DYNAMISM

Doctrine according to which all phenomena can be reduced to forces and their activity. Leibniz sees matter as a form of representation of forces, in opposition to Descartes, who defends mechanism. For the latter, matter is a reluctant mass which has to be moved from outside by pushes. Dynamism is also the term used to indicate systems which reduce the existence of bodies to the existence of forces. This involves believing that there are in empty space nonextensive elements, in the form of points, which wield power over each other. A perceptible continuous body is only a constant equilibrium in a group of these elements.

DYSTELEOLOGY

Study of the particular biological phenomena from which a well-ordered result seems to be missing, as in atrophies, monsters, etc. In a broader sense, the term indicates all phenomena in which an imperfection of the final result is supposed, justly or unjustly, to exist, e.g., useless organisms, harmful insects, etc. The word "dysteleology" was introduced in biology by *Häckel.

E

E

Symbol for absolute negative propositions; e.g.: no plant has senses.

EBREO, Leone (Jehuda Abrabanel)

Born in Lisbon between 1460 and 1463, died in Ferrara between 1520 and 1535. Jewish Platonic philosopher, later became Christian (probably forced). In his love dialogues (*Dialoghi d'amore*) philosophy is concerned with love, an intellectual love of God, which influenced Spinoza's *amor Dei intellectualis*.

ECKEHART

See Joannes Eckehart.

ECLECTICISM

A way of thought which takes ideas from different philosophical systems and tries to constitute a logically coherent unity, omitting the elements of those systems which do not fit into that unity. We can then speak of the eclecticism of all great thinkers, since all of them use theories of their predecessors or contemporaries in their own systems, based in their own principles ,(e.g., scholastic principles in Descartes), or they assimilate the seemingly, contradictory principles of several systems in a more perfect viewpoint (e.g., the theory of Heraclitus of the eternal becoming with that of the Eleats of the unchangeable and imperishable essence, brought together by Plato in the dualism of the physical and suprasensory world). In the time of the Enlightenment eclecticism was considered the highest and most independent form of philosophical thought. "Eclecticism" was used for the first time in the strict sense in the 19th century by the school of *Cousin, with which the term has been definitely connected. F.S.

ECOLOGY (oecology)

Part of biology dealing with the relationship between living organisms as they are found in nature. In nature many plants and animals live and work actually together. The ecology has often given cause to opinions about the super-individual functionality in nature.

ECONOMY

(*See* Mach). The science which studies how the best possible results can be achieved with the least means. In political economy this theory is applied to the material goods of the state. In philosophy, economy of thought is achieved when one tries to determine as wide a knowledge as possible with the least possible concepts and propositions.

EDUCTION

Of *form from *matter, is an actuation, in substantial or accidental changes, by means of a cause. This means that through this cause no form is introduced from outside.

EDWARDS, Jonathan 1703-58.

American idealistic theologian and philosopher.

120

EFFECT

What comes after an action as proceeding from it. Although a conscious action contains the knowledge of what is going to be effected, the effect does not belong to the action but it is outside of it. The relation "action-effect" is causal, not final; the effect is united with the action; it is not wanted, either for itself as the end or as the means. The effect is exterior to the action, essentially connected with it or only accidentally, foreseen with absolute certitude or only as being possible, accepted reluctantly or willingly.

EFFICIENT CAUSE

See cause.

EGO

Indicates for the person who speaks, thinks or acts, one's own person. One has to investigate how I realize my own person as opposed to other persons and the entire reality. One has also to investigate how I see myself. For if originally the own person in its totality was called the "ego," it is now only the case for my psychic being, or even for the source, in which my activities of consciousness continuously originate. We speak of an "ego" in the strict sense of the word, inasmuch as this source, characterized by subjectivity, immanence and freedom, forms a self-conscious unity. This "ego" can, from a critical point of view, be limited to a pure subject of knowledge, which can as such not be objectivated and which has a natural relation of knowledge with the domain of the objective world. It is in this last sense that the "ego" is an important topic of discussion in contemporary philosophy. Descartes considers it the unshakable rock on which philosophy can be built, and its existence con-

stitutes the first certitude. But while Descartes teaches that we catch this "ego" intuitively, Kant says that we can only affirm it (and not see) as the strict logical subject of our thought. Nothing allows us to see in it more than a function of thought. (instead of an existing substance). Kant, on the other hand, confers upon the "ego" a creative activity, which Descartes does not. This power of creation is still limited, in as far as the "ego" has to receive the content of its thought from the experience and produces only the form in which it knows. The idealists however accepted already that the "ego" itself produces its own content of thought. It has at the same time again an ontological character, although it can't be reduced to its empirical reality. The question finally arises: is the "ego" as subjectivity confined to itself and not approachable by an other being, so that it has to lead to a solipsistic existence; or has it, on the contrary, access to the other "egos" and to the world, as the phenomenology and the existenz philosophy clearly defend? The question in fact is what relation is there between subjectivity and the world, and what limits are necessarily imposed, because of this relation, to knowledge and striving, objectivity and freedom. See also subject(ivity). — J. Gr. - L.D.R.

EGOCENTRISM

The attitude of remaining confined to oneself. Knowledge and action are meaningful exclusively in terms of the ego and its needs. Characteristic of the attitude of animals.

EGOISM

Conscious pursuit of profit for one's own sake, without concern for what is objectively proper, and with indifference to the pursuits of others. Egoism is therefore different from *egocentrism, which is generally unconscious, and is more than *selfishness, since it does not care about others. It is evident that man is, in fact, very often egoistical; Hobbes teaches that this attitude is the only proper attitude. Bentham thinks that *altruism is a specific form of egoism: since man is weak, he can only gain by helping others, who will answer this aid with their help.

EHRENFELS, Christian Freiherr von 1859-1932.
Austrian psychologist, disciple of Brentano, founder of *"Gestaltspsychologie."*

EIDETIC
Pertaining to the *eidos. In psychology, the ability to evoke again with all its characteristics that which was seen previously. Investigated especially by Jeansch.

EIDOS
(Visual form, figure) For Husserl, the *essence of a given thing. *See also* idea.

EINFUEHLUNG
Psychological theory to explain the aesthetic experience. Its main defenders were Theodorus Lipps and Joannes Volkelt. They consider as the essence of the aesthetic experience a certain sentimental sympathy, the pleasure-producing identification of oneself with the sensible forms and motions. *Einfühlung* certainly sheds light on a real element of the aesthetic experience and also describes a specific type of aesthetic pleasure. It does not, however, explain completely the experience. In itself *einfühlung* is not yet specifically aesthetic; it becomes so only through aesthetic contemplation, in which it is then integrated as a more material component. Outside of aesthetic contemplation, *einfühlung* is nothing else than a phenomenon of naive inner life.

EINSTEIN, Albert 1879-1955.
German physicist, founder of the theory of relativity. Although this theory is in the domain of physics, and not of philosophy, it still had a great influence on philosophy. In his later writings Einstein is also directly interested in philosophical problems.

ELAN VITAL
Philosophical concept developed by *Bergson, in connection with biological data. Organic life is characterized by the *élan vital* as a stream of life, which creates itself continuously notwithstanding the opposition of the physical, quantitative world. *Evolution of the species has to be seen as a series of efforts in which life gains victory over matter and attains self-consciousness. This evolution lead in the animals to instinct, in man to intellect. The theory of the *élan vital* is historically important as a reaction against the *machine theory and the *materialism of the second half of the 19th century, which was very much under the influence of the natural sciences.

ELEAN-ERITREAN SCHOOL
Shows much affinity with the school of Megara, but was still more interested in the dialectical play of the *Eristics. Was founded in Elis by Phaedo, disciple of *Socrates, who went to Eritrea with Menedemus and Asclepaeus.

ELEATIC SCHOOL
A group of philosophers, who lived first in Elea (Italy). The most important are *Parmenides, *Zeno of Elea and *Melissus. *Xenophanes of Elea was consid-

ered their precursor. They teach that the real essence is absolutely immobile, unchangeable, and "one"; that therefore all change in the world is only semblance. This change is observed by the senses, while reason alone knows the "one" and the essence.

ELEMENT(S)

This concept is very generally used in philosophy (*hylomorphism) as well as in the sciences to indicate the simple, irreducible components of something. In general, an element is that which is present as a component in more complex things and to which they can also be reduced. Therefore in mathematics the simple quantities which are the basis of a specific system and its axioms are called the elements of that system, e.g., the axioms and definitions of Euclidean geometry. In chemistry since Lavoisier, these chemicals are called elements which because of the known chemical means of analysis, could not further be analyzed into chemicals of another sort.

The term "element" remained even when it was later discovered that these elements could be further analyzed (see theory of atoms); because the concept had so clearly proven its fruitfulness in chemistry. Therefore the term "element" now has in the natural sciences an expressly relative value. On the other hand in chemistry it is more a qualitative than a quantitative concept. It is equally used for the atom of an element as for larger unities. A.G.M.v.M.

ELENCHUS

See refutation.

ELIOT, George 1819-1880

English novelist (Mary Ann Evans) whose major themes were always of an ethical nature. Works: *Middlemarch* (1872), *Silas Marner* (1861), *Adam Bede* (1859), *Mill on the Floss* (1860).

EMANATION (outpouring), EMANATISM

(Doctrine of emanation). While evolution indicates generally a development from lower to higher, emanatism means a development from higher to lower, from the infinite to the finite. The overfull absolute being would overflow out of inner necessity, to create on different levels man and the things of the world. A related doctrine teaches that philosophical wisdom is reached when one proceeds from the lowest things, through all levels, to the absolute. This outflowing absolute is called the One (Plotinus) or spirit (Hegel) or will (Schopenhauer) or the unconscious (Ed. v. Hartmann). In the philosophy of India it appears under different forms. Emanatism excludes real creation (although Thomas Aquinas uses the word emanation for creation), because this overflow is generally connected with an inner necessity. In this reality and essence God is not distinct from the world; this is near to *pantheism. H. R.

EMERSON, Ralph Waldo 1803-1882.

American idealistic philosopher. His main work: *Nature*, 1836. The idealism of Emerson is lightly *neo-Platonic. It tries to grasp God, the world and the ego in one intuition. The only moral law he accepts is the realization of the self, which is essentially identical with God and the world. The philosophy of Emerson became very popular in America as well as in Europe, especially among the general public. His works contributed much in America to the development of the philosophical life, though thought is considered by him to be inferior to experience. B.D.

EMOTIONALITY

Susceptibility to emotions. One of the three basic principles of the temperament, in *Heyman's theory.

EMPEDOCLES

Born in Acragas or Agrigentum (Sicily) about 490, died 430 B.C. Wrote a work on natural philosophy and another of an ascetical-religious kind. Was renowned as medicus, miracle-worker and philosopher. He taught the doctrine of the four substances, as "roots" of all things in the universe: fire, air, water and earth. These elements were and are always mixed and separated by two opposite forces: friendship and hate. In the beginning the universe was like a sphere, totally homogeneous, non-differentiated. Hate created differences which become continuously larger and larger, but love is always working to keep the universe together. The evolution of the universe can be divided into periods, in which hate and love triumph successively. Knowledge is possible because fine particles radiate from things into man through appropriate pores. The religious view of Empedocles is close to that of the Pythagoreans (See Pythagoras). F. D. R.

EMPIRICAL

That which belongs to experience or is founded on it, or originates from it. Sometimes wrongly identified with *experimental.

EMPIRICISM

Doctrine teaching that *experience is the only source of knowledge. Empiricism does more than contend that experience is a presupposition of all our knowledge; it contends that the intellect can

regulate only the data of experience. All so-called general concepts (see universalia) and all judgments in which man speaks of the essence of that which is perceived by the senses or the general conditions of experience are reduced to syntheses of a series of data given by experience, by association or by induction, so that their value remains purely hypothetical. Furthermore, experience is very often understood in a very narrow sense, namely, the immediate data of the external senses (see sensualism). Or the experience is limited to the totality of existing facts and the way they are discovered by the positive sciences. (See Positivism.)—J.P.

Historically, Empiricism had its origin in England. In the Middle Ages some scholastics (Robert Grosseteste, Roger Bacon) turned toward more experimental methods in the sciences; Francis Bacon wants to exchange the deductive method in the sciences for a new inductive system. *Hobbes constructs a philosophical system on the empirical method, *Locke develops it to explain the problems of knowledge. In this way it is opposed to *rationalism, which was developed at the same period on the continent. The main question concerns the origin of ideas and the content of consciousness. The rationalist teaches that they are innate (see inneism); Locke thinks that they are acquired by inner or outer experience. Locke is still, however a semiempiricist, and he accepts the difference between so-called primary and secondary *qualities. *Berkeley rejects this distinction: reality is what we immediately imagine it, reality is nothing else than what is represented. Berkeley arrives at the position of subjective *idealism. *Hume applies empiricism insofar as experience presented not only as the source but also as the standard for all knowledge. On the metaphysical level this leads naturally to complete skepticism. H. R.

EMPIRIO-CRITICISM

The system of *Avenarius and *Mach. "Pure experience," critically purified from all additions on the part of the subject, is the only point of departure in philosophical thought. The sole role of philosophy is to give a pure description of the evolution, content and cohesion of (sensory) experiences, avoiding all metaphysics, that is, all dualism between the physical and psychic, subject and object, consciousness and essence.

EMPYREUM

(Greek: afire, aglow) In the medieval world picture, the highest heaven of light. In Dante's work, Paradise and the place where nine choirs of angels float around God.

ENCYCLOPEDISTS

The bookseller Le Breton asked *Diderot in 1746 to translate the *Cyclopaedia or Dictionary of Arts and Sciences,* which had been published in 1728. With a group of collaborators with d'Alembert as editor, Diderot did more than translate it, and from 1751 began publication of the *Encyclopédie ou Dictionnaire raisonné des arts et des métiers, par une société de gens de lettres.* Voltaire was also among the collaborators. Around the *Encyclopédie* gathered the group known as the Encyclopedists, which included Rousseau (who opposed the group later), Grimm, d'Holbach, Turgot, and Helvetius, who became the exponents of the philosophy of the French Enlightenment. In this work were laid down the concepts of nature, religion, ethics, state and society which partially prepared for the

French Revolution. Several articles defended materialism and opposed revealed religion. When several parts had been published, the state prohibited further publication but Diderot managed to have 28 volumes printed (1751-1772); later, 5 volumes of supplements were published and a two-volume set with the *"table analytique."* H.R.

END

Final point of an effort, or what draws an effort to a close by satisfying it. The effort has been made for that reason (*see* final *cause) and is directed toward the same. But such direction cannot be determined by this final point, if this latter is not present in the form of an image. The image of the pursued is also called an end.

The question is raised whether all activity, as every conscious effort does, is directed at an end (*finality). Aristotle says that it is: everything which acts, acts for an end—not all, however, in the same way. Unconscious beings act only under the influence of consciousness trying to reach the end. Conscious beings with a knowledge of the end: either imperfect knowledge (so that they know the final end, but not in its capacity of end), or—like man—with complete knowledge, i.e., with knowledge of the end as end, its meaning for the acting being, its relation to the means.

If an end is pursued, everything which led us to it will be pursued, i.e., the means. The end has its own value, however, while the means have only meaning in relation to the end. Several ends can be pursued at the same time, each because of its value; sometimes one remains independent of the other, sometimes all of them are arranged in a hierarchical order (e.g., with a prime end and subordinate ends), without one or another becoming pure means. (E.g., we can give donations for several reasons: this does not mean that we have to use one end as a means to another end.) God, infinite End, is not a prime end next to which other ends can be found, but a transcendent end, which embraces all other ends in an eminent way so that in this respect the other ends become pure means, receive their value from the supreme end. (*See* also *Kingdom of ends.) L.D.R.

The end to which human action is directed determines, according to Thomas Aquinas, its morality. This is as true for an inner act of the will as for external action: in the first, the end is the *intention; in the second, the object on the *content of the *action. When it is a question of the action as a totality, the intention seems to be determining, although not without content. This is the *ethics of the end.* This is opposed to the ethics of intention (Kant), and also to the morality of *value. But this last opposition is not complete, since the end does not exclude the value. For when something is pursued as an end, it is because it embodies, in the last instance, a value. The opposition with ethics of the intention is, on the contrary, complete. Not because, next to the intention, the content would be considered determining. Even the fact that for Kant the intention is purely formal does not explain this opposition. The end, however, is not able to determine from itself the morality of the action, but only insofar as it is related to the last and supreme end of the effort: it is from the relation to this final end that every end derives its moral excellence. In other words, the excellence of the end is never abso-

lute, and that is exactly what opposes the ethics of the end to the ethics of the intention, which tries to achieve excellence in the observation of the formal moral law, which is absolute, for it is unconditional. J. Gr.

END, FINAL

The end toward which efforts are naturally directed as that which must completely satisfy them. Effort is not only naturally but also necessarily, directed toward the final end, because without a final end there would be no reason to realize the several limited ends. These latter constitute more than a succession: a concatenation of moments subordinate to each other. Even if the final end is the last in the order of realization, it is the first to be conceived. The final end of an effort is at the same time the first condition of this effort.

The question arises now: Of what does the final end consist, more specifically the final end of man? This question is significant. If the final end as the condition for the possibility of effort has to be affirmed, then as such it is not, or hardly, conscious. It can only be determined through reflection, in which we have to take account of the complexity of the end. One distinguishes in every striving the *finis qui,* the *finis quo* and the *finis cui.* As *finis qui* or as object which is pursued, the final end does not lie in external goods such as wealth or power, nor in internal goods such as virtue or knowledge. No one of these can satisfy human striving completely except the good which embraces all good: God. But we have to ask at the same time how or by what act we can reach God. The scholastics, who returned to Aristotle for the final end as *finis quis,* do not agree in their definition of the final end as *finis quo.* The more intellectual Thomas Aquinas thinks that we reach God through knowledge. J. Duns Scotus, however, who is more inclined toward voluntarism, thinks that knowledge is only a condition for the act of charity, by which the unity with God is formally achieved. In any case, a feeling of total satisfaction follows the possession of God, as well as a state of pleasure which is called *beatitude. The final end can thus be defined as the *beatitudo,* wrought by the possession of God.

We will mention two remaining problems. The first is related to the *finis cui.* When man strives toward God—as he does in everything he pursues—he can do so only because of his own perfection or "for himself." Is the love of God not necessarily abolished by this striving since it seems to be selfish? We think that this striving cannot be called selfish since it happens unconsciously. Also striving toward God and one's own perfection are parallel: It is in his effort to reach God a definite being, that man also realizes himself. Here a second difficulty is created: How can a finite being reach an infinite being, who surpasses him infinitely? How otherwise than through an intervention of the Infinite Being Herself? This intervention (which Christianity considers a supernatural gift, thus making the problem still more acute) can only prevent the necessary striving toward the final end from being vain (*see* desiderium naturale.) *See also* supreme *good.

ENERGETISM

The doctrine of natural philosophy which, in line with the central place which energy had in the natural sciences, found the essence of matter in energy alone. *Ost-wald was a well-known representative of this school.

ENERGY

The power to perform labor. Originating in mechanics, in the narrower sense, this concept became one of the main physical concepts. In the beginning it meant the mechanical ability to work. It received this meaning from the law which states that the sum of motive energy and potential energy are constant. (For a pendulum at its lowest point potential energy is zero, and motive energy maximal; the situation is exactly reversed when it is at its highest point.) This is not exactly true in practice, since energy is lost through friction. The concept "energy" received its fundamental meaning when the heat produced by friction was also considered a form of energy, so that the law of the conservation of energy still holds. Later, quantities were discovered in electrical, magnetic and chemical phenomena which were directly related to the concept, so that can indicate exactly how much of a specific quantity is equivalent to a specific quantity of energy. The theory of relativity gave the concept of energy a final extension: the quantity of mass also represented a specific quantity of energy. The importance of the concept lies in the fact that by it phenomena of different domains can be related to each other in a rather simple way. A.G.M.v.M.

ENGELS, Friedrich

Born in Barmen 1820, died in London 1895. With Marx the founder of socialism and dialectical materialism.

ENLIGHTENMENT

The 18th century is called the period of the Enlightenment; there are however many people of the second half of the 17th century who can be considered belonging to the Enlightenment. The Enlightenment ends with Kant. It is the period in which the human intellect frees itself from authoritative coercion and traditional prejudices. The Enlightenment called itself the philosophical age; in no other period did philosophy become so popular. The Enlightenment tried to extend the renewal of the sciences, begun in the 16th and 17th centuries, to the entire society; it did not build new systems but emphasized the self-satisfaction of the human reason (*rationalism). It opposed strongly the belief in authority in religion; and defended natural religion.

The origin of the Enlightenment can be found in England, and has its roots in the empiricism of Bacon and Locke. Newton's idea to reduce the several natural phenomena to a few general discerned laws, had left a great impression. The rationalism of Descartes, which tried to deduce the factual from general clear distinguishing concepts, the criticism of Spinoza on the revealed religion, which was made from the point of view of reason, and Wolff's faith in the power of the human intellect, had prepared the Enlightenment. The *deism and the free thought, both coming from England into France, have imposed on it their seal. There are however still many differences in the Enlightenment, differences between individual philosophers and differences between the French, English and German Enlightenment. In France the Enlightenment does not limit itself to the intellectual circles and opposes strongly the traditions of the society, the politics and the Church, it leads to the French Revolution. The ideas of the Enlightenment have spread from France into the entire European continent.

There is immediately a counterstream next to the rationalism: in England Shaftesbury evokes the enthusiasm for the beauty; Rousseau in France for the natural instincts of life and he warns against the misleading intellect; in Germany there will also be later a philosophy of feeling. The transcendental criticism of Kant takes both these rational and irrational moments and finishes the Enlightenment in Germany.

The spirit of the Enlightenment in France is determined by the Cartesian analysis and the philosophical synthesis, begun by Leibniz. With clear concepts they want to go to the origin and the individuality; from mechanism to organism, from the principle of identity to the continuity and the harmony. This line of thought is found in Diderot, who wants to give an hylozoistic interpretation of nature, also in the voluminous natural history of the evolutionist Buffon, in Voltaire's works, d'Alembert and the other *Encyclopedists, notwithstanding their original criticism of Leibniz. With this attitude they try to solve the problems of the epistemology, psychology, natural sciences, theories on state and society and the philosophy of religion.

In Germany: Leibniz's philosophy helped indirectly the rise of the Enlightenment. His ideas of harmony, sufficient ground and continuous evolution had their influence through the changes Wolff brought to them. Wolff's first disciple, Al. Baumgarten, returned in his metaphysics and especially in his aesthetics to the individuality of Leibniz's theory of the monads and the preestablished harmony.

In England: the empiricism of

Locke and the mechanism of Newton are here the main schools, but the many interpretations are very divergent. We can hardly unite under one common title such different theories as the deism of many philosophers and especially the *pantheism of Toland; the moral conceptions of Shaftesbury; who gives as eudaemonia: a satisfaction of oneself without expectation of retribution for the human virtue in another life; the idea of Hutcheson, who accepts a moral feeling. H.R.

ENS

See being.

ENS RATIONIS

Something which exists only in the human intellect and cannot exist outside of it, such as logical predicates, judgments and reasoning. The *ens rationis* is the object of logic.

ENTELECHY

Concept used by Aristotle to indicate the animating principle in a living being. It means "turned to an end." According to Aristotle we should conceive it as a real principle of being, realized in the *"hyle," materia prima,* and composing with it a completely undivided unity. Entelechy is dynamic, directed toward a being's own development and preservation, and toward the preservation of the species through propagation. The same term was later used by H. *Driesch in another sense, to represent a supernatural factor which directs the lower physico-chemical forces in a practical way. This is a dualistic theory which does more or less violence to the totality of the organism. The doctrine of Driesch is still accepted by some biologists.

ENTHUSIASM

To be completely engrossed with a specific person, idea or ideal. Originally a religious event. Was brought into philosophy by the neo-Platonists; the basis of philosophy also for Bruno and Shaftesbury.

ENTHYMEME

A shortened syllogism, in which one of the *premises has been left out because of its self-evidence. E.g.: All mammals give birth to living young; therefore the whale gives birth to its young.

ENTITY

A real being; also used in a pejorative sense to indicate a realized abstraction.

ENUMERATION

A series of cases to prove a general basis, of which the cases are particular instances (*induction). There is complete enumeration when all possible cases have been introduced: I establish successively, for instance, that all the children of my sister are able to walk. There is complete enumeration when only the known or observed cases are included in the series: I ascertain that I never saw a swan other than white swans. However extensive this enumeration may be, it never justifies a universal conclusion.

EPICHEIREMA

A syllogism with established premises. E.g.: Every reasonable being has a free will, because it possesses intellect; every man is a reasonable being; therefore every man has free will.

EPICTETUS

Born in Hieropolis (Phrygia) *ca.* 50 A.D., died about in the middle of the reign of Hadrianus (117-138). Went early to Rome and as a slave followed the lessons of

129

Musonius Rufus; after the death of Musonius he taught himself Stoicism, was expelled by a decree of Domitianus in 94 and retreated to Nicopolis (Epirus), where he opened a school. One of his disciples was Arrianus, who preserved for us his master's teachings.

EPICURUS

Born in Samos 341, died 270 B.C. As a young man was familiar with the doctrine of *Democritus, settled in Mytelene and in 307 founded in his garden at Athens the Epicurean School. He was so respected that his disciples said, "Act as if Epicurus saw it." Only a few fragments of his many works have survived. We know his system mostly through the writings of his disciples.

The philosophy of Epicurus is pre-eminently ethical. It contains, however, a sensualistic theory of knowledge. Sensual observation guarantees the authenticity of its object. From things, images are driven to the senses. Through the intellect we deduce the unseen reality, e.g., the existence of the atoms, but these deductions are true only insofar as they are confirmed by observation. Concepts are recollections of many similar perceptions (nominalism). Next to sensations and concepts, feelings form the criteria for truth: delight and taste are the norms of that for which we strive or avoid.

This sensualistic ethics later became the basis of the hedonism of the school of *Cyrenaica. Epicurus, however, made a distinction between physical pleasure and spiritual enjoyment; he seems to prefer the latter, so that his ethics differ from those of his disciples, who attached to the term "epicureanism" a less sublime meaning. For Epicurus the ideal consists of *ataraxia, or perfect peace of mind, which is attained by weighing carefully joys and sorrows in their actual extent as well as considering possible consequences. Life becomes an egoistical art, to defy unpleasantness, to renounce many pleasures, and to attain in this way the highest delight.

Like Democritus, Epicurus accepts in physics the principles of the atoms and empty space. But instead of speaking of an original motion of the world, he thinks that the world is formed through the fall of the atoms in space. However, they have the ability to deviate freely from their path (the "clinamen") and so collisions occur, and accumulations, which form, if they have enough stability, lasting natural bodies. For Epicurus the soul consists of fine, circular and smooth atoms, dispersed through the entire body. By death those atoms of the soul are dispersed, so we do not have to fear death. The gods are composed of still finer atoms; they are not concerned with the direction of the world, so we should not fear them. F.D.R.

EPIGENESIS

Relates to the development of an organism. The fertilized female cell shows new structures, which were previously not visible. So epigenesis means "something is added."

EPIPHENOMENON

Physical reality considered as an accompanying phenomenon of matter. According to the doctrine of physiomonism, a materialistic doctrine about man (see monism).

EPISTEMOLOGY, or theory of knowledge

In the broader sense, epistemology embraces all inquiry about knowledge. Psychology studies the activity of knowledge as a function of the consciousness; it is especially interested in the evolution of knowledge in the growing man and in the relation of knowledge to other functions. Sociology inquires about the part of knowledge in society and the influence of society on knowledge. Ontology inquires about the essence of knowledge as a way of being, while in logic the way is indicated by which we can attain real knowledge.

In a narrow and strict sense, inquiry into the conditions under which real and certain knowledge is possible. In this case we can also speak of criticism of knowledge, criteriology or gnoseology.

The question of the value of knowledge was discussed in the Middle Ages; in modern times, however, it became a more acute problem. In Kant's philosophy this question governed everything, and in the 19th century philosophy was very often reduced to epistemology. Since contemporary philosophy reasserts the *intentionality of consciousness, epistemology is no longer so important and is certainly not the central problem.

These are some of the questions posed in epistemology: Must we pose the question of the value of knowledge (see dogmatism, criticism)? Can this problem be solved (see skepticism)? What is our initial attitude when we ask the question: *certitude, *doubt, *epoche? Is certitude something subjective or objective? What is the first certitude? In what sense do we understand the existence of the subject (see cogito)? Or the data of the sensual *experience? Or the first absolute *principles? What is *evidence? Is it the criterion by which we recognize truth or are there other criteria?

How is *error possible? Why is it so frequent? Why is knowledge primate? What is the part of the *subject, what the part of the *object, in knowledge? Is knowledge dependent on essence or essence on knowledge? Is truth the concordance of knowledge with itself (*idealism) or with that which is (*realism), and do we not in the latter case have to make a transition from the idea to reality? Do we have in all domains of knowledge the same certitude? Do we have true and certain knowledge only of what can be attained through the senses (see agnosticism) or of the suprasensual (see metaphysics) as well? Of the relatively only or of the absolute also? How is it possible, under the last supposition, that we can say something about immaterial and infinite beings by means of concepts borrowed from physical and finite beings (see analogy)? J.P.

EPISYLLOGISM
    See polysyllogism.

EPOCHE
    Abstention from all judgment, either because one doubts the possibilities of human knowledge (*skepticism) or because one suspends a judgment temporarily in order to judge with more certitude after an inquiry. This is done in the methodical *doubt of Descartes, in the *phenomenology of Husserl.

EQUALITY
    R being a relation having the following qualities: (1) each element x has the relation R to itself, thus $R(x,x)$; (2) if x has the relation R to x, then y also has the relation R to x, thus: if $R(x,y)$, then $R(y,x)$; (3) if x has the relation R to y and if y has the relation R to z, then x has the *relation* R to z,

131

thus: if $\underline{R}(\underline{x},\underline{y})$ and $\underline{R}(\underline{y},\underline{z})$, then $\underline{R}(\underline{x},\underline{z})$. Such a relation $\underline{R}$ is called an equality. We award a quality to each element $\underline{y}$, to which a given element $\underline{x}$ has the relation $\underline{R}$. We indicate it as $[x]\underline{R}$. To each of the elements $\underline{u}$, one quality $[x]\underline{R}$ is

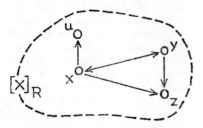

due, and it has this quality with all the elements to which it has the relation $\underline{R}$. It is said, therefore, that the qualities $[x]\underline{R}$ form together a system of characteristic features, which is determined by the relation $\underline{R}$. E.W.B.

EQUIPOLLENCE

Logical equivalence of propositions with the same propositional terms. It is obtained through a logical conversion. Equipollence of concepts: concepts which have the same extent.

EQUIPROBABILISM

Principle of casuistics, according to which the one who has doubts about the moral value of an action can follow one opinion as being as probable as the contrary.

EQUIVALENCE

Deductibility of a system of *axioms from another system, or of a *proposition from another proposition on the grounds of a system of axioms; is therefore not the same as *equipollence or logical equivalence.

EQUIVALENT

Two *propositions are equivalent if, for the same equality-values of their variables, they themselves

have the same equality values. In a specific system are called equivalent or deductive-equivalent two *assertions from which, in this system, the same conclusions proceed. In general we can use equivalent *expressions the one for the other.

EQUIVOCATION

(Latin: *aequia-vox,* same name) Ambiguity of a term which can be applied to two or more totally different meanings and therefore indicating entirely different concepts and things. E.g., the term "bear," indicating on the one hand a kind of animal, on the other hand a constellation. Equivocation is one of the causes of many paralogisms.

ERASMUS, Desiderius 1466-1536

Dutch scholar who at first favored the Reformation and then opposed it, advocating reform within the Catholic Church. Edited New Testament and wrote *In Praise of Folly.*

ERDMANN, Johann Eduard 1805-1892.

German Hegelian, disciple of Hegel, belonging to the medium group. His work is, on the one hand, an introduction to the thought of Hegel and, on the other, a history of philosophy.

ERISTIC

Art of arguing, generally used in a pejorative sense: a vain, dialectical game. Was very much in use in the school of *Megara. They discussed, for instance, the following case: A liar says that he lies: thus he lies and does not lie at the same time.

ERIUGENA

See Joannes Scottus Eriugena.

EROS

Initially the god of love. In Plato's works: the urge toward the "good" as it is expressed in philosophical knowledge, which proceeds from the sensual world to the ideas.

EROTEMATIC
The teaching which is given by means of questions and answers. Opposed to *acroamatic.

ERROR
Approval of a *false judgment. While falsehood means the (known) nonconformity of the content of a judgment with that which is, error excludes the subjective stand of the person who judges, and who posits the false judgment with the pretense that it is true. Although error occurs often, it is difficult to understand in the theory of knowledge how error is possible. Judgment is an act of thought leaning on (because it will be the expression of) experience and insight, thus on knowledge. But observation and insight, as acts of knowledge can only be knowledge of something which is. How can they then lead to knowledge that thinks beings are otherwise than they are —which, in other words, thinks that is which is not, and thinks that is not which is? We must therefore explain how pretended knowledge is possible. Since the intellect as such is directed toward truth, the cause of error has to be found herein, that the judging man is not determined in his thought by observation and insight. Where *evidence exists, error seems to be excluded: the immediate cause of error can only be lack of evidence or ignorance. The reason, however, why the ignorant man falsely agrees with what he does not see or realizes springs from a lack of attention and laziness in thinking, as well as from precipitation and impatience in judging. The lack of respect for the truth which he thus expresses can only be explained by an unjustified influence of the will (compare with *belief), which therefore is the distant cause of error. That is to say, the will is led by passions instead of leading them.

ESOTERIC
Designed for the initiated alone and understood only by him (opposed to *exoteric). Used especially for the strict scientific writings of Aristotle.

ESSE
To be, have reality, exist. A judgment of being does not state what is: Esse is not a quidditative predicate, its meaning does not belong to a *category, it is transcategorical, in this sense *transcendental. No category however has sense without an existential relation (man or good is being man or being good), everything is characterized by beingness and one can therefore say that esse is transcendental in the sense of allembracing: it is the opposite of nothing, therefore also the opposite of no term of comparison, and as such it is unique and *absolute. One should not consider the being, the beingness in the things, as an abstract concept or as a concrete shell around the things, because they only exist in their individuality, with what it contains concretely, so that they belong innerly, with all that is proper to them, to the absolute unity of being.

Outside of the domain of the *beings can we nowhere come into contact with the "esse"; we only recognize beingness in present beings. Since the "esse" appears there only transcategorically, we do realize that "esse" and being really are in tension, i.e. constitute a real relation of two (therefore not identical) terms. The question arises:

In what consists this tension, and how can we explain that it continues to exist in spite of the total unity of all in the "esse"? Or, reversed, how does it happen that this existential unity does not exclude this tension?

This problem received mostly only a seeming solution: by erasing one of the terms of the problem, the "esse" or the being, they thought to be able to take the tension away. Parmenides, the first to become interested in the "e s s e," was so blinded by the omnipresence of the "esse," that he negated the beings and fell into the monism of "esse." It is however mostly the contrary: One tries to reduce completely the "esse" to being and comes to an essentialism that namely only gives sense to the essence, i.e. to the being within the limits of what can be expressed of it with quidditative predicates. With "esse" or existing is meant then only the pure fact, i.e. misunderstood reality, as it appears when one collides with it without seizing anything of it with the intellect. They were therefore led to call the (quidditative) table of species and genus (also the so called *tree of Porphyry) the list of the degrees of being; or also, following here the neo-platonici, to consider the "esse" as the lowest point in the hierarchy of the (quidditative) perfections, which does however appear in the more perfect beings, but supplied with other, higher forms of perfection, as life and thought.

Some philosophers have constantly been anxious to emphasize the necessity of keeping both terms "esse" and being separated: "esse" appears in every being, it is not a being, and not the sum of all beings, since it has no quidditative meaning at all; every being participates therefore only in the "esse" (*Participation), possesses it according to its quidditative definiteness, in a way which differs from all other ways. The essence is therefore integrally relation to "esse," way of "esse;" the "esse" is ground perfection, only source of sense and value.

Participation in "esse" contains implicitly multiplicity and *order: The fundamental unity of the beings is therefore in an ordered principle that is none of these beings, i.e. in the absolute *identity of the subsisting "esse," creative (because independent) source of participation for all that possesses reality.

Many questions should be posed about this: a.o. about the origin and nature of the ideas "esse" and being, about the structure of the being and the order of the beings, about the relation of the beings to the subsisting "esse" and about the nature of the knowledge which we could obtain about it. L.D.R.

ESSENCE

That which makes a thing what it is. Essence differs from accidental definiteness, by which a being becomes different without becoming something else. Essential (as opposed to accidental) is that which relates to the essence as such, especially the necessary band by which elements are united to a significant essence. A real essence is concrete and individual. Very often the term "essence" is used for an abstractly considered essence, as it responds as quiddity to a definition.

Many idealists think that we only can reach the real ground of reality by means of categories created by our mind. The realists, however, assert that knowledge of the essential in things can only be reached through the data of experience, although they don't agree about the manner in which this happens. If we stick to the pure empirical observation of data, we can establish actual groupings of phenomena, but we cannot discover their essential connection. This would, however, as many philosophers assert, be in the realm of the abstracting intellect; because, they say, in abstracting we not only forsake individual characteristics to attain general characteristics, but we also distinguish between the essential and the accidental, so that we can give a definition of the essence. In about the same direction go those philosophers who describe phenomena phenomenologically, based on insight into the essential structural connection of the data. The question, however, remains: With what techniques we can obtain fruitful results? In his knowledge of essential structures, the phenomenologists say, especially those who tend toward existentialism, man is controlled by the situation in which (because of his nature) he exists in this world. They therefore question the so-called essentialism of the realists and idealists who neglect this existential situation, in the appreciation of abstract essences and by trying to look at the sphere of the (eternal, unchangeable, absolute) essences from a neutral (absolute) point of view.

This term is also used, especially by the Thomists, to indicate the metaphysical principle of structure which a being has, the real reason of its essential definiteness. Being and essence, taken in this sense, do not differ from each other as concrete does from abstract, and not as the actually existing differs from the possible, but as act differs from potency, two real (thus concrete) but metaphysical principles, which are integrally and correlatively united to each other. Potency receives its definiteness from its corresponding act: essence then borrows, as pure way of being, its sense and value from the principle of being. In this conception, priority belongs completely to being. If, however, one rejects this distinction between essence and being, the full accent is put naturally on essence as the unique source of value and intelligibility, independent of whether one considers essence as concrete or abstract; through the devaluation of being one comes to what is called, in this particular sense, essentialism.

L.D.R.

ETERNAL

Reality without beginning (an eternally created world) and also reality without end (an eternal soul). Eternal especially is God, creator of time and therefore above time; i.e., above the beginning, end or lapse of time. There is no past and no future in God, only an absolute present: an absolute independent, always actual and in unlimited possession of Himself.

ETHICAL

1) indicates what is related to morals, either actual conduct, object of positive, social approval, or the ideal actions, judged according to the unconditioned principles. 2) value, characteristic of man inasmuch as he, through his free voluntary decisions, in accordance or not with his independent insight and what seems to him objectively decent, constructs his own personality. 3) generic concept which contains both the good and the bad acts as subspecies. Ethical is often used for ethically good deeds; the

135

ethically bad deeds are then called unethical.

ETHICS
Philosophical study of the moral life. This study develops gradually in three stages. The first involves pinning down the essence of the ethical phenomenon. This seems to be self-evident, but very often all that is given is an "explanation" of what has not even been discovered in its appearance. Sometimes these explanations cover the fact as it really appears. More important, therefore, is the phenomenological analysis of the ethical, as it appears in the immediate consciousness. But such analysis is naturally not sufficient and the question remains whether the difference between good and evil, which forces itself on us as a fact, is also to be justified critically. A critical-transcendental analysis is therefore necessary which will discover the conditions under which the affirmation of the ethical is intelligible. Finally, a synthesis of the results of the successive analyses is necessary. This synthesis must guide us toward the metaphysical meaning of ethics. Ethics can only be explained in relation to the essential basis itself. *See also* morality. J.Gr.

ETHOS
The totality of the conceptions held by a specific community in relation to ethics.

EUBULIDES
Ca. 400 B.C. Philosopher of the School of Megara. Assiduous student of *eristics. Known for his dilemmas, of the liar who says that he is lying, of Electra who recognizes and does not recognize her brother, etc.

EUCKEN-RUDOLF
Born in Aurich 1846, died in Jena 1926. German spiritualist and university professor. Tried to find a solution for the spiritual needs of his time, which science, with its high achievements, could not provide. The element of universality and necessity in our knowledge shows the existence of a higher spiritual world, inaccessible to reasonable concepts, but open to the complete human experience of life, in which the opposition of subjectivity and objectivity, of the empirical Ego and the objective-ideal not-Ego, is abolished. Because of the existence of the spiritual world, human life becomes meaningful and valuable, and egoism and eudemism are conquered. The acceptance of this existence is called by Eucken "universal religion." When man chooses to rise into the spiritual world rather than to remain in an easy sympathy with the "purely human," he will experience the help of a higher force, which reaches toward him and attracts him. In this way man reaches God, not as the conclusion of a syllogism, but as the result of an experience. In Christ Eucken finds the most perfect image of human life, and the answer to the question whether He and His disciples can still be called Christians is in the affirmative. He rejects the supernatural character of Christianity, but recognizes in the entire story a revelation of the spiritual world. F.S.

EUCLID of MEGARA
5th-4th century B.C. One of the first disciples of *Socrates, founder of the School of *Megara. United the Socratic ethical doctrine with the doctrine about the *Eleates about the One, which he previously, however, had considered to be the Good. He is also the founder of the *eristics of Megara.

EUDAEMONISM

Doctrine that ethics is the pursuit of eudaemonia or *happiness. Happiness is however a complex datum: if it exists in a situation of pleasure which completely satisfies the being, then it follows the condition of perfection which man reaches by acting according to the requisites of human nature. Out of this follows a double interpretation of eudaemonism according to the importance given to one or the other factor. Perfection can be dependent on pleasure, as when one gives his life for his fatherland because of the pleasure of being a hero, or pleasure can be dependent on the pursuit of perfection. In the first case the eudaemonism is formally hedonistic, and it appears under this form in Aristotle's works; in the second case *hedonism is surpassed: perfection is no longer pursued as a means to pleasure, but for itself. In this sense Thomas Aquinas recognized eudaemonism, which he borrowed from Aristotle, and elevated to a principle of morality. J.Gr.

EUDEMUS OF RHODES

Disciple and collaborator of Aristotle, wrote an history of mathematics and of astronomy. His thought is closer to the doctrine of Aristotle than that of Theophrastus, and when it deviates from Aristotle it shows a rather theological inclination; the *Ethica Eudemia* of Aristotle was probably published by Eudemus after the death of his master.

EUDOXUS OF CNIDUS

Ca. 408-355 B.C. Mathematician and astronomer, *ca.* 368 moved his school from Cyzicus to Athens, where he lived in the *Academy and replaced Plato as head of the school while the latter was on his second voyage to Sicily. He an-swered Plato's question as to how one could explain the seemingly irregular course of the planets by the theory of the regular motion. He put together a system of 26 concentric spheres, which was later expanded by Callipys and Aristotle. In the field of geometry he is well known for his invention of the general *theory of proportions,* which he applied to measurable as well as immeasurable quantities. He also invented the *method of exhaustion,* very important in Greek geometry, and the tensor for the doubling of the cube. C.J.d.V.

EUHEMERUS

Ca. 300 B.C. Known especially for his theory about the gods. They were nothing else than powerful rulers of previous times, who, to impose their authority, accepted a religious cult and therefore received a place in Greek mythology.

EULER, Leonhard

Born in Basel 1707, died in Petersburg 1783. German mathematician and natural philosopher. Deviates from the physical theories of Newton; proposes a theory of ether, and to explain light, a theory of waves. Space and time, logical foundations of mechanics, are not deduced from experience, but are only concepts of the intellect.

EUSEBIUS OF CAESAREA

Born in Caesarea (Palestine) *ca.* 265, died Bishop of Caesarea in 339 or 340. Historian and apologist, introduced a great number of Platonic and neo-Platonic ideas in Christian thought.

EVIDENCE

The quality of a being insomuch as it reveals itself to the knowing subject. Although we presuppose in this a proportion between the ability of knowledge and the object thereof, the evidence is still a quality of the object itself; that which follows in the knowing subject is not called evidence but certitude. It is not necessary for evidence that the object manifests itself completely; to the respect and in the measure in which it is given, it is evident.

One distinguishes *immediate* and *mediate* evidence. Immediate evidence can concern the content of a general essential relation (e.g., the first principles), or as an individual factual relation. In the latter case judgment is based on experience, and so-called predicative evidence is anticipated by a prepredicative evidence: the evidence of an individual object of experience as a possible substratum of express recognition. The first evidence in this sense is the existential evidence of the knowing subject in its existence.

Mediate evidence is obtained by intervention of the aspects in the object, which are themselves immediately evident, e.g., in reasoning. If the connection between immediate and mediate evidence is strictly necessary, then the mediate evidence is also absolutely (or metaphysically) evident. If not necessary, the evidence is called physical or moral; it does not exclude all possibilities of the contrary.

Immediate and mediate evidence are both *inner* evidence. To this, one can oppose *external* evidence: when certitude is obtained by the intervention of a means of revelation which does not belong to the object of the knowledge itself. Evident is then only the credibility of the witness (his reliability and capacity for knowing) in whose authority we *believe. But for this witness the object is evident. Evidence is therefore always eventual-

ly inner, as it is always eventually immediate. In mathematics, *see* *philosophy of mathematics. J.P.

EVIL

Is disorder in the spiritual activity. This can appear by man in his free act. With his will man is certainly inclined towards the good, but a particular good can sometimes be strived for without respect for the hierarchy of values. This is, if we consider everything, wrong. Because man, immortal in his spiritual existence and therefore oriented towards a personal final end, injures his own completion, creates disorder in relation to his own eternal end. Their is then *sin or malice (malum simpliciter).

Physical evils are called pain, illness, death. For the animal, who is striken with it, it is an evil (at least secundum quid). Since an animal is only temporily existing, and has no personal final end, we have to consider evil, with everything which happens to it, from a broader point of view: is physical evil still a disorder when you consider it in the whole of the cosmic evolution? The answer is not easily found. It is still more difficult to discover the meaning of physical evil in the undying existence of man; could it have some positive value and therefore be eventually good or in order?

Many philosophers have studied the nature and the meaning of evil, its origin, its relation to the fundaments of being; it has however always remained an unsolved problem. Some used a fundamental dualism; a good and evil divinity; some others said that a good God succumbed under the load of his work. When one declares however that the being as such is good (ens et bonum convertuntur) in other words when one declares that

138

metaphysical evil is impossible, then the existing evil can not be reduced to a divine essence, but it has to originate in a finite being, without affecting the being as such. Many therefore underline the privative character of evil, which has no positive nature, but is only the absence of something. L.D.R.

EVOLUTION
In living nature the term applied to the appearance in the course of the earth's history of ever new kinds of organisms, which proceed from each other. The whole presents the image of a development from "low" to "high." There is no strict proof that there was such an evolution, but many arguments drive us to accept it. These arguments are primarily deduced from the study of fossils of extinct species and from the theory of heredity which shows a certain variation. Most biologists now accept evolution, but do not agree as to its causes.

*Darwinism teaches that evolution proceeds from an accidental play of different factors, without plan. Lamarckism declares that organisms react actively and appropriately to the environment, and that the resultant changes in them are hereditary. It is certainly clear that progress in evolution, the appearance of always higher forms, can only be explained by causes which are proper to living nature, and by the existence in these causes of potencies which developed over the course of time (e.g., during a period of 1,500 million years). The study of fossils, however, teaches us also that the great structural types in living nature (e.g., vertebrates, molluscs) have always been distinctly separated, which would support the theory of more than one initial form. Many questions remain unsolved in the evolution theory, but this does not mean that the evolution itself is not accepted by most biologists.

According to the theory of emergent evolution, constantly new steps were realized in nature, which were quantitatively higher than the preceding ones on which they rested. This theory (defended by Alexander and others) also has philosophical implications, as do all theories of evolution (*see* Bergson).

Its influence on the general world view was important: the theory of evolution has often been used as a weapon of materialism and atheism; falsely however, since he who accepts evolution has to accept the existence of a First Cause, who regulated everything according to plan. M.B.

EVOLUTIONISM
The view that all reality can only be explained by an evolution from "lower" to "higher."

EXACTNESS
The conformity of a concept with the essence of a thing, as opposed to the truth of a judgment about the same; also the fact that the form or construction of a reasoning satisfies the conditions, required by the formal logic for obtaining a reasonably justified conclusion.

EXCLUDED THIRD, Principle of the
There is no middle between being and not-being.

It refers to contents of thought which are contradictory to each other, as is the principle of *contradiction. The latter however states that the contradictory contents of thought can not be *affirmed* together of the same being, while the principle of the excluded third states that contradictory principles of thought can not be both *denied*. In other words: every proposed fact (proposition) is either true itself, or its contradiction is true: one or both has to be true, both can not be false. It is indeed impossible to have about a proposed fact the attitude of neither affirming nor denying. Without deciding that the affirmation with the negation is definitely true, one has to agree that at least one or both is true; if the one is true, then the other is false (principle of *contradiction). No other true attitude is possible because "being", which excluded already a second possibility (not-being) excludes also a fortiori a third possibility. Thought however (real thought) has always reference to "being"— relation of conformity or non-conformity—, so that it can not remain neutral.

The principle of the excluded third, different from the principles of *identity and contradiction, has reference to finite beings, inasmuch as we do not know them yet in particular. The formulation of the principle which, we mentioned above in a logical way, will therefore in ontological form read: everything which is thought (represented) to be, is or is not; everything which is thought not to be, is not or is. Since being-thought is also being, we can not understand being in this case as simply being, but as being in the specific ways in which the represented is thought to be.

No logical system can lack the principles of identity and contradiction, some however do not use the principle of the excluded third. See intuitionistic *logic.—J.P.

EXCLUSION

Of p and q is the *proposition: or not-p, or not-q (it is excluded that p and q are both true). Sheffer has proved that by means of the exclusion all *truthfunctions can be defined. If we write p/q for the exclusion of p and q, then is the negation: not-p equivalent to p/p, the conjunction p and q, equivalent to (p/q) / (p/q) etc.; All truthfunctions can also be defined by means of a conjunction of negations: not-p and not-q.

EXCLUSIVE

See judgment.

EXECUTION

That moment in the action when the proposed content is realized by the acting subject. This moment, in the order of the physical reality, is certainly an integral part of the action which it indeed completes. But what about the moral order? The execution is for Kant completely valueless: the morality is entirely in the *intention. We can certainly not deny that the intention is decisive in moral respect, but it is not the only one. It is indeed not so much a question to know if the execution adds something to the *intention but to the *resolution. The resolution (which is, as is the intention, completely dominated by the will) is certainly more important than the execution, but the latter is not arbitrary. The resolution is, firstly, only perfect if it goes into execution as soon as the occasion arises (because the execution requires other faculties than the will). The execution, on the other hand, affirms the seriousness of the resolution and influences it by weakening or strengthening it.—J. Gr.

EXEMPLARISM

(Latin: *exemplar*, example, prototype or archetype) Theory which accepts the existence of prototypes (ideas) of things, existing outside these things, and according to which they are realized. Augustine, Bonaventura and Thomas

Aquinas teach that in God (or in the Word of God) is the prototype of all creatures, and that the purpose of every being, as it is created according to its prototype God, is to realize this archetype completely.

EXEMPLARITY

Characteristic of the archetypal idea, according to which an intellectual cause works. Plato emphasizes especially this aspect of causality in the explanation of tangible things, so that it seems that their cause exists in this only. Exemplarity has its role in all the work man does, in the light of his consciousness. As soon as one proves that all causality, eventually at least, has to be based on the activity of an intellectual cause, then exemplarity acquires an absolute ontological value. The Christian authors used it very often in their explanation of the world by the creative activity of God.

EXISTENCE

In the Middle Ages the prefix is sometimes emphasized: *ex-sistere,* meaning "placed outside of;" *sistere extra causas,* "placed outside its causes." In this sense the not-created cannot be called a real existing reality: God does not exist; He is.

Contemporary *existentialism also puts the accent on the prefix but attaches another meaning to it. Existence for this philosophy is not only "existing," but the form of existing proper to man. In this sense man alone, not animals, exist. What is meant is that man, in his complete reality, is characterized by intentionality: it is his nature to be open to his environment, to be as *da-sein* in the middle of persons and things. He is not simply a thing, whose attitude and position are brought about by physical,

physiological and sociological factors, from outside; he is also not an isolated monad, an idealistically conceived ego, a delimited subjectivity whose psychism is dependent on the environment and complete immanent activity; he is, on the contrary, incarnated inferiority, naturally bodily-conscious. Existence is this fundamental relation between subjectivity and the world, and it appears necessarily, find its affirmation in all human activity, in feeling as well as in the knowledge. This inevitable duality, of which the terms form a unique substantial unity, is the basis of a series of characteristics of the existence, among others, perspectivity, temporality, historicity.

Perspectivity: The existing man is, from the beginning, in a situation which conditions him from which he cannot separate himself and which rules his acts. His view of and reaction to the world are therefore perspectivistic, varying and always progressing.

Temporality: His existence is spread out in the dimension of time: past, present and future are disintegrating moments, which are however, completely terminated in their correlations; man never lives outside his projects, outside his future that is, but he is always carried by the presence of his past.

Historicity: His activity is the fruit of dialectical tension between subjectivity and the world; he develops himself and discovers his own meaning, but only through cultivating the world and discovering its meaning; this limited freedom, which rests neither on pure receptivity nor on complete reflection and creative power, impresses upon human acts the stamp of historicity. L.D.R.

EXISTENCE (logical)

Quality of a specific concept, when it (in a whole of concepts) indicates a class, which is not empty. If the class is empty i.e. if no individual of this class is existing or can exist, the concept has no logical existence.

EXISTENCE, Mathematical

In mathematics we very often ask ourselves the question if there exists a mathematical entity with given qualities; sometimes we reach a negative answer. In other cases we find an affirmative answer, and to justify this answer we have to prove the existence of a mathematical entity (number, straight line, point, etc.) with prescribed qualities. It very often happens that we construct a mathematical entity and that we prove that this entity has the prescribed qualities. The method of construction depends on the field of mathematics: in geometry a point is constructed by the crossing of two straight lines or circles, a number is constructed through calculation, etc. One can explain the term "construction" in two ways: One can first conceive that the entity was previously ready, available among a number of entities of a specific kind; construction would then be the isolation of one of these entities; one can also conceive that the entity did not exist previously and that it was created by the construction. It is clear that philosophy is interested in learning which explanation is the most probable, but elementary mathematics is not concerned with it. In modern mathematics, however, there are cases where a proof has to be accepted or rejected according to what explanation is accepted.

As an illustration of this: in the article "Continuum" we gave under No. 1 a proof of the existence of a limit A for a climbing and at the top limited series of real numbers. We started from the division of real numbers into two functions, P and Q. In this division the number A (whose existence had still to be proved) was not left out of consideration; for further along in the proof we noted that A had to be part of Q. If you accept the term "construction" in the second definition we gave, then you cannot accept the foregoing proof.

It is often possible to change the proof and avoid the problem; but there are cases—even cases of fundamental importance—where a change is not possible. E.W.B.

EXISTENTIAL

That thought which does not consider the truth without its relation to existing being, through which it is thought. In the course of history there have always been philosophers who followed this path: one thinks of Socrates, Augustine, Pascal, Newman, Nietzsche, etc. In the strict sense, *existential philosophy is dependent on Kierkegaard: Kierkegaard not only thinks truth in relation to existing man; he also deduces from it specific characteristics of the truth.

EXISTENTIAL PHILOSOPHY

The philosophy of existence inasmuch as, closely connected to Kierkegaard, it thinks existentially. It will therefore not as much describe or explain or present universal truths, than give insight into the problem which existence naturally poses. More specifically still in *Jaspers.—J. Gr.

General term to indicate a group of philosophical schools, in which existence takes a central position. The term "existence" is here used in the particular sense of the specific human form of existence. It was Kierkegaard who first shed light on this way of existing. What distinguishes man from God on the one hand and from things on the other hand is that he is never completely himself: a thing is simply what it is, but since it is unconscious it cannot be itself; God is completely Himself because He is what He thinks; man is placed between the two and has to realize himself by constantly acting according to what he thinks. Only in this way does he exist, and this way is called existence.

Although existential philosophy had its origin with Kierkegaard, the question remains whether there is an inner unity in this philosophy. The fact is that many of the philosophers who belong to this school deny for one or another reason the existence of a school. The movement originated historically with Kierkegaard, but one can become disloyal to his inspiration (Jaspers) or be influenced by other philosophies (Heidegger, Sartre) or deny any influence of Kierkegaard (Marcel). There is finally no agreement either in regard to the end or in regard to the results. According to the end we distinguish an existential and an existentialistic school. The first, to which Jaspers and perhaps Marcel belong, limits itself to throwing light upon the meaning and the task of human existence; the latter analyzes human existence but with the eventual purpose of finding the meaning of the "esse." The first is, in fact, more practical, and the latter holds more to theory (it developed from *phenomenology, as feeling is for Heidegger and Sartre). As for the results, one sometimes thinks that all existential philosophy is atheistic, yet Marcel, Jaspers and Heidegger (to some degree at least) are theistic. Atheism is found only among a group of French existentialists, such as Sartre, de Beauvoir, Merleau-Ponty and Camus. Existential philosophy is also essentially limited to French and German language territories. In Germany there are Jaspers, Heidegger, Binswanger, Bollnow; in France, Marcel, Wahl, Sartre, de Beauvoir, Merleau-Ponty, Camus. There are also the Russian thinkers living in the West: Berdiaiev and Chestov. B.D.

If we consider, however, existential philosophy as one movement, we do so because of the above-mentioned conception of human existence: in every case the "esse" of man seems to contain an inner division to be determined (positively or negatively). It is therefore necessary for existence, at the risk of not being, to exist: to be outside oneself as related to the other, which is for Jaspers transcendency (God), for Heidegger the world, for Sartre the "en-soi." However existence appears, it is no more than the necessity of existing. Existential philosophy can therefore be defined as being that philosophy which catches existence as pure task or considers existence as existing. At the same time it is very clear that existential philosophy possesses an edifying character, or at least, even when it describes, analyzes and explains, it always appeals to authenticity. Therefore the curious fact that many of these philosophers are also literary writers, such as Marcel, Wahl, Sartre, de Beauvoir and Camus.

It should be emphasized that existential philosophy has had its influence on theology, psychology, psychiatry, psychosomatic medicine, sociology, literature and linguistics. The influence of existential philosophy is very important in the attitude to life of the European man. J. Gr.

EXISTENTIAL PROPOSITION

The logic of Aristotle uses general *propositions: all a̲'s are b̲'s, in which is implied that there are a̲'s (and that there are b̲'s). Such general propositions are called existential propositions.

EXISTENTIALISM

In a large sense, the philosophy of *existence, inasmuch as this is more absolutely a "doctrine" of human "esse" and the "esse" in general. Historically, existentialism can be explained by the contact of phenomenology with the philosophy of existence, or even by the autonomous development of phenomenology, in which the central concept of *intentionality seems to rest in *existence (ek-sistentie). It is without doubt under the influence of phenomenology that human existence is analyzed and described, rather than exposed as a problem: from this human existence then, which is naturally related to the "esse", the philosopher looks for the meaning of the "esse" —*Heidegger (at least according to some commentators) and *Sartre (independent of Heidegger). According to Merleau-Ponty, existentialism takes over the original intention of phenomenology.

In a more strict sense, existentialism is applied to the philosophy of *Sartre, or the view of life to which the philosophy of Sartre tries to give concrete form, especially in literary and other milieus. One cannot, however, consider this view of life as the concrete form of Sartre's philosophy. It is first of all spontaneous, and finds its expression rather in Sartre's philosophy. Sartre brought a clearer realization and philosophical justification to a world view which existed before, although not explicitly. On the other hand, not all the philosophical aspects of Sartre's theory appear in this attitude toward life. The social character of existence and the positive problem of the existence are completely absent.

The basic form of this philosophy, as it is lived in several circles, is despair in the face of the absurdity of existence, despair which tries to conquer itself, rather than to run away from itself, toward the bourgeois way of life, because of a lack of honesty (mauvaise foi). The belief of the bourgeois in absolute norms and truths serves only to cover his own despair and that of others.

We find therefore in existentialism as a view of life, an antibourgeois attitude in ethics, social life and art, a despair so complete that it affects even the liberty which creates the motives or values according to which it acts. Weariness with life, embitterment, revolt follow. They are experienced and described in Sartre's works. There is a brutality in this attitude to life, and it is always bathed in a sultry atmosphere. The importance of sexuality is accentuated (through *psychoanalysis) since it is here that despair is most strongly felt, for the possibility of the abandonment of lovers is completely excluded. J. Gr.

EXOTERIC

Initiated people, laymen, outsiders.

EXPERIENCE

To be conscious in such a way that the conscious subject and the conscious object are melted together, or that the subject in his entire being and with all his abilities, more specifically his feelings, is connected to the conscious content. In this latter case we mean the personal experience of consciousness (Strauss). *See* aesthetic experience, religious experience.

That which one obtains as knowledge and skill while wandering through the world. To have experience one has to be a knowing being, which receives the object of knowledge in a certain passive way. One immediate impression is not experience, but one event which occurred in the past and is presented as actual by the memory, and therefore is included in the now present situation, can be called a source of experience. This is always knowledge which is related to the concrete present and preferably to the practical. Next to this meaning of experience which is used in daily life, there is philosophical experience. This is receiving knowledge on the level of observation and is opposed to further assimilation by the memory, the imagination or reasoning. Although the object of experience is the total concrete essence, and although this essence is also apprehended intellectually through observation, the term "experience" is used preferably for qualities which are perceptible through the senses. So in *empiricism.

One can distinguish between *exterior* and *inner* experience; inner experience is related to one's own psychical condition, exterior experience is related to the so-called *outer world.

For *Kant experience is the totality of judgments of perception, created through the a priori forms of the intellect and therefore having strict necessity. J.P.

EXPERIMENT

(Latin: *experiri*, to test) Empirical scientific investigation, in which the investigator, often with the aid of technical means, creates important phenomena by dividing related facts and things. Experiment is different from observation, for the investigator intervenes actively in the creation of the object of his study; he uses different methods to create, when he wants these phenomena in different circumstances of location and time. It is especially the study of relationships according to laws and the formulation of these laws; also the testing and verification of provisional explanations (*hypotheses) by the facts.

EXPLICIT

Opposed to implicit, expressly indicated.

EXPONIBLE

Obscurely compound. *See* judgment.

EXPORTATION

Is the operation in which one concludes from: if p and q, then m, too: if p, then, if q, m. In this operation is the *proposition p exported from the antecedent as independent supposition.

EXPRESSION

Is a succession of symbols; the rules of the theory are actually only applicable to well-formed expressions, which represent, according to the rules of the system, objects of thought. An expression is *variable* if it contains free variables; it is *constant* in the contrary case.

EXTENSION

Of a concept or class is the collection of all the individuals on which the concept can be applied. The extension can, in this sense, be an empty collection. In formal logic the class is not an extension but indeed the concept.

145

In logic, the extent of a concept: the totality of things which a concept can be applied. E.g., the concept "man" can be applied to all men, wherever they live, have lived or will live. Extension and *comprehension of concepts are inversely proportionate.

In natural philosophy extension is the quality in material particles of being separate in space as well as in time. *See* continuum.

EXTENSIVE

A quantity is called extensive when it can be, in the strict sense, bigger or smaller. Extensive quantities can be added to each other. So is length an extensive quantity. Two lengths together give a greater length.

Opposed to extensive is intensive. An intensive quantity can be more or less intensive, but not larger or smaller. When one adds two intensive quantities, the result will not be a larger intensity. Two quantities of water of 40° do not give water of 80°.

EXTENSIVE QUALITY

Although qualities are intensive quantities, they have a certain ex-tensivity because a quality is always present in a specific extensum. A specific color can be not only more or less intensive, but can also cover a larger or smaller surface. A.G.M.v.M.

EXTENSUM

That which has extension. An abstract concept which embraces concrete physical things under the quality of their extension.

EXTREME TERMS

(Final terms), the subject and predicate terms of the *conclusion of a *syllogism, in which they are successively compared with the *middleterm.

EXTRINSIC

From the outside and without inner connection.

EXTROSPECTION

Observation from the outside. Opposed to introspection, the inner view of personal experiences. Extrospection has more importance than introspection because more than one person can experience that which is seen, so that there can be more objectivity, while the object of contemplation remains untouched.

F

F

As capital letter, symbol to indicate the possibility of a direct reduction of the mood in *Festino, *Felapton, *Ferison, *Fesapo and *Fresison to the mood in *Ferio of the first syllogistic figure.

FABER STAPULENSIS, Jacobus
See Lefevre d'Etaples.

FACT

What is, what happens, what presents itself. A fact can, as the only real thing, give us absolute certitude. This is accepted by positivism, which appeals only to pure facts, however difficult they may be to discover. Fact can also, however, be considered that which simply is, i.e., without explanation and necessity. Thus Leibniz called factual truth (*vérité de fait*) that truth which, in opposition to necessary truth (*vérité de droit*), could also have been otherwise or not been.

FACTUM RATIONIS, or fact of reason

Called by Kant the paradoxical fact that pure practical reason produces from itself the moral law. See autonomy.

FACULTY

Force to do something. In narrower sense: active *potency in the psychic life to develop oneself in a specific direction. We have traditionally made a distinction between organic and spiritual faculties in man: sensory knowledge and striving, on the one hand, intellect and will on the other hand. The question about the ontological nature of the faculties, their number, their real distinction, their mutual connections does not belong to empirical science but to philosophy.

FAIRNESS

Special form of justice, applied where a positive norm of justice is absent. Judicial arrangements are necessarily general, so that by every application of the juridical norm on specific cases fairness is imposed. In this sense fairness is opposed to (positive) law, although it imposes itself, says Binder, as a new law and so changes to (positive) law.

FALCKENBEG, Richard 1851-1920.

German historian of philosophy.

FALSE (ness)

Opposite of *true (truth). False is in the first place said of a proposition in as much as it does not coincide with that what is, as it is. This not-coincidence (in *adaequatio) should not be understood as an imperfect coincidence (i.e. imperfect truth) but as a positive deviation, so that is said to be what is not and not to be what is. As is the case for truth, there must be a question of *known* not-coincidence. How this knowledge is possible while one still states a proposition with the pretension of being true, how in other words error is possible, is one of the most difficult problems of the epistemology. A distinction should certainly be made between untruth and *error, and say that for the latter an implicit true knowledge exists, which contradicts the explicitly false proposition. One can by *reflexion on these fundamental experiences and insights return to the false proposition and correct it. False is also said of the being, in as much as it is not in itself as it presents itself to us: untrue.—J.P.

FANTASM

Representation, constructed by the imagination with the help of the memory from previous sensory observation.

In scholasticism, the still individual, schematic representation by which sensory experience reaches a conclusion. Is opposed to the general abstract *concept of thought.

FANTASY

The ability to form by oneself new representations. One should distinguish the analyzing (or abtracting) form and the synthesizing (or combining) form. The prior has a relation to the creation of something new through analysis; the latter is the more general form: reaching something new through given data.

FARBER, Marvin

Born in 1901. American phenomenologist, university professor in Buffalo.

FATE

That which governs the course of events. Originally and in Greece, fate was conceived as a supra-divine force, but the Stoics reduced it to the immanent law of nature. This is again personalized in Christianity, where it is affirmed as divine providence.

Fate weighs on man. For existentialism it becomes identified with what, in the last instance, weighs on man: the limitedness of his existence. Nietzsche learned to accep. this limitedness heroically through the *amor fati.*

FEAR

An emotional state, characterized by a concern and unrest over a vague threat, in which one feels incapable of resisting the threat. In psychological terminology there is a tendency to use the word "anguish" when the anxiety has no specific object, and fear when a specific object exists, e.g. fear of pain, of height (Goldstein). Fear is often a neurotic reaction-form. The meaning and cause of this fear are then not known to the patient. Fear also has bodily aspects (turning pale, stomach contractions) which can lead to bodily (psychosomatic) deviations. Contemporary psychology and anthropology are much concerned with fear and explain it in terms of different sources. The psychoanalyst speaks especially of its unconscious origin. According to existentialism fear brings man back to himself and to the possibility of a real existence, because of the indefiniteness of its object.

FECHNER, Gustav Theodor

Born in Groszärchen 1801, died in Leipzig 1887. German psychologist and metaphysician, founder of the experimental examination of psychical phenomena with the help of physical methods. By generalizing the results of experience Fechner wants to go beyond that which can be experienced. In accordance with the analogy of the phenomena of the consciousness he explains that natural happenings are one side of a reality the other side of which has a psychical character: the universe is animated as man is. The human soul is a part of the soul of the earth, which itself is part of the universal soul or the Omni-spirit, which is the principle of all order and causality in the universe. The omni-spirit of God and the world belong together as necessarily as soul and body. Their difference lies only in the point of view from which they are considered, as an arc of a circle is convex when it is seen from the outside and concave when it is looked at from the inside. The happenings in the world are further explained as an interaction of atoms, which were considered by *Leibniz as centers of energy. F.S.

FEELING

The capacity of the emotions in a physical or spiritual sense. Characteristic are subjectivity, the relative passivity of the subject and the influence upon the entire person. Some theories, such as sensualism (Stumpf), reduce the feelings to characteristics of *sensation. Scheler reserves for feelings the central place in the psychic life (emotionalism). For the modern psychologist the feelings are irreducible data of experience, a particular category of psychical phenomena. P.S.

Appears as an experience of totally proper nature, in the threefold division of the faculties: knowing, feeling, willing. The *dichotomy on the contrary recognizes only knowing and willing, and reduces the feeling to the cognition. Scholasticism therefore studies the feeling under the sensory faculties of striving, namely the passions. The physiological psychology reduces the feeling to a way of expression ("we are sad because they cry"). In sensualistic sense we see in the feeling a sensory experience, in intellectualistic sense we see in it a quality of representa-

tion; in biological sense it is a useful experience of profit or harm. The modern psychology emphasizes again the total-quality of the feeling but endangers therefore the proper nature of feeling. This is the subjective being proportionate to the inner or outer world, relatively passive in regard to the active gathering of the knowledge and the intervention of the will. In the intentional feeling exist however together a subjective undergoing and an objective involvement. In any case is the feeling predominantly connected to an act of knowledge, however much the content of this act be free from the reflexive intellect, as for instance in the humour. There exists on the other hand a close connection between the biological and the constitutional ground of the personality and the nature of the feeling. On this are based most of the feeling-typologies.

One distinguishes sensory and spiritual feelings. The latter are defined as being related to a value (intellectual, moral, social feeling etc.) Scheler distinguishes four levels 1. the sensory (sensational) feelings (e.g. pain) 2. the vital feelings (life) (e.g. weakness); 3. The psychic (motivating) feelings (e.g. joy); 4. the personal feelings (e.g. despair). The scholastic division of passions leads to three pairs; love and hate, desire and repulse, joy and sadness.

The close connection between feelings and physical situations has led to psychosomatics: the theory of the chronical functional disorders on the grounds of or in connection with specific situations of the feeling.

The susceptibility for emotions is called emotionality.—P.S.

149

FEELING OF DEPENDENCE

For Schleiermacher, the immediate consciousness of dependence upon the divine. It is the source of all religiosity.

FEELING OF NATURE

The aesthetical experience which finds its origin and its object directly in nature. The feeling of nature is at the same time intuition of nature, although one prefers to call the aesthetical experience of nature, *feeling*, because of its more subjective character. In its pure form feeling of nature is the fact that one feels himself one and in harmony with the life and the scene of nature. In this context nature, being a landscape or in its diversity of forms, the immediate illustration of an absolute essential sense, although this illustration remains more in the domain of undetermined feeling than that it becomes a structural intuition. Pure feeling of nature becomes more an artistic contemplation of nature, when it is structured intuition and nature is then brought in closer relation with a possible artistic creation. Nature is therefore often, with its unlimited possibilities for contemplation, the fruitful milieu in which the artist arrives at artistic inspiration. L.V.K.

FETISHISM

(Portuguese: *feitiçao;* Latin: *factitius*) Used the first time by Ch. de Brosses (1760) to indicate reverence for animals and inanimate objects. It is, according to A. *Comte, the first phase of the so-called theological stadium, in which things in nature are revered for themselves and not for the spirits who live in them. John Lubbock considers it as the third phase in the religious development of mankind, after atheism and magic. This theory is entirely forgotten today. The cult of things in nature or objects made by hand is found among animistic peoples, either because they believe that a genius lives in the object or because it contain relics of their ancestors; it is found with totemistic people who believe that these things possess special forces. Sorcerers use fetishes because they believe that avenging spirits live inside them.

FEUERBACH, Ludwig

Born in Landshut 1804, died in Rechenberg near Nürnberg 1872. German naturalistic thinker, adversary of Christianity. In his widely circulated book, *Das Wesen des Christendums* (1841), he calls it a product of the mind and therefore incompatible with philosophy, which is the fruit of reasonable thought. The origin of religion, he thinks, is to be found in the fact that man, because of his urge for happiness and other inner needs, creates for himself an image of God, in whom he thinks that his wishes and desires will be realized. Feuerbach's epistemology is sensualistic: only sensory perception can give us knowledge of reality; only what we perceive with the senses is real. He therefore comes close to materialism, without accepting it in toto. He considers man as being part of nature. Feuerbach's ethics are also naturalistic: the urge for happiness, given by nature, is the origin of ethics as well as of religion. Morality consists therefore in promoting one's own happiness and the happiness of others; it is man's duty to recognize and honor the urge for happiness of others.

FICHTE, Johann Gottlieb

Born in Rammenau (Oberlausitz) 1762, died in Berlin 1814. German idealist, university professor at Jena 1794, at Berlin 1810.

Helped the German people to become nationally conscious of German unity through his *Reden a. d. deutschen Nation* (1807-1808)

Starting from the principles of °Kant, Fichte attempts to construct in his *Grundlage der gesammten Wissenschaftslehre* a system of idealistic philosophy on one basic principle only. This principle can be looked for only in the subject. We have to find it through reflection and it is nothing else than the self-consciousness of the Ego—not the empirical, concrete Ego, but the abstract, general and supra-individual Ego, which produces the synthetic unity of appreciation, as Kant calls it.

The self-consciousness of the Ego is the "esse" of the Ego; by thinking it creates itself. From this first act of thought come all other acts of thought and they produce the full content of consciousness and thus total empirical reality. The first act of thought is expressed in the thesis: "The Ego set itself" (thesis). With this first act of thought a second one is immediately connected, expressed as: "The Ego sets a not-Ego against itself" (anti-thesis). On the one hand Ego and not-Ego belong necessarily together, but on the other hand the propositions in which they are expressed are opposed to each other. This opposition is lifted by a third act of thought, expressed as: "Ego and not-Ego limit each other," i.e., they lift partially and mutually their reality (synthesis).

On these three acts of thought are founded the logical principles of identity, contradiction and sufficient foundation, as well as the categories of reality, negation and limitation. All further propositions depend on the first three and have to be deduced dialectically from them, like the development of the Ego to the not-Ego and their mutual limitation. The third proposition, however, has a double element: inasmuch as the Ego set itself as limited by the not-Ego, it is theoretical, but inasmuch as it sets the not-Ego as limited by the Ego, it is practical. These two elements form the starting points of theoretical and practical philosophy.

Theoretical philosophy shows that the Ego constructs its world by unconscious production and gradually creates a content of consciousness, which finds its end and highest reward in knowledge of itself and in the insight that the not-Ego is determined by the Ego; by this the transition to practical philosophy is also indicated.

Practical reason has in Fichte's philosophy, as it does in Kant's, primacy over the theoretical. For practical philosophy teaches that the self-limitation of the Ego and the edification of the world in consciousness happen only because of practical motive and for practical ends. The Ego sets the not-Ego exclusively, because it wants to act and needs an object for this action. The Ego, however, has to push further away the limits which it has erected for itself, with complete independence and freedom reveals itself now to the ethical consciousness as a categorical imperative, formally defined as "Act always according to your conscience," but which, in regard to the content, is directed toward the absolute valid end of independence and freedom. The original passion, however, is opposed by natural passion, which pulls the Ego toward the object and tries to subject the Ego to this object. The Ego can only overcome natural passion by taking over the object and using it for its own ends.

The legal order according to

Fichte, as it is for Kant, is different from the ethical order because it is not related to the will or mood, but only to external action. Individual consciousness accepts the recognition of a community. This is only possible, however, when the rule applies that everybody has to limit his freedom in such a way that others also keep their freedom. The original rights of the individual (free command of his own body, property and self-preservation) are therefore necessarily limited by the rights of the other members of the community. When these rights are disregarded by both sides the state authority intervenes with its laws in order to impose respect for the rights of individuals. The state borrows this right from the common will of all, uniting for the protection of their rights. The question of the factual or historical origin of the state is therefore of lesser importance.

The concept of the state in the thought of Fichte is of one larger than the pure constitutional state, and has a totalitarian aspect. Labor must be organized by the state in such a way that everybody can live from his labor. The most important duty of the state, however, is to bring the people, by ethical and spiritual education, to the point when they will do by conviction what they previously did out of obedience to the laws. By means of instruction and education the state must create in the people a strong will to do what is good. In the individual this has necessarily to be prepared for through the love of country, because he has first of all to be convinced that the good will be realized in his own community and only later in the human race as a whole.

The final end of all theoretical and practical activity of the Ego is the absolute Ego, in which freedom and independence are realized without limitation. This end certainly exists in an endless perspective, but it gives a direction and therefore contributes form and shape to the moral order. In the last period of his life Fichte added realistic views to his idealism. The end of action is further determined as being the becoming Divinity, Who is the only reality, in comparison to Whom anything else is only a figure and to Whom man must give himself in love. F.S.

FICINO, Marsiglio

Born in Figline 1433, died in Careggi 1499. Friend of Cosimo de Medici, who founded the neo-Platonic Academy in Florence. Ficino translated the works of Plato, Plotinus, Porphyrius and other neo-Platonic writers. Originally Ficino wanted to re-establish Platonism in its neo-Platonic form, but later he attempted to harmonize this philosophy with Christian doctrine; the doctrine of ideas of Plato as integrated into Christianity by Augustine. God is the "One" above all being; matter, the completely changeable, comes last in the hierarchical system of the world; the human soul is in the middle and partakes of everything.

FICTION

(Latin: *fictio*, invention). An explanation which is incorrect, improbable or even impossible when taken by itself, but which is however considered methodically true (*hypothesis) in order to better understand facts and situation, things and their mutual relation; very often one hopes that the incorrectness is the effect of accidental elements, coincidence or special points of view.

FICTIONISM

Doctrine advanced by *Vaihinger: all human knowledge which goes beyond sensory perceptions is fiction or the creation of the human mind, and no reality corresponds to it. Knowledge, however, which is conducive to life, has pragmatic value.

FIDEISM

(Latin: *fides*, faith). The philosophical theory of knowledge according to which the individual human reason is not able to reach certitude on its own at least in the religious and ethical field. Certitude can only be achieved by leaning on the authority of divine revelation or faith. Fideism and *traditionalism generally go together.

In a less strict sense, fideism is also applied to the theory that certitude is found in an irrational belief or sentiment. We find it in the sentimental philosophy of the Scottish school, in the *Glaubensphilosophie* of Jacobi and Schleiermacher.

FIELD

The space around an electrically charged body is in a special situation which shows in this way: another charged body will in these particular surroundings undergo a force which it would not undergo if the first body were not charged. This changed space around an electrically charged body is called the electric field. There are also magnetic fields. The field produced by the *gravitation is called gravitation-field.

Fieldtheory, the theory that electrical, magnetic and gravitation forces work via a field and do not work from a distance (*actio in distans).

FIGURE

In a philosophical sense: the form or the qualitative way of being, proper to a specific quantum, exactly because of this definiteness. In this sense: the figure of a human being, an animal, a plant, or organic matter.

In logic: the structural outline of a *syllogism. It is determined by the place of the middle term (*M), which in the first figure is subject of the major and predicate of the minor (sub-prae), in the second figure predicate of the major as well as of the minor (prae-prae), in the third figure subject of both (sub-sub), and in the fourth figure predicate of the major and subject of the minor (prae-sub). The first one can be applied according to four valid *moods, which have, respectively, as conclusion an $\underline{a}$, $\underline{e}$, $\underline{i}$ and $\underline{o}$ proposition. The second figure also has four moods, having always a negative conclusion; the third one has six moods and always has a particular conclusion; the fourth figure or figure of *Galenus with its five moods is often not considered a separate figure, but as an indirect first figure, for it is only grammatically different. The moods of the first figure are evidently correct and are therefore called perfect; the others are imperfect, but can be reduced to the moods of the first figure (*reduction). The moods of the second figure are especially used to refute an argument, and the moods of the third to dispute their universal value.

FIGURE OF PROOF

Is in the systems of logic with natural deduction a rule of deduction according to which a sign of operation (either in the antecedens or in the consequens of the assertions) is introduced.

153

FINAL CAUSE
See cause.

FINALISM
Opposed to °mechanicism. Theory which underlines the final (*see* finality) character of the natural processes, or at least of the organic processes (°organicism).

FINALITY
Ordering of a being toward its end, which is in this being (*intrinsic* finality) or outside this being (*extrinsic* finality). The finality is immanent when it is not introduced from outside, but results from the nature itself of the finalized being.

We can consider finality as being an essential aspect of causality: a specific being will inevitably act in a specific way, according to its nature, and reach a result which answers to its activity. It is an order, imposed by nature, between cause, act and effect, where no place is left for chance. This general sense can also be applied to the *principle of finality*: every being has an aim. This happens, however, in different ways, which have to be clearly distinguished from each other.

In relation to lifeless nature, finality implies, first of all, that every activity takes a certain direction. A motion has a direction, a chemical reaction creates a specific final result, etc. It is also apparent that these directions have as a common characteristic the quality of following specific laws, e.g., of being directed to a situation of minimal energy. For instance: streaming water searches for the lowest place. We can therefore speak of a *universal* tendency toward an end in the processes of lifeless nature.

In living nature the different, extremely complex, physical and chemical processes seem to be oriented so that individual and species are conserved (although this conservation is not absolute). While it is often very different to follow these processes *in concreto*, their final character is very apparent. The final view plays, therefore, an important role in biology.

Man, in his conscious acts, represents himself as good, has insight into this value, feels that he is attracted to it, orders his acts so as to reach it with appropriate means: this is finality, which is based on insight and which consists of the actual influence of the proposed end on the man who acts and orders his acts. The question now is: what remains of this human finality in all casuality; and, among other questions: how far can we go with the analogy between man and matter in this respect? Can physical and biological order exist free from all physical intervention? Does blind ("blind" meaning not enlightened by knowledge) striving suffice if the physical element is necessary? Is instinct, which develops in the sphere of organic perception, sufficient? Do we not have to appeal to reason, which understands order as such and which is not only able to comprehend it but can also devise it? One must certainly watch out for anthropomorphism. We have to inquire whether the ordering intellect in the universe is unique or multiple (which, because of the limited insight of mutually independent intellects, leaves room for accidents), and whether there exists a fundamental being on which all causality leans and from which all finality emerges. L.D.R.

FINALITY OF KNOWLEDGE
Its inner tendency toward an end, which completes its existence.

This end is the *truth, considered as the conscious harmony of thought and "that which is." This pointing of thought toward being is used for instance, by *Maréchal in order to solve the critical problem of the dynamism of our finite and not-intuitive intellect, which, in judgment, opposes subject and object to each other, but searches further in reasoning thought, so that it goes farther than the phenomena toward an absolute reality. See also Blondel, Rousselot. J.P.

FINITE

That which does no possess everything and therefore has a limit. In this way the parts limit each other in matter which is divisible. One part lies outside of the other; but the limit between both is not only a dividing line, it also connects both. Even if the parts differ from each other, they belong to the same order and form together a totality. Finiteness implies "alterity" (or relative negation, i.e., distinction and relativity). Because of its limitation finiteness also has an exterior side, points toward an exterior domain, next to it. One cannot know this domain as long as one is locked in the finite: to recognize a limit one must have crossed this limit; in a certain way at least he must know that there is an exterior side which refers to something beyond.

The same kind of observation can be made, *mutatis mutandis*, in every case where there is diversity and many terms are connected to a totality or to an order: space, time, species and genera, finally also reality considered in its entirety. Finality has, in any case, to be studied: the nature of the terms discovered, the importance of their differences weighed, the nature and intimacy of their relations determined. It is self-evident that human beings differ from each other in a different way than inorganic matter, and the individual terms which belong to an order of participation are differently connected with each other than the quantitative parts of a totality. The finiteness of man, especially, has to be proved in all its dimensions, (physical and spiritual) and has to be investigated accurately.

The correlation of the finite and the infinite raises an important question: Are they implicit in each other and in what sense? If the finite requires the infinite, does the infinite also require the finite? See infinite. L.D.R.

FISKE, John

Born in Hartford (Conn.) 1842, died in Gloucester (Mass.) 1901, American historian and philosopher. In his "cosmic theism" transforms the doctrine of evolution of *Spencer to a dynamic view of the world.

FLUID

Fluids are supposed imponderable particles, which were considered to be carriers of specific qualities, such as heat, magnetic characteristics and electricity.

In the eighteenth century the increase of heat was explained by an increase of heat-matter. A better knowledge of the essence of heat, namely, as related to the motion of molecules, made the theory of "heat-fluid" superfluous. Magnetism was reduced to electrical factors, and the "fluid" of electricity was more or less identified with the *ether.

FORGET

To lose the remembrance of, neglect. Forgetting happens for mechanically learned senseless material according to a specific function of the time (Ebbinghaus). For

155

Freud it is a Fehlleistung (*Psychol. des Alltagslebens*) an action which develops because the conscious motivation is influenced by unconscious factors or is foiled by them. (*memory)

FORM

Means first of all figure, the lines of a body; from there in general the definiteness of a subject, in substantial or accidental domain. Opposed to the subject which receives definiteness in itself (and is usually called matter) is the form, as the act against the potency. The form principle, as the real reason for definiteness in a being, is also called formal cause (cause formalis): an inner cause therefore, which namely participates in this being (e.g. the soul as substantial form of man). The exemplar cause is called external formal cause (causa formalis extrinsica) i.e. the image according to which inner definiteness is given to a being.

The aristotelian principle that the form is connected to the being, means that no real existence can be found outside of the real definiteness: the question then remains if one should consider form and being as one and the same or as two separate principles belonging to the same structure. Another statement is: one always acts according to his form—i.e. according to the definiteness of his *nature.

As real principle is form considered in many different ways: there has always been a tendency to exaggerate the difference between form and matter and to consider the form as an incomplete being (chosism); the reaction brought the distinction back to a purely logical domain; Thomas Aquinas considers it as a distinction existing in reality, but between two purely correlative terms, which

have namely, outside of their relation, no sense at all. For the same reason (the unity of the being) he accepts only one substantial form in every being. — L.D.R.

Opposition matter-form is applied, in an analogical way, to many other cases, for instance to the human activity and its work.

In *logical* respect. In a logical *judgment we should consider the subject as a material to be judged and the predicate as the form in which the judgment happens. In a *reasoning are terms and theses the material; structure and consequen._ are however the form, which makes this reasoning: this form is studied in "formal" logic.

In the *knowledge* is the form for Kant a priori. *Form a priori.

Also in the moral action, in the juridic attitude, in *art are matter and form often distinguished. In all these cases points the word formalism out the over-estimation of the form.

FORM, A PRIORI

The formal element in the knowledge, which is, according to Kant a priori. In the first place they are the forms of time and space, the time is the a priori form of the internal sense, the space the form of the external sense. They are applied by the knowing subject to that what the sensations (which originate in the affection of the senses) produce and make therefore, while being dependent from the experience, the experience possible. They also explain the necessity and absoluteness of mathematics. They are also the categories or pure concepts, through which the *intellect* makes the phenomena to objects of knowledge. They also explain the necessity and absoluteness of the natural sciences. There are finally the ideas, through which the *reason* brings the objects of thought to unity. J.P.

FORMAL

What concerns only the *form as such or results from it; also the point of view which is taken after studying the form.

FORMALISM

Tendency to give meaning, principally and perhaps only, to form. It is characteristic of Kant's thought and after him dominated philosophy until *phenomenology again focused attention on the value of content.

Formalism in Kant is first of all attached to thought: thought is effected when the data of experience are accepted in the a priori *forms (or categories) of the intellect. These forms explain the absoluteness and necessity of the synthetic a priori propositions on which science is constructed. But while for Kant form affects only a given content, idealism teaches that it produces content from itself.

It is especially in the domain of ethics that formalism was accepted by Kant. The ethics of human activity should not be determined by the pursued *content. This content is necessarily connected to the striving for happiness and is therefore foreign to the ethical order. No content can, because of its empirical character, provide grounds for an absolute or a law valid for everybody. If the action is not ethically determined by the content then it is ethically determined by the manner in which it pursues the content; in other words, the content is ethically indifferent; only the form or *intention is the carrier of morality. And in this intention the entire moral law can be realized. The moral law is formal and orders, independent of con-

tent, because of its *form* alone, its form of universality: "Act in such a way that the maxim of your action can become the principle of a general law." In other words, in order to know whether a specific rule of conduct is ethical, I have to investigate whether it can be generalized without abolishing itself. Scheler reacts against this formalism by saying that there are contents which are not empirical, namely, *values. J.Gr.

In the field of aesthetics, formalism also comes from Kant. In this field there is a tendency to place, the value of aesthetics, exclusively or at least mainly on form. This means that the value depends on the way in which an aesthetically enjoyable content is rendered. Since both the spiritual and the sensual are elements of the aesthetic relation, this doctrine is not able to explain the total phenomenon of aesthetic experience.

Formalism can not be identified with *Symbolism*. It is a symbolism connected with axioms and rules, so that all reductions happen only from axioms, according to the rules, and do not proceed from intuitions about the meaning of the symbols. (This would, for instance, be the case if specific diagrams correspond to the symbols, and if the proof would rest on the graphic observation of these diagrams).

It is neither desirable nor possible that the whole content of formalism, rules included, happens by means of symbols. Rules are related to the use of the symbols, and can therefore not be expressed by means of the use of the symbolism. The transparency and the certitude of the deductions in a formalism do not depend on the fact that one speaks *through* symbols, but that one speaks *of* symbols (in this sense, that the meaning of the symbols do not have a role in the deduction).

The most general formalisms are the *general-deductive* (in which there is no question of specific constants) and especially the *logical* formalism (*see* meaning). R.F.

FORMALIZATION

Of a scientific domain is not only the fact that a °symbolism is used, but also that the content of this domain is rendered as a deductive °theory (and even as purely deductive theory), that later this deductive theory is translated by means of a °formalism.

The scientific work of the formalization is therefore not the same as the invention or choice of proper symbols; it is principally this: All theses are inferred from a small number of axioms and rules and these °axioms and rules are so expressively formulated that nothing remains implied. Formalization is not suitable for elementary teaching of a science, but for the research into its foundations. R.F.

FORTUNATUS A BRIXIA, O.F.M.

Observant, born in Brixen 1701, died in Madrid 1754. Wrote a *Philosophia* (1749) with a mathematical-mechanical view of the world, in which he takes up the view of nature common in his time.

FOUILLEE, Alfred

Born in La Poueze (Maine et Loire) 1838, died in Lyon 1912, French evolutionist. Tries to join naturalism and spiritualism through his theory of *idées-forces*, an evolution theory with a spiritualistic character, close to the idealism of the later Platonic school and influenced by the dynamism of °Leibniz. By *idées* Fouillée means all psychic conditions, which are conscious of themselves and of their content. The power immanent in ideas pushes towards realization and transposition into action. In this, the possibility is given of the unlimited development and progress of the world: only to this is real causality due. Mechanism in nature is only its external appearance; it is only the way in which we represent in space and time the relations between things.

FOUNDATION RESEARCH
(Mathematical)

The evolution of mathematics since 1850 led to (1) an important expansion of the domain investigated by mathematics, (2) a striving toward unification, and (3) a more abstract approach. At the same time (4) the limit between pure mathematics and its applications was more clearly drawn, and therefore (5) the influence of empirical and graphic data became more limited and (6) the formal character of mathematics became more important. All this led to efforts to construct a pure mathematics independent of all intervention of graphics, so that as a basis only (7) logic (*see* Frege) or (8) the theory of a system of numbers (*see* Cantor) was accepted. These efforts lead (9) to the discovery of the °paradoxes of logic and the theory of the system of numbers. Thus originated (10) formalism and °intuitionism, which, in its own way, gives a certain importance to graphics. We now explain these points.

1. It was only in this century that a theoretical basis was found for work with real and complex °numbers, and this led to the introduction of new sorts of numbers; next to the three-dimensional space of Euclid, more-dimensional and non-Euclidean spaces have been introduced and studied.

2. The expansion of the domain

required summarizing views. An-analytical geometry had already led to the conception that one can *represent* a point in the three-dimensional space of Euclid by an ordered trio (x,y,z) of real numbers. Pure mathematics, however, can easily *identify* a point with such an ordered trio. Geometry is therefore interpreted in terms of the theory of real numbers and becomes a part of it.

3. Nothing keeps us from conceiving a number of four (x,y,z,t) real numbers as a point in four-dimentional space. The graphic representation which is connected with the term "point" has therefore been abstracted.

4. This abstract way of presentation is only to be retained as long as we do not apply geometry.

5. As long as we do this, we must abstain from appealing to any empirical or graphic datum about real space.

6. If we keep strictly with the abstract presentation, we must also renounce the conception that natural numbers represent concrete count results.

7. As a basis for pure mathematics all that is left is logic, or, what is the same thing:

8. The abstract theory of a system of numbers (*see* Cantor).

9. The effort to construct pure mathematics on this basis, however, was crossed by the discovery of the *paradoxes.

10. The main idea of the formalism of *Hilbert: We have to see his program as a minimum program; an abstract construction of pure mathematics in such a way that the absence of paradoxes can be *demonstrated*, if necessary with the most primitive graphic data. To arrive at this, all terms of pure mathematics are replaced by symbols; enunciations of pure mathe-matics are replaced by formulas, consisting of these symbols; the laws of mathematical proof take the form of rules establishing under which conditions a specific formula can be added to another formula as its conclusion. We can even think these formulas as numbered; the rules then connect the numbers of the premises and the numbers of the allowed conclusions. We may suppose that for a mathematical theory a numbering is received which satisfies the following conditions: (1) If the number of a given formula is odd, then the number of its negation is double; if the first number is even, then the second half is the first. (2) From premises with numbers p,q,r only the conclusion with numbers $p+q+r$ is possible. (3) The axioms have the numbers 7, 17 and 93. This theory is free of contradiction. Indeed if p, q and r are odd, then $p+q+r$ is also odd. The axioms have odd numbers. As far as we go, we will always have conclusions with odd numbers. No two conclusions can exist of which one is the negation of the other, because the first would then have to be an even number. E.W.B.

FOURIER, Charles

Born in Besançon, 1772, died in Paris 1837, French utopian socialist. Teaches that the fundamental principle of the harmonic ordering of society is the rational satisfaction of all human inclinations and needs; transposed into work, this will be a source of happiness for man; the only question then is to make work attractive. Every member of a society therefore has the right and the duty to do the work which is suitable for him.

FRANCISCANS, School of the

The order of the Minorites was founded *ca.* 1210. In 1219 the

Franciscans came to Paris, where they received in 1236 a chair in the theological school, when a secular magister, *Alexander of Hales, entered the order. Robert *Grosseteste received them in 1224 at Oxford and their magister in the theological school was *Adam of Marsh, who taught from 1247 or 1248 on. In the 13th century the school of the Franciscans followed its own theories, in Paris with *Bonaventure and in Oxford with Thomas of York. In 1270 it opposed the new Thomism, from which resulted a long philosophical rivalry between the two orders. In the 14th century the Franciscan School was divided into Bonaventurians, Scotists and Ockhamists.

FRANCK, Sebastian (1499-1542)
German mystic, heretic of the Reformation period. Defended the heretics and the inner word against the orthodoxy and the letter of Scripture.

FRANK, Philipp
Born in 1884, Austrian neo-positivistic physicist and theoretician of science, member of the *Wiener Kreis (Vienna Circle). Has lived since 1938 in the U.S.A.

FRASER, Alexander Campbell, 1819-1914
Scottish religious philosopher, professor in Edinburgh. Main work: *Philosophy of Theism*. Gifford Lectures, 1895-1899.

FREDEGISES
Born in England, 8th century, died in France 834, disciple of *Alcuin and his successor as head of the School of Tours. His philosophical ideas were quite primitive.

FREEDOM OF THE *WILL
The faculty of the will to determine itself and to act of itself, without any coercion from in- or outside. Freedom of will means a principal (not necessarily actual) independence from the sensory striving and the psychological mechanism, while the sensory striving is determined by its object.

The *materialistic *determinism* denies freedom of will in the frame of a general theory about man. He is seen as a physical mechanism, determined by necessary natural laws (Epicurus, de Stoics, Taine, Stuart Mill, Ribot). Denied also by the psychophysiological parallelism (Ebbinghaus). The *psychological determinism* teaches that every choice is always determined by previous representations and feelings (Leibniz, Wundt, Herbert, Hartmann). The *metaphysical or theological determinism* teaches that God and man are determined by the fate (Manicheism), or that the necessary evolution of one substance (Spinoza) or the absolute spirit who is immanent to all phenomena (Hegel) excludes the free will's act; or that our actions are necessarily determined by concupiscence or grace (Luther, Calvin). Kant thinks that the free will is theoretically unprovable, but the free will is postulated by the categorical imperative ("Du sollst"), evidently therefore not for the world of the phenomena but only for the world of the noumena.

The freedom of the will is proved 1) through the consciousness man has of the freedom of his actions. That unconscious, therefore unknown influences can direct the will (Leibniz, Wundt, Freud) is not denied, because the will stays above the motives and only chooses among them (Lindworsky). The free action has as such no physical causes, but has the will itself as cause. The will determines itself by the light of reason. 2) through the moral nature of man, so that every will's act has for the subject the aspect of obligation and responsibility. 3) through the metaphysical consideration that the reason reaches the concept of the absolute good. This absolute good is however not in this world, so that it is not able to determine completely the will of man, so that man always is before a choice. Therefore exists the necessity of a choice. Thomism, in relation to the omnipotence of God, teaches the participation-theory.

The modern anthropological and psychological theories avoid the formal philosophical question and state the experience of the freedom of the will as a central problem of anthropology. The interest in the problem of freedom in regard to the causes of this freedom is thereby diminished and one considers the freedom as a task which man has to fulfill. "Man is condemned to freedom" (Sartre). Herewith is the question about the aim of freedom emphasized. P.S.

FREGE, Gottlob, 1848-1925

German mathematician and philosopher, professor in Jena, disciple of *Lotze. Tried to make pure mathematics a part of *logic, and therefore contributed much to the development of mathematical logic. *Whitehead and *Russell studied his work, which at first did not interest many people.

FREUD, Sigmund, 1856-1939

Austrian psychiatrist, professor in Vienna, founder of *psychoanalysis. The importance of Freud lies not in the philosophical interpretation he gave to his psychological discoveries, but in those discoveries themselves and in the analytical method of curing which he himself devised. Although much criticism can be made, philosophically as well as psychologically, of Freud's interpretation of the psychic life, his discoveries of the unconscious, of the importance of sexuality, of repression and many other aspects of the psychic life remain of exceptional value. Psychology without psychoanalysis is no longer possible; psychiatry is indebted to Freud for most of its methods of treatment; the theory of education, sociology, the study of literature and literature itself have been greatly influenced by Freud's work. With this influence a certain fashion in these fields has been created. Philosophy, and especially existential philosophy, was directly or indirectly influenced by Freud. Moral theology and ethics cannot ignore the discoveries of Freud. B.D.

FRIES, Jakob Friedrich

Born in Barby 1773, died in Jena 1843. German idealist. Adds to the Kantian critique of knowledge a psychological basis by establishing it in an a priori empirical way. Trust is best certified by immediate feeling, which lets us also recognize the Infinite in phenomena. It connects phenomena and reality, experience and metaphysics, knowing and believing.

FROBENIUS, Leo, 1873-1938

German ethnologist and philosopher.

FUER SICH SEIN

For Hegel the second moment in the development of the idea, in which the idea, out of itself, is placed for itself. It can be considered characteristic of consciousness. See pour-soi.

FULBERT OF CHARTRES, 960-1028

Founder of the well-known School of *Chartres (990), Bishop of Chartres after 1006.

FUNCTION

Suppose that between the elements of a quantity A and the elements of a quantity B exists such a connection that by each element x of A belongs one distinct element

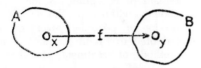

y of B; then we say that there is a function f, which makes an element y of B correspond, to each element x of A, and we write $y=f(x)$. The elements of A are also indicated as arguments and the corresponding elements of B as values of the function, for f. E.g., if A is the ordered set of the natural numbers 0, 1, 2, 3, . . . ,k, . . . and B the ordered set of the rational numbers. Let the rational number ½ belong to the natural number 0, to the natural number 1 the rational number ¼, . . . , to the natural number k the rational number ½k+1 . . .; we have then a function f, which makes the rational number ½k+1 correspond to the natural number k and its notation is therefore $f(k)=$½k+1.

If the natural numbers 0, 1, 2, 3, . . . k, . , , are the arguments, then the notation for the value of the function corresponding to k is generally ak and one says that the values of the function ao, a1, a2, a3, . . . , ak . . . form in this succession a series:

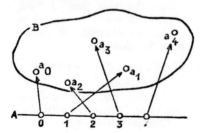

It is not necessary that the elements of the quantities A and B be numbers. If A is an ordered set of any given things, and B an ordered set of values of truth T (True) and U (Untrue). Be f a function, which makes an element $y=f(x)$ of B correspond to each element x of A. This function creates in A a distinction between two sorts of things; the first sort has the elements x, so that $f(x)=T$, the second sort has the element x, so that $f(x)=U$. The function f determines therefore a predicate F, which does apply to the things of the first sort, and does not apply

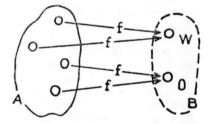

to the things of the second sort. As *Frege was first to establish, one can consider each predicate F as concrete through a corresponding function f of the sort considered here (a function of a sentence). *See also* appendix.

Is an expression with variables or *arguments, which receives a specific value when the argument or arguments receive a specific value. In our terminology we call functions what others call an indefinite value of a function, for they use the term function for the law, according to which values of the whole expression correspond to values of the arguments.

The functions of mathematics correspond to a specific sort of logical functions, namely the descriptive functions, or to functions of the combinatory logic.

One distinguishes the different

162

logical functions according to the expressions which are formed by these functions. One can therefore have *proposition-forming functions* (sometimes called by others, but with less clarity: propositional functions), *classforming, relationforming* functions.

FUNCTOR

A function is actually the result of a (perhaps complex) operation of arguments. If this operation is expressed by one symbol, then we call that symbol a functor. One can always make corresond to a function, a functor in the form of a *lambda-functor.

Functors can, as do the functions, be divided according to the expression (function) which proceeds from their application on arguments; we have therefore *propositionforming, classforming, relationforming* functors.

Functors can also be classified according to the place which they occupy in respect to the arguments. A functor with one argument is called a *preceding* functor (in the contemporary formal logic no functors exist which are written *after* the argument). Functors with more than one argument can also be written before the argument; with two arguments one writes often the functor between the arguments (*medial* functor). R.F.

FUTURA CONTINGENTIA

The future which is dependent upon specific circumstances. A special place is taken by the choice of a created free will, which could be in a specific situation in which it in fact is not. Christ knew that the inhabitants of Tyre and Sidon would be converted if He performed miracles among them, which, however, He did not do. The omniscience of God also has to include the *futura contingentia* of all possible creatures and not merely actually existing ones.

G

GABRIEL BIEL
See Biel.

GAIUS
First part of the 2nd century A.D., was converted to the Platonic school, wrote a work in nine books about the most important theories of Plato, which was published by his disciple Albinus.

GALENUS, 131-200
Personal physician of Emperor Commodus. Supposedly the inventor of the fourth, so-called Galenic syllogistic *figure, although, according to Leibniz, it is not found in his known works.

GALILEI, Galileo
Born in Pisa, 1564, died in Florence 1642. Mathematician and physicist, follower of the system of Copernicus and opposed to Aristotle's theories of the solar system. He therefore came in conflict with the Inquisition, abjured his own theories outwardly and was confined to his country home for quite a long time. He energetically defended the method of accurate observation, experiment and measurement in physics. The natural sciences, too closely connected with the nonscientific language of the Scriptures and with the Ptolemaic world view, became, thanks to Galilei, freer from the authority of the Church.

GANDHI, Mohandas Karamchand 1869-1948
Indian leader, mainly respon-

sible for the liberation of his country from British rule through the now familiar technique of nonviolent resistance. Works: *Indian Home Rule, Young India.*

GARCIA, Episaeus
Carmelite, disseminated through his work, *Cursus philosophicus juxta mentem Bacconii* (1700-1704), the doctrine of his fellow friar, *John of Baconthorp (died 1348).

GASSENDI, Pierre
Born in Champtercier 1592, died in Paris 1655. French priest, professor at the Collège Royal in Paris, concerned with the mathematical, astronomical and philosophical sciences. He admires Galilei, does not accept the world view of Copernicus but rather that of Tycho Brahe and Kepler. He attacks Aristotle as well as Descartes and tries to construct in physics an atomism similar to that of Epicurus, and thus opens the way to the mechanistic interpretation in physics. The smallest particles, *corpuscula*, are impenetrable; they possess size, weight and external shape. Next to atoms and motion Gassendi accepts the existence of a third element in nature, namely, empty space. Space and time are individual realities. Gassendi accepts, as opposed to Epicurus, the existence of an immortal soul and a creator—God—who directs the world with providence. In epistemology, in which he initially was

164

very close to skepticism, he rejects the Cartesian innate ideas. Observation occurs because little images (*idola*) in the shape of minute bodies are ejected by objects and received by the sensory organs and thence assimilated by the intelligence. In ethics Gassendi defends an Epicurean hedonism. Happiness is rest for the soul and the liberation of the body from pain. Happiness is obtained through virtue, which protects us against emotions. H. R.

GEGENSTANDSTHEORIE

Name given to the theory of the Austrian *Meinong, a disciple of Brentano. Meinong starts by saying that every object can be investigated scientifically, whether this object exists or not, whether it can exist or not. We can therefore ask the question about the square circle, which cannot exist: *what* cannot exist? Object therefore have to be known purely in their being so, disregarding their factuality; such knowledge is a priori.

GENERALIZATION

Is the operation which forms from a *proposition *P* a *universal proposition* (for all *x*'s one has *P*) or a *particular* proposition (for some *x*'s one has *P*).

GENERATIO AEQUIVOCA, or GENERATIO SPONTANEA, or ABIOGENESIS

The creation of living beings by dead matter. In antiquity and in the Middle Ages the *generatio aequivoca* was generally accepted for worms and the like. Later, especially through the experiments of Pasteur (died in 1895), it was established that life always proceeds from life. One can say, in general, that the lower cannot generate the higher, unless the potential for the higher is already present in the lower. It seems, therefore, very improbable that in the history of the world *generatio aequivoca* could have taken place, although this is accepted by some biologists and philosophers. The characteristics of the virus are at present used as an argument for proving the existence of *generatio aequivoca,* but this is in our opinion, wrong.

GENERATIONISM

The doctrine that the human soul is created by the parents. The simplicity of the soul excludes, however, the splitting of the soul of the parents. Is opposed to *creationism.

GENERICAL

Concerning a specific genus. E.g., a horse and a color are generically different things, because they fall under another genus, another class or group of things. Opposed to determining a specific *sort.

GENETICAL

Following the historical development of becoming. In the theory of knowledge the genetical method as a psychological method is opposed to the analytical "transcendental" method; in history as the "prospective" method it is opposed to the "retrospective" method.

GENTILE, Giovanni, 1875-1944

Italian neo-Hegelian philosopher, professor in Rome. Gentile has elaborated in an original way the influence of *Hegel. He continues the interpretation of Hegel in the same manner as *Vera did. His main work: *Teoria generale dello spirito come atto puro,* 1916. The philosophy of history and the history of philosophy form, for Gentile, a complete unity, because thinking is the only reality. The entire world is nothing else than the self-unfolding of thought.

Thought is the divine spirit which creates the world in its self-realization. But this self-realization happens by means of man, who carries the divine spirit in him. The world is therefore nothing else than thinking the divine spirit, inasmuch as it is thought by man. Everything therefore exists in the ego's act of thinking. Does this mean that only the individual ego exists? It has this meaning as long as one does not understand the real nature of the ego. The ego is always more than the purely individual and subjective ego. The ego always transcends itself, because in the ego lives and works the divine spirit. Only this spirit is *atto puro*, pure act—therefore the name °"actualism" given to Gentile's philosophy. His influence was very great in and outside Italy. B.D.

GENTILI, Alberico

Born in San Ginesio 1552, died in Oxford 1608. Italian scholar of the philosophy of law. Became Protestant and professor in Oxford. Defends the natural law and the law of nations, which is also valid in time of war.

GENUS

A °universal concept, which can be applied to several °specifically different things and which indicates a common essential part thereof. The genus "organism" can, e.g., be applied to trees and bacteria, to horses and flies. The supreme or most general genera are called °categories (predicaments). The lowest or proximate genus (*genus proximum*) is that genus which determines the entire essence of something with "*differentia specifica*" or specific differences. E.g., the square is an equilateral rectangle (lowest genus).

GEOMETRY

Had originally as object the investigation of particular qualities of the "real" space, and had therefore to take in account the graphic and empirical data which are available. More and more in modern times, in as far as it has been studied as a section of the pure mathematics, it has freed itself from such data and become therefore more and more an abstract science.

The germ of this evolution was however already laid in Antiquity, which, according to the "elements" of Euclid, strived already towards a purely deductive construction, in which indeed the ground principles and axioms were borrowed from the intuition and/or the experience, but in which they build further on these so obtained ground principles, using the pure logic. In its details is the work of Euclid sometimes very insufficient; a pure deductive construction of the geometry is only given by °Hilbert in his "Grundlagen der Geometrie" (1899).

Much earlier the studies of the question if some of the axioms accepted by Euclid could be deduced from the others, had already led to the construction of geometrical theories, in which these axioms were left aside or even replaced by others; in the beginning were these theories (metageometry, non-euclidian and more-dimensional geometry), in which naturally partly other theses were defended than in the usual geometry, not received without scepticism, but later one had to acknowledge that these theories, were from the point of view of pure mathematics, as scientific as the "usual" geometry.

With these metageometry has indeed in common, that it studies the *homogeneous* space, i.e. the space in which a particular group of representations of the space is indicat-

166

ed in itself, so that figures, which can be transformed in one another by such an image, can be considered as equivalent; herein is reflected our conviction of the homogeneity of the "usual" space, and this is again based on the experience of the free mobility of the solid bodies. E.W.B.

GEORGE, Henry 1839-1897
American social philosopher, preacher of the "single tax," whose *Progress and Poverty* (1880) had wider influence on British and continental socialistic movements than in his native country.

GERARD TERSTEGEN VAN 'S HERENBERG (de Monte), 1424-1480
Disciple of Hendrik of Gorcum, professor at Cologne, one of the leaders of the Thomistic group in their opposition to the *Albertists.

GERARD OF BOLOGNA,
Ca. 1250-1317. Carmelite, professor in Paris, after 1297 superior of the order. In philosophy he followed *Godfried of Fontaines.

GERARD OF BORGO SAN DONNINO
13th century Franciscan, published in 1254 *Introductorius in Evangelium aeternum* of *Joachim of Fiore, in which the Franciscan friars are presented as the heralds of the new Gospel. This work was condemned in 1255 and 1263.

GERBERT OF AURILLAC, 950-1003
Monk in Aurillac (Auvergne), later professor in Rheims (972), in 982 Abbot of Bobbio, Archbishop of Rheims in 991 and of Ravenna in 998, became Pope in 999 (Silvester II). Very cultivated man, with a special interest in the quadrivium (mathematical sciences).

GERSON
See John of Gerson.

GERSONIDES 1288-1344
Fourteenth-century astronomer, who wrote on physics, physiology, mathematics, logic, ethics, psychology, the Bible and Talmud. Much of his work lost or still unpublished; major work: *Milhamoth Adonai* (*The Wars of the Lord*).

GESTALT
Gestalt (shape or form) is an integrated whole, which is more than the sum of its component parts (moments) and which precedes these elements. It is this *"Gestalt"* which we primarily observe; later we can discover its composing moments. The same applies to motion. This is the teaching of *Gestalt* psychology, which originated as a reaction against psychological atomism (whose doctrine is that the unity in observation originates in the mechanical junction of elements), behaviorism and introspectionism. It was introduced in an article of Christian von *Ehrenfels and gained importance through the Berlin School (Wertheimer, Koffka, Köhler); and in France, among others, Guillaume. In America *Gestalt* psychology was stimulated by Lewin, who chose as the object of his study the process of the will in social and psychological relations. V. von Weiszäcker launched the *"Gestaltkreistheorie,"* in which he emphasized the unity of observation and motion, originating initially in pathological anatomical data. The *"Gestalt"* originates in phenomenal organization, and some psychologists (as, e.g., Köhler) look for its cause in the central nervous system. P.S.

As applied in physics and biology the *"Gestalt"* is the unity which is higher than the sum of its parts; these parts lose some of their qualities as soon as the higher connection, the *"Gestalt,"* resolves itself. This is valid for many psychic processes, and also for many things which occur in nature. The biological concept of *"Gestalt"* (Köhler, 1925) provided a reaction against machine theory, as well as the concept of totality; it indicates a characteristic of forms of life and of processes rather than defining the proper nature of an organism. The English word configuration is used for a *Gestalt* and configurationism for *Gestalt* psychology.

GEULINCX, Arnold

Born in Antwerp 1624, died in Leiden 1669. Follower of *Descartes, professor in Louvain and Leiden. The philosophical system of Geulincx is based on the principles of Descartes and uses the method of rationalism. It is characterized by its strong emphasis on the striving of created things and their dependence upon God as First Cause. First, the agreement of specific phenomena in the body with specific phenomena in the soul is explained by the intervention of God, who uses the physical process, e.g., the activity of the sense organs, to produce a matching process in the soul, observation and the contrary. There is therefore no interaction between body and soul. God is the only true cause of man's experiences; His activities follow definite rules. Geulincx here uses the example of two clocks, which run exactly alike without having any causal connection between them. This conception is then extended to all reality: no created being has his own causality; all created things work only as instruments in God's hand. The being of created things is for the most part lost in the being of God.

The ethics of Geulincx are an effort to construct, in the spirit of the Stoics, a purely natural ethics, which leave the revealed moral law intact. They have a strongly intellectual character. Since reason teaches man what a small place he occupies in the world, the most important virtues will be humility, self-contempt and resignation. F.S.

GEYSER, Joseph, 1869-1949.

German neo-Thomist philosopher, professor in München. Geyser was interested in several fields of philosophy, and became the leading figure in German Thomistic circles. He tried to give the practice of experimental psychology a well-considered basis. He also worked in logic and epistemology. Here he dealt with the problems of evidence, sufficient ground, causality and substantiality. The heart of his thought therefore appears in the ontological reflection: *Einige Hauptprobleme der Metaphysik*, 1923. His versatility and profundity brought him in contact with all important schools of philosophy.

GILBERT DE LA PORREE (Porretanus)

Born in Poitiers 1076, died there 1154. Disciple and friend of Bernard of Chartres, professor and chancellor of the School of *Chartres, in 1141 professor in Paris, in 1142 Bishop of Chartres; author of the *Liber sex principiorum*, an exposition of the last six categories of Aristotle. This work had a great influence, and became one of the official textbooks of the liberal arts. Gilbert is also the author of commentaries on the *Opuscula Sacra* of *Boethius; he was a convinced defender of moderate *realism.

GILSON, Etienne

Born 1884, French Thomist, professor at the Collège de France.

Gilson had a great influence in the revival of the study of medieval philosophy. His great merit lies not in his study of sources, although he stimulated many historians and trained them to engage in it. His great strength lies in the original way in which he views medieval philosophy. This is especially found in his works on Augustine, Bernardus, Bonaventura, Thomas and Duns Scotus. He always has a clear idea of the connection and the difference between philosophy and theology. He was therefore influential during the debate over *Christian philosophy. He also has a steady interest in the relation between philosophy and general intellectual fields, as is clearly shown in his work on Dante. Important is his view on the part medieval philosophy plays in modern philosophy, as he showed in the case of Descartes. Philosophical actuality for Gilson, a disciple of *Bergson, is always interesting, so that he engaged in discussions about the foundation of *realism, and later expressed his position against the ontological questions raised by *existential philosophy. He wrote his *L'Etre et l'Essence* in 1948, in which we can most clearly distinguish Gilson's own thought. B.D.

GINZBERG, Asher 1856-1927

Known also under his pseudonym, Ahad Haam, Ginzberg was a contributor to the revival of the Hebrew language and Hebrew literature. Was opposed to political Zionism in favor of a genuine Jewish culture throughout the world.

GIOBERTI, Vincenzo

Born in Turino 1801, died in Paris 1852. Italian priest and philosopher, liberal politician, founder of *ontologism. According to Gioberti the intellect apprehends directly through thought that Absolute Essence which is God. But God is only the first and immediate object of contemplation, inasmuch as He is the Creator of finite and contingent beings. God remains unknowable in His deepest essence, even in this contemplation. On the other hand, all knowledge is a revelation of God, so that a philosophy independent of theology is impossible for Gioberti. He thinks that only the Catholic can be a good philosopher. Knowledge finds its limit in something which is supraintellectual, which is only attainable by God and which man has to accept as a mystery. God therefore opposes all man's attempts to bring the mysteries of faith closer to the intellect. On the other hand, Gioberti does not consider the dogma of faith as established truths, since they develop in accordance with the level of civilization. F.S.

GLAUBENSPHILOSOPHIE

Philosophical school in 18th century Germany, established as a reaction against the Enlightenment and the unilateral importance given to reason. It rejects all methodical and scientific treatment of philosophy, and limits its tenets to the suggestions of feeling, with which belief in the mysteries of Christianity is closely related. Followers: *Hamann, *Jacobi, *Herder, *Fries.

GNOSIOLOGY

See epistemology.

GNOSIS

"Enlightened" belief, which claims to have penetrated literary or immediate meaning to the symbolic or real meaning of the content of faith. See Gnosticism.

GNOSTICISM

Philosophical and religious school in the 2nd century, which originated through the combination of Hellenistic philosophy and the Christian religion. This name is given to a group of doctrines which have the common characteristic of attempting to absorb Christianity into the Greek and Eastern religious views of the period. Gnosticism is therefore not so much a heretic transformation of Christian doctrine as an attempt to incorporate Christianity into some form of pagan religious thought. According to the gnostics, faith is only a step toward the "gnosis," higher knowledge of God, mystical experience which achieves complete unity with God. The main representatives of gnosticism were: Marcion of Rome, Basilides of Alexandria and Valentinus, first in Alexandria and later in Rome.

GOD

For the philosopher the deepest principle, which is the foundation of everything, to which finite reality points. Insofar as it tries to penetrate the deepest grounds of all that is, philosophy is also "theology"—what Aristotle called the "first philosophy," which has to accept the existence of a God, the final ground founded on itself (*aseitas) of all the things in the world and of all worldly relations.

Things in the world have an existence, but it is not an essential characteristic of them; otherwise they would exist necessarily. Since God's existence is the deepest explanation of all things in the world, it cannot lie outside of His essence. His essence or nature is to be (*esse*) and therefore He exists absolutely (independent of all relations or conditions), necessarily, so that he cannot not-be. He does not, therefore, exist as a realized possibility (which can or cannot be realized), but as pure reality (*actus purus*), which lays the foundation for all possibilities that

are to be realized (potency). Since all becoming and changing are the realization of possibilities, God is the unbecome, the unchangeable.

Being the deepest principle of explanation of everything, God cannot belong to the series of things of the world (otherwise He would have to be explained by them, and would not be the principle of this explanation). He rises therefore above all things (transcendent) but is at the same time the bearing ground present in everything (immanent). This is also true for our own most personal being, in which God is immanent and above which He still rises infinitely.

The existence and essence of infinite God can never be completely comprehended by the intelligence of a finite being. We know Him only philosophically, insofar as the things of the world, because of their finiteness, point toward a final ground. What we understand to be the pure existential qualities of these things we also apply to God, such as good, nature, truth, knowledge. Qualities which contain in their definition some imperfections are only figuratively applied to God (hearing, wrath, regret). Our abstracting intellect thus forms many concepts about the essence and *attributes of God, but understands at the same time the inner unity in this multiplicity and the richness-embracing simplicity of the divine essence. H.R.

GODFRIED OF FONTAINES

Born in Liège *ca.* 1250, died in 1306 or 1309, canon in Liège, Paris and Tournai, studied the liberal arts in Paris *ca.* 1270, *magister regens* of theology in Paris 1285-1304. He wrote fifteen *Quodlibeta* which show us clearly the various disagreements among the philosophers of the period. He was very much under the influence of

Aristotelianism and *Thomism*, but followed his own way. His authority was as great during his lifetime as afterward. His main opponent was °Henry of Ghent.

GOEDEL, Kurt 1906-

Mathematician, he discovered nondemonstrable mathematical theorems which can neither be proved nor refuted.

GOETHE, Johann Wolfgang von

Born in Frankfurt a.M. 1749, died in Weimar 1832. German poet and politician, in philosophy influenced by °Herder and °Spinoza.

GOLDEN EDGE

An ideal aesthetic proportion between two unequal parts, in which the smaller part is related to the bigger one as the latter is to the totality. The golden edge or golden proportion occurs in all the arts; it creates a very harmonic impression, because it unites in a singular way unity and diversity. It is not, however, to be considered as an absolute norm of aesthetic proportion.

GONSALVUS OF BALBOA (Hispanus)

Born in Balboa (Galicia) *ca.* 1250, died in Paris 1313, Franciscan, *magister regens* in Paris (1302-1303), provincial of Castile in 1303, general minister in 1304. Gonsalvus was the teacher of J. Duns Scotus in Paris, and vividly defended the traditional theses of the Franciscan school.

GOOD

That which pleases or satisfies; therefore what responds to a striving, what is its final end, what brings completion, fulfillment, perfection; therefore what is suitable, orderly, perfect, completely determined.

The good is therefore found in the development of a being. The good is an end and result of his activity; and it is freely reached. Related to this freedom are morality and duty. But the good is also the essential care which is, in its determination, the source of activity. This is especially true for beings which are endowed with spiritual life: their goodness dominates and rules all other.

As a final reason for goodness (or °value) one can consider the *"esse."* Thus the different forms of goodness are reducible to the substantial ways of being with their accidental changes; here is laid the foundation for the primacy of good over evil, because, as such, every being is good (*ens et bonum convertuntur*).

In the substantial determination of its nature, every being is fundamentally good; it is also good within the properly limited expansion of its active forces; it becomes completely good when it comes into possession of its final end. L.D.R.

Good, in a strict moral sense, is opposed to evil. It indicates a correspondence between correct human action and the moral law—either the °moral law creates the order which the good presupposes (Kant) or the moral law expresses this order (Thomas Aquinas). As for the order's origin, there seems to be a fundamental opposition which, up to a certain point, carries on the opposition between °voluntarism and °intellectualism. In any case, insofar as human action freely respects order, it acquires a new perfection, which makes it a moral good. *See also* morality. J. Gr.

GOOD, HIGHEST

A good which is good without exception or without any further condition. In Kant's conception this applies only to the virtue of morality. Virtue, however, cannot satisfy such a complex being as man without being connected with the happiness which belongs with it. In other words, the highest good is not the absolute good. The latter is rather complex, and consists of elements which are mutually irreducible and even opposed to each other. The question arises how the good that man naturally tries to achieve is possible. In scholasticism the dialectic of the perfect or absolute or complete good is also developed, but in relation to the final *end. The supreme good, according to scholastic interpretation, is that unlimited act of goodness in which God exists. J.Gr.

GOODS

Things which not only incarnate a value, but whose unity is created by the *value. Thus a painting only exists insofar as it expresses an aesthetic value. Traditionally the distinction between a good and its value or the reason why it is a good (the goodness of a good) was not made and only the term "bonum" was used to indicate both good and value. The real basis of this is that traditionally the good as goodness was supposed to exist in the "esse," while now its value has been opposed to the "esse." J.Gr.

GORDON, Andrew, 1712-1751

Scottish O.S.B., defends an empirical philosophy (1745). In epistemology he is close to nominalism, in ethics close to the philosophy of the Enlightenment.

GORGIAS

Born in Leontitni in Sicily 483 B.C., died 375 B.C. One of the most important *Sophists. Was especially interested in the art of rhetoric

He found many figures of speech, such as the antithesis, the *homoioteleuta*, and other tricks.

GOUDIN, Antoine, O.P.

Born 1639, died in Paris 1695. Wrote philosophical works according to the principles of Thomas Aquinas; he connects these, however, with obsolete principles of physics.

GRABMANN, Martin, 1875-1949

German neo-Thomist, historian of medieval philosophy, professor in München. Grabmann had a very great influence on the study of the history of medieval philosophy, especially in Germany but elsewhere as well.

GRACE

The benevolent condescension of God toward man, as taught by all religions. In the Bible and Christian theology: the supernatural inner gift, which God gives to man in order that he may reach his supernatural end.

GRACIOUS, THE

Aesthetic category, which comes into being when a beautiful appearance is somewhat underlined by a spiritual sense. The gracious differs from the beautiful because of its greater mobility, lightness, charm, spontaneity and playful simplicity. A defect in a gracious motion can change the gracious into the comical, and the smile with which the gracious is always accepted is changed to real laughter.

GRATRY, Alphonse

Born in Lille 1805, died in Montreux 1872. Was first officer, later priest, reformed the Oratory in France, which he later left. He is a moderate ontologist influenced by *Malebranche. Man has, according to Gratry, an innate knowledge of the Infinite and when he lets himself be attracted to it by love through consciousness of his own insufficiency and his desire for the better and higher, he will be able to form a correct judgment of the Infinite, i.e., God. Knowledge and love, poetic vision and adoration go together here. Gratry thinks that this proves the existence of God as absolute, transcendent, infinite being. Further knowledge, however, is not dependent upon God's knowledge. F.S.

GREEN, Thomas Hill, 1836-1882
English neo-Hegelian, professor at Oxford.

GREGORY OF NAZIANZEN
Born in Arianzus, near Nazianzen (Cappadocia) cs. 329, died there 389 or 390, friend of *Basil, bishop of Constantinople (379-381), Platonist.

GREGORY OF NYSSA
Born in Caesarea in Cappadocia ca. 335, died after 394, brother of *Basil, bishop of Nyssa, important theologian, knew and used Plato, Philo and neo-Platonism, but was much influenced by the School of *Alexandria (Clemens and Origenes).

GREGORY OF VALENTIA, S.J.
Born in Medina del Campo 1549, died in Naples 1603. Professor of Döllingen, Inglostadt and Rome. Unites Thomas Aquinas and Suarez. Gregory of Valentia makes a clear distinction between theological and philosophical elements. Philosophical teaching in Catholic and Protestant universities in Germany was very much influenced by him. He was a follower of *Molinism.

GROOT, HUGO DE
See Grotius.

GROTESQUE
As a variation of the comical the grotesque is the rude-comical. As opposed to the fine-comical it is expressed with a special sudden vehemence and is responded to with loud laughter. In a more general sense, one can call grotesque anything which has a peculiar, fantastic and extravagant form.

GROTIUS, Hugo (Hugo de Groot)
Born in Delft 1583, died in Rostock 1645. Dutch jurist, politician, theologian and philosopher, Aristotelian, in aesthetics influenced by the stoicism of the later scholastics, in philosophy of law by Suarez.

He is especially important in philosophy for his conception of natural rights, for which he sought a basis in the natural aspiration of human nature for a society in which man has to live according to stoic principles. The rules of action, which his aspiration imposes on him naturally, would continue to exist even if God did not exist (which Grotius rejects for various reasons). The factual disposition of human nature can, however, find its basis only in God's created order. Next to human nature, therefore, the will of God forms a new source of rights. The rules of natural rights for relations among individuals are also valid for relations between people. The rightfulness or illegality of a war and the admissibility or inadmissibility of acts of war will depend upon these rules.

Grotius is also called the founder of the law of nations, although the main principles of this law had already been formulated by Francisco de Vitoria and Francisco Suarez. He intends it as a positive law, based on an agreement, but presupposing the claim of justice founded on natural right and the duty of bona fides in international relations.

The original community of goods, given to humanity by God in the beginning, has been transformed later, by mutual agreement, into private property. The state was created because human beings freely obliged themselves for reasons of social necessity to a civil society, and subjected themselves to authority. Because of this submission the community definitively tranesfers its original power to the sovereign. He is responsible only before God. The power of the public authorities is still limited by the boundaries of natural right and positive divine right, as well as by the will of those who gave them the power and who can limit it.

GROUND

That on which a thing is based in order to be. Also, what justifies an opinion, a method, an argument, a system.

GROUP

Union of men who are conscious of their being united.

GUERINOIS, Jacques Casimir, O.P.

Born in Laval 1640, died 1703. French defender of Thomistic philosophy against Descartes and his contemporaries.

GUILT

The sense of guilt, as it exists in primitive society, is the feeling to be (mechanically —by inadvertent touch— or because of his own stupidity and curiosity or by any other way) the cause (culpa) of a moral debt (debitum): this latter is indeed very materialistically conceived as a stain which makes impure. The causality is here however not total, because not formaly-ethical. King Oedipus for instance, by marrying his mother, has made a serious moral fault which he can never undo, but he is, formally ethically, not guilty, because he did not want the incest in its unethical character, because he did not know that he married his mother. He therefore has no real *remorse. The sense of guilt is therefore not remorse, although no remorse is possible without a sense of guilt. They are however generally considered the same, for instance in scholasticism, which still underlines the idea of staining or soiling through the lack (of morality) in the one who is its cause. — How can man however be the cause of a lack or source of negativity? Heidegger answers: by existing, i.e. by accepting an existence which is negative, because finite and in its origin and in its possibilities. Man is therefore, as the *conscience reveals him, from nature guilty and this primitive guilt is the basis of all moral or other guilt which he shoulders. J.Gr.

GUITTON, Jean

Born 1900, French spiritualistic philosopher, professor in Dijon. Guitton works especially in the border region between theology and philosophy.

GUNTHER, Anton

Born in Lindenau 1783, died in Vienna 1863. Austrian priest theologian and philosopher. His thinking was dominated by the problem of the relation between natural knowledge and revelation. He attributes to the dogmas of the Catholic religion a supernatural character, but only under presupposition of the fall of man. These dogmas can then be converted into concepts in the philosophy of Descartes and of German idealism.

GUYAU, Jean-Marie

Born in Laval 1854, died in

174

Menton 1888. French evolutionist and sociologist. Wants to reduce philosophy to its practical and social function: which is to give guidance to people and individuals in their striving for better conditions. He wants to achieve this by finding the solution to actual problems in the results of the positive sciences. The problems of philosophy can be simplified by looking at them from a sociological point of view. The problems of ethics lose their difficulties when the individual learns to consider himself as a member of a body, in which solidarity is a law and in which the concensus of the members represents the highest good. Life itself creates duties and sanctions. The task of art is to infuse the spectator with sympathy for the totality. The idea of communication between man and universe is the basis of all religion; it will therefore survive all particular religions. F.S.

H

HABIT

Is acquired by the repetition of separate acts. It has an individual character, as opposed to the *customs, which are collective.

HABITUS

Inner definiteness, by which spiritual capacities (intellect and will), and sensual capacities insofar as they come directly under the influence of the spiritual (*appetitus concupiscibilis et irascibilis*), are inculcated with a permanent inclination to act in a specific sense. Some habiti are innate (*intellectus principiorum*: spontaneous knowledge of first theoretical principles; *synderesis*: spontaneous knowledge of first practical principles), others are acquired (e.g., virtues). Like ability, which is enriched by it, habitus is a quality; its growth is therefore qualitative.

HADEWOCH

Flemish mystical author, lived *ca.* 1250, wrote visions, letters and verses. Her writings show the influence of *Augustine and *William of St. Thierry.

HAEBERLIN, Paul

(1878-1961), Swiss philosopher, is mostly interested in questions of philosophical anthropology and pedagogy. His philosophical starting point is the "I am." Man therefore has to be an experience, and with that of the "*esse*" as such. Every individual being is a manner in which the "*esse*" expresses itself.

The "*esse*" is not absorbed by the world, because God rises above the world. There seems to be a tension between body, soul and mind. The mind rises above the vital sphere and pursues the objective as such.

HAECCEITY

In the conception of *Joannes Duns Scotus, what this and that as such characterizes, and what therefore gives individual definiteness to specific perfection.

HAECKEL, Ernst Heinrich, 1834-1919.

German naturalistic philosopher and zoologist. Main work: *Die Welträtsel*, 1899. Matter is for Haeckel the only reality. It is, however, constantly in evolution and, as the physiology of the brain shows, produces the mind. This continuous evolution gives mankind constant hope for a better future. Haeckel had considerable influence on the general public.

HAECKER, Theodore, 1879-1945

German existential cultural philosopher and philosophical anthropologist.

HAERING, Theodor, Ludwig

Born 1884, German neo-Hegelian.

HAGERSTRUM, Axel

Born 1868, Swedish Kantian philosopher, professor in Uppsala; his special interest: ethics and philosophy of law.

HALDANE, John Scott, 1860-1936.
English biologist and philosopher, founder of "Holism." His starting point is not the individual-concrete but the totality. This leads to the situation that the lower can only be explained through the higher. Haldane firmly opposes all mechanistic explanation of life.

HALEVI, Judah c. 1080-1140
Jewish poet and philosopher of the Middle Ages. His *Kitab Al Khazari,* written in Arabic and translated into Hebrew, *Sefer Ha-Kuzard (Book of the Khazar)*, is a defense of Judaism against Christian and Islamic criticism.

HALL,Granville Stanley, 1844-1924
American philosopher, psychologist and educator, who tries to combine ethical idealism and psychological realism.

HALLUCINATION
An experience, for which no adequate stimulus exists in the outer world. Delusion: also negative (sensory amnesia). Hallucination is different from illusion, because the latter has a basis in reality but falsifies it.

HAMANN, Johann Georg
Born in Königsberg, 1730, died in Münster in 1788. Founder of *Glaubensphilosophie.*

HAMEL, Jean Baptiste du
Born in Vire 1624, died in Paris 1706. French oratorian, later secular priest. His book on philosophy and astronomy is often called *Philosophia burgundica.* Inclined toward *atomism. Since him the name ontology has been given to general metaphysics.

HAMELIN, Octave, 1856-1907.
French idealistic philosopher, professor at the Sorbonne. Hamelin tried in his *Essai sur les éléments principaux de la représentation,* 1907, to present a philosophical system in which all known and to-be known facts would find a place. This system can only be a system of relations, because there is no other reality than relationship. Relationship itself is nothing else than an act of thought. So Hamelin concludes that thought is the only reality. The system of relations leads from the abstract to the concrete, according to the dialectical way of thinking, in which an opposition is always overcome on a higher level. One finds on top of dialectics the concrete human person. But man seems to be a limited being. Thought therefore has to acknowledge above a perfect reality human reality. This also has to be a person. In this way Hamelin arrives at a theistic concept of God. Hamelin had a great influence on French *spiritualism. B.D.

HAMILTON, Alexander 1757-1804
One of America's Founding Fathers, he was still an admirer of the British monarchy and the House of Lords. His great contribution to American political philosophy is contained in his articles in the *Federalist,* expounding on the U.S. Constitution.

HAMILTON, William
Born in Glasgow 1788, died in Edinburgh 1856; professor there. In the beginning he followed the realism of commonsense philosophy, but under the influence of Kant he later put some limits to this philosophy. All knowledge is dependent upon the conditions to which the possibility of our knowing is subject; only "the conditioned" can be observed or thought by us; knowledge is powerless in regard to the absolute, but it leaves a place open for belief.

HAN FEI TZU

Died 233 B.C., Chinese "legalistic" philosopher. Society and individual must function as mechanically as the processes of nature. The means to this are strict laws, absolute authority, rewards and punishment. Philosophical absolution receives its most characteristic expression in the theories of the politician and legalist, Shang-Yang (died 338 B.C.).

HAPPINESS

A situation in which *complete* satisfaction fills the consciousness. Happiness is the immediate acquisition of beatitude, but in such a way that the experience has its own meaning. The question therefore arises in what such a happiness consists or by what it is created. The thinkers of antiquity especially sought an answer to this question. They make the distinction between happiness as favorable fortune (with the so-called goods it offers) and happiness as subjective feeling. And this feeling is opposed to *pleasure, because it is lasting and not immediate, complete and not partial, not purely subjective but supposes the assimilation of objective goods. For some thinkers it is the sum of all goods; for others it is the fulfillment of the highest human capacities.

The enjoyment created by the striving towards the possession of a good. In scholasticism is the happiness a passion. Reaction of the mind to a satisfaction; in strong measure: ecstasy.

Happiness is one of the emotions and is an expression of spiritual lust. This term is rarely used to indicate sensual pleasure.

HARDENBERG, Friedrich von

See Novalis.

HARMONY

Quality of the aesthetic or artistic object, through which a multiplicity of elements are connected to each other in such a way that a graceful unity of balanced mutual proportions is created. Harmony was originally a musical concept. In a broader sense, one speaks of harmony in lines, colors, images, shapes and motions. This externally perceptible balance is also the expression of a more hidden harmony of the mind and sensibility, of sense and form, of man and cosmos, of insight and striving, of finiteness and infiniteness.

HARMONY, PRE-ESTABLISHED

The plan set up by the Creator which, according to Leibniz, would contain everything and dominate it appropriately. Because the elements of nature evolve separately according to that plan, together they form a well-ordered unity, although they cannot influence each other.

HARRIS, William Torrey, 1835-1909.

American idealistic philosopher and educationalist.

HARTLEY, David, 1705-1757.

British psychologist and doctor, gives a physiological explanation of psychic phenomena. External objects influence our sense organs, which transport ether vibrations to the brain so that perceptions are created. Hartley developed an association theory and applied it to the spiritual life, thereby noting the parallel between spiritual and physical phenomena; he did not, however, subordinate the former to the latter. This his disciple Priestley did later.

HARTMANN, Eduard von

Born in Berlin 1842, died in Groszlichterfelde 1906. First an officer, later because of infirmity without a job. In his *Philosophie des Unbewuszten* (1869) he proceeds from the observation of the instincts of living beings to the conclusion that the absolute original ground of things must be the unconscious. This unconscious has no connection with the unconscious of empirical psychology. It is an individual, impersonal, all-embracing being, and its attributes are the active, irrational, infinite will, the basis of existence, and the passive, finite representation of the idea, ground of the essence of the world. In the creation of the world, the unconscious acted purely irrationally and without aim; the will has transformed itself to image, by subduing the idea and making it its content. This now tries to rectify the error of the will, using consciousness on its different levels. Therefore the world now has an aim, by which all happenings are directed toward the final end: liberation from the miseries of existence, the peace of not-being. Pessimism, founded on the inexpediency of the origin of the world, is changed to optimism, founded on the appropriateness of its constitution, which makes it seem the best possible world. Man has the duty of adopting the aims of the unconscious and, by raising his consciousness, helping to attain the final end of the world.

Hartmann calls his epistemology "transcendental realism." This means that the *"Ding an sich"* is independent of the knowing subject, but is still dependent upon the forms or categories of knowledge. These are unconscious functions of knowledge, but let themselves be known in the consciousness as the formal elements of knowledge, which give the real world of phenomena its logical character.

The individual's mystic feeling of unity with the unconscious forms, according to Hartmann, the basis of religion. The religion of the future is "concrete monism," which considers the divine unity both transcendent and immanent in the world at the same time, and which includes the abstract monism or pantheism of the Indian religions as well as the monotheism of the Jewish-Christian religions. This religion dictates us to be more and more conscious of our unity with the unconscious in will and love.

HARTMANN, Nicolai, 1882-1950.
German philosopher. He received his first education in Russia, graduated in Marburg (1907) and taught in Marburg, Cologne, Berlin and Göttingen. Educated in the idealism of the School of Marburg, under the influence of Husserl, he developed a more realistic philosophy. The phenomenological method of Hartmann contained three steps: (1) a faithful description of phenomena, *phenomenology* in the narrow sense; (2) from this dependable material we dig up the problems: aporetics; (3) an effort to give a solution to these aporia, theory.

The natural consciousness of relativity is, according to Hartmann, a fundamental phenomenon and as such not to be disputed. For Hartmann knowledge is therefore an activity in which something is apprehended which is independent of that knowing. From Hartmann's epistemology follows the necessity of an ontology, because the object of knowledge presupposes a being.

The object of knowledge is the real *"esse"* and the ideal *"esse."* The real *"esse"* exists in different spheres, in which the higher sphere always has its own legality, which is not to be deduced from the lower sphere. The higher sphere rests, however, on the lower as on a physical basis and its existence depends on it. In the real *"esse"* we make a distinction between the physical sphere, the organic sphere, the psychic and the spiritual sphere, i.e., the cultural life of man and everything connected with it. The ideal *"esse"* contains concepts and judgments, laws of logic and mathematics and values. All these have an *"ideales Ansichsein,"* i.e., they are not real, yet are independent of the knowing subject. Values determine matter not directly, but only through the intervention of man, who on the one hand has the capacity of knowing values intuitively, and on the other hand the power to realize them. Aesthetic values are values of relations between the real and ideal sphere. Since Hartmann limits human knowledge strictly to phenomenological experience, his philosophy remains absolutely *"diesseitig."* The newer schools of philosophy, especially existentialism, he cannot really appreciate. According to him, philosophy is no more when it concedes that it is no longer a science. A.P.M.K.

HECATON OF RHODES

Disciple of Panaetius, who lived in Rome during the 2nd century B.C. In ethics he emphasized the importance of inner strength, from which he deduced the self-sufficiency of the virtues for the happiness of man. He also accepted the fundamental unity of the different virtues and the possibility of acquiring them. Under the influence of the Roman milieu he became interested in casuistic and juridical questions.

HEDONIC

That which relates to pleasure and pain.

HEDONISM

Doctrine according to which pleasure is the only and highest value, the value which is actually strived for in fact and for which we have to strive. Historically, it presents itself under three different forms. Gross hedonism was taught by *Aristippus. Remaining free of all external goods, man will be entirely taken up with the pleasure of the moment. *Epicureanism and *utilitarianism, on the contrary, teach that man should not be seduced indiscriminately by just any pleasure, but should take all aspects of the sought pleasure into account. 'Eudemism, finally, cares not so much for pleasure as for complete and lasting happiness.

Hedonism is based on the proposition that in all that he seeks man strives for pleasure. Although pleasure determines the striving of man, it is not the only determining factor. First, man strives before he has experienced pleasure: hunger, for instance, makes the newborn baby seek food, and not the pleasure of its taste, which he does not yet know. Pleasure is rather the subjective sign of the objectively satisfied striving. Moreover, pleasures themselves cannot ultimately be determined without indication of the object which causes the pleasure. It is through the quality of the object that the pleasure of eating differs from the pleasure of drinking, and that these sensual pleasures differ from aesthetic satisfaction or religious bliss. Pleasure is not only determined by the object of the striving, but, since man is reasonable, he can strive at an object because it is fitting in itself, rather than for the pleasure it gives. J.Gr.

HEGEL, Georg Wilhelm Friedrich

Born in Stuttgart 1770, died in Berlin 1831. German idealist, professor in Jena 1805, Heidelberg 1816, Berlin 1818. He was first a follower of the philosophy of the *Enlightenment, to which he added a sentimental religion with social tendencies, in line with *Rousseau. Later he was influenced by *Kant and *Schelling. The basic ideas of his own system, absolute idealism, were theoretically expressed in his *Die Phaenomenologie des Geistes* (1807), and he gave a complete exposition of this theory in the *Enzyklopaedia der philosophischen Wissenschaften* (1817).

German idealism reached its ultimate consequences in Hegel's absolute idealism. His extensive knowledge of practically the entire value of science of his time was included in Hegel's explanation of the *"esse."* The irrational elements of *romanticism were also adopted. It is a closed construct of concepts, in which every element finds its justification in the whole, which is dominated by the basic idea of the identity of thought and being. Starting point and foundation of Hegel's system is the Absolute Consciousness, in which thought and being completely coincide. This consciousness creates, through thought, the general and ideal, which are the essence of reality, but at the same time identical with thought in its self-motion. Reality is thus a being: thought or better-thinking thought. Hegel calls it *"die Idee, der logische Begriff, der absolute Geist, die absolute Vernunft."* The idea-reality has an immanent activity, through which it is necessarily involved in an eternal development, in which the progress of the *"esse"* answers to the dialectical development of concepts from each other. The logical categories also have the function of being forms of the *"esse."*

The characteristic of the dialectical process, according to Hegel, is the creation of oppositions and the absorption of these oppositions in a higher unity, from which in turn new oppositions generate. The thesis contains the ground of its being otherwise, or antithesis, and both seem to be one in the synthesis. In every following phase, the prior is lifted, inasmuch as its reality disappears, but it is also brought to a higher level, by which it can form a link, in the course of the absolute process, to further realization. Because of this new dialectics, which rejects identity and contradiction as grounds of thought, Hegel is capable of unifying the most diverging elements of reality. All thinking and all development of being follow the scheme of the "triad." All moments of the world and its history can be explained through dialectics.

According to the development which occurs in the idea following the scheme of the triad, Hegel divides philosophy into logic, natural philosophy and *"Philosophie des Geistes."*

Logic, which is at the same time general metaphysics, is concerned with the idea, as it exists in itself without revealing itself in the world. It is divided into the doctrine of being, the doctrine of the essence and the doctrine of the concept.

The *philosophy of nature* is interested in the idea in its other-being, i.e., inasmuch as it has become part of the world which can be experienced. The process of change from idea to nature is completed in three phases, a mechanical, a physical and an organic phase. The idea cannot, however, realize itself completely in nature, so there is left an irrational remainder which forms the domain

181

of the unlogical, the inappropriate, and the accidental.

The *"Philosophie des Geistes"* is concerned with the idea inasmuch as it finds itself in a higher unity; this process occurs in man, but as a phase of the self-realization of the Absolute. Spirit directs itself first toward itself as *subjective spirit*, which works its way up to consciousness of freedom. Then spirit tries, as *objective spirit*, to realize freedom in the general goods of mankind: right, morality, ethics. Right is not a limitation of freedom, but its reality; it contains the conditions for an ordering of society and only resists arbitrariness.

Morality is the stiuation of the individual will, which knows that it is bound by the reasonable and limits itself accordingly.

Ethics is the unity of legality and morality. It is found in the family, the civil community and the state.

The *state* offers the complete realization of ethics and the highest realization of the idea of freedom in the world. It has unlimited authority over its subjects and no duties toward them. There is no legal order possible between states; their relation is based solely on arbitrariness.

History is the self-revelation of the mind in its process toward freedom. The strivings, interests and intentions of individuals and peoples are subjected to the plan of the Spirit, which is the absolute final end of the world.

In the *Absolute Spirit* subjective and objective spirit reach a synthesis. In it the oppositions between subject and object, thinking and being, are removed. The Absolute Spirit develops itself in art, religion and philosophy.

Art expresses in the beautiful the unity of idea and image, thought and realization, form and matter.

Religion gives man a representation of the Absolute, a representation which lies between contemplation and concept, and speaks to the heart as well as to the intellect. Christianity is the absolute religion of truth and freedom, in which all previous religions are lifted, but we cannot speak of either a personal God or a supernatural character in Christianity; it is only a phase in the development of the Absolute Spirit. The facts of the history of salvation are only sensual representations, used by the Spirit to express eternal suprasensual truths. Dogmas are the garb of irrationality, in which the Spirit dresses itself in behalf of the irrational mass; they can be solved in rationality.

In *philosophy*, finally, the Spirit conceives itself and becomes conscious of the infinite content which it generated in itself in the course of its evolution. Philosophy can only realize this task when it understands its own history and views each philosophical system as the realization of a specific moment in the course of the evolution of the idea. It has its starting point in the most abstract (the pure being of the Eleatics, the becoming of Heraclitus and the being-for-oneself of the atomists), proceeds through the "existence" of Plato and the "concept" of Aristotle to the "consciousness" of Descartes and the "consciousness of oneself" of Kant and Fichte, and arrives finally at the Idea with Schelling and Hegel. The philosophy of Hegel is, according to him, the closing synthesis, the absolute system, in which all prior systems are condensed in an all-comprising totality. In this philosophy Absolute Spirit becomes conscious, of itself. The high point of evolution is reached.

Consequently, it should stop here. But also consequently this synthesis will again change into its opposite, and the process of evolution enters a new phase. F.S.

HEGESIAS, 4th century, B.C.
Philosopher of the School of *Cyrenaica. In ethics he defended the theory that human happiness can have no positive content, but exists only in the absence of evil—which seems to be identical with death. Some of his disciples committed suicide, so that he received the nickname "instigator of suicide."

HEHASID, Judah Ben Samuel of Regensburg 12th and 13th Centuries
Jewish mystic, teacher, and leader of the Jewish community of Regensburg. Works: *Sefer Hasidim* (*Book of the Pious*) and *Sefer Hakahod* (*Book of Glory*).

HEIDEGGER, Martin
Born 1889, German existential philosopher. Professor in Freiburg i. Br. The main work of Heidegger, *Sein und Zeit* (1927) inquires about the existence. In order to know what the question (Seinsfrage) means, one has first to investigate who is the man who poses that question. Man appears to be a being, which is taken up by the world, which is interested in the things of the world and acts, feels, wills and thinks as *one* acts, feels, wills and thinks. Because of his interest in the world and in the other human beings, man (das Dasein) can best be characterized as *Sorge* (concern). Such is man in his daily life. He has thus a certain concept of the existence. This concept is however pre-philosophical. It is contained in all his activities, but it is not expressed thematically. The question arises now if man can express it thematically, is he not so taken up by his daily activities that he is unable to think in an other way? This can only happen when a specific emotion, among others *Angst* (Dread) and *Freude* (joy), detaches man from commonness. In *Sein und Zeit* he explains what he means by *Angst:* it is not the same thing as fear; it bursts on us, whereas fear has always a specific cause. The cause of dread can not be determined. Man feels dread *for no reason,* for *nothing.* This shows that man in his emotion of dread is standing before nothingness. The entire active world, all the beings disappear. What remains is nothingness. This nothingness *nichtet* (makes nothing of) the beings: i.e. nothingness shows the nullity of all beings and of all human activity. In his later works: *Über den Humanismus* (1947); *Holzwege* (1950); *Einführung in die Metaphysik* (1953), Heidegger contends that this nothingness is the same thing as the existence. Existence can only show itself to the common man, who is used to be only associated with the beings, as nothingness exactly because it is no being. Herewith one finds that approach to the existence. The discovery, of existence, by turning away from the beings, fills man with joy. One can not say exactly what existence itself is. It is that what makes that being exists. It is not the sum of all the beings, it is not God, because God transcends the existence. One can not express in a positive way, what existence is, but each human life and the entire history of humanity is however determined by the way in which man approaches the question of existence. The influence of Heidegger's thought is very important in and outside Germany, especially in

France. This influence is not only felt in philosophy, but also in psychology, psychiatry, sociology, literature and linguistics.—B.D.

HEIM, Karl

Born 1874, German theologian and philosopher, professor in Tübungen. Especially interested in the epistemological foundations of theology.

HEIMERIC VAN DE VELDE (de Campo)

Born in Son (Holland) end of 14th century, died in Louvain 1460, studied in Paris ca. 1415 under *Joannes de Nova Domo, and in Cologne in 1422. Taught theology in Cologne and became in 1435 professor at the new theological school at Louvain where he played a very important role. Wrote many commentaries on Aristotle and was the leader in Cologne of the Albertists.

HELMHOLTZ, Hermann von 1821-1894

German physicist, known for his invention of the ophthalmoscope, theory of color vision, determination of the velocity of nerve impulses, theory of electricity and many other accomplishments, but especially famous for his paper on the principle of the conservation of energy, *Uber die Erhaltung der Kraft* (1847).

HELVETIUS, Claude Adrien

Born in Paris 1715, died there 1771. From German descent (family of physicians). Joins the French Encyclopedists. His book: *de l'Esprit* (1758) was condemned by the Sorbonne. Helvetius is a sensualist and materialist. The only incentive to our actions is self-interest. Education and law must see to it that egoistic ends be always in agreement with the public good.

HENRICISTS

Are called some writers who wanted to revive the philosophy of Henry of Ghent (died 1293). They were all members of the order of the Servites, and lived in the seventeenth century. They thought wrongly that Henry of Ghent was a member of their order. Among them are Henricus Burgers (died 1630), M. Angelus Cosius and Angelus W. Ventura (died 1716).

HENRICUS SUSO

Born in Germany 1295, died 1366, Dominican, disciple of Eckehart, author of many works of mystical theology.

HENRY OF GHENT

Born in Ghent before 1250, died (Paris?) 1293, magister artium in Paris before 1270, magister in theology in 1275, magister regens 1276-92. *Doctor solemnis.* Henry of Ghent was one of the many theologians who reacted with Bonaventura, John Peckham and the bishop of Paris, Etienne Tempier, against radical Aristotelianism and Thomism; he belongs therefore to the movement which we have called neoaugustinism. He wrote many yet unpublished philosophical works, and is especially known for his 15 *Quodlibeta* and his *Summa theologica.* He is a very independent thinker and clever dialectician and had therefore an important role in the theological discussions of the end of the thirteenth century. His most important opponents were Gillis of Rome and Godfroy of Fontaines. His philosophy is based on the neoplatonic metaphysics, clearly influenced by Avicenna; he tries to correct Avicenna by protecting the freedom of God's creation. The existence of God can be proved as well, and even better a priori than a posteriori. God is the only *Ipsum Esse,* and the concept of being is therefore necessarily analogical, but its necessary consequence is not the real difference between *esse* and *essentia* in the created things. Henry of Ghent attacks here the theory defended by Gillis of Rome, but which the latter took from Avicenna; Henry of Ghent is therefore in the same group as Siger of Brabant and Averroes against Avicenna. The free act of creation posits difficult problems about the divine attributes (immutability, simplicity, will, wisdom). Henry studied the questions very carefully and tries to resolve them in the light of the platonic-augustinian doctrine of the divine Ideas. He had also very personal notions about the substantial forms: he finds in man two substantial forms: the *forma corporeitatis* and the immaterial soul. In epistemology he appeals to the theory of abstraction (which investigates the origin of our concepts) and also to a special illumination by God in order to explain our knowledge of the eternal and necessary truths. He is therefore a representative of the avicinian *augustinism. F.V.S.

HENRY OF HARCLAY

Born in England ca. 1270, died in Avignon 1317, magister in theology in Oxford, chancellor there in 1312. He borrowed many elements from thomism, but attacked it in many points, following then the franciscan school of Scotus. He has wrongly been called a precursor of the nominalism of Ockham.

HERACLIDES PONTICUS

Ca. 390-310, disciple of Plato and member of the Academy. Wrote about ethical problems and natural sciences. His dialogues were much read in Antiquity and they influenced the later veneration for Pythagoras and the cosmic religion. He teaches that the soul is an ethereal body, related to the stars. His astronomical theory of the movement of the earth, revolving around its axis is important. He probably also taught that Venus and Mercurius rotate around the sun. In physics he teaches a kind of theory of atoms, however not mechanical as Democritus did.

HERACLITUS OF EPHESUS

540-ca. 475 B.C., one of the most important presocratic thinkers. He expressed his ideas in quite difficult aphorisms, and received therefore the name of Heraclitus the Obscure. He was searching for the first principle of being; he considered as first natural element fire. From fire came, through a process of condensation or dilution, all the other elements: water, air and earth. But Heraclitus surpasses all other philosophers of his time, because of his clear consciousness of the changeableness and mobility of the things. "All things flow" has become a classical expression. "In the same stream we descend and we descend not, we are and we are not" (fr: 49). Motion is necessary, because of the oppositions, which evoke each other. "It is always one and the same: be living or dead, sleeping or awake. Because the one turns into the other and the reverse." (fr: 88). "Sickness makes health pleasant; so makes evil the good, hunger the abundance; tiredness the rest" (111). No wonder that he considered fire as the primitive element of being, because "fire can be exchanged with everything and everything with fire, as merchandise with gold and gold with merchandise" (90). These antitheses in things were also expressed in the image of the war: "War is the father of everything, king of everything" (33). The battle of these antitheses is however not fought in a chaotic multiplicity. There is on the contrary a more deep harmony: "the antitheses strive towards each other and out of different tunes originates the most beautiful harmony, and everything happens through the struggle" (8). This deep unity of the antitheses is not always very patent, but "an invisible harmony is better than a visible one" (54). In the continuous motion of the universe exists thus a specific and very strict order, as is shown in this fragment: "the sun will not transgress its limits, and if it does the Erinyes, daughters of the justice, will know where to find it." (94). The question if Heraclitus called this immanent law of the world-events a reason or "logos," is not yet solved. In later literature he has always been honored as the inventor of this concept, which will have such an important role in later Greek philosophy. In the most ancient sources, namely in Plato and Aristotle, Heraclitus is only considered as the philosopher of the changeable and the antitheses. It is possible that the stoics, who borrowed the theory of the fire from Heraclitus, also ascribed to him the concept of the "logos," which has a central place in their own philosophy.

As did all the philosophers before Socrates, Heraclitus connects his conception of the human soul with that of the first element; the fire. The soul is a subtle fire, which enables us to know. We therefore say that "a dry glittering is the most wise and best soul" (118). The characteristic of the human soul is the knowledge: "To all man is given to know himself and to think" (116). This self-knowledge is how-ever not subjective or individual. Truth is only found in that what is in common: "If one wants to speak intelligently, he has to arm himself with that what is only common to all, in the same way as a city arms itself with the law—and still much stronger. Because all human laws are fed with the one divine law" (114). Heraclitus seems to have had a vague notion of the divine transcendency: With respect to his wisdom, beauty and all the rest the wisest man appears to God as being a monkey, (83). Many of his aphorisms hit the reader because of their antithetical expressiveness. They are sometimes more suggestive than clear, as for instance: "Time is a boy, who plays with checkers. Kingship of a boy!" (52).—F.D.R.

HERBART, Johann Friedrich

Born in Oldenburg 1776, died in Göttingen 1841. German realistic philosopher and educator, professor in Königsberg and Göttingen. His basic conviction is that the experience can show us the way, from the world of the phenomena, to the essence of reality, without which the phenomena would not exist. Reality consists in a multiplicity of absolutely simple and unchangeable phenomena, which are not extensive in space and are called *reals*. Each of these reals has a specific quality. Because of the opposition of these qualities among each other, it is compelled to defend itself against the disturbances provoked by others. This action for self-preservation, which has only the meaning of a mechanical reaction, is the only real happening in the world. The soul is also a simple being of specific quality, which defends itself against disturbances, through representations. They function as forces, whose ac-

186

tion is produced with mechanical necessity, if the right conditions are fulfilled. They melt with each other, unite themselves in groups, hinder or even push each other aside. The entire physical life, feeling and striving inclusive, is reduced to the representations and their activities. Psychology traces the laws of these activities and fixes them in mathematical formulas. Herbart is therefore the founder of the mathematical psychology.

Education has its center in the instruction. It is principally a producing of these ideas, which can guide our will and action in the desired direction. Education is only the acquisition of positive knowledge; Herbart does not attach any importance to formal education. Herbart had, with his didactic materialism, a very profound influence on the pedagogy and the school—affairs of the nineteenth and twentieth centuries.

His ethics proceed from the experience and becomes, as for *Shaftesbury, a doctrine of the ethical taste, which judges will and action according to the feeling of pleasure or displeasure, which it creates in the impartial onlooker. F.S.

HERDER, Johann Gottfried

Born in Mohrungen 1744, died in Weimar 1803. Follower of the *Glaubensphilosophie. Mostly known through his *Ideeen zur Phil, der Geschichte der Menschheit*, in which he explains that the history develops itself in the same way as the natural history, under the influence of specific physical causes and according to specific and stable laws. He explains history as being the progress of the human species towards "humanity," i.e. towards the harmonious unfolding of all abilities and forces of the human nature.

HEREDITY

The phenomenon in which living beings, through reproduction, pass their characteristics completely or largely on to their offspring. Heredity obeys specific biological laws, which are of great importance in practical life (agriculture, cattle-raising) and to the inquiries of evolution.

HERILLUS OF CARTHAGE

Disciple of *Zeno of Citium, founded a dissident school and criticized very much the theories of his master. The final end of human existence was defined as a life which is not lived in ignorance, but which is illuminated by scientific knowledge; next to this ideal of wisdom he accepted a secondary final end, which is in fact pursued by the masses.

HERMENEUTICS (Greek: the art of explanation)

The scientifically justified method of classical philology for the explanation of the ancient texts. Considered by *Dilthey as a mental science and has to bring us to *"verstehen" the data of culture.— *Heidegger considered it as the phenomenological analysis of the human existence, as conceived in *Sein und Zeit*.

HERZEN, Alexander

Born in Moscow 1812, died in Paris 1870. Russian Hegelian, revolutionary, hoped that anarchism and nihilism would bring the victory of the Slavic world over the German world.

HESS, Moses 1812-1875

German Socialist, who broke with Marz and Engels to become a follower of Lassalle. Also an early champion of Zionism. Works: *Rome and Jerusalem* (1862), *Holy Story of Humanity* (1837).

HETEROGENEOUS
What is not everywhere the same. Opposed to Homogeneous. see Continuum.

HETEROLOGICAL
Is according to Grelling an adjective which is not applicable to itself. The adjective "cold" is heterological, because "cold" is not cold: "English" however is an English word.

HETERONOMY
Characterizes, according to *Kant, the will which let itself be determined by something else than by the natural law, which is formal and a priori. Opposed to Autonomy.

HETEROTELIC
Related to ends which are outside of the own person. Especially used in American literature, also in connection with types of character. Opposed to Autotelic.

HETEROZETESIS (Greek: heteros-zetesis)
The philosophical search for an other and higher principle or cause of something.

HEURISTIC (Greek: heuriskein, to find)
Method of finding. For Aristotle the method for finding a definition, thanks to the irony or feigned ignorance through which the questioned person feels embarrassed (see aporia), and the maieutic, through which one helps him to find by himself the right answer—Also *Raymundus Lullus' *Ars magna:* to find methodically new truths.

HIEROCLES OF ALEXANDRIA
5th century A.D., member of the neoplatonic school of Alexandria,

most known for his commentary on the neo-pythagorean *Carmen aureum.* A very simple metaphysical system: speaks only of the Demiurge as the transcendent divinity; he does not create the world from a preexisting matter, but from nothing and through his will (influence of christianity).

HILBERT, David, 1862-1943.
German mathematician, professor in Koenigsberg 1893-95, in Göttingen 1895-1929; represented the formalistical school in the mathematical *foundation research.

HIPPARCHIA
Second half of the 4th century B.C., sister of the cynic philosopher Metroclus and wife of Crates. Born in a rich family, she followed however the poor philosopher. She wrote perhaps apophthegmata or, according to others, a philosophical book against *Theodorus Atheus.

HIPPIAS
Sophist in the 5th century B.C., official orator in the panhellenistic meetings, versed in all the sciences of his time. The end of life is the selfsatisfaction or *autarchy. The wise man as universal man, is above all the particular laws of the state.

HIPPOLYTUS
Died 236, probably a disciple of Irenaeus and opponent of *gnosticism.

HISTORICISM
Can be negatively defined as the rejection of all absolute, rational and moral norms in the judging of the creations of history. Positively as the proclamation of the creative power of the human mind, for which no other world image, art work, system of justice, religion has value, than the ones he creates himself or wants to make valid by recreating it. It is founded in an

irrationalistic idealism and, if it is consequently thought, it does not escape scepticism.

HISTORICITY

of man, as it is emphasized by the *existential philosophy, means: negatively, that man is not attached to an absolute truth and any absolute norm of life, because all norms are dependent from the fluctuations of historical life; positively, that man is always in a continuously changing situation in the world and therefore determines, in complete freedom, his attitude in and towards this situation, independently from any super-historical norm.

HISTORY

In the objective sense, everything that happens in nature as well as in the world of man; generally, however, limited to the latter. In the subjective sense, the science which investigates this happening. As such, history limits its object to a systematic investigation and description of the activity of mankind in the past, inasmuch as it was expressed in society. The difference between the history of peoples who wrote and of peoples who did not is only of a methodical, and not of a principal, nature. Because of its extent, history is very often limited in space, time and practical content of human activity. But even the most limited history always strives toward universal history, the interest in the becoming and development of the world of man. Methodically, history is divided into the search for and criticism of sources, and the writing of history or synthesis. The ideal of the latter is to show the past as it was (Ranke) and therefore to try to establish and understand the inner connection of the facts. Since the historian is always interested in human values, he has to assess their factual realization, and will therefore be more or less influenced by his own views on life and world. K.L.B.

HOBBES, Thomas

Born in Malmesbury 1588, died in Hardwick 1679. English philosopher. During his voyages on the continent he met the renewers of the natural sciences (Galilei and Gassendi). His doctrine is mechanistic and materialistic. Reality is of a physical nature, and the laws of the natural sciences, especially those about the motion of the bodies and the smallest particles, can completely explain all occurrences. Hobbes is empiricist; knowledge originates by unification and separation of sensations and remembrances; the latter are deducted from the former. Thought is a kind of cipher with concepts and symbols, because concepts are names of symbols which we attach to the things.

Hobbes is determinist: he negates the existence of a free will in his main work *Elementa philosophica* (I. De corpore; II. De homine and III. De cive). *Leviathan* is the title of a book in which he expresses his views on politics: human nature is naturally selfish and inclined to fight the fellow man. The state has been created because one understood that a struggle between all and all had to be avoided. Therefore men undertook by contract to live in community and to subject themselves to a government. Hobbes defends absolutism, as the best form of government, which can retain order and peace.—F.B.

HODGSON, Shadworth Hollway, 1832-1912.

English critical realist. Main

work: *The Metaphysics of Experience,* 1898.

HOFFDING, Harald, 1843-1931.
Danish positivistic philosopher, professor in Copenhagen, whose influence as critical historian of philosophy was very strong, also outside his country.

HOHENHEIM
See Paracelsus

HOLBACH, Paul Henri Thiry d'
Baron de Heese et de Léande, born in Heidesheim 1723, died in Paris 1789. Associated with the encyclopedists, especially in the field of chemistry. He is strongly anti-religious and atheistic. Selfishness, love and hatred are, in moral domain, identical incentives as attraction, inertia and repulsion are in the physical world. These passions are to be used by the state in favor of the public good.

HOLISM
Theory about the peculiar character of the human beings. Was first posited by general Smuts, and later elaborated by others (J. Haldane, A. Meyer). Holism underlines the connection of all parts and activities of an organism, which clearly seems to be a coordinated whole. There is here therefore a connection with the concepts *"Gestalt" and *totality; their connection exists also in the fact that holism does not go as far as to give definitions of the nature of life. In further analysis holism also underlines the connection between several living beings in nature, and also between living and inanimate beings. Holism has shown, in biology, the peculiar nature of organic life.

HOLMES, Oliver Wendell, Sr.
1809-1894
Professor of anatomy and physi-ology at Harvard Medical School who became popular through his book of commentaries, *Autocrat of the Breakfast Table* (1858).

HOLMES, Oliver Wendell, Jr.
1841-1935
U.S. Supreme Court Justice, known as "the great dissenter" because he often dissented from the majority opinion of the Court. Works: *The Common Law* (1881) and *The Dissenting Opinions of Mr. Justice Holmes* (1929).

HOLY, THE, (das Heillige)
Especially used by R. Otto as the essential characteristic of that what is religious. It is for Otto about the same thing as the divine. Other authors use this term to indicate only that what is excluded from daily use (taboo). All writers however underline the opposition with the profane. In its primary meaning is the holy an attribute of God and therefore everything which is in one way or another connected with God: 1) all things which are dedicated to God and therefore excluded from profane use, the inaccessible; 2) What is possessed by superhuman, superworldly power; 3) quality of men who prove their special unity with God by their heroic virtue and are therefore, but not necessarily, bestowed with a special gift of miracles.

HOMEOMERIES, (literally with identical parts)
Is the name given by *Anaxagoras of Milete to the "seeds" which constitute the world. These primitive beings are infinite in number, qualitatively different, everlasting, but they can be divided. All matter contains all kinds of seeds, but the matter gets its name from the seeds which form the

majority. Change happens by mixing or taking away these homeomeries.

HOMOGENEITY
See geometry.

HOMOGENEOUS
Two functions are homogeneous if each element of the one is connected with an element of the other by means of a *correlator, which is a one-one relation. Homogeneous functions have the same cardinal *number.

Are two relations if their elements are connected through an ordinal *correlator. Homogeneous relations have the same relation *number.

HOWISON, George Holmes, 1834-1916.
American philosopher, idealistic personalist.

HSUN TZU
Ca. 300-238 B.C., founder of the "realistic school" of confucianism. Culture is the ennoblement of the (originally bad) human nature. The value of morality lies in its practical usefulness for the community.

HUGO OF SAINT-VICTOR
Born in Saxony 1096, died in Paris 1141, founder of the theological school of Saint Victor; entered in 1115 the abbey of St. Victor in Paris and taught there from 1125 until his death. Hugo of St.-Victor is firstly theologian and his works are mainly devoted to dogmatics and mystical theology. He was also interested in the liberal arts, which were considered as being a necessary introduction to the theology, and in his works he touched many philosophical themes. His most interesting work, in this respect, is his *Didascalion*, a kind of summary of the knowledge of his time in 7 books. The first three are devoted to the liberal arts. Later he changed those three books into the *Epitome in philosophiam* (unpublished). His most important philosophical themes are: the classification of the sciences (inspired by Aristotle) the proof of God's existence (augustinian tendency), nature and activity of the soul (augustinian influence together with an aristotelian conception of knowledge)—F.V.S.

HUI SHIH 4th Century B.C.
The teachings of Hui Shih are preserved only in the book of Chuang Chou, brilliant precursor of Taoism. His aphorisms express awareness of eternal change and emphasize the paradoxical.

HUIZINGA, Johan, 1872-1945.
Dutch historian, professor at Leyden. The works of Huizinga are all penetrated with a philosophical spirit. Are especially important for philosophy: *De wetenschap der geschiedenis* (The science of history) 1937, in which Huizinga forms a clear idea of the nature and culture of the historical science; *Homo Ludens*, 1939, a contribution to the philosophical anthropology, in which Huizinga analyzes the element of play in human existence; *In de Schaduwen van Morgen* (In the shadow of tomorrow), 1935 and *Geschonden Wereld* (Violated world) 1945 are a contribution to the meditation of the contemporary image of man and world.

HUMAN ACT
An operation which does not so much happen to man (like reflexes or automatism) as it is completed by man, i.e., with spiritual consciousness and free will. Because of this human character, the human act belongs to the *ethical order.

The human act can be *imman-ent* or *transitive*. The former occurs when the operation creates a change which is limited to the subject e.g., physically or morally. The transitive human act, however, leads to a change in reality outside the subject. In this case two moments can be distinguished: progress in the will itself (the desire, the decision, etc.) and change in the outer world with the collaboration of other functions than the will. These moments are called, respectively, *interior* and *exterior* human acts, or the *elicited human act* or act of the will and the *commanded act*.

The question then imposes itself: by what is the human act morally or ultimately determined? Is it determined by the manner the content is strived at (*see* intention) or by the pursued °content? If the latter is true, is it because of the end or because of the value which embodies the content? In the latter case the human act can be considered as the sum of all the operations for the realization of a value which is present in the consciousness. *See also* action. J.Gr.

HUMANISM

Movement for the defense of man against all that could threaten his complete development, from outside or inside, from above or underneath.

Humanism designates firstly the movement, originated in the early Renaissance, which tried to revive the ideal of Humanity as it existed in Antiquity, through study and imitation of the Latin literature. It is ultimately a self-affirmation of man against the authority of the Church which limited in many ways the human freedom. It is therefore in the period of °Enlight-enment that humanism will be completed.

Feuerbach and Marx think that man has to be more defended against specific economical situations (namely private property), because these are the real reasons for his alienation. Only communism can guarantee the divine character of man.

Sartre's existentialism wants also to be considered as a humanism. He uses this appellation first of all to point out that his existentialism is not a °nihilism, although he wants to liberate man from all self-deception and lead him towards authenticity.

There exists also a *christian* humanism. Man is only completely man, when he opens himself to the divine. It is however rejected by many philosophers who see in it an inner contradiction, either because humanism would exclude all transcendency, or because christianity rejects all that is purely human as perverted. J.Gr.

HUMANISM or HOMINISM
See pragmatism.

HUMANISTS

Followers of the humanism. The cult of the literature of Antiquity never disappeared completely in Western Europe after the fall of the Roman Empire. It existed in the Schools of the liberal arts (episcopal and conventual schools) and had two flourishing-times during the Middle Ages: the *Carolingian Renaissance* in the 9th century and the renaissance of the 12th century, which has been called the "spring of the mediaeval civilization" and which occurred together with a remarkable social, religious and cultural revival. In this time the School of °Chartres was the main centre of the humanistic movement.

The real humanism began however in the 15th century in Italy (Florence, Rome and Venice) and was favoured by the immigration of Greeks after the fall of Constantinople (1453). By the end of the 15th century humanism spread over all Western Europe. In philosophical respect humanism favored the revival of several antique systems especially platonism and aristotelianism. The best known humanists were: Rudolphus Agricola (1443-1485), Erasmus of Rotterdam (1467-1536), Luis Vivès (Valencia, 1492-1549)—F.V.S.

HUMANITARIANISM
Enthusiastic defense of the interests of the whole humanity.

HUMANITY
The complete and harmonic unfolding of the abilities and forces who make that man is man. Cicero defined this ideal for the first time, and gave the first humanistic education, which leads to it.

HUMBOLDT, Wilhelm von
1767-1835
German philologist and diplomat, philosopher and historian. Major work: *Uber die Kawisprache auf der Insel Jawa*, published posthumously.

HUME, David
Born in Edinburgh 1711, died there 1776, British philosopher and historian. Studied law for a few years but left for France in 1734, where he studied at la Flèche (where Descartes also studied) and prepared his masterpiece *A Treatise of Human Nature*. The two first parts of this work were published in 1739 and the third part in 1740. In 1741 he published his *Essays, moral, political and literary*, which had a greater popularity in the intellectual circles than his philosophical work. He made between 1746 and 1748 trips to Vienna and Turin, became in 1752 librarian in Edinburgh, which permitted him to write his famous *History of England*. From 1763 to 1765 he was secretary and chargé d'affaires at the English Embassy in Paris, where he was at once received in the French intellectual and philosophical circles (the *Encycloped-ists). He returned to London in 1766, with Rousseau; he was first his friend but had later some differences with him. Until 1769 he was undersecretary of State in Edinburgh and remained there during the last years of his life.

Hume is rightly considered as one of the most important philosophers of Britain; he completed the theory of knowledge developed by Locke and Berkeley with a positivistic-empirical doctrine. While in the doctrine of Locke and Berkeley still rational elements are to be found, is Hume's philosophy purely empirical, because he not only deduces the material of our knowledge from the experience, but bases this knowledge, formally and fundamentally on this experience. He rejects all metaphysics which, by definition, transgresses the experience. Human knowledge is limited to contents of consciousness, which he divides in *impressions* i.e. impressions of the external and internal experience, and the *ideas* i.e. representations or images of reminiscence, which can best be considered as copies of impressions and are less clear and lively than the original impressions. This material is connected in consciousness according to the laws of association; when these connections are only related to representations and are independent from reality, as this is for instance the case in mathematics, then knowledge can have some necessity and certainty. But our judgments of the reality, our knowledge of facts can glory only in a little certitude. The so called rational judgments are from force of habit created by association of impressions and ideas. They are expectations that specific facts will take place. Hume asks: what is the value and validity of our judgments, when they surpass the sensual impressions? or in his own words: "What is the nature of that evidence, which assures us of any real existence and matter of fact beyond the present testimony of our senses or the records of our memory?" Since our conceptions of the identity and the relation of the objects in space and time are based on the concepts of cause and effect, Hume will analyze this concept of causality. He denies to this concept absolute value. When we establish repeatedly a succession of specific happenings, the habits will lead us to consider one of these happenings as cause and the other as effect. (E.g. with the perception of a flame the phenomenon of heat is connected) The causal connection is not in the objects themselves, but is given to them by the human mind.

A similar criticism is applied by Hume to the concept of substance and to the concept of psychic subject. The continuous and repeated connection of specific representations in a thing-representation, has led to the belief in a material substance, independent from the consciousness. Nothing, however, exists in the experience which gives us the right to conclude from the visible sensual qualities to an exponent of these qualities. He not only denies, with Berkeley, the existence of a physical substance, but he denies also the existence of a spiritual substance or of a personal identity. One can only establish in oneself a ceaseless flux of contents of consciousness and perceptions, "a bundle or collection of different perceptions." Hume denies thus, against his predecessor Berkeley, the existence of one's own ego, a spiritual substance.

In his ethics Hume teaches that our ethical activities are determined and have to be determined by the agreement or rejection of these activities by our fellow-men. The highest virtues are: kindness, sense of justice and to make oneself useful for the social entity. These virtues favor not only the happiness of mankind but also the happiness of the individual. He does not find evidence for the rational and absolute norms for good and evil (as did Locke and Cudworth).

His views on religion are found in his *Dialogues on Natural Religion* and in his *Natural History of Religion*. He opposes an anthropomorphism that defines God's nature and being, according to an analogy with the human qualities. He develops a kind of scepticism in regard to the demonstrability of the existence of God and the immortal soul. He admits however that the acceptance of a religious conviction, although not proved by the intellect, can be of great value in daily life.

The historical importance of Hume lies in the solution he gave to the cardinal problems. His criticism of the principle of causality has incited Kant to look for a renovation of the theory of knowledge. Hume's doctrine concluded the philosophical school of English empiricism and is a very important link in the evolution of the European thought. F.B.

HUMOR

The most deep-human form of the °comic. The object of humor is naturally all that is human, it knows that in all human things, greatness and littleness go together. It is essential that the humoristic subject does not exclude himself from this. The usual form of expression of humor is a soft irony, in which the bitterness has given way to the sympathetical appreciation of the human littleness. This sympathy is still present in the more capricious and cold forms of humor as in grim or sardonic humor, for instance.

HUNEIN IBN ISHAK 809-873

A Nestorian Christian who was born in Syria, who wrote in Syriac and Arabic, and whose masterwork, *The Sayings of the Philosophers*, was translated into Hebrew, Spanish and other languages—a curious work subject to the errors and confusion attendant upon the decaying state of Greek culture and the manuscripts of his time.

HUSSERL, Edmund, 1859-1938.

German philosopher, founder of the phenomenology, professor in Freiburg i. Br. The thought of Husserl went through a long evolution: *Logische Untersuchungen*, 1900-1901, 2nd ed. 1913-21; *Ideen zu einer reinen Phänomenologie und phänomenologischen Philosophie*, 1913; *Formale und transzendentale Logik*, 1929; *Méditations cartésiennes*, 1931; *Die Krisis der europäischen Wissenschaften und die transzendendentale Phänomenologie*, 1936. Husserl was originally interested in problems of mathematics. These problems brought him however to more deep thoughts so that he was brought to the question of the foundations of philosophical thinking. He reaches a solution quite similar to that of Descartes. In philosophy there is a complete lack of agreement, because one does not realize sufficiently the origin nor the method of philosophy. We have to find a method which enables us to think without prejudice. One begins most of the time to think, going out from a specific theory or a specific point of view. One should however first look with an unprejudiced mind, at the things themselves: Zu den Sachen selbst! Herefore one needs an analysis of the consciousness. This analysis shows us that the consciousness is essentially intentional: it is as such always directed towards an object. Since we consider the structure of the consciousness in itself, we have to investigate the appearance of the object in the consciousness (the phenomenon) and the real existence or inexistence of the object does not matter. This existence is therefore left aside: (phenomenological reduction, epochè). Remains now the multiplicity in the manifestation of the objects. We have to find now the essential in the phenomenon. All what is not essential has to be left again aside (second, eidetic, reduction) so that only the pure being remains (eidos). This is however not a process of abstraction, as we find in thomism, but a matter of intuition: the essence is seen by the intellect (Wesenserschauung). We find in this way the essential structure of consciousness. This does not coincide with the empirical consciousness. Everything which is empirical in consciousness has again to be disregarded. (Third, transcendental reduction). We find so the transcendental consciousness. Phenomenology is in the last instance the description of the transcendental consciousness. This way of thinking (from the time he wrote the *Ideen*) brings Husserl more in an idealistic line, although it is not so sure that his idealism can be identified with classical idealism. Most of Husserl's disciples are convinced that phenomenology has to justify realism. Next to this idealistic trend in the later works of Husserl we can find in Husserl's philosophy another tendency which brings him in line with many simultaneously evaluating trains of thought, as are the existential philosophy, the logistics and the psycho-analysis. Husserl investigates in this case more and more the presuppositions, which are present in any idea and action.

The influence of Husserl's phenomenology was exceptionally wide. The publication of his posthumous works (*Erfahrung und Urteil,* 1939; the German text of his *Méditations,* 1950; the edition of parts 2 and 3 of his *Ideen,* 1950-52) opens new perspectives. Very important are the Husserl-Archives at Louvain, where all his manuscripts are kept. His influence was great in two different periods: the first after the publication of the *Logische Untersuchungen,* the center of the phenomenological school was in München, with as central point the Wessenschau; the second period of influence came after Husserl's death during which especially his posthumous works were very influential: the centers of these new and partly differently oriented phenomenologies are in Louvain, Paris and Strassburg. In the U.S.A. the influence of Husserl was mostly felt during and after World War II, because of immigrated German philosophers and some American philosophers as Marvin *Farber.— B.D.

HUTCHESON, Francis, 1694-1746.
English philosopher and moralist, was, in many respects, a follower of Shaftesbury. Is however more known as one of the first founders of the aesthetics, of a doctrine about the nature and origin of our concept and feeling of beauty, harmony and virtue. He influenced several German thinkers as Kant, Lessing and Herder.

HUTCHISON STIRLING, John, 1820-1909.
English neo-Hegelian. His book: *The Secret of Hegel,* 1865, introduces the neo-hegelian movement in England. Hutchison explains Hegel's idealism in a theistic sense; as many contemporary Hegel-scholars do, he underlines more the concrete aspect of Hegel's thought than well the abstract aspect.

HUXLEY, Thomas Henry
Born in Ealing 1825, died in London 1895. English biologist, positivist and evolutionist. He invented the appellation "agnosticism" for the recognition of our ignorance about everything which transcends our experience.

HYLEMORPHISM
(hyle—matter; morphe—form)
Doctrine of Aristotle that all physical beings are composed of two principles of being: the prime matter or materia prima, which is an undefined primitive matter, and the substantial form, or forma substantialis, which is a definite form of existence. Every single kind of matter has its own specific form of existence, while all matter has the same primitive matter. In other words all concrete matter is *this particular* sort of matter thanks to a specific form of existence, and it is *matter* thanks to the prime matter. The latter should therefore not

be considered as an elementary sort of matter, but only as disposition to matter, which is brought to realization by one or another form. The primitive matter does therefore never exist in itself, but always in one or another concrete form, i.e. defined by a concrete form of Hylemorphism can be defined as the doctrine of the not-simplicity of the physical existence. It is based on two universal characteristics of matter: the changeableness and the different individuals of a species (see species-individual-structure). Both characteristics can only be explained if matter, in its most profound nature, is not simple.

Until the 17th century hylemorphism was the most important principle to explain the scientific natural phenomena and was used to solve the problems of natural science and natural philosophy. Because it was fruitless in the theories of natural science, hylemorphism was abandoned in the 17th century. It is more than ever actual as philosophical principle in the explanation of matter, because contemporary physics are more than in any previous century confronted with the fundamental changeableness of matter. — A.G.M.v.M.

HYLOZOISM (literally: animation of matter)

Is an older doctrine which attributes animation to all matter, and also thinks that all life is tied to matter. Defended by the Ionic cosmologists, the Stoics, the cosmologists of the Renaissance and the French materialists of the 18th century (Diderot). They reject the distinction between matter and spirit, but do not accept a purely mechanical thought. Closely related is the pantheistic hylozoism of the neo-platonici and of the Renaissance (Paracelsus Bruno), which considered everything as animated and as emanation of the divinity; in this theory life is a higher emanation than matter.

HYPOSTASIS (literally: that which stands under)

Was used by the stoics in the sense of substance or ousia; had later also the meaning of person. This last meaning has been kept in theology. The *Unio hypostatica* is the union of both natures of Christ (the human and the divine) in one single person.

HYPOTHESIS (Greek: supposition)

A temporary, more or less probable and not yet as thesis verified explanation of a perceived fact or regular natural happening. It may never be in conflict with definitely established truths, nor be considered as definite results of science. Its probability increases in proportion as the given explanation is rational, better and more simple than other hypotheses, but it decreases in proportion as more additional hypotheses have to be used to make it admissible. We can distinguish between *general* and *particular* hypotheses; *Physical, moral* or sociological and *hermeneutic* Hypotheses etc., also between *explanatory* and pure *workhypotheses* (see fiction). see also theory.

HYPOTHETICAL

See proposition, syllogism.

HYSTERON PROTERON (Greek)

The postulating of a thesis which can only be proved afterwards; more specifically a paralogism by which a thesis is deduced from a truth which can only be proved through this thesis. Descartes, for instance, tries to prove the reliability of our senses through the veracity of God, who could not have given us deceitful senses. See petitio principii.

197

I

Symbol of the particular affirmative proposition; e.g. some animals can be easily trained.

IBN-BAGGA
See Avempace.

IBN-ROSCHD
See Averroes.

IBN-SINA
See Avicenna.

IBN-TOPHAIL
See Abu-Bakr

IDEA (Greek idein, to see)
Originally, the appearance or visible form (see species) of the things, and therefore also their for the mind accessible essential stature. It became then for Plato, the by the intellect considered eternal and unchangeable essence, that is opposed as the true reality to the changeable phenomena which can be approached by the sensual experience. In the doctrine of ideas the relation between ideas and phenomena and between ideas themselves is described (see participation) and it explains how one can achieve the institution of the idea (*anamnesis). While for Plato the ideas form a world of their own they are considered by Augustine, under the influence of neo-platonism, as the thought of God's Spirit, according to which He creates the things (*exemplarism). God's nature itself is, as in many limited ways imitable, the Idea of ideas.

In modern philosophy the Idea is reduced to a content of consciousness, either from sensual or intellectual origin, or innate (see inneism) or acquired by experience. But already with Kant a turning appears: idea is the metempirical object that consciousness necessarily conceives, namely the world, the soul and God. Hegel, finally, comes back to the original meaning of the idea. It is then, as thinking thought, the real reality, or the Absolute in its steady evolution.—J.P. —In a less strict sense, the representation we form of a being. The normative aspect is here more important. The idea becomes thus the conception which we form about the ethical and social realities, in order to act accordingly. In connection with art, the idea is the essential view and the knowable essential value, which appears in sensible artistic form and representation. It is immediately apprehended by intuition, not in an abstract generality, but in the sensibly perceptible form itself. The intuition of the idea does not happen outside of, but in the more subjective feeling. The idea brings this feeling to a sort of clear insight, while the feeling builds the intuition into an esthetical and emotional discovery of the lasting values of existence and life.

IDEA OF GOD
The concept man forms of God can, as is shown in the history of

religion and philosophy, be very different in content and in color. Thomas Aquinas makes a distinction between: (1) An obscure and vague idea of God, which does distinguish Him enough from other things. (2) A distinguishing but still somewhat vague idea of God, which is enough to distinguish Him from creation, but does not express anything specific about His inner nature. It expresses only God's activity toward the outside, as suggested in the terms, the Creator, the Highest Lawmaker, etc. The essential characteristics of such an idea of God are His more or less absolute transcendence and His personality. (3) A distinguishing and clear idea of God, which originates in philosophical thought about God. Although it does not penetrate to His inner nature, still it distinguishes clearly His nature from creation and the finite—e.g., God exists in Himself, and is infinite, simple, necessarily one, the absolutely highest being. (4) The Christian idea of God, which says something, although only analogically, about the inner nature of God—e.g., God is one nature in three persons. The problem of the historical and psychological *origin* of the idea of God differs according to the distinctions given above. The answers will likewise be different (*see* origin of *religion).

IDEA OF LAW

This philosophy, introduced by the professors H. Dooyeweerd and D. H. Th. Vollenhoven in Amsterdam. So called because (1) according to this theory a subjective pre-theoretical idea about the (generally valid) law of the study of science underlies every scientific doctrine, (2) it wants itself to submit to the law of God, under whose sovereignty also the theoretical thinking

must bow. The philosophy of the idea of law teaches that an answer is given, in the idea of law of every science, to three basic questions, which are unilaterally dependent from each other, namely, the question about the origin, the unity of root and the cohesion in the diversity of the creature. It states strongly the mutual irreducibility as well as the universality in the own circle of distinct facets of the cosmos. It has also developed a theory about the modal aspects and individuality-structures of the temporary existence, which have the character of a law. In its transcendental criticism of thought it requires above all from the theoretical thinking an appreciation of its archimedic point.—M.

IDEAL, adj.

Is opposed to real. That what exists only in thought, inasmuch as it is feared. It is however not necessarily dependent from thought.

IDEAL (moral)

Coincides with the fullness and absoluteness of the ethical. As opposed to duty, which composes a minimum, the moral ideal forms the maximum of the morality to be actualized. It is therefore expressed not in a negative way, (this is forbidden) but in a positive form (this is wished) as e.g. "Be perfect." The question is now if man is obliged to pursue the moral ideal, at the risk of being faulty against morality: in other words, can we philosophically make a difference between ideal and duty? Kant rejects this idea in any case: morality and duty are for him one and the same. The scholastics however accept it, although they only give a solution after much hesitation. We do not speak here of the absolute ideal, or abstract ideal, i.e. the maximum morality which can be attained by man, but the concrete morality, or the maximum which a concrete individual can achieve, taking in account his physical and psychical nature.

—The incarnation of the so described moral ideal in the representation of a human figure: this representation is either historical (as Socrates or Jesus), or is a pure construction (as "the Just"). The moral practice is then reduced to the imitation of such an ideal or example.—J. Gr.

IDEALISM

In the broad sense, doctrine or at least attitude of mind, which gives a central place to the ideals or ideas. In *art idealism is opposed to realism. In ethics and pedagogy it refers to the attitude, which believes in the power of ideals to overcome the imperfection of the actual reality. In a more narrow sense and in the field of epistemology: the doctrine that the *idea* or the *thought* has priority to the *reality* or the existence. Historically we find it first in the *acosmic idealism* of Berkeley. He reduces the world of time and space to a representation of man: the existence of such a world is only in the fact of being-perceived. Opposed to this theory, Kant developed the critical or transcendental idealism. There exists a given reality, but we do not know how this reality is in itself, for we know it only through the a-priori forms of our senses and intellect. These a-priori forms, which make a given thing to an object of knowledge, are not fixings of the empirical subjects with their accidents, but of a general, in all subjects identically present function, called the pure consciousness or the transcendental subject. The idealism of Kant coincides therefore with a certain measure of realism. This is also true for many other thinkers and systems with idealistic tendencies. In the most strict sense the term idealism applies to the systems of Kant's successors. The "Ding an sich" is now abandoned, so that the object of knowledge can be explained, in form and in content, through the transcendental subject. The latter has therefore not only a critical but also a metaphysical function. The system of Fichte is called *Subjective idealism.* Fichte sees in the (not yet reached) ideal of the autonomous (moral) subject the motive of the entire evolution of reality, from which "that what is given" can be completely explained. For Fichte the question if idealism is related to the individual, human subject, to the community or to the human subject in general, is already decisive. Schelling's idealism is called *objective* idealism. The transition to an absolute subject is clearly achieved. In his first period (see *Identity, philosophy) he identifies it with the absolute object. Hegel called his system *absolute idealism,* and considers it as the synthesis of the objective and subjective idealism. For him reality is the self-unfolding of the Idea as the absolute.—J.P.

IDEALITY

Quality of a being, inasmuch as it exists or only exists in the human mind.

IDEAL-REALISM

Also real-idealism, can be called all doctrines in which existence and thought (knowledge) are essentially involved with each other, so that the principles of thought are realized in the beings. The nature of this connection between existence and thought differs greatly according to the different systems. See *realism, *idealism, *Wundt.

IDEATION

Forming of ideas. In Husserl's phenomenology it is the intuitive catching of the essence of an object of consciousness, by disregarding its factual existence. In a later evolution the object of consciousness is reduced to the intentional datum of a pure consciousness.

IDEE-FORCE

Is called by *Fouillée the idea which contains in itself the force to it's own realization.

IDENTICAL PROPOSITIONS

Logically equivalent propositions, in which the same thing of the same thing is affirmed or negated on the grounds that a double negation equals an affirmation (*equipollency); e.g. everything is changeable and nothing is unchangeable; it is necessary that the world perishes, and it is impossible that the world would not perish.

IDENTITAS INDISCERNIBILIUM

A principle formulated by Leibniz: two realities with exactly the same qualities can not be distinguished. In other words, a purely numerical difference would not be a real difference.

IDENTITY

Quality of that what is one and the same. Things which are many and therefore different from each other, are relatively the same inasmuch as they are considered the same from a specific point of view, i.e. they are caught in the same thought. *Relative identity* can differ in degree and nature. If only accidental characteristics are involved, we have accidental identity; if, however, it involves identity in the definiteness of the species, then we have substantial identity (as, for instance, exists between men);

if it is concerned with the lasting factor in our course of life, then we have the individual and substantial identity of our person. In these cases an abstraction is made, since we do not consider concrete differences. There arise constantly problems: what is the real ground of this identity and what is its relation to the ground of the differences?

Another question is: do we have to penetrate an *absolute identity*? It is a fact that we can think of the whole reality and that we, spontaneously, evoke contents of thought, which are, as for instance the thought of existence applicable to all things without exception. Many different answers have been given. Sometimes they deny the lasting identity of the meaning of existence: it would therefore be the identity of a mere world. If one however agrees with the all-embracing identity of this content of knowledge, then we have to ask the question: what reality answers to it? Some think that it was the origin of everything, but it disappeared in the emanation of the multiplicity (whether this is considered as a decadence or as a growth). Some others think that it is a non-existing but to be pursued end (and this can be considered as a to be reached final end or as an eternally unreachable ideal). Some others again think that absolute identity actually exists, namely in God's eternal and unperishable perfection, which also has to include in its simple unity, all the perfections of the finite beings, for God is the total cause of everything and He therefore possesses, in an eminent way, all what the creatures, through the participation on his perfection, possess: the absolute identity remains then, without harming the (created) multiplicity.—L.D.R.

IDENTITY-PHILOSOPHY

Is the philosophy of *Schelling in the second period of his life: highest and unique reality is the Absolute Indifferent, absolute unity of subject and object. It is also all philosophy in which subject and object, thought and being, matter and spirit, as different aspects of a same reality, are ultimately identical. They come together in the Absolute.

IDEOLOGISTS

Name of the members of a philosophical group in France (early 19th century) who continued the sensualism of *Condillac and wanted to limit philosophy to the analysis of the psychical life in sensations and its expressions. The Ideologists assembled regularly at the home of *Helvetius' widow at Auteuil, later at the home of Mme. de Stael. The main spokesman: *Destutt de Tracy. The Ideologists represented during the first Empire the idea of freedom of the Enlightenment and Revolution.

IDEOLOGY

The whole of the conceptions about the spiritual, defended by a person or a group of persons. In pejorative sense used to indicate constructions of thought which stay far from reality. In this sense Marxism calls ideologies all conceptions about the spiritual, because the spiritual is nothing else than a result of the physical, especially the economical facts.

IDEOMOTOR ACTION

The actions of the voluntary muscular system, inasmuch as they are directly conducted by representations (of motion) (Carpenter). The momentum of the separate innervation of the motions by the conscious person is absent.

IDOLS

Are called by F. *Bacon the prejudices which make sane judgment difficult. The most important are those which originate in human nature, the individual natural ability, the milieu and the reigning opinion.

IGNORABIMUS

Expression of E. Dubois-Reymond, indicating that there are specific problems which man never will be able to solve (e.g. about the nature of matter).

IGNORATIO ELENCHI

A faulty counter-argument (see elenchos: refutation) On the grounds that one overlooks the "cardo quaestionis," the specific point which is the basis of a specific dispute. One reasons therefore outside of the debated question, i.e. one proves something different from what has to be proven (see paralogism); e.g. contradictory conceptions can not be both true at the same time; philosophers and theologians have always fought against each other; therefore philosophy and theology, science and faith, teach contradictory things and can not both be true at the same time.

ILLUMINATION-THEORY

Adopted by Augustine from neoplatonism. According to this theory knowledge is absolutely and necessarily valid as created by an illumination of God. The augustinism of the 13th century (Bonaventura and others) followed Augustine in this idea. Thomas Aquinas harmonizes this theory of illumination with the abstraction-theory and the active intellect.

I-LOGIC

See *logic, systems of the formal logic.

IMAGINATION

The more personal form of *fantasy. As a characteristic of the personality it is a favorable quality, provided that it be inside specific limits (phantasia non homo).

In scholastic sense is the vis imaginativa (imagination or fantasy) the ability to retain the sensual cognitive images when the object is no longer before the senses, or to renew these images.

IMITATION

See imitative art.

IMMANENCE

What is particular to the immanent. Blondel calls *method of immanence* the method of showing in man a point of contact for all what has to penetrate his life and can inform his knowledge. All this has to respond to an "appeal" or need in man.

IMMANENCE PHILOSOPHY

The doctrine according to which the object of knowledge has no own existence outside the knowing activity, but is entirely absorbed by it. This knowing activity is however not the activity of the concrete knowing subject, but of the world consciousness (Bewusstsein überhaupt). Immanence philosophy indicates sometimes also the fact of being included in the sensory experience. What is not a part of it, but is transcendent can in no way be known (Hume, Kant).

Also the doctrine that God is immanent in the world and in no way transcendent. This immanence philosophy becomes *pantheism and *monism (Spinoza). It denies the existence of a free chosen act of creation of a personal God. From the scholastic conception that God's existence is analogical with the existence of the world, follows that God is immanent in the creation, but transcends at the same time this creation.—H.R.

IMMANENT

What belongs to the structure of a being and therefore remains inside this being. The activity which comes about inside the subject; e.g. the activity of life, or cognition or love. This immanent activity is opposed to the *transitive activity, which tends to the realization of an effect in another being. (*Action).

Kant calls immanent principles, those principles whose application has to be limited to the domain of the possible experience; the appropriate use of these, this is inside the limits of the experienced world, is then called by Kant the immanent use. The opposite is *transcendent.

IMMATERIAL

What does not belong to the physical order or what can not be reduced to matter. Immateriality is what characterizes the immaterial as such.

IMMATERIALISM

The idealistic doctrine of Berkeley that no material things exist, but only spirits with their spiritual ideas. Esse est percipere aut percipi: only knowing or being known is real-being.

IMMORAL

What is contrary to morality or ethics.

IMMORALISM

Doctrine which negates the existence of a *moral value, or at least wants to exchange the existing morality with a morality in which good and evil are arbitrarily defined. So, for instance, in Nietzsche.

IMMORTALITY

Of the soul can be deduced from the fact that the soul, although directed towards the physical as a constituting principle of the human existence, transcends the physical in the activities of intellect and will. Also from the striving of the soul which remains unsatisfied in every finite good.

IMMOVABLE MOVER

Is the name given by Thomas in the first of his five proofs of the existence of God, to God. The name comes from Aristotle, who comes from the motion and the change in the physical things to a primitive principle that as principle is not moved. Otherwise it would not be a principle that explains but which had to be explained.

IMMUTABILITY

See relativism.

IMPENETRABILITY

The quality of a body which makes it impossible for another body to penetrate it in such a way that both, in a strict sense occupy the same place.

Most scholastic philosophers accept that from the *extension immediately can be concluded impenetrability. Other philosophers think that it is a result of an active force, there exists therefore the possibility that this force be overcome by another force. See penetrability.

IMPERATIVE

In strict sense the grammatical mood in which an order is expressed. This order itself in as far as it contains a necessity. (See commandment) Kant distinguishes between the *categorical* and the *hypothetical* imperative. The latter is conditional inasmuch as it makes the response to the order dependent upon a preceding condition: do this or that if you want to be happy. It is therefore more a *prescription that contains good advice, than strict commandment. The categorical imperative however is unconditional; for it orders the will as will, and not in function of a preceding condition which is after all subjective. The categorical imperative constitutes therefore laws which are objective and absolute, in fact the natural *law.

IMPETUS (literally: the fact of rushing upon, fast movement)

In the Middle Ages the active, inner quality which is considered to be the cause of the continuous motion of a projectile. Synonym of *impulse and nisus.

The *theory of impetus* was opposed to the theory of Aristotle, who ascribed the impetus to the medium in which the projectile traveled; the medium would be able to transfer this impetus to the next layers. His commentator Philoponus (early 6th century) placed this impetus in the body itself. The impetus-theory was completely adopted in the 14th century by the Parisian nominalists. They taught that the impetus was greater in the body when a greater initial velocity was given to the body and according to the primitive matter of the body. They knew that the impetus was opposed by the resistance of the medium, and; in case of throwing the object upwards, by the gravity. Contrary to Aristotle they accepted that the impetus remained undiminished. (see law of inertia).

IMPLICATION

The *material* implication between the *propositions $\underline{P}$ and $\underline{Q}$ is defined as follows: P is untrue, or Q is true. This does not fit with the intuitive sense of: if P, then Q, which is usually translated into: P implicates Q. If P is untrue, then one has P untrue or Q true, from this follows for instance that: if $2 = 1$, then all humans are trees.

To avoid the disadvantages of the material implication, Lewis translates: if P, then Q, by a *strict* implication which can be defined as: necessarily is P untrue or Q true. This however is not yet a satisfactory translation. We have, on the other hand, not any more: if $2 = 1$, then all humans are trees, but only: if necessarily $2 = 1$, then all humans are trees.—R.F.

IMPLICIT
What is contained in a proposition without being explicitly mentioned e.g. the proposition that something exists now, includes implicitly that always something must have existed.

IMPORTATION
Is the rule according to which: if p, then if q, one has m, the °proposition: if p and q then m, proceeds. p is here introduced or imported in the hypothesis from which m proceeds.

IMPOSSIBILITY
The °modality of an inference, in which a predicate is negated in such a way to a subject, that it never can be affirmed, e.g. a thing can not be, and not-be at the same time and under the same respect. Is opposed to °possibility and °necessity.

IMPREDICABLE
Is called in the most generally used sense a quality which can be applied to itself. So is "number" impredicable, because the quality of being a number is not a number; the quality "class" is on the contrary a class.

IMPRESSION, SENSUAL
The change in the sensual capacity of knowledge as a result of the affecting of the organ by the surrounding physical world, so that an idea of these surroundings can arise.

IMPRESSIONISM
See art.

IMPULSE
1. sudden instinct for action without any previous deliberation. The impulsive act appears frequently in pathology, where the spiritual superstructure is often eliminated. *Impulsive* is then inclined to reactions with impulses. In neurology this term is used for the stream of action in the nerves. 2. First used in mechanics by Descartes, for the "quantité de mouvement," the quantity of motion of a body; this is then equal to the product of mass and velocity of that body.

The origin of the impulse-concept is found in the Middle Ages, where it was used as a synonym of °impetus. The Parisian nominalists of the 14th century taught already that the impulse of a projectile was greater as it had more primitive matter and as it received a greater initial velocity.

IMPUTATION
The act by which a person is also made responsible for the specific moral good or bad action, which he did not only cause physically but also freely and, more definitely, in moral respect, which he has willed. In fact however animals and other unfree beings are often considered and treated as being responsible; sometimes also people are made responsible (e.g. lunatics) for not-free actions.

INADEQUATE

See concept.

INCENTIVE

In the strict sense of the word, the feeling from which action arises: love or hate, respect for the moral law (from which, according to Kant, moral action has to arise), etc. Opposed to °motive, which is in a certain sense the final cause of action, while the incentive is its efficient cause.

INCLINATION

Lighter form of desire. It is related to preference, as a partly intellectual, partly emotional attitude to something or somebody; or also as habitual preference, i.e. a light form of habit. One distinguishes *basic-inclination* or innate directions, analogous to instincts in the animals, e.g. the impulse for procreation, the desire for happiness, in general the search for the truth, the beautiful and the good, and *special inclinations* which appear in the course of evolution. In pathological sense (sometimes also innate): kleptomania etc. . . . Also cravings, e.g. for a drink.

INCLUSION

Is a relation existing between the classes a and b if all a's are b's so that it remains true if there are no a's.

INCOMMUNICABILITAS

Proper to every °suppositum, i.e. to every subsisting reality. Since it forms itself an existing whole, this reality is not a part or structural element that, united with other parts or elements in one whole, could only exist in this whole.

INDEPENDENCE OF THE SUBJECT

In realism is taught that the °object is ontologically independent from the subject: the being, which is object, exists itself. If therefore the fact of being known is created by the subject, certainly not the possibility of being known or the self-being of the object. In idealism, on the contrary, is the independence of the subject limited to a certain gnoseological independence, in as much as the object, as object, makes of the subject a knowing subject, specifies the knowledge and therefore limits.

INDEPENDENT

A °proposition is independent from another proposition in a specific collection of propositions, if it can not be inferred from the other. The °axioms of a system are independent from each other if none of them can be inferred from another. The independence of axioms is most easily proved, by indicating for each axiom a model (an example), which satisfies all other axioms, but not the intended axiom.

INDETERMINISM

Opposed to °determinism. It denies the validity of the law of causality. In physics it holds that the natural phenomena are not strictly determined (uncertainty-relations of Heisenberg); in the field of psychology it holds that the will is free, in its decisions, from all inner or outside factors, especially from the motives. This doctrine was more explained by examples than proved. So was the example of the ass of Buridanus: put at the same distance of two hay-stacks with exactly the same qualities, the ass has no reason to choose one above the other. He therefore will die if he waits for a rational motivation. He does however not die, which proves that he moves to the right or the left without motivations. The example of the coins, used by Thomas Reid, is of the same kind. See also freedom of the will.

INDIAN PHILOSOPHY

Its main characteristics are (1) an uninterrupted continuity. During ± 30 centuries, generations and schools of thinkers, building on each other's work, although often violently arguing, wrote in the same language (Sanskrit) about a complex of central problems (nature of the human soul, nature of the phenomenal world, relation of both to the non-phenomenal; sense and end of life, existence in the world, etc.) (2) The adherence to specific axiomata: cyclic character of all what is empirical, the psychosomatic life included (transfiguration, by which every soul returns to the earth in always different bodies; earth and universe have successive periods of existence and non-existence); strong tendency to break, as individual, the cycle and to "save" oneself from death and regeneration. (3) In connection therewith a strong accent on the method of practical mysticism (*Yoga) in order to obtain the liberation, and a practical objective of the thought, whose duty it is, not so much to want to know the per se unknown, which lies behind the phenomena and the state of being saved (to which the mystic-intuitive unification can lead), but whose duty it is to purify the spirit of misconceptions and fallacies, which are a handicap for the realization of the great end; systematic treatment of ritual and other duties, at the risk of preventing the salvation; interpretation of the Veda according to philological and logical rules (especially studied by the school of darsana of the Mīmāmsā), logic and dialectics (Nyāya-darsana), cosmology (Vaisesika-darsana), psychology, and a discussion, on the intellectual level, of the final cause of the world, its eventual eternal character, the relation between the soul and its origin, the ways and means to the salvation. (4) The Indian thought is also characterized by a strict authoritative religion. Each author tries to prove that his doctrine is in complete agreement with the Veda and other essential writings based on the Veda; later authors write frequently commentaries on the works of a well known predecessor. Indian philosophy is not very much inclined to confront its conclusions with perceptible facts. See Upanishad, Vedānta, Brahman. —J. G.

INDIVIDUAL

A being, complete and undivided as such, which itself can exist and subsist: a *suppositum. In a narrower sense, a suppositum with the same specific nature as many others. In other words a being, particularized or individualized in its species.

INDIVIDUAL PSYCHOLOGY

Psychological system according to which man is in-dividuum i.e. inseparable from the community. The community-feelings are opposed to the "Wille zur Macht", which is the basic tendency of the human striving (Adler).

As a therapeutic system the individual psychology tries to show the unconscious passion for power and to liquidate it, by substituting for it the community-sense. The inferiority of an organ or also a psychic inferiority can be for man (especially for the child) an incentive to abolish it (compensation). If a person goes too far in this compensation then we speak of overcompensation.

The Individual psychology, as

207

does Freudian *psychoanalysis analyses the motives of conduct. The "Leitmotif" is here however not the sexuality but the passion for power.—P.S.

INDIVIDUALISM

Is the philosophical theory or conception, which considers the individual as that what is most essential in the order of reality or highest in the order of values, and it subordinates therefore the community to the individual. The community has indeed no own reality; it is nothing more than the sum of the individuals who compose it. The state, according to the doctrine of the Enlightenment, has its origin in a contract: the individuals abandon partially their liberty, to defend themselves in the state. Opposed to *universalism.

INDIVIDUATION

That what confers to a reality the characteristic of individuality. Beings of the same species, e.g., men, although they are the same for what their species is concerned, differ from each other because of their individuality. The first question which arises: can it here only concern numerical differences, as Thomas Aquinas thinks, or are they necessarily qualitative, as Joannes Duns Scotus considers the haecceitas, and also many others, as for instance Leibniz (identitas indiscernibilium), teach? Another metaphysical problem arises: Is there in such beings a *real* difference between the ground of the specific perfect and the ground of the individuality? Many thinkers answer in the negative, because the idea of species is the result of an abstraction process. There is a real basis, in the beings considered, for the logical distinction between that what is specific and that what is

individual, and which originates from it, but there is under no circumstance a corresponding real distinction. Thomas Aquinas, on the contrary, basing his answer on the answer he gave to the first question, answers affirmatively: the substantial *form, principle of specification, is correlatively connected with the prime *matter, purely potential principle which fullfills the role of *individuation-principle;* in the accidental order, there is then also a same correlation between the *quality, formprinciple, and the *quantity, accidental and individuating potency.—L.D.R.

INDIVISIBILITY

A distinction has to be made between *physical* and *mathematical* indivisibility. An atom can not be divided physically, although, in mathematics, it can be further divided, because it has *extension.

A distinction has also to be made between *absolute* and *relative* indivisibility. Relative indivisibility means that a thing can not further be divided in parts of the same sort as the whole. Absolute indivisibility is only had when no division at all is possible. An *atom is therefore relatively indivisible but not absolutely.

INDUCTION (Lat: in-ducere, lead in)

In broad sense every transition from the concrete-individual data of experience to abstract-absolute intellectual knowledge. In narrower sense a reasoning, in which from a sufficient number of particular cases (see enumeration) is concluded to a general thesis. As in *deduction (see syllogism) we have here generally two premises and a conclusion, but a real *middle-term is missing and is replaced by a sufficient number of cases, which are then considered as parts of a logical unity. We use daily inductions but logic is only concerned with scientific induction. Its own field is in the natural sciences. One can distinguish between the *real* induction, which teaches us something new, and the *apparent* induction, which is no more than a pure enumeration. The real induction is *illegal*, when it is not based on a "sufficient number" of cases (sufficient according to the nature of the newly discovered truth). The *legal* induction is, according to some, an *inauthentic* induction, when it is based on a complete enumeration (*complete* induction), and an *authentic* induction, when there is an incomplete, but still sufficient enumeration of cases (*incomplete* or scientific induction). See method. I.v.d.B.

To prove, that every natural number has a certain property E, one often uses this method. One proves: (A) the natural number o has the property E; (B) if n has the property E, then also n+1. One concludes then: (C) every natural number has the property E. That this *proof by complete induction* is valid can be explained as follows: according to (A) o has the property E; then also 1(=o+1), according to (B); then also 2 (=1+1), according to (B); etc. Related to this is the *proof by transfinite induction*. One demonstrates: (A) if there is no natural number smaller than k without the property E, then k has the property E. One concludes: (B) all natural numbers have the property E. If (B) were not valid, there would be natural numbers without the property E; among these natural numbers one is the smallest, let us say k. k would miss the property E, but there would not exist a smaller number without this property, contraction with (A). In this proof we utilize the fact that the ordering of the natural numbers is such that the series of natural numbers is either empty, or has a smallest element. In every series, whose ordering has this property, we can use the proof of transfinite induction. E.W.B.

INERTIA, Law of

Says that a body on which no outside forces work, persists in its position of rest or motion. This principle of the classical mechanics is in clear opposition to the idea of Aristotle that all motion stops by itself. See Impetus.

INFERENCE or illation

The resulting of one truth from another truth, which can not be true without the first one being true. See consequence.

INFINITESIMAL

See continuum.

INFINITY

Contrary of *finity. Infinity is therefore characterized by *unity and *absoluteness. The divine Being is in all respects infinite. Something can also be called infinite in a relative sense or under a certain aspect: e.g. the infinity in time and space; an angel, at least as he is conceived by Thomas Aquinas, unique in his species and therefore possessing completely, without limits, i.e. infinitely the perfection of his species; the series of numbers, which can indefinitely be continued and therefore potentially infinite.

This following question comes immediately to mind: would a complete and, in this sense, infinite order (which by definition would contain all actual and also all possible terms belonging to this order) always, sometimes or never consist of a number of terms which is countless and, in this other sense, infinite? (Would, for instance, space consist of a countless number of simultaneous places, time of an innumerable number of successive moments, the whole creation of a countless number of existing and possible creatures?) One can not determine a priori that in all these cases the answer should be the same.

Another question follows: is the unlimited-complete order of finite beings also unlimited-complete reality? A negative answer to this question can only make sense when one accepts that this order is only a relatively infinite order, namely if one accepts that there is an absolute-infinite Being or a transcendent Divinity. The reason is that, by definition, no other limited reality can exist outside of the complete order of the finite beings. This problem is certainly the most fundamental one in metaphysics. —L.D.R.

—As a divine attribute, infinity negates, in every respect, the limitation of positive perfection. Although the word expresses a negation, the thing for which it stands is very positive: the actual completeness of the divine esse and the divine perfection. This divine infinity does therefore not belong to any limiting category, and can not be compared with the mathematical infinity. It is also to be distinguished from the potential infinity; which consists of a never-ending process of becoming always more perfect. God's actual completeness is really and essentially different from the totality of the things in the world, and is therefore not a pantheistic infinity.

In the quantitative order infinity means only the absence of a quantitative limitation. One can again make the distinction between *actual* and *potential* infinity. It is in this sense possible to complete the series of natural numbers into infinity. The series of so obtained numbers does not actually exist: the infinity is only potential. An extensum, e.g. a line can be divided in infinity, since every partition produces other lines. The lines which are obtained are then not actually existing in an infinite number. Here again we have only a potential infinity.

In mathematics the terms infinitely big, infinitely small or infinitely far are often used. It means something which is smaller, bigger or farther than any arbitrary small or big value or arbitrarily far distance.—A.G.M.v.M.

—Systems of numbers can be called infinite, when it is not possible to characterize their °number by a natural number. The theory of the system of numbers enables us however to give a number to a system and even to determine this number by addition; in such operations one uses the transfinite induction which was found by Cantor.

INGE, William Ralph, 1860-1954

English philosopher, oriented towards neoplatonism, Plotinus-scholar. Defends a theistic metaphysics, which he especially studies in connection with the philosophy of religion and with a kind of neoplatonic view.

INGERSOLL, Robert Green 1833-1899

American agnostic who was a prolific and popular lecturer in the second half of the nineteenth century. Among his works: *Some Mistakes of Moses* (1879) and *Why I Am an Agnostic* (1896).

INNATE

Given with birth as a differentiating quality. It is broader than hereditary, which applies to what is transmitted from parent to child via the genes (potencies, dispositions). Innate is also what has been acquired between conception and birth. Contrary of *acquired. See also innate *idea, *inneism.

INNEISM

Doctrine that the human mind receives not at least some ideas from the *experience, but that these ideas are innate, in embryo, or are given to man with the human mind. The experience is then, at the most, an occasion for making the subject more conscious of the already existing ideas.—Plato explains this independence from the sensual experience through the survival of the soul; Descartes, Spinoza, Leibniz through an appeal to the nature of the mind itself.

INNER

What is situated inside something. The question is: in what thing? In connection with the humans relates to the inner psychic element as opposed to the physical element. Also what is naturally related to the consciousness as opposed to that which has also its own existence outside the consciousness. In psychodiagnostics: "inner are the problems which are inside the personality" as opposed to the conflicts with the outer-world.

INSTINCT

Originally "animal impulse." It it now used in many meanings; the less pure is the adjective form: instinctive. One can distinguish three kinds of meanings: (1) the biologically fixed way of knowing of man and animal; the parallel in inner life is the intuition. (2) the innate impulse to act with a triple aspect: the cognitive factor, conative factor, and the affective factor (Mc Dougall). The construction of

always new instincts has discredited the instinctpsychology. (L. Bernard has about 500 instincts to explain the different forms of behaviour). (3) The hereditary, biological disposition to act or these actions themselves, belonging to the passionsphere of the organism. We use for this kind of instinct now preferably the terms motive, striving, desire, need.

Going back to the regular meaning, we can define the instinct as the complex of dispositions to behaviours, which are innate and determinate and which are unchangeable in all individuals of a same species, to ordinate the adaptation to specific ends, without the cooperation of the consciousness. This definition puts a limit to the adaptability of this concept to the human behaviour. This behaviour has often an instinctive incentive, but surpasses, as human behaviour, immediately the determinism. Many instincts are indeed innate, but develop themselves only during the maturation.—P.S.

INSTRUMENTALISM

Doctrine that knowledge is an instrument in behalf of the acting. To direct his actions man projects hypotheses, whose truth value is determined by the measure in which they favor the action and show to be exact in the experienced effects. According to the founder of this doctrine, *Dewey, the action does not have to satisfy the emotional instincts of the individual, but the general-human needs. Instrumentalism is one of the forms of *pragmatism.

INTEGRATION

A biological concept, generally used in connection with *differentiation. When there is a greater complexity in form and function, there is also, in the living beings, a stronger tying together of the many parts and activities; this happens mostly through a stronger development of and control by the nerve system.

INTELLECT

Faculty of man to understand the beings i.e. to comprehend them in their essence. The Greek philosophers have already put next to the perception, by which we have access to the beings in their actuality, the intellect, through which we can catch what the beings are or seize their essence. We try however also to explain why they are and why they are what they are: we try to penetrate the grounds of being and essence of the beings, to their active cause, final cause. The human intellect does however not have a complete *intuition of the essence of the beings, but must through *abstraction catch something of the essence in *concepts (active or passive intellect). These concepts have a way of being which does not coincide completely with the way of being of the individual beings; they only express abstract aspects of the reality. We must therefore connect them with the concrete-existing, which is in the *judgment the subject of the predicates. The judgments however are also deficient; the human intellect must therefore, as reason, proceed by reasoning from judgment to judgment to arrive at a deeper insight. Our infinite intellect will however never reach on its own the perfect insight in the reality as a whole. — J.P.

Intellect is defined by experimental psychology as the ability to put a connection between the parts of our knowledge. If we hold that herefor abstraction and reflection are necessary, then we deny it, as a spiritual faculty of knowledge, to the animals. Intellect is often opposed to intelligence, analogous with intellectual as opposed to intelligent, and analogous with educated as opposed to gifted.

In thomistic philosophy: the knowledge which, surpassing the sensual knowledge, reaches towards objects which are independent from all material conditions. On the outside is the acting intellect (intellectus agens) the first activity of the intellect. It takes the sensual impressions, which are impotent against the immaterial intellect, and makes them actually knowable, by depriving them from their individual and concrete conditions, and elevates them in that way to the level of the immateriality. The passive intellect (intellectus passivus) is the real intellect, which accepts in itself the thoughts formed by the active intellect. This latter only poses the act of understanding or the act of intellectual knowledge. —P.S.

INTELLECTUALISM

Doctrine which underlines strongly the value of the human intellect and even over-estimates it. It is therefore the doctrine which teaches that the intellect is able to penetrate completely the reality or considers even the intellect as that what determines the reality (idealism); it is thus the doctrine which gives the primacy to the intellect, above feeling and will (as opposed to *voluntarism) or even wants to reduce the latter to pure moments of the intellect (Herbert); also the doctrine which teaches that the sufficient and necessary ground for moral actions is the intellectual understanding of that what is morally good (Socrates).

INTELLECTUS PRINCIPIORUM

The habitus with which, according to thomism, the intellect knows the first theoretical principles. Opposed to *synderesis.

INTELLIGENCE

The ability to adapt oneself to new situations (Stern). Older definitions call it the capacity to have an insight in two or more data of experience. Without defining more clearly the concept intelligence, some philosophers in America have formulated it (operationism): intelligence is that what we test. A so-called operative concept, by which we make the things more operational but not more discernible. The factor-analysis (Spearman) tried to isolate in mathematical sense the different elements with which the intelligence is composed. One can distinguish different sorts of (or facets of the) intelligence; theoretical, practical and social.

INTELLIGIBLE

Or knowable by the intellect, is the being inasmuch as it has a ground or reason of being, which reveals itself in the knowledge. In this way is the *intelligible world* the basis of explanation for what is given to us in the (sensory) experience. Extreme *realism tends to give this intelligible world its own reality (Plato), while *nominalism and *conceptualism cut the ties between the intelligible world and the beings and consider it only as a product of thought.

INTENSITY

The greater or smaller measure in which a quality is present in a body. This intensity can be measured by comparison with the same qualities in other bodies and by numbering the stronger or weaker presence of these qualities. For accurate measuring the quantitative effect of the quality is mostly used; e.g. the volume-expansion of a liquid by higher temperature (thermometer). As opposed to *extensive quantities, we can not make a sum of intensive quantities.

INTENT

The presented *content of an action. This is actually that moment which produces the action, i.e. the specific change in the reality, through which the value to which one strives is to be realized.

INTENTION

Of an action, is the meaning to which the acting subject strives in the completion of the action. It is *simple* when the meaning to which is strived corresponds to the meaning which the action as such has (e.g. when I steal to steal). In the opposite case it is *complex,* either because one meaning is subordinate to the other (e.g. I steal to enrich myself), or they are heterogeneous. The intention gives the form, so that the person who steals to commit adultery is an adulterer, more than a thief. Is it indeed not because of the intention that the *content of an action is realized? In the order of morality is the intention also decisive: next to the other moments, says Thomas Aquinas, but Kant says the intention is exclusively and completely decisive. But Kant considers the intention also more as the striving towards the value which will be realized in the action. See also resolution—J.Gr.

—In scholastic philosophy: fact that one being is directed towards another in order to complete or enrich it. More specifically, the fact that knowing and striving are directed towards their object, namely when this object differs from the object and has to be reached in a kind of tension. They contain the object intentionally. That what is known is intentionally present in the one who knows, the one who is loved in the one who loves. This *presence coincides indeed not with the real existence of the object in itself, but it is related with that real existence.

In connection with knowledge, the scholastics distinguish the intention prima (first intention) attention to an immediately or mediately given object, from the intention secunda (second intention) or the attention to the first intention as to an object: the reflexion on the intentional way of being of the known objects in the subject. The object of the second intention is an ens rationis, a being that is constituted by the relations between contents of thought as such; e.g. the logical arrangement of gender, species etc.

In connection with the striving, intention indicates especially the attention to an end that has to be realized through the means; also the intentio finis as opposed to the execution. The striving has indeed an intentional character, and is therefore motivated by the object; it is not purely an unfolding of the subjective situations.—J.P.

INTENTIONALITY
Indicates in the mediaeval philosophy the intentional character of knowledge and striving. Brentano and the *phenomenology made it the essential characteristic of the consciousness. The consciousness is thus not a subjective situation, as had been thought for a long time; it is always the consciousness of something. In other words, it contains essentially a certain aiming and relation to an object, this object can exist or not. In existentialism this intentionality seems to be the expression of the existence itself, which, as ex-sistence, is essentially directed towards the world.

INTERACTION
The phenomenon that when A influences B, B for that reason also influences A. — In psychology interaction means the mutual influencing of soul and body.

INTERCHANGEABILITY
See substitution.

INTERDICTION
A *commandment with negative content. An interdiction is actually made to oppose the inclinations which prevent man to submit himself to the moral law. The interdiction is therefore more a protection of the morality, rather than a positive promotion. See *duty, *obligation.

INTEREST
The spontaneous attention for an object which comes at the foreground. It is self-evident that this "inter-esse" (to be between) presupposes that the object has some meaning for the subject. Not only what presents itself as a source of advantages or pleasure has meaning, but all that touches man in one or another function. Because he is a thinking being, man is interested in the grounds which will explain why reality is as it is, or also in the forms in which reality shows itself; as an acting being he is interested in reality itself; either because reality is pursued for the enrichment of one's own being, or for its own goodness. Interest is therefore not the same thing as *self-interest: the interest can be selfish or not and is in fact mostly a gestalt of selfish and not-selfish elements. J.Gr.

214

INTERPRETATION (Lat. interpretatio, rendering; explicatio, unfolding; explanatio, explanation)

In general a clear enunciation, elucidation; it gives an answer to a further question about facts or things. A satisfactory interpretation happens through referring to previous and better known things: such an interpretation is for instance a *definition as compound concept for explaining a simple concept. In daily life one will often try to give an interpretation of something by building *analogies with that what the questioner knows.

The scientific interpretation, by *Dilthey opposed to the humanistic "understanding" (see science), tries to explain something by indicating its connection with other things, e.g. by giving the aim or intention of something, or by showing that something is the particular case of a general rule or empirical legality, which can then again be explained causally from one or other deducted law, and the latter finally from a basic law. Some modern students of the natural sciences reject this causal interpretation as being pre-scientific and they limit themselves to a pure but accurate description of the facts and their statistical assimilation, or to a so called constructive description from which namely other facts can be deduced and foreseen, and which therefore have some resemblance to a theory or hypothesis. —I.v.d.B.

INTERPRETATION, true—,

The true interpretation of a *formalism is given when we give such a *meaning to the symbols that the *assertions are true assertions. True interpretations can give more or less profound meanings.

INTERPRETATIONISM

Doctrine that man in the sensory perception has an immediate contact with what he perceives, but that he does not perceive that object according to the qualities which he gives to it on the grounds of the impression which received the perceiving organs from that object. Also *perceptionism, *conceptionism.

INTERPUNCTION

Is often used in modern *formalisms as the simple interpunction. It exists however only in a number of points; special rules determine the degree of interpunction. An interpunction accompanies a sign of operation and determines the expression on which the operation can be applied, this expression forms the *domain* of the interpunction.

INTERSUBJECTIVE

Valid for many subjects, as e.g. the science.

INTROJECTION

Originally a form of spiritual assimilation: the transition from objective data to subjective data. In psychoanalysis opposite to projection (transfer of one's own experience to the outer world): the unconscious acceptance of data of perception from the outer world in one's own personality. This is related especially to the psychic particularities of other persons (the parents for the child), which become then elements of the personality of the child ("psychic cannibalism"). For Szondi, the inner building of the ideals.

INTROSPECTION

Methodical process in the experimental psychology for the study of the psychic processes through their inner perception (School of Würzburg). The introspection had a very important role, but it encountered much opposition, because of its lack of objectivity and its unverifiable nature. The behaviourism developed a method based purely on extrospection (which can be perceived from the outside). On the other hand build the "verstehende" and phenomenological psychology in a certain sense on the subjective methods of the introspectionists.

INTUITION (Lat: intueri, to look at)

Knowledge by which, as in the vision, the object is immediately apprehended. It can be apprehended directly and completely, in what it is, or it can be apprehended in its concreteness. In the former the intuitive knowledge is opposed to the discursive, in the latter it is opposed to the abstract.

To be complete, the intuition (as opposed to the discursive knowledge) must actually create it's object, because, as long as this is not the case, it remains in a sense transparent. Intuitive is then in the first place the knowledge God has of Himself and of the world: possessing Himself completely He also apprehends Himself completely, as He looks into the world which He, thinking, creates. If the human consciousness can be intuitive in the same sense depends on the meaning which one gives to this consciousness. In any case Fichte gives to the Ego (but to what extent can this be identified with the empirical Ego?) an *intellectual intuition*, through which it comes into being as an Ego. It is the immediate consciousness that I act and "that" I act; here I know something because I produce it. According to Kant however, can the intuition in man only be sensual. It is therefore only through the senses that objects are given to man.

This limitation (which concerns also the inner structure of the intuition), is not accepted by everybody. Plato teaches that the ideas are directly and immediately seen, form which we can conclude that also the transcendental is an object of intuition. Some others defend the same thing in connection with the first principles of thought, the moral norms, the natural laws etc. . . . The *phenomenology, on the other hand, against Kant showed how, provided a particular attitude of the consciousness exists, the nature of what is present is not thought but seen. Here intuition is therefore also used in the sense of spiritual vision.

As opposed to abstract cognition intuition has an all-embracing character. The intuition of existence embraces all what in one or another manner, is, even if all the different aspects of existence are not explicitly shown. But the intuition gives a global knowledge of a limited object, before it is divided by the different cognitive functions, as thinking, feeling, perceiving etc. . . ,in different aspects. The intuition remains however susceptible of nuances. For Croce it is more the apprehension of the spiritual *in* the sensual; for Bergson it is a thought which is strongly affective and therefore opposed to the intellectual cognition. The intuition is as a "sympathie vécue," which helps us to penetrate much more easily the things. It is therefore the best instrument in philosophy.—J.Gr.

Forms of intuition, according to Kant, are *time and *space. They regulate all that is given through the vision. These forms of intuition are themselves not given, but, in this sense, a priori. See also a priori.

INTUITIONISM

Doctrine which gives to *intuition the main place in human cognition, generally at the expense of the *abstracting and *discursive cognition. — In mathematics, the school, inaugurated by *Brouwer, in the mathematical foundation research. It defends that the *existence of a mathematical entity with given properties, can only be proved by construction—taken in the sense of production. This has very important consequences. We can then try to remove the objections given under "existence" for the proof given under *"continuum," by giving an indirect argument, as follows. Suppose that the number A which was sought, was not there, there would then be no objection to divide all the real numbers in two series P and Q. Then would either P have a last or Q a first number. But we know already that P can not have a last number; and if Q had to have a first number, this number would have to be A, which does not exist, according to our supposition; this supposition is therefore absurd, and the number A must therefore exist. This argument is for Brouwer untenable, because there is no question about a generation of A; but on the other hand accepts Brouwer that the non-existence of A is refuted. On the grounds of the principle of the excluded third (middle) we can conclude from the absurdity of the non-existence of A to the existence of A, and this principle must also be rejected by Brouwer.—E.W.B.

INVENTION

Or modus inventionis, form of reasoning, through which a new truth is found; is opposed to the *proof or modus iudicii, in which a truth is judged. Also the fact of finding a medium in a syllogism.

INVERSE

Of a relation is the relation which exists between y and x if the original relation between x and y exists. "Bigger than" is the inverse of "smaller than"; equal "is its own inverse.

IRENAEUS OF LYON

Born ca. 140 in Asia Minor, bishop of Lyon where he died martyr ca. 202. Was the main opponent to gnosticism in his famous work, written in Greek but of which only the Latin translation reached us: *Adversus heareses.*

IRONY

More sharp form of the subjective *comic, very close to wit. In the irony, wit directs itself, with a kind of playful hostility, to the person who is its object. We can distinguish these main forms: 1) an ironic structure in which *qualities* are ascribed to the victim, which it, in fact, does not have, but this does not show until, because of the growing emphasis and generosity one puts in describing these qualities, the absence of the qualities is suddenly seen and the subject, who accepted them eagerly, is now in a shameful situation. 2) a structure, in which the real value of a victim is praised, but for *reasons* which are not real, so that in the sudden realization of the groundlessness of the reasons, also the groundlessness of the value is accepted. Irony loses its esthetic character, as soon as it loses its playfulness and turns to real hostility. An extreme form of this irony is *sarcasm.*

IRRATIONAL

Is a form of thought which withdraws in a certain sense from reason. This term can be used in many different nuances.

IRRATIONALISM

Doctrine according to which reason would not be able to explain reality, either because other faculties and namely the feeling are the fundamental source of knowledge, or because reality originates in a not rational source: e.g. from the irrational will (Schopenhauer) or from the Absolute (Schelling). Some writers underline the irrationalism of the contemporary *existenz-philosophy, which does indeed not use the traditional forms of thought.

ISAAC OF STELLA

Cistercian, born in England, abbot of l'Etoile (Stella) in France, 1147-1169. Wrote a treatise, in form of letters, about the soul. (*Epistola . . . de anima*) directed to Alcher of Clairvaux who wrote a similar treatise. It is a resumé of the augustinian doctrine about the soul (higher and lower part of the soul, through the lower part union with the body; higher faculties: intellectus, intelligentia, directed towards the immaterial beings and God) with aristotelian elements (the senses know the particular, reason knows the one real, doctrine of abstraction). In his sermons also proofs of the existence of God as super-independent being.

ISOCRATES 436-338 B.C.

Skilled Greek orator and author of pamphlets on philosophical and political subjects. Attacked the Sophists and advocated peace among the Greek states.

ISODORUS OF SEVILLA

Born ca. 560, died 636, archbishop of Sevilla, author of an encyclopedia (*Etymologiarum libri XX*) through which he introduced many elements of the culture of Antiquity into the Middle Ages.

ISOMORPHIC

Or ordinally *homogeneous are two relations between which an ordinal correlator exists.

ISRAELI, Isaac c. 850-950

Famous physician and founder of a medical school, his treatises were later used as textbooks in early European universities. Principal work: *Kitab al Istiksat* (Arabic), translated into Hebrew as *Sefer Hayesodoth* and into Latin as *De Elementis*.

ISVARAKRSNA Fifth Century A.D.

The name of Isvarakrsna is connected with the *Samkya Karika*, probably the oldest of the six traditional systems of Indian philosophy, which inspired Buddha about a century later.

J

J-LOGIC
See Logic, systems of formal—.

JACOBI, Friedrich Heinrich
Born in Düsseldorf 1743, died in München 1819. Follower of the *Glaubensphilosophie. Attacked Spinoza and Kant, and thinks that only "belief" can overcome the mechanism, materialism and atheism to which the doctrine of the former leads, and complete idealism, to which the criticism of the latter must arrive. Belief, is for Jacobi the immediate feeling of certitude without intellectual grounds.

JACOBY, Gunther
Born 1881, German metaphysicist: *Allgemeine Ontologie der Wirklichkeit*, 1925.

JAMBLICHI
See Anonymous Jamblichi.

JAMBLICHUS
3rd-4th century A.D., died ca. 330, originally from Chalcis in Coelesyria, disciple of *Porphyry, founder of the Syrian school of *neo-platonism, the same tendency as we find in *Amelius, to multiply the supra-sensual hypostases and so to remove still further the Absolute from the world of experience: above the One he places the absolute Primitive Being, who transcends all oppositions and can not be expressed in qualities; Jamblichus adopted in his system as much as he could Greek and Oriental elements; he is also important for the neoplatonic exegesis of the dialogues of Plato.

JAMES, William, 1842-1910.
Son of Henry James, American psychologist and philosopher, founder of the pragmatism, professor at Harvard. Main works: *The Varieties of religious experience* (Gifford-Lectures), 1902; *Pragmatism*, 1907; *The Meaning of Truth*, 1909; *Essays in radical Empiricism*, 1912. According to James a concept or judgment is true, when it is manageable, in other words when it is active. A not active judgment is false. Truth is a quality of concept or judgment, not of the things themselves. A concept or judgment is not only true when it proves it's meaning for the physical existence, but also when it is active in the fields of science, art or religion. The world itself is, without any doubt, real, but the reality is tied to nothing, is consists of many separate beings, which are always in motion and evolution. The "radical empiricism", which James holds, wants to follow the continuously changing relation between the things in their moving evolution. Spirit and matter, psyche and nature are the two aspects under which the one, but always variable reality shows itself to us. James is a deeply religious thinker, who has always much attention for the problems of psychology and the philosophy of religion.—B.D.

JANET, Pierre, 1859-1947.
French psychologist and philosopher.

JASPERS, Karl
(1883-1969) German existense-philosopher, professor in Heidelberg and later in Basel. Main works: *Philosophie*, 1932; *Von der Wahrheit*, 1947. Jaspers makes a distinction between *world orientation* (Weltorientierung); *elucidation of existence* Existenzerhellung) and *metaphysics*. Every elucidation of existence requires a world orientation and metaphysics is only possible on the grounds of world orientation and elucidation of existence. World orientation happens in the positive sciences. Study of the positive sciences is a necessary condition for the study of philosophy. One reaches hereby the limits of the positive sciences. Many problems arise which can not be answered by the science concerned, but which still require a further investigation.

The elucidation of the existence put us from the beginning before philosophical problems. Firstly: what is existence? It is the realization of oneself in the world and it is therefore, at the same time, going beyond this world. There is possible and real existence. The possible existence is the whole of the conditions, by which the real existence can originate; real existence is however limited to the rare moments in which man can completely transcend himself. The possible existence is not a general thing, as the positive sciences. The existence has to be realised by each one in its own particular way. Philosophy can only indicate the generally necessary conditions. The existence is, on the first place, always *geschichtlich*, i.e. every man is determined by the situation in which he lives. This situation is for each man different. But no man can be satisfied by a pure domination of his situation. The question of existence is especially forceful when man is in one of the border situations, i.e. when he is confronted with struggle, guilt, suffering or death. Then he inquires about the sense of his existence. This happens in *communication*. Man is naturally directed towards the other. Only in communication with the other man do I penetrate the most profound questions about myself.

We enter then in metaphysics. Metaphysics analyses the transcendence of man above the world and himself. This transcendence happens when man really exists. It can happen in different ways. The formal transcendence is the thinking transcendence of that what can be thought. It is the intellect itself which compels us to transcend that what can be thought. Then I come to myself in the border situation and discover that I have a relation to the transcendental, i.e. to that what transcends man and world. I can then transcend, when thinking by means of symbols (chiffren), in which man, in the course of history, has laid down his transcending. I have then to understand the language used by myths and religion. The transcendental itself can not be said, but it can be indicated by the term God. The idea of God evolutes by Jaspers more and more in a theistic sense. Also of central importance is Jaspers' idea of the *Umgreifend* (embracing), which he sees present in different ways. Umgreifend, is firstly the Ego itself. This expresses itself already in life as such, but it shows better when The Ego is seen as consciousness, as spirit and finally as existence. Umgreifend is also the "esse", that shows itself as world and also as transcendence. The connection between all these forms of the Umgreifende is put in us by the intellect (*Vernunft*). Jaspers is more and more interested in showing that his thought is in no way an irrationalism, but a rational philosophy, which comes as such in contact with what surpasses the reasonable. His thought is an appeal (*Appell*) directed to man to realise his existence. This existence is to be grasped at once and not in preconceived categories. One can however distinguish several attitudes to life, the most important distinction between these attitudes is based on the distinction between philosophical and religious attitude. One can not be at the same time christian and philosopher. One has to choose. This does however not exclude the fact that christianity and philosophy need each other: one can not stay pure without the other.—B.D.

JEANS, James Hopwood, 1877-1946.
English astronomer and physicist, noted especially for his works popularizing new advances in science. Among his works: *Theoretical Mechanics* (1906), *Radiation and the Quantum-Theory* (1914), *The Stars in Their Courses* (1931), *Through Space and Time* (1934).

JEFFERSON, Thomas, 1743-1826.
Third President of the United States, he wanted his tombstone to read: "Author of the Declaration of American Independence, of the Statute of Virginia for Religious Freedom, and Father of the University of Virginia." His political philosophy is still espoused by American economists, politicians and voters.

JEWISH PHILOSOPHY

One can not find a pure philosophy in the Jewish writings (neither a systematical construction: there is always a certain lack of order). There is only a judaizing philosophy: application and adaptation of the Western (Greek) philosophy to the data of the Jewish religion. The first period belongs really to the Greek philosophy: Aristobulus (2nd century B.C.), Philo (died 1st century). The second period in the Middle Ages, with a few precursors in the Talmud-literature, is mostly developed under the influence of the Arabic philosophy and mostly written in Arabic. It is the flourishing-time of the Jewish philosophy. There are two branches in this period: the real philosophy and the mysticism (which uses many neoplatonic and other themes of the philosophy). A diverging school is the one of the Karaites, anti-rabbinic and anti-traditionalistic. Still more divergent was the case of some "heretics" as Hayyawaih of Balkh (9th century).

The evolution of the real philosophy of the orthodox Judaism goes from the neoplatonism to a kind of aristotelianism, which remains however always in the shadow. The period of preparation is theological and is parallel with the Arabic kalam (see Arabic philosophy). The first main figure is *Saadia of Fayyumi* (882-942) contemporary of Asari (see Arabic philosophy) and opponent of Razi (Arabic phil.) but himself influenced by Mu'tazila. About at the same time lived *David ben Marwan a-Moqammes*, also influenced by the Arabic kalam. More systematic philosophy is found in the works of the neoplatonists *Isaac Israeli* (860-950) and especially *Salomon ibn Gabirol* (see Avencebrol) about 1020-1050.

221

In the same period lived *Bahya ibn Paqouda* (11th century) whose work is more ascetic, but still continues the rationalistic religious conception of Saadia. Other neoplatonic authors are: the anonymous author of a Book about the soul (doctrine of the emanation, survival); Abraham bar Kiyya (12th cent.) who taught a kind of doctrine of the original sin (christian influence); Joseph ibn Saddiq (died 1149) who is very dependent on Avicebron; Abraham ibn Ezra (±1092-1167). More independent is Juda Halevi (±1085-1140) who depends, in his somewhat fideistic thesis, on Algazel's criticism on the philosophy. (The *Liber de Causis* is perhaps also a Jewish work)—The more aristotelian (Avicennian) trend is expressed in the work of *Abraham ibn Daud* (died ca. 1180) namely in the proofs of the existence of God and the psychology. The great figure is *Moses Maimonides* (1135-1204). In the works of his disciples and later, we find a greater influence of Aristotle because of the translations and commentaries of Averroes, so that one can speak of a Jewish averroism. *Hillel ben Samuel* (12th cent.) comments especially on the intellect-doctrine of Averroes, uses the criticism of Thomas Aquinas, and tries to find a middle way. *Isaac Albalag* (13th cent.) teaches the doctrine of the double truth. *Lev ben Gerson* (1288-1344) follows the averroistic aristotelianism, but rejects the externity of the universe; he accepts the one intellectus agens and has an unclear explanation for the personal immortality. *Moses ben Nahman* (ca. 1270) is rather a reaction against intellectualism. *Hasdai Crescas* (±1340-1410) criticizes severely Aristotle's physics and rationalism (God is goodness and will; the origin of things is voluntaristic.) He is the last great figure of the Middle Ages. Of less importance are Simon Duran (1361-1444), Joseph Albo (died 1444), Elia del Medigo (died 1493), Isaac Abrabanel (1437-1509), Leone Ebreo (ca. 1460-1521); Joseph Sal. del Medigo (1591-1655) and others. The third period belongs again to the general Western philosophy with figures as Spinoza, Mendelssohn, Cohen etc.

The *mystical* (gnostic and neoplatonic) *tendency* starts already with the allegories of Philo and the cosmological speculations of the Talmud-literature and the Jewish gnostic sects. One of the earliest documents is the Book of the Creation (Sefer Yetsira, between the 3rd and 4th cent.). This trend was especially strong under the name of the so called Kabbala, of which the most important figures are *Abraham Abulafia* of Saragossa (1240-after 1291), *Joseph Gikatila* (1248-1305) and others, and the main books, the Bahir (12th cent.), the Zohar (end of 13th cent.). Next to it there was the more ascetic and social school of the German *Hassidim* (12th-13th cent.). After its expulsion from Spain, the Kabbala became more apocalyptic and messianistic in the Orient (Moses Cordovero, Isaac Luria, Vidal Calabrese), and heretic sects were founded such as the sect of Sabbataï Zevi (1625-1676) who became a Moslem. The last mystical form is the new Hassidism of *Israel Baal Shem* (died 1760). Philosophers as M. Mendelssohn and S. Maimon reacted against it as representatives of the "enlightened rationalism." The kabbalistic ideas had some influence on christian thought already on Raymundus

Lullus (1325-1315) and later in the Renaissance.—J.V.

JOACHIM OF FIORE

Born in Italy 1145, died in Fiore (Calabria) 1202, Cisterican abbot, author of several works on the Bible, especially known for his theology of history, in which he distinguishes three periods: the era of the Father (O.T.), of the Son (N.T.) and of the Holy Ghost, whose arrival he predicts, and also the reformation of the Church. This last era will be the definitive period of the "Eternal Gospel." In the 13th century the spiritualists (the radical faction of the Franciscans) considered the work of Francis of Assisi the realisation of the prophecy of Joachim of Fiore.

JOAD, Cyril, E.M. 1891-1953.

English neo-realistic philosopher, professor in London, wrote for a broad audience.

JOANNES A. S. THOMA, O.P.

Born in Lisbon 1589, died in Fraga 1644. Spanish philosopher and theologian, one of the main figures in the revival of Spanish thomism. In many essential problems he opposes Suarez by asserting that the human intellect can only know, indirectly and incompletely the individual material things. He opposes also Molina's conception of the connection between human freedom and the fact that God is cause of everything. He differs from Thomas Aquinas because he sees the essence of God in the understanding. In other problems he follows Thomas Aquinas faithfully.

JOANNES BURIDANUS

Born in Béthune, died shortly after 1358, magister artium in Paris for 25 years; leader of the ockhamists in Paris. His *nominalism was moderate; disapproved the phenomenalism and atomism of *Nicholas of Autrecourt. As a physicist he had a main role in the liberation of the experimental physics from the oppression of the Aristotelian physics.

JOANNES CAPREOLUS

Born in Rodez (France) ca. 1380, died there 1444, Dominican, studied in Paris and taught in Toulouse. Obtained the title *Princeps Thomistarum* because of his main work: *Libri IV defensionum theologiae divi Thomae de Aquino.*

JOANNES DE JANDUNO

Ca. 1280-1328, magister artium in Paris till 1326, friend of Marsilius of Padua, with whom he composed the *Defensor Pacis* against John XXII, and with whom he fled in 1326 to Louis of Bavaria. Founder of Latin *Averroism in Paris, left many commentaries on Aristotle, inspired by Averroes; called himself the "ape of Averroes and Aristotle."

JOANNES DUNS SCOTUS

Born in Scotland between 1263-66, died in Cologne 1308. Franciscan in 1281, studied in Cambridge, Oxford and perhaps in Paris (1292-97), taught in Oxford from 1297-1302, taught the *Sententiae* in Paris from 1302 until 1304, promoted to magister in 1305; returned in 1306 probably to Oxford and was sent in 1308 to Cologne, where he died the same year. *Doctor subtilis.* Main works: *Quaestiones in Metaphysicam, De primo principio,* and especially his commentary on the *Sententiae,* of which many redactions have been saved and the most important of these are: *Opus Parisiense* (or *Reportata Parisiana*) and *Opus Oxoniense* (or *Ordinatio*), i.e. the text prepared for publication by Scotus himself; he never finished his redaction; it was continued after his death by his disciples, which gives us quite a lot of difficulties to reconstruct the original text. Four volumes of the critical edition of the *Opera Omnia* have been published since 1950.

Joannes Duns Scotus is one of the most subtle minds in the history of philosophy, and he had the opportunity to apply his precocious genius on the end of the brilliant period of scholasticism, so that his critical work investigates the ideas of the second half of the 13th century. The criticism which he had for thomism for instance, is very important, but the line of his thought is difficult to follow, not only because of the state of the texts which came to us, but also because of the succinct and even obscure style. He underwent the influence of many predecessors, and he can therefore not be put in one definite school; from the pagans he took much from Aristotle and Avicenna, and because of this influence his doctrine was in many aspects different from that of the franciscan and augustinian schools. In some other respect is his thought often the result of the franciscan thought of the 13th century and especially of the neoaugustinism, founded by John Packhamn, edited by William of Mare and illustrated by such masters as Henry of Ghent and the English Franciscan Roger Marston. On the basis of these sources, Joannes Duns Scotus has built a strong and personal synthesis.

Main trends in Scotism:

1. *Epistemology.* In the beginning point of the abstraction exists an intellectual intuition of the concrete, which reaches loosely the individual definiteness of the object (*haecceitas*); it is the work of the abstracting intellect to make this intuition explicit. The formal object of the intellect is the "esse," and the concept of being is "univocal." Thanks to this fact the human intellect is able to know realities which transcend the bodies and especially the infinite Being. Duns Scotus underlines thus the immediate realism and the metaphysical realism of Thomas.

2. *Metaphysics.* Duns Scotus tries to give a solution to the problem of the essential structure of the finite beings, which was very much discussed in the 13th century, by the famous *distinctio formalis a parte rei,* which is a link between the real and logical distinction. It is however not clear what kind of distinction exists between this distinction and the virtual logical distinction (*cum fundamento in re*). Whatever it may be, Duns Scotus uses this formal distinction to solve many problems. All real distinction between essence and existence is rejected. Primitive matter is not only capacity and God could let it exist without any form. The principle of individuation is not matter, but *haecceitas,* i.e. the last *formalities* by which an individual distinguishes himself from another individual of the same species. We can know God thanks to the univocal concept of being: God's existence can be proved a posteriori and also a priori (Duns Scotus tries to give an acceptable meaning to Anselm's ontological proof of the existence of God). Infinity is God's metaphysical essence. i.e. his fundamental attribute.

3. *Psychology.* As does the entire franciscan School, Duns Scotus underlines the importance of the autonomous and active character of the will as opposed to the cognition (see voluntarism), as a reaction against the aristotelian intellectualism; in all possible occasions

he shows the excellence of the will. The spiritual soul is the form of the body, but this latter is already composed by the matter and the *forma corporeitatis.* The immortality of the soul can only be indicated, with probability.—F.V.S.

JOANNES ECKEHART

Born in Hochheim near Gotha ca. 1260, died in Cologne 1327. Became Dominican, was in 1300 in Paris as *baccalaureus sententiarius* and obtained the licentiate in Rome (1302). He held high office in the order of the Dominicans in Germany and Bohemia, was perhaps magister regens in Paris from 1311-14 and taught afterwards in Cologne. In 1326 he was accused of heresy by the bishop of Cologne. In 1327 he appealed to the pope, but died the same year, so that the condemnation by John XXII came after his death. On March 27, 1329 this Pope condemned 27 theses drawn from Eckehart's works. Eckehart wrote in Latin and German, he was very erudite and was influenced in many ways by Albert the Great and Thomas Aquinas, but he used still more the neo-platonic sources: Proclus, Pseudo-Dionysius, Joannes Scotus Eriugena. He was a deep thinker and a great contemplative, he brought in words, but using in paradoxal and equivocal formulas, the souverain perfection of God, the contingency of the creatures and the unity of the soul with God in the mystical life. Some honored him as the representative of the neo-platonic pantheism, while others venerated him as the founder of the German orthodox mysticism. The national socialism greeted him as one of the creators of the true German idea, and began a popular edition of his works. The critical edition, partly published, will help us to describe his doctrines more clearly.

JOANNES FIDENZA

See Bonaventura.

JOANNES OF BACONTHORP

Born in England ca. 1280, died 1348, Carmelite, studied in Paris ca. 1320, taught in Cambridge and Oxford, in 1327 provincial of England. *Doctor resolutus.* Wrote worthwhile commentaries on Aristotle, Augustin, Anselm and Petrus Lombardus; critical and independent mind; followed Averroes where he was not opposed to the christian doctrine. Nifo (16th century) considered him the best interpreter of the Arabic philosopher (*princeps averroistarum*).

JOANNES OF BASSOLES

Died in 1347, French Franciscan, wrote a commentary on the *Sententiae* (published in 1617), disciple of J. Duns Scotus.

JOANNES OF DAMASCUS

Born in Syria 7th century, died in Palestine 749, author of an important work *Born of the knowledge*, which has an introduction to the philosophy, a history of the heresies, a systematic explanation of the theology, which is a real summa of the conceptions of the Greek Fathers of the Church. This latter part was translated in the 12th century into Latin (*De fide orthodoxa*) and was one of the main Greek sources for the western theologians. In philosophy Joannes of Damascus based his doctrine mainly on Aristotle (via Nemesius of Emesa) and on *Platonism.

JOANNES OF GERSON
(Jean Charlier)

Born in Gerson (Champagne) 1362, died in Lyon 1428, magister in the theology in Paris in 1392, disciple of Petrus of Ailly, became afterwards chancellor of the University (1395), dean of the chapter of Bruges (1397-1401). Had an important role in the council of Constance (1414) that put an end to the great schism, was as philosopher a more moderate ockhamist than Petrus of Ailly; as mystical theologian he followed the augustinian tradition, especially against the school of St. °Victor and °Bonaventura. He saw a danger for pantheism in the doctrine of Ruusbroec.

JOANNES OF MIRECOURT

Cistercian, explained the *Sententiae*, in 1345, at the College of St. Bernard in Paris; in his commentary 63 suspicious theses were found, and in spite of his defense 40 of these theses were condemned by the chancellor of the university. His criticism degenerated into a nearly complete scepticism and agnosticism; on the other hand he defended the divine determinism of °Thomas Bradwardine.

JOANNES OF RUPELLA
(de la Rochelle)

Died 1245, Franciscan ca. 1230, magister regens in Paris from 1238 or 41 to 1245, author of a *Summa de anima* and other works. Disciple of °Alexander of Hales, and promoter of the *Summa universae theologiae*, known as the *Summa Fr. Alexandri*, but greatly composed by Joannes of Rupella. He made an eclectical aristotelianism serve theology.

JOANNES OF SALISBURY

Born in England, ca. 1110, died in Chartres 1180. Studied in Chartres and Paris, one of the most cultivated men of his time. He travelled a good deal and became bishop of Chartres in 1176. Main works: *Entheticus de dogmate philoso-*

phorum (introduction to the doctrine of the philosophers), essay of a history of the ancient philosophy, followed by a philosophical poem; *Metalogicus,* about dialectic; *Polycraticus,* remarkable treatise about political philosophy.

JOANNES PECKHAM

Born in England before 1235, died in Mortlake 1292, Franciscan, magister regens in Paris (1269-71) and in Oxford (1271-75), lector at the pontifical curia ca. 1277, archbishop of Canterbury in 1279; faithful disciple of Bonaventura and prolific author; opposed to the renovations of Thomas Aquinas; can be considered as the founder of the neo-Augustianism, founded to set a limit to the influence of Thomism. As archbishop he continued accusing the Thomism of the English Dominicans. In 1284 and 1286 he condemned their theses.

JOANNES PHILOPONUS

Born at the end of the 5th century, died in the first half of the 6th century, grammarian in Alexandria, monophysite, commentator on Aristotle and Porphyry, also influenced by Platonism and stoicism. In the Middle Ages known under name of *Joannes Grammaticus.*

JOANNES SCOTUS ERIUGENA

Born in Ireland between 800-815, died in France ca. 877. Descended from the Irish branch (Eriugena) of the Scottish nation (Scotus), he went to France where he went into the service of Charles the Bald. ca. 850 he taught at the palatial School in Paris. Because of his interference in the theological dispute about the predestination, he came in conflict with his superiors. He had learned Greek in an Irish monastery and in 858 he began the translation of the writings of the °Pseudo-Dionysius, on which he later wrote a commentary. Main work: *De divisione naturae,* composed between 862-866 in the form of a dialogue between master and disciple. This work has been considered as a peculiar continuation of the pagan neoplatonism in the middle of the christian Middle Ages and the historians ascribed to Joannes Scotus Eriugena a monistic and pantheistic conception of the universe. The falsity of this interpretation has been definitely proved by the studies of the sources of *De divisione,* which are all christian: especially Pseudo-Dionysius and Augustin. This work is in fact a speculative theological synthesis in which the author wants absolutely to bring the data of the Revelation under neo-platonic schemata, without sometimes being concerned, with the literal meaning of the catholic doctrine; this is surely a proof of rationalism. The title of the work could be translated as: "About the differentiation of the real": the author wants to prove how reality, from the unity of God, multiplies itself and is made intricate through the participation, to find its unity again in the reunification with it's Origin. He distinguishes between four successive levels in the reality: God in His eternal and inaccessible perfection *(natura quae non creatur et creat);* God who expresses himself in the world of the ideas, exemples or prototypes of the things *(natura quae creatur et creat;* this world is very much related to the Logos, which is also described by S. Paul as the Image or the Idea of the Father); thirdly God who expresses himself in the created world, i.e. our universe, which is a theophany *(natura quae creatur et non creat);* finally God as final end, who takes things up in his unity *(natura quae*

nec creatur nec creat).—The vision of Eriugena recalls the ideal of S. Paul: "that God be: everything in all" (1 Cor. 15, 28). We have here a theocentric conception of the universe, still more than with Augustin or even Pseudo-Dionysius; as in the works of these thinkers, we find in Eriugena a philosophy of the participation. The *De Divisione* is a great but obscure work, because the expression of the author is still awkward and inadequate. Therefore his daring formulation, which led his disciples in the Middle Ages astray, as well as his first biographers.—F.V.S.

JOANNES TAULER

Born in Strassburg ca. 1300, died there 1361, Dominican, studied in Cologne and was one of the greatest preachers of the Middle Ages. His mystical theology, although influenced by Eckehart, is completely orthodox.

JODL, Friedrich, 1849-1914.

German positivistic philosopher.

JOHNSON, Samuel, 1696-1772.

American idealistic philosopher, influenced by Berkeley.

JOHNSON, Samuel, 1709-1784.

English writer and eminent figure of his time. Author of a unique dictionary and *Lives of the Poets,* but now best known through the work of his biographer, James Boswell.

JOHNSON, William Ernest, 1858-1931.

English philosopher, specialist in logic.

JOLIVET, Regis

Born 1891, French neo-thomistic philosopher, professor in Lyon. He has an important place in French Thomism. He wrote systematical and historical studies. Jolivet is convinced that modern Thomism has much to learn from the contemporary philosophy, among others from the *existential philosophy, but that these philosophies can also learn from Thomism. He had an important role in the dispute about christian philosophy.

JONSON, Ben, 1573-1637.

Elizabethan playwright, known principally for his satiric comedies, *Volpone* (1605), *Every Man In His Humour* (1599); also the composer of critical essays on the life of his time.

JOSCELLINUS OF SOISSONS

Died 1151, disciple of P. Abaelard, probably the author of *De generibus et speciebus*.

JOSEPH, H. W. B. 1867-1946.

English critical realist, professor at Oxford.

JOUBERT, Joseph, 1754-1824.

French moralist in the style of Montaigne and La Rochefoucauld, he preferred an Epicurean aestheticism to more traditional ethical concerns; he was also remarkable as a psychologist of morbidity.

JUDA HALEVI

Born in Castile ca. 1080, died 12th cent.; Jewish poet and thinker, attacked the Greek philosophy because of religious convictions, as did Algazel with the Arabs.

JUMP, LOGICAL

A formal *paralogism or *sophism: a fault in the form or structure of a *syllogism, so that the *consequence is lacking. E.g. the vicious *circle and the *post hoc, ergo propter hoc.

JUSTICE

One of the four cardinal virtues or virtue containing all virtues. Justice, holding the middle between doing injustice and suffering injustice, is an attitude which gives everybody what belongs to him. Justice as virtue is, in other words, the will to realize justice, i.e. to give each human being what he deserves according to the positive and natural right. With Aristotle we divide Justice in *commutative* and *distributive* justice. The latter is exercised by the authorities in the repartition of pleasures and duties according to the merits of each; the former on the contrary exists in the equality of the commodities of exchange or the equivalence of the mutual obligations in contracts. As such it excludes the intervention of a third party, while this intervention is the condition for the distributive justice.

JUSTINUS

Born in Flavia Neapolis (Samaria) ca. 100, died as martyr in Rome ca. 166, Greek apologist, converted from platonism to christianity, author of the *Dialogue* with Trypho and two apologies of christianity.

K

KAFKA, Gustav, 1883-1953.
German psychologist and historian of the philosophy, professor in Wurzburg.

KALLEN, Horace Mayer, 1882-
German-born educator who came to America as a child and eventually became professor of philosophy at New York's New School for Social Research. Interested especially in civil rights, freedom of conscience and the rights of labor. Works: *The Liberal Spirit* (1948), *The Education of Free Men* (1950).

KANT, Immanuel
Born in Königsberg 1724, died there 1804, founder of the °criticism, critical or transcendental idealism. Born from a simple family, educated in the spirit of pietism, studied in Königsberg, was private tutor (1755) and professor (1770) there.

In the first period of his activities, he studied natural sciences and natural philosophy in the spirit of Newton and Wolff; then followed a sceptical period under the influence of Hume, and he lost then the confidence in the traditional metaphysics; the third period, the critical one, started with the publication of the *Kritik der reinen Vernunft* (1781, 2nd edition 1787); in this period he wrote his most important works, among others: *Kritik der praktischen Vernunft* (1788), *Kritik der Urteilskraft* (1790) and *Die Religion innerhalb*

der Grenzen der Blosen Vernunft (1793).

In the K.d.r.V. Kant wants to establish the conditions from which depend the possibilities of absolute and necessary knowledge. This problem is changed into the question about the possibility of physical and mathematical sciences, to which such a knowledge is certainly due, but for which he wants to lay the epistemological foundation, and still examining the question if metaphysics, as a general and necessary knowledge of an extra-intellectual reality, is possible.

Against the empiricism of his day Kant objects that it, by sticking to the individual in concrete, can not guarantee the possibility of a general and necessary knowledge. Against rationalism he objects that it can not realize the transition between the order of cognition to the order of being. He therefore uses a middle way and assumes with empiricism that our knowledge goes no further than the phenomena, so that metaphysical knowledge of a reality outside of ourselves is absolutely excluded. He agrees with the rationalists that the knowledge derives its character of generality and necessity from the ability of knowledge only, independent from the experience. Ability of knowledge is however for him not a real ability of the human mind, but the inclusion of the synthetic functions of our cognition by means of elements a priori (i.e. independent from the experience given in the subject itself).

The main principle in Kant's epistemology is therefore, that we only know of the things that what we ourselves award to it, through the form-giving function of our ability to know. He persistently teaches the real existence of a world outside our consciousness (realism in ontology), but it remains for us a secret what this outer-world is in itself, independent from our cognition: the *Ding an sich* is and remains for us the unknown x.

The phenomena originate in a synthesis of the impressions from outside, which activate the ability of knowing without determining it, with the a-priori sensual ability of knowledge of space and time.

The experience as such is possible only through the knowledge of the intellect. This originates in the synthesis of the phenomena, as physical, indetermined element, and the a priori intellectual forms of knowledge or categories, as formal, determining element. The result of this synthesis are the synthetic propositions a priori, propositions which enlarge our knowledge and are at the same time general and necessary and in which our entire scientific knowledge is taken up.

As conditions for the possibility of such a knowledge, the categories are called "constitutive"; the world of experience and its laws are constituted by the knowledge which they form, but they will not lead us behind the limits of the experience.

The knowledge of the reason, finally, originates in the synthesis of the synthetic propositions a priori with the three ideas a priori, and the result is: the three "Vernunfteinheiten" or "Noumena," the soul, the world, God. The ideas are called "regulative" as conditions for the ordering of our knowledge as a whole; they indicate how we can explain the phenomena; as if they formed a coherent whole and were based on the absolute. The "Vernunfteinheiten" are purely unities in our thought; they do not inform us at all about the real existence or the positive possibility of the world, of the soul, of God. When man gives way to the "transcendental semblance" or the natural impulse to relate his knowledge to the things outside him, then he necessarily falls into paralogisms or contradictions.

Highest and final condition for the validity of theoretical knowledge is found in the "transcendental apperception," i.e. the connection of the given representations in the unity of consciousness. This is necessary if a subject wants to know an object; on the other hand nothing could become, without it, the object of knowledge. The synthetical unity of consciousness has however no metaphysical or psychological meaning: it is a pure idea.

The practical knowledge is for Kant more important than the theoretical knowledge. It opens the way to the noumen and the metaphysical, which can not be reached by the theoretical knowledge and which delivers the certitude on a-logical grounds, which logical knowledge can not reach.

Kant's ethics, especially described in the *K.d.pr.V.* and the *Metaphysik der Sitten*, is purely formal: human action is according to its object or content completely indefinite; it receives its ethical character only through the formgiving of the practical reason or the reasonable will, which entirely autonomously, becomes its own law. This law makes itself known as a requirement for the action, as the "categorical imperative," the absolute must, that independent from all condition keeps its validity. It is formulated as: act in such a way that the maxim of your will always can count as the principle of a general law.

The ethical good coincides with that which is imposed; on the other hand is only this action good, which is posed in respect of the law of one's own will. All other motivations disturb the moral character of the action. The morality is only in the will or the disposition; the exterior action has therefore no meaning.

Moral order presupposes human freedom, the immorality of the ethical subject and the existence of God, truths, which transcend the theoretical reason, but are postulated with absolute certitude by the practical reason.

Justice is entirely outside the moral order, because it has only a connection with the exterior actions in the community, of which it limits the arbitrariness. Justice is the whole of the conditions, by which the arbitrariness of the one can coexist with the arbitrariness of all the others, ascending to one general law.

Religion finds its touchstone for its truth and value in the practical reason. Kant thinks even that by abolishing the knowledge of the suprasensual things, he made a place for religion. Religion as such has no independent meaning; it is completely reduced to morality and consists only in the fact that man considers his moral obligations as divine commandments. He therefore denies all positive elements and revelation in religion: with the Enlightenment he believes only in a "natural religion," within the limits of reason.

In the *Kritik der Urteilskraft* Kant finally tried to bridge the gap between theoretical and practical reason by means of a teleological view of the reality. "Urteilskraft" is namely the ability to think the concrete in connection with the absolute, while more particularly the "reflektierende Urteilskraft" deduces the concrete from the absolute, by which concept it can be judged. The order of nature is thus seen, with it's mechanical causality, as being in the service of the order of morality, where freedom reigns. When the concept of causality is applied to the content of our representations, i.e. the things of nature, then we see that organic beings have an inner appropriateness. This can then only be explained by considering that, what was effect, in connection with the mechanical necessity, can be considered cause in other connections. When this concept of causality is applied to the form of our representations, we recognize in the work of art an extern or esthetic appropriateness, which consists in the coincidence of our satisfaction with the representation.—F.S.

KARMAN (literally the action)

In Indian thought especially the accumulated effect of the actions of a living being in a specific existence; the factor of retribution immanently attached to the actions, by which it has for the life after death a decisive value. The doctrine of the karman is on the one hand an effort to explain the mechanism of the transmigration (so called regeneration), on the other hand an hypothesis to justify grief and unhappiness. There are in Indian philosophy many theories about the origin of the karman, how it adheres to the living being and how it works.

KEPLER, Johannes

Born in Weil 1571, died in Regensburg 1630. German astronomer, discovered the laws of the motions of the planets, follower of Copernicus's system, which he wants to reconcile with the Holy Scriptures. His study of nature is based on Plato and Nicholas of Cusa.

KEYSERLING, Hermann von, 1880-1946.

Philosopher of culture, well known for his *Reisetagebuch eines Philosophen*, 1919. The Eastern philosophy and culture surpasses according to Keyserling, the Western philosophy and culture, for which he predicts a rapid fall. The Orient has a notion of the deep identity between thought and life; the Occident with its intellectualism stays always on the surface.

KIERKEGAARD, Soren Aabye, 1813-55.

Danish theologian and philosopher, who laid the foundations for all contemporary existential philosophy. Kierkegaard does not want to be a theologian nor a philosopher, but someone who reflects on the sense of his existence. His reflection shows him his own inner division. This he explains in his many works, which are published under different pseudonyms. Each work shows another aspect of Kierkegaard's personality. Under his own name he published only a few very simple sermons. His sermons, his books and the private papers constitute the three sources for the study of his thought.

Kierkegaard opposes definitely *Hegel. He objects to him that he has built a system of ab-

stractions, in which there is no place any more for the concrete existing man. All abstractions have only a value when they serve the concrete existing man, Hegel's system loses therefore the only thing which is important. How can man exist? Kierkegaard distinguishes three forms of existence: the esthetical, the ethical and the religious existence. The first one is the existence of the man who ties himself to nothing but wants to experience everything. The second one is the existence of the man who becomes responsibly conscious and subjects himself therefore to the ethical laws. The third one is the existence of the believer, who recognizes, in a strict personal way, in Christ the Godman and who receives therefore, transcending the general laws, a personal relation with God. The prototype of the religious man is Abraham, who wants to sacrifice his own son by order of God, although this is against the ethics. Faith is a completely paradoxal attitude; it is for reason completely absurd. It is therefore a very difficult thing. The full existence is however only reached in faith: exist is therefore a venture. The religious ideas of Kierkegaard influenced very much the dialectical theology of Karl *Barth. It is amazing that Kierkegaard's influence was only felt in the 20th cent., first in Germany, then in France and now also in Italy and the Anglo-Saxon countries. During the 19th century he was only appreciated, as a good author, by the Scandinavian countries. Works: *Enten-Eller* (Either-Or), 1843; *The Repetition*, 1843; *Fear and Trembling*, 1843; *The Concept of Anguish*, 1844; *Philosophical Fragments*, 1844; *Stages on Life's Way*, 1845; *Concluding unscientific Postscript*, 1846; *Sickness unto Death*,

1849; *Exercises in Christianity,* 1850; *The moment,* 1855.—B.D.

KINGDOM

Domain formed by beings, things or concepts, in as much as they are linked by common structure and laws. One speaks then of the three kingdoms in nature (animal, vegetable, mineral kingdom). See also realm.

KLEIN, Georg Michael

Born in Alitzheim (Bavaria) 1776, died Würzburg 1820. Follower of the °identity-philosophy of °Schelling.

KNOWLEDGE

Situation of me, by which I am conscious of an object with the certitude that is in itself as it is in my consciousness; by which the "being in itself" is "for me." This description is necessarily reflexive, since it is the knowledge of knowledge. The spontaneous knowledge is entirely oriented towards its object, it is a certain, not more explicable identification with the object.

Knowledge has a relation to *all* being, *as* being; it constitutes the highest, all-embracing and in itself eternal way of being, which coincides with the complete unfolding of the existence itself. This has to be proved.

Knowledge appears as a relation to an object: this object is involved in the immanence of the knower, but in such a way that it remains what it is in itself. This makes the difference between knowledge and the different forms of thought, which all have only sense when they proceed from the knowledge (as the central attitude) or are oriented towards it. These activities have first of all an immanent object which is constituted by the subject as an object, something "of

me": a representation, an idea, a judgment, a reasoning. Knowledge is however only present when the idea is correct, when the judgment is true, in other words when °truth is achieved. If truth is not reached there is only a supposed knowledge. The object is therefore not considered as being constituted by the relation of object and subject, but something which is made object. The object is not only a "being object for me," but the knower knows that it came to his attention because it is "in itself" such and because it is knowable by me in itself on the grounds of its existence.

We oppose thus to the purely-being-for-me the being-in-itself, which, optically, is the "being" as such. The question is now if the pretention of existence of the object of our knowledge is justified. Objections are made by °scepticism or °relativism. Do we not have to conclude from the undeniable influence which has the subjective disposition on the knowledge, that we only know our ideas (representations)? Firstly (°Descartes and others), my representations, as the immediate object of knowledge, are opposed to what-is-in-itself. One still tries to include this what-is-in-itself in the domain of knowledge through reasoning (°indirect °realism) or one just leaves it aside because it is unknowable (°agnosticism, °Kant). Secondly: the representations are not opposed to what-is-in-itself, but being-in-itself is itself made to a representation, it is made objective by the subject (°idealism). This subject can be the definite, individual subject from which the reflexion proceeded (subjective °idealism) or can be a general, absolute subject (mostly called °transcendental subject), that produces the objective reality through thought: all "cognition" is then reduced to "thought." We must however ascribe eventually to this absolute subject, a "being-in-itself," which has to coincide with the knowledge of oneself, so that there is still a being which does not coincide with being-object-for.

One can only decide about idealism or realism after a return to the phenomenon of dependence of cognition from the transobjective being, as it reveals itself in the conscious knowledge. As soon as it is undeniably established that there are judgments (acts of knowledge) which are based on knowledge (experience and insight) i.e. that there is *evidence*, as the self-revelation of the being as it is in-itself (and only the absolute sceptic could deny this), then we have to accept this phenomenon and we must search for its fundamental basis. We have to look for the secret relations between the being (in-itself) and the knowing subject, who makes the act of knowledge possible.

Idealism has then to accept that the (same) subject, in a deeper unconscious layer -as "transcendental" subject- is the cause of that from which it -as "empirical" subject- shows itself dependent in the conscious activity. If one accepts that there is a contradiction in sticking to the identity of what is cause and effect, and if one does not want to (in the way of the naive idealism or empiricism) explain knowledge as a passive acceptance of that what comes from outside (because this is contrary to the immanent activity), then one has to consider the knowing beings, not as specific beings, next to others, but as beings who—in a however imperfect and potential manner—include in their immanence, because of a certain identity, all beings as beings, in their total-

ity and as they are. In this case would the evolution of the cognition be the self-unfolding of the subject in his "being-everything" i.e. in his fundamental relation of embracing the transobjective being as being.

The evolution of the intellectual knowledge from the sensory experience has to be understood in the same way: the receptivity is a deficient form of activity. Because man is an imperfect knower, and has therefore an imperfect subjectivity, he can only come to actual self- and being-consciousness through his orientation towards others, with whom he is together. The senses are accentuated by the received impression (*species impressa) which results from the vegetative relation of man, as organic being, with his environment. If the sensory *intuition wants to become knowledge in the real sense, then the *phantasma (final result of the sensory meeting) which is only potentially intelligible, has to be spiritualized by the intellect (*intellectus agens); then only can the datum be understood *as* being. For this understanding cognition, an intermediate help is again needed; concepts, judgments, reasoning are immanent representations, *intentionally related to the real object of knowledge, that what-is-in-itself.

Are thus (with idealism) maintained; the relation of the mind as mind with all beings, and (with realism) the dependence of the human spirit-in-matter to the "given" physical world. Our knowledge is at the same time, as knowledge of being, universal and as knowledge of experience, particular; determined by our place in the world and our perspective. The self-unfolding of our knowledge depends on the being with which we are together, and some of them (the physical) are accessible in their exterior by our senses, while some others (the spiritual) want to communicate themselves to us only in their inner being, when our cognition begins to recognize them.

The finiteness of the human becoming knowledge—which reveals itself in the intentionality or orientation towards the other as first object of knowledge—points towards an absolute knowledge, with which it participates in a partial way: God's self-presence, where no distinction between subject and object of knowledge exists, but the complete identity of knowing-being and known-being in the subsisting existence itself as the pure Act. J.P.

KNOWLEDGE, Theory of
See epistemology.

KORPERGEOMETRIE
See theory of space.

KRAUSE, Karl Christian Friedrich
Born in Eisenberg 1781, died in München 1832. Founder of the °panentheism. His thought is fundamentally the "Grundanschauung" of the Ego, which recognizes in itself the mutual limitation of spirit and nature and also the limitation of itself by beings of the same necessarily towards an highest unspecies. These oppositions point limited or absolute being, God, whose reality is therefore immediately known by intellectual vision, so that the certitude of the "Grundanschauung" is dependent on it. God embraces all oppositions in Himself. Spirit and nature are two sides of his eternal being, which is the only basis for their union and interaction in man. The essence of God can however not be considered in the way of Spinoza. We have to ascertain to God self-consciousness, freedom and personality, as to the Ego. All is however in God, but also under and through Him. F.S.

KROPOTKIN, Peter, 1842-1921.
Russian socialist, philosopher, favored anarchism.

KUELPE, Oswald, 1862-1925.
German philosopher and psychologist, founder of critical realism and the psychology of thought. Main work: *Die Realisierung* 1912-22. In every observation of the observer are independent elements, which can therefore not be explained through the process of observation only. Observation requires with a subject also an object. The object is therefore cocause of the observation, in other words: the object has to be considered real. (argument of causality). The fact of observations outside of our conscious will can also be only explained by the reality of the object (substratum argument). Külpe has been inspired by Riehl. He was very influential in the victory of idealism.—B.D.

L

LABEO
See Notker Labeo.

LACTANTIUS, Caecilius Firmianus
Ca. 250-ca. Ca. 325, rhetor in Nicomedia. Latin apologist; author of many works, influenced by Cicero; opposes Christian wisdom to the false wisdom of the philosophers.

LAIRD, John, 1887-1946
English neo-realistic philosopher, professor in Aberdeen. Main works: *A Study in Realism*, 1920; *Theism and Cosmology* (Gifford lectures), 1940; *Mind and Deity* (id), 1941. Laird is convinced that in our knowledge we touch a reality, independent from it; that we really can know things as they are in themselves. This includes however that the subject must surround his knowledge with all the precautions of empiricism and careful analysis. The subject is always limited and can therefore only reach a part or aspect of the reality. The experience forms thus the basis of his knowledge, and all further assimilation of this knowledge in remembrance and imagination, judgment and reasoning goes back to this experience and, with that, to the experienced reality itself. Reality offers a physical and spiritual aspect. The spirit can not be reduced to matter. From here is a philosophical estimate of the Divine Thought possible. B.D.

LALO, Charles, 1877-1953
French philosopher, professor at the Sorbonne, specialist in aesthetics.

LAMARCK, Jean 1744-1829
French naturalist, the forerunner of Darwin in his concern with the concept of evolution, especially as a consequence of environmental influences upon the species. Works: *Recherches sur les Causes des Principaux Faits Physiques* (1794), *Système de la Nature* (1795), *Philosophie Zoologique* (1808).

LAMB, Charles, 1775-1834.
English essayist whose *Essays of Elia* (1823) is a type of intellectual autobiography; friend of Coleridge, Hazlitt, Leigh Hunt and other literary figures of his time.

LAMBDA DEFINITION
Defines a symbol as a synonym of a °lambda functor. We give, for instance, a lambda definition of the combinator T, by considering it equal to $\lambda x y. (y x)$.

LAMBDA FUNCTOR
Has the form of $\lambda x (M)$ or $\lambda x y z (M)$. With $\lambda x (M)$ one expresses what applied to x, produces the expression M; with $\lambda x y z (M)$ what applied to x, y, z (in this sequence), produces the expression M. The lambda functor $\lambda x y (y x)$ expresses that what applies to x and y, produces the expression y x.

LAMBERT, Johann Heinrich, 1728-1777
German mathematician, astronomer and philosopher; entertained

236

correspondence with Kant who esteemed him highly. He built an epistemology, in which Kant did find the distinction between matter and form of knowledge.

LAMENNAIS, Felicite-Robert de
Born in St. Malo 1782, died in Paris 1854. French priest, apologist, journalist, later apostate. With his *Essai sur l'indifférence en matière de Religion* (1817-23) he became the leader of a movement of young catholics who expected from the liberty of religion and politics all good for the Church and the religion, and who had in view an amelioration of the social situations through christianity.—The philosophical views of Lamennais are *traditionalistic: certitude can not be received by the human reasoning only, but has to be found in the general conviction of the entire human race, expressed in the testimony or the word. Since, however, most essential and fundamental truths are given by God to the humanity, the authority of God is the last ground of all certitude. The existence of God, affirmed by general consent of the humanity, is the most certain of all truths and the basis of all other truths. F.S.

LA METTRIE, Julien Offray de
Born in St. Malo 1709, died in Berlin 1751. Physician, was banned from France and the Seven Provinces, because of his materialistic publications. He was received by Friedrich of Prussia. Thought originates in the bodily functions; matter can move and perceive. His morality is hedonistic; good is what gives pleasure, but private pleasure has to remain subordinate to general pleasure.

LANGE, Friedrich Albert
Born in Wald near Solingen man critic, well known through his *Geschichte des Materialismus* (1866) and his defense of a "Psychologie ohne Seele." Opposes, on the grounds of kantian principles, German idealism and materialism and he does not conceive the a priori elements in a purely epistemological way, but he tries to justify them with the help of the physiology of the senses and a psychological analysis of the intellectual functions. He rejects the real existence of the Ding an sich, which Kant defended: for Lange it is only a concept of knowledge, that the knowledge has to accept as an unknown cause of the phenomena.

The practical reason of Kant disappeared completely in Lange and therewith also the practical philosophy. Ethics are not accessible for scientific justification, he says; with aesthetics, religion and metaphysics it belongs to the domain of poetry, which is considered by Lange as a necessary expression of the deepest essence of the mind. Religion is the elevation of the mind above the world of reality; it is independent of all reasonable fundaments and can therefore not be refuted with reasonable arguments, as little as one can "refute" a Mass of Palestrina. F.S.

LANGUAGE
In general, every system of signs used as means of understanding and which therefore presupposes a community. In a more specific sense: the language of words. This language is a system of phenomena (vowels and consonants), words, rules for the formation of words, 1828, died in Marburg 1875. Ger-schemata for sentences and intonation of sentences. As system is the language opposed to the *speech (the use of the language). By

combining elements of the system and applying them in a specific situation, the user of the language will express ideas and feelings (1), communicates something to others and evokes in them reactions (2), and aims at "things" (in the most broad sense of the word) and relations between things (3). The philosophers have mostly interest in the latter.

There are many theories about the origin of the language. They are dependent from the view on life and of that what one considers central in man, but also does it depend on the conception about the relation between the sound-form of a word and its meaning or the thing which is named with that word. Is this relation natural (according to "nomina consequentia rerum") or determined by pure convention? The discussion is since a long time in favor of the conventionalists, although one can not deny a natural connection in some cases (soundimitation). The thought about the arbitrariness of the signs has favored the opinion that man, with his thought attached to language, never can reach knowledge of the reality.

The *philosophy of language,* which studies a.o. the relation between language and thought and tries to determine the value of the language for science and philosophy, becomes often language criticism. It is interested in the *metaphorical use of the language and in the metaphoric character of many words. Also in the vagueness and equivocity of the language signs: logical thinking in a natural language is difficult if not impossible. Therefore the need to invent other systems of signs, which would be free of the named faults. Opposed to the natural languages are the artificial languages, namely the universal languages a priori (*Leibniz) and a posteriori (Esperanto)—C.S.

LAO TZU (literally: the old master)
A vaguely historical figure; according to the tradition contemporary of Confucius and author of the (certainly much later written) "Canon of Reason and Virtue": *Tao Tê Ching.* See Taoism.

LA ROCHEFOUCAULD, François VI, Duke of (Prince de Marsillac) 1613-1680.
French writer of maxims and friend of Mme. de Sévigné and the Comtesse de La Fayette. The full title of his most famous work: *Réflexions ou Sentences et Maximes Morales* (1665).

LASSALLE, Ferdinand
Born in Breslan 1825, died in Geneva 1864. German economist, founder of the German social-democracy, follower of the historical materialism.

LAVATER, Johann Kaspar, 1741-1801.
Swiss mystic, philosopher and theologian whose longing for manifestations of the supernatural made him the victim of numerous charlatans and fanatics. He is considered the founder of physiognomy, which, though not scientifically based, stimulated many psychologists: *Physiognomics* (1774-78).

LAW
(1) Absolutely binding rule for the human actions, imposed through the habit, the social authority, or expression of the divine Will. 2) Rule according to which the human thought should evoluate to reach absolutely valid and objective values (law of thought). 3) natural law in the moral meaning,

or reasonable insight which dictates to man what he should do or omit in order to act as a man. 4) natural laws in the scientific sense, i.e. regularities in the phenomena of nature, perceived in the observation and expressed in a general formula. 5) in analogy with 4) psychic, social, phonetic, semantic, historic laws.

LAW OF IDENTITY

Can be formulated as follows: a is a, a thing is what it is. This judgment is not a tautology, nor is it originated through a pure analysis of concept: it expresses rather the necessary identification of all what is with itself.

Expressed in a purely logical manner, the law of identity means that in a specific line of thought a same term has to have and keep it's specific sense. It is therefore the main law of all thought, and precedes even the law of contradiction. Because, when we, because of the imperfection of our cognition, make the identity clearer starting from the diversity, then the fundament of the negation of the diversity is still that what is positive. Taken that the law of identity regulates the form of all thought, then the question still remains if it also governs the content of thought. This seems to be the case. The necessity which it possesses, is founded on the identification of the being with itself in the existence. The existence is absolute self-sufficiency and directed towards itself, which is clarified for us by the fact that the existence is only opposed to the non-existence, the non-existence is however not an antipole, and therefore is the existence opposed to nothing. The identity of existence with existence is the original identity in which the being, inasmuch as it is, participates.

In the last instance the law of identity has to be expressed in all-comprising terms or in terms of being: existence is existence. Herewith one expresses the necessity of an absolute identity, as it imposes itself on us in all that appears to us, unclearly but imperatively. At the same time the fundamental metaphysical question is posed about the reduction of the many beings in what is absolutely one and identically the same. J.P.

LAWS OF PRESERVATION

Physical laws which declare that by mutual reaction of chemicals total amounts of specific quantities are preserved, such as energy, weight, etc. Eventually all these laws are subsumed under the law of the preservation of *energy.

LAXISM

Laxity in the observance of the laws, especially of the moral law. Therefore the thesis of some casuists that one who doubts the moral value of an action, can follow the meaning which has only a small probability. Is opposed to *rigorism.

LEGALITY

Is called by Kant the agreement with the moral law, which is purely exterior. So is the attitude of the businessman who is only fair because he does not want to lose clients. Is opposed to *morality.

LEIBNIZ, Gottfried Wilhelm von, 1646-1716

Universal mind of the first importance, jurist and mathematician, historian and politician, eminent philosopher, who had, until Kant, a very great influence on German thought. Also a man of peace and compromise, who vainly tried to reconcile protestants and catholics or certainly lutherans and calvinists. He was also a very good organizer. His doctrine which was created in a constant contact with Descartes, Malebranche, Bayle and Spinoza, but had also much to thank to the influence of Aristotle, has never been put by Leibniz himself in one system: all his works have been written because of a concrete exchange of ideas, and his most important ideas are often concealed in his extensive correspondence, among others with Arnauld, De Volder, Des Bosses and Clarke. Main works: *Discours de métaphysique,* 1685-86; *Système nouveau de la nature,* 1695; *Nouveaux essais sur l'entendement humain,* 1704—in connection with Locke's *Essay* of 1690, but printed in 1765—; *Essais de Théodicée,* 1710; *Principes de la nature et de la grâce fondés en raison,* 1714; *Monadologie,* 1714.

In epistemology Leibniz holds the middle between rationalism and empiricism. He distinguishes in our cognition factual truths, which are based on the experience, and immediately evident truths which do not rest on experience. The latter are in a certain way innate, subconsciously present in our soul, and they become conscious under the influence of the experience; Leibniz uses for this theory a psychological discovery he himself made, namely the existence of unconscious, weakly conscious ideas, which also influence our spiritual life. Because of this aprioristic structure of our thought and because of the construction of our senses, our experience has a double subjective character: We learn only to know the phenomena, not the things themselves, and so originates the problem about what the substance or the reality itself is.

Leibniz thinks that he found it in the concept of force; the last indivisible unities of the actual reality are immaterial centres of force, and unities of consciousness without extension, which he called since 1696 the monads (Greek: monad-unity). These simple, indestructible, immortal concentrations of being extend from complete unconsciousness (lifeless objects) via weak consciousness (plants and animals) and clearer consciousness (man) to the clearest consciousness (the divinity). Causal interaction between these non-spatial monads is according to Leibniz impossible: each monad is a world, closed in itself and evoluting according to its own laws without "windows" to the outside.

In order to explain the empirically perceptible interaction between all and all, especially between spirit and matter, he rejects the dualistic, pantheistic and occasionalistic conceptions of Descartes, Spinoza and Malebranche; when two watches are running regularly on the same time, it is not necessary that one influences the other, or that both are images of a third motherwatch, neither that a watchmaker put them both right again and again—it is also possible that the watchmaker (the divinity) organized them once and for all in such a way that they always will run on the same time. Leibniz has drawn up for that solution the formulation of the Pre-established Harmony (harmonie préétablie), in this form since 1696. This unique "wonder" can explain the fact that the things influence each other apparently and that every consciousness sees the things in about the same way as the others, all monads reflect, each in its own way, one and the same universe. Their individuality lies in this "each in their own way", the unity of the reflected subject limits their subjectivity.

One thing is not understandable in this causally bound world which is however oriented by the divinity to a unique end, in this carefully harmonized construction of ideas: the existence of evil. The solution of Leibniz of this perennial problem, that of the theodicy, is typical of the optimism of the Enlightenment. There is firstly in the world more good than evil, evil (pain, sorrow and sin) is actually something negative, namely the absence of the good because of the finity of the creature or even of our free will which God does not cause but only permits. It is often a means to attain a greater good, while pain and sorrow are often an harmonic punishment for sin. Evil can therefore be absorbed in the harmonic universe, although we can not always diagnose this harmony. And— his main argument—this world is not an absolute good but the "best of all possible worlds", since God is bound in his creation by the laws of his own intellect, the eternal truths which render the genesis of an absolutely good universe impossible.

The ethics of Leibniz are also typical for the Enlightenment. Man's moral end is aching according to the will of God. We can best achieve that by following the commandments God has put in our hearts, namely the commandments of the reason, and by favoring the constantly progressing enlightment of this reason in us and in others. But to achieve this our will has to be free, which seems to be in contradiction with the causal determination of the universe.

The solution of this difficulty has been found by Leibniz in the fact that we ourselves can determine our will, surely not in the sense of the absolute arbitrariness, but always driven by (sometimes subconscious) motives, which determine our acts but not with absolutely logical necessity, no more than omniscient providence of God. We are in any case "normaliter" free of all external coercion and we therefore possess freedom of action and freedom of choice between the possibilities offered, and the highest moral freedom would then exist in the fact that we can not act except well.

The concept of God, which is the foundation of the entire system of thought, is the concept of an extra-worldly and supernatural God-creator, a primitive monad, who can be compared, in his relation to the world, with a clever manual labourer or a creative artist, who organized the entire world in such a way that direct intervention (miracles), if not entirely excluded, is still limited to a minimum; God's greatness is especially expressed in the law abiding order of the universe.—Th.C.v.St.

LEMMA (Greek: lemma: from lambanein: to take)

A proposition, borrowed from somewhere else and assumed to be true, which is used for instance as a premise in a dilemma, trilemma, etc.

LEONTIUS OF BYZANTIUM

Ca. 475-ca. 543, Greek theologian, influenced by neo-platonism, but used also the logic of Aristotle and the *Eisagoge* of Porphyry.

LESSING, Gotthold Ephraim, 1729-81

German poet, essay-writer and thinker. In philosophy his aesthetics are important (*Laokoon*, 1766), but also for the further development of the system of Leibniz. Also influenced by Spinoza and therefore in some aspects critical of Leibniz. Convinced of the lack of liberty in the human will, he preaches in *Nathan der Weise,* 1779 the ideal of tolerance, in *Die Erziehung des Menschengeschlechts,* 1770-80 the moral evolution on the basis of the belief in the human immortality, in the form of the metempsychosis.

LEUCIPPUS OF MILETE
Teacher of *Democritus of Abdera and with him last founder of the school of the *atomists. Leucippus is for us not much more than a name. He is always named together with Democritus and his writings were published in the same book as the writings of his great disciple.

LEVY-BRUHL, Lucien, 1857-1939
French positivistic philosopher, sociologist, whose work had much influence on specific domains of the philosophy.

LEWES, George Henry
Born in London 1817, died there 1878, made the positivism of *Comte known in England.

LEWIS, Clarence Irving
Born 1883, American philosopher, specialist in modern logic and epistemology.

LIAR
The well-known logical paradox of Eubulides, basic form of all others: If you are a liar, but say that you are lying, then you lie but say at the same time the truth.

LIBERUM ARBITRIUM (literally: free judgment)
Is used by the scholastics to indicate the free property to dispose of something, or the freedom of choice, in short the freedom of the will. The freedom of the will consists indeed, in the first place, in the judgment of the different motives which incite to action. As soon as the judgment is pronounced that in this particular circumstances a particular motive is stronger than another, it is necessarily chosen. But it is exactly in the construction of the motive that the freedom exists. In as much as the choice is an act of the will, will and the ability of free choice fall together, although the will is also referring to acts, where there is no question of choice (e.g. the desire for happiness) and has therefore a broader meaning. The will, on the other hand, refers also to the striving of the will towards an end; the ability of free choice on the other hand refers to the choice of the means to reach the end. The freedom, as the possibility itself to choose, is not a property of man, but a quality of the will, by which this is a free ability of choice.—P.S.

LIBIDO, sensual desire.
In a narrower sense (Freud), the psychical energy of the sexual strivings which are oriented towards the Ego (Ich—or narcissistic libido). For Jung: The energy which is the basis of the psychic processes. The modern term is close to the "Sexual desire" (libido sexualis), seen especially in connection with the intensity and the stadium of evolution between the infantile libido and the psychosexuality.

LICHTENBERG, Georg Christoph, 1742-1799.
German physicist and satirist who ridiculed Lavater's theories of physiognomy, the *Sturm und Drang* writers, and other pomposities, and expressed himself best in brief aphorisms.

LICHTGEOMETRIE
See theory of space.

LIFE
The exclusive characteristic of the living beings. The concept life is often limited to *organic* life, realized in matter and found in plants, animal and man. In such an organism one finds also the structure of different parts, each with its particular task (see organ). Aristotle gave already as characteristics of organic life the following: feeding, growth and reproduction; the scholastics accepted this. These characteristics could still be used but one speaks now more of "metabolism" rather than of feeding.

These characteristics point all to the completely special activity or dynamics in the living being. One finds here a cycle of processes, which keeps itself into being and itself actively creates the conditions for its own survival. The result, also end of this special dynamics, is the own development, one's preservation and the preservation of the species. One can therefore define life as "self-motion", but one fails more or less to appreciate, in this older term, the own activity of the lifeless nature. A good, but not strict definition would be: "selfmotion through incentives" in which one expresses that a particular activity always appears in connection with influences from the (inner or outer) milieu, which act as incentives.

With Aristotle and Thomas Aquinas we still distinguish three levels of life: vegetative life with only metabolism, growth and reproduction, animal life, in which we find also observation by senses and consciousness, and intellectual life only found in man and in which are present the spiritual properties: intellect and free will. With each of these functions are also connected the corresponding organisation and the interaction with the environment.

From these characteristics we can conclude that life is more perfect than the lifelessness, and that it can not be reduced to it. Vegetative and animal life are studied in biology, which comes close to philosophy in its most general conclusions. The philosophy will have to answer the questions about that what is particular to life and about the functionality of it.—M.B.

LIGHT-METAPHYSICS
Can already be found in Philo's philosophy, where he teaches that God is the original light or the spiritual sun, from which many rays, which can be intercepted by the intellect, go out. In neo-platonism the light of the world is considered as a lower degree of the divine light, and it participates by emanation in that divine light. Decisive for the light-metaphysics is the conception of God held by Augustine: He is the uncreated light that literally enlightens everything. In the 13th century the light-metaphysics reached its highest point with Robert Grosseteste, who taught that God is the light preeminently, while also the created things, through their participation in God, are essentially light; also held in Latin neo-platonism by Witelo. Outside of the Augustinian tradition (Malebranche) we find the lightmetaphysics in modern philosophy in the theories of Bohme, Herder, Schelling. Also *illumination-theory.

LIMIT
See finite, continuum.

LIMITATIVE or limited
See proposition.

LINCOLN, Abraham, 1809-1865.
The American President probably most admired for his character, integrity, and devotion to the political idealism upon which the American "way of life" rests. A master of expression of American political philosophy in his addresses and state papers.

LINNAEUS, Carolus, 1707-1778.
Swedish botanist who is considered the father of modern systematic botany. Works: *Systema Naturae* (1737), *Philosophia Botanica* (1750), *Species Plantarum*.

LINSENMANN, Franz Xaver
Born in Rottweil a.N. 1835, died in Lauterbach 1898. Catholic German moral theologian and ethicus, bishop of Rottenburg, disciple of *Kuhn and follower of *Jacobi.

LIPPS, Theodor 1851-1914
German psychologist and aesthetician, defender of the psychologism.

LIPSIUS, Justus (Joest Lips)
Born in Overijse (Belgium) 1547, died in Louvain 1606. Flemish philologist, historian and philosopher, professor in Jena, Leiden and Louvain.
Lipsius wanted to apply the philosophy of the Stoics to the doctrine of christianity (especially the philosophy of *Seneca). In his earliest works he remained in the limits of christian stoicism, which belonged to the tradition of late *scholasticism and *humanism in the Netherlands. In later writings he united the philosophy of Seneca and the christian dogmas to an harmonic whole. The theistic elements in the doctrine of Seneca have been extended, the christian idea of creation is introduced and a meaning is given to the stoic concepts *providentia* and *Fatum*, which coincide with the christian

ideas. Lipsius thought that this christian stoicism would provide a better view of the world for modern times, better than the scholastic synthesis of christianity and aristotelianism.—F.S.

LITT, Theodor
Born 1880, German pedagogue and philosopher, professor in Bonn. Has been influenced by several schools, especially by *Hegel, *Dilthey, and the *phenomenology. Litt refuses to accept the irrationalism of Dilthey and tries through a phenomenological-dialectical way to arrive at the understanding of the structure of the mental sciences. Main work: *Denken und Sein*, 1948.

LOCKE, John
Born in Wrington 1632, died in Oates 1704, English philosopher. Studied medicine, natural sciences, theology and philosophy at the Christ Church College in Oxford, went in 1666 into the service of the Earl of Shaftesbury and was in charge of the education of his grandson, the well known moralist and philosopher. He stayed many times on the European continent, in 1675 in Montpellier and from 1683-89 in the Netherlands, where he became a friend of the Remonstrant, clergyman and scholar Philip of Limborch; there he also prepared the publication of his main work. After his return to England he held many important official posts but he prefered a calm and retired life in the country. The last years of his life were spent in the home of Sir Francis and Lady Masham, the latter being a daughter of the philosopher Cudworth.
The special importance of Locke in the history of philosophy is his systematic investigation of the origin, the certitude and extent of the

human knowledge. Because of his method, the analysis of the empirical consciousness, he can be considered as the founder of the modern psychology. His main work, published in 1690 has therefore the title: *Essay concerning Human Understanding*. He wants to establish the content of our knowledge, and he finds that knowledge only exists in the "ideas", the representations which descend from the experience through the medium of our senses. They are "ideas of sensation" and "ideas of reflexion". Consciousness is at the origin as a blank piece of paper, it has no innate knowledge. The ideas are simple or complex, and man can on the basis of simple ideas arrive at complexes of representation, which represent the real things. But to guarantee the cohesion between the representations of things, Locke thought he had to accept the existence of a material substance. We can not form an idea of this substance, because we can only observe qualities; it remains therefore completely unknown to us. Without it there can however be no place for continuousness and identity of things. It is the "supposed, but unknown support of those qualities we find existing".

Locke makes the historically important distinction between secondary qualities (colours, taste, smell, noise) and primary qualities (solidity, extension, shape, motion, rest and number) of the objects. The former do not agree with the reality of the things, they are subjective representations, which originate in the action of invisible particles upon our senses. The primary qualities are identical to the reality: "their patterns do really exist in the bodies themselves". The problem how our knowledge could be objective and true depends therefore on the conformity of our ideas, our representations, with the reality. Locke accepts three forms of knowledge: an intuitive knowledge of ourselves, a demonstrative knowledge of God and a sensory knowledge of the phenomenal reality, which latter can only glory in great probability.

Locke left also important ideas in the field of politics and ethics. His *Epistola de Tolerentia* preaches tolerance in the religious questions. His *Two Treatises of Government*, published in 1690, opposed the absolute monarchy and defended the sovereignty of the people and the freedom of the citizens. *Thoughts on Education* is a very important work, published in 1693. Locke emphasizes the possibility of forming and developing innate qualities and character by early influence and acquisition of good habits. His ideal is that the education would be oriented in the first place to society and life, in the second place to the university or science.—F.B.

LOGIC

Or theory of thoughts, comes from Aristotle, although the term itself was first used by the stoicist Zeno of Citium. Aristotle used *"analytica" but his works on logic were united by Andronicus of Rhodes under the name *"Organon" or "instrument". Logic gives the rules for orderly, correct and easy thought, or, more specifically, reasoning (Greek logikè, in connection with reasoning). The object of its study is therefore the *reasoning and in connection therewith the *propositions (assertions) and *concepts (terms) with which it is built. It does not consider it as psychological acts of thought, but as its result and product: as

245

constructions of thought or *"entes rationis".

Logic means now also the whole of ideas concerning the way in which we reach the truth, especially in connection with the sciences. These ideas are formulated in a theoretical as well as in a normative form, or in the form of an art of reasoning. Since the logic as an art of reasoning and as normative science presupposes the logic as theory, this latter is considered as the logic as such.

In the (theoretical) logic we can distinguish between formal and material logic. *Formal* logic is interested in the right form or structure of a reasoning; *Material* logic studies the requirements necessary for their materials, i.e. their assertions and terms. A good reasoning requires a good form as well as good materials which are reliable; on the first is based the correctness of the conclusion, on the latter its truth. These two parts of logic evoluted later into two more or less independent subjects: a so called *Minor* logic, where methodical thought is studied, and a *major* logic, so called because of its much greater content, in which all kinds of special logical problems are treated. When the problem of certitude became important another part of logic was formed, a kind of *critical* logic, which was often but wrongly, identified with the major logic, in which the theory of certitude has an important place. This critical logic is however not really a theory of thought but more a theory of knowledge.—I.v.d.B.

Logic however remained in its great lines unchanged for twenty centuries and kept the form given to it by Aristotle and his immediate followers. This *traditional* logic uses mostly the usual language and is based on the terms of the usual language; it is not deduced completely from axioms.

In the 19th century a new form of logic came into being, and the terms used are: *Formalized* logic, *mathematical* logic and also *logistics*. We speak of a new form of logic, not of a new logic, in the sense that this logic is indeed not rejecting the principles of the traditional logic; it is an extension of the older logic, on the same basis but with new methods. Its relation to the older logic is about the same as the relation between the modern mathematics and the mathematics of the Greek, not the relation between the modern physics and the physics of the Antiquity.

The new form of logic is also called *symbolic* logic. This term should be avoided because it gives an incomplete idea of that what is characteristic for the contemporary logic. One can already find in Aristotle a certain amount of logic symbolism; those who use symbols as a pedagogical means, do not penetrate the spirit of the contemporary logic. Characteristic for contemporary logic is its formalisation, the use of symbols with axioms and rules, so that all deductions rest exclusively on axioms and rules and not on a meaning of the symbols, neither if this meaning is the object of a certain abstract intuition, nor if one tries to clarify it with diagrams.

Around 1900 the name of logistics came into being. This term is however used now in an entirely different meaning, and it gives the impression that one has to do not with logic, but with something entirely different from logic.

The term *mathematical* logic can be used as synonym of formalizing logic. This appellation was in the 19th century perhaps not recommendable, when the mathe-

246

matics were identified with the theory of the quantities; there is now no strict separation any more between mathematical logic and the modern abstract algebra, in its logical interpretations.—R.F.

LOGIC (Systems of the formal)

Are inferred from axioms and rules, which are more or less arbitrarily chosen. There is therefore place for different systems (as there are now different systems for geometry) which we can call different *logics*. These systems are however not incompatible; they use different logical operations or different conceptions (interpretations) of the logical operations.

We distinguish: A. systems with different *propositionlogics*: B. systems which use different sorts of concepts.

A.–1. *Classical* logic is called today the *bivalent* logic in which *propositions can have only two *validityvalues or *truthvalues, namely true and untrue (false). This logic is actually the same as the logic of the stoics; it is different from the traditional logic because it does not consider modalities. In this logic principles, as the principle of contradiction, of the excluded third and the *ex falso sequitur quodlibet*, are valid. This logic can be deduced according to different methods, either by *valuation with two values, or from a series of axioms.

2. In the so called *intuitionistic logic* of Brouwer and Heyting (it would be better to speak of a logic of intuitionism) is the principle of the excluded third not used. This principle is however not rejected, neither is it considered false; it is simply not used, not taken as an axiom. This logic teaches that a disjunction can not be proved,

except if one or another *alternative is proven.

The intuitionistic logic is different from the classical logic, especially in the fact that the double negation not-not *p* does not coincide with the affirmation *p*. It corresponds in certain respects to a logic in which *p* is everywhere changed into: *p* is provable; it is clear that: *p* is provable, contains a stronger operation than: it is provable that *p* is unprovable.

A radical form of the intuitionistic logic is the *minimal* logic of Johansson, in which not only the principle of the excluded third is not deductible but also the *ex falsum sequitur quodlibet*. Often are used, for the intuitionistic logic, the term I-logic and for the minimal logic the term J- or (better) M-logic.

It should be noted that the intuitionistic and minimal logic are partial systems of the classical logic, because they use only a part of the axioms of the classical logic and do not add any other axioms.

There is room, within the classical logic, for other partial systems, in which not only some axioms but also some operations are absent. This is the case for the many forms of a *positive logic,* in which no negation appears.

3. In the *modal* logic, on the other hand, we have an expansion of the classical logic, in this sense that the simple *proposition logic is completed with the addition of new operations, which change the proposition *p* into the proposition: *p* is necessary, and *p* is possible. One can already find *modalities in Aristotle; the formal logic has deduced a series of modal systems with a finite or infinite number of modalities.

4. We should mention, next to the intuitionistic and model logic,

the *multivalent* logics. These logics are most easily explained as systems with more than two *validityvalues*, where the usual functions (negation, *alternation, *conjunction, *implication) are *validityfunctions. Let us indicate the values of a trivalent logic as true, false and a value between both. The most used trivalent logic is then the negation of true and false, false and true, the negation of the value in between again the value in between.

In the multivalent logic about the same theses are found as in the bivalent logic; we must however make a distinction between *categorical* and *shaded* functions. The negation can therefore have the value in between: to be more or less true; a categorical negation of the value in between would produce a false proposition.

According to the same principle of the multivalent logics one would be able to construct *topological* logics, in which no determined number of values but only a determined order of values would be established.

B.—The traditional logic did not study any other abstract concept than those which we call now classes. In each of the above mentioned logics one can introduce next to the *logic of concepts* a *logic of relations*, and also logics *of higher * abstraction*. (These logics do not rest on different axioms and rules; we have here more or less high degrees in the concepts).

A last form of logic should be mentioned separately, namely the *combinatory* logic, which depends on the propositionlogic. This logic exists in two forms: the logic of the *lambda-conversion* which uses *lambda-functors,* and the simple *combinatory logic,* using *combin-*ators and which can take the form of a logic without variables or with empty operations.—R.F.

LOGIC OF CONCEPTS

or logic of classes, the section of the modern formal logic that corresponds approximately with the logic of Aristotle (the modalities excluded). It operates with concepts—in the narrow sense of the word, not containing individuals and relations)—or with qualities which can belong to individual objects of thought, or with aggregates of individuals which have a specific quality. Concepts or classes are for instance: red, big etc. . . . We will notate the indefinite concepts by means of variables a, b, c . . .; the contemporary logic uses also the total class (aggregate of all individuals, concept which can be applied to all individuals) and empty class (empty aggregate, concept which can be applied to no individual).

From concepts are formed by means of logical operations, other concepts. By negation proceed from the concepts a and b, the concepts *not-a* and *not-b*. By means of *conjunction originates the concept: a and b, by means of *alternation: a or b (a or also b). Such operations can be applied in infinitum to compound concepts.

From the classes are constructed the *propositions. The most common are universal propositions: all a's are b's (in this sense that all is either *not a,* or also b), and also propositions: there are a's, there are a's which are b's.

The theses of the logic of concepts are either rules of operation with negation, conjunction, alternation, or comparable to the immediate inferences and syllogisms of the traditional logic.—R.F.

248

LOGIC OF RELATIONS

Was especially developed by Schröder in 1895 and by Russell before and in the *Principia Mathematica* (1910). Its point of departure is formed by elementary propositions rxy, starting that a relation exists between two things x and y; the relation r is considered as a predicate of a pair of things. Operations of these relations are, as in the logic of concepts, negation, *conjunction, *alternation, but also *inversion* (if r exists between x and y, then exists the *inverse of r between y and x), and *relative conjunction* r/s; this exists between x and y if there is a z, so that *rxz* and *szy*. Powers are $r^2 = r/r$, $r^3 = r/r^2$ etc. A relation can also be *limited* to specific domains; e.g. the relation between parents and children can be determined into male or female antecedents, consequents or both. By means of relations r it is possible to define *relative classes:* the r's of x, the r's of the a's, the r's (the r's of whatever could be). The logic of relations is a necessary tool for the logical analysis of scientific domains. —R.F.

LOGICAL

(1) what belongs to the life of thought, as thought-constructions (e.g. reasonings) only exist and can exist in the human intellect. Is then opposed to ontological, belonging to the world of the existence. (2) What is reasoned correctly and according to the laws of thought.

LOGICISM

Is the striving to construct pure mathematics with only logic as basis. After *Frege was stopped, in his attempts in this direction, by a paradox, *Russell, in cooperation with *Whitehead, resumed the study of this question. The precursors of the modern logicism are Leibniz and Bolzano.

LOGISTICS

See appendix.

LOGISTICS

See logic, formal.

LOGOMACHY

A battle with words and for words instead of for things.

LOGOS (Greek: lego, read)

Originally collection, in any sense (Heraclitus); later the principle which produces the collection or ordering, the intellect or the reason (Aristotle). Logos indicates for the Stoics the immanent law of nature, which soon will be made independent as a law-giving intellect. In christianity the Logos (or the Word) is identified with the second person of the Trinity.

LONERGAN, Bernard

Born in Canada, entered Society of Jesus in 1922 and was ordained in 1936; obtained his S.T.D. from the Gregorian University in Rome; Professor of Dogmatic Theology there. Wrote *Insight*, a modern inquiry into the nature of understanding, considered a restatement in modern terms of a large area of scholastic metaphysics, ethics and psychology — a new version of Thomist philosophy.

LONG-CHAMP, R.

See Radulphus de Longo Campo.

LONGINUS, CASSIUS, Third Century A.D.

Greek Platonic philosopher and rhetorician whose major work, *On the Sublime,* influenced aesthetic and literary criticism for centuries —yet it is probably the work of another writer. Known works: *Philological Discourses, On First Principles.*

LOSSKY, Nikolai

Born 1870, Russian philosopher, since 1922 in the West. Lossky accepts a threefold reality: the real world, the ideal world and God. The real world is the physical, time-space world. The ideal world which is also real, is man's world and the world of all spiritual things created by man. Man transcends through his knowledge the real world and in this the ideal world reveals itself, and shows that it is irreducible to the real world. The knowledge of the real world is real realistic knowledge, in which we reach the things themselves, as they are given to us. Lossky calls his theory therefore sometimes intuitionism, because this character of being given is also proper to the ideas and to the way in which God shows himself to us. Religious reflection forms the center of Lossky's thought and the source of his ethics, in which the highest value is that of the Kingdom of God. —B.D.

LOTZE, Hermann

Born in Bautzen 1817, died in Berlin 1881. German realist, professor in Göttingen and Berlin.

The philosophy of Lotze, related to the philosophy of *Herbart, is on the one hand connected with the spiritualism of *Leibniz, and on the other hand with the monism of *Spinoza, and is also closely connected with the natural sciences. Dualism and monism are combined.

The "external" or empirical contemplation of things leads, according to Lotze, to the anatomic-mechanical explanation of the whole physical world, from which the spiritual world is excluded. The unity of the consciousness and of every expression of the psychic life forces us to the acceptance of an independence of the soul, essentially different from the body, which has an interaction with the body and directs the course of the psychic life. In the psychic life the feeling holds a special place (against Herbart). The freedom of the will is a postulate of the practical reason, which can theoretically neither be proved nor refuted.

The "internal" or metaphysical contemplation of the things leads to a spiritualistic monism, that the carriers of the worldly happenings let know as *monads,* simple, immaterial substances, of which space and matter are only phenomenal forms. The monads are as *modi* contained in an eternal, immaterial substance or all-spirit, who through his own immanent activity brings the monads in communication with each other. The mechanical laws in nature are the reflection in the empirical world of the natural necessity in the activity of the All-spirit.

The needs of the mind give the right to represent the All-spirit as the divine original ground of the things and to apply to him such predicates, which made him become, from a metaphysical concept, the living God of religion. Metaphysics leaves a place for the further definition of the divine concept in accordance with the personal needs of each person.

Lotze introduced in ethics the concept value and its validity. He distinguishes therefore the domain of the existence and that of the property (Sein-Sollen). In the first one lays the factual empirical action as phenomenon of the time; in the second we find the supratemporal values which have to be realized through the actions. The values have their own form of existence, the "validity," which consists in the fact that the action must conform itself, as temporal phenomenon, to it. A value is however only valid when it is felt by the subject, in some way, as a lust. The absolute character of the values is therefore limited by an element of relativity. F.S.

LOVE

Striving towards a real union between two beings who are involved with each other. As in the Indian philosophy it is for Empedocles a cosmic force by which the uneven elements, in which the cosmos is fallen, are reunited. Plato keeps the difference as a basis for love. Love is then the desire of an imperfect being for the good a perfect being can give him. It appears in two different forms, which will dominate the spiritual life in the Middle Ages. The "amor concupiscentiae" (love of concupiscence) is the love of another thing or person for one's own sake, it is opposed to the "amor benevolentiae" (love of benevolence or love of friendship) in which the lover is concerned with the one he loves as such. One of its forms is the platonic love (in the Middle Ages the *Courtly love*): without any selfishness one is interested in the union with the loved lady. (see also platonic *Academy; Ficino) It should be noted that christianity has reversed the motion of love which in Greek philosophy went from high to low; God is even pure love, i.e. purely giving gift.

When love becomes sexual love, it unites in itself selfishness and unselfishness, physical and spiritual tendencies. One can therefore not speak, as does Freud, of sublimated passion. Passion is on the level of the instinct and strives blindly towards a biological end, without any respect for the value of the human act. In modern psychology however love is often reduced to erotics. There is even a particular terminology. "Binding" instead of the love relation, "narcissism" instead of sensual self-love. The opposite of love is then not the hatred but the "frustration," the disappointment in desire of love. Love and hatred become two aspects of the same relation; from an analytical point of view even often unconscious interchanges with each other.

Love is identified traditionally with the striving, either with the lower or with the higher properties of striving. This is justified in as far as love is more than an emotion. It can not be considered a higher lust, because it surpasses the passivity of the passionate experience and because it is essentially a moment of the will which recognizes the value of a good. Love is much more that momentum in the striving in which the satisfaction of the value or the good (complacentia) leads to the real striving towards it. The contemporary existential anthropology however sees love only in its existential meaning, as the fact of opening oneself for the other. For Marcel and Jaspers this existential communication must make possible that one becomes oneself. Sartre considers love, the mutual possession in freedom, as impossible, however much it may be practiced.

In christian ethics is love (caritas) one of the theological *virtues. Love is commanded as well towards God as towards the fellow-man (friend or enemy); the love for God, who is himself love, becomes from itself love of the fellow-man. Outside of the religious context, love becomes humanitarianism or philanthropy, and altruism. Innerly Schopenhauer reduces love to *compassion.

There exists from old a discussion about the primacy of knowledge and love. Can we only love what we know, or is it the love which makes knowledge possible? Augustine and the augustinian tradition affirm the primacy of love. For Pascal it is also the love ("the heart") which opens for the intellect the way to things and men. It is however Scheler who emphasizes the fact that the essence of things is only revealed in love. In addition every man characterizes a particular "ordo amoris" under which he orders all different values and according to which he acts. See also *emotionalism. J.Gr.—P.S.

LOVEJOY, Arthur Oncken, 1873-
American critical philosopher who called his position one of "temporalized realism," rejected monism and idealism, and was greatly influenced by his interest in historical thought and research.

LUCRETIUS, Carus T., 95-55 B.C.
Author of a didactic poem *De rerum natura*, in which he renders accurately the system of Epicurus, in its entirety. In this poem he tries especially to liberate man from the fear of the gods and death. The poem was not completed by Lucretius and was published by Cicero.

LUKASIEWICZ, Jan, 1878-1953
Polish logician, professor in Warsaw 1920-45, one of the protagonists of the modern logic in Poland.

LUL (LULLUS)
See Raymundus Lullus

LUNEN NATURALE
Natural ability of the human mind, through which specific truths are immediately evident to one. Aristotle and Thomas Aquinas identify it with the *intellect (us agens).

LUST
If used in a very general sense, can have several meanings: pleasure or delight (voluptas), zest for work (studium), sexual lust (libido) etc. . . . One can distinguish the physical lust feelings from the spiritual ones. The lowest grade of spiritual lust is the apathy. The highest possible level of physical lust, especially in a sexual sense, is the complete sexual satisfaction (culminating in the orgasm); the lowest degree of lust is the insensibility, in a sexual sense, frigidity. Another form of lust is the lust for life (animo). Lust originates in the satisfaction of the striving or desire, which reaches its adequate object. The goal of lust is found in the motive power, which proceeds from the desire to provoke a specific action (e.g. the sexual intercourse, which leads to procreation) (Aristotle). For Wundt is the experience of lust and unpleasure one of the *dimensions of his tri-dimensional theory of feeling. For others (among others Ebbinghaus, Lehman) is the experience of lust and unpleasure the only dimension and every other feeling can be reduced to it. Freud speaks of the *Lustprinzip:* the instinctive, unchecked sexual desire, which clashes with the limitations imposed on the children by the parents (Realitätsprinzip). The Lustprinzip is here the main principle of the unconscious.—P.S.

LU WANG (Lu Hsiang-Shan) 1139-1192.
Confucianism became scholastic in the philosophy of Lu Wang, who was imbued with the spirit of Buddhism though his terminology remained Confucian. He considered mind as the embodiment of reason, and taught training of the mind by "tranquil repose," in which state

the essences of truth and goodness will be perceived by intuition, and the individual will be united with the universe. Neo-Confucianism revolted against Lu Wang's metaphysics which regards moral conduct as a mere consequence of intuitive insight into the essences of reality. In recent times, Lu Wang's philosophy was revived by Liang Sou-ming whose book *The Civilization and Philosophy of the East and the West* (1921) was a great sensation in China.

LUZZATTO, Moses Hayim (1707-1747). —
   Some occurrences in Luzzatto's life show a parallel to that of Spinoza. Just as Spinoza earned his living by grinding optical lenses, Luzzatto did the same by lenses. Like Spinoza, he was ex-communicated from his coreligionists. But Luzzatto remained a faithful Jew, ardently devoted to the cause of Judaism. He even felt himself, like the Messiah, bound to rescue the Jewish people from danger and misery, and he believed that the study of the Cabbala would enable him to perform that mission. Notwithstanding pressure on the part of orthodox rabbis, Luzzatto did not turn his thoughts from the mysticism that not only incited his loftiest aspirations but also inspired him to the conception of high ethical principles. Luzzatto was a versatile and gifted writer whose Hebrew style is much admired: He composed a drama, many liturgical poems and philosophical treatises in Hebrew, while his mystical works were written in Aramaic. His best-known book is *Mesillat Yesharim* (Path of the Upright, 1740) which has been compared with Bunyan's *Pilgrim's Progress* though it was not influenced by the latter. In 1746, Luzzatto emigrated to the Holy Land where he died shortly after his arrival.

LYCOPHRON, 5th-4th century B.C.
   Sophist, not much is known about him. Aristotle ascribes to him the sentence: the law is the safeguard of justice. In this he opposes other *sophists who contend that the law restricts the natural law of the strongest.

M

M

Symbol for the *middle term, with which, in a *syllogism, both the final terms are successively compared.

MACARIUS THE GREAT

Ca. 300-395, Egyptian hermit. He is not the author of the stoicly inclined homelies which were accredited to him.

MACH, Ernst, 1838-1916

Austrian physicist and philosopher, professor in Vienna, founder of the *Denkökonomie*. Main works: *Die Analyse der Empfindungen* 1886; *Erkenntnis und Irrtum*, 1905. The duty of science, according to Mach, is only the description and ordering of the observations. In this ordering it is led by the principle of the economy of thought. The most simple ordering of the known facts is the best, because it can most easily be handled in the further work of the thought. Mach therefore termed his philosophy: "Economy of thought". Metaphysical concepts are also nothing more than means to ordering. Their value can therefore only be measured in regard to their use. Philosophy and all other sciences are at the service of life: it is their duty to orient man in life. B.D.

MACHIAVELLI, Niccolo

Born in Florence 1469, died there 1527. Italian political philosopher. Going out from Livy and Polybius he comes to a Roman concept of state, which he wants to see realized in an Italian unified state by a monarch, in whom the Roman will of power relives. According to this Renaissance paganism which was strongly opposed to the corrupt policies of the ecclesiastic State, the ideal state consists in a republic, independent from all other power, even from moral norms, because morality and religion only generate within the limits of the state. To restrain the always threatening corruption, there has to be a regent who knows the human passions and uses these stronger passions for the good of the state, without any scruple and in sober calculation.

MACHINE-THEORY

In biology a conception according to which the living beings differ only from the lifeless matter because of a greater complexity. There is therefore no essential difference between an extremely fine machine and a living being and it would therefore be possible to make a living being. The machine-theory, already present in the works of *Descartes, was developed especially in the second half of the 19th century (Büchner, Loeb), but further studies in the biology have always indicated the particular character of the processes of life and the organization of the living beings, as well as the existence in them of an inner appropriateness, which is naturally negated by the machine-theory.

MACKENZIE, John Stuart,
1860-1935

English idealistic philosopher, professor in Cardiff. The world of our experience shows systematics. On these grounds the cosmos can be seen as order. We have however to recognize the existence of accidents. The order is then broken through the spirit of nature. God surpasses the spirit of nature, he has to be thought as personal or supra-personal.

MACROCOSM (the large "world")

The world as it can be observed by the senses as opposed to the °microcosm.

In the old philosophies which accept a correspondence between the parts of the universe and the parts of the human body, the macrocosm was the universe and the human body was the microcosm.

MAGIC

Collective term for a series of conceptions and customs in the societies of primitive people and also of civilized nations, which would have their origin in a supersensual impersonal power, which the sorcerer would be able to master and use for helping his fellow-tribesmen and also for harming his enemies. *Magism* is the theory which considered the magic as the forerunner of all religious life. °Dynamism made a distinction between the magic attitude (which is compelling) and the diffident, respectful and pious attitude, which became the source of the feeling of dependence and of the feeling of being safe (Beth, Soderblom, V.d. Leeuw)

MAGNIEN, Jean Chrysostome
(Magnenus)

French philosopher but professor in the medical sciences in Pavia; defends an atomic view of nature in his *Democritus reviviscens* (1646), influenced by Sennert.

MAIEUTICS

(Greek mai eutikè, art of the midwife), term used by Socrates, Son of the midwife Phainarete, for the method of interrogation (see heuristics)

MAIMON, Salomon

Born in Nieszwicz (Lithuania) 1753, died in Nieder-Siegersdorf (Silesia) 1800. German philosopher, developed the criticism of Kant in an idealistic sense.

MAINE DE BIRAN
Marie-Francois-Pierre

Born in Bergerac 1766, died in Paris 1824. French official, politician and spiritualistic philosopher. Was first moving in the circle of the °ideologues, but formed later with °Ampère, °Royer-Collard and others a philosophical society which freed itself from all sensualism and materialism.

The experience, according to Maine de Biran, is the only reliable point of departure for philosophical speculation. Although in his youth he was very much interested in the sciences of the external experience, he especially investigated the inner experience, and he became more and more convinced that all philosophical investigation has to start from the constatation of that what the latter, the *sens intime*, produces. The first immediate datum, "the primitive fact", in which all consciousness has its origin, is the effort in which the ego learns to know itself as a superorganic power which acts directly on the body, produces the movements of the muscles and presupposes a passive antipole in the inertia of the muscles as necessary resistance. The importance of the knowledge which is acquired in this manner lies in the fact that it let us penetrate into a real causality, as well in the Ego as in the not-ego, and therefore surpasses the domain of the phenomena.

All further knowledge must be deduced from the "primitive fact" of the consciousness. The certitude of its bases is guaranteed by an instinct of the reasonable nature, the *croyance*, which fills the insufficiencies of the reason.

The essence of the ego is further determined as activity, and especially as willing. The concept of the substance can not be applied on the supraphysical reality of the ego. Maine de Biran however speaks of an independent unity of soul and body in man and he rejects all dualism.

Through his thought and will man surpasses nature, of which he forms a part through the fact of his being sensory. Higher than human life is the life of the spirit, i.e. life with God. Here the *croyance* gives certitude to some truth of religious nature, which man learns to know through reasonable reflexion. This truth can only be reached if man frees himself of all lower inclinations and turns towards God. The "life of the spirit" is completed by the *sentiment,* initially considered as the cooperation of all properties of the soul, later as the grace of the Christian doctrine. The spirit of God works together with the human spirit to bring about the autonomy of the soul, as opposed to the sensuality, and in order to receive peace, light and sanctity.

These ideas brought Maine de Biran by the end of his life to the Catholic Church, in which he found the content of the own innerly experienced divine revelation; the method of the immanence was for him the way to the intelligent acceptance of the dogma. F.S.

MAJESTIC
Variant of the sublime; this latter becomes majestic when it appears as noble, impressive form of a tempered motion. A weaker form of the majestic is the worthy, which has often a moral nuance.

MAJOR
Firstly the greater propositional term or the predicate's term (see P) in the conclusion of a syllogism: it has in a proposition a logically greater extension than the subject term (see S). Also the premise of a syllogism in which the greater end term is compared with the middle-term.

MALEBRANCHE, Nicolas
Born in Paris 1638, died there 1715, French Oratorian. Not satisfied with the union of Aristotle and Scholasticism, he thought that cartesianism united with augustinism (what was lauded by Berulle, the founder of the Oratoire) could be the philosophy of the catholic Church. Writing in a literary, sometimes verbose and often subtle style, he wants scarcely to separate philosophy and religion. He does not deduce the philosophical truth from the religious dogmata, but he thinks that the same Divine Reason illuminates us on the one hand through inner evidence and reasoning, and on the other hand through revelation from the outside. All our cognition is an immediate contemplation of the divine Ideas. Malebranche rejects the innate ideas of Descartes and thinks, under the influence of the *illumination theory of Augustine, that the divine ideas illuminate our intellect immediately. Malebranche starts from two Cartesian principles to reach this *ontologism. 1) That one only has to consider to be true that what one sees in a clear idea in evidence 2) the idea of the infinite (taken not

only in negative, but also in positive sense) is the highest, most clear idea. From the first principle comes the a priori character of Malebranche's philosophy and his contempt of knowledge through experience. From the second principle he derives that we contemplate only and immediately, in God, the object of all our intellectual ideas. There is no need for a proof of the knowledge of God's existence; a simple inquiry into our intellectual life gives us the intuition that we cannot think without affirming that the existence—and that is the infinite existence—is. Under the influence of Arnauld and Bossuet, Malebranche accepts later the existence of created ideas in us, but their real object is God. Our vision in God is however not a perfect one; it is a limited vision of a particular aspect: the extent for instance, from which our entire geometrical science derives, is the divine being in as far as all possible bodies can be part of it.

Through our senses we have a vague contact with the outer world. But certitude about its existence is only given through the dogmata of the incarnation and the redemption. The world is also limited in its existence as creature of God. Not only can matter not affect the spirit, as taught Descartes' dualism, but every creature lacks also activity. God, as the infinite, is unique cause, who makes all other causes unnecessary. God creates in the beginning an unchanging amount of motion in the world, which was also taught by Descartes. Physical things receive parts of this motion, but can not convey them, because they do not know anything about a goal; through their presence they are only an occasion (*occasionalism) to the revelation of the causal activity of the divine wisdom. Since

this wisdom does everything in the most simple ways for its own glorification, it organizes only a few general tendencies, which are, because of the multiplicity of the occasional causes, ready for many applications. S c i e n c e investigates these special laws and applications in order to see them taken up by these general strivings. This world is the best, not absolutely, but in as much as the optimal good is reached through these most simple paths (Optimism)

While he let us see the essence in God of the extensive physical things in an idea, Malebranche rejects, against Descartes, the possibility of such a knowledge of our own spiritual soul. He is afraid that there would be pantheism in the assertion that I would contemplate myself as thinking Ego in the thinking, eternal, necessarily all-unique-Idea. We have therefore only an obscure experimental feeling of our own spiritual existence. A parallelism between the motions of soul and body is brought about by God in a freely constituted law.

The danger that the freedom of the will, basis of all morality, would be lost, if God is unique active cause, is bypassed in Malebranche's philosophy, since he distinguishes in the act of the will the immanent act of consent and the so-called reality of the act. The latter is of God, the former is in the power of the will, by which we do or do not make present the occasional cause, as result of which God works.

Since Malebranche denies any other working cause than God, he prepared the way for the pantheism of Spinoza, in whish God is the only substance and reality. H.R.

MAN

Has been considered in the most diverse ways. The traditional def-

257

inition of man is animal rationale (reasonable animal): reason would therefore distinguish man from animal. Seen in this light man would be a spiritual-physical entity, who comes into being through an immediate and direct information of the physical principle by the soul as form of substance. The *soul is not only a form of substance but also the carrier of its own existence. This aristotelian-thomistic conception has been attacked by the theory of *dualism and *monism. Since the latter is materialistic, it sees and explains man essentially as a physical being or at least as a bodily being, never more than nature; the spiritual nature of man is completely negated.

In the empirical psychology the concept man is completely avoided, while one limits himself to the concepts of person and personality. This has been stopped by the *phenomenology. This philosophical school gives also preliminary considerations on man, which bring about entirely new views on the formal and physical object of the empirical psychology. One borrows formally the classical separation subject-object, which is in the nature of the case not possible in the "self perception as fundament of all knowledge of man". Knowledge of the innerness, but also of the other and of the world comes about through a dialogue with the other. Man is physically represented as carrier of values or as subject. Man is not related to the objects of physics, he is not an object. "Man is not a "thing" with qualities, but an initiative for relations to the world, which he chooses and by which he is chosen" (Buytendijk). One wants to understand man starting from his world (see body).

Hereby becomes the man-in- the-world again object of psychology.

This world is his world, on the grounds of his own interpretation, which the individual man gives to the world and to his own existence. The community of all men, from all eras is defined as mankind. Also genus humanum. P.S.

MANDEVILLE, Bernard de

Born in Dordrecht 1670, died in London 1733, French physician in London. He wrote an anonymous work, later published under his name: *The fable of the bees* in which he attacks the moral conceptions of Shaftesbury. The state, he contends, is destroyed by disinterested perfect virtue. Selfishness and egoism is the secret and open source of all activity, through which the community flourishes as a bee-hive.

MANICHEISM

The doctrine, defended by the Persian Mani (died 276), which explains the world from two independent last principles: a good and an evil one (dualism). To explain evil in the world manicheism made from evil an independent god next to a good god.

MANISM

Term invented by Spencer, deduced from *manes* and not from *mana*, to indicate the adoration of the names or spirits of the ancestors. This would be the origin of all religious life.

MARCEL, Gabriel

Born 1889, French existenz-philosopher. Main works: *Journal métaphysique*, 1927; *Le Mystère de l'Etre* (Gifford Lectures), 1951. Marcel poses the question about the existence of man. This existence can however not be grasped in a simple way since its characteristics are that it forms itself in spontaneous freedom. This does not mean that man would only be himself,

258

he is on the contrary only being in the world (être-au-monde). In this he always is in a situation which is determined from his corporeity (incarnation). This situation is however not given as something unchangeable, but undergoes also the influence of the acting man. He can adopt either of these two attitudes: The other can be object for me in the same way as a thing is an object: the other is then for me only an *"he"* (lui), the other can however also be for me a *presence;* then he is for me a *"you"* (toi). The ego forms itself especially through the I-you relation. Decisive is here the fidelity. If I have confidence in the other and am myself faithful to the other, then I create my own existence (fidélité créatrice). This fidelity is in fact only possible because every "you" has part in the absolute "You" (God). Every man can fail, God never fails. The creative fidelity means therefore in last instance a participation in the creation of God.

It is clear, through this, that philosophical thought is of an entirely different nature than the positive-scientific thought. The positive-scientific thinking poses *problems,* i.e. problems which can be solved in principle, and which disappear as soon as the solution is found. Philosophical thought is placed before *mysteries,* i.e. before problems on which light can be thrown and in which we therefore can penetrate always deeper, but which are not susceptible of a solution, so that they always will remain problems. The philosophical problems come necessarily always back: they present themselves to every period of history and to every single person. So is for instance the problem of the corporeity a philosophical problem: do I have my body or am I my body? It is clear that the relation to my body can not be expressed in terms of possession nor in terms of identity. The corporeity itself, through which I am in the world, keeps always the character of mystery. The same thing applies to our relations with the others and our relation to God. Philosophical thinking can certainly throw some light on it, but can never penetrate it completely. The influence of Marcel on the French philosophy and even outside his country is considerable. The problems of the corporeity have been posed by him in an entirely new way as well as the distinction between being-person and being-object. B.D.

MARCIANUS
See Aristides.

MARCUS AURELIUS, 2nd century A.D., reigned 169-180
Author of *Meditations* (Ta Eis Heauton). Became interested in philosophy under the influence of the stoic philosopher Diognetus, and came later in contact with several stoic philosophers, especially with Junius Rusticus. He then knew the writings of Arrianus on Epictetus: both had on him a decisive influence. He was also in contact with the platonists and peripatetici, and his thought underwent also the influence of their schools. Philosophy is for him an art of living; therefore the importance attached to the ethical problems.

MARITAIN, Jacques
Born 1882, French neo-thomist, since 1948 professor in Princeton. According to Maritain can the metaphysical ontology of Thomas Aquinas not be changed or deepened, but our times have brought many questions into discussion which did not exist in Thomas'

times and which have to be resolved in the light of the principles given by the thomistic thought. In three domains he worked thomism out. In many of his works he made a study of the philosophy of culture. In his most extensive work, *les Degrés du Savoir*, 1932, he treats the subject of a natural philosophy adapted to the modern natural sciences. He had also a very great influence on the social politics because of many works, especially his *Humanisme intégral*, 1936, and other small works written during the war in France and America. He defends in these writings the inalienable rights of the individual and the necessity for more just social laws. In this domain his ideas are very closely related to the teachings of the *personalism of *Mounier, with whom he continuously collaborated. He took part in the discussions about the *christian philosophy with his *De la Philosophie chrétienne*, 1933. B.D.

MARSILIUS OF INGEN

Ca. 1340-1396, magister artium in Paris (1362-85), first rector of the university of Heidelberg in 1386. Disciple of *Joannes Buridanus and his successor as leader of the ockamism in Paris; convinced follower of the *via moderna, as well in logic as in physics.

MARSTON

See Roger Marston.

MARTINEAU, James, 1805-1900

English personalistic philosopher·

MARX, Karl

Born in Trier 1818, died in London 1883. German economist, socialist, founder, with the publication of the *Manifesto of the communist party* (in collaboration with *Engels, 1848) and *Das Kapital*, of the historical *materialism; he is influenced by the theory of Hegel about the dialectical evolution of history and by the materialism of Feuerbach.

According to Marx is the human activity entirely dependent on economic factors, in this sense that in the structure of the society, because of the economic infrastructure of the process of production, is the ideological suprastructure: morality, law, politics, philosophy, art and religion, are completely determined. The phenomenal forms of the spiritual and cultural life have therefore no independent character, but change with the evolution of the physical factors.

With this conception Marx connects a theory about the evolution of the social relations. This evolutes, in his opinion, according to the scheme of the Hegelian triade in thesis, antithesis and synthesis: the original classless society has evoluted towards the bourgeois society of today, in which private property, capitalism and the struggle of the classes are necessary elements, and this will again make way for a higher form of society, in which on the grounds of the collective ownership of the goods of production, all differences between the classes will be abolished. The downfall of capitalism and the disintegration of the bourgeois society can only be achieved through the struggle of the proletariat against the propertied classes. This struggle is, taken in itself, fought independently from the will and consciousness of the individuals; it is, as is the growth of communism, a necessary link in the evolution, but it will be the duty of the socialism to make this struggle conscious in the mind of the people and thus collaborate at this revolution. F.S.

MASARYK, Thomas, 1850-1937

Czech politician and philosopher, theistic realist.

MASS

Distinction is made between the inert mass and the heavy mass. The *inert* mass has to do with the resistance which a body offers to the setting in motion. When a same force gives to one body a smaller acceleration than to the other, then we say that the latter has a smaller mass than the former.

The *heavy* mass is the mass which has a role in the general attraction between bodies. The mutual power of attraction is proportional with the mass of the bodies. Since the fall of a body is based on the mutual attraction of the earth and that body, the heavy mass of a body also determines its weight. The weight is however also dependent from the distance of the object from the center of the earth. It is experimentally proved that the heavy mass is identical to the inert mass.

The mass of an object has been considered in earlier times as being unchangeable, which is however not exactly so. The mass seems to be dependent on the speed of a body. There are also processes known by which a body loses mass and gains energy. This plays indeed a role in the reactions between *atom nuclei. On this loss of mass are also based the enormous quantities of energy which appear in nuclear fission (atomic bomb). The equivalence between mass and energy is expressed in the formula $E = m.c^2$, in which c indicates the speed of light (300,000 km per sec.)—A.G.M.v.M.

In sociology, mass is an unordered group of people, in which the individual let himself be absorbed. It comes into being and acts according to its own laws, which the mass-psychology has tried to determine (social *psychology). Because of the evolution of the contemporary civilization, the mass gets more and more meaning and is at the same time more and more dangerous. The individual who has to give way in all domains for the mass loses himself the more easily in this mass as he tries to flee from his own responsibility.

MATERIAL

The external matter, in which the artist brings the form into perceptible and for the greater part independent shape and existence. The material has however to be seen in its immediate own qualitative way of being, by which it differs from other sorts of artistic material. In a broad sense the material contains all exteriority, which contains possibilities of giving form as well therefore the sounds, the human voice, the motion, the light as solid raw materials. In a narrower sense the term material is only used for the material of the plastic arts: marble, granite, kinds of wood, of paints etc. There is a close relationship between the sort of the material and the sort of artistic conception. Not every sculptural conception can be realized indifferently in wood, marble or bronze. The kind of material determines therefore not only the technique, but also in a great measure the internal intuition and the inspiration. It is in this connection easy to understand that specific materials in themselves already and because of their own natural qualities can produce an inchoative aesthetical sensation. L.V.K.

MATERIALISM

Teaches that the whole reality consists of matter or is based on matter, while all happenings present themselves as functions or actions of matter. Matter is then all that presents itself to the experience as being extensive in space and measurable; the activity of the matter is explained as motion.

Historically materialism is most pure in France during the Enlightenment with °Lamettrie, Helvetius and Holbach; in Germany in the 19th century, on the one hand with °Moleschott and Buchner and on the other hand with °Marx and °Engels. It identifies itself also with the °sensualism, °positivism and °monism, or takes many different forms.

Biological materialism considers more life and the living as phenomena of matter, and teaches that the expressions of life, even the highest (Thinking and willing) are completely determined by the physical factors, which play a role in the processes of life: descendance, heredity, nutrition, climate.

The *anthropological* materialism rejects the existence of all supraphysical factors in man and sees in the psychic and conscious only a quality, effect or representation of matter and its activities.

Historical materialism teaches that the actual economic structure of the society forms the real basis by which the suprastructures of the institutions of justice and state, in the domain of religion, philosophy and general culture in a given era are completely determined. According to Stalin it differs from the dialectic materialism by the fact that it holds on to mechanical evolution of history and therefore can not see that a new production-relation came into being, except if the conditions for such an evolution germinated already in the old society.

Dialectic materialism considers the process of growth as a whole,

in which quantitative relations, as for instance the accumulation of richness, turns into qualitative relations.

In esthetics materialism sees the highest good for man in the satisfaction of his physical and economic needs.

MATHEMATICS, Philosophy of

The development of the mathematics in formal and abstract direction, the evolution of the mathematical logic and the mathematical °foundation research, and the discovery of the °paradoxes, has opened a new period in the philosophy of mathematics. In the past (Aristotle, Plato, Descartes and Kant) the philosophical problems, which are inherent to the mathematical thinking, were already discerned but no specific philosophy of mathematics was ever constructed because a sharp distinction was made between the problems of mathematics and the problems which are posed by the philosopher about the mathematical thinking.

Mathematics, they thought, was based on a series of *evident principles*. The duty of the mathematician is to find as completely as possible the conclusions drawn from these principles. He should simply accept the principles themselves as evident insights, which form therefore an unassailable and unchanging basis. The philosopher can, on the contrary, leave to the mathematician the tracing of the conclusions from the principles; these conclusions have no interest to him. He must however give an explanation for the fact that we have insights at our disposal to which such a kind of evidence applies and he has to indicate the objects to which these insights have relation. They agreed that the mathematical objects could not belong to the world of matter and that the mathematical insights could not be based on empiry, because such kind of evidence could never belong to our empirical knowledge, as is proper to the mathematical principles. The answers, for the rest, were divergent: Plato states that the mathematical objects belong to a domain between the physical world and the kingdom of the ideas and our mind rises therefore to the land of its origin, when it is rising above the physical world, acquires knowledge of the principles of mathematics; Aristotle thinks that the mathematical entities are forms, immanent to the physical world, and we learn to know them through an abstractive insight; that certainly starts from the sensory perception but surpasses it. According to Kant are the mathematical entities forms which the mind imposes to the sensory perceptions: in the pure contemplation of these forms we acquire the evident insights, which give the principles for the mathematics. This idea was still held by *Brouwer, who does however not apply a fundamental meaning to the spatial contemplation and thinks that the time-intuition is sufficient as basis for the pure mathematics.

The above drawn problem is not in accordance with the contemporary state of the mathematics. The pure mathematics constructs its deductive theories without attaching too much importance to the question if evident insights are the basis of these theories. The evidence, which *Cantor ascribed to his comprehension-axiom, appeared, through the discovery of the *paradoxes, deceptive. In some cases do the problems, important for the philosophy, only appear when one deduces the con-

clusions from the principles which are the basis of the mathematics; I name the problem of the mathematical *existence. The previous distinction between the task of philosophy and mathematics can therefore not be accepted any more. The philosopher is not satisfied with the knowledge of the mathematical principles; he has to follow closely the evolution of mathematics, and makes the construction of a philosophy of mathematics necessary. This philosophy will be a mediation between mathematics and the general philosophy. E.W.B.

MATRIX

Is, in the most usual sense of the word, a table which indicates the *validityvalue of a function (from the *propositionlogic) for all the validityvalues of the arguments.

MATTER

In general that of which the sensory perceptible world is composed. Is opposed to *spirit.

In philosophy matter is often used in opposition to form. It has then the meaning of what can be formed. Distinction is made between second matter (materia secunda) and prime matter (materia prima). *Materia prima* is the general bent for matter, which through a form of existence is actualized to this or that sort of matter (also *physical). *Materia secunda* means the concretely existing matter, abstraction made of its form. In this sense the chemistry speaks of matter; copper, iron, water etc.

In natural sciences the term matter is sometimes limited to the ponderable, that what has *mass and weight, as the atoms and the bodies composed of atoms. Light and other radiation phenomena are then called immaterial or incorporeal. This term, which is disappearing gradually because of the recently developed atom theories, is in philosophical respects unwise, because ponderable matter as well as light have all the qualities which are relevant for the concept matter. These qualities are: extension in space and time, changeability, several qualitative qualities, through which the physical can be perceived, a *species-individual-structure. A.G.M.v.M.

MAUTHNER, Fritz, 1849-1923
German positivistic philosopher of language.

MAXIM
Is according to Kant the rule of conduct which, as opposed to the objective and therefore absolutely valid *law, is subjective i.e. can only be valid for a specific individual. Inside the same person a conflict is even possible between maxim and law: the law is also based on the pure reason while the maxim is dominated by the capacity of desiring.

MAXIMA
As the division of a physical extension is mathematically possible in the infinite, but is physically tied to a minimum limit, so can also the size of a physical extension be thought mathematically into the infinite, while the question is to what extent this is physically possible. For instance, the physical speed of something can never be greater than the speed of light.

MAXIMUS CONFESSOR
Born in Constantinople 580, died 662 as expatriate in the Caucasus, author of the *Scholia* (commentaries) on Pseudo-Dionysius, whom he always interpretes according to the catholic doctrine.

MAYA
Sanskrit term for "special power", especially when it gives the ability to the possessor to create something in an incomprehensible way or to delude people with artificial and deceptive (pseudo-) realities. The Indian philosophers used this word to express the impossibility for man to understand the essence and the power of the creator or the origin of the world. Under the influence of the Buddhistic idealistic schools who considered the maya as the power which let us believe in the pseudo-existence of the phenomenal world, the *Vedānta taught originally that the universe is as a dream or a maya (it is not as it presents itself to us): all phenomena are dreamlike projections of the One, who is able to project himself thanks to the maya. In other words, the maya is the formula for the absence of any relation, in the sense one can attach to this term, between the world and *Brahman or the One. Still in other words: maya is the formula which expresses that the diversity of the empiricism is neither identical with Brahman, nor exists in itself as free from Brahman. Later in *Sankara, maya is an undefinable and inexplicable quantity, which neither exists nor not-exists, and conceals for us the reality, and leads us to believe in a pseudo-reality. The maya is then the postulate necessary to explain the "reality" of the universe or the pseudo-existence of the empirical reality, while only the One exists. According to *Rāmānuja however is maya the expression of the marvellous in God's creation and creative ability. J.G.

MAZZINI, Giuseppe, 1805-1872
Italian patriot who associated himself with all the European revolutionary movements in the first half of the nineteenth century and was active in the various Italian rebellions in the 1850's and '60's.

McCOSH, James, 1811-1894
American philosopher of the Scottish common-sense School.

McDOUGALL, William, 1871-1938
American psychologist and philosopher, born in England, professor at Harvard University. McDougall has great merits for the development of the social psychology.

MEAD, George Herbert, 1863-1931
American pragmatic philosopher, professor in Chicago.

MEANING
What is hidden behind the representative form and is understood as such: sense, value, essence. Consciousness of meaning refers to the apprehension of the meaning of a word or gesture. If this is lacking, we speak of asemia.

Can be attached to the expressions of an *axiomatica or formalism. If the formalism is conceived as a natural or pictorial symbolism, then it has a *combinatory* meaning. If we call general-deductive formalism a formalism that has no relation with specific constant things, then can the *purely logical meaning* be closely defined as the purely combinatory representation which corresponds to a general deductive formalism. It is however also possible to consider next to purely logical meanings, the *logic-psychological, logic-physical, logic-ontological meanings,* in so far as one considers the intuitive psychological, physical, ontological content. R.F.

MEANS
What helps us reach a specific goal. In itself it has only meaning and value when considered in relation to that goal. Indirect, what only by means of a third term is deduced from a specific term; in a more general sense: what is not immediate or unconditional but mediated by something else.

MEASURE
A standard, with which quantities and also the intensities of the qualities are compared in order to measure them. The measurement of the qualities is simple and happens with the help of extensive measures as measures of length, surface and content; for time are used astronomical measures as e.g. the year, month or day, the latter being divided in hours, minutes and seconds.

For the measurement of intensity many methods are used, the most important being the measurement of a quantitiative effect of a quality e.g. the volume extension of a liquid by increase of warmth. The standard-measure is then given by a quantitative standard-effect. In art measure means especially the physical and static aspect of the artistic harmony. The measure is that by which this harmony can be reduced to a certain mathematical and even geometrical proportion. In poetry and music for instance, is the measure the divisibility of the motion in equal or at least proportionated parts. The measure is the most quantitative element of the aesthetic harmony and bases it on a physical ground of regularity and reiterability equal to itself. Reduced to pure measure, the harmony loses its aesthetic character and falls into mechanical and lifeless egality. The measure has only an aesthetical meaning in the *rhythm which overcomes it qualitatively, but- in order to be authentic rhythm- can not do without measure, if it does not want to lose its bound freedom in favor of a senseless arbitrariness. L.V.K.

MECHANICISM
The philosophical theory which is based on the assumption that the

only possible changes consist of changes in place and the only possible differences between the things are of a quantitative nature. (see machine-theory).

One of the oldest forms of mechanicism is *atomism. Mechanicism made great progress in the 17th century when it succeeded to explain many changes with the help of the mechanics. It received however a very important setback in the 20th century as an absolute method of explanation, when the evolution of the *atom theory proved that the mechanical representation was only usable in a limited way.

MECHANICS

Mechanism, mechanical, mechanisation. All these terms come from mechane: instrument.

Mechanics means therefore originally: the skill in the production of tools. Later it took the meaning of a division of the natural sciences, namely the theory of the equilibrium, motion and strength. The development of the mathematics since the 17th century has also developed the theory of the mechanics.

MECHANISM was originally the way in which the different parts of a compound instrument gear into one another and move one another. The concept was later enlarged and applied to all compound entities whose uniform development can be compared with the mechanism in the original sense, one speaks then of the mechanism of the economic process, the mechanism of the state.

The derived term MECHANICAL has undergone a similar evolution. Originally: what happens by means of a tool: later: all that happens in a uniform way without thinking. (Mechanical activities).

Mechanisation means the attempt to explain everything through mechanical laws and to make all processes in the technical sciences evolute according to the mechanics. One speaks therefore of the mechanisation of the world-picture to indicate the tendency, originated in the 16th century, to describe and explain the entire nature with mechanical laws and representations. See also Mechanicism. A.G.M.v.M.

MEDIATION

For Hegel the passing of thesis and antithesis into synthesis, in which both are reconciled. The possibility or impossibility of the mediation is the difference between the closed and open dialectics.

MEGARA (School of)

Unites the ethic ideas of Socrates with the ontology of the *Eleates: the *good* is one and unchangeable; evil can not exist and is only appearance. The experience, which seems to indicate the contrary is argued away by emphasizing the contradictions. This school therefore ends up in the *eristics. Its founder was Euclid of Megara, a disciple of Socrates. His successor *Eubulides is known for his dilemma of the liar and others.

MEINONG, Alexius von, 1853-1920

Austrian philosopher, disciple of *Brentano. He built a philosophical discipline which he called *Gegenstandstheorie*, because it is its job to be interested in the things as such. Thing, is everything which the intellect can in any way mean (meinen), therefore as well the existing as the not existing, the possible as well as the impossible. Opposed to this "meinen" of the objects stays the understanding (erfassen) of the objects, and the question about possibility and reality are then very important. This is however not the duty of the Gegenstandstheorie but of the Erkenntnistheorie. B.D.

MELANCHTHON, Philip

Born in Bretten 1497, died in Wittenberg 1560 (called Schwarzerd), humanist, friend and collaborator of Luther. After having been averse to philosophy, he turned towards the philosophy of Aristotle, expurgated from scholastic additions. This philosophy is for him the basis of the revealed doctrine. He completes aristotelianism with stoic elements of the "natural light", taught by Cicero, on which he founds his philosophical ethics. He holds a traditional conception of the natural law, but does not think, with Aristotle, that it can be deduced by reason from the human nature. He accepts the idea of the state of Aristotle.

In the conception of the *universalia is he nominalist; he accepts the physics of Aristotle without the eternity of the world; he rejects the copernican world-image. In psychology he softens the servitude of the will as it was held by Luther. In dialectics he often follows Petrus Hispanus. Because he was the first in the Reformation to give a systematic and philosophical foundation on scientific life, he was called Praeceptor Germaniae and is the founder of a protestant scholasticism.

MELIORISM

Conception according to which the world can always be bettered.

MELISSUS OF SAMOS

5th century B.C., admiral of the fleet of Samos, defeated in 442 the fleet of Pericles. He wrote a philosophical work, in which he explains the theories of Parmenides. The only change which he introduces is that the being is not presented as finite but as infinite.

MEMORY

The ability to fix, keep and revive experiences. There is *mechanical* or sensual memory (remembering without insight, associatively) and *logical* or intellectual memory. Some memory is involved in the formation of a habit and in automatization. Memory has an important predicting function. Herein lies most of its meaning for the entire personality.

MENASSEH, Ben Israel, 1604-1657

Jewish theologian and scholar who interceded with Oliver Cromwell in 1655 to abolish legislation excluding Jews from England (since 1270). His *Hope of Israel* (1650), dedicated to English Parliament, and *Vindication of the Jews* (1656) were written for political purposes; the *Statue of Nebuchadnezzar* outlined a mystical philosophy of history.

MENCIUS (Meng Tzu, Master Meng)

Ca. 371-289 B.C., founder of the "idealistic school" of *confucianism. Man is naturally good. The really perfect man comes, through self-ennoblement, in union with the highest ethical principle, Heaven.

MENDELSSOHN, Moses

Born in Dessau 1729, died in Berlin 1786. Jewish philosopher according to whom philosophy must serve the happiness of man. He accepts the immortality of the soul and mingles rationalistic elements of Wolff with empirical ones of Locke. He invented the *ontological argument, which Kant attacked.

MERCIER, Desire-Joseph

Born in Braine-l'Alleud (Belgium) 1851, died in Brussels 1926.

267

Belgian Philosopher and prelate, professor in Louvain, founder of the Higher Institute of Philosophy, archbishop of Malines, cardinal.

Through his teaching and his many writings Mercier gave the initiative for the renovation of the scholastic philosophy and its adaptation to the philosophical needs of the time as well as to a *neo-scholastic school, which originated in Louvain and had much influence all over the world.

The point of departure of Mercier's ideas is that the philosophy has to be studied for its own, as an independent, purely reasonable explanation of the world, in close contact with the different professional sciences, and that we always have to take in account the actual problems. His philosophy is therefore built independently on an aristotelian-thomistic basis, strongly oriented towards the natural sciences and it therefore also has in its question and defense the characteristics of the philosophical problematics of his time.

In the ontology he holds the strict-thomistic ideas, in which he emphasizes very much the dualistic character of the substance. In epistemology he had to find his own way, opposing the *criticism and he thinks to have found the point of departure in the testimony of the consciousness that we form the judgments, which we spontaneously consider to be true and certain, on the grounds of the insight in the obvious objective connection of the terms, while the content of the concepts, which have the function of terms, are abstracted from those of the sensory experience; that the latter are determined by things from outside, can be proved by the principle of causality (mediatism)—F.S.

MERIT

The happy or unhappy effect (or *sanction) which is due to an action because of its moral or immoral character. Here is understood that there exists an harmony between the moral order and the physical order or world of happiness. This—spontaneous—belief is not irrational: God the creator of both orders must have created, in his simplicity, the ethical order in such a way that it has a perfect response in the physical order. One order is however not the other, neither the pure expression of the other; their bound is much more synthetic. The moral action is therefore meritorious, claims a merit.

METAGEOMETRY

See geometry.

META-LANGUAGE

If one considers a formal system as a play with symbols—to which a sense *can* be attached, which has however no role in the deduction—one must use a language about symbols to determine the rules of the operations with symbols. If this language has a technical symbolism, then it is a metalanguage. In such a language can, for instance, for the symbol which is written p the name 'p' be used, in rules about a class of symbols, e.g. about symbols of propositions, these (undetermined) symbols are represented by letters as P, Q, M, p, q, m.

It is possible that for theories or studies of matalanguages the use of an higher metalanguage is necessary, etc. Curry proved that a meta-language is not necessary for the use of a formal theory, if this theory is considered as a theory of indefinite objects of thought and not of symbols.—R.F.

METALOGIC

Term used in logistics to indicate a complementary theory necessary for a symbolic logic, in which the laws for the logical use of symbols are explained and clarified.

Under this term one can place all the metatheories about logic. It is, without doubt, about metalogic that the most spectacular results in the domain of logic and especially of the simple classical logic have been achieved. This in two ways. 1) the formal qualities of systems have received a strict definition (and not only of logical systems), which has made possible to discover interesting nuances. 2) In regard to the results themselves: in the domain of the logical theory proper the traditional logic did receive important extensions; one can however not contend that logical theses have been reached which were not supposed to exist by the simple common sense.

In the domain of the metatheories, especially of the *decisionmethods and of the *completeness, *unforeseen* results have been reached. Decisionmethods have been worked out for the *proposition—and classlogic (one never doubted the existence of such methods, but these had never been clearly worked out). One had however never suspected (what Church proved in 1936) that the *logic of relations is undecidable. In the domain of the completeness is the theorem of Gödel about the completeness of the logic of predicates most important. This theorem should be distinguished from the well known incompleteness-theorem.—R.F.

METAMATHEMATICS

See foundation research.

METAPHOR, (alienation, transference, imagery)

The use of a term in the broader sense, in as far as it is applied by comparison to other things than according to its strict linguistic meaning. E.g. Clemenceau was the political "tiger" of the first World War.

METAPHYSICAL DEDUCTION

Is, for Kant, the process by which the a priori categories of the intellect are deduced from the forms of judgment (e.g., the category of substance from the categorical proposition a=b).

METAPHYSICS

Originally a collective noun for the 14 books of Aristotle, which were placed by Andronicus of Rhodes (1st century A.D.) *after* (meta) the treatises on physics. All these writings comprehend investigations into the last grounds, lying out of the reach of the experience, of the reality. Therefore the term metaphysics to indicate the study of that what goes *beyond* (meta) the natural things.

There seems to be in Aristotle's writings a certain hesitation about the object of the metaphysics. Once it would study the "esse as such" and therefore be part of the *first philosophy*, sometimes it would be concerned with the study of the "divine esse" and therefore be a *theology*. There is in fact no contradiction since the first philosophy as study of the principles and causes of the esse empties itself in the theology, by the affirmation of the existence of a divine being.

The distinction between those two aspects of the metaphysics remains however through the Middle Ages. It is still found in modern times, especially in Wolff, be it under another form. The study of the esse as such, now called *ontology, is *general metaphysics,* to which the theology answers as being the *particular metaphysics.* The latter develops into the application of the general principles of being to the particular beings; as are the divine being, the conscious being, the physical being. It embraces therefore the (natural) theology, the (rational) psychology and the cosmology.

Seen formally, metaphysics, in its explanation of the reality, surpasses the experience. Whatever it has as object, the reality in general or in particular, it always penetrates their last and deepest grounds. It could even be identified with philosophy, inasmuch as the philosophy surpasses the limits of the experience (as opposed to the sciences). It can even work in a double way. It either explains the reality in the light of a preconceived general principle (*speculative metaphysics*), or it concludes from the experience to such a general principle (*inductive metaphysics*).

Because exactly of its non-empirical character, metaphysics has often been attacked in the course of history, first by empiricism, later by criticism and finally by positivism. The influence of the positive sciences in the 2nd half of the 19th century, leads to the ruin of metaphysics. But the 20th century has brought a new life and even a new flourishing of the metaphysics, especially by Heidegger. He renovates in so far as he tries to penetrate the being of beings, especially in the experience of the anguish.—J.Gr.

META-THEORIES

Are theories about a formal theory (Curry proposes to call them epi-theories, when no meta-language is used). The meta-theories are usually interested in the research of theories according to their formal qualities.

During the last twenty years most of the research in formal thought was spent in the investigation of the meta-theories, especially the meta-theory of mathematics. The research of Hilbert and his school was devoted to proving the contradictionlessness of mathematics, which supposed a *decision method. Since such a method can not universally exist (which has been proved by Gödel in 1931) it was impossible to reduce the proof of the contradictionlessness of mathematics to the one of the elementary arithmetics.

One has also invented techniques to reach proofs of completeness (in the several meanings of the word) and of independence.—R.F.

METEMPIRIC

That what surpasses the empirical, understood in the sense of the sensually perceptible.

METHOD (Gr. meta-hodos, pursuit)

In general: all systematical progress in our thought and action. In science we distinguish between *general* and *particular* method, the latter being more used for specific sciences (e.g. physical, mathematical, philosophical method). They are either *handling-methods* or *investigation-methods.* In the former we teach or study already acquired science according to a specific plan; in the latter a deeper foundation or expansion of our scientific knowledge is aimed at and in which we use then again different inductive and deductive, analytical and synthetic methods. The scientific progress is often principally obtained through the application of a useful new method on the grounds of new experiences and new ideas.

The *inductive methods* (nomological methods), were, after Bacon, developed especially by J. St. *Mill. They give the point of departure for an *hypothesis and the real *induction, and comprehend the method of *agreement*: the *observation of a regular being together present and absent of particular facts and things, so that a causal connection can be put as hypothesis. The method of *difference*: an experimentation (see experiment), by which one tries to verify a similar hypothesis (see verification) also for others than the usual observed cases, especially as complement of the previous method (joint method of difference and agreement); the method of *concomitant variations;* by which simultaneous quantitative changes of the hypothetical cause and its effect are determined and which is again a further completion of both previous methods, but presupposes, that the studied facts and things are quantitatively comparable. The method of *residues;* by which one, reducing different elements of a factor or thing to its known causes, concludes that the remaining elements have to be attributed to a remaining known or unknown cause, which sometimes has led to great scientific discoveries.

The *inductive* method is pre-eminently the physical method, the *deductive* method is the mathematical method, and the *inductive-deductive* method, is a combination of both, the philosophical method. In the *analytical* (see analysis) method or regressive method, one goes from the *concrete to the *abstract, from the particular to the general, from the effects to their causes; in the *synthetic* (see synthesis) or progressive method on the contrary, one goes from the abstract-known to the concrete-existing, from the general to the particular, from the principles and causes to the effects.

The goal of all these methods is the acquisition of new knowledge. Many other subdivisions of methods can be found (see methodology). The *critical* method however tries to investigate the value and the limits of our knowledge (see proof): it can be only the defensive refutation of the arguments against the reliability of our capacity of knowledge (*apologetical* method) or a psychological analysis of our actual acts of knowledge (*psychological* method), or also a critical investigation of the conditions which make these acts possible. (*transcendental* method) See also dialectical method. I.v.d.B.

METHODOLOGY

Or theory of methods (see method), is that part of logic in which the rules are given for proceeding according to a particular plan, orderly, easily and faultlessly in the study of the sciences and the scientific research according to the different goals (see theory of science). The *general* methodology discusses, as the theory of the handling method, for instance the different sorts of definitions, divisions, and argumentations, which will be under discussion in the study of every scientific subject as the three fundamental methods of knowledge. As the theory of investigation the general methodology discusses for instance the application of the *induction and the *deduction, of *analysis and *synthesis, the use of the authoritative arguments and comparisons (see analogies), of *hypotheses and *fictions, the use of statistics and their value. The *special* methodology explains the methods of the different professional sciences, e.g. of the method of teaching (acroamatic and erotematic method), the mathematical method (axiomatic, hypothetic-deductive method) the method of the natural sciences (the inductive investigation method), the psychological method (extrospection and introspection, descriptive and phenomenological method), the historical method (prospective and retrospective method) and of the possible application of these on special objects of study. I.v.d.B.

METRODORUS OF LAMPSACUS, 330-270

Most important and best liked disciple of Epicurus; wrote several polemic works. According to Seneca Epicurus did not esteem his originality and independence very highly.

MICROCOSM (small world)

In the biology: the world, which is only visible with the help of a microscope. In physics: the world of molecules, atoms, electrons, etc. . . ., i.e. the world of those entities which are not visible with the naked eye, but of which the visible things are constituted. (see macrocosm)

MIDDLE TERM (M)

One of the three terms of a syllogism with which the two others are compared (comparison term) and so called because its extension holds the middle between that of the greater (*maior) and that of the smaller (*minor) extreme terms. The middle term has the function of a proof and is as if it were the "heart of reasoning."

MILL, James

Born in Montrose (Scotland) 1773, died in London 1836. Precursor of the English positivism, gave the *utilitarianism of *Bentham a psychological basis with his association-theory, where the unconscious has also its place. The entire psychic occurrence is then reduced by him to perceptions, which have the ability to combine themselves into complexes; when complexes can not further be separated, strong convictions are formed, which Mill, as well as *Hume, calls belief.

MILL, John Stuart

Born in London 1806, died in Avignon 1873. English positivist, son of James Mill, followed in the beginning, because of the influence of his father, the utilitarianism of Bentham, but he soon changed the basis of this theory in the sense that he began to recognize a graduation in the values according to which the ethical subject, driven by self interest, orients his actions. More than his father, he was attracted by social problems.

The main importance of Mill is however found in the fact that he gave a firm form to the epistemological positivism of Comte. Experience is for Mill, the only source of knowledge, induction is the only method of all sciences. The value of knowledge is found in the fixed relation of the representations.

On the ground of these principles the terms and propositions used in logic, had to receive another meaning. The general term means only the sum of a series of representations; the general proposition is only a summary of particular propositions, in which the objective relations between two phenomena are indicated. The deductive syllogism of the classical logic loses therefore its value, since the conclusion is already presupposed by the major and therefore not can be deduced from it.

The first principles of being and thinking do not go beyond the experience: they are won by a simple addition of the facts and have in the framework of the experience a statistic value.

By the end of his life Mill lost some of his agnosticism in regard to metaphysics; he agrees then that one can conclude from the imperfection in the world to the existence of a finite deity. F.S.

MINIMA NATURALIA (the smallest particles of matter which can be found in nature)

Aristotle pointed already out that, as opposed to the mathematical divisibility of the continuum which is possible ad infinitum, the physical division of the physical things only can be achieved up to a certain limit, and that passing this limit the nature of the specific thing can not exist any more.

Aristotle himself thought especially of living things, his commentators in Antiquity and in the Middle Ages accepted also the minima naturalia in the lifeless matter and pointed out that the minima naturalia of a same species had to be of the same size. The minima naturalia differed from the *atoms of Democritus, because the minima of the different matters had different qualities.

The Medieval theory of the minima naturalia melted together with the atom-theory into the corpuscular-theories (see corpuscule) which influenced Dalton for the erection of his chemical *atom-theory.

MINOR

Firstly the smaller term of a proposition or the subject term (see S) in the conclusion of a syllogism: it has indeed in a proposition a smaller *extension than the predicate-term (see P). Also the premise of a syllogism, in which the smaller end term is compared with the middle term.

MISES, Richard von

Born 1883, German neo-positivistic mathematician and philosopher. Died 1953.

MIXTA

The old name for all compound bodies. Is opposed to element. A distinction was made between *mixta imperfecta*, in which the elements are next to each other but free from each other. This can sometimes be seen by the naked eye (as for instance sand and sugar) or only be found out after investigation (as for instance in the mixture of air). In these mixtures the elements are present in the same way as they appear outside of the mixtures.

In the *mixta perfecta* a mutual union of the elements has taken place. A new whole has been formed as in a chemical compound or a living body. The elements are still present but in a somewhat different way. They can however still be separated from the compound. The mixtum perfectum was considered as a totality, a new substance.

MNEME (Gr. Mnemosyne, goddess of the memory)

The *memory in broad sense, as well of the individual as of the species. (Semon). *Mnemotechnics*, initially the art of memory, now used to indicate the means for memorizing.

MODAL

See proposition, syllogism.

MODALITY

The necessary or not necessary way in which, in a proposition the predicate of the subject is affirmed or negated; it is divided in necessity, impossibility, possibility and contingency.

MODEL (of a system)

Is had when one exchanges the symbols of these systems into such an appellation of things, that after the exchange all valid propositions of the system become true propositions.

MODERATION

For Plato one of the four cardinal virtues. It requires such a presence of mind that the given condition and the problem can be considered in all its aspects.

MODERATUS OF GADES

1st century A.D.

Belongs to the platonic school of the neo-pythagoreanism; well known for his symbolic theory of numbers as expression of metaphysical theses.

MODERNISM

Movement among catholics in the beginning of the 20th century, born of the conviction that the modern philosophy as well as the modern biblical criticism had definitely undermined the theses of the natural theology and the historicity of the Holy Scriptures. They were looking for more modern and new ways to bring again faith and reason together. The dogmas, in their opinion, had therefore to be considered as symbols, and their meaning could change according to a change of culture. Pope Pius X has condemned modernism in his encyclical *Pascendi Dominici Gregis*.

MODIFICATION

Change in the way of being or acting (*modus). Modification is generally used for changes which do not touch the essence itself.

MODUS

The manner in which something exists or acts; also the ontological reason of its action or existence. When a definiteness or perfection appears more than once, it differs from case to case and is realized in different ways: the difference between definiteness and way or modus is then clear. Neo-platonism and thomism take this difference in account in their theory of participation: the members of one and the same order are, in different ways, participant to one and the same definiteness. The modus is therefore principle of being such, of alterity, limitedness and distinction. It is a natural relation to the definiteness which is changed by it and the question arises again and again if the distinction between them is real or only logical.

All this applies to the quidditative or essential perfections, namely the substantial and the accidental; but, according to Thomas Aquinas, it applies also, even primarily, to the *esse, the perfection of being, whose modus (i.e. *Modus essendi*) is called *essence.

Many followed the example of Descartes and reserved the term Modus for the qualities of the substance. The *modal distinction* (which Descartes opposes to the real distinction "inter rem et rem" and also to the purely logical distinction) appears between the substance and its modus, and also between the different modi of a same substance.

Among the modi which have created controversies, are those which have relation to the ontological ground of the suppositality: Modus subsistentiae (Cajetanus), Modus substantiae (Suarez), Modus unitivus (Mercier). L.D.R.

MODUS PONENS ET TOLLENS

The affirmative and negative form of reasoning in an hypothetical *syllogism. From the affirmation of the condition of the conditional proposition follows the affirmation of the conditioned and from the negation of the conditioned follows the negation of the condition. E.g. If the premises of a correct reasoning are true, the conclusion is true; well the premises are true, therefore also the conclusion; or the conclusion is not true therefore also not the premises. In a disjunctive syllogism the affirmation of one member of the disjunction produces the negation of the other member, and opposite the negation of the first produces the affirmation of the other. E.g. bacteria are plants or animals, if they are plants they are not animals, if they are not plants they are animals.

MOHAMMED, 570-632

The founder of Islam, his original name was Ubu'l Kassim. Mohammedanism dates from 622, the year of Mohammed's flight, or hegira, from Mecca to Medina, where he became both a spiritual and military leader. Wrote the Koran, the holy book of Islam, under the presumed inspiration of the archangel Gabriel.

MOLECULE

The smallest particle of matter, which still has the qualities of this matter and can be found in free condition.

Only in the so called inert gases is the molecule composed of one *atom only in the other matters the molecule is composed of several atoms, from one or from more elements. One agrees that the molecules in the gaseous state of a matter, are relatively far from each other and therefore move freely and sometimes bump into each other. From this so called kinetic theory of the gases one can deduce the phenomenological laws of gases (Law of Boyle, Gay-Lussac). In liquids however the molecules are united in more or less great complexes.

It is for the philosophy a very interesting problem to investigate if the molecules have to be considered as aggregates of atoms or as substantial unities.

MOLESCHOTT, Jacobus

Born in 's Hertogenbosch 1822, died in Rome 1893. Dutch physiologist and philosopher, materialist, professor in Zurich, Turin, Rome. Matter is the only reality and the explanation of all happenings in the world is to be found in the transposition of matter, which in the circular course of nature comes to life; life becomes thought, thought becomes will and this returns again to matter, which remains the same in all changes of mass and energy.

MOLINISM

A theological explanation, invented by Luis de Molina S.J. (1535-1600), about the collaboration of God's grace and the free will of the creatures. This theory led to a long fight with Dom. Banez (1528-1604) and his disciples.

MOMENT

Point in a dialectical development. See dialectical moment.

MONAD

Is called by *Leibniz the last, further indivisible and innerly simple element of the All.

MONADOLOGY

Theory of the monads, derived from Leibniz' work with the same title.

MONARCHOMACHI

Those who fight, for religious motives (catholics and protestants) against the absolute right of the kings.

MONISM, (Theory of unity)

Term used firstly by *Wolff to indicate every theory which wants to reduce the multiplicity of things to a real physical or spiritual unity.

Also: theory which reduces everything to one cause: God (see theism). One mostly thinks however while speaking of monism, of the reduction of everything to one substance (Spinoza), which is the real unique reality, or of the reduction into a spiritual evolution and logical process (Hegel, German and English idealism), or into a physical energy (Oswald). *Haeckel, who founded the *Association of the monists*, rejects all *dualism and teaches the unity of the universe without distinction between matter and spirit, world and God. The world is then not created, it evolutes according to eternal laws. He also reduces life to physical and chemical processes, and accepts a unity of psychic and physical. From that unique source originates everything (see emanation) because of a continuous evolution. This one is impersonal. Although monism seems to be close to pantheism (as in Hegel and Spinoza) is the monism of Haeckel better called atheism. H.R.

Psychic monism teaches that the spiritual principle in man has to be reduced to a physical process, or that matter only exists seemingly and has to be counted in the spiritual order of being. The first conception has a materialistic flavor and has been followed by Democritus, Lamettrie, Feuerbach; the latter is more spiritualistic and can be found in Berkeley, Spinoza, Heymans. Both points of view are opposed to the aristotelian-thomistic conception of the real unity which exists between soul and body.

From the monistic trend of thought came also the psycho-physical parallelism (Fechner), which does not accept a mutual influence of soul and body, but only one reality, whose phenomena present themselves as spiritual or physical, according to the point of view one takes. In such a monism no place is left for the freedom of the will. P.S.

MONOPSYCHISM

The theory that there are no individual principles of life, but that there is only one world soul, of which all other souls are parts or expressions. In a more narrow sense, that the intellect is not a property of the individual soul, but a joint property.

MONOSYLLOGISM

A syllogism with simple structure, from two premises a conclusion is drawn. Opposed to polysyllogism.

MONOTHEISM

Recognition and worship of one omnipresent God with negation of the existence of other gods. To be distinguished from the henotheism or the worship of a divinity without negation of the existence of other divinities, and from *deism, which affirms the existence of one God, creator of heaven and earth, but rejects all positive cult. See original monotheism.

MONTAGUE, William Pepperell, 1873-1953

American theistic neo-realist, professor in New York.

MONTAIGNE, Michel Eyquem de

Born in Montaigne 1533, died there 1592. In his *Essais,* masterwork of the French literature, he points out, going out from himself, the ferment of the coming new era; he also avows a scientific scepticism and a morality based on the submission to nature. He wants to unite Epicurean pleasure and stoic impassivity. Religious truth is the more strong since it goes in against reason. He defends a fideism, which shows that he wants to remain in the catholic faith. He does not want to dislocate the traditional bonds. He only wants to fight for the independence of the moral consciousness, which is based on the natural laws of all the beings. He defends in his *Apologie* the rational argumentation of Raymond de Sabunde's *Theologia naturalis,* but does not think that the human intellect can reach the truth about God. Because of the relativity of the sensory knowledge, the intellect gives at the most probability. H.R.

MONTESQUIEU, Charles de Secondat, baron de la Brede et de

Born in Brède, near Bordeaux 1689, died in Paris 1755. According to his famous work *De l'Esprit des Lois* (1748) the system of the positive laws rests necessarily in all nations, on some natural relations. The public mind, named here for the first time, which is reflected in the spirit of the laws of each nation, is determined by factors of soil, climate, religion etc. The English form of government is considered by him as an ideal against arbitrariness to guarantee the maximum of freedom, because of the separation of the legislative, executive and judicial powers. This notion of the *Trias politica* (threefold power) has had much influence on the development of the parliamentary demonstration.

MOOD

Disposition of the mind. The mood is closely related to the temperament and the humour. The two extremes are euthymia (cheerfulness) and dysthymia (depression).

There are *anomalies of mood,* as for instance the morbid deviation: melancholy.

MOORE, George Edward

English neo-realist, (1873-1958), professor in Cambridge. In 1903 he wrote his article *Refutation of Idealism* that gave the impetus for the realistic movement in England and America. Moore is a strong analytical mind, who looks very carefully for the inner contradictions of the idealism. He often pursues his analysis to the point that he comes close to scepticism. To avoid this, Moore tries in his *Defense of Common Sense,* 1925, to defend the world image of the common sense as unquestionable. The realism of Moore underwent a certain evolution. He initially admitted that the things themselves are immediately given in the perception. Later he limits this thesis by considering only the "sense-data", the qualities of things, as given. These make us however also know the things themselves. Moore did not write much; but his influence in England and in the United States is especially great. B.D.

MORAL, adj.

In connection with the *morality; more definite in agreement with the morality, moral *good.

MORAL FEELING

Prevalent especially in England during the 18th century with Shaftesbury and Hutcheson as major sponsors. Moral feeling or the *moral sense was believed to be the central principle of morality. Thanks to this capacity man immediately feels what is morally good and approves it, just as he immediately feels what is beautiful and joyfully agrees with it. Moral feeling is entirely independent of any prospect of retribution; harmony, in which the good (and the beautiful) exists, has its own value.

MORAL LAW

The whole of the unconditional and absolute rules which determine the morality. It is either spontaneously ordered or logically thought; is either accepted or felt without criticism or rationally justified; contains in the strict sense the commandments and especially the prohibitions which *oblige* man to do or omit certain actions; in a broader sense it contains all the norms in connection with the realisation of the *ideals* of the moral perfection.

MORAL SENSE

The property by which man, according to Hutcheson and others, immediately would feel what is good and not good.

MORALITY

Opposed to *legality, is called by *Kant the agreement with the natural law, in as much as this law does not stay only extrinsical but is even concerned with the incentive. The action happens therefore according to the natural law, as it also happens because of it or out of reverence for it. So is the businessman who is honest because the natural law requires it, although this attitude is not necessarily profitable.

MORALS

Indicates firstly the manners, which actually are observed in a specific community at a specific moment. Also the ethical conceptions (or the *ethos) which are realized in these manners. It finally also indicates the natural law, not as it is actually accepted, but as it imposes itself.

Morals can also mean the reasoned knowledge of the ethical. It is here not concerned any more with actions or conceptions, but with the study of these actions and conceptions. In as much as this study forms a whole it is called moral system. This moral system can be positively scientific: purely theoretical (as the ethics) or more practical (as the study of the morality). The moral philosophy remains often normative and is limited to the deduction from the different moral prescriptions, but it can also contain an explanation of the spiritual phenomenon. In this latter case the term *ethics is mostly used. J. Gr.

1) habitual conduct or behaviour of an actual society, as opposed to the habitual judgments of the value of these conducts (ethos). 2) Habitual conducts which are the object of a moral judgment of value. This is based a) on a positive fact of social approval or disapproval, followed by a moral or juridic sanction, b) on unconditional principles or criteria which are imposed on man, as being supra-social and supra-individual.

The STUDY OF MORALITY is a normative science which, based on the ethics wants to give practical rules for the action. It is a) a technique which prescribes how a lawmaker in a community can improve the morals (e.g. diminution of the crime rate by regulations of the sale of alcohol); b) the study of the prescriptions which every individual must apply in conscience on his actions, in accordance with the unconditioned principles of the moral law.

Ethics, on the other hand, is a logically built theory about the fixed rules, measures, grounds of the moral activity (morals 2 b)). The principles and also the ethics are philosophic when they are discovered by reflexion on the acts and contents of the natural consciousness; they are theological when they are based on faith in a supernatural revelation.

The *science of morals* (translation of "science des moeurs", Lévy-Bruhl) is the positive science of the moral and ethic forms in specific societies. E.D.B.

MORE, Henry, 1614-1687

British philosopher. Originally correspondent and disciple of Descartes, he develops a mystic theology and philosophy, much influenced by platonism and neo-platonism. The reality can be penetrated according to More, by intuition, which can obtain confirmation from reason.

MORE, Thomas

Born in London 1478 died in London 1535. English politician and humanist, chancellor, under Henry VIII, decapitated because of his opposition to Henry's church politics, canonized martyr. In his *Utopia* More describes an ideal state, in which a common possession of goods exists; without finance the goods are exchanged and divided among the families. The leaders are chosen from the best ones. There exists freedom of religion but the people who would deny the truths of the natural religion (divine providence, immortal soul, reward for the good and punishment of evil) are considered inferior and can not occupy an office. The art of war is accurately described.

MORGAN, Conwy Lloyd, 1852-1936

English biologist and neo-realistic philosopher. The neo-realism is developed by Morgan in a metaphysical way. He teaches a form of evolution of the reality (see Alexander, Broad), in which the new stadia of the evolution always add an aspect to the previous stadium, which can not be reduced to it. *Emergent Evolution* (Gifford Lectures), 1923 *Life, Mind and Spirit* (id.), 1926.

MOSES MAIMONIDES

Born in Cordova 1135, died in Egypt 1204, most influential person in Jewish philosophy. Tried to combine the doctrine of the Mosaic religion (with the additions of the Talmud) and an expurgated and theocentric aristotelian philosophy, into one complete system, as the Scholastics of the Latin Middle Ages did with the christian religion. His main work: *Dux perplexorum*, is a treatise, not always very well ordered, of the philosophical doctrine about God and morals, with much exegesis of the Scriptures. He gives a long explanation of the names given to God in the Bible, of the divine attributes and the way we know Him. He is however not very clear about resurrection and immortality. The celestial bodies are reasonable living beings, while the angels are incorporeal. Maimonides shows further that the proofs of Aristotle for the eternity of the world have no compelling value and he remains at about the same point which Thomas Aquinas, one century later, will reach: it is not impossible that the world be created in the time, but the so called proofs for this temporality, given by so many theologians are nevertheless not compelling. The prophecy has a natural explanation, as in the epistemology of *Avicenna and *Averroes. Maimonides speaks also of the origin of evil, the knowledge God has of the singularia and the providence; providence is only personal for man, it is specific for the other lower creatures. He gives then a rational explanation for all the moral prescriptions of the biblical law. The ethics are indeed an aid to achieve perfection, which really consists in the reflection. His epistemology and the theory of the soul are not very extensively elaborated. The intellectus agens appears however as a separately existing being and mediator between God and man, e.g. in the prophetical knowledge. Maimonides gives also many indications about the Greek and Arabic philosophers, which were used by the Latins.

Dux perplexorum was during Maimonides' life already translated into Hebrew. A great controversy among the Jews was the result and they questioned if profane sciences should be taught to the children. The Latin Scholastici attacked the negation of all multiplicity in God (therefore of the Trinity), his negation of a real analogy in the attributes of God and of the positive attributes, the fact that he taught that the celestial bodies were living beings and the eternal movement, the natural prophecy, the limitation of the omnipotence, of the providence, the ignorance about grace, and a point of his ethics. J. V.

MO TI (Mo Tzu, Master Mo)

Ca. 400 B.C., Chinese philosopher and moralist, taught the principle of the "all-embracing love", rejects the confucian ideals of "sense of duty" and "decorum". Attacks the war of aggression. His argumentation is utilitarian; strong religious influence. In later phases Mohism has special interest in the dialectical and epistemological investigations.

MOTION

This concept in philosophy differs from contemporary colloquial and scientific language, where it means only a change of place, for in philosophy qualitative and substantial changes are also implied. This appears clearly in the definition of matter as *"ens mobile"* in natural philosophy (*ens mobile*: being which is subject to motion, change). It is also clear from the definition Aristotle gave of motion: *actus existentis in potentia in quantum in potentia*, the act through which a potential thing becomes actual, inasmuch as this actualization is not completed. Motion is thus being on the way to actualization. So is an arrow in motion, when it leaves the bow but has not reached its goal. As long as the arrow is still in the bow, it is only aimed at the goal, and when it reaches the goal, this aim is achieved; only during the time in between we can speak of a not-yet-completed realization of the aim. Although the example is deducted from local motion, it is clear that the definition also applies to other forms of motion; e.g., a chemical element can be considered tending toward a solution before it mixes in a solution; when the solution is achieved, the tendency is also achieved. It is only during the act of reaction that the chemical element is in motion, moving toward the realization of the solution.

The Aristotelian concept of motion is thus broader than the meaning of motion in contemporary language. There is also another difference. Behind the Aristotelian concept of motion a postulate is hidden which states that there is an absolute difference between the condition of motion and rest. This is especially clear in the conception of local motion. When an object is in motion, this means, according to Aristotle, that it changes places in regard to the earth, which is in absolute rest in the center of the universe. Since the natural sciences abandoned the idea of a resting earth, and nothing has taken over the role of that which is in absolute rest, the concept of motion received a relative meaning. We can only speak of motion in regard to something, which is considered in rest in relation to the motion in question, without being in rest absolutely. A.G.M.v.M.

MOTIVE

That which determines someone to act, i.e., to realize a proposed content. The motive can coincide with the content of the act but the acting subject can also have his own reason to act (motive in a narrower sense). It is then opposed to the content of the act, and the motive coincides with the intention. The emotion of the acting subject also leads to the act as a *vis a tergo;* e.g.. his love or hatred, his respect, etc. (*see* incentive).

In psychology the motive as incentive for human action is limited to the intellectual domain. It has now, however, a broader meaning and indicates the affective-conative factor which regulates actions. By underlining the affectivity in motive the way has been opened for the concept of "unconscious" motives. Stern opposes genomotive (real motive) to phenomotive (the apparent motive).

MOUNIER, Emmanuel, 1905-1950

French personalistic philosopher. Founder of *Esprit,* 1932. Mounier asks for a social reform in which the individual can achieve a complete development. He does not expect this from an individualistic society, but from a social society, in which the individual is at the same time for himself and for the others; this is only possible when one recognizes a personal God. Otherwise man becomes the slave of the state, money or a specific social class. Mounier calls his philosophy personalism. Main work: *Révolution personaliste et communautaire,* 1934. B.D.

MUENSTERBERG, Hugo, 1863-1916

German neo-Kantian, later in the United States. In his *Philosophie der Werte,* 1908 he developed further the theory of values of the School of *Baden.

MUIRHEAD, John Henry, 1855-1940

English neo-Hegelian, professor in Birmingham. Muirhead is especially interested in ethical questions.

MULTATULI, pseudonym of E. Douwes Dekker

Born in Amsterdam 1820, died in Nieder-Ingelheim 1887. Dutch man of letters, though his *Ideeen* he popularized the contemporary ideas of positivism, agnosticism and free thought.

MULTIPLICITY

Combination of unities, i.e. diversity tempered by unity, and therefore relative diversity. It is unthinkable that terms should not be susceptible of comparison under any aspect, this means that they would differ absolutely from each other or be an absolute multiplicity: the fact only that this question can be treated, shows implicitly the possibility of calling up these terms before a similar mind, of understanding them both and in this sense at least to unite them. Unities can be united superficially or thoroughly, through *relations of different nature. The following question arises: are the terms of a multiplicity necessarily countable, do they always form a specific number or is it not impossible that either simultaneous terms which constitute a whole, or successive terms of a series, would be in an *infinite number?

MUNK, Kaj, 1898-1944

Danish pastor of orthodox Lutheran faith who defied Nazi tyranny during the German occupation until he was murdered by the Gestapo.

MUST

Expresses a necessity, either of a physical nature (=mussen) or of a moral nature (=sollen.) In the first case it is a necessity of this nature that what has to happen can not not-happen; in the latter case it is something which should be, which is proper to be but is not.

MUTATION

Is called in the theory of heredity a sudden change in a living being, which maintains itself in the reproduction, and seems therefore to be hereditary. The perceived mutations have a relation to smaller changes within the limits of a species.

MYSTERY

In religion for the Greeks secret rituals, by which one was initiated in order to obtain a blessed existence in the hereafter in the presence of a specific divinity: In the Scriptures the term mystery is used in the profane sense; a secret thing, but more in the religious sense: divine secrets. The Fathers of the Church use the term more in particular for the effects of the redemption, applied to the christians in baptism, confirmation, the Eucharist (in Latin: sacramentum). In the 19th century the Church gave a statement about the relations between the mysteries and reason: they are 1. truths hidden in God; 2. truths which we can only know through the divine revelation; 3. truths which, even if they are imparted to us by divine revelation, still remain covered with the veil of faith, and can not be reduced to the evidence of natural principles. K.L.B.

MYSTICISM (Greek: mystikon, secret, mysterious)

Immediate experience of the action of God on the soul, and in connection therewith also the theory and explanation of this action.

In the not christian religions mysticism is generally explained in a pantheistic manner, it is the experience of the identity of the most inner being of man with the divine, or as in Buddhism, of a still beyond the divinity lying not-being (Nirvana). Very often in christianity images are used as: the drop which loses itself in the ocean, or the candle which is completely consumed by the flame, or the bride who loses herself completely in the divine bridegroom; christianity has however often stated that man cannot possibly reach the mystical experience through a natural way. It is a special grace, in which God imparts himself to the soul and enables the soul to experience his action. Linked to the antique theory it is called also infused contemplation. Next to the real forms of mysticism there exist many forms of imitations. K.L.B.

MYSTICISM (Mediaeval).

The historians distinguish between two parallel and in some respects opposite forms of mediaeval thought: scholasticism and mysticism. The mediaeval mysticism belongs actually more to the history of the theology and the piety, and one should rather distinguish between scholastic philosophy and scholastic theology. The mystic theology is important for the history of philosophy in so far as it is speculative and contains philosophic ideas about God, nature and the life of the soul, the way in which we know God through our natural properties. Such philosophical ideas can be found by all great mystical theologians (Pseudo-Dionysius, Augustine, Joannes Scotus Eriugena, Anselm, Joannes of Ruysbroec and the Dutch School and Joannes Gerson and the French School, Bernard and the Cistercians, the Victorians, Bonaventura, Thomas Eckehart and the German School). The history of philosophy is generally much interested in *heterodox* mysticism, because it is generally the result of rationalism, i.e. of an exaggerated reverence for the philosophical reasons for the higher forms of contemplation. Heterodox mysticism is actually very little represented in the christian antiquity and in the Middle Ages. Some elements could be found in the gnostics, Joannes Scotus Eriugena, Joachim of Fiore, Eckehart, the unknown author of the *German theology*, even in Joannes of Ruysbroec and Nicholas of Cusa, but one does not consider the heterodox character of most of these writers very important. F.V.S.

MYTH, (Greek: word, story)

In Plato a phantastic story showing more profound truths, which can not be reached by strict logical argumentation. E.g. the myth of the grotto. In the modern religious science, story about the primitive times, in which older peoples by means of personification give an imaginary expression to their view on life and world. Some even speak of the christian dogma as of a myth. One means by this to negate the historic character of the redemption by Christ, without however always negating its truth as symbolic expression of the real relation of man and God. In our times myth means also the ideal image of a movement. In Rosenberg's *Mythus des 20 Jahrhunderts* myth means the summary of all the irrational forces of the German people.

N

NAIVE

(Lat. nativus, innate, natural), appellation, sometimes used in a pejorative sense and applied to our natural conviction that the things are as we see them; opposed to the more critical conception about that what we know, in a scientific theory of knowledge.

NAME

Sometimes used for word. Since a proper name does not call something by its meaning, it is also called: word without meaning, which can not point to a reality. The writings about the "names" of God, treat his attributes.

NATION

Community of people which acquired an inner unity in the domain of culture and often also of politics. There is no definite answer to the question if the first or second factor is decisive. Since the romanticists (Fichte) the idea of a national *state has become more important; this state would best guarantee the further development of the nation.

NATIVISM or innatism

The theory that the innate properties are determining the further evolution. Is opposed to empiricism, which teaches that the influences of the milieu and exercise are decisive for the determination and development of the conduct. In psychology this opposition is solved by the *convergency law* (Stern): the interaction of ability

and milieu determine the evolution.

In the psychology of observation nativism refers to the theory that the optic observations of space are an innate quality (Helmholtz). See also inneism.

NATORP, Paul, 1854-1924

German neo-Kantian of the School of *Marburg, professor in Marburg. Natorp rejects the duality of thought and observation: all knowing is thinking and all reality is only content of thought. This identity of thought and reality is however not given, but proposed as a duty to the one who thinks, as a continuous process. This way of thinking brings Natorp gradually closer to *Hegel. The ethics are for Natorp ethics of the will, the ethical action is an action answering to norms, so that the ethics can be considered as a logic of norms. In later years Natorp became more and more convinced that the complete reality can not be grasped in the logical system. He was then under the influence of the *philosophy of life and the *phenomenology. Natorp's thought is put in simple form in his *Philosophie*, 1911. His *Platos Ideenlehre* in 1903, is important for the history of philosophy and for the understanding of the purpose of the School of Marburg. B.D.

NATURA

Nature i.e. the All. It is identified by *Spinoza with God. As creating cause God is then Natura naturans, while the natura naturata indicates the All as existing through God.

NATURALISM

Philosophical doctrine, in which nature is considered as the only being: while spirit and the spiritual are related to nature, this latter resting only on itself. One has to note that nature is very often limited to the physical world or the world of the sensual experience, so that naturalism is close to *materialism, *sensualism or *positivism.

In ethics naturalism deduces morality also from nature. Morality is then: act according to the requirements of nature or unfold the natural impulses. This unfolding is then strongly encouraged in social and pedagogical connections.

Naturalism as a school of art by the end of the 19th century, taught that real art is the reproduction of nature. Nature does not mean here any more the reality as opposed to the ideal, but the reality inasmuch as it is different from the ideal. J. Gr.

Naturalism in the philosophy, and especially in the philosophy of history is the use of the scientific method on history. In this respect naturalism is opposed to *historicism, which emphasizes the opposition of nature and history.

In theology naturalism is used to indicate the identification or too close union of the divine and nature.

NATURAL LAW.

This term indicates a firm order in the occurrences in nature. A superficial investigation of nature shows us already that next to great varieties one can find a specific regularity in the occurrences in nature. There is however a long way between the discovery of the regularities and the formulation of a

natural law. A natural law has indeed to be absolutely valid. This absolute validity can be obtained by studying a specific concrete occurrence, e.g. the fall of a stone, in such a manner that those aspects are discovered which have this specific character that they follow a law. The fall of the stone is different from the fall of another stone, but *each fall* appears to satisfy a natural law. The natural laws are therefore not only absolutely valid but also abstract. The different natural laws can be brought in relation with each other. The laws of the fall and laws which govern the movements of the celestial bodies can be united into the one *law of attraction of *Newton.

The natural laws show thus mutually a certain order and dependence. As soon as the fundamental law is found, e.g. the law of Newton, it is possible to deduce from this fundamental law a specific law, e.g. the law of the fall. This does however not mean that man has a real insight in the necessity of the natural law. The necessity is always hypothetical. If the general law of attraction is valid, then the law of the fall is also valid, but the law of attraction itself is not really understood. The natural laws have therefore always a certain character of actuality; from the analysis of the facts they are found in a certain hierarchic order and remain then in the last instance always based on these facts. A.G.M.v.M.

NATURAL RIGHT

The legal ordering of the human society, which would be borrowed from the nature of man itself and therefore would have absolute validity in space and time. The Stoic School was the first to elaborate on this subject. In the scholastic school it is considered as the expression of the ordering laid by God in the creation. Natural right however had its main development, outside of all ecclesiastical relation, in the 17th and 18th centuries during the Enlightenment. The founders were Hugo de °Groot, Pufendorf, Thomasius; next to them Leibniz, Wolff and Kant, who however followed a somewhat different line.

The theory of De Groot is that the natural right does not only contain an ideal ordering, to which the positive right has to conform, and it does not only form the basis for the validity of the positive right, but natural right itself has juridic validity, at least when positive right fails. It is absolutely unchangeable, even God could not change it and it would be valid even if God did not exist.

After the natural right had had a deep influence on the legislation and had helped to the humanisation of the administration of justice, it lost very much of its meaning in the 19th century. The historical school of law underlined indeed the dependence of the legislative order on the people and their history, and, under the influence of positivism, positive right became the only valid right. In contemporary studies of law the interest for natural right is again growing. J. Gr.

NATURAL SCIENCE

Is interested in the study and discovery of the fundamental laws of nature, in order to obtain through this way, an insight into the concrete occurrences in nature. This insight is always relative, because we do not have an a priori knowledge of the natural laws, but have to find them in the concrete natural occurrences. This finding of the occurrences happens via observation and experiment, which make it possible to analyse the many factors so that through that analysis one can find out what factors are essential for a specific occurrence and what factors are not. The basis of the natural science is therefore the inductive method.

The deductive method however has also an important role, because the different discovered laws of nature can be put in an hierarchic relation. In this deductive part of the natural science mathematics plays a very important role. The modern natural sciences contain next to each other a more theoretical and a more experimental section. The theoretical natural science e.g. is concerned with the connection of natural laws found by experiment, so that it can deduce from them new laws which again have to be tested experimentally. For the relation between natural science and natural philosophy see cosmology and physics. Also science. A.G.M.v.M.

NATURAL THEOLOGY

Differs from supernatural theology because of its object and method. Its object is not the data of revelation, but the religious life of people inasmuch as it is a phenomenon which is liable to "empeiron" or observation. Its means are the normal natural means of knowledge: empirical investigation of factual data, psychological and phenomenological penetration of the sense of religious conceptions, attitudes and actions, philosophical investigation as to the final causes of the religious life and as to its truth and value.

NATURE.

This term, very closely related to kind and sort, has a different meaning according to the context in which it is found: one thinks of the pairs of concepts natural-supernatural and nature-culture. In compounds as natural science and natural philosophy the term nature points to the physical being as distinguished from the spiritual being. The characteristic moment in the use of this term in this connection, is that it points towards something which exists independently from man's free will. Nature is a datum which we can study, use, change but never change essentially. We have to take nature as it is. All use or change of a natural datum can only happen on the basis of the fundamental laws which govern nature.

A distinction can be made between the *organic nature*, or the nature of living beings, and the *inorganic nature*, nature of the not-living beings. A.G.M.v.M.

NECESSARY

What cannot be otherwise. In reality as well as the order of thought, necessary can be taken in an absolute, i.e. unconditional sense, or in a relative, i.e., hypothetical sense.

In thought is *absolutely necessary* that which imposes itself as thought, it is not based on anything else, so that it in no case can be thought away. Namely the most fundamental ideas and principles. *Hypothetically necessary* is all that is dependent on a specific idea which is postulated and as soon as it is postulated, and which can not be otherwise thought. Such are the conclusions of an inference. The question is now if in the order of thought the hypothetically necessary requires inevitably the absolutely necessary.

In reality is *absolute necessary* what is completely independent and can therefore not be destroyed by anything else; *hypothetically necessary*, is all that is dependent on specific causes, as soon as they are presumed, and which have to exist. The relation between cause and effect is twofold: The effect can follow necessarily from the cause, i.e. that the cause is forced from nature to produce this effect; or the cause can be free and determines autonomously its actions, so that the effect is produced in a contingent way. If a cause is free and still dependent on a higher power, the laws which are imposed to it, as a necessary rule, will not be force but obligation. The question is here again if hypothetically necessary reality presupposes the existence of absolutely necessary reality. One has also to pose the question if and in what sense °necessity in the order of thought is based on real necessity, how and to what extent it reveals it. L.D.R.

NECESSITY

The °modality of a judgment, in which a predicate is applied in such a way to a subject that it never can be denied to this subject. E.g. every human being holds a metaphysical view. Is opposed to °contingency and °impossibility.

NEED

A desire for something because of a shortage. This can either be sensual or spiritual. Need is generally transitory; it can return when another shortage is experienced.

NEGATION (in formal logic)

Of the °proposition p is the proposition not-p (equivalent to: p is untrue). The negation of the concept a is the concept not-a.— In the minimal °logic, the negation not-p of a proposition can be defined as: p results in the untrue; herein is a specific (arbitrary) proposition chosen as the untrue.

NEGATION

As of judgment which determines the not-presence of something which could be present. This act is actually twice relative. It presupposes on the one hand a positive term A which is rejected, in order to make room for another term B; it is, on the other hand, based on the alterity of A and B. To negate that A is, means that one replaces it by something else. The *relative* negation has therefore sense, but the *absolute* negation is senseless: the absolute negation or the negation of everything would be an idea from which all content is rejected; but an idea without content is the negation itself of this idea. It is therefore on a basis which is absolutely impossible to negate or on an affirmation, that all negation eventually rests.

Negation serves for the distinction or limitation of content and size of the concepts. Through a negative *concept we know what something is not: it serves often as a preparation for a positive concept. It can also be purely negative (as the concept nothing) or privative, as the negation of something which should be there (e.g. blind). In a negative judgment we deny one or another predicate to a subject, e.g. grass snakes have no venom-teeth.

NEMESIUS OF EMESA

Ca. 400 A.D., bishop of Emesa in Phoenicia. His work: *De natura hominis* is an important source for the knowledge of the Greek philosophy. His personal ideas: an eclectic neoplatonism with christian influence.

NEO-AUGUSTINIANS

Form a not clearly defined school in contemporary thought. There is in their thinking a growing influence of *Augustine, for instance as a result of the affinity which we can find between the thought of Augustine and the *phenomenological and *existential views. Neo-Augustinian elements can especially be found in the *spiritualistic thinkers in France and Italy, in the *neo-thomists of Germany, France and Italy.

NEO-CRITICISM

The renewal of the *criticism of *Kant, firstly created in Germany by *Liebmann, *Lange and others, in France by *Renouvier, *Lequier, *Lachelier and others. In the schools of *Marburg and *Baden neo-criticism was further developed.

The followers of neo-criticism are in general quite independent from Kant and each of them emphasizes specific aspects of Kant's system; some emphasize the role of theoretical reason, others the practical reason. Many efforts have been made to solve definitely the problem of the real existence of the *Ding an sich*. The realistic interpretation has sometimes the upper hand, although the possibility to know the *Ding an sich* is not accepted, and sometimes is the D.a.s. considered as a pure concept. Opposed to empiricism and positivism, they point out the a priori elements in knowledge. Many follow Fries and give a psychological basis to this a priori.

NEO-FRIESIAN SCHOOL.

This neo-Kantian school gets its fundamental inspiration from Fries. Its founder is Nelson. It tries to lay a basis on Kantian criticism through psychology. The influence of this school remained quite limited.

NEO-HEGELIANISM.

This term indicates the renewal of the Hegelian philosophy, as it appeared in several European countries in the last quarter of the 19th and the first quarter of the 20th centuries. Most important was the revival in England and Italy. In England it began with *Hutchison Stirling, was defended by some important philosophers as Green, J. and E. *Caird, *Bradley, *Bosanquet and others. In Italy it was prepared by *Spaventa and *Vera and achieved complete evolution with *Croce and *Gentile, whose influence was felt far outside Italy. Neo-Hegelianism has never had a strong root in Germany; with Lasson, *Kroner, Hearing, *Litt it had partly a more historic partly a very free character, as opposed to the strict neo-hegelianism in England and Italy. There was no neo-Hegelianism in France, but there is since 1940 a growing interest in Hegel. B. D.

NEO-KANTIANISM

The revival of the study of *Kant, which happened at the end of the 19th century. It rejects the *positivism and the speculative philosophy of *Hegel, although it often, especially in the School of *Marburg, reapproaches Hegel. The neo-Kantians want to develop thought, farther than positivism and materialism permit. They therefore go back to Kant. With him they find on the one hand the victory over positivistic and materialistic attitudes in thinking, and on the other hand the critical aversion for premature speculation. Neo-Kantianism was prepared in the 19th century by thinkers as *Lange, Liebmann and Riehl. In the 20th century it finds its complete development in several schools, the most important being: the Schools of *Baden and *Marburg. Also the *neo-Friesian School and in a certain way also the critical *realism. Neo-Kantianism remained always a typically German school. It had not much influence in England, France, Italy or the United States, but in the Netherlands the official philosophical thought between the two world wars was practically completely neo-Kantian. This was in a certain measure also true for Belgium. Neo-Kantianism disappeared in Germany, the Netherlands and Belgium after the second World War. The School of Baden and the critical realism left important impulses in the modern way of thinking, the School of Marburg on the other hand gave an indirect help to the advent of *neo-positivism and the new undogmatic interest in Hegel. B.D.

NEO-PLATONISM

The revival of platonism, which was the dominating philosophy of the pagan world since the middle of the 3rd century till the closing of the philosophical schools in Athens in 529. Neo-platonism had a long preparation from Antiochus of Ascalon and Posidonius to *Plotinus, who gave it its definitive form. In the 4th century it became the bastion of paganism against the growing christianity, with its main centers in Syria and later in Pergamum. Iamblichus belongs to this period. In the 5th and 6th centuries the schools of Athens (Syrianus and Proclus) and Alexandria (Hypatia, Synesius, Olympiodorus) became important.

Since the 19th century neo-platonism is opposed to the doctrine of Plato, as the theory of the hierarchy of being which has a strong dynamic character. One considers now however that neo-platonism is in its essential characteristics a legitimate platonism.

About the influence of neo-platonism in the Middle Ages, the Renaissance and later, see platonism. C.J.d.V.

NEO-POSITIVISM

Distinguishes itself from the older positivism and empiricism, because it abandons the striving towards an empirical foundation of the pure mathematics, in connection with the results of the °mathematical °foundation research, and especially in connection with the °logicism of °Frege and °Russell. The theses of logic and mathematics have a purely conventional and tautological character, they do not represent an independent content of knowledge and do therefore not need an empirical foundation. The neo-positivism was before 1933 especially defended by the "Wiener Kreis" (°Schlick, O. Neurath, °Carnap) and the "Berliner Gruppe" (°Reichenbach, R. von Mises), but has followers in the entire world. E. W. B.

NEO-PYTHAGOREANISM

Renewal of the old Pythagoreanism. This took place in the 1st century B.C. and was carried through by mixing with it platonic, peripatetic and stoic elements; depending on the representatives of this school one of these influences will be stronger. In metaphysics they emphasize very much the transcendence of the divinity, so that they believe in the existence of several demons who bridge the distance between the physical world and the divinity; in psychology they emphasize the duality of body and soul; in ethics much attention is paid to asceticism. Main representatives are: Nigius Figulus, Apollonius of Tyana, Moderatus of Gades, Nicomachus of Gerasa and Numenius of Apamea. G.V.

NEO-REALISM

The return to realism as it was started by °Moore in England and the United States. Neo-realism meant in England by the end of the 19th century, separation with the contemporary d o m i n a t i n g °neo-hegelianism. From the beginning it appears in England in two different schools. The first one is neo-positivistically oriented: among others °Broad, Nunn, Russell; the other is oriented towards °metaphysics: among others °Alexander, Ewing, Laird, Morgan, Whitehead. In the United States are also different forms of neo-realism.

NEO-SCHOLASTICISM.

One can speak of neo-scholasticism, since in the 19th century a number of philosophers and theologians went back to the great figures of the mediaeval thought: °Bonaventura, °Thomas Aquinas, °Duns Scotus, in order to find there inspiration for a renewal of philosophical and t h e o l o g i c a l thought. This movement has its origin in Italy and Thomas Aquinas was especially studied: °Buzetti, Tarapelli, Liberatore, Sanseverino, Cornoldi, Zigliari. A similar tendency originates in Germany, but has from the beginning a freer conception: °Clemens, Kleutgen, Stöckel, Gutberlet, H a g e m a nn, Werner. In 1879 Leo III writes his Encyclical *Aeterni Patris* in which he recommended for the catholic philosophers the study of the great scholastic thinkers, especially Thomas Aquinas. This encyclical influenced many important initiatives. The Franciscans began to work in Quaracchi at the critical edition of the writings of Bonaventura and Duns Scotus; the Dominicans in Rome at the critical edition of the works of Thomas Aquinas, de *editio leonina*. None of those works is completed. Next to that there was the initiative of the foundation of a thomistic center in Louvain, the initiative was taken by Leo XIII and executed by *Mercier. From this initiative came the Higher Institute for Philosophy in Louvain, one of the most important philosophical centers in the world. Since then neo-thomism has forgotten its original, quasi academic character and has been in contact with the modern philosophies and sciences. France had in this a leading role: *Garrigou-Lagrange, Maritain, Sertillanges, Gilson, Jolivet. In Germany it is *Geyser who began a new phase of neo-scholasticism. The main school of neo-scholasticism is neo-thomism, there is however also a neo-scotism which has many followers among the Franciscans. Neo-Suarezianism (see Suarez) which had in the 19th century a few followers, is now practically dead. B. D.

NEO-SCOTISM
    See neo-scholasticism.

NEO-STOICISM
    See Stoicism.

NEO-SUAREZIANISM
    See neo-scholasticism.

NEO-THOMISM
    See neo-scholasticism.

NEWMAN, John Henry, 1801-1890
    English theologian and philosopher, cardinal. Main philosophical work: *An Essay in Aid of a Grammar of Assent*, 1870. Newman has an empirical practical mind but is most interested in the inner-life of man. His epistemology is a view on the concrete human way of knowing: his ethics an ethics of innerness, of the conscience. Newman refuses to make science subordinate to usefulness. Science finds its goal in itself, because it answers the highest claims of the human mind. In all sciences are philosophical presuppositions. Philosophy is therefore a synthetic science, which gives us an insight in the whole of reality. It has therefore also to consider the question of the existence of God. In philosophical questions a twofold assent in a judgment is possible. A notional assent is the purely intellectual agreement with a judgement; a real assent is the agreement to a judgment with the entire being. There can therefore be a conceptual unfruitful recognition of the existence of God and a real recognition, which touches man in the deepest part of his being and which transforms him. The difference between assent and inference is also important. Inference is a connection of propositions, the assent is the recognition of a proposition. Assent comes generally into being in a complicated way. Feeling and will have an important part, but it is therefore not unreasonable. Thought is indeed always an aspect of the entire personality. Feeling and will can therefore as well lead as mislead the thought. The insight in life is therefore not in first instance the product of the formal correct inference, but of the attitude of the entire person. This property to come to an insight without formal reasoning, is called by Newman the illative sense, because it works the same way as a direct illation. In this study of the concrete thought a major role is given to the conscience. Conscience is the implicit insight, which shows the right direction to

291

action and thought, will and feeling. Conscience is that what is most personal in man, but in this most personal element man surpasses himself and comes to the recognition of God. Newman's influence was limited during his lifetime but became very important after his death. He can be considered as a precursor of *phenomenological and *existential thought.

B.D.

NEWTON, Isaac

Born in Woolsthorpe 1642, died in Kensingron 1727. English mathematician and physicist, his work had a great influence on philosophy. He holds a mechanical-mathematical explanation of nature (law of gravitation). The method of science is the mixture of mathematical postulates, induction and experiment. In physics he limits himself to the phenomena and does not want to think of (metaphysical) hypotheses (hypotheses non fingo). Since Newton accepted the objectivity of an absolute space which would be the sensorium of God and an absolute time, he placed metaphysical beings as fundaments of an experimental philosophy.

NICHOLAS OF AUTRECOURT

Born in Autrecourt (Verdun) ca. 1300, died after 1347, baccalaureus in theology in Paris ca. 1340; retired after the condemnation of 60 theses in 1346 in Avignon. Because of his criticism on the principle of causality he has been called the "Hume of scholasticism". He taught a strong scepticism. In physics he followed the atomism of Democritus; in ethics is the divine determinism of Thomas *Bradwardine dominant.

NICHOLAS OF CUSA

See Cusa.

NICHOLAS OF ORESME, 1323-1382

Magister in the theology, in Paris ca. 1360, Bishop of Lisieux in 1377. Contributed to the development of the experimental physics.

NICHOLAS OF PARIS

Middle of the 13th century, taught logic at the University of Paris, author of many commentaries on works of logic.

NICOLAI, FRIEDRICH 1733-1811

German bookseller, publisher, editor, and philosophical writer who was a friend of Lessing and Mendelssohn and a critic of religious orthodoxy as well as the philosophy of Kant and Fichte. His Sebaldus Nothanker (1773) gives a picture of Berlin under Frederick II.

NIETZSCHE, Friedrich

Born in Röcken (Thüringen) 1844, died in Weimar 1900. German classicist and philosopher, professor in Basel 1869-79, in 1889 he became mentally ill.

The philosophical views of Nietzsche can not be better described than with the term individualism. His writings are the expression of his own most individual experiences; he does not want to adhere to any philosophy. Because of his sharp, bitter and violent form of expressing himself, he came continuously in conflict with the established convictions in all domains and found himself gradually left alone by his friends, so that he eventually was left in spiritual solitude. His exaggerated selfconsciousness alternated continuously with a feeling of complete failing. The question whether his passionate attacks against God and religion had to be understood as an expression of the hatred of an apostate or as the desperate cry of a seeker of God is still debated.

The language used by Nietzsche is full of unexpected turns, alliterations and plays on words, full of wit and decorated with a very personal imagery.

One can distinguish three periods in the spiritual evolution of Nietzsche. In the first one he is influenced by the pessimism of *Schopenhauer and he sees as origin of all suffering the will to exist and as only a means to free oneself from suffering the negation of life; the world is created by the Original Will only for the sake of art, which Nietzsche find embodied, in its highest form after the Greek tragedy, in the musical dramas of Richard Wagner.

In the second period the negation of life has given way to the most open affirmation of it. Life should be lived and it is worth living, but not for the sake of the art any more, but for the sake of science and truth; With *Montaigne, *Diderot and *Renan he comes close to a rationalism in the manner of the rationalism of the Enlightenment. Romanticism, religion and metaphysics are bad, only the positive has value. Nietzsche finds in *Spinoza his predecessor, not only because he feels himself related to him in the general tendency of Spinoza's thought, but also because he thinks to discover in his own thought the main points of Spinoza's doctrine.

In the third period the artist and romanticist subdued again the rationalist. Nietzsche's extrasensitive mind could not be satisfied with the methods of reasonable thinking. He teaches the belief in life, the "neuer Glaube" and rejects the belief in the God of christianity. In his main work, *Also sprach Zarathustra* (1883-85) he ex-

pressed his final conviction about culture and life in the symbolic forms of a prophetic didactic poem.

He seems to have gone back to the basic ideas of the first period, without however rejecting completely those of the second. Science keeps its place next to art. The real human being is at the same time free thinker and artist; free thinker because he rejects contemporary culture and with it the entire past; artist, because he wants to create a new, higher human type, that of the *Uebermensch.* The main importance of Nietzsche in his third period consists in his sharp and bitter criticism of the contemporary culture and society. Christianity, he claims, is cause of all this degeneration of culture in pessimism and negation of life, it made man slave because of the morality of pity, humility and submission. Nietzsche wants to change the entire order of values: the highest value is for him life in all its force and evolution. Instead of pity and weariness of life he defends the consciousness of power and the will to live. The highest goal of culture is the creation of *Uebermenschen,* and in them an higher form of life will be realized, they will not be limited by the laws of morality or decency, "jenseits von Gut und Böse", and hindered by nobody and nothing in the free exploitation of their instincts of force.

In Germany the ideas of Nietzsche were very much appreciated because of an extreme consciousness of the race and the haughty consciousness of superiority which was encouraged by the state and systematically spread by press and radio. Nietzsche became therefore one of the precursors of the *Weltanschauung* of national-socialism.

NIHIL EST IN INTELLECTU QUOD NON PRIUS FUERIT IN SENSU (Nothing is in the intellect what was not previously in the senses)

It expresses the dependence of intellectual cognition from sensual cognition, and of knowledge from experience. If one understands the saying literally, then the intellect is only a property of ordering the sensual experiences (sensualism, empiricism). One can however also mean that the intellect has its origin in experience, which has always a sensual starting-point, although it is as such, supra sensual. One therefore adds sometimes to the saying: *nisi ipse intellectus* (except the intellect itself).

NIHILISM

Doctrine which teaches the non-being in absolute or at least in relative sense. Truth is denied in the domain of knowledge, the validity of values and norms is negated in ethics, in politics it holds the refusal of all society (see anarchism). The term nihilism has been spread by Turgenev, who called in his novel "Father and Sons" (1862) the Russian revolutionists nihilists. Especially Nietzsche taught nihilism. He rejects radically the values, which the European man, under the influence of christianity, considers absolutely valid. He even is not afraid to teach the senselessness of the existence, but accepts it in an heroic pessimism. Existentialism appears also as nihilistic. This seems however not to be exact, because Sartre teaches more and more a social humanism: The human existence finds its sense in the fact that it is an example for the other human being. Heidegger himself wants especially to avoid nihilism, to which the Western philosophy was brought through its subjectivism. The *nothing experienced in anguish reveals eventually also the being.—J.Gr.

NIRVANA

(Literally to be blown out, as fire) or to be extinguished (as the fire of delusion or passion) for the Buddhists the name of the undefined "goal" of striving: to obtain definite salvation from the worldly existence. It is often described as follows: the position where neither water nor earth etc. . . , nor the illimited space is, neither the nothingness, nor consciousness nor non-consciousness, neither the world, nor the other world; there is neither come nor go, remain nor leave. It is an unborn, unbecome, non-compound something. If it did not exist, there would be no escape from the birth, becoming, making, compoundness. Or also: "It is a beatitude without feeling, an absence of feeling with consciousness, the certitude that the unrest of the earthly existence is definitely past."—J.Gr.

NOEMA

In phenomenology, the content to which consciousness is intentionally directed. Opposed to noesis.

NOESIS

In phenomenology: the conscious act which is intentionally oriented towards a content or noema.

NOMINALISM

In the Middle Ages: *Roscellinus (11th century) and *William of Ockham (14th cent.)

As a reaction against ultra-realism, which makes realities (res) of general concepts, Roscellinus reduces them to words (voces) or general terms. He does not proceed further, he does neither negate the existence of absolute concepts, nor their objective value and prepares

more the moderate realism of
*Petrus Abaelard. Ockham reacts
even against this moderate realism
and rejects the thesis that the absolute concepts would represent
real natures, multiplied in the individual things. The absolute concepts are for him only symbols of
the things, not purely conventional
signs however as the words in a
language, but natural signs, since
the evolution of a concept to such
a category of objects does not happen arbitrarily but on the ground of
the correspondence which we establish between the individual
things. Since they are "signs" for a
series of individual objects whose
place they take in the propositions
and the reasonings, one can consider them as terms (terminism) or
names (nominalism). F.V.S.

Later nominalism indicated all
theory that denies absolute validity
to human concepts. The so called
concepts would only be signs or
words which give a certain schematic coherence to a multitude of
individual data of experience, but
without expressing a "being" (present in each of the beings). The
peculiarity of the language which
brings together in signs the multiplicity of individual data, has been
explained in different ways: mechanism (Hobbes), associationism
(Locke, Hume, sensualism), pragmatism (James), conventionalism.
See also neo-positivism.—J.P.

NON-BEING

The negation of being is in an
absolute sense impossible: if one
denies everything, then remain
neither content of thought, nor
thought (see negation). But the
negation of being in a relative
sense is possible and rests namely
on the positive basis of alterity and
distinction: the one is *not* the other;
what *is not* (such) (is otherwise);
what *is not* (here) (must be there).

NON-EGO

What is not a *Ego and does not
belong to an Ego structure; more
specifically, what appears outside
of the limits of the selfconscious
and free acting (or the unbound,
independent being).

Ego and non-ego are correlative
in man, penetrate each other and
are united in a fundamental unity;
man is indeed not a mere ego, but
a subjectivity which exists, from
nature, in the world.

Fichte on the other hand holds
that the non-ego is produced by
the ego. The independence of the
world is then abolished and the
way is open for idealism.

NOOLOGICAL

Related to noology: mental science as higher psychology. See
Pneuma.

NORM

Indicates what has to be or has
to happen. Norm is therefore and
the standard to judge a factual
datum and the principle which
compels to factual realization. The
norm is essentially characterized
since that what ought to be is expressed. See also commandment,
rule, prescription, law.

In philosophy one can distinguish between norms for thought,
action and artistic creation. They
are respectively studied in logic,
ethics and aesthetics.

NORMAL

What agrees with a norm; average.

NORMAL FORM OF A PROPO-
SITION

A *proposition in *disjunctive
normal form* is an *alternative
whose terms are conjunctions of

variables $p,q, \ldots$ and of negations of variables, $Np, Nq, \ldots$ A proposition in a *special disjunctive normal form* according to specific variables, $p, q, \ldots$ is a proposition in disjunctive normal form, equivalent to it, and in which every conjunction, $p, q, \ldots$ appears once (as affirmation or as negation). The *complete disjunctive normal form* is a special disjunctive normal form, according to all the variables which appear in the proposition.

Conjunctive normal, special normal, complete normal forms are defined as above, changing the word conjunction into alternation.

One proves that for every proposition all normal forms exist; on the normal forms are based the decisionmethods.—R.F.

NORMATIVE

Having a value of norm, or prescribing norms. It is especially said of those sciences which give more a basis to what has to be than explain what is.

NOTA NOTAE EST NOTA REI IPSIUS

(The note of the note of a thing is a note of the thing itself): if for instance the immortality is a note of the spirituality, then the spiritual soul is also immortal. According to some who put the basis of the syllogism not on the extension but the comprehension of the concepts, this would be the ground principle of all deductions. Also dictum de omni et nullo.

NOT-COMPLETABLE

Is a system when a proposition, which can not be deduced from the axioms, can not be adopted as an added axiom, without causing contradictions in the conclusions. Not-completable and not-ramifiable are equivalent qualities.

NOT-CONTRADICTION

See contradictionlessness.

NOTE

In a broader sense all that by which something can be determined and known or distinguished from other things (see distinction); more especially the essential qualities or essential characteristics and the strictly accidental qualities, namely the seven "individual notes" (Lat. notae individuantes), by which a human individual is permanently distinguished from any other individual and which are therefore generally put on a passport. Namely: physical exterior, mathematical figure, date and place of birth, nationality, last and first name.

NOTHING

The non-being as independent thought. Bergson pointed out that the human mind again and again considers the nothing as that what precedes the being, although it follows the being since it is the negation of the being. That God created the world from nothing, as the christian philosophy with Augustine teaches, is only a means to emphasize the absoluteness of God's creative power. Even the principle *ex nihilo nihil fit* (from nothing originates nothing) expresses only the necessity to explain the being through the being.

Nothing has more meaning for °Hegel. In the dialectic evolution of the idea the nothing is produced as antithesis through the pure being: the opposition is abolished in the becoming, which is at the same time being and not being. Nothing has no less importance in existentialism, which ascribes to it a specific activity (nichten, néantiser). The nothing is for Sartre as much in the pour-soi, that the lack of fullness itself characterizes the pour-soi positively. Heidegger teaches that the nothing is lived in the anguish: then disappear all the specific objects or beings, who gave support. But while the nothing or not-something remains, the being can reveal itself, if the esse is not being but that by which all being is.—J.Gr.

NOTION

In scholastic philosophy about the same as note. Kant however thinks that notion is pure concept free from all elements of experience, in as much as it has its origin only in the intellect.

NOT-PREDICATIVE

Are qualities whose expression supposes all elements of a class. So is: "to have all the qualities of a good soldier" a not-predicative quality.

NOT-RAMIFIABLE

Is a system when it can not be completed in any way without contradiction. So are the elementary arithmetics and the proposition logic not-ramifiable, while the geometry is a ramifiable system. To the axioms of a general geometry, we can indeed add the axioms which make this system an Euclidian geometry, or a geometry of Riemann, Lobatschewsky, etc. . . , this is then a ramifiable system.

NOUMENON

(Greek, from nous-intellect), for Kant that what could be surveyed by an intuititive reason. Opposed to the phenomenon of that what appears to us in the senses. In ontological sense, that what as °"Ding an sich" stays behind the phenomenon. Against this distinction between noumenon and phenomenon the scholastics and phenomenologists claim that also that what appears to us (but not in the more narrow sense of the phenomenon in Kant) "is" in another way, and therefore belongs to the noumenon or intelligible knowabilities.

NOUS, (Mind)

In Plato and Aristotle it is the higher soul or reason, for Plotinus it is the Selfconsciousness as first emanation of the One. (See Intellect).

NOÜY, PIERRE LECOMTE DU 1883-1947

French scientist who applied mathematics to biology and introduced the concept of "biological time" as opposed to physical time. His best-known work, *Human Destiny* (1947), emphasizes his "tele-finalism," the doctrine that finality dominates evolution and that mankind is progressing more rapidly both psychically and morally than biologically.

NOVALIS

Pseud. of Friedrich v. Hardenberg, born in Oberwiederstedt 1772, died in Weissenfels 1801. German poet of the Romantic School. The philosophy of the German idealism is put in the form of a poetic imagination.

NUMBER.

If A and B are two aggregates, we say: A is homogeneous with B —and we write $GS(A,B)$—, if there exists a depiction f of A on B. The relation of homogeneity is now an °identity, and we can therefore use the method of definition by °abstraction. The characteristic element $[A]_{GS}$ which belongs to every aggregate B homogeneous with A, is called the *number* of the aggregate. —One is used to determine the *number* of an aggregate A, by representing A in a aggregate B whose number is already known. This operation is called *count;* the elements of a counted aggregate are sometimes called *unities*.

In daily life, the natural sciences and technology, many different sorts of numbers are at present used, the most common being:

1. *Natural* numbers: 0, 1, 2, 3, 4, . . ., which we find when we *count* a function, i.e., when we determine its *sum*.

2. *Whole* numbers (or *integers*): . . ., -3, -2, -1, 0, +1, +2, +3, . . .

3. *Rational* numbers, which are generally written as quotient m/n of two whole numbers m and n, in which n has to be different from 0.

4. *Real* numbers.

Each of these has one function, ordered according to the quantity of the numbers. In the function of natural numbers addition and multiplication are possible without limit. In the function of whole numbers subtraction is also possible. In the function of rational and real numbers division is included, if the divider is other from 0. Investigation of the qualities of numbers belongs to pure mathematics. Philosophically it is interesting to know that the existence of real, rational and whole numbers can be proved if the existence of natural numbers is accepted; if and how the existence of natural numbers can be proved is a matter of discussion among philosophers. E.W.B.

NUMBERS

Frege and the *Principia Mathematica* have defined *cardinal* numbers those which correspond to the usual whole cardinal numbers. When we consider two functions, so that the elements of those functions correspond one by one, by means of a correlator, to each other, then the functions have the same cardinal number; this number is thus a quality which belongs to all similar functions (or the function of all these functions). Cardinal numbers of finite functions are the cardinal numbers in the usual meaning of the word; the number of a finite function is never the same as that of one of its own partial functions. One can however also ascribe to infinite functions cardinal numbers; and the number of an infinite function can be the same as that of one of its own partial functions. So is the cardinal number of all finite cardinal numbers the same as that of all even cardinal numbers.

One will define *relation-numbers* according to the same method. One considers here ordered functions (they are relations, taken as functions of pairs of things). If all elements of two such functions are connected by means of an ordinal *correlator, then these functions have the same *structure* or the same *relationnumber*.

The relation is serial if it is a *transitive, irreflexive (and asymmetric) relation, so that the relation or the *inverse relation exists between the elements which are in relation to something (this corresponds about to the intuitive concept of a series). The number of a serial relation is a *serial number*. We can define approximately a well ordered relation as a serial relation with a beginning and without interruptions. The serial number of such a relation is an *ordinal number*.—R.F.

NUMENIUS OF APAMEA

2nd half of the 2nd century A.D., belongs to the neo-pythagorean school, gives Pythagoras the highest authority and makes Plato dependent on him. In his interpretation of Plato, Numenius speaks of the theory of the three highest principles; the highest divinity is good by itself, pure activity of thought and origin of the being; the second god or demiurge exists through participation to the first, surveys the supra sensual Ideas and is principle of the World. The third divinity is the world itself. In psychology Numenius accepts in every man two souls a rational and an irrational one, bringing therefore dualism to its extreme.

NUMINOUS

Word formed by R. °Otto from the Latin *numen*, indicating the irrational element in the holy. Characteristic of the numinous is its two-sidedness: it rejects and it attracts. It appears as a *mysterium tremendum* (etrrifying) and at the same time *fascinans* (attractive).

O

O

Symbol for the particular negative propositions; e.g. some mills do not mill.

OBJECT

Literally what is thrown over against; the following relation is here essential: the object is opposed to the *subject, while the subject turns towards the object.

In the order of thought object is primarily that to what an act of cognition is directed. As a pure correlate of the intentional act of cognition, the object specifies the latter. It does not make any difference if this object has or has not a real existence outside of this act. All forms of cognition have an object: the observation that what is observed, the remembrance that what is remembered, the imagination that what is imagined, the understanding, that what is in a concept, the judgment and reasoning that what is posed in judgment or reasoning.

In a narrower sense object is not as much that what is posed actually as object, but that what is posed rightfully by a subject and for the subject. In this sense thought has as object the truth even if it does not reach it. The latter can then be a correlate of a subject or consciousness-in-general.

Not only the property of knowledge but all properties are directed to a specific object. One can here distinguish between the *material* and *formal* object. The former is the being which is object, while the latter indicates the respect in which the being, which is object, is grasped. In a still narrower sense the object is the correlate of the act of cognition, in as much as it has its own structure, not only independently from the knowing subject but also remaining identically the same, although different acts are related to it. Criticism and idealism limit the esse of this object to the fact that it is an object. Realism lays the foundation of this being-object in the fact that it itself is: because it is itself, something can become object of knowledge.

Only in knowledge is the object taken up by the immanence of the subject. In his love for an object is the subject attracted to affective union; in the striving towards an object is the subject attracted to effective drive, which in action comes to the realization or at least the change of the object. See action, content.—J.P.

OBJECT OF AN ACTION
See content.

OBJECTIVATION
Make or become *object. For Kant, the process by which the sensory impressions, which are moments of the subject, in the observation, are opposed to the subject and are made objects or contents with their own structure.

OBJECTIVE
What has a relation to or belongs to an *object, as far as the

300

latter is, in its structure, opposed to the subject. Opposed to *subjective.

In the Middle Ages the existential dependence was emphasized. The object being, as the ens rationis, has only existence in the thinking subject, it does not have real existence.

OBJECTIVISM

Opposed to *subjectivism. The conception that the *object has its own structure.

In epistemology the objectivists affirm that truth is objective, i.e. independent from the subject. Objectivism can also be used to indicate pejoratively an epistemological theory, which applies real existence to that what has only existence in thought, or intersubjective value to that what has only subjective value.

In ethics objectivism teaches the objective character of the *values. They therefore do not express human desires or decisions, but impose themselves on man.

OBJECTIVITY

Property of being *objective. Especially used for thought, which would orient itself to that what characterizes the object as such. The question is however to what extent objectivity is possible for thought, and to what extent it is necessary. Phenomenology for instance teaches the possibility and necessity of the objectivity, but Nietzsche laughs at objectivity which brings us to a completely impersonal relation to the facts; Kierkegaard and other existential philosophers emphasize the fact that objectivity does not apply where truths are involved which are essentially interesting man.

OBLIGATION (CONSCIOUSNESS OF)

Is a particular form of the consciousness of *application. Both are rationally based, the latter is however more general and indefinite while the consciousness of obligation contains some moral value, valid for my concrete will. I feel obliged to act in a certain way in the moral order: this necessity is however such that I can always avoid it, not only physically but also and especially in the inner will. And this is exactly the obligation: a necessity which is not physical but moral. Consciousness of obligation is however more than that, it contains also a feeling of inner disharmony. The moral value obtrudes itself indeed on the person more than values which are, as for instance the pleasant, immediately seen as attractive. It obtrudes itself without actually or necessarily being felt in its own meaning. The tension is therefore augmented, tension which exists already between that what is only valid, although one could see that it aims at a value, and what is felt as valuable. This latter content seems to me very intimately connected to me, while the other seems to me foreign, intruding, dominating and limiting me. Obligation is the best felt when its object is duty. As opposed to the moral ideal, is duty valid in an absolute way. The duty intrudes however very often on me as "in spite of me." Therefrom comes the negative form in which it is in the last instance expressed. An order as "Thou shalt" directs itself as a matter of course to a subject which does not do the moral act spontaneously, but who is much more dependent on other inclinations. That he has first of all to combat these inclinations is expressed in the "Thou shalt not."
—J.Gr.

OBSCURE
See concept.

OBSERVATION
An accurate, more or less systematic perceiving of specific facts and things for which one has a special interest. Scientific observation presupposes some pre-knowledge in relation to the object and is used in several sciences as physics, biology, psychology, pedagogy, economy, philosophy, etc.; in some sciences where no place is made for experimentation (e.g. geology, astronomy, meteorology) observation is the only possible point of departure for further scientific studies. The use of technical instruments is in the observation not completely excluded (e.g. telescope, microscope).

OCCASION
Cause which has a real influence on the effect but is insufficient to originate it.

OCCASIONALISM
Theory which explains the interaction of soul and body. They can, according to the cartesian dualism, not influence each other directly. This interaction is therefore explained as follows: God would intervene when an occasional motion happens in the soul and creates a similar motion in the body, and the contrary.

The exclusion of own causality of spirit and matter in man was then extended to the entire order of the creation and led eventually to the acceptance of an existential independence of the created world, in this sense that the created things lose their own independence in their opposition to the One substance of God and are conceived as the images of God.

Both notions found their final consequences in the theories of *Spinoza.

Historically we find occasionalism in a few followers of *Descartes in the 17th and 18th centuries (Claubert, de la Forge, Cordemoy, *Geulincx, *Malebranche).

OFFENCE
Special feeling of oppressed anger, or what produces such feeling. For Kierkegaard, the truth which is not only incomprehensible (*paradox) in its appearance for us, but is really incomprehensible: e.g. the existence of the God-man as eternal-temporal being. In this sense is offence characteristic for christianity.

OMNIPOTENCE
Attribute of God through which He can realize everything which does not contain an inner contradiction. Inner contradiction is exactly that which is excluded by the divine being.

OMNISCIENCE
Attribute of God, through which He knows Himself and all that exists, is possible or in certain circumstances could be chosen by free creatures.

ONTOGENESIS
The evolution of any living being from the fecundated ovum to the stage when all organs are formed. In this evolution of the germ a specific plan is followed and there exists a great possibility of adaptation to different circumstances. There is also a clear *differentiation.

ONTOLOGICAL ARGUMENT
Name given by Kant to the proof of God's existence, firstly formulated by *Anselm in his *Proslogion*. This proof starts from the concept of God, considered as most

perfect being, and argues that such a being has to exist in reality. It has been taken over, under a more or less different form, by Bonaventura, Duns Scotus, Descartes, Leibniz and Hegel; it was rejected by *Gaunilo, Thomas and Kant. It is still disputed in certain circles. See also ontological *proof of God's existence.

ONTOLOGISM

Doctrine according to which the intellectual knowledge has its origin in the immediate insight in God and His ideas: as first principle in the order of being (primum ontologicum) is God also the first known (primum logicum)

Even if God is immediately viewed, He is however not grasped with a clear knowledge. It is more the idea of the esse only which is viewed immediately in the consciousness (see Rosmini) or understood immediately by thought (see Gioberti, Ubaghs). The idea can further be grasped as the idea of the esse as such, eternal, uncreated, unchanging, simple, but further completely indetermined, which then breaks up in a multiplicity of ideas, which make for us the things of the experience intelligible (Rosmini), or as the idea of the Absolute Esse, the highest reality, God, in Whom the eternal truths and the essence of things are immediately viewed (Gioberti, Ubaghs).

Ontologism refers often to *Augustine and returns directly to *Malebranche and his successor H. S. Gerdil (1718-1802). It had most of its followers around the middle of the 19th century in Italy. Connected with *traditionalism it had some influence in the Netherlands through Ubaghs (19th century). F.S.

ONTOLOGY

Philosophical subject investiga-ting the being as a being and used, since Parmenides until today, in many different ways. In any being one can make, at least logically, the difference between that what it is and the fact that it is, and emphasize in a philosophical investigation one of the two aspects. Most philosophers were only interested in the investigation of what the being is and tried to reduce all ontological opinions to that (essentialism), they oriented therefore their ontology to a theory of *categories. Some did it in a realistic others in an idealistic sense. It mostly was done starting from a not-situated, i.e. from a purely absolute point of view. Contemporary existentialists reject this, because they think it impossible to have any other than a humanly situated point of view. Some emphasize in the being that it is: they try to discover the being itself and to reconcile the many beings with the unity of being. Parmenides did it already but at the cost of the multiplicity of the beings. Thomas Aquinas put complete emphasis on being itself and explained the beings, in everything they possess, through their participation at the esse, the only fundamental value. Lavelle also followed the road of the participation. Heidegger remarks that the esse is not a being, and that the beings, which certainly really exist, only can be explained on the ground of the unique esse, which is not a being. Kant thinks that all ontology is evil, because it would go, in an irresponsible way, and on the grounds of a purely logical assimilation of concepts, from the order of thought to the reality; and the proof of the existence of God by Anselm is therefore called by him an *ontological argument. L.D.R.

OPERATION

There is no reason why we should put a strict separation between an operation and a °function, except that the word operation is used as well in metalogic as in logic, or that with the word operation sometimes is meant the act of operating and the meaning of the sign of operation, function, on the contrary, indicates the entire expression.

By means of an operation, applied to an *operanda*, is reached a result or *operatum*. The operanda are mostly of a specific sort. So originates for instance in the simple algebra, by means of the operation of addition, applied to the numbers a and b an other number $a + b$ (operatum), and in the logic of proposition, by means of the operation of negation, applied to the proposition p, the proposition not-p. R.F.

OPPOSITION

A specific incompatibility of concepts by a same datum, or of propositions with the same subject and predicate: all opposition presupposes a certain conformity. For the CONCEPTS we distinguish: *relative* (see relation) opposition, where the relata presuppose each other e.g. father-son *contrasting* opposition (see contrast), were the opposed elements exclude each other, e.g. love-hatred; *privative* (see privation) opposition, between presence and absence of that what has to be present e.g. seeing-blind; *contradictory* (see contradiction) opposition, in which only one of the terms, can be present and has to be, e.g. something-nothing. For the PROPOSITIONS: *subalternation*, which has only to do with the quantity between A- and I-, and between E- and O-propositions; *contrast*, has only to do with the quality between A- and E-propositions, which exclude each other; *Subcontrary*, which has only to do with the quality between I- and O-propositions, which do not exclude each other; *contradiction*, has to do as well with quantity as with quality between A- and O-. and between E- and I-propositions, of which only one can and also has to be true. I.v.d.B.

OPTIMISM

Attitude according to which the world is basically good: the world is certainly not perfect and evil even exists, but this is all temporary or accidental and does not touch the world in its last ground. Optimism has been put in theory by Leibniz. In his *Théodicée* he shows how God is obliged by his Wisdom and Goodness to create, of all possible worlds, the "best possible": the fact that the world is not the best in an absolute sense depends only on the fact that the world forms a whole of possibilities which have also to be mutually possible (compossibilitas), and the fact that the world is imperfect goes necessarily together with its finiteness. As immediate view on the world was optimism especially lived in the period of the Enlightenment; therewith was connected the belief in an unlimited possibility of perfection for the world, for man in the world, through the enlightenment. J. Gr.

ORDER

Arrangement of many things in a whole, in as much as the relations unite the terms in unity. On the grounds of this unity the laws of the whole apply to the parts and creates regularity. Where relations exist there is order: as well in the domain of knowledge (logical order) as in the domain of reality (real order). The nature of the order depends on the nature of the relation. Real order exists on different levels, superficial and fundamental, it can be wider and narrower according to the fact that it unites real principles in a constructed being or unites parts in a whole, or subsistent beings in groups and society. The same terms can also be grouped in different ways; ordered totalities contain the one and the other and all together can finally compose an hierarchic whole. (see participation) It is the nature of our intellect to look everywhere for order and to create it: all kinds of organizations and also the scientific research are the proof. The order brought about by man is always based on finality. The question arises then if all order, also the order in nature, comes from the finalizing action of the intellect; and if all order does point eventually towards a divine ordering Principle. L.D.R.

ORGAN (Gr. Organon=tool)

Is called a part of an organism or living being, with a special form and function. Aristotle already pointed out that living beings always have organs (e.g. eye, heart) corresponding to a series of functions which are all together necessary to keep *life. This is clear when one isolates an organ; it can sometimes remain alive for a while (e.g. a heart or muscle + nerve) but it soon dies completely, because the harmony and the connection with the whole is broken. It is in the division of duties in an organism that one organ completes the other, but it can not exist separately. Life, in the strict sense, is only applied to the whole organism. This latter term means: living being consisting of organs and using them. One can not consider it as a sum of organs (summative concep-

tion), but the organs exist in and through the *totality.

Distinction can be made between: organs of the vegetative functions: the organs for metabolism and reproduction, present in all organisms; organs of animal functions: senses, nervous system, muscles, present in animals and in man. The spiritual functions of man, intellect and free will, are certainly dependent in their activities, on the activities of the organs and of the total, physical state but do not have specific organs in the strict sense. Memory and fantasy, however, on which the intellect is based, are specially connected in man with the cerebrum.

The life of organisms realised in matter is called **Organic**, i.e. bound to organs. One speaks also of **Organization** of the parts in a living being, and one should see that the connection is here closer and more necessary than in human organizations. We should finally point out that in unicellular organisms all functions are present in the one cell, which sometimes has visible organs, which are then called "organells." M.B.

ORGANICISM

A theory in biology which recognizes and looks for the unique character of the living beings in a specific relation of forms and functions, as the investigation in fact proves. The followers of this theory (among others von Bertalanffy) do not want to give a philosophical definition of life and do also not want to speak of finality and appropriateness in the living nature. Organicism brought a valuable criticism of the machine-theory.

ORGANON (Organ of thought or instrument of thought)

Name given by Andronicus of Rhodes to the logical works of

Aristotle, because they have to do with definitions, distinctions, argumentations, which are as the organs of the mind and compose the scientific apparatus of thought for the acquisition of new knowledge.

ORIGENES

Born in Alexandria 185 or 186, died in Caesarea (Palestine) 254 or 255; disciple of *Clemens of Alexandria and possibly of *Ammonius Saccas, founder of the neoplatonism. He headed the christian school of *Alexandria from 203 to 231, when he had to leave because of heterodoxy. He is one of the strongest minds in the christian antiquity. As did his master Clemens, he made his knowledge of the Greek philosophy subservient to christianity and designed an extraordinarily speculative theology. Sometimes however he left the orthodoxy because of his exaggerated confidence in reason. (see Platonism)

ORTEGA Y GASSET, Jose

Born 1883, died 1955, Spanish philosopher of culture. Main work: *La Rebelion de las Masas*, 1930. Ortega thinks that the European civilization is threatened with ruin, because of the ever growing pressure of the average man on the spiritual aristocracy.

OSTWALD, Wilhelm, 1853-1932

Energetic monist, professor in Leipzig. Energy is the only principle of reality. Nature as well as mind are constructed from energy. This energetic monism, originated under the influence of the natural sciences, had for some time followers in a limited circle.

OTHER

That which is not identical with something, but is different from something. When the other is a *person, the question, in modern philosophy, is posed if we can be sure of his existence and how we can get in touch with him as a person. For Sartre one can be contacted only inadequately by another (*autrui*) because we are always contacted as an object; on the other hand, we can only be sure of the existence of the other insofar as we can ascertain that it is part of our human constitution to be directed toward others.

OTTO Rudolph, 1869-1937

Phenomenological philosopher of religion, professor in Marburg. His work *Das Heilige* was epochmaking.

OUSIA (substance)

The first of Aristotle's *categories; that what functions as a subject of attributes, but is itself not an attribute pointing to a subject.

OUTER WORLD

The world as existing outside or independent of the subject which knows it. It is first a matter of the observing subject. Then the outer world is the totality of what strikes through the senses (sight, sound, taste, etc.). This totality exists in itself and is ordered in space. To it the body, through which the subject observes, does not belong, since it is not observed but experienced. But one's own body can be observed by the senses. There are even peculiar sensations, such as pain, hunger, thirst, etc., which are related to the situation of the body. So one's own body belongs to the outer world, where it is seen as part of the totality opposed to the psychical subject: Kant would speak of the phenomenal world or the world of phenomena. In a broader sense: opposed to the pure nonobjectivating ego, the outer world comprises also the psychical activities and passivities which compose the so-called empirical ego. For a long time the existence of the outer world, however it may be described, has been considered evident (*see* realism). Descartes made this evidence dependent upon one's own existence. Berkeley denied the independent existence of the outer world. In *idealism the existence of the outer world is dependent upon the subject. Contemporary thought, more specifically under the influence of *phenomenology, has returned to the original evidence of the existence of the outer world. J.P.

OWEN, Robert 1771-1858

Welsh socialist who pioneered in the cooperative settlement and by protesting early industrial abuses influenced British social legislation. His *New View of Society* (1813) contended that existing evils were not due to lack of religion but to the wrong distribution of wealth and deficient regulation of production.

OXFORD, SCHOOL OF

Was founded by Robert Grosseteste, who also gave it a specific orientation: interest in the experiment and the experimental sciences, with as effect, inclination towards empiricism; interest for mathematics and the conviction that it is fruitful for the natural sciences. In the 13th century *Roger Bacon was the most typical disciple of Grosseteste. In the 14th century the school followed the same direction which explains the good reception the theories of William of Ockham received in Oxford. This orientation remained until the end of the Middle Ages and can be found in the doctrine of Francis Bacon and the modern English empiricism.

P

P

Often used to indicate, as symbol, the predicative term of a *proposition; also used as a symbol to indicate the possibility of an incomplete logical inversion of a proposition, the so called *conversio per accidens.

PAIN

The irreducible experience of bodily affliction. To explain pain thinkers have sought, in the causal direction, for bodily processes. In teleological sense they emphasized the utility of pain as warning. Modern psychology thinks that pain is a datum, that developed together with intelligence as product of a higher evolution (Pradines). Hattingberg considers pain as an independent morbid symptom. See also sorrow (spiritual affliction).

PAINE, Thomas, 1737-1809

American philosopher, follower of the *Enlightenment.

PALINGENESIS (Literally: becoming again)

Is either the regeneration of the soul taught by the Pythagoreans, or the moral regeneration, or also the periodic renovation of the world by the fire (see Stoics). In connection with evolution the term palingenesis is used to indicate the repetition of the philogenetic evolution of the individual.

PALMER, George Herbert 1842-1933

American neo-idealist.

PANAETIUS OF RHODES, 2nd cent. B.C.

Lived in Rome together with Polybius and was the friend of many Roman aristocrats as Laelius and Scipio Aemilianus. Only fragments of his works have been saved. In some points he deviates from the orthodox doctrine of the older *stoics and accepts some elements of Plato and Aristotle; he rejects the mantics, the periodical worldfire and the immortality of the soul; on the other hand he defends a psychological dualism, because he accepts a rational and irrational part in the human soul; his political ideal is a mixture of the three forms of government.

PANENTHEISM

The doctrine of *Krause about the relation between God and world. Everything is in God but also under and through Him. God or the Being is the unity which contains everything, but surpasses everything through its unity. One tried sometimes to call panentheism the philosophy of Spinoza or the occasionalism of Malebranche. But since Spinoza teaches the complete immanence of God in the world, this term can not be used for his philosophy; and Malebranche, who recognizes in God only an efficient cause, sees God in a more transcendental way than Krause. The scholastic philosophy says also that God is in everything and everything in God, but considers God so transcendent that God is still God without world-creation. The term panentheism is not a very expressive term. H.R.

PANLOGISM

Doctrine according to which the entire reality is logical i.e. understandable, in this sense that it can completely be constructed according to the laws of thought. The beings would then be moments in the selfunfolding of the logos. Panlogism is mostly used for the system of *Hegel "all reality is rational and all that is rational is real".

PANPSYCHISM

Doctrine according to which everything is animated. All things are alive or have even consciousness. See Hylozoism.

PANTHEISM (literally: all in God).

This term was created by J. Toland (1705) to indicate philosophical systems which identify God with the things in the world or with the world as a whole. God is however never identified completely with the world, but there exists always a certain difference. In poetry only or other literary works vague expressions can be found in which the author calls himself or things in the world, God. In the philosophy of Spinoza is the reality of God so emphasized that the reality of an *all*, different from God, is omitted. The world as something its own and as opposed to God does not exist here. (*acosmism)

The pantheistic theory contains three points: 1) Not enough distinction is made between God and the world, at least not a real and essential difference. 2) God is not accepted as a personal being or has at least, without man, no consciousness of himself; 3) the world

does not originate from God in a free creation.

Pantheistic are the monistic systems of the Indian Vedanta. The emanation doctrine of Plotinus, although very often explained in a pantheistic sense, could perhaps be excluded. H.R.

The earliest historians thought that many elements of pantheism were present in the Middle Ages: in Joannes Scotus Eriugena, in the School of Chartres, in Amalric of Bena and David of Dinant, in Eckehart and Nicholas of Cusa. The opinions today are more careful, because one sees these authors in their historical context and take their real intentions in account, which were often expressed unclearly because of unclear formulation. Only Amalric of Bena and David of Dinant can be called pantheists. Amalric taught a *formal* pantheism, which made of God the form of all beings; David defended a *materialistic* pantheism, inspired by the Greek atomism and by Alexander of Aphrodisias. The doctrine of Amalric and David is not very well known and had only a limited influence. F.V.S.

Spinoza's opinions are pantheistic, when he identifies God with nature; both distinguish themselves only in the fact that God is the interior and the world the exterior; God's "thinking himself" produces nature as expression. There is no essential difference and one can not call God a personal being. This divine being has, with inner necessity, to express himself, so that the existence of the world does not depend on an inner free choice of God. In the entire world reigns absolute necessity.

Hegel, who claims not to be a pantheist, distinguishes God or the Absolute and the world or the relative. But according to Hegel the

309

Absolute does not exist except when it relativates itself and makes itself finite in the world. The finite has to be there as the other (antithesis), to make the Absolute (thesis) real. In this Hegel omitted to make God sufficiently transcendent and distinguished from the world. Creation belongs as a process to the becoming of this Absolute, which therefore does not exist without the world. Only in man, says Hegel, does God arrive at the consciousness of himself. H.R.

PARACELSUS (real name: Theophrastus Bombastus von Hohenheim), 1493-1541

German philosopher of nature and physician, born in Einsiedeln in Switzerland, died, after a life of wandering, in Salzburg. He was more a practical empirical physician than a theoretical scientist. He broke definitely with the mediaeval-galenic medical "science". He considers man as a microcosm, formed with all the elements of the big world, composed of an "elementic" body of flesh and blood, a sideric body which has its origin in the stars (the seat of the mind and thought, of the natural light which makes us philosophers) and a soul created by God (the seat of the eternal light, which brings us to the theology). The principle of Life of the individual man is called the "archeus;" health and sickness are dependent on the harmony or disharmony of this central principle. His main works: *Paragranum* (1530), *Opus paramirum* (1532) and *Astronomia magna oder die ganze Philosophia sagax* (1538). Th.C.v.St.

PARADOX (literally: against expectation)

Is for Kierkegaard a datum which, although actually unexplainable, is not innerly contradictory and therefore not essentially unexplainable. Opposed to the *absurd.

PARADOXES

We start here from the comprehension-axiom, (silently) agreed to by *Cantor systems are mathematical entities and can therefore also appear as elements of a system. If x is a system we can inquire if x appears among its own elements. The systems which do not appear in their own elements have between them a specific characteristic in common. They form thus a system which we call R. We now pose the question: does R appear among its own elements? (a) If R appears among its own elements; R has to possess the quality by which we characterized the elements of R, and thus also the characteristic not to appear among its own elements. This is thus in opposition with the made hypothesis; (b) if R does not appear among its own elements, then R can not have the characteristics of these elements—R must therefore appear under its own elements—This paradox of *Russell proves that we can not accept the comprehension-axiom without impunity; we can therefore not introduce first a system according to clause (a) as a *multiplicity* of elements, and then promove it, according to clause (b), to possible element, thus to *entity*. On the other hand would the important results of the theory of systems of Cantor be lost through an absolute interdiction of this way of doing. E. Zemerlo (1908) pointed the way for a possible compromise, which exists in the acceptation of a more limited comprehension-axiom: (1) mathematical entities, which have a specific quality in common, form a class determined by this quality, of which they are the elements;

310

(2) if the quality is definite, then the classe determined by it, is a system; systems are mathematical entities and can therefore appear as elements of a class; (3) Classes which have the same elements are identical. One has then to define more clearly which qualities can be considered definite. E.W.B.

PARADOXES (in formal logic)

A) Paradoxes or better "antinomies" are ways of reasoning, invented or rediscovered ca. 1900, and which show that through an unlimited (but not imposed) application of the rules of the formal logic one reaches contradictory conclusions, and that therefore the formal logic, as it was then formulated, is contradictory. A few examples: 1. Paradox of the liar. A man states: I lie. Here he states that he is lying when he affirms that he is lying, therefore, that actually is not lying. 2. A variant of the above. In a book is the sentence: the sentence on page x, rule y (only the page and the rule of the sentence between quotation marks) is false. This sentence is therefore not false. 3. I define k as the quality: not to be applicable to itself. (This does not seem to be an abnormal quality, because most predicates are clearly applicable to other realities than to themselves). A definition is universal. Therefore, if we apply this definition to k, then is: k is a k, equivalent to: k is not a k. 4. A variant (Gonseth) is the following: A library can have a catalogue of all the catalogues in a specific language or published in a specific region. We suppose that this list is published in that particular language or in that particular region, and we limit the list to the catalogues which do not mention themselves. Should this list be mentioned in the catalogue? If it has to

be mentioned, then it does not mention itself.

B) The first reaction of the reader to the above mentioned "popular" paradoxes will certainly be: that we have here age-old subtleties (this is indeed true for the paradox of the liar), which nobody wants to consider seriously because we have here clearly a vicious circle. This answer is however superficial. To the ways of reasoning, used in everyday life, reasoning is more an orientation rather than a proof in itself decisive, and we can very easily see that this or that way of reasoning leads to an absurd conclusion. But the formal logic has been invented to enable us to have unlimited confidence in its conclusions, even if we do not have graphically verifiable things. Of such a nature were the applications of the formal logic to the infinite aggregates. One can indeed infer mathematical paradoxes with the same method as those used in the "popular" paradoxes. One can for instance prove that the greatest number of a specific sort is *not* the greatest number.

If one can not have complete confidence in the formal rules, they lose their basic meaning. The rules must therefore be corrected in such a way that they exclude the paradoxes. This correction can not be such that it touches the intuitive meaning of the terms, or cannot contain an intuition of bad faith, so that is understood what one wants to determine (and that is what is meant by vicious circles). There has to exist a formal rule which excludes the paradoxes.

C) After many attempts in different directions a solution was found in the so called *theory of types*. The limitation of types is very natural on first view, but it has many difficulties as will concede those who try to understand the *Principia Mathematica*. These difficulties have been diminished by the elimination of the ramified theory of types, but they remain nonetheless great. There have been therefore efforts made to make the theory of types less strict (among others the effort of Quine in *Mathematical Logic*) or even to lose the types. There have been up till now no definite results. R.F.

PARALLELISM

Doctrine which explains that man's body and soul, or more in general, the physical (which can be reached by exterior observation) and the psychic (which can be reached by inner observation) form two completely correlated appearances of one, unknowable reality. The physical and the spiritual are to each other as a text and its translation or as two translations of the same text. (Fechner, Wundt).

In one respect the psycho-physical parallelism appears as a dualism, in another respect as a form of monism. In Leibniz' theory of the harmonia praestabilita, according to which body and soul have only immanent activity, but are so tuned to each other by the Creator that they seem to influence each other constantly causally, a dualistic tendency comes to light. Also in the occasionalism of Malebranche, who explains the connection between body and soul by the repeated incidental intervention of God. The monistic tendency is however clear in the theory of identity of Spinoza, in which the physical is a modus of the eternal substance extended in its attribute, and the spiritual a modus of the same Substance, according to its attributive thought. J.P.

PARALOGISM (Lat. fallacia)

A fallacious *syllogism, either because of a misconception of the terms and propositions of which it is built, or because of its wrong structure. As opposed to *sophism, the paralogism is not made to deceive.

Kant calls paralogisms the dialectical reasoning, with which psychology thinks that it can prove the independence of the soul, its simplicity, personality and the perfection of its representations.

PARETO, Vilfredo 1848-1923

Italian economist and sociologist, contemptuous of metaphysics and religion, he attempted to raise sociology to a logico-experimental science. Much of Italian Fascism claimed to be based on Pareto's ideas. Best-known work: *Sociologia Generale* (1916), translated into English as *The Mind and Society* (1935).

PARMENIDES

Born in Elea (colony of Phocaea in the South of Italy) ca. 504—died ca. 456 B.C. founder of the "school of Elea". Wrote a didactic philosophical poem in hexameters, usually called *"On nature."* It contains two parts: the first part (mostly saved), about the eleatic theory of the being; the second (only fragments are saved) about the theory of the appearance.

The being is, and outside the being nothing can be; therefore what is, is; what is not, can not be. From these premises all the characteristics of the being are deduced. It is eternal (it can not originate from the being, which would not have existed, and not from the not-being from which nothing can proceed); it is also a whole and is indivisible (because the divisibility presupposes the not-being, in which the parts would be spread); it is also completely immutable: it rests in and on itself; it finally is limited (a thing which has not yet reached its limits is imperfect and as such not-being). Parmenides represents this perfect being as a perfectly round sphere ("sphairos"), everywhere identical to itself. He seemed therefore not to have considered the being as purely spiritual, but as an extremely fine physical, perfect mass. This being is however identical with the thinking "because thinking and being are one and the same" (fr. 3). We have here to make abstraction of our modern categories of materialism and idealism, which are concepts acquired much later in the distinction between matter and spirit. This held for Parmenides no contradiction that the being was considered as spatial and at the same time as pure thinking. As for all the presocratic writers who preceded him, the universe consists of one element, in which physical and spiritual beings are included—and this element is the immutable and eternal being, who has the extensiveness of the universe and the depth of the thought.

Although he put it in a very crude form, Parmenides penetrated the idea of the being, which will become not only the basis of Greek philosophy but also of Western thought. He formulated a first law which dominates the being and the thought: the law of *not-contradiction. He used also in his didactic poem a *dialectical method of reasoning, which we did not find in his precursors. They tried to make their theories accepted by intuition or, as for the Pythagoreans, by vague analogies. Parmenides however deduced other truths from the idea of being, by means of the principle of not-contradic-

tion, and excluded the contradictory theses. From the fundamental thesis of identity he deduces dialectically that the being did not become, is eternal, unmoved, limited and thinking.

The second part of the didactic poem has a theory of becoming and decay, about the not-being and the fallacious meaning. Although the change can not "be", but "appears" only to be, we still can find a certain order in the evolution of the cosmic changes. Some critics think that Parmenides wants to give in this second part, which we know only fragmentarily, a kind of doxology of the different natural philosophies of his time. It is however more reasonable to accept that he took more or less for his own the theory which was the most probable. For as far as we can see, his doctrine of light and night, as principles of change, and his cosmogony have many resemblances with the *Pythagorean opinions. Parmenides has been influenced in his youth by the Pythagorean Ameinias. It is not clear how much influenced he was by Xenophanes. F.D.R.

PAROUSIA

The presence of the *ideas, not as they are in themselves, but in as much as they are in the sensory-perceptible that participates in them (Plato)

PART

A part is by its nature correlative with the whole. Both concepts, considered as a pair, part-whole, can be applied to different things, but not always in the same sense. A heap of stones is a whole in another sense than a human body is. Therefore the corresponding parts are "part of" in a really different sense. A stone remains the same stone when it is removed

313

from the whole; an eye outside the body is not an eye any more.

In natural philosophy, °atomism and °mechanism have always defended the actuality of the parts, so that all wholes were really °aggregates. Aristotelianism, on the other hand, always emphasized the potentiality of the parts in a whole. In physics the actuality of the parts has for a long time been accepted, especially under the influence of mechanism, but the evolution of the theory of °atoms brought scientists to accept the fact that parts and particles such as atoms, electrons and neutrons have less actuality; their behavior seems to be determined by the whole. A.G.M.v.M.

PARTICIPATION

Participation shows on the one hand a resemblance to the part: this latter is as such pure proportion to other °parts, with which it forms an independent whole. The participation differs on the other hand with the part, because it is itself already a subsisting reality; but, as the part, it is completely in proportion to other participating terms, to form, together with them, a whole, namely an order. All these terms are identical in this sense that they all belong to the same order; and they differ from each other in the uncommunicable way in which all of them have their place in the whole.

The theory of participation is an attempt to conceive clearly °order, as such, and to explain it. It can therefore be applied whenever the problem of the one and the multiplicity or the problem of the finite exists: multiplicities of being, species, accidental orders. When different beings (e.g. John, Peter etc. . .) answer to a same definition (man), they have unmutilated the same (human) perfection.

They can however not be identified as such with this perfection, since they are many and they therefore mutually differ: every one has his perfection only in a particular, i.e. finite way (°mode). By the fact itself that a being is characterized in such a way, it leaves a place for others: it exists then, thanks to its own reality, in an order; his entire activity will bear witness of this and show inevitably a social aspect.

Where participation appears the question rises on what inner structure it rests in every participating term; and also the question about the ultimate basis of the participation-order, and if an exterior cause is necessary to create the parts of the order and to maintain them. L.D.R.

PARTICULAR

See concept, proposition.

PARTICULARIZATION

Is the operation through which from the proposition p: p is true for a few X, proceeds.

PASCAL, Blaise

Born in Clermont 1623, died in Paris 1662. French mathematician and physicist, philosopher, apologist and religious thinker.

The philosophical importance of Pascal is especially found in the epistemological conception of the *Pensées*. They tend to conteract all over-estimation of the reason (raison) and to limit it to its legitimate expressiveness. Next to reason (*raison*) another source of knowledge of truth exists, which Pascal calls le *coeur* or *l'intelligence* and which is used by God to teach us the truths which are necessary for our salvation and which our own strength of thought can not reach. It is not a pure function of our feeling, but as a spiritual instinct, in which go together an immediate insight and an irrational emotional certitude.

The ideal of the purely rational certitude can be found in mathematics, in physics also (*ordre des corps*) one can reach certitude through reason. In the *ordre des esprits* however reason reaches for the first time its limits: for the knowledge of the first principles, space, time, motion, numbers, man has to follow *le coeur*. The distance between these two orders to the *ordre de la charité* can only be reached with God's help: the truths which man needs for his eternal salvation (*vérités divines*), can only be had through grace, which will bring them close to the coeur. The traditional arguments for the existence of God, for the immateriality and immortality of the soul can only give man human certitude; they have no religious value and can not bring man closer to God, but can only prepare man's mentality necessary for the acceptance of the supernatural insight.— F.S.

PASCHASIUS RADBERTUS

Ca. 800-ca. 860, Abbot of Corby since 842, distinguished author, exegete and theologian. His philosophical ideas are especially clear in his *De corpore et sanguine Domini* (831), a speculative theological essay which was primarily inspired by Augustin.

PASSION

One of the ten aristotelian °categories. In the philosophical psychology, motion of the sensory strivings; in the general psychology, strong motion of the soul which directs man towards an object. As tendency of an higher intensity it proceeds from nature and is, as the instinct, innate. It can also be acquired and then intensity and strength are added to the tendency. Passion in this sense breaks the emotional balance and has the character of a crisis.

PASSIVE

What undergoes an °activity, more definitely as it happens in the physical nature. °Matter is naturally passive: every physical thing lacks the ability to create activity independently or of its own power; only in connection with its surroundings and with the entire cosmos and, because of the influence of other physical factors, it received the necessary completion to react and to act itself on others. It is therefore thanks to its passivity that its activity exists. The passiviy in the physical things shows the unbreakable bound which brings them together in a cosmic whole and makes them dependent, as so many parts of a whole, from the determinism of the same physical laws.

PATER, Walter Horatio 1839-1894

English essayist and critic who spent most of his life interpreting Rennaissance art and literature. An Epicurean in spirit, his best-known work is *Marius the Epicurean* (1885), a philosophical romance of the era of Marcus Aurelius. Also wrote *Plato and Platonism* (1893).

PATHETIC, THE

Variant of the category of the °sublime, in which the experience of the sublime is dynamically intensified by the certain subjective consciousness one has of this experience itself. The pathetic gives the sublime a kind of warm grandeur, it can however easily fall in bombast or affectation.

PATRISTIC PHILOSOPHY

The philosophy developed in christian circles during ca. the five first centuries of christianity. This period is called patristic because of the fathers of the church, who had as it were a fatherly influence through their teaching on the young church and who began the first theological education of the christian people. This period comes at the end of the antiquity and the ancient philosophy, which gives it also specific characteristics. The patristic philosophy is then the first meeting of the christian thought with the pagan thought of the Antiquity.—The christian intellectuals of the first centuries were aware that they stood on the crossroad of two entirely different worlds. On the one hand the *Hellenic world,* the most perfect result of the pagan antiquity and inheritor of the knowledge, acquired by the human reason after centuries of efforts. On the other hand *christianity,* completion of judaism and inheritor of the divine Revelation, which began in the time of the patriarchs and prophets, and was completed by the "glad tidings" of the Gospel of Christ. The contrast between the purely rational wisdom of paganism and the christian wisdom, which comes from God and is received through the faith, strikes them. The one could however not deny the other, because, even if christianity was not a new philosophical sect and even if it did not want to bring a new philosophy in the strict sense of the word, it did however contain a philosophy in the broader sense, a "Weltanschauung", which did put it in radical contradiction with paganism. The problem which interested the patristic minds the most was thus the relation between both wisdoms. Three opinions were outstanding: *absolute opposition* against pagan wisdom in the name of christian wisdom, which replaces the former and makes it unnecessary (e.g. Tertullian); *unlimited agreement* with the pagan wisdom (so the relationistic attitude of the gnostics: it leads to the preeminence of philosophy over faith, which has to be transformed into gnosis, or higher knowledge); *harmonic collaboration* of both wisdoms, in which philosophy remains subordinate to the revelation. Most christian thinkers followed this conciliatory attitude, which was in fact clearly the best one. They understood that the pagan philosophy could render christianity important services: one had to follow it to *defend christianity* against the attacks of the pagan and Jewish philosophers and to make the Gospel acceptable for the pagan intelligentia (especially the work of the *apologists); one had also to *defend the orthodoxy* against specific heresies, inspired by the pagan philosophy (e.g. gnosticism, arianism, manicheism); one had also to *define more clearly* the content of the revelation, *explain* it and *study* it which was impossible without philosophical notions (the work of the School of *Alexandria, and especially of the great Greek and Latin teachers of the 4th and 5th centuries). —The patristic period did not give us a really original philosophical system; it used the systems of the pagan antiquity, mainly platonism, stoicism and neo-platonism. Among the christian thinkers of this period we do not find professional philosophers, who are as such interested in philosophy: mostly all of them had religious solicitudes and used the philosophy to express their christian vision of the world or their theological doctrine. They already applied the famous motto of the scholastics: *philosophia ancilla theologiae.*— F.V.S.

PATRIZZI, Franciscus, born in Clis-

sa 1529, died in Rome 1597.
Opposed aristotelianism, drew up a neo-platonic, mystic conception of nature. In the emanation is light the principle. With this doctrine he hopes to win the protestants for the Church.

PAULSEN, Friedrich, 1846-1908
German psychic monist, professor in Berlin, was working especially in the domain of ethics.

PEANO, Giuseppe 1858-1932
Italian linguist and mathematician who devised an international language, known as *Latino sine flexione,* consisting of words common to Latin, French, German and English. Considered an originator of the science of symbolic logic.

PECKHAM
See Joannes Peckham.

PEILLAUBE, 1864-1934
French neo-thomist, professor in Paris.

PEIRCE, Charles Sanders, 1839-1914.
American physicist and philosopher, gave the impulse to the evolution of logistics and *pragmatism in America.

PENALTY
Punishment to obtain the balance which was broken through an unethical action. Penalty is the natural effect of *contrition, or, better, it is its body.

PENETRABILITY
In the strict sense of the word, the capacity of a body to coincide with another body, so that both bodies touch each other point by point innerly, without losing their own continuity. Both bodies would in that case occupy the same space. It is admitted in general that this is impossible for ponderable matter. Lorentz, however, believed

ponderable matter can be penetrated by *ether. In a less strict sense, penetrability occurs when one matter penetrates the pores of another.

PENN, William, 1644-1718
English Quaker who petitioned King Charles II for a grant of land in America as payment of a family debt and founded the State of Pennsylvania, which he called "a holy experiment" where he could establish a "theocratic democracy." Religious tolerance was the heart of his political beliefs, and he is legendary for his successful dealing with the American Indians.

PEOPLE
Community of men based on common descent, language and culture. The concept people is therefore less broad than *race, which has only relation to physical characteristics and not to cultural. Many people can therefore belong to a same race. See also *nation, *state.

PER ACCIDENS
See per se.

PERCEPTION
Is in philosophical sense distinguished from *sensation by giving to the former a broader meaning, namely the sensation (the act of the exterior senses) with all that at the same time appears spontaneously in the representation through the activity of the other faculties (memory, intellect etc. .) The sensation is then limited to the sensory contact; in the perception are also present a.o. the size, the distance, the reputation etc.
The empirical psychology emphasizes the objective pole, represented by the object of the perception (passive) and the subjective pole, in the perceiver himself and

determined by the special aptitude (types of perception), the previous experiences, the situation in which the perception is happening etc. (active). When the perception shifts strongly from the objective-documentary to the subjective-interpretative pole, then we speak of *projection. Perception becomes then the adjudication of values, an active action, in which the entire personality is involved. Among the subjective conditions for the perception are most often named the schemata of perception, which represent a certain anticipating activity, so that the perception happens in a specific way.—P.S.

PERCEPTIONISM
Doctrine teaching that perception gives only immediate certitude of the real existence of the spacially perceived. Cfr. E. J. Hamilton. Gredt teaches that the sensory experience is an immediate (intuitive) perception of the objective qualities of the perceived.

PERFECT
Finished, what does not show any lack and is therefore completely determined. Used in a narrow sense (one does then not use it in the etymological sense: per-fectus, formed by) it means definite: perfection is definiteness. This means firstly: what answers to the terms of a definition and is at the same time clearly limited by the limits of the definition; the indefinite is then the unlimited, in the sense of general, vague, unclear. But perfect or definite, can also be applied to an *Infinite Being, to the unlimited therefore, but in an entirely different sense, to the absolute perfection of a reality, which does not answer to any limiting definition because it clearly transcends all limitation, and in whose unity all perfections fuse into pure positivity.

There are many definitenesses: first the quidditative perfections, which are, in a being, the ground of what that being is; but St. Thomas sees in them only modi of being, which point from nature, to a deeper ground, the perfections of being, so that being must be called the fundamental and omnipresent definiteness. A being can be completely defined in a certain respect, while it shows in another respect some lacking: it is then relatively perfect and at the same time relatively imperfect. So does a being, which differs from other beings, not have the definiteness of other beings; it has therefore not all perfection and is considered imperfect. It is however in this being's nature to be only itself and therefore to be limited (that it does not have the perfection of other beings is a pure negation not a *privation). The imperfection is here thus not a lack. The question is: is there a being which transcends not only all privations but also all negations and therefore contains completely all perfection: the purely perfect or the divine *Absolute. —L.D.R.

PERICLES, 495-429 B.C.
Athenian statesman whose name is given to the period considered the height of Greek civilization. Made his city-state the center of art, literature and philosophy, and gave a memorable address on Athens' democratic way of life in 430, during the Peloponnesian War.

PERIPATETIC SCHOOL
Contains the Greek philosophers, followers of the doctrines of *Aristotle. He taught sometimes while walking (Greek: peripatein), from which the school derived the name

of peripatetism. One distinguished the *older* peripatetics or immediate successors of Aristotle and the *younger* peripatetics, who live in the hellenic-Roman period. In the first group of philosophers we find *Theophrastus of Eresos, successor of Aristotle, as head of the school, he was especially interested in the history of the sciences and the philosophy; *Eudemus of Rhodes, developed especially the theory of the syllogism; Aristoxenus of Tarente wrote a theory of music; Dicaearchus tried to reconcile aristotelianism and platonism; Demetrius of Phaleron was especially interested in politics. The younger peripatetics were involved in the struggle between the later Greek systems and produced scientific works in the spirit of the Alexandrian period. Straton of Lampsacus developed the empirical side of the aristotelian philosophy of nature. Among them are also Hieronymus of Rhodes, Ariston of Keos and many authors who are important for the history of the Greek philosophy: Hermippos, Sotion, Heracleidos Lembos, Antisthenes of Rhodes.—F.D.R.

PERISH

Cease to be where one is, by changing places; cease to be what one is, by changing into something else; cease to be completely, i.e. to be annihilated.

PERSEITAS

That what characterizes per se or naturally valid as such. It often is used in a narrower sense of *aseitas, the fact of being from-itself which is inherent to the divine Absolute.

PER SE, PER ACCIDENS, naturally as opposed to accidental.

Man is naturally gifted with reason, but he is accidentally a painter. Sometimes also: in first line, directly, for itself as opposed to in second instance, indirectly, for something else: theology for instance is per se dealing with God, per accidens with the creatures.

PERSON (Lat.: persona, mask, later actor, post and dignity, also man as juridical being: this latter under the influence of stoicism, which preferred to emphasize the role of man in the world)

Indicates somebody who, having rights and obligations, takes his decisions freely so that he is responsible for his actions. The person is therefore in the first place characterized by his spiritual activity (intellect and will and more specifically self-consciousness). In this self-consciousness the person experiences himself as a unity in the differentiation of the functions or the succession of the moments of time: this unity appears further to be completely peculiar and incommunicable and is at the same time lived as its own source of activity. All this is found in the classical definition given by Boethius: persona est naturae rationalis individua substantia (a subsisting reality with rational nature) or in the definition of Thomas Aquinas: subsistens in aliqua natura intellectuali (a *suppositum gifted with intellectual life). Modern definitions follow the same trend but emphasize the self-consciousness: some shed light on the activity of thought, others on an element from the mind (e.g. love), still others on the will.

In the metaphysical order the scholastics look for the **constituting** principle of the completeness of being which is characteristic of the person: many thomists find it in their own principle of being; others (*Cajetanus) in a mode which cuts off the substance and orders it in

319

accordance with its own way of being; *Suarez appeals to a mode which affects the being as existing reality.

Because the person is responsible for his actions, he has necessarily a place in ethics. Kant teaches that he is not only the subject of the ethical order, but that he produces the moral law to which he has to submit himself (*autonomy). In any case the *personal value is absolute. Since people live actually in community, the question arises how and in what measure a person keeps his independence in the community. L.D.R.

PERSONALISM

Way of thought, which was developed in the French philosophy by *Mounier and de *Rougemont. It is primarily not speculative, but directed towards action: it is interested in the reform of the community. It emphasizes the particular meaning and unalienable value of the individual human person and is therefore opposed to *Marx. The opposition between the personalistic conception of the society and the contemporary bourgeois conception is however more often underlined. B.D.

PERSONALITY

What characterizes the *person as person, —namely self-consciousness and self-control. In narrow sense: person is opposed to personality as the principle is opposed to the term of the formal spiritual life. The person develops himself to a personality thanks to the use of his abilities, more specifically on a moral level, the person becomes a personality thanks to his (good or bad) actions. In strict sense is personality only applied to those people who show, in their development, a great originality of vision together with an extraor-

dinary will-power. The personality is then mostly determined by innate aptitude but also developed by exercise.

PERSONAL VALUE

The *value which is due to the *person, as formal spiritual being. This value is absolute: the person has not only value in himself and for himself, he has an infinite value. He can therefore never be used as a pure means.

In a derived meaning, personal values are values which are related to the person. In the hierarchy of values they are the highest. Since the person is the principle of moral life, personal values are necessarily moral values. In other words: as soon as values are brought in relation to the person as a formal spiritual being, they have a moral character. In the strict sense are only personal values those values which constitute the moral *ideal of a *specific* person, and as such impose themselves more specifically on him.

PERSPECTIVISM

Doctrine which teaches, with Nietzsche and others, that all knowledge is perspective, i.e. is in relation to the needs, and more specifically the necessities of life of the knowing subject.

PESSIMISM

Attitude according to which the world is fundamentally bad. It appears most clearly in the fact that no human striving can be completely satisfied. It is already defended in Buddhism, but with Schopenauer and E. von Hartmann it became a real doctrine: the world is so evil that not-being is better than being. The world, in last instance, is evil because it is the expression of an irrational "Will". Existentialism is also pessimistic because it emphasizes the finity

320

and the failing. See Nihilism.—J. Gr.

PESTALOZZI, Johann Heinrich, 1746-1827

Swiss educational reformer, generally considered the father of modern European pedagogics. Established famous school, based on the theories of Rousseau, which failed, but Pestalozzi continued to teach and learn. His doctrines contained in the novel *Lienhard and Gertrude* (1785).

PETITIO PRINCIPII

A paralogism, in which is accepted as premise of a reasoning, that which only can be a *conclusion of it or a subsequent *corollarium. E.g. when Descartes proves the reliability of our senses from the veracity of God, who can not have given us deceitful senses. See also Vicious circle.

PETRUS AUREOLI

Born in Cahors, after 1250, died in Aix (Provence) 1322, Franciscan. Studied in Paris ca. 1304 (under Duns Scotus-), magister in theology in 1318, provincial of Aquitania in 1320 and bishop of Aix in 1321. Main work: commentary on the *sententiae* (two redactions). Critical and independent thinker, he disputed scotism, emphasized the value of the individual and the knowledge of it, and he was a precursor of the *via moderna.

PETRUS DAMIANI

Born in Ravenna 1007, died in Faenza 1072, professor and later hermit (1035), finally cardinal-bishop of Ostia (1057). He participated actively on the gregorian reformation and considered the profane sciences a danger for the faith; he clearly defended anti-intellectualism and condemned the use of dialectics in theology.

PETRUS HISPANUS

Born in Lisbon ca. 1220, died in Viterbo 1277. Physician and philosopher, professor in logic at the facultas artium in Paris ca. 1240, professor (in medicine?) in Sienna ca. 1246, archbishop of Braga in 1272, pope in 1276 (John XXI); imposed soon after his election the study which brought about, in 1277, the condemnation of aristotelianism. He is the author of the *Summulae logicales*, for centuries the official textbook of logic.

PETRUS JOANNES OLIVI

Born in Sérignan (Hérault) 1248, died in Narbonne 1298, Franciscan, studied theology in Paris ca. 1268 and knew there Bonaventura; he was in constant conflict with his superiors because of his theological and philosophical ideas, but especially because of his relations with the spirituals; left us a great number of literary works. His philosophy underwent a strong influence of the franciscan neo-augustinism, but contains also original ideas; especially in physics and phychology. The council of Vienne condemned in 1311 his theory about the *pars intellectiva of the soul*.

PETRUS LOMBARDUS

Born near Novara, ca. 1100, died in Paris, probably 1160. Studied in Italy and France, became in 1140 professor of theology at the School of Notre Dame in Paris and in 1159 bishop of Paris. His *Sententiarum libri IV*, probably completed in 1153, are one of the first efforts to systematise theology; in the beginning of the 13th century it became the official textbook of the theological schools; the baccalaurei had to explain it during two years before receiving the title of magister. Since this rule remained until the end of the 16th century, we have hundreds of commentaries on the work of the *Magister sententiarum*. His philosophy is superficial.

PETRUS OF AILLY (Pierre d'A.)

Born in Compiègne 1350, died in Avignon 1420. Professor of theology in Paris (1380), chancellor of the university (1389), later bishop (1395) and cardinal (1411). Wrote several works, influenced by the nominalism of Ockham. Was also suspicious of reason: the traditional arguments for the existence of the outer world and the existence of God are, in his opinion, only very probable (valde probabiles).

PHENOMENALISM

Doctrine that the knowledge man can reach is never more than the knowledge of phenomena, because man's limited ability to know necessarily deforms objects according to his own subjective nature.

PHENOMENISM

Doctrine that human knowledge attains only a subjective seeming, to which no reality corresponds. This doctrine is identical to °conscientialism: to be is nothing else than to be experienced (*see* Berkeley). In Indian thought, phenomenism is found in the doctrine of the Maya. *See also* phenomenalism.

PHENOMENOLOGY (Literally: doctrine of what appears)

The term was introduced by Lambert in 1764. The introduction to the system of Hegel is called *"Phänomenologie des Geistes,"* because in it he examines the kind of exteriorization by which knowing develops from absolute knowledge. In Husserl's philosophy phenomenology is first of all a method to reach *"den Sachen selbst"* (in order to establish a foundation for scientific philosophy) as it reveals itself to whoever experiences it immediately and personally in consciousness. This method brings us such an original attitude toward beings, that their appearance becomes the self-revelation of their essence to the contemplating man. Thanks to eidetic reduction, by which the individual appearance as well as factual existence of the data, is put between parentheses (*Einklammerung*) immediate conscious (*Wesensschau* or °intuition) of the essence of the data becomes possible (°ideation). On the grounds of this insight into concrete being one can reach general conclusions and deduce apodictically from them new conclusions by means of other, also immediately evident principles. In this way one can reach the science of being.

Later on, phenomenology developed from a method to a system; it is not the science of things as they appear to the conscious being, but the science of revelation itself and of its roots in consciousness. Next to the eidetic comes the phenomenological and finally transcendental phenomenological reduction, in which the object is reduced to an act in which it appears; it is only "being-for-me in my acts." While the objective or noematic aspect of knowledge is taken up by the gift to the subject, the noetic is formed by the "pure consciousness" (*see* cogito) that as transcendental subjectivity constitutes the objects to which it is directed, and their totality (the "world"). This "transcendental idealism" tries to avoid solipsism, however, it is proper to the noematic to appeal to the complexity of transcendental subjects. The objectivity of the world is in this way phenomenologically constituted by a "transcendental intersubjectivity." J.P.

Many philosophers adopted Husserl's method, not his system, but it has been explained by each of them in his own way. The first big phenomenological s c h o o l was founded in Munich after the first publication of Husserl. For this school—to which belonged *Conrad-Martius, M. Geiger, von Hildebrand, Pfänder, and Reinach—the *Wesensschau* is the center of phenomenology. Phenomenology takes an entirely different direction in Heidegger, and still another direction in some French philosophers after the Second World War: Sartre, Merleau-Ponty, Ricoeur. The latter uses the posthumous writings of Husserl and shows the influence of Heidegger and Hegel. In the large sense of the term, many other writers belong to phenomenology, although they do not belong to one of these groups, e.g., *Jaspers and *Marcel. In Holland there has been for some time a phenomenological psychiatry under the direction of H. C. Rümke, professor of the university of Utrecht. Here phenomenology is used to indicate the description of the inner situation. *Buytendijk has been the leader of phenomenological psychology. B.D.

PHENOMENOLOGY OF THE MIND

Called by Hegel, in his work *Phänomenologie des Geistes*, the study of consciousness in the different forms under which it appears during its dialectical movement from naive consciousness, through self-consciousness, reason, morality and religion, to absolute knowledge of the Mind.

PHENOMENON

(Greek: *phainomai*, appear) That which appears to the consciousness. It can be considered as pure seeming, to which no reality corresponds (*phenomenism), or as the appearance of reality (*phenomenalism). For Kant the *Ding an sich* is the basis of the phenomenon: in the phenomenon the *Ding an sich* finds its expression, although deformed by its relation to a subject and its laws.

When it is not pure seeming, the phenomenon can indicate the external aspect that a thing exhibits in sensory experience. In this sense, for instance, it is opposed in Plato to the noumenon or to the stricter reality which can be known by surpassing sensory things. Finally, it means the inner, real self, insofar as it reveals itself to the consciousness. This latter meaning is held in *phenomenology.

PHILODEMUS

1st century B.C., wrote a treatise *on piety* and another *on the gods*. Is most known through the papyri which were found in the 18th century in Herculanum.

PHILOLAUS

5th century B.C., Greek philosopher, disciple of *Pythagoras. He teaches that the world order consists in the harmony between the limited and the unlimited, and this harmony rests on specific numbers. The soul is punished to be united with the body and locked up as in a jail.

PHILO OF ALEXANDRIA

Ca. 20 B.C.-ca. 50 A.D., lived in Alexandria, descendant of an important family, in 40 he accompanied a mission of the Alexandrian Jews to the emperor Gaius. Left many writings, few of them are purely philosophical. He left also several commentaries on the *Pentateuch* (method of allegorical explanation), and a few historic-apologetical works. Main characteristics of his thought: union of

Jewish doctrines with the Greek philosophy. He emphasizes strongly the transcendence of the divinity: God surpasses the idea of the good and can not be reached through a scientific argument but only through immediate evidence: one can also come to a certain knowledge of God through esthetic and teleological considerations, but this knowledge is of minor value. To create the worldly God uses some immaterial forces, or Ideas, which are considered independent beings. All these forces are however submitted to the *Logos;* he conceives it as the place where the ideas remain and as the highest force of which all others are dependent; a distinction has to be made between the logos in man, which is not purely interior or can be expressed in the word, and the logos in the universe which exists as intelligible world of ideas or is expressed in the perceptible reality. The logos has thus for Philo the role of the demiurge in Plato's *Timaeus,* with this exception however that it is considered as the place of the Ideas. It is however difficult to determine the exact place of the Logos in the philosophy of Philo, especially for what concerns its independence and its relation to the divinity. Philo rejects the creation *ex nihilo:* next to the Logos and the divinity there is matter, which is conceived in a platonic sense as a not-being and which can not be deduced from the divine being. The world began but will continue to exist eternally. The human soul is composed of two heterogeneous elements: one is physical and inseparable from the blood, the other is pneumatic and a result of the divine logos. The duty of the human existence is: to become identical with God, which will actually mean to live according to the logos which is present in every man. Man can reach the highest perfection in the ecstasy, in which he completely and immediately is taken up by the divinity, so that all personal consciousness disappears.–G.V.

PHILO OF LARISA
Was the successor of Clitomachus as head of the *Academy. (110-80) He still rejected the stoic criterion of truth, but learned that the things can be known in their own nature. This was a first regression from scepticism. Philo is therefore not counted among the followers of the New Academy but of the fourth Academy.

PHILOSOPHEME
Philosophical assertion, question or doctrine. For Aristotle an apodictic *syllogism.

PHILOSOPHER
The philosopher: is in the Middle Ages Aristotle.

PHILOSOPHES (Les)
French thinkers of the 18th century as Condorcet, Condillac, Rousseau, Voltaire.

PHILOSOPHY (Greek: philein- to love; sophia- wisdom)
As Socrates mentioned: the philosophy does not possess wisdom but has only the desire to possess it. It is the whole of the efforts, either in a certain period or for a specific people, to reach *wisdom. Therefore the philosophy of antiquity, or the philosophy of the Greeks. –In what does this effort consist? Philosophy is firstly a form of *knowledge*: it aims therefore at acquiring insight or giving explanations. This insight can be desired for itself, but can also be simply a means for enlightened action or one's own existence, as in stoicism or the existential thought. The ex-

planations given by philosophy must be *rationally* justified. The reason is the measure for the philosophy, and so does it make philosophy different from *Weltanschauung and revealed religion. This does however not indicate the conditions and the manner in which it works: for Aristotle philosophy avoids all contradictions, for Hegel it abolishes all contradiction; for Plato it penetrates, from nature, the suprasensual, while for Kant it needs the help of the sensuality; for some it is pure receptibility, for others, it is creative. Philosophy finally tries to give an explanation which is *total*, either by seizing a datum in all its aspects and relations or penetrating into its last grounds. This makes the difference between philosophy and science, and even Comte agrees to this when he calls the philosophy: "la haute systématisation des sciences". Only philosophy reaches the All as All, and its highest ideal seems to be going through the evolution of the All, beginning with its primitive principle. In conclusion we can say: *philosophy is this knowledge of the All* (or of a content of the All) *which is rationally justified and totally explained·* It should be added that this explanation should necessarily happen in a specific cohesion, so that the philosophy only exists as the philosophy of Aristotle, of Kant etc.

History of philosophy, is not accidental to the philosophy but belongs to its essence, because it is more desire than possession. We can here not discuss if, as Hegel states, the history of philosophy shows a necessary evolution and if it, in its repeated efforts to explain the All, always remains at the same place or makes a steady progress. It should however be noted that the philosophy in the

three circles of civilization (China, India and the West) had originally a similar evolution.

The Western philosophy had its origin in Greece since 700 B.C., it was an explanation, through reason, of that what was only explained through mythology. Several periods can be noted in its evolution: 1) the *philosophy of antiquity*: reaches very soon a height which is difficult to equal, and reaches such a multiplicity of views, problems and solutions which seem to exhaust the possibilities of the human mind. 2) The *philosophy of the Middle Ages,* also called christian philosophy because it has its origin in the contact between the pagan philosophy and the christian revelation and because it is determined by the conflict which follows this contact. 3) the *modern philosophy,* under influence of the spirit of the time it put forward the subject (the Ego), more specifically the thinking subject. 4) the *contemporary philosophy* is characterized by the existence of different schools next to each other.

Division of the philosophy in philosophical fields is immediately dependent on the philosophical views one has. In every division however we find the following schema: 1) the *Philosophy of the instrument*: of the thinking (*logic or theory of thought; *epistemology or theory of knowledge) 2) *Philosophy of the data*: a) of the All as totality of the data (*metaphysics, *ontology) b) of the special data:—nature (natural philosophy or *cosmology); culture as transformation of nature by the human mind (*moral philosophy, philosophy of *art etc.) J.Gr.

PHILOSOPHY OF ART
See theory of art.

PHILOSOPHY OF FEELING
See Glaubensphilosophie.

PHILOSOPHY OF HISTORY
The term *"philosophie de l'histoire"* was first used by Voltaire, but before him Vico had already spoken of the "reasoned theology of civil affairs." Herewith he established a very clear distinction between a theological view of history, which in the light of faith tries to penetrate the plans of divine Providence for the supernatural salvation of humanity, and the philosophical view of the history, which, without taking account of revelation, tries to indicate in the light of reason alone, the general causes or factors in the historical life of humanity, and also to discover the sense or direction of human evolution. D i f f e r e n t philosophical schools, from rationalism, idealism and positivism to contemporary historicism, have developed their own vision of history.

Historicism, which considers reason as well as the conscience of man in historical change, cannot avoid absolute relativism: every era has its own truth and its own norms of life, and can therefore be understood only by those able to think and live intuitively in the norms of truth and life of a given era. But thought and life cannot be identified. The human being rises above life when he thinks. All historicists therefore search for absolute norms which direct and lead human life and with it history. In the absence of methaphysics they cannot succeed. A history without metaphysical basis cannot be realized. But the metaphysican also has to concede that the final meaning of history escapes him. God, the Lord of history, leads it according to His inscrutable will, and reveals only to mankind what man needs for his eternal salvation. The theologian who looks at history in the light of divine revelation can satisfy only himself with the contemplation of what God revealed to mankind about His plans. K.L.B.

PHILOSOPHY OF LAW
This philosophy which has more specifically the *right as object. Plato considers the philosophy of law as the political philosophy, it is however mostly considered as a part of ethics. Hegel identifies it with the philosophy of the objective *spirit.

Positivism saw the right as a purely historical phenomenon, and reduced the philosophy of law to an absolute doctrine of law which describes purely empirically the phenomenon of right. Often the philosophy of law is nothing else than a *theory of law,* in which the conditions are investigated which make the right, or better the conception of right, possible. Kelsen arrived even at a pure doctrine of law. The neo-kantian philosophy of law follows the same direction (Stammler). Others try also to define the right by its content, while the neo-hegelian (e.g. Binder) can only define it dialectically. Only the thomistically oriented thinkers (Cathrein) use the philosophy of law still in the traditional sense, as the doctrine of the natural right. J. Gr.

PHILOSOPHY OF LIFE
A philosophy which inquires about the sense of life; more specifically the school in contemporary thought which tries to reach the original reality of the stream of life in an act of immediate experience. This school has its origin with Nietzsche; Dilthey has developed it into *historicism, while it was reduced by Spranger to a psychology of the forms of life and

by Spengler to a typology. Simmel underwent clearly the influence of Bergson, who himself in intuition, is open to the stream of life. It reaches also in this theory a certain *relativism.

Life, in this case, is not the organic life of plants and animals, but the stream of life itself, which, in creation, produces the reality in it's diversity. In philosophy it has to be seized in its original force, while the existing idealism as well as positivism limit themselves to the justification of the culture, or even the science, which is still only one of the forms in which life, as spiritual life, became, as if it were, rigid. All philosophy of consciousness, on the other hand, with its construction of concepts, remains on the surface of reality. Only in the immediate experience it reveals the stream which nourishes it. In this sense is the philosophy of life irrationalistic. Dilthey, finally, considers life itself or the historical existence of man. This can only be "understood" in experiencing its sense. It is in this perspective that we have to see the intention of the *Verstehenpsychologie, w h i c h leads already in Jaspers to the existenz-philosophy. J. Gr.

PHILOSOPHY OF NATURE
See cosmology.

PHILOSOPHY OF RELIGION
Investigation of the final grounds which determine the religious life of humanity, and of its truth and value. Its first duty is to investigate the natural factors, i.e., man and his milieu, in order to give a satisfactory explanation of the origin and historical development of the religious life of humanity, to determine whether an appeal has to be made to the special intervention of God. Thus the philosophy of religion is forced into its second duty: to determine the norm according to which the religious life has to be judged, not only as to its relative truth and value, but also as to its absolute truth and value. This metaphysically based philosophy of religion is rejected on the one hand by idealistic and positivistic philosophers, who deny the possibility of any intervention of God in religious life, and therefore reduce every judgment of the truth and value of religion to judgment of its relative function in historical, psychological, social or spiritual and cultural domains. It is rejected on the other hand by some theologians, who invoke the Christian tenet that faith is a gift of God and therefore not open to philosophical criticism, neither in its essence nor in its content. The first group can only be refuted in general metaphysics and epistemology. To the second group it can be said that insofar as their objections are not philosophical faith necessarily penetrates all conscious human life, a penetration which presupposes an acceptance of God's revelation on the grounds of the so-called *motiva credibilitatis*—reasons which prove the credibility of God's revelation on reasonable grounds and therefore are subject to philosophical criticism. K.L.B.

PHYLOGENY or PHYLOGENESIS
The biologist's term for the creation by evolution of a series of organisms which descend from one primitive form. From this the biologist tries to build a genealogical tree. The concept of descendance is very closely connected with phylogeny. However, it is used more frequently in connection with an existing species of which one tries to find the genealogical tree in the past.

PHYSICAL

Predicate which applies to all material things, i.e. things which are extensive in space and time. Physical can also be applied to all structural elements belonging, as such, to the material things, and to their qualities and accidental definiteness. Because every matter always consists of a correlation of *quantitative and *qualitative characteristics, according to scholasticism its substantial ground is composed of two correlative principles; a potential and an actual principle. They are called respectively prime matter and substantial *form. Prime (i.e. fundamental, substantial) matter is in the scholastic terminology the (not empirically perceivable) *potential principle, whose correspondence with a corresponding form-principle makes a physical *substance. According to Thomas Aquinas is the prime matter in no case source of definiteness, but only principle of determinability, purely potential principle: it has, outside of its structural connection with the substantial form, no possibility to exist. It is, as such, the fundamental reason of *quantiy and of all what originates from it (as extension, passivity and inertion). It is also the *individuation-principle or the substantial reason for the not-formal things which belong to the same species and are therefore specific. L.D.R.

PHYSICO-THEOLOGICAL

*Kant's term for the argument for the existence of God through the finality and final striving of nature. He does not attach any value to this argument, because it would contain the ontological proof, which is only in the order of the concepts. He thinks, however, that we can reach God through a physico-theological way.

PHYSICS

Initially, the study of nature (*fysis*) or of that which is experienced by the senses. It is therefore the same thing as natural science (*see* science). Physics is now considered a specific part of the natural sciences, comparable to chemistry, biology and other natural sciences. In philosophical works the term "physics" is still used in its primitive meaning.

Physical theory can refer to the theories of physics in the broader sense, i.e., theory of the natural sciences as opposed to philosophical theory, or can mean the theory of physics in the modern meaning.

The particularity of a physical theory (in a broader sense) is that from such a theory conclusions can always be drawn which are susceptible of experimental proof. The structural theories of chemistry, for instance, reveal something about the mutual situation of the different atoms. Their spatial configuration is something which is open to sensual observation, although the objects in this case are too small to be directly observed. One has to find an experiment, a specific one, for instance, the röntgen rays, which will permit us to receive specific data about the spatial configuration of atoms. This example shows how closely theory and experiment are connected in physics. For the experimental proof of structural theories is only possible through specific theories of the röntgen rays. Natural philosophy, as opposed to physical theory, is never open to experimental proof, because this theory is concerned with the characteristics of matter (e.g., the structure of *species-individual), which is already presupposed in every experiment according to the experimental method. See Cosmology.

PICO, Giovanni della Mirandola

Born 1463, died in Florence 1494, one of the main figures of the neo-platonic academy of Florence. He joins phantastic elements with profound ideas. The knowledge of God, of Whom we can only speak without knowing him and only negatively, is the highest bliss. There are three worlds, which proceed from God: the suprasensual world of the angels, the heavenly and the sublunar world. Man is a microcosm in which the three worlds are joined. Human thought is fundamentally one in all its forms of expression, as in the H. Bible, Kabbala and the different philosophical visions.

PIERRE D'AILLY

See Petrus of Ailly.

PLACE (Lat.: ubi)

One of the ten aristotelian *categories. The presence in a place is however different for a physical being (circumscriptive: every part of the latter answers to a specific part of the occupied place); for a spirit (definitive: the place of our soul is determined by the body, in which it is active); and for God (relative: He is active in the entire creation and "fills" it therefore with His presence)

The spoken language determines very often the place of a physical being inexactly. To the question: "where is this object?" we answer quite often e.g. in this city, this house, this room. It is clear that a strict determination of place requires the data of the most immediate surroundings. In the natural sciences the place of an object is often schematized e.g. to a point in a system of coordinates. This is however also only practical approximation of the concept, since the place as well as the object has *extension.*

Aristotle defines the place of an object as the inner, immobile limit of that which surrounds immediately the object. It is noteworthy that Aristotle defines the place as a surface. If one accepts the existence of the *ether of Lorentz, place can be defined as a specific part of the ether. The immobility of the place is clear through the fact that the place occupied by an object, remains even when the object is removed. This immobility must not be absolute, for a good definition of the place. It is obvious that the place of an object, defined in this way, is not in the object but in something else. The described conception of place follows the *contact-theory. For another conception see the *position-theory. C.J.M.v.M.B.

PLANCK, Max, 1858-1947

German physicist and philosopher of nature, professor in Berlin, founder of the quantum-theory (see quanta).

PLANT

Is called an organism that has the lowest level of life, without consciousness, but with vegetative functions (see life). The limit between plant and animal is sometimes difficult to determine, especially for lower forms. Other, but not exclusive characteristics of plants are the possession of chlorophyll and therefore ability to synthesis of organic matter; an "open" structure with never finished growth; more automatic reaction on stimuli than in animals, a strong ability to a sexual propagation.— If one identifies soul with principle of life, one can rightfully speak of a *vegetative soul.*

PLATO

Athenian philosopher, 427-347 B.C., profoundly influenced by *Socrates. After the latter's death

(399) he moved with other disciples of Socrates to Megara. He certainly was around 388 in Southern Italy and in Sicily, at the court of Dionysius I. In 387 he returned to Athens, founded the °Academy, and headed it for 40 years. He returned twice to Sicily in the hope to make of Dionysius II a king-philosopher, whom he considered the real ruler. Both trips (367/6-361) became failures. He himself wrote about his experiences in Sicily in his 7th letter, which most scholars of Plato consider today as being authentic.

We have 25 dialogues of Plato which are undoubtedly authentic, the *Apology* (of Socrates) and a collection of 13 letters, the 6th, 7th and 8th are now generally considered authentic.

The dialogues (next to the *Apology*) are divided chronologically in three groups:

I. *The period before the foundation of the Academy* with the *Apology, Crito Protagoras, Hippias, Minor, Euthyphro, Laches, Charmides, Lysis, Io,* the first book of the *Republic* and the *Gorgias.*

They are (exception made for the *Apology*) conversations in which Socrates is the main character and in which he interrogates somebody else, mostly about the nature of one or another virtue (bravery, piety, modesty etc.). A definition is put forward which can not stand up under the questioning of Socrates. With a second and third definition the same thing happens. At the end they conclude with a confession of not-knowing and intend to repeat the conversation "sometime later".

In these conversations they are looking systematically for the unique essence of the different phenomena. This method of Socrates has brought Plato to his *Theory of Ideas,* which is explained in the dialogues of the middle period and which are again submitted by the end of the period to a very critical scrutiny.

II. *From the foundation of the Academy to the second trip to Sicily.* In the beginning of this period we have the *Menexenus,* a manifest of Plato, as head of the Academy, against the rhetors. Then the *Meno, Euthydemus, Cratylus Phaedo, Symposium* and the *Republic.* By the end of this period we place the *Phaedrus* (in which we find for the first time the Plato's concept of the soul as cause of motion) the *Theaetetus* (an extremely critical study of the nature of knowledge) and the *Parmenides,* which begins an entirely new critical reflection on the theory of Ideas.

III. *From the second trip to Sicily till Plato's death.* Sophistes (possibly written immediately before his second trip to Sicily), *Politicus, Philebus, Timaeus, Critias,* and finally the *Laws,* with the *Republic* the most important work of Plato. The interest of Plato is in these latter works more directed towards the experience.

All these dialogues are without doubt authentic. The authenticity of the *Hippias Maior,* the *Alcibiades Maior* and the *Epinomis* is not so sure. Other dialogues transmitted under Plato's name (there are 12) are inauthentic.

The theory of Ideas: The reflexion on ethical concepts leads us to the theory of Ideas. Plato asks for the one *eidos* or the one *idea,* through which all pious actions are pious (*Euthyphro*). The theory of Ideas is certainly not limited to this kind of concept. That the things are beautiful, great or small, rests also on this one concept as on a basis: they are beautiful or great because they participate at the beautiful-in-itself and the great-in-itself (Phaedo). Even for the concrete things which we call table, bed, tree, animal etc., we accept every time one single *eidos* (Republic X).

Plato thinks that these ideas are really existing beings, more real (because more fundamental) than the concrete things, which only exist because of their participation at the "ideas". The ideas are that what they are in *the complete sense;* they are the complete and original. They are "examples" and the concrete things, in their multiplicity, are always behind them. The "identical" in concreto is never really and completely identical, the one never completely one. They are stable and unchangeable essences, which for that reason make knowledge (*Cratylus*) and reasoning (*Parmenides*) possible.

The Ideas are grasped through pure thinking. The education of the philosophers, as described in the *Republic*, is therefore a long training; the mind has to be averted from the sensible and directed to the suprasensual. Mathematical thinking is a first step in this direction.

The welfare of the human society depends on those who learned to focus their attention to this reality; which can only be contemplated with the mind. Only those who have "seen" something from the highest existing Reality: the Idea of the Good, they alone are capable to realize something good in concreto.

Plato later submitted his doctrine of the Ideas (*Parmenides and Sophistes*) to a critical analysis. Essentially, however, he still agreed with it. In the *Sophistes* he added this new vision: we can not deny the life of the mind, therefore in a certain way motion, to the Intelligible Reality. This means that the intelligible world is considered as a living organism, dominated and ordered by higher ordering principles: the transcendental Spirit. It is then also understandable that Plato, in the *Timaeus,* wrote about the creation of the world: the Demiurg (who is a transcendental Spirit) created the world as a living and animated organism, *according to the example of the intelligible world.* This is for Plato not so unusual: a cosmos is as such always ordered by a Spirit; the physical world with its ordering Spirit is however not the last and deepest reality. It depends on an intelligible cosmos, which, as "original image" is also an organism, ordered by a Spirit.

The late dialogues of Plato have to be completed with the information we find in Aristotle and some other writers about the theory of the first principles: the One and the undetermined duality to which Plato in his later period reduced everything. We know those principles from the *Philebus,* in which Plato describes them as the "specifying" (péras) and the "indeterminate" (apeiron). In between is the "mixture", and a fourth principle has to be accepted, the "cause of the mixing". In the *Timaeus* we find these four principles in a somewhat mythological form, consciously used by Plato: they are by the origin of the sensible world the Ideas (the determining) and the space in which the things originate (the in itself indetermined); the sensible world, the "mixture" of the *Phil.* becomes here "the child" and the Demiurge appears as an ordering cause. We have to remark that Plato in the *Timaeus* does not go as far as the final principles. He certainly considered the intelligible world to be hierarchically ordered: above the Ideas is one principle, which he calls in the *Republic,* the Good and later preferred to call the One.

The *immanent soul* occupies in Plato's philosophy an intermediate place, between the transcendent world of the Ideas and the sensible world of the physical, it is then also clear that the hierarchy in being which we find in the writings of the *neoplatonists is already present in Plato's works. His immediate successors, Speusippus and Xenocrates, and later Posidonius, define the soul as a mathematical principle; which is comprehensible if we consider that Plato saw the objects of the mathematical thought as an intermediate sphere between the purly intelligible and the sensible (although closer to the first).

It is not true, although sometimes heard, that Plato abandoned in his last big work, the *Laws,* his *theory of Ideas,* this work is on the contrary animated with the same spirit as his other big work: the *Republic*: we find here also the burning desire to give form to the human society according to the requirements of the highest good. Only for the possibility of achieving it he became more sceptical. He does not believe any more in the education of philosophical rulers, to whom we could entrust without danger to human society. He therefore wants to achieve as much as possible through specific prescriptions. "The Good has to be done, even with force"—this is Plato's opinion in the *Laws,* a work in which he is interested, not less than in the *Republic,* with education, and in which he gives it very specific rules.

From the beginning to the end, Plato remained a passionate educator, animated with the ardent will to radiate and make active in the world of man that what he experienced as deepest Reality. C.J.d.V.

PLATONISM

(1) the philosophy of Plato himself; (2) the philosophy of Plato in the course of history. One can speak of platonism of the old *Academy, in Aristotle (in his youth), in a certain measure in the stoic Posidonius (especially in his conception of the soul). In the 1st and 2nd century A.D. platonism can be found in Philo of Alexandria, who explains the ideas as thoughts of God (a conception which we find principally in Plato, but not in these terms; Philo was certainly not the first one to use them), in Plutarch (who teaches a very transcendental concept of God, under Him a Spirit and then the soul) and in the so called middle platonism of Albinus (also *Origenes* and his doctrine of the soul). In the 3rd century comes the so called neo-platonism of Plotinus and those who followed him. The christian writers of the 4th century and later were very much influenced by this form of platonism. Augustine knew Plato's philosophy through the neo-platonici of his time. Through Augustine and through Pseudo-Dionysius who was very much influenced by the neo platonici, platonism came into the Middle Ages (Anselm and the School of Chartres, Bontaventura and most philosophers of the 13th century). The platonism of the Renaissance-man Marsilius Ficino was also neo-platonic. The same thing can be said of the *Cambridge-platonists of the 17th century, Henry More and Ralph Cudworth. We can also speak of a platonism of Whitehead and of some French mathematicians as Bouli-

gand, Desgranges and especially Lautmann. The theory of Ideas of Plato is revived by them in a kind of metamathematical t h e o r y. C.J.v.V.

PLAY

Free physical or intellectual activity, lead by no aim outside the activity, but lead only by the desire in the activity itself. The specific play character is not lost when a game is played according to specific rules, in a specific space and time; but it is lost when monetary reward is the main aim. Huizinga called also the sacred liturgical acts a play. It is different from the usual meaning of the play, although the comparison is true in many aspects, because of the consciousness of the faithful that they take part in a divine reality.

PLEASURE

Pleasure can take different forms. It is enjoyment when it more definitely follows the possession of the pursued; it can be delight or joy, the first being more superficial, the latter touching the deepest essence. When it concerns sensual emotions, we call it lust; when spiritual emotions are satisfied, we speak of felicity; and bliss or beatitude is achieved when the pleasure satisfies completely.

Pleasure is in any case an affective condition, in which the true meaning of reality is revealed. It is thus a value. For the hedonist it is the only value. However, since man, who is a rational being, does not have to be absorbed in the subjective sensation of satisfaction, but can judge for himself the objective suitability or propriety of this sensation, hedonism can be challenged. Pleasure, objectively judged by the mind, can be considered *proper or improper.

PLEKHANOV, George, 1857-1918

Russian Marxist who, in 1904, sided with the Mensheviks against Lenin, and after the Revolution of 1917 fought Bolshevism, even though he was dying of tuberculosis. Works: *Anarchism and Socialism* (1894), *Essay on the History of Materialism* (1896), *Fundamental Problems of Marxism* (1908).

PLETHON, Georgios Gemistos

Born in Constantinople 1389, died in the Peloponnesus between 1450 and 1464. He accepts Aristotle's Physics, but attacks vehemently his metaphysics. His platonism convinced Cosimo de Medici to found the neo-platonic Florentine Academy.

PLINY THE YOUNGER, 62-113

Roman statesman under the Emperor Trajan; best known for his *Letters*, some of which are essays and which give valuable information on the political, social and literary life of his time.

PLOTINUS

Born 204-5 in Lycopolis in Upper-Egypt. 28 years old he meets with Ammonius Saccas in Alexandria and participates in an expedition to India (ca. 243) to come in contact with the Indian philosophy. He returns and opens a philosophical School in Rome: his first disciple is Amelius Gentilianus who becomes the first director of the school and secretary of Plotinus. In the beginning Plotinus refused to write; because he wanted to keep his promise not to divulge the doctrine which he learned from Ammonius. Later however, 50 years old, he began to put his thoughts into writing (253-4). Among his audience we can name Amelius and Porphyry, Eustochius, a physician who was very devoted to the master and who took care of him during his last illness; Zethos, also a physician, of Arabic descendance; the senator Rogatianus. Plotinus was also an educator of boys and girls who were entrusted to him. During an epidemic Plotinus became ill, he retired on a domain of Zethos in Miturnae and died there in 270.

The philosophical treatises were written *currente calamo,* the text was not reread or corrected. The oldest edition was published by Eustochius: it has been lost but we can reconstruct it from some fragments kept in the *Praeparatio evangelica* of Eusebius and from a scholion on *Enn. IV,* 4, after cap. 29. The edition we still have and in which the treatises are ordered in six Enneads (6x9) comes from Porphyrius: We can see from the comparison with the old fragments that Porphyry did not make many changes and that the lectures which he renders are generally better than those in the old edition.

Plotinus sees the philosophy as a systematic explication of an initial datum which is present in the human spirit; he will therefore incite the soul to investigate itself, its own essence, so as to become conscious of what it is in the hierarchic structure of the universe. The basis of this philosophical method is the conception about the growth of the human knowledge: this does not happen though elements which come from outside but through the gradual elucidation of a datum of knowledge, which is from the first moment present. This method is also based on the doctrine of emanation: a reflexion of the soul on itself is not limited to the essence of the soul but can lead to the first principle, because this principle is present as formal essential part in all what is.

Plotinus shows herewith that the three highest hypostases are present in every man, and arrives therefore to the ground intuition of his system. This is the unity of the universe: all multiplicity is reduced to unity; this unity is realised on every level of perfection and the lower grades of perfection are connected with the higher ones.

METAPHYSICS. The suprasensual reality contains three hypostases: the One, the Intellect and the Worldsoul. The first principle is elevated above all multiplicity and above all determination, also above the "esse", the good and the beautiful. We can however not reach it positively, because we would thereby limit its plenitude; it is then also conceived as infinite, which represents a great progress in the evolution of the Greek thought, where the idea of infinity was always connected with imperfection. The One, as highest reality, can therefore not be expressed in a positive proposition, but can only be approximated by negations. From this first principle everything originates through a necessary process: perfection has necessarily to propagate itself; so originate the less perfect beings, which show already a certain definiteness. Immediately from the One comes the Intellect or the Nous, as its first image, which also strives back to the One. The Nous is unity, but already multiplicity, because it contains the multiplicity of the ideas; this multiplicity presupposes an intelligible matter. It is furthermore conceived as an *ousia* or something which is, a being and even the first being. The worldsoul occupies the third place, which, mitigated image of the Nous, unites the suprasensual world with the physical world. As a product of the Nous, is the worldsoul identified with the reason or the *logos*: it does therefore not contemplate immediately the ideas, but has to form a number of concepts or *logoi*, which are a reflection of the ideas. These logoi are then further the cause of the physical reality as *rationes seminales* (see Stoics); they have about the same function as the forms of being for Aristotle.

Cosmology. To be able to communicate itself the world soul needs to find beneath itself a lower reality, which proceeds from it, namely matter: the world soul can give form and existence to this matter. Matter is conceived as being purely negative: it is completely indefinite and also undefinable, so that Plotinus goes still farther than Aristotle, who thought that the material principle was pure potency. The union of matter and soul is a purely exterior union: from both elements no real unity originates. The material principle is considered to be the cause of all evil, which means that the world is completely good, since evil is considered to be something completely negative. Following the Stoics, Plotinus says that the world is a big organic whole or a living being, and everything which exists in the world is also animated and living; although the cosmic reality is constantly submited to an evolution, the whole is still eternal and imperishable. He justifies fortune-telling on the grounds of the mutual oneness of the different parts of the cosmos (the universal sympathy), here again he agrees with the Stoics.

Psychology. Plotinus thinks that there are as many human souls as there are living people. Each of these souls had a preexistence in the world-soul as one of its *logoi*: there it contemplated the pure Spiritual. Later it descended into a body because of a certain meta-

physical necessity, while, on the other hand, it naturally strives back to its origin. In the human compositum three elements can be distinguished: the intellect, the soul and the body; the soul is the bond which unites the other two elements. The intellect permits man to stay in connection with the ideas of the divine Nous; the soul also has in some way part in this higher activity, namely through the activity of reason. We can therefore, by contemplating that what is sensibly perceptible, reach the knowledge of the suprasensual; there is indeed in this manner, a kind of revitalisation of the immediate knowing of the ideas, as it existed previously when the individual soul and the world soul were united. The sensory knowledge is considered as an activity of the soul only; the body intervenes only to grasp the physical impression. Freedom of the will has only a small place in the philosophy of Plotinus, if he follows the logical construction of his philosophy, he would have to reject it; he does admit it however on moral grounds.

Ethics. Plotinus teaches that the final end of man and of the entire universe is the return to the first principle; the striving of man has therefore to be directed to the spiritualisation of his existence; he has to disengage himself from all what is physical, to be able to give himself to the ideal of the contemplative life. Man can still go farther up through uninterrupted exercises, higher than the contemplation of the reason could bring him, even higher than his own intellect; he can reach a kind of mystical union with the First Principle. This is to be considered as an *ecstasy*, an immediate contact and an identification with the divinity. According to Porphyry Plotinus would have experienced six times this ecstasy during the six years they stayed together in Rome. The rise to the highest is described by Plotinus as a long and difficult way, with three different stages, which were later borrowed by christian mysticism (purification, enlightening and union). G.V.

PLURALISM
Doctrine according to which reality is composed of different principles. In Antiquity they are mutually irreducible principles: as the four elements of Empedocles, or the qualitatively different homoeomeries of Anaxagoras, or the atoms of Democritus, which all have the same nature. For Leibniz they are the different independent monads. In a less strict sense and in modern philosophy, pluralism is accepted by all those philosophies which accept the existence of different, independent and even personal beings (*personalism), of different forms of definition, and different realms of being. J. Gr.

PLUTARCH OF CHAERONEA
45-ca. 125 A.D., disciple of the platonic philosopher Ammonius in Athens. Visited many countries, e.g. Rome, where he had friendly relations with many important personalities. Was very interested in the politics of his city, was for many years priest of the sanctuary of Apollo in Delphi. Wrote many works; for his philosophy several treatises of the *Moralia* are of interest. He is eclectic with platonic elements prevailing; there are however also stoic, pythagorean and peripatetic elements; scepticism had also influence on him. In metaphysics he strives for a concept of God as pure as possible: he therefore accepts two principles for the reality, a good and an evil principle, to avoid that the divinity be considered as the cause of evil in the world; on the other hand he emphasizes very much the transcendence of God; the demons form the bond between God and the human beings. Plutarch has a very liberal attitude in regard to the popular religion of the Greeks as well as that of the barbarians: he uses therefore allegorical explanations. In psychology Plutarch emphasizes the separation of soul and intellect (*nous*) and holds the survival of the soul after the death. In ethics he is mostly dependent on Aristotle. G.V.

PNEUMA
For Aristotle the "life-giving bloodgas". Later more generally the spirit of life; also in the New Testament "the Spirit who vivifies". PNEUMATOLOGY, the part of dogmatic theology which teaches the doctrine about the Holy Spirit. In psychology, the speculative psychology from a theological point of view.

POETIC, THE
In a general sense, the particular aspect of art, in which the artistic form in its esthetical value as well as in its physical reality is realized and as if it were created by the artist in matter. In narrower sense: indicates the quality of a special verbal art, which is distinguished from prose. Poetry, as opposed to prose which is more attached to the objective ideas, accentuates more the esthetical elements of rhythm and of the subjective-original intuition.

POIETIC
Related to action in as much as it produces something with a destinctive existence.

POINCARE, Henri, 1854-1912
French mathematician and philosopher, professor at the Sorbonne.

He studies criticism of science in the same way as *Boutroux. Physics is not only based on experience but on hypothesis as well. We have to accept as hypotheses the principles, which permit us to order the phenomena in the most simple manner. We should therefore not seek truth in it: we do not know in what measure we will get a rendering of reality. Physics does not have laws in the strict sense, only statistical rules. Axioms in geometry are only arbitrary creations of our mind. B.D.

POINT or STEP OF PROOF

Is *elementary* when it can be proved by means of principles (groundrules and definitions).

POLARITY (Greek polos, pole)

Presence or absence in one and the same principle of two poles, i.e. two opposite attitudes which, however, presuppose each other. Goethe saw already in the polarity the basic law of the course of the world. Schelling was the first to use it as philosophical concept: he considered the subjective or ideal and the objective or real, in other words the spirit and nature, as two opposed poles in the one absolute. They produce in the one a dynamic tension: nature is, as the sensible spirit, the negative or real pole, and the spirit, as the invisible nature, the positive or ideal pole. Hegel dissolved this opposition in a higher *synthesis.

One speaks now also of polarity in the sense of oppositions in the one man or of the seeming opposition (antinomy) between the truths as the allcausality of God and the own activity of the creatures. This term is also applied to concepts in general between which exists a relative *opposition. Polarity is however especially used for the phenomena, in which a contrary effect of direction is existing: so the polarity of a magnet (North and South pole). In biology polarity of plants means the quality according to which the buds develop only at the top and the roots only at the lower part of the stem.

POLEMO OF ATHENS

Head of the Acedamy after Xenocrates (341-270), he was converted by Xenocrates from a licentious life to philosophy. He was mostly interested in ethics and spoke, as did the stoics, of "living according to nature".

POLIN, Raymond

Born 1910, French philosopher, professor in Lille, especially interested in the problem of *values.

POLISH SCHOOL

(Lwow-Warschau).

The logical school founded by Lukasiewicz and S. Lesniewski. To this school belong K. Ajdukiewicz, T. Kotarbinski and *Tarski. L. Chwistek, for instance, did not belong to this school.

POLITICS

(Greek: politikè, things of the state), the statesmanship as the ability in the governing of a *state. Politics indicates also the science which studies political life with its foundations and rules. It remains an open question if statesmanship can be scientifically based and justified. Many philosophers, in any case, have designed an ordering of the state, which appeared to be, in every case, purely utopian.

POLUS

One of the later *sophists, disciple of *Gorgias, and rhetor. He used in his speeches the oratorical artifices of his master. He has no real importance for the philosophy.

POLYSYLLOGISM

Or chain reasoning, a chain of

syllogisms, in which the conclusion of the first or *prosyllogism* is used as the *major or *minor of the next one or *episyllogism*. If it is used as the major, we speak of a *progressive polysyllogism*, when it is used as the minor the polysyllogism is *regressive* e.g. intellectual acts have spiritual objects of knowledge; spiritual objects of knowledge suppose spiritual acts of knowledge; therefore intellectual acts are spiritual acts of knowledge; spiritual acts of knowledge suppose a spiritual ability to know, intellectual acts therefore suppose a spiritual ability to know; a spiritual ability to know supposes a spiritual individuality; acts of intellect require therefore a spiritual individuality. See Sorites.

POMPONAZZI, Peter (Pomponatius)
Born in Mantua, died in Bologna 1525. He combats the revival of the averroistic interpretation of Aristotle, which considers the active intellect as being one. He can not find any philosophic argument for the immortality of the soul, thinks that miracles are impossible and teaches a stoic determinism of the will. Thanks to the double truth, which he defends, he can accept the christian doctrine even if philosophy is opposed to it.

PONS ASINORUM
Or asses' bridge, in the scholastic logic a scheme attributed to Joannes *Buridanus which helps to find easily the proof (see M) for a conclusion; so called because the "passage of this bridge" distinguished the keen student from the slow learner.

PORPHYRY, born 232-3 A.D.
Disciple of Plotinus in Rome in 262-3, stayed for a long time in Sicily from 268, died beginning 4th century. Published an edition of the works of Plotinus with a bio-graphical introduction; wrote commentaries on some works of Plotinus and also on Plato, Aristotle and Theophrastus; very well known is his introduction to the logical works of Aristotle; title *Eisagoge* or *Quinque voces;* He also wrote a work to prove the harmony between Plato and Aristotle. The philosophy of Porphyry shows mostly a more practical and religious importance than the philosophy of Plotinus: the end of the philosophy is the salvation of the soul, which can be reached through asceticism and philosophical knowledge of God. When he was in Sicily he wrote a work in 15 books against the christians, especially in connection with the divinity of Christ; a few fragments of this work have been kept. G.V.

PORT-ROYAL, LOGIC OF
A kind of Cartesian "Art de penser" (1662), edited by Antoine Arnauld (1612-94) and Pierre Nicole (1625-95), based on the manuscripts of *Pascal. They were in close relation with the Cistercian abbey of Port Royal-des-Champs, of which Angélique Arnauld, the mind of French Jansenism, was abbess.

POSIDONIUS, 135-51 B.C.
Born in Apamea in Syria, Disciple of Panetius. Travelled much, lived on the island of Rhodes, founded there a school, had among others Cicero and Pompeius as auditors; much discussed and many-sided man. Tried not only to unite the philosophy of Plato and Aristotle with stoicism, but also the opinions of earlier philosophers (presocratici), tried to integrate the Eastern thought in his system as to give the universal Roman Imperium also a universal philosophy. Opposed to his master, Posidonius accepts the universal world-fire

and the sympathetic cohesion of the universe, basis of manticism. In the philosophy of culture he accepts a progressive decadence of humanity in morality in direct relation to material progress. G.V.

POSITION-THEORY

Says that a body, through the fact of being there, is "somewhere", has a place, and only as a result of its position makes contact with or is at a specific distance of another body. The fact of having a position is considered for a body as its own inner quality, independent from its relation to other bodies.

There are different modifications of the position theory. The *absolute* position-theory says that a body has already a position or place in the empty space and that one therefore can speak significantly of the motion of this body. The *relative* position theory also confers a first phase to the body, but if we want to speak significantly of motion, there has to be another body in relation to which the first one moves. See also contact-theory.

POSITIVE

See science.

POSITIVISM

The conception that knowledge does not reach further than the "positive", that what is given to the inner or outer experience. This actual is also the source and norm of human thought. One has to limit oneself to the observation of facts and the investigation of their relations. Positivism therefore supposes *empiricism as the theory about the origin of knowledge, and it rejects metaphysical t h o u g h t, which does remain with the factual but, because it discovers a priori elements in the human experience, which permit to have an insight in the necessary grounds of the fac-

tual, indicates that what makes a fact.

It is Comte who gave the name of positivism to the philosophical theory which limits the duty of philosophy to the ordering and synthesizing of the experimental sciences. Others positivists are Taine, Stuart Mill, Spencer, and others. See also neo-positivism. J.P.

POSSIBLE

What can be. In narrow sense: what is purely possible, what could have been although it actually does not appear (neither in the past, nor at present or in the future). It is then opposed on one side to the impossible (i.e. what in no case could be) and on the other side to that what actually exists. In a broader sense: what really can be, setting aside the fact if it really exists or not. It is then only excluding the impossible and including the purely possible and the actually existing. (The following reasoning is therefore sometimes used: ab esse ad posse valet illatio; something is or exists actually, it is therefore not impossible)

What characterizes that which is possible can be seen from a double point of view; the *extrinsical possibility* (i.e. the relation to a cause which has the power to realize it) and the *intrinsical possibility* (i.e. the absence of contradiction between the elements of a specific notion). This intrinsical possibility is then relative or absolute, the former when based on a limited order of thought (e.g. so far as I know this man, this is possible: it is conceivable for me that he acted this way) and the latter when one refers to an absolute system of thought (e.g. it is for everybody completely unconceivable that two and two *would* not be four).

Something is negatively possible

when one does not see its impossibility, although one does not see its possibility. The possible is sometimes also called the objective *potency.

The philosophical p r o b l e m s about the possibility are threefold: what is the fundamental basis of the intrinsical possibility? What is the relation between intrinsical and extrinsical possibility? (This is related to the problem of the reduction of the principle of causality to the principle of identity). Does it make sense to speak, (outside of the case of free causality) of pure possibility and therefore of *contingency? L.D.R.

POSSIBILITY

The *modality of a proposition, in which it is not considered impossible that a specific predicate belongs to a subject; e.g. happiness in work is possibly of more importance than the wages for work. See contingency.

POST HOC, ERGO PROPTER HOC

A false inference in which one concludes from the purely temporal succession to a causal connection; according to Hume the fundamental *paralogism of all metaphysicists.

POSTPREDICAMENTS

Concepts which can be said in a proposition as *predicate of all or of different *categories of things as their common quality. As possible predicates of heterogeneous things they are analogical concepts, which can not be put at the same level as a *univoque determined category. Aristotle distinguished five post-predicaments: *opposition, order, simultaneity, change and possession.

POSTSCHOLASTICISM

The common name for the philosophical schools of the 16th, 17th and 18th centuries, which were inspired by scholastic basic theories, but made an effort to renew and reform the philosophy as to free themselves from the extravagant subtleties used in later scholasticism, and writing in a perfected Latin they tried to build a more or less closed system of philosophy adapted to the modern times. In the beginning this movement did not take the modern natural sciences and the heliocentric view of the world too much in account, they held therefore the cosmology of Aristotle. It was only under the influence of Descartes' and Newton's views on nature that the postscholasticism freed itself from the cosmology of Aristotle.

In the 16th century the Dominican fathers tried to renew thomism. Following the examples and the influence of Cajetanus they tried to remain as close as possible to the tradition of the scholastic school. The Jesuits, with Fonseca and Suarez especially, and under the influence of the spirit of eclecticism, renewed several fundamental principles or even dropping them sometimes entirely.

Scotism, as well as Thomism, underwent a renewal.

In the 17th century the first efforts were made to bring the scholastic philosophy in agreement with the natural sciences. This was in Paris. The postscholasticism received gradually an eclectic character and was until the end of the 18th century taught in this form in the catholic schools.

In Germany and in the Netherlands a protestant postscholasticism was founded, which stayed close to Aristotle, but underwent on the one hand the influence of P. Ramus and on the other hand the influence of Suarez and the members of his order. In the Dutch universities the protestant postscholasticism remained opposed to cartesianism until the 18th century, but there has been a gradual shift from Aristotelian to Cartesian Scholasticism. F.S.

POSTULATE (Lat. postulatum, claim or demand)

In broad sense a thesis which, although as such unprovable, has to be accepted to understand specific facts. Kant spoke more specifically of *postulates of the empirical thought*: the necessary conditions for a possible, actual and necessary object of experience; he spoke of the *postulates of the practical reason*: theses which are theoretically unprovable but still have to be affirmed to explain moral action: namely freedom, immortality of the soul, existence of God. They are, says Kant, the object of (rational) faith, in as much as they are affirmed in their reality without being conceived in their nature. In a narrow sense and in legal respect postulate (or convention) is a scientific principle, which we accept without compelling reasons; acceptance or rejection of such principle will depend from the considerations of opportunity; a clear example can be found in the acceptance of a specific system of unities or of a specific system of notations.

According to *neo-positivism all scientific principles, in as much as they are not based on empirical grounds, have such a conventional character; this is especially true for the principles of logic and mathematics. One is therefore free to accept or reject such principles (principle of tolerance).

POSTULATION (Lat.: propositio)

The first *premise and generally the *major of a *syllogism. In connection with the second (assumption) it produces the *antecedens,

from which the *consequens proceeds.

POTENCY

Capacity of being determined. Aristotle underlines in his study of the process of motion, this essential aspect in all what changes (*Become); it is really directed towards that what it still misses, i.e. a definiteness which it has to reach through the change. Potency is therefore characterized by a *privation or lack, which includes not only the absence of the specific definiteness, but also supposes a real capability to receive it. In such a relation to the definiteness (ordo ad actum) exists actually the potency. The term potency means also the structural principle which, in not-simple beings, is the real reason for their definability. In the physical things this is, on the *substantial level, the prime *mater; in all beings which change on the *accidental level, it is the *accidental* potency, which has to be distinguished according to development in specifically different directions of the activity of a being. Here we have also *passive* or *active* potency: the former is in the physical things, the real reason of their passivity, while the latter is the capacity to develop an activity. (e.g. intellect, will, organic forces). When one conceives all structural bounds, as does Thomas Aquinas, according to the model of the correlation potency-*act, the concept potency is strongly characterized by analogy and appears under different forms: the relation of prime matter and substantial form, of essence and existence, of substance and accidence, of capacity and action, are always relations of potency and act.

This potency is always called *subjective* potency, because it appears in the real subject (i.e. be-

341

ing); it is opposed to the *objective,* potency or to that what is *possible but does not exist and only appears as object of knowledge. L.D.R.

POUR-SOI

Is called by Sartre the being which, as opposed to the *en-soi,* is innerly split, namely by the Nothing: actually the consciousness.

POWER

This concept is originally borrowed from the human activity, in which several concepts as force, possibility, labour are still undistinguishably united. Power has later been identified as the cause of the origin or change of the motion of a body. One can distinguish *mechanical* (as the gravity) *magnetic* and *electric* power. A constantly active power gives a body a more rapid motion, which is inversely proportional to the *mass of the body.

POWER

The possibility, not as much of being something, as well as of realizing something. There are constantly obstacles to be overcome, which can be of different natures. *Nietzsche considers the *Wille zur Macht* to be the fundamental tendency in man.

In social respect is power the possibility to impose one's will, and not only through force. For what? The question is not solved but many contemporary thinkers indicate the demoniac character of the power.

POWERS (OF A RELATION)

If we write R/S for the relative conjunction of R and S, then is $R^2 = R/R$, $R^3 = R/R^2$, and we can define in this way R^e for every number n.

PRACTICAL

Refers to the activity in as much

as it produces no changes in the outer world but only in the acting being itself. *Practical philosophy*: the philosophy which is interested in the activity, among others ethics. *Practical reason*: reason in as much as it illuminates the activity.

PRADINES, Maurice

French pychologist and philosopher, professor at the Sorbonne;

PRAEDICABILIA (Gr. kategorem; Lat; preadicabile)

The way in which something can be said, in a proposition, as the *predicate of a subject, namely as *genus, *species, *difference determining the species, essential and individual *characteristic. All logical disputes are, according to Aristotle, questions about the way a predicate is said of a subject; e.g. is the freedom of the will man's essential or individual characteristic. *Porphyry considered therefore the theory of the five predicables or ways in which the concepts are *universal, as one of the most fundamental problems of logic.

PRAGMATICISM

The first autochthonous American philosophy. Its most prominent defenders are *James and *Dewey, it had however also soon influence in England (see Schiller). Pragmatism can also be found in other countries, but there it is generally mixed with other theories. In Germany *Avenarius (empirico-criticism); Mach (e c o n o m y of thought); P e t z o l d t; Vaihinger (Als-ob-Philosophie). Pragmaticism finally had some influence on the *criticism of science in France. In contemporary philosophy its influence is greatest in the *neo-positivism. B.D.

Pragmaticism negates the possibility of purely theoretical knowledge and reduces truth to usefulness. The effectiveness of that which is known for the acting existence of man is the norm of truth. This effectiveness is understood in different ways and can mean: be affirmed through a possible experience, but can also mean: reach a personal profit. Understand something means for *Peirce, in whose works pragmaticism is already rudimentarily present, foresee the practical effects of something, and by practical he understands: that what appears in the human experience. James, who developed further the theory, teaches that an enunciation is true when its acceptance produces satisfying results for the development of man and society. *Schiller calls the form of pragmaticism he developed: humanism: man is the measure and gives form to the reality. "What is reality?" is a senseless question. Senseful is however the question "what man can make from it?" See instrumentalism. PRAGMATIC: what is related to human activity. J.P.

PRAGMATICS

The *semiotics or science of *symbolism is generally divided into *syntax, semantics and pragmatics, in which nothing is spoken of the relations of the symbols between each other, nor of the relation of the symbols to their meaning, but of the relation of the symbols to their use (to the acts of the logical thought and reasoning). Pragmatics has not yet been systematically developed.

PRATT, James, 1875-1944

American personalistic realist.

PRAXIS

Activity (as the change of the reality in me or outside of me) as opposed to knowing. Also the ability which is acquired through repeated activity. Praxis is then opposed to the purely theoretical command of a datum.

PRECEDENCE

Priority. Especially the priority of the practical reason over the theoretical reason, as defended by Kant.

PREDESTINATION

Indicates the destiny with which God in his omniscience and all-causality determines the eternal and temporal fate of every creature. There are different interpretations of the way in which this predestination works, the free will of the creature is also connected to this question.

PREDETERMINISM

The thesis that God cooperates with the free activities of man on the strength of an immediate and preceding determination.

PREDICAMENT

See category.

PREDICATE

The propositional term which, considered in its *comprehension, is said of the *subject and, considered in its *extension, is called the major. See category.

PREDICATION

Is the operation in which from an individual x and a predicate a, the *proposition: x is an a, proceeds. More in general, x can be a term of type n, and a a term of type $n + 1$.

PREEXISTENCE

Doctrine according to which the human soul had already an existence before the birth (Plato, Origines, Leibniz), either as spirit or in a previous body (plant, animal, man). Also *creationism.

PREFORMATION

A conception in the biological theory of the evolution of the embryo, according to which in the fecundated egg cell all later organs are already present in a simple form. Preformation was defended especially in the 17th century, but was later surpassed by the theory of the °epigenesis.

PREJUDICE (Lat: Praeiudicium)

A judgment about a thesis which precedes the proof and is not rationally justified.

PREMISS

One of the preceding theses from which, in a °syllogism, the conclusion is drawn. See Enthymeme.

PRESCIENCE

Because God is outside and above time, there is no question in God's knowledge of a "before" or "after" of the facts of the world. Past, present and future are all present for the divine cognition; which knows all the possible and the real, and also what free creatures in specific circumstances, which will never be realized, would choose (°futura contingentia). God's supercausality and complete independence knows all what is knowable in his own divine essence. This cognition is called prescience.

PRESCRIPTION

Is called by Kant a general rule of conduct which does however not determine the will as will (as does the law), but in connection with a preceding condition. The prescription is therefore a hypothetic °imperative.

PRESENCE, INTENTIONAL

Through knowledge, an immanent activity of the knowing subject, real objects are also attained.

The develoment of knowledge thus implies that objects existing outside the active subject are also found in the subject, but in a way proper to the order of knowledge and characterized by reference to the outside, the "intentio" (tendere in).

PRESENT

That which appears. Existence itself is present, says Heidegger, insofar as it is considered as an appearance. In a more restricted sense, that is present which not only is in a definite space or at a definite moment, but which also imposes itself on us by its existence. In this case we think primarily of a person who is present.

PRESERVATION (IN EXISTENCE)

In existing reality one can distinguish between coming into being in the sense of the principle of being and continuing to exist or preservation, and ask questions concerning both. If the reason why a finite being in an entirely dependent (and thus created) reality is situated in the finiteness of its existence, then this applies as much to its continuing to exist as to its coming into existence: its preservation in existence is then a mere effect of the one act of creation.

PRIESTLEY, Joseph, 1733-1804

British chemist and philosopher, who developed the theory of Hartley into a materialism. The mind is, for Priestley, not an independent principle of its own species, but rests on and is an accompanying phenomenon of complicated physical and organic processes, especially of the nervous system and the brains. He considers the life of the mind as built from simple psychic elements through association and mechanical connections of the elements, of representations and remembrances. As did the utilitarians after him, he considers the good of the majority of a society the measure for the moral attitude and political management.

PRIME MATTER
The specific matter of which all matter is built. Greek antiquity considered, for this, different elements: water, air, fire. *Anaximander had a more philosophical concept of the prime matter, it was the *apeiron. *Aristotle taught that it was a principle of being (materia rima). See Hylemorphism.

PRINCIPLE
From which something originates or through which something is, mostly through which something in last instance is, either in the order of being, or in the order of activity or in the order of thought. In the latter it is then the first principles of thought as for instance the principle of identity, without which thought is impossible or at least without which a specific kind of thinking is impossible, as mathematical thought is not possible without the principle (see axiom) that the whole is bigger than the part; or also the first specific principle on which a specific science rests, as the definitions and postulates of mathematics. In the order of being it is the principle which explains the whole reality. What it is actually, however, is explained in different theories: for Thales it is water, for Fichte, on the contrary, it is the Ego. The activity, as the realisation of thought, is also dominated by principles. Kant opposes here the principle and the *maxim, which, because of its subjectivity, can not have absolute validity. J. Gr.

PRINCIPLE OF TOLERANCE
See postulate.

PRITCHARD, H. A., born 1871.
English neo-realist, professor in Oxford. He is mostly interested in the problem of knowledge. He firstly admitted that the things exist independently from our consciousness and are directly grasped by our knowing ability. He later however mitigated his realism and makes the secondary qualities of the things originate firstly in their relation to the subject.

PRIVATION
Lack of that which should be present. That the plant does not have a sense of sight is purely a negation; for the blind man however it is a privation, which is then a privative negation or lack. PRIVATIVE, indicating a lack. See concept.

PROAERESIS
The (free) choice as decisive moment in the activity (of the will). According to Aristotle it requires reasonableness and discernment, while it has only bearing on that what is in our power. See Liberum arbitrium.

PROBABILIORISM
Principle of casuistics: when in doubt about the moral value of an activity one has to follow the opinion which is more probable than the contrary.

PROBABILISM
Doctrine according to which human knowledge can not reach farther than enunciations which have a more or less strong appearance of truth. Man is not able to find in knowledge an (absolute) criterion of truth. (*scepticism) Probabilism was defended by the New *Academy (Carneades), *Cournot. —principle of casuistics: when one doubts about the moral value of an activity, one can follow the opinion which contains probability,

even if this opinion is not as probable (*equiprobabilism) or not more probable (*probabiliorism) than the contrary.

PROBABILITY

The more or less great possibility, that a not absolutely certain thesis will be true. There are several degrees. It is bigger when more grounds in favor and less against the truth can be introduced. A *proof by probability* is had when the truth of the premises is not absolutely certain. A *proof by authority* is one of them, it rests on the testimony of people, and the knowledge and love for truth of the people has to be established: it can be based either on the general feeling of the people, or on experts or on the best experts. Belong also to the same proofs by probability the *analogy-reasoning* ("no comparison goes on all fours") and the *hypothesis, a more or less probable supposition based on too few or too weak grounds to be accepted as a thesis. Also the *chance-calculation*, in which from a multiplicity of possible cases is concluded the probability of one specific case: the degree of probability can here be calculated very accurately, when there are mathematical greatnesses; less accurately when there are physical contingencies; and least accurately for conduct of the free acting man. *Newman points out that we can often come, in daily life, to certitude on the grounds of a complex of probabilities. I.v.d.B.

PROBLEMATIC

Undecided, uncertain, see proposition.

PROCESS

Systematic evolution.

PROCLUS

Born in Constantinople 410 A.D., disciple of Olympiodorus in Alexandria and of Plutarch and Syrianus in Athens, headed from 438 on the Athenian School, died 483. Wrote many commentaries on Plato; among his original works we mention especially the *Elementario Theologica,* because of its great influence in the Middle Ages. He had characteristically an unlimited confidence in dialectics and a tendency to split and distinguish the philosophical concepts; even further he is indeed convinced that to every distinction of the intellect a reality corresponds.

PRODUCT (logical)

Of the *propositions p and q is the proposition: p and q (p and q are both true). The logical product of the concepts a and b is the concept: a and b.

PRODUCTIVITY

Aspect of the causality: a *cause is firstly productive, i.e. produces something. Its effect, participating in its definiteness, shows therefore some resemblance to it; in other words, since one acts according to his nature, the effect gives always something away about the cause. Causes are connected to each other in series; according to an order in which coordination and subordination go together.

PROGRESS

Motion towards a specific goal; in figurative sense applied to the evolution of the cosmos, which would evaluate from not-differentiated to always more differentiated forms; or to the human history, which would always generate higher forms of culture. The judgement of this progress depends always on the scale of values used in forming this judgment.

PROJECTION

The more or less unconscious

346

act of attributing that what is his own to another. ("he measures my corn by his own bushel"—"he measures another man's foot by his own last"). The projection concept comes from Hume. Psychoanalysis has underlined the unconscious factor in projection.

PROLEGOMENON

Temporary remark as introduction in a science. Are very well known Kant's *Prolegomena zu einer jeden künftigen Metaphysik*.

PROLEPSIS

The anticipating answer to an expected objection. The *Stoics called prolepses those presuppositions which were considered so basically and generally accepted that one did not expect any objections against them.

PROOF

The reduction of a thesis to previous and better-known truth. While an argument is looking for a new truth, starting from the previous truth, proof is a judgment of a new, not yet established truth, by reducing it to the previous truth. In deductive proof (*see* deduction) the *middle term functions as means of proof; in induction a sufficient number of cases are the means of proof. In classical logic, we distinguish: demonstration (certain proof), *dialectic (probable proof) and *paralogism (fallacious proof).

The aim of a proof is to deduce, according to laws, a thesis from theses (which are already proved). In a broader sense it can also be used to indicate proofs of deduced rules.

PROOF OF GOD'S EXISTENCE.

Such a proof is never parallel with other proofs, which always deduct one finite from another finite. Some (among them Kant) deny therefore the possibility of such a proof, because our finite knowledge can only know the finite experienced world. We have to agree that although scholasticism and some other philosophic schools (among them Aristotle, Descartes) accept the possibility of arguing from the world to the existence of God. God as cause is only known in the functioning of the created world; as the infinite—functioning perfectly among the limited qualities of the things around us; as the absolute—necessary in order to give meaning and reason for existence to the worldly relativities which are dependent upon many conditions; as final end, toward which all things which are limited in their striving eventually strive. In other words, the proof can never give us more than an analogically known God (*analogy of being).

All proofs of the existence of God originate in our intellect, which looks for completely satisfying explanations. This intellect is directed toward the comprehension of reality. Since the things in this world are always related to each other and belong to a higher order, no worldly being can explain itself completely; also, the series of all finite causes, however extensive they may be, give only caused causes, or a causal being which is caused. As an eventually satisfying ground one has to come finally to an uncaused being outside of the series, to that which is related to nothing, absolute, transcendent being. Also, the *processus in infinitum*, mentioned by Aristotle and Aquinas, does not give a satisfactory answer; one does not give a satisfying explanation by indicating a numerically infinite series of grounds. One still has to prove that this deepest ground of all wordly things and wordly relations is a personal God. This same structure is the basis for all valid proofs of God's existence. However, it is not only the aspect of active causality which gives the proof value. The well-known five ways of Thomas Aquinas have as their starting point the physical processes of nature (argument from motion; cosmological proof), or finality in the finite world (theological or finality proof), or the steps in which the finite being is realized. The starting point can also be man's striving toward happiness (eudaemonical argument), the moral order (ethical argument), or reality insofar as it is dominated by laws of thought, historical and other laws (ideological argument). Starting from the principle of causality, Anselm, Descartes and Leizniz tried to make a proof of God's existence from the content of our concept of God (ontological proof; this term dates from the period of Kant). Thomas Aquinas, Kant and others reject this argument as insufficient: one does not reach the real existence of God. Spinoza and Hegel, however, adopted it in their philosophy. H.R.

PROOF (purely constructive).

A proof is called purely constructive when no operation symbol, used in the theses of the proof, disappears. In the proof new symbols are gradually introduced, but never eliminated. The "Hauptsatz" of Gentzen (1934) proves that in some systems the proofs are purely constructive.

PROOF THEORY

Has developed more and more since Hilbert, parallel with the pure logic. It investigates not only the proofs of the pure logic, but also those of logic applied to the sciences (especially and about exclusively to mathematics). The aim of the proof theory is not to accumulate proofs but to investigate proofs, according to their formal qualities (*contradictionlessness, *completeness, *determinability, *independence). The main aim of Hilbert was to proof the contradictionlessness of the existing mathematics; the theorem of incompleteness of Gödel has however shown that such a proof can not be given without limitations. R.F.

PROPAEDEUTICS, (Greek: propaideusis, preparative instruction)

Preliminary instruction, preknowledge required for a science. The philosophical propaedeutics is intended as an introduction to the different fields of philosophy and a training in philosophizing.

PROPER

Is that what is objectively befitting for a being in one of its components, as the nutritive is objectively right for the human being (as bodily being). The proper is therefore a value, without being necessarily the only value, because the pleasant is also a value. Although the pleasant presupposes always a minimum of propriety and although the propriety be always eventually delightful, they are as such different. While the pleasant contains only a subjective satisfaction, the proper means an objective ability for the entire being, as is affirmed by an implicit or explicit judgment. And while the pleasant can be called universal (inasmuch as it has meaning for all affective beings) but is really individual and changeable, for it is subjectively related—what is pleasant for one is unpleasant for the other and what pleases today displeases tomorrow—the proper has, in what it is, universal validity. The pleasant is therefore not the proper, and where both go together, as for instance in the happiness, the bond can only be synthetical. J. Gr.

PROPERTY

The right of a person or group to possess a thing or an animal, and the right to manage it at his own discretion, under the condition however that this is not against the rights of the community. Right to property is based on natural law, but is worked out by positive laws.

PROPORTION

The relation of two quantities to each other (2 to 4); also of two qualitative terms (two tones: do and sol).

PROPORTIONALITY is the relation of two proportions (2 is to 4 what 3 is to 6; the intellect is for the mind what the eye is for the body). The distance between the terms can be measurable, or unmeasurable (e.g. between Creator and creature).

The proportionality plays a role also in the evolution of the thought. The question is now if one can, on the grounds of proportionality, use ideas which are drawn on the °finite to indicate the infinite. This is the main metaphysical question about the analogy.

PROPOSITION

Logically an expression which is the result of a psychological judgment. Essentially an expression, by which something is affirmed or negated as predicate of something else as its subject. According to its essential quality an expression which can be true or false. The two terms of a proposition are called subject and predicate and are generally indicated by the symbols S and P: S is also called the

matter and P the form of the proposition, because the proposition is in a way constituted as such by the two terms. Since P in a proposition has a logically greater °extension than S, P is called the major term (Lat: terminus °major) and S the minor term (Lat: terminus °minor); S and P are sometimes also symbolized by t and T. The connecting and separating, as well as the judging function is done by the copula; the binding-verb "to be", is, at least silently, supposed in every proposition, since all propositions are an enunciation about the being of the things.

The propositions can be divided on the ground of their content. (a) according to the content of the predicate: *determinative* proposition ("helium in gas"); *existential* proposition ("God exists"); *attributive* proposition ("swans are white"); *relation* proposition ("John is a brother of Peter"). (b) According to the source of knowledge: *apriori* or purely intellectual proposition (the whole is bigger than the parts"); *a posteriori* or experience proposition ("water conducts electricity"). The former, says Kant, are universal and necessary, the latter however never. (c) according to the value of knowledge: *analytical* or explicative proposition ("all bodies have extension"); *synthetical* or extensive proposition ("all bodies are heavy"). In the former, says Kant, P is already present in the notion of S, so that nothing new is taught; which is not the case for the latter. All analytical propositions are a priori, but according to Kant, not all synthetical propositions are a posteriori, some of them are a priori. These synthetical propositions a priori learn something new and are also universal and necessary ("all what happens has its cause"); they would constitute the real scientific propositions. (d) According to the grade of certitude: *evident* propositions ("if two things are equal to a third, they are mutually equal") *not-evident* proposition ("old trees can not be transplanted")

Propositions can also be divided on the grounds of their logical form. (a) According to their quantity: *universal* proposition ("all physical things are transient"); *particular* proposition ("some philosophers are evolutionists"); *singular* proposition ("this novelist is a doctor"); if the extension of S is not given one speaks of indefinite proposition. (b) According to their quality: *affirmative* proposition ("man is responsible for his free chosen actions"); *negative* proposition (man is not only a citizen). Some prefer the division in positive and negative propositions. Kant adds to that the *limitative* or infinite proposition, namely the affirmative proposition with a negative P-term, ("the soul is immortal"): belongs to the infinite group of things which remain after the exclusion of the mortal things. (c) According to their relativity: *categorical* (predicative) or unconditional proposition ("the earth moves around the sun"); hypothetical (suppositive) proposition. The latter are subdivided in: *copulative* proposition ("John *and* (or *nor*) Peter can drive a car"); *conjunctive* proposition ("one can *not* serve God and the Mammon"); *conditional* (strictly hypothetical) proposition ("if something exists now, something must have existed always"); *disjunctive* proposition: in the complete or real disjunction only one term can be true (bacteria are plants *or* animals); in the incomplete or unreal disjunction both can be true ("you will get your arms *or* legs broken"); also

alternation. A *causative* or explanatory proposition is not an hypothetical proposition; it is not a complex proposition but a complex of propositions. (d) According to their modality: *absolute* (attributive, assertoric) proposition ("you did do that"); *modal* proposition, which can be *apodictic* ("that what is dependent necessarily depends from something else"; "something can not" be and "not-be under the same respect and at the same time"); *problematic* ("it is possible that you were there" —"you possibly did not do it") I.v.d.B.

PROPOSITION (in formal logic)

Is what (rightly or wrongly) can be ascertained. A proposition should not be confused with its expression or with a sentence. (In the traditional logic is the word proposition used in the meaning of sentence and the term judgment in the sense of proposition). A proposition should also not be confused with the assertion itself. The proposition is that what is asserted and is often translated by (the content of) a sentence in the indicative mood.

Propositions are *universal* when they determine something for *all* individuals: *all* humans are mortal; they are *particular* when they determine something for *some* individuals. (The reference to all or some individuals remains implicit, when the proposition, as it is expressed, does not mention all or some, but is equivalent with a proposition with the expressed mentioning). *Individual* propositions are those propositions which are neither universal nor particular. Individual propositions can be *compound* when they are in fact the negation of another proposition, or composed of other propositions.

350

Propositions are also divided in *analytical* and *synthetical,* in a sense which reminds us of Kant. *Analytical* propositions are those which are valid according to the logical laws, *synthetical* are those which are valid in fact.—R.F.

PROPOSITION LOGIC

Term used in modern logic for that part of formal logic which reasons only on *propositions and not on the elements of propositions which themselves are not propositions. This is expressed in this way: in the propositionlogic appear no other variables than the variables for not-analyzed propositions.

To the propositionlogic corresponds, in the traditional logic, the theory of the hypothetical reasoning. In the systems of the modern logic the propositionlogic (with only a few exceptions) has a basic role; from it are inferred the *logic of concepts and of relations.

The theses of the propositionlogic can be proved following the method of the *truthvalues and *matrixes; they can also be inferred from a great number of systems of *axioms and rules (which are however deductively equivalent). In the classical propositionlogic are theses valid which express the principles of contradiction and of the excluded third; *conjunction, *alternation, *implication, etc.; can be defined by each other. For not classical propositions see *Logic. —R.F.

PROPRIUM

See essential quality.

PROSOPON

Greek word which means: face, mask; later: seeming, figure, player or actor. Under influence of Stoicism it became in legal and philosophical respect the same as *person.

PROSYLLOGISM

The first syllogism of a *polysyllogism.

PROTAGORAS OF ABDERA: 485-415 B.C.

Knew the Ionic natural philosophy, but rejected the speculative thinking, in order to croos Greece as a famous *sophist. He stayed also several times in Athens, where he became the friend of Pericles, but had to leave the city because he was convicted of atheism. He is a relativist and sensualist. Every experience is what it is and depends on the immediate situation of the observer. Therefore his famous "homo mensura" phrase: man is the measure of everything.

PROUDHON, Joseph

Born in Besançon 1809, died in Paris 1865. French utopian socialist, founder of the theory of anarchism. Philosophy has for him the duty to search for the principle, which can guarantee the general human certitude about thinking and acting, and this principle is Justice. This is a cosmic reality, which is, at the same time, rule and norm of activity, for individuals as well as for societies, even the end of the existence.

PROVIDENCE

The execution of the plan of creation, formed by God and with which he directs the creatures towards their final end, each separately and all in their mutual connections. God, in the execution, uses the creatures, each according to their nature, in such a way that the rational creatures direct themselves. Chance does not exist in the Providence, because it includes everything. *Fatalism sees blind necessity opposed to a world attending Providence.

PSEUDO DIONYSIUS THE AREO-PAGITE

Mysterious personality, author of 4 famous theological works: *On Mystical Theology, On Divine Names, On the Heavenly Hierarchy,* and *On Ecclesiastical Hierarchy.* The text indicates as author: "Dionysius, priest", and the apostles are considered contemporaries; it seems that the author ascribed his works, in a kind of literary fiction, to Dionysius the Areopagite, converted by St. Paul in Athens (Acts: 17.34). Quite early the fact was generally accepted that they were the authentic works of Paul's disciple. The treatises were translated in the 9th cent. by Joannes Scotus Eriugena, other translations were published in the 12th, 13th and 15th centuries, and the Dionysian *corpus,* had in the Middle Ages about the same authority as the Holy Scriptures. The author lived actually ca. 500, probably in Syria. He depends on Proclus and explains his vision of the universe with the help of *Proclus'* neoplatonism. The Pseudo-Dionysius created therefore in the East a *christian neoplatonism,* as did Augustine in the East, and neoplatonism was favored thanks to the authority of these works.

God is the summit of this synthesis: we reach Him through a double, positive and negative, way. The "positive" theology applies to God the perfection which we discover in the creatures, because He is their creator; the negative theology recognizes that we can not apply those attributes in a deeper meaning to God, because He is absolutely transcendent. Following the example of the divine processes, the creatures proceed from God and participate in different ways in his perfection: we have therefore the existence of the heavenly hierarchy (the angels), the hierarchy of the earthly world (from Christ to the simple believer, imitation of the heavenly hierarchy). The created world tries, as a whole, to return to its Maker, but the complete return is only possible for angels and for man, who is able to reach through grace real divinisation (*theosis*). Ecstasy and beatific contemplation are its summit.—F.V.S.

PSYCHE

Soul. The Platonists use this term to indicate, as opposed to *nous, the lower soul of the vegetative and sensitive operations; for Aristotle: the principle of life as well for plant as for animal and man. One can distinguish it from *soul, as a more metaphysical concept of Psyche.

PSYCHIC

Belonging to the *psyche. This term is used in contemporary psychology in different and often not very clear meanings. Is often opposed to physical or physiological, or also to psycho-logical (belonging to the science of the psyche or psychology).

PSYCHISM

Psychological phenomenon or aptitude. Also psychic life, the whole of the psychic phenomena.

PSYCHOANALYSIS

Was developed by *Freud, initially only as a psychological theory for the explanation of the syndrome of the hysteria. Freud's well known "Vorlesungen" awoke interest and became the beginning of the diffusion of the theory, especially in the Anglo-Saxon countries. Adler, who initially was a collaborator of Freud, detached himself from the orthodox doctrine. The main controversy was the Freudian primacy of the sexuality to which

352

Adler opposed the "Wille zur Macht". In an effort to synthesis, Jung created a third form of psychoanalysis, which found an entirely different background in the philosophical, anthropological and ethnological studies of Jung. In and outside of the group of analytics, further changes in the orthodox doctrine were developed and they grew into an independent school.

In any case, the psychoanalysis has been for the official psychology of extreme importance because of its pressing questions and its extensive terminology, also because of its little formal-psychological character. Integration of the psychoanalytical theories in the official psychology is now achieved and in the United States there are even efforts made in experimental research.

1. According to what precedes psychoanalysis can mean the psychiatric-psychological *theory* about man. One starts here from the thesis that the °unconscious life of the soul is of utmost importance. The main character of the unconscious is according to the early works of Freud the libido, according to Adler the "Wille zur Macht". Jung speaks of a collective unconscious which contains the experiences of the family, race and even the entire human race. The strivings of the unconscious (Lustprinzip) collide with the society (Realitatsprinzip) and with the ideals of the individual (Ich-Ideal); From this a conflict can arise. In connection with this theory, Freud and his school have contributed much in other fields of science and culture.

2. Psychoanalysis can also indicate the *treatment, through conversation,* of neuroses. The above mentioned conflict can indeed be eliminated by the analysis of unconscious motives for the behaviour. When the not-accepted tendencies of man are repressed (frustration), they form a complex. This complex dominates then the entire psychic life. Treatment is here elucidation, make conscious of the disturbing elements of the unconscious.

3. Psychoanalysis is finally the *system of a philosophy of life,* although this is mainly indirect. In this meaning, but also in the two previous senses, psychoanalysis had to endure much resistance and scientific criticism. The modern American (Horney, Alexander) and Austrian (Frankl.) forms of psychoanalysis are however more acceptable, but their relation to the original concepts is very limited. —P.S.

PSYCHOID

Term used by the biologist-philosopher °Driesch for what he calls a superphysical factor, which directs the physical processes in a living being. °Entelechy is limited to a factor which directs the evolution, and Psychoid for the "soul" in a grown organism. He sometimes also speaks of several psychoids in one organism. He certainly does not agree with the Aristotelian concept "psyche" or soul, which he however uses, because he replaces the complete matter-form unity by a dualistic structure.

PSYCHOLOGISM

The theory which considers psychology as the basic science. It teaches that the factors, with which the empirical psychology explains the origin of human cognition, as a subjective occurrence, are also determinative for the truth value and the objectivity of this cognition. In as much as the truth of the cognition would be dependent on the empirical factors, which produce the cognition, this psychologism is a form of *relativism. There are several forms of psychologism, depending on the specific factor to which the effective influence on the human cognition is attributed: the own nature of man leads to a truth which has only value for man (anthropologism); every circle of civilization creates its own truth (historism); belonging to a specific race (biologism); the decisive factor is found in the social-economical relations (marxism).

In contemporary philosophy, *Husserl reacted strongly against the psychologism and underlined in the human cognition the differences between act and content of knowledge, so that the content of knowledge is independent from the act.—J.P.

PSYCHOLOGY (lit. study of the soul)

Can be understood differently according to its object and method.

Aristotle and the scholastics: the study of the principle of life, vegetative sensitive, intellective.

Descartes: the object of psychology is the res cogitans (consciousness), while the body, as the res extensa, is the object of physics. This dualism of Descartes created two streamings: 1. the psychology of consciousness, which chose as main method the introspection and as object the phenomena of consciousness; 2. the behaviourism, which considers as object of psychology only the externally perceptible behaviours. It looked for a close relation with the positive sciences. The latest evolution has returned to the interest in the whole man. Body and soul, exterior and interior, are not considered separated, sometimes even not different. The separation between man and the (his) world is not accepted in modern psychology as a methodical starting point. Herewith is then also the method changed, which from objectivating becomes subjectivating.

All these different streamings have produced specific contributions to the knowledge of man. Making a specific point of view absolute, produces always inaccuracies and conflicts.

The *philosophical* psychology (this part of philosophy which under the aspect of the last causes of being, is interested in the phenomena of life and therefore treats the substance, spirituality, immortality etc.) in modern sense can be defined as the doctrine of the soul as a transcendental being. The *empirical* psychology is then the doctrine about the expressions or the incarnation of the soul (Strasser). The substantiality of the soul is however opposed by the actpsychology (see Act and consciousness).

One divides the psychology according to the different fields: patho-Psychology, animal-psychology, child-psychology, physiological psychology. One can also distinguish them in introspective psychology, behavioural psychology, statistical psychology, analytical psychology etc. . . . according to the method used.

Next to the *theoretical* psychology an *applied* psychology was developed which led to a system of investigation in the individual (psychothechnic) or to a series of separate auxiliary sciences (pedagogical psychology, pastoral psychology, medical psychology etc.).

Modern psychology develops under rather strong influence of the *existential anthropology and

354

the, in philosophy accepted, *phenomenological method.—P.S.

PSYCHOLOGY OF RELIGION

The methodical investigation of the psychical aspects of religious phenomena. The methods are no different from those of psychology in general, except for the special interest in the dispositions of the religious man. A distinction is made between the *general* psychology of religion, or investigation of the general characteristics of the religious consciousness; the *typological* psychology of religion, or investigation of the typical character of religious consciousness in its relation to specific generations, races, cultures, temperaments, religious sects, etc.; the *genetic* psychology of religion, or investigation into the conditions which influenced the origin and the early development of religious life; the *social* psychology of religion, or the investigation of the influence members of the same religious sect have on each other in their religious life. Since this influence differs with the sect investigated, different forms of psychology are to be discerned here.—K.L.B.

PUFENDORF, Samuel

Born in Chemnitz 1632, died in Berlin 1694. Influenced by Hugo de Groot and Hobbes, defender of the natural *right, based on the divine will and known through the light of the intellect. The state came into being through a *contract.

PYRRHO OF ELIS

Ca. 365-270 B.C., went with Alexander to the East and met there the atomist Anaxarchus of Abdera. He came thus under the influence of Democritus; underwent later the influence of relativism and scepticism through the sophists and the Cyrenaic epistemology. Only the impressions we undergo would be knowable to us, not the stimuli which create these impressions; he defends a similar relativism in ethics: nothing is morally good or bad *from* itself or from its nature; but the moral value depends from the human definitions and habits. Since the things are impenetrable by the human cognition, man will have to reserve his judgment (*epochè*); for each judgment exists opposite grounds which are as strong as the first judgment. This is true for the theses of the dogmatists and also for the ground principles of scepticism itself: this doctrine therefore undermines eventually its own principles. He has also a sceptical attitude in his appreciation of the things and events: everything is indifferent; nothing therefore may be able to disturb the human peace of mind (*ataraxia*).—G.V.

PYTHAGORAS, Ca. 582-Ca. 507 B.C.

Greek philosopher. Not much is known about his life. Later biographies, especially those of *Porphyry and *Jamblichus, have been adorned with so many legends that it is impossible to distinguish truth from invention. We don't even know for sure what he himself taught, because his theories are only known through the works of his disciples, so that it is difficult to separate Pythagoras from the PYTHAGOREANS. He certainly was a very important personality, who knew how to link his philosophical research to his deep religious attitude. When his disciples were in disagreement the word of Pythagoras himself was sought as a final argument: "Autos epha": he himself said it.

For the Pythagoreans the principle of the universe is not a natural element as for the older philosophers, but the number. Only the number can explain the order in nature. They did however not know the number as an abstraction, but as a number of concrete, extensive points. They discovered several remarkable relations between the numbers and distinguished them in square (even) and oblong (odd) numbers. The most beautiful and most holy number was the tetractys or the decimal, which contains the first four numbers. They discovered mathematical relations between the length of the cords of a lyre and their sound-value; between the distances of the celestial bodies and the harmony (inaudible for us because of habituation). Every phenomenon of the cosmic, human and divine life was eventually a substantial number. Justice was 4, because four is the sum of two even quantities; soul and mind were the number 6, etc. The number is not only the principle of the being, but also of the knowledge; it is the guarantee for the truth: "the number does not lie", wrote Philolaus.

The Pythagoreans adapted the cosmogony of *Anaximander to their theory of the numbers and explained thereby the origin and evolution of the universe. Everything originates in the opposition of the limitating and the unlimited: The limitation, which poses therefore a definiteness, is considered as the odd and perfect element; the illimited is even and imperfect. The world is therefore created by a gradual limitation or determination of the indefinite. The categories one, right, male, at rest, straight, light, good, square (cfr. the numbers) belong to the sphere of the perfect or odd; to the sphere of the even or imperfect belong the opposite: many, left, female, moved, bend, darkness, bad, oblong. The universe, formed by these oppositions, contains three zones: the Olympus or the sphere of the solid stars; the cosmos with the five planets; the ouranos (heaven) or the sublunar, place of birth and death.

The Pythagoreans accept also the theory of the *metempsychose. A Greek play upon words condensed this theory: the body is the grave of the soul (soma-sêma).

The Pythagoreans formed also a religious community, which was devoted to an aristocratic, ethical attitude and self-control. They were also actively interested in the political life of the cities of the South of Italy. They administered the cities: Crotona, Sybaris, Acragas, Katana, Rhegion. An insurrection of the democratic parties obliged them to leave Crotona and to flee to Greece. Some of them remained in Southern Italy but their houses were burned down. Archippus and Lysis moved to Thebes, where *Philolaus, the most important Pythagorean of the 5th century, and Archytas received their education.

Pythagoreanism, which continued as a secret religious sect, was revived in the first century B.C. in the so-called neo-pythagoreanism—F.D.R.

Q

QUADRIVIUM

The whole of the four sections (arithmetic, geometry, music, astronomy) which formed in the Medieval schools the higher cycle of the education. It was taught at the Faculty of Liberal Arts.

QUALITY

In a broad sense everything that can be added to something to define it better, namely, all its accidents.

We distinguish *necessary* or *essential* quality, or quality in the narrower sense (Latin: *proprium*), which, proceding from the essence of something, can only be applied to all the individuals of a specific species—as for instance the freedom of the will in man—and *occasional* or *individual* quality, the strictly accidental quality which can be present or absent without affecting the essence of an individual, either always, e.g., John is a native American (individual *character*istic) or temporarily, e.g., John is reading a book.

Following Democritus, Locke makes a distinction between *primary* and *secondary* qualities. The prior cannot be detached from bodies (such as extent, density, shape, rest or motion, etc.); the latter are actually nothing else than the ability to create in us sensations, with the help of primary qualities, such as colors, sounds, etc.

Answer to the question: how is it? In narrower sense: how is something in the *accidental order. Accidental qualities are: the faculties with their *habiti; the way (colour, sound, etc.) in which sensual objects appear; the definiteness in the physical dimensions (e.g. the *figure). In the 17th century a distinction was made between the primary quality (the geometrical and mechanical, rather quantitative qualities) which were considered the real qualities of matter, and the secondary qualities (colour, sound etc.) which were considered as being purely subjective.

—In logic the quality of a proposition is the connecting or separating way in which the *predicate is said of the subject (affirmation, negation). It is thus determined by the predicate and is essentially proper to every proposition.

QUALITY, (formal)

Is a quality which can be defined by means of the primitive concepts of a deductive system. E.g. the *total reflexivity* of a relation r is a formal quality in the *logic of relations; it can indeed be defined as: the quality for a r, that rxx is generally valid.

QUALITY, PRESERVATION OF

The preservation of the qualities of elements in a chemical solution. Of old there was disagreement as to how the elements remained in the solution. Some Aristotelians hold that the elements disappear entirely in the solution, so that their qualities also get lost. The atomists, on the other hand, think

357

that there can only be juxtaposition, the atoms remaining next to each other in the solution, so that the qualities of the elements are completely preserved, while the qualities of the solution are determined by the combination of them.

QUANTA

In classical physics, it was universally accepted that matter was composed of *corpuscles, so that they thought that matter could not be indefinitely divided. Transmission of energy could however be divided indefinitely. M. Planck (1858-1947) however found that specific deviations between physical theory and experiment could only be bridged if he accepted that also the transmission of energy was bound to specific minima. This lead to the introduction of the well known constant of Planck (h). In radiation-energy the minimum of energy which can appear (the indivisible energic quantity), the so called quantum, is rendered by the formula E=h2, in which 2 represents the frequency of oscillations of the wave. From this comparison one can see that the light quanta for light of different colours are also different, because every colour is characterized by its own frequency of oscillations.

Quantum theory. Distinction has to be made between the old and the new quantum theory, also called quantummechanics. Bohr developed the older quantum theory in his atom-theory. It uses mostly the classical mechanics, but introduces a few hypotheses, which take in account Planck's constant.

The most important hypothesis is that the electrons which move around the atomic nucleus, do not radiate continuous energy, but only discontinuous, actually when they spring from one path to another.

The new quantum-theory (Heisenberg, 1926) developed a mechanics which took from the beginning account of the appearance of the quanta. The quantum mechanics say that the classical mechanics do not have to take the existence of quanta in account, because the processes which it studies in the macrocosm are so big that the discontinuities, which happen on an atomic scale, have no influence on it. The processes can therefore be considered as continuous. Quantum mechanics passes then automatically into the classical mechanics. For the quantumtheory as for some other modern theories, e.g. the theory of *relativity, the modern theories contain the older theories as particularisation of the universal theory. This also proves how strongly the classical theories are moored in the experience. Mathematically the quantum-t h e o r y seems to be equivalent to the *wave mechanics. A.G.M.v.M.

QUANTIFICATION

Of the predicate. Term invented by W. *Hamilton, meaning that one indicates the extension of the *predicate expressively in a grammatical form: e.g. not saying "all whales are mammals", but "all whales are some mammals". Many laws of logic, among others the law of *conversion, could then be simplified and logic could then be more mathematically constructed.

QUANTITY

Quality of all physical things, which forms the basis of their spatial extension, divisibility, localisation and therefore their relation to other stimultaneous places in space (answer to the question: where?), passivity and inertia. Special motion gives continuous time and therefore relation to successive moments of time (answer to the question: when?). Real quantity is always in correlation with *quality and becomes then specific quantity. *Quantitas continua* means continuous quantity, *quantitas discreta* is graduated quantity.

—In logic: quantity is the extent in which the *extension of a *subject is taken when one applies to it a *predicate. It is therefore determined by the extension of that subject. The quantity is essentially proper to every proposition, but is not necessarily expressed, in this case one calls the proposition indefinite, e.g. women are inconstant (= some women are inconstant). See also number.

QUANTOR

Is either universal or particular. A *universal* quantor is an expression for: all (e.g. for all x), a *particular* quantor is an expression for: some (e.g. for some x).

QUATERNIO TERMINORUM

The fact that a syllogism has four terms. This is the most common form of a paralogism; especially because one of the terms is used in a twofold sense. E.g. from nothing comes nothing, create is produce something from nothing, create is therefore impossible.

QUIDDITY

Answer to the question: quid est? what is something? Mostly, in narrow sense, what is expressed in the definition; and because the definition is always abstract, quiddity is then the abstract essence.

QUIETISM

Practice of an attitude to life which, averse to all activity, is only interested in the contemplation of the divinity. Molinos taught quietism: according to him the soul can come easily to a state of continuous union with God in love. God gives the soul such a peace that it is not necessary to follow any moral or religious practice.

QUINTESSENCE (Lat. quinta essentia=fifth essence)

Matter of which according to Aristotle the fifth sphere of the universe was made. The quintessence had totally different qualities than the four elements: it was everlasting and followed its own laws.

QUODLIBET

Is in scholastics a work which treats many problems in the form of question and answer.

R

RACE

Is called in biology a demonstrable division within a *species. A race acts more or less independently because of hereditary transmission. Examples of races: all "species" of dogs, all "species" of dahlia, human races. One can cultivate new races through crossbreeding and other means.

RADHAKRISHNAN, S., born 1888.

Most prominent Indian philosopher and scholar, professor in Calcutta and Oxford, now Vice-President of India. His great merit has been the understanding he brought in India and in the West for both philosophies. In his many works he tries always to understand and to appreciate the Indian and Western thought and their relations.

RADICAL

Penetrating the deepest grounds or proceeding from them. Radikal Böse (das), the radical evil, is according to Kant not only absence of goodness but the corruption of human nature itself.

RADULPHUS DE LONGO CAMPO

Born in France 12th cent., died after 1215, disciple of *Alanus ab Insulis, author of a Summa philosophiae and of a commentary on Alanus' Anticlaudianus.

RAHNER, Karl, born 1904.

Austrian neo-thomist.

RAMAKRISHNA, 1834-1886.

Indian mystic, follower of the Advaita, but also convinced that all philosophical theories are essentially the same.

RAMAUJA, ±1050-1137.

Very important religious leader and thinker, belonging to the *Vedānta, but, as opposed to *Sankara, a faithful Vishnuite, under strong influence of *bhakti trends, founder of the visistadvaita (monism of the distinct). He accepts as well *Upanishads as Bhagavadgītā as basis, teaches a theistic metaphysics and an indestructible individuality of the soul, also after the redemption. *Brahman is completely identical with the Highest Soul or God, and not without attributes; it (or He) is among others object of that insight which leads to salvation: his "body" is causa materialis and his "soul" causa efficiens of the world. Brahman, the totality of the conscious and the totality of the unconscious in the universe are all evenly real and form also a unity of body and soul. As body and soul are not independent from each other, so do Brahman and universe not exist independently from each other. The conscious, i.e. the totality of the individual souls, and the unconscious in their subtle state, form the body of Brahman. Brahman transforms itself in immanent processes in brahman, with as body both of them in their rude state: nothing comes into being and nothing perishes; what we call birth and death is nothing else than a change of condition of the same causal substance. One can also say: the conscious and the unconscious, both, form brahman's "modus"; in a logical sense: its attribute; in metaphysical sense: part of the universal whole; in ethical sense: sudordination and dependence of the limited on the infinite, which is the first principle and final end of the limited. But this distinction is Western. God, souls and world are one, but at the same time three; souls and world are contained in the unity of God as parts of a whole—J.G.

RAMIFICATION

Is used in two entirely different contexts, namely in the so called ramified theory of *types and in not-ramified *systems (systems to which no *axioms in different directions can be added, because of their *completeness).

RAMON LUL

See Raymundus Lullus.

RAMSEY, Frank Plumpton, 1903-1930.

English philosopher who died at 26 but showed promise of becoming a leading thinker in the fields of philosophy, mathematical logic and economic theory.

RAMUS, Petrus (Pierre de la Ramee).

Born in Picardy 1515, died in Paris 1572 (murdered during the Massacre of St. Bartholomew). Taught in Paris, later, after his conversion to protestantism, in Germany and Switzerland. He wants to exchange Aristotle's logic, which he considered unnatural, for a logic adapted to the mind, purified from scholastic obscurities and subtleties. Logic and rhetoric form together the ars disserendi.

RAOUL DE LONGCHAMPS

See Radulphus de Longo Campo.

RASHDALL, Hastings, 1858-1929.

English personalistic idealist. The community of persons is the only reality. It finds its perfection in the person of God. God is as such part with man of the one ideal reality. On this basis is Rashdall's ethic theory constructed. Man has to realize the good, i.e. pleasure, happiness and value. This is only possible on the grounds of his conviction of the freedom, the existence of God and the immortality.

RATIO or °reason.

The human understanding, inasmuch as it reaches knowledge through discursive reasoning. It is opposed to intellectus, i.e. the understanding inasmuch as it knows by immediate insight. Ratio and intellectus together form the human understanding.

RATIONAL, Reasonable: belonging to, resting on or related in general to the human reason.

Rational psychology, see psychology.

RATIONALISM

Doctrine which teaches that human reason can, with the help of its concepts and reasoning, at least in principle, know all what is as it is. Human reason would therefore possess specific fundamental concepts: through these concepts it would reach by reasoning the real knowledge. Rationalism is then in this respect radically opposed to *empiricism, which considers experience to be the only source of knowledge. Historically rationalism was embodied in the theories of Descartes, Spinoza, Leibniz, Wolff. Rationalism is here at the same time dogmatic (because the reliability of the reason is simply accepted), inneistic (because the real ideas, which reason possesses, are innate), aprioristic (because true knowledge, is obtained independently from the sensory experience, by means of the ideas).

This isolation of human conceptual thought leads, on the one hand, into an explanation of all what is, through concepts which are empty in their generality, and, on the other hand, into the elevation of rational discursive conceptual thought to the norm of all knowledge. More specifically: rationalism denies all power to other human faculties, as mind and will, denies even their ability to reach the Holy and religious. Rationalism can in this respect be identified with *intellectualism, although the latter points more the intuitive knowledge out, and it is then also opposed to *irrationalism as it is found in traditionalism, fideism and Glaubensphilosophie.

Rationalism holds that only is true, what is seen by the human reason. Religion, based on revelation, is therefore rejected in favor of a natural *religion. Kant also wants to limit religion within the borders of reason.

In Ethics: rationalism teaches, as did Socrates, that the moral attitude of man should be measured by his reasonable knowledge. This, again, is intellectualism, although rationalism emphasizes more the *autonomy of the human reason. J.P./H.R.

RATRAMNUS OF CORBY

Died after 868, monk in Corby, author of two psychological works: *De anima* and *De quantitate animae*. In the first one he defends the immortality of the soul, in the second he attacks the doctrine of the one and universal soul for all men.

RAYMOND OF SABUNDE

Born in Barcelona, died in Toulouse 1437, physician, mystic, professor of theology in Toulouse. In his *Theologia naturalis* he gives rational grounds to the dogmata. Montaigne disapproved of it.

RAYMUNDUS LULLUS

Born in Palma (Majorca) 1232 or 1235, died at sea 1316. After a worldly youth Raymundus decided in 1262 to devote his life to the conversion of the infidels. With indefatigable fervour he made many travels, tried to obtain the support of several sources and wrote 150 to 200 works in Catalonian, Arabic and Latin. He wrote in 1274 his *Ars magna* in order to create a common basis for discussion with the Mohammedans. It is an extremely original work of logic, in which he uses a particular combination-technic which was intended to lead to a really universal science, acceptable by all men. His philosophy is however not as original as it seems by first reading; it is much indebted to the franciscan tradition.

REALISM

Doctrine which required as condition for human cognition, an object which is independent from the knowledge.

Depending from the domain to which the knowledge is related we can distinguish *conceptual realism, realism of the *outer world* etc. The latter recognizes the existence of being, independent from thought, for which the unfortunate term outer-world is used (unfortunate because this suggests special). Conceptual realism on the contrary, which is mostly found in Antiquity and in the Middle Ages, confers reality to ideas (Plato) or universal concepts.

Considering the manner in which reality is known, realism can be immediate or mediate. In the former, consciousness would reach reality itself, in the latter, it would remain enclosed in itself: it "reaches" only reality, inasmuch as the content of the consciousness renders them adequately. How can this theory be justified? Descartes appeals to God's veracity, others appeal on the one hand to the sense of passivity and on the other hand to the principle of causality. In the immediate realism one should determine clearly what the immediate datum is. For *Noel it seems to be a reality which is created through the collaboration of the surroundings and the observing sensory organ.

The manner in which one recognizes the knowledge of reality is the basis for the division of realism in naive, methodical and critical realism. *Naive* realism does not find any problem in the fact that thought recognizes independent beings: this is in agreement with the natural attitude of man in regard to reality. *Critical* realism, which sets in when idealism has shaken the realistic certitude, tries to justify philosophically the natural realistic mental attitude. In *methodical* realism, realism justifies itself as a philosophical method in the practice of its method. Because of the onesided emphasis put on the problem of the physical world, realism did not pay enough attention to problems of the real existence of other knowing subjects next to the individual knower; the intersubjectivity must also be justified critically against monistic idealism; some found herein a possibility to fight down idealism.

When one finally put the problem of realism on the absolute level of the knowledge of existence, and when one sees that human knowledge is pointed towards the being *as* being, one will then on the one hand guard against the (very often in realism made) mistake to identify being and really being (because the only-possible and the only-thought is being), and one will on the other hand (against some forms of realism) hold that the finite knowledge which is necessarily the starting point of criticism of thought, can not be the complete cause of the being in its totality, and therefore presupposes a given reality. J.P.

—In the Middle Ages realism keeps pace with the solution to the problem of the *universalia. This evoluted gradually from Boethius to Abaelard. Under the influence of platonism and augustinism the philosophers of the first centuries of the Middle Ages were very much inclined to ultra-realism, which was for that reason called *doctrina antiqua*. One was inclined to contend that the genera and species were real things (*res*). But how? Where are those *res*? The answer to this question was by some more platonic than by others. Some members of the School of Chartres contended that they existed in themselves, while Anselm and the Augustinians contended that they existed in the idea of God. The theory of the *identitas*, originally taught by William of Champeaux answered: they exist in the physical world as unique substances common to all individuals, and these individuals differ from each other only because of accidents.

Little by little the reaction against this ultra-realism was created. Originally the reaction was too strong, Roscellinus for instance reduced all absolute concepts to words (*sententia vocum*) and most of these thinkers turned to radical nominalism. Later a more founded reaction came up with

363

Abaelard, who introduced the *moderate realism;* he recognized that the absolute terms are *nomina* (*sententia nominum*), i.e. words which represent concepts which take the place of real qualities, which are however multiplied with the individuals. It is called 'moderate realism' because it recognizes, on the one hand, the real value and importance of the absolute concepts, but on the other hand concedes that the absolute as such exists only in man's abstracting thinking. F.V.S.

—In modern philosophy realism is opposed to idealism. The question of idealism shocks indeed the realistic certitude, which characterizes as well the natural attitude of man as the older philosophy. Since Locke accepted the subjectivity of the so called secondary *qualities (colour, sound etc.) Berkeley reduced all sensory experiences to pure subjective representations. Kant only agrees to a *transcendental* realism which can as well be called transcendental idealism (ideal-realism); in our cognition appears to our thinking a being which is independent from it, but which in itself cannot possibly know. In the 19th century, and mostly in Germany, idealism was the prominent philosophy, until the end of the century when realism came again into view. The break-through of realism was that of a *critical* realism. It was strongly defended by *Külpe and also by *Mercier. In the thirties the neo-thomists discussed the problem vehemently, *Noel taught an "immediate" realism and *Gilson a "methodical" realism. *Maritain and *Jolivet took also part in this dispute. Realism has in a short time pushed idealism away and dominates practically the entire

philosophical world. See also neo-realism.

REALITY
What characterizes the real as such. Also: the real itself, it is the opposite of pure seeming, of fictive, of imaginary. So is the real order opposed to the logical order i.e. the order of existence against the order of the ideas.

REALIZABLE-NESS OF A PROPOSITION
A variable *proposition is realized if a true proposition is had, by substitution of the variables.

REALIZATION OF A SYSTEM
See model.

REALM
Or *kingdom, domain formed by beings, things or concepts, in as much as they are linked together by common structure and laws. E.g.: the realm of values, the realm of dreams etc. . . *Realm of ends*: for Kant the systematic link of rational beings by common objective laws. Each rational being treats himself and the others always as an end in itself (*person) and never as a pure means.

REASON
(Lat. ratio, connected to basis or ground), the human ability to discover the ground of the beings, their cause and end, meaning and sense. Reason is sometimes identified with *intellect, and has then the broader meaning of: ability to know the beings and to understand them in their essence. Reason is sometimes opposed to intellect, and does then not express so much the contemplated and recognizing activity (Lat: *intellectus) but rather the searching and progressing: *thinking in a narrower sense.

In kantian sense also is reason

opposed to intellect. Intellect is the capacity to unify the *phenomena into objects of thought; reason is, in its unifying activity, searching for the unconditional. Kant speaks here often of *pure* reason, by which he means that the reason transgresses the experience or abandons the supply brought by sensuality, it does however not repeal itself.

One can distinguish the *theoretical* reason from the *practical* reason. The former is interested in the question: how are the beings; the latter (which is not adequately distinguished from the former) is interested in the question: how do we have to act? In the thomistic ethic it has an important role, because it determines what belongs to the essence of man (who is a rational being) and what activities lie or lie not therefore in the line of the human self-realization. In the Kantian ethics its role is still more important, because it is at the same time legislative (see autonomy).

Or ground, what speaks to the reason or the intellect: what makes intelligible inasmuch as it puts a basis, proofs or explains. This applies to the reality (a cause, for instance, is the real reason for its effect), but also to the order of thought (the premises of the syllogism for instance are the reason for the conclusion). *Principle of sufficient reason* (Leibniz): nothing exists or happens without *sufficient reason.

REASONABLE

1) what is gifted with reason. 2) what proceeds from reason and is connected to it: e.g. the will. 3) what is in agreement with the reason or what follows the order proposed by reason. what therefore is suitable and equitable.

REASONING

Logically the thought-construction, (see ens rationis) made with several propositions, which is the result of a psychological act of reasoning. As an *instrument* of thought, devised by the intellect to proceed from present knowledge (*antecedens) to new knowledge (*consequens) the reasoning has not only to be good in its form but has also to be built with reliable materials (see logic)

In a simple reasoning this material consists of three propositions or theses as nearest elements, namely two introductory elements or *premises and a final proposition or *conclusion; and three concepts or *terms, as remote elements, namely the two *extreme terms (i.e. subject or *terminus *minor and predicate or terminus *major of the final proposition) and the middle term with whom the extremes in the premises (major and minor) are compared.

The required form is given to this material by the *consequence. As for the conclusion, one can distinguish between the *mediate* and *immediate* reasoning. The latter, in which no middle term is used, means the obtaining of an *equipollence or opposed proposition by using the rules of the *conversion or *opposition. But the mediate reasoning is the only real reasoning. On the grounds of its form or structure it is divided in *deduction (see syllogism) and *induction; on the grounds of its content or matter in *proofs giving certitude* (demonstration), *proofs giving probability* as for instance the *analogy-reasoning, and *seeming proof* (*paralogism, *sophism). I.v.d.B.

RECEPTIVITY

Openness to impressions and influences, in cognition, feeling and striving. Especially used for reception of sensory impressions.

REDUCTIO AD ABSURDUM

An indirect argumentation which indicates the *absurd consequences of a specific thesis; e.g. when one denies the principle of contradiction, no assertion makes sense.

REDUCTION

The reduction of the imperfect or not-evidently-true inferences of the second and third syllogistic *figures to the perfect or evidently-exact inferences of the first figure. This reduction can be achieved directly or indirectly by proving that the contradictory *conclusion of one of the imperfect inferences is opposed to one of the premises which were considered true. (*reductio ad absurdum)

REFLECT UPON

Let the thought wander over something, while contemplating successively the pro's and the contra's. Also: consider, take into consideration.

REFLECTION, REFLEXIVE

The bending of the human thought over itself. Attention is expressively put on one's own thinking, which in its natural tendency (*intentionality) reaches towards the "others", in order to discover what in the act of thinking itself is implied. Every proposition contains already a certain reflection, because the absolute concept is seen in its relation to the sensory experience of the individual with which it is connected in its origin and for which it has value in its application. In science a further reflection happens. Psychology explains the origin of thinking through the nature of the subject, logic orders the contents of thought as such; metaphysics reduces the

distinction between subject and object in the thinking to the common origin, because subject and object are ways of being. J.P.

REFLEX

An unchangeable answer to a specific stimulus, acting in the body, without necessary cooperation of the consciousness. One distinguishes *temporary* reflexes (phasic) from *lasting* reflexes (tonic). Pavlov created reflexes in dogs; he trained them in the perception of, successively, an arbitrary stimulus and the stimulus necessary for the awakening of the reflex, making them react eventually only to this arbitrary stimulus (*conditional* reflex). Reflexologism has, on the grounds of this principle, brought forward a reduction-d o c t r i n e, which reduces the psychic phenomena to reflex-answers to selected stimuli (among others Bechterew). P.S.

REFUTATION (Greek: elenchos).

A syllogism, wherein the contradictory of the conclusion of a specific reasoning is proved. When it is not the same predicate of the same subject, then one speaks of an *ignoratio elenchi.

REGRESSUS IN INFINITUM

Elucidation of something conditional by an infinite series of conditions; and of an effect by an infinite series of causes. Aristotle says that a regressus in infinitum does not elucidate, no more than a *vicious circle does.

REGULATIVE, regulating.

Kant opposes it to constitutive, as that what, although not required for proper thinking, still provides in the subjective needs of thinking. So are the transcendental ideas regulative principles: they answer indeed to the subjective needs of thought, which intend to bring the many conditioned things under the unity of an absolute unconditioned something.

REICHENBACH, Hans, 1891-1953.
German-American philosopher, professor in Berlin (1926-33), in Istanbul (33-38) and (until his death) at the University of California in Los Angeles. Directed the "Berliner Gruppe" of neo-positivism and wrote important works on natural philosophy, symbolic logic and the basis of the theory of probability.

REID, Thomas
British philosopher, born in Starchan 1710, died in Glasgow, 1796. Is considered the most important figure in the Scottish School. Originally a follower of the philosophy of experience of Locke and Berkeley, rejects later the idealism of his predecessors because of the sceptical and even absurd consequences as given by Hume. He is opposed to the idea that our consciousness could only have representations as material for knowledge. Our mind concludes directly and justly through the experience that objects independent from our consciousness or realities exist. From the observation of a colour or form we conclude to the evident existence of the colored and formed thing. Reid formulates 12 unprovable but fundamental tenets on which the so called *Principles of Common Sense* are based and which have to lead us in our search for knowledge and truth. The theories of Reid and the Scottish School were categorically denied by Kant, but they had great influence on the American philosophical thought and in France until about 1870. F.B.

REIMARUS, Hermann Samuel
Born in Hamburg 1694, died

there 1768. Follower of the deism of the Enlightenment; defends a natural religion against the revealed religion. His philosophy is influenced by Leibniz and Wolff.

REINCARNATION
Teaches that the souls of the deceased regain a physical appearance. The religion of the Hindus is largely based on this doctrine, with in addition the idea that reincarnation, in a higher being, is a reward, reincarnation in a lower being is a punishment. See Metempsychosis.

REININGER Robert, 1869-1955.
Austrian idealistic philosopher, professor in Vienna.

RELATION
One of the ten Aristotelian categories. A *real* relation (e.g. paternity) supposes two real terms, namely the subject or carrier of the relation (e.g. father) and the relatum or final term of the relation (e.g. son) but also a real fundament (e.g. procreation). If the latter is missing we speak of a *logical* relation. Between the creature and his creator exists, for instance, a real relation of dependence, but between the Creator and the creature only a logical: the relation of dependence is not mutual, but one-sided. For a mutual relation we use the term correlation or correlates. Also relative *opposition.

Reference of one thing to another, *ad aliquid*. Logical relations connect thoughts, real relations are encountered in reality. Predicamental or *categorical relations, which occupy the fourth place in Aristotle's list of categories, are called *accidental relations, which on the grounds of quantity and quality (they are, between the accidents, the so-called absolute categories) belong to substantial reality. When, in this connection, it is a matter of real relations, then the question is whether they differ ontologically from their quantitative and qualitative ground. In any case, they belong as real accidents ontologically to their substance; they exist in their subject, *esse in subjecto,* and as accidental relations they put their subject in a certain relation to another, and they consist in "to be something in relation to another", *esse ad terminum.*

°Transcendental r e l a t i o n is called, in scholastic language, a reality (this can be a real being or substantial or accidental elements in which the structure of a real being consists) which is integrally relative to another; so is a creature integrally dependent on and relative to its Creator; generally the Thomists give also as definition of a potential principle its relation to a corresponding act principle.

In Kant's division of the categories into four parts, relation has the third place and is the relation of substance and accident; cause and effect; and of interaction, to which respond the categorical hypothetical and disjunctive propositions.

Hamelin uses the term to indicate the connection between thesis, antithesis and synthesis. L.D.R.

RELATION (in formal logic).

As such, means binary relations, i.e. qualities or predicates which can be applied not to one thing but to two things. Peter is older than John: the relation "to be older than" exists between Peter and John, so that the expression "Peter is older than" or "is older than John" is incomplete. The same thing is true for relations as: protect, precedes, follows, is the father of, etc. . . It should be noted that in the terminology of the modern logic "father" is no relation but forms the characteristic of the domain of the relation: father of.

One can also have relations which concern, in indivisible way, more than two things: e.g. the ternary relation between x, y, z: x gives z to y; the quaternary relation between x, y, z, w: x exchanges z for w with y.

A relation is *totally reflexive* when it exists between each individual and itself; this is the case in the identity, equality. This relation exists however mostly between an individual and itself when this individual belongs to a specific broad class. x is of the same color as itself, if x has a color; x is of the same weight as itself, if x has a weight. One speaks therefore rather of a *reflexive* than of a total reflexive relation. A relation is irreflexive, when it never exists between something and itself e.g. difference, sequence in time.

If a relation exists between x and y, then exists also the inverse relation between y and x. A relation is symmetric if it coincides with its inverse or if both exist between the same things: resemblance is symmetric, because if x resembles y, y also resembles x. A relation is *asymmetric* when it excludes its inverse: if x is higher than y, then is y not higher than x.

A relation is *transitive* if everytime a thing z exists, this relation exists between x and z, so that x has the relation with z and z with y. The relation is *intransitive*, if this latter supposition excludes the existence of the relation between x and z. Parallellism is a transitive, "father of" an intransitive relation.

A relation is *one-many* if not more than one thing has the relation to that particular thing: "father of" is a "one-many" relation. A *many-one* relation is a relation which a thing can not have with several things: the relation son-father is "many-one" relation. The *one-one* relation is the relation which exists between not more than two different things: e.g. the relation of the oldest son with his father. R.F.

RELATIONNUMBERS
See numbers.

RELATIVE
That which is defined by its relation to another, and is often limited by it, e.g., the term "father" is relative to the term "child"; a creature is a relative being, entirely relative to its creator; the value of our knowledge is relative to many, often unrealized, conditions. Opposite of *Absolute. See also: Concept.

RELATIVISM
Doctrine defending *relativity, in a specific domain or in general. It is therefore the doctrine which, although not denying human knowledge all ability to know the truth, still denies it the ability to know the unconditioned and all-valid truth, because the relativity of the disposition, situation and point of view of the one who knows is determining his insight and conviction. Relativism negates that in every human judgment a relation exists to the existence of the being as such. In this relation is, at least implicitly, a drawing closer to the absolute being included, as the unconditioned momentum of the human knowledge exceeding all dependence from experience or subjective influences.

The not-absolute condition, from which human knowledge remains eventually dependent, according to relativism, is found e.g. in the regularities which explain the origin of knowing as a subjective occur-

rence (*psychologism); in the effectiveness of the knowledge; in the experience (*pragmatism); in the sensual experience (*sensualism). Relativism, as an absolutely valid thesis about the limitation of all human knowledge, contradicts itself. If relativism itself is only considered relative, then it comes close to *scepticism. J.P.

RELATIVITY
What is proper to the relative as such, in the many meanings of the word. (see *relation) See also *proposition.

RELATIVITY OF THE HUMAN KNOWLEDGE, means its limited value, which again is differently evaluated by different philosophers. It is especially understood that knowledge can only occur from a specific point of view and in a varying situation. If and how one still can, under those circumstances, reach the *absolute, is the basic question.

RELATIVITY OF THE ETHICS, is the expression used to indicate that morality is dependent from time and space: what we consider good can be condemned elsewhere; what we accept today can have been condemned in earlier times. This is a fact which can not be negated, but the question remains: can we therefore conclude to the complete relativity of ethics, so that the distinction between good and evil disappears? (relativism). We think that in spite of this fact, ethics has an unchangeable root. We therefore agree that the moral consciousness takes part in the evolution of the individual and the humanity, we also agree that the moral consciousness differs according to the psychic structure of the individual or the civilization of the society. The moral law is then every time seen in a different light: there exists not only a different *"ethos",

369

the differentiation takes even place inside the ethos. To realize a same value, different prescriptions can sometimes be necessary. Sometimes also is the personal conscience opposed to prescriptions which are generally accepted. Thus, if the difference in prescriptions does not prevent that christianity and Islam have the same respect for honorability, so does the relativity of ethics not prevent the absoluteness of ethics, at least in its root. And this root is intimately connected with the essence itself of man, who, being a spiritual being, recognizes what is true and decent. Relative are only the conditions under which that what is decent has to be realized. J. Gr.

RELIGION

From *religere* (Cicero), the contemplation or the concern for something which surpasses the human being; from *religare* (Lactantius), the feeling of attachment to a divinity. Both etymologies say something about religion. They are both, however, insufficient to explain its human as well as its specific character.

Unless we want to include in the definition of religion conceptions and usages which differ from it essentially, we cannot be satisfied with the minimum definition of Tylor—religion is the belief in spirits—nor the more subjective definition of Van der Leeuw—religion is the striving toward expansion of force. The definition of religion must include a sufficient concept of God, and at the same time a sufficiently distinct description of the attitude of man. The definition therefore cannot be other than: religion is a complex of concepts and usages through which man expresses his belief in a personal transcendent Power, upon which he knows that he is dependent and from which he hopes to receive protection in his life struggle.

The question as to the source of religion can have an historical as well as a psychological, a philosophical as well as a theological, emphasis. All historical documents presuppose the existence of religion. Indeed in between these historical documents, which suppose the existence of religion, and prehistoric monuments are several millennia. An effort has been made to bridge this great distance, first of all through comparative linguistics and mythology, but all that has been found, is that something can be said for a common basis to the religions of the Indo-European peoples. Second through ethnology, which started with the assumption that still existing, so-called primitive peoples really represent the primitive stages of human culture. But it was discovered that the religions of these peoples showed remarkable differences. How can one discover the oldest form of religion or the germs from which all others were derived? Since only contradictory responses to this question have been given, we must conclude that ethnology does not penetrate the origin of religion. Its answer, indeed, is not always purely historical. It always depends upon specific psychological insights, which themselves are generally dependent upon philosophical and theological postulates. If we accept the notion that the first human beings were like us, we must also accept the notion that their religion originated in the same grounds of mind and feeling as our religion does. If we believe also that there was primitive divine revelation, then we must also believe that God, in His goodness, met the same needs of mind and feeling in such a way as man never can understand.

RELIGION, NATURAL

Whereas revealed religion contains a belief in revealed truth, natural religion reduces itself to a "rational" belief. Man believes only what can be investigated by his natural reason, such as the existence of God, the immortality of the soul and the existence of good and evil. Natural religion has been very much honored since the Enlightenment. See also deism.

RELIGIOUS

A subjective characteristic of the human being, of which the sense and meaning are described differently according to whether or not one accepts the objective value of religion. In the first case, man is called religious when he is ready to render God the adoration, the thankfulness and the love which He deserves; in the second, such dispositions as the feeling of dependence, of being above everyday life, etc., are called religious.

RELIGIOUS PHENOMENOLOGY

Investigation of religious phenomena. It is not a question of the historical development or the origin of religious phenomena, but the investigation of their meaning, structure and essence. And the answer is sought by engaging in original religious experience, leaving aside all questions as to its truth or value. Religious phenomenology, however, has to overcome one difficulty. It supposes that all experience is the witnessing of something, the living relation between a subject and an object, in this case the divine. But the divine is not an object which can be grasped through contemplation, it is not a phenomenon which reveals itself in its essence. There is, therefore,

no other solution but to make of the religious experience an intuition, or to take refuge in the belief that the man who tries to inject the religious phenomenon into his life is seized by the object, God. In this case religious phenomenology cannot avoid the philosophical question as to the reality of the religious object. K.L.B.

RELIGIOUS SOCIOLOGY

Investigation of the relation between social and religious phenomena, in order to determine the social function of religion. This investigation can be empirically descriptive, phenomenological or philosophical.

REMEMBRANCE

The more personally tinted memory. To be distinguished from reproduction (active) and recognition (passive). Remembrance is wider than those, and has not only reference to the object but also to the circumstances and the sphere of the earlier imprinting.

REMIGIUS OF AUXERRE, ca. 841-ca. 908.

Successor of Heiricus as head of the School of Auxerre, author of commentaries on the *De Consolatione* of Boethius and on the pseudo-augustinian *De decem categoriis*.

REMORSE

C e n t r a l moral phenomenon which concerns the entire person, even into his physiological structure. In its deepest nature is the remorse affective: an atrocious grief, proceeding from the laceration of one's own nature which experiences his own identification with an action posed by the free will, which it intellectually condemns and rejects. This laceration is stronger when the Ego, which created itself completely and actively in the free act, now, passively, must undergo itself however much it wants to free himself from himself or shake off his laceration.

RENAN, Ernest
Born in Frégmer 1823, died in Paris 1892. French orientalist and historian of religion. Tried in his well known *Vie de Jésus* (1863) to bring back the origin of christianity to a series of naturally explainable facts. Renan's ideas are interesting for the philosophy because of his scepticism. The truths in which philosophy is interested are for Renan not to be proved, so that they can neither be affirmed nor negated. Only a certain belief can give a solution. He explains the natural events through the law of the eternal becoming, an eternal metamorphosis, in which the Infinite reveals itself in finite forms, in which nature rises gradually from mechanism to consciousness, and in which humanity rises gradually to the concept and exercise of perfection. F.S.

RENOUVIER, Charles
Born in Montpellier 1815, died in Paris 1903. French critic, rather independent from *Kant, also influenced by *Hume. Renouvier does not believe in a closed philosophical system. His thought proceeds from three mutually independent points of view: the conviction that the actual-infinite is impossible; that freedom is an element of the empirical world and the basis of all ethical life, science and philosophy; his relativism: he rejects the *Ding an sich* and retains only phenomena or representations of the consciousness, which have always a relative character. These basic ideas are not postulates of the practical reason, but theoretically provable theses; its certitude is only affirmed by the "moral conviction", through which reason is elevated to a higher insight and which has always the last word in every choice of view on life and world. The strongest "moral conviction" is that of the moral destination of the individual human personality, for which society has to create the necessary conditions. Pure morality is for Renouvier the definition of the law of reason, analogous with the categorical imperative of Kant, which free men have to impose on their passions either by themselves or in common with others. The pure law of justice prescribes the realization of a common good for the members of the community. Man and society have actually failed in this duty because of a decadence of humanity, which originates not in God, identically with the moral order, but only in the free will of man. About the future history of humanity Renouvier had some theories which coincide very much with the christian doctrine, and in which the free will of man has an important role. The human personality remains the same during all changes in the world. It is per saldo the only reality as opposed to the phenomena of the world (see personalism). F.S.

REPRESENTATION
In philosophy the living image, given with the act of cognition, of an object: species expressa.

In the old psychology an element of consciousness, found in the analysis of the processes of consciousness. The representations are of different nature, according to specific domains of the senses.

REPRESENTATION (in formal logic).
In a theory which attaches a natural meaning to the symbols, as

in the theory of Wittgenstein, (a natural symbol) *represents* that which it resembles.

A symbol represents something *satisfactorily* for all qualities in which it resembles that something, and insatisfactorily for all other qualities. A satisfactory representation is superfluous if between the symbol and the represented thing still other resemblances exist; if a representation is satisfactory but not superfluous then it is exact. (the opposite of exact in the sense used here is not inexact but superfluous).

A *symbolism produces a *combinatory representation* of a connection of objects of thought when to each symbol an object of thought, to each combinatory relation a deductive connection between the objects of thought corresponds. The representation is *purely combinatory* if it represents exactly the deductive connection (in the above mentioned sense). The purely combinatory representation which produces a universally deductive formalism, is called a *purely logical* representation. The representation is called *logical* and not purely logical if the representation is combinatory but not purely combinatory. R.F.

RESENTMENT

Feeling of revenge which leads to minimize the worth of a certain value which cannot and because it can not be realized. This kind of resentment is, according to Nietzsche the basis of the christian morality: unable to assert himself by force in the eyes of the neighbor, the christian will recognize love for the neighbor as a value.

RESISTANCE

From outside imposed to our actions. Was brought out by Destutt de Tracy and Maine de Biran, but only by Dilthey was it analyzed in detail. According to N. Hartmann the resistance gives us certitude about the existence of the reality, and according to Scheler is it the reality itself.

RESOLUTION

The will to pose an action which is defined in the essential characteristics of its content. It is therefore a moment in the action. It is however often incorrectly identified with the *intention: when both remain inner, the intention has relation to the value which is pursued in the action, while the resolution is related to the change in the reality, by which the value should be realized. If the resolution without the *execution is sufficient morally, is questionable, especially when the execution is possible.

RESPECT

Feeling directed toward that which possesses in itself an infinite value. Respect for the moral law, says Kant, which he defends as being the motive for ethical activity, is not a sensual feeling but a reasonable feeling, produced in the moral subject by the action of the moral law itself.

RESPONSIBILITY

Is in moral content more narrow but also more profound than in juridic content. One who acts in complete freedom and with moral consciousness, must also vouch for his action for himself and for others. Responsibility is therefore a faculty of man as man or as moral subject. It presupposes freedom and is the basis of the *imputation. Responsibility is also the act by which a moral subject imputes his own actions to himself or also takes the responsibility of his own actions.

REST

When the distance of one body in regard to another body does not change, we say that this body is at rest in respect to that other body. Rest, as well as motion, is a relative concept. If one wants to use these concepts in practice, one has, by definition, to consider one or another body or group of bodies at rest. When one says that there is motion on earth, one considers the earth to be at rest, in astronomy one considers the fixed stars as being at rest.

RESTRICTIO MENTALIS

Silent restriction in a statement, which limits or even alters the sense of this statement.

RESTRICTION

The use of a *term in a narrower sense than the linguistic meaning; e.g., Eve is the mother of all living (meaning "of all men").

REVELATION

The meaning of this concept depends on the fact if one accepts or rejects the existence of a transcendental personal God and the receptibility of the human mind for God's communication. In the first case revelation means the supernatural communication by God or by his envoy of religious truths. One has to exclude essentially from this revelation the natural revelation in which God reveals himself through his creation. If one rejects the relation God-man, then the revelation is the rational knowledge of God who manifests himself in nature and/or in history, or is the fact of breaking through the infinite spirit, through the limitation of the finite spirit or the fact that the absolute Spirit is himself in the human spirit, etc. K.L.B.

REVERSAL

Sometimes identified with the *conversion, sometimes in broader sense: every exchange of subject term and predicate term, through which a judgment is obtained which is equivalent to the initial one or which is the opposite of it: one speaks then generally of reciprocal judgments.

REWARD

See sanction, pleasant.

RHABANUS MAURUS

Born in Mainz 776 or 784, died there 856, disciple of *Alcuin in Tours, founder of the school of Fulda, later abbot of Fulda, and finally archbishop of Mainz. Author of works of compilation (*De clericorum institutione, De rerum naturis*) with which he obtained the title of *Praeceptor Germaniae*.

RHYTHM

That by which the artistic harmony becomes a spatial and temporal movement. Rhythm frees the esthethic ordering of the individual elements of form from the severe static and monotonous repetition of the pure measure. It gives form to the material measure-movement with a principle of spiritual freedom and originality. Rhythm recreates the artistic movement uninterruptedly into esthetic newness. As opposed to the purely quantitativeness of the measure, is rhythm the qualitative diversity. This qualification can however only happen on the grounds of a certain metric regularity, because the connection with this meter only can make evident the rhythm as rhythm and therefore the originality as originality. In more temporal arts, as music, dance and poetry, the rhythm is more clearly visible. In the spatial and plastic arts however rhythm detaches itself in the interplay of lines, forms, light and colours. To the objective rhythm which can be shown corresponds always the subjective rhythm of the showing. The perfection of rhythm lays, in fact, in the proper melding of both these aspects. L.V.K.

RICARDO, David, 1772-1823.

British economist known as the father of the classical school of economics. Developed his theories of rent, profit and wages in *Principles of Political Economy and Taxation* (1809).

RICKERT, Heinrich 1863-1936.

German neo-Kantian of the School of °Baden, professor in Freiburg i. Br., later in Heidelberg. Main works: *Die Grenzen der naturwissenschaftlichen Begriffsbildung*, 1896; *Kulturwissenschaft und Naturwissenschaft*, 1899. Rickert is especially interested in the question of the values and their meaning for the sciences. There is, he found, a very clear difference between the natural sciences and the cultural sciences. Natural science is free of values, it is interested in establishing facts and drafting laws. Cultural sciences on the other hand are evaluating: a science as for instance history is only possible on the grounds of judgment of values about what is and what is not important. Philosophy has to investigate what values give guidance to scientific investigation. Because of this difference in the importance of the values the natural sciences are always directed towards the absolute, whereas the cultural sciences are directed to the particular. Philosophy has here a second duty: it has to deliver the logic which makes possible the study of the absolute and of the particular. The first form of logic is the classical logic; the second will have to be a

normative logic because the particular can only be seen under the aspect of the norm, the value. B.D.

RIDPATH, John Clark, 1840-1900.

American author of popular histories and history textbooks; by temperament an encyclopedist, surveying the whole range of knowledge of his time. Works: *Encyclopedia of Universal History* (1880-85), *The Great Races of Mankind* (1884-94), and the 25-volume *Ridpath Library of Universal Literature* (1898).

RIGHT

The whole of the norms which regulate the relation between men (actions and property). The right does not only prescribe that what can not be done (interdiction) but also what has to be done (order). Accurately determined sanctions (criminal law) can support the application of the right. The goal of the right is to order society in such a way that individual and society have the liberty which is due to them.

Natural right is had when the ordering lays in the nature of man, *positive right* when the ordering is expressly determined by the human society (lawmaker or legislative body). *Public* right concerns the interests of the society; *private* right orders the relations between private persons.

RIGORISM

The extreme severity in the observation of the law and especially the natural law. Therefore the principle in casuistics that in the slightest doubt about the moral value of an action, this action can not be taken. (opposed to °laxism). Also the attitude which can only affirm that what is morally-proper as a value, and even only that what is morally-proper in the painful coercion of the obligation. This attitude is found, among others, in the Stoics and Kant. Kant thinks that the moral purity of an action is only saved when this action is taken against all natural inclinations.

ROBERT GROSSETESTE

Born in Stradbroke (England) before 1168, died in Lincoln 1253. Magister artium in Oxford until 1209, studied probably theology in Paris until 1214, returned to Oxford where he was magister in theology until 1235 to become bishop of Lincoln. While magister in theology and first chancellor of the young university of Oxford, he received there the first Franciscans, organized their studies and was from 1229 till 1235 the first magister regens of their *Studium*, without being himself a Franciscan. Robert Grosseteste was especially successful in the impulse he gave to the studies in Oxford and his importance lies also in the many philosophical and scientific writings which cover about all the then known profane sciences, especially the natural sciences (his great merit was that he foresaw the importance of mathematics in the development of the natural sciences). He translated from the Greek the *Ethica Nicomachea* of Aristotle, the works of the Pseudo-Dionysius and John of Damascus; he also incited other writers to translating. Robert Grosseteste is a typical representative of the eclectic aristotelianism. F.V.S.

ROBERT OF MELUN

Born in England, end 11th century, died in Hereford 1167, professor of logic in Paris after Abaelard, in 1142 professor of theology in Melun, finally bishop of Hereford in 1163; is more important for theology than for philosophy.

ROBIN, Leon, 1866-1947.

French philosopher, professor at the Sorbonne, specialist in the history of Greek philosophy.

ROGER MARSTON

Born in England before 1250, died there 1303, Franciscan. Studied in Paris ca. 1270, taught in Oxford since 1277, later in Cambridge, and was provincial of England 1292-98. Typical representative of the Franciscan neo-augustinism, also a very personal thinker; he composed under influence of Avicenna, an epistemology in the line of the *augustinism.

ROLAND OF CREMONA

Born in Cremona end 12th cent., died 1259, magister artium in Bologna, Dominican in 1219 and first magister regens of the Dominicans in Paris (1229-30). Wrote around 1234 a *Summa theologiae*, which is a commentary on the *Sententiae* and shows an extensive knowledge of Aristotle.

ROMAINS, Jules, 1884-

One of the major French novelists of the early twentieth century, he was an exponent of unanimism: the idea that unifying principles in human societies are more significant than personalities. His masterwork is a series of novels under the general title *Les Hommes de Bonne Volonté* (*Men of Good Will*).

ROMANES, George

Born in Kingston (Canada) 1848, died in Oxford 1894. Biologist and psychologist of animals, positivist. Introduces in *Darwin's theory of evolution a teleological element; agnosticism has in Romanes' works a religious character.

ROMANTIC SCHOOL

Is in philosophy a group of German thinkers of the first half of the 19th Cent., who, reacting against the rationalism of the *Enlightenment and following the irrationalism of *Herder and the idealism of *Fichte, consider the phantasy of the artist to be the creative factor of the origin of the world; in addition they have a very great respect for the imagination in general, for the individual feeling of life and for the emotion for the beauty of nature and art, also an inclination towards religious mysticism and symbolism and a sense of the primitive and the popular, which led some of them to an exaggerated veneration of the Middle Ages. F.S.

ROMERO, Francisco, 1891-
Latin-American philosopher of the Gestalt school, he is influential as a critic. Works: *Old and New Concepts of Reality* (1932), *The Problems of Philosophy and Culture* (1938), *Program of a Philosophy* (1940).

ROSCELLINUS OF COMPIEGNE, ca. 1050, died between 1123-25.
Taught in several schools. Reacted against *ultra-realism by defending, in connection with the problem of the universalia, the *sententia vocum*, a point of view which is close to *nominalism.

ROSENZWEIG, Franz, 1886-1929.
German scholar who devoted his life to the elaboration of a new conception of Judaism based upon historical, linguistic and philosophical research. His book *Der Stern der Erloesung* (*Star of Salvation*) was published posthumously in 1930.

ROSMINI-SERBATI, Antonio
Born in Roveredo 1797, died in Stresa 1855. Italian priest, politician, founder of monasteries, one of the main defenders of *ontologism.

Following *Malebranche and *Augustine, and the entire Platonic tradition, he is convinced that truth is not primarily sought in the realm of experience, but in the world of the ideas. All human knowledge of truth has however its basis and origin in a "first truth", on which all other truths are dependent, namely the Idea of being as such; this is innate to man, in this sense that man is immediately and by an inner experience conscious of it. The Idea of being opens into a multiplicity of ideas, who make understandable for us the objects of our experience. The relation of these objects to the ideas is presented by Rosmini as a participation, in the sense of *Plato; the object is certainly connected with the idea but is still different from it. E.S.

ROTHACKER, Erich, born 1888.
German philosopher, professor in Bonn, especially interested in the problematics of the mental sciences.

ROUSSEAU, Jean Jacques
Born in Geneva 1712, died in Ermonville 1778. Rousseau belongs to the Enlightenment, but objects to its rationalism. He defends the rights of emotion and feeling, and the natural, unspoiled human intellect. Man is created with good abilities, but is spoiled by the unnatural and artificial culture. The ideal in education is to follow, as closely as possible, the natural state and remove all coercion, which hinder or deform the forces of the personality which are from nature directed towards the good. No place is left, in education, for a commanding authority. The moral norm is the language of the function of feeling of the conscience, not the intelligence which deceives. Rousseau is a deist. We know God

only as a supreme cause, through our voluntary and intellectual natural religion, in a complete surrender to the truth which satisfies the feeling. The soul is immortal; punishment and penalty exist only in this world, not in the other world. Because the natural state can not be kept, man has a (silent) contract, *Contrat social*, in which the individual obeys the general will (*volonté générale*) which is something else than the will of all. This general will is the impersonal law, in which no personal profit is found. All other contract means personal profit and laws to be guaranteed. In this state freedom and equality must reign, as close as possible to the natural state. The sovereignty belongs to the people, who give to the government only the executive powers. Rousseau had much influence in France and Germany, for instance on Kant. H. R.

ROYCE, Josiah, 1855-1916.

American idealistic personalist, professor at Harvard. Royce is an original thinker, influenced as well by *Hegel as by *pragmatism. It is possible that these very different influences have brought him to look for a synthesis of speculative thinking and practical action. An idea has only practical meaning when man has mastered it completely and has therefore given it its own individual character. Only these individualised ideas are real ideas. They are all different from each other according to the particular nature of the individual who thinks them. The generality is only a lack. This does however not mean a complete individualism, because the unity of all ideas is in God. God expresses himself in the infinite variety of the individuals, who choose, each for themselves and in freedom, their own existence. God

is the truth who is recognized in all knowledge of the human individuals. Only this knowledge, which is perfect in God himself, is the true reality. Main work: *The World and the Individual*, 1900-1902.—B.D.

RUGGIERO, Guido de, 1888-1948.

Italian neo-Hegelian, professor in Rome.

RULE

In objective sense the logical expression of a conformity, whether this conformity concerns facts (theoretical rule), or imposes itself to the actions as a request (practical rule); in subjective sense *prescription or norm.

As opposed to the *law, the rule is mostly but not always valid. In other words a rule permits exceptions: next to the general cases with which the rule is concerned, exist exceptional cases which, although fulfilling the required conditions, still depend on other conditions. When the rule was made, one did not think of these cases, so that they do not fall under the rule.

RULES OF STRUCTURE

Are, in formal systems, rules which determine the expressions (of the objects of thought) about which, in the system, can be reasoned.

RUNES, Dagobert D., 1902-

American philosopher. Among his works are *Dictionary of Philosophy, The Art of Thinking, On the Nature of Man, Pictorial History of Philosophy, Treasury of Philosophy* and *Philosophy for Everyman.*

RUSH, Benjamin, 1745-1813.

American social reformer and writer on medicine, social problems, natural sciences and philosophy, as well as an active politician and practicing physician. His *Med-*

ical Inquiries and Observations (1789-98) and *Medical Inquiries and Observations upon the Diseases of the Mind* (1812) were long considered standard works on psychiatry.

RUSKIN, John, 1819-1900.
English sociological writer and art critic. Books: *Modern Painters* (1842-60), *Stones of Venice* (1851-53), *Sesame and Lilies* (1865), *Bible of Amiens* (1885).

RUSSELL, Bertrand
(1872-1970), English neo-realistic philosopher, very close to neopositivism. He wrote together with °Whitehead the *Principia mathematica* (1910-13). Mathematics and natural sciences are for him the only scientific forms of thought. Philosophy is only a temporary study of problems which can not yet be treated methodically and scientifically. Russell's work is twofold. On the one hand he is interested in the basis of the exact sciences and, in connection therewith, in the structure of the physical reality and our knowledge of it. On the other hand he discusses problems of anthropological nature, in the most broad sense of the word: ethics, religion, human happiness, education, freedom and social order. Russell's work in the former domain shows generally great scientific carefulness; his work in the domain of philosophical anthropology has rarely profound ideas. The world in which we live is a world of sense-data. These sense-data are real and form together the real world, which is then however for each individual different. Many relations exist between the sense-data, but these relations are purely exterior. We can not speak of a real Ego; the Ego is only the actual and constantly changing whole of the sense-data. The sense-data have neither a psychic nor physical nature. We can only say that they are in a certain respect physical, in another respect psychic. This whole reality is then neither physical nor spiritual, because it is withdrawn from the physical and the psychic. In this whole reality man is only an insignificant part. Immortality and the existence of God are fiction, and are only used by man, when his existence is too hard, to alleviate it. On the other hand however we have to say that man is important, because he is free and his freedom makes his ideal of life. The only ideal towards which man should strive, is a life led by science and love. This ideal leads man to his own happiness but puts him, at the same time, in the middle of the community. The prosperity and freedom of the community must be pursued by all men.—B.D.

RUUSBROEC
See Joannes of Ruusbroec.

S

Much used symbol indicating the subject of a proposition (without content). Also a symbol to indicate the possibility of a completely logical transposition of a proposition, namely of the conversion, which happens *"simpliciter"* (simply).

SAADIA ben JOSEPH

First great Jewish philosopher (Egypt 882-942). Wrote on linguistics, bible studies, theology. Under the influence of the philosophical methods of the Mutuzilia, Saadia defends a certain rationalism: the revealed truths can be completely known by reason; reason is the highest criterion; the existence of God and the creation from nothing in the time are proved; the revelation has a more practical value (later developed by Moses Maimonides, and in another light by Thomas Aquinas). The same applies to the ethics: reason proves the immortality of the soul and drafts the ethical laws, the revelation is, here again, only an aid.

SAD

A weaker form of the tragic. Tragic becomes sad when the presented subject lacks greatness or when his failure remains limited. A more sentimental or at least affective form of sad is *moving*.

SAENZ D'AGUIRRE Cardinal Joseph, 1630-1699.

Spanish Benedictine, published a thomistic philosophical course (1671-1678).

SAINT SIMON, Claude Henri de,

Born in Paris 1760, died there 1825. French utopian socialist, precursor of positivism. Hopes that a new science, in which natural science and the science of man come together into one set of laws, will bring the renovation of the social order and the transformation of the political state into an industrial state, organised exclusively on the basis of work and production, so that a lasting peace can be achieved.

SALOMON ben GEBIROL

See Avencebrol.

SAMKHYA

Indian form of thought, characterized by a consequent dualism: the everlasting matter and the spiritual principle exist from all eternity. The latter exists in the animated beings as an infinite number of mutually equal "souls". The world is an evolution from the prime matter. The physical (the psychic included) is in eternal motion, the spiritual is at rest and viewer of this motion, but because of our blindness we consider it as being active. In every world-period the components of the being develop themselves from the prime matter, in a specific series, i.e. on the one hand the elements from which matter evolutes, on the other hand the psychical apparatus of the animated beings. The most representative Sāmkhya-school is atheistic and represents the events in the world as purely mechanical, i.e. according to eternal nature laws. —J.G.

SAMSARA

See Indian philosophy

SANCHEZ, Francisco

Born in Bracara before 1552, died in Toulouse 1662. French physician, born in Portugal. Being a sceptic, he objects, in science, to authority and syllogistic dialectics. The connection between all things and the continuous becoming of things is the reason why some things cannot be known.

SANCTION

Is the happy or unhappy effect of the ethical value or disvalue of an action. In the first case one speaks generally of compensation, in the second of punishment. Sanctions should be divided in: 1. individual sanctions or sanctions in the own essence of the acting person; 2. social sanctions, or sanctions in the social relation of the acting person; 3. Cosmic sanctions or sanctions in the acting person as a natural being; 4. religious sanctions or sanctions on the part of God Himself.

SANKARA

Indian thinker, around 800 A.D., he was in many aspects rather a teacher of a method of salvation; an organizer of the not-buddhistic religious life, an opponent of the heterodox and extreme schools, than he was a philosopher. He wrote very personal interpretations of the Vedanta to which he belonged and this interpretation was very much followed in the centuries after him. His doctrine shows a great speculative courage, a very sharp intellectual capacity, a subtle

consequent logic and a straight thinking out of his ideas. This doctrine will lead to insight in the distinction between that what is eternal and that what is transitory, and will learn to reject the latter. His point of view is the pure monism (kevalōdvaita). Nothing is exactly real except *brahman, which is being, pure and unqualified intuitive consciousness and salvation or beatitude; those three are identical. Brahman, which can not be defined in a manner known to man, can only be reached in an integral mystical experience which transforms the entire essence of man. All this however is valid on the level of the absolute reality. There exists a lower level, the level of the empiricism, relatively true and real, but not not-being. Those who do not penetrate the true insight, as, for instance, the followers of other schools of thought, stay in a world view of the empiricism and the science which is based on it. They can only clarify the complete dependence from brahman through myths, as the myth of the creation, and their mutual relation only through symbols. The Creator they imagine, the Lord (Isvara), is however the qualified and differentiated brahman, brahman in the phenomenal level, as are matter and the souls. Brahman is called in an image "nothing than light" and the Lord "light in the darkness." Isvara is the causa materialis and causa efficiens of their own emanation, (see Vedānta). His "creating" services to make possible the adjustment of the *karman. There is, for this reason, no arbitrariness in the creation.—*Maya is for Sankara the formula which expresses that space, time and causality are not, as we think naturally, the eternal fundaments of objective reality, but forms of our experience, subjective forms

381

proper to our understanding of the reality.—Sankara tries to explain the relation between brahman and the world through the hypothesis of the seeming-transformation: brahman can manifest himself as something else without really transforming himself. Brahman is that of which the world is, in time and space, the relative manifestation. There is no causality between them, but a metaphysical connection, an eternal coexistence.—J.G.

SANSEVERINO, Gaetano

Born in Naples 1811, died there 1865. Priest and neo-scholastic philosopher, most important figure in the movement to re-establish thomistic philosophy in Italy. Wrote several textbooks in Latin and had through them great influence on the philosophical education in the seminaries.

SANTAYANA, George, 1863-1952.

American philosopher, professor in Harvard. Main works: *The Life of Reason*, 1905-06; *The Realms of Being* (1927-40). In Santayana two ideas are united: thought sees in the essences the reality par excellence, and the conception that the consciousness is only a result of the corporeity. Religion has no sense as a doctrine, only as the recognition of a sense of life. Philosophy is necessarily a reflection on the finiteness.

SARTRE, Jean-Paul

Born 1905, French existentialistic philosopher, psychologist, essay writer and littérateur. Main work: *L'être et le Néant*, 1943. Sartre wants, as did °Heidegger, to investigate the question of existence. The first phenomenological analysis teaches us that existence breaks up into two domains: the "être-en-soi" (in itself) and the "être-pour-soi"

(for itself). The "être-en-soi" is the existence of the physical things. This existence is without further definition. The "être-pour-soi" is the existence of the consciousness. Consciousness is characterized by intentionality, i.e. it is always directed towards the other. Consciousness is even nothing else than this being directed towards the outer. This means, that consciousness is always a consciousness *not* to be what the other is, this is called by Sartre "néantisation" (making nothingness). Outside of this "néantisation" consciousness is nothing: it is the existence through which nothingness comes into the world. This means also, that consciousness never coincides with itself. Because I can never identify myself with what I am *now*. I always rise above it and make therefore always nothing that is "actual to me." This means that I am *free*.

Consciousness can coincide with itself, but it can not coincide with the consciousness of another. What one calls love is a vain effort towards it. One makes either of the other a thing and then one does not have a real contact with the other any more, or one makes of oneself a thing so as to be dominated by the other, and then it is also impossible, from nature, to speak of contact. Consciousness does however not only have the desire to coincide with the consciousness of another, it desires also to coincide with itself, in other words it wants to be at the same time thing and consciousness. Since this can not be realized, man projects this in the idea of God: God, on the other hand, is sufficient to Himself, but He is, on the other hand, pure consciousness. This however is an inner contradiction. God can therefore not exist. B.D.

SATANISM

The conception which considered as only value the negation of all values.

SATIATED

A system is satiated if it is so complete that a contradiction arises when, as added *axiom, is accepted a "proposition which is not provable in the system.

SCHELER, Max

Born in München 1874, died in Frankfurt a.M. 1928, German philosopher. Very complicated personality with a very productive activity in different domains: ethics, epistemology, history, philosophy of culture, psychology, pedagogy, God and religion . . . with solutions which contradicted themselves in the course of the years. This multiplicity in thought can however be brought into a unity. Scheler speaks always of one mystery: what is man, starting, in his concrete way of thinking, from the question: What is the man Scheler? To live and to philosophize are inseparably one, so that one to know his doctrine has also to know his life.

He was the son of a protestant father and a Jewish mother and converted during his studies in the "Gymnasium" to catholicism. In 1898 he breaks—because of a woman—with the catholic practice but his thought continues to evolute in a christian direction. In 1897 he graduates in Jena under Eucken but the separates himself definitively from Kant in 1901, according to his own declaration, because he gets in touch with the phenomenological method of Husserl. He gives of Husserl his own interpretation. The method of the direct experience of consciousness is bent by Scheler into its more emotional side: philosophize with

as basis the own rich experience in the most complete sense of the word. He chooses realism, opposing here Husserl. Private problems force him in 1910 to leave München, where he taught at the university. He moves to Berlin, where he holds many lectures and writes his main works. His *Der Formalismus in der Ethik und die materiale Wertethik* (1913-16) brings about an entire renovation of the ethics. In this work Scheler opposes Kant by emphasizing the values which are objectively valid, independent from man, and which we have to realize according to a certain order. Man who has to realize these values is composed of two extremes: spirit-life or also nature-grace, but spirit, grace, finally God are emphasized, God who gives unity to man. Man can only be understood by God: Theomorphismus. In 1916 he returns to the practice of the Catholic religion, he deepens this image of man in still more christian sense and one seems to expect, through his publications in ethics, religion and culture that a new Augustine was born. In 1919 however, he becomes professor of sociology in Cologne, three years later he is separated from his wife and leaves again the Church because of another woman. From 1922 on, his philosophy is a reflection of this new attitude in life. He constructs a dualistic philosophy in which the weakness of the mind and the strength of the passion is taught for man, world and even God. "God" is now only to be understood by man, he is freed by man from the initial contradiction in which he exists. We can therefore call this phase in Scheler's life the pantheistic period, or, in connection with the impersonality of this particular conception of God: religious atheism. Just arrived in Frankfurt, where he was named professor, Scheler dies suddenly after a very tumultuous life. The publication of his posthumous works, prohibited during the Hitler regime, has been taken up in the series of his collected writings begun in 1954.

Scheler has directly and indirectly a great influence on contemporary thought, in Germany and elsewhere, in the christian and nochristian thought. His best works are in the domain of ethics, psychology, cultural philosophy and philosophy of religion. In his *Vom Ewigen im Menschen* (1921) he shows, for instance how "the holy" is the highest value and how the religious act is constitutive for man. A fault of Scheler's works is his lack of systematics. J.N.

SCHELLING, Friedrich Wilhelm
Born in Leonberg, Würtenburg 1775, died in Ragaz (Switz.) 1854. German idealist, professor in Jena, Würzburg, Erlangen, München.

Four periods can be distinguished in the thought of Schelling. In the first he is interested in natural philosophy, in the second he builds the system of objective idealism or the philosophy of *identity, which is an important link in the history of German idealism. In the third he defends a syncretism of neo-platonic inspiration, and finally in the fourth period he goes over to theosophic speculations in the spirit of *Boehme.

In the first period Schelling holds that the not-Ego or nature is as positive as the Ego and therefore object of philosophical investigation, which is summed up in the natural philosophy. He then explains the entire happenings in the world in the spirit of *Paracelsus, i.e. as a dynamic activity of the world soul.

In the second period Schelling is looking for a highest principle, from which all reality can be deduced. Since he can not find it in the Ego nor in nature, he let both originate in a common original ground, the Absolute Indifferent, which constitutes, as undivided unity and absolute identity of subject and object, mind and nature, the ideal and the real, the highest reality, the only *Ding an Sich*. The Absolute Indifferent can only be reached through the intellectual contemplation, which is the special privilege of the philosopher. It unfolds in the contradictions mentioned above; the concrete things in nature and mind are only its representations. Through this theory of the relation between the Absolute and the concrete, Schelling comes very close to the theory of *Spinoza about the Infinite Substance and its modi; the religious aspect of this is also found in Schelling.

In the third period he does not consider the Absolute as being Indifferent but he shows it as the divinity, whose ideas realize themselves in platonic sense, in the development of the being.

In the fourth period, finally, Schelling describes the origin of the finite and imperfect as a defection from God, which is possible because of his concept of freedom. The extreme point of this defection is reached in the human Selfness, in which however also the return to God, who is the cause of everything, begins. God reveals his nature in the mythology or natural religion, his personality in the revealed religion. Since the absolute is essentially irrational and is absolute freedom, the rational explanation of being can only be negative, and Schelling counts in this also his own philosophy of identity. He also concludes that the philosophy of the mentioned double revelation opposes it as a "positive" philosophy.

Schelling had very close relations in the first part of his studies, with the leaders of the *Romantic School. F.S.

SCHEMA

Sketchy representation of the imagination which originates in the emphasis on the similarities between different objects of sensual knowledge. There arises then, by approximation, an image of each of the objects of a group. See Phantasma. In Kant's philosophy the schema is the middle between the a priori concepts of the intellect and the sensory phenomena and makes therefore the application of these concepts to the phenomena (data) possible. The schema can be the middle because it is on the one hand sensory and given in the time, on the other hand close to the concept because of its generality. See also the appendix.

SCHEMATISM OF THE INTELLECT is called by Kant the uses of these schemata by the intellect.

SCHILLER, Ferdinand Canning Scott, 1864-1937.

English pragmatist, born in Germany, taught in England and the U.S.A. Main work: *Humanism*, 1903. The question; "what is reality," is senseless. The only thing which makes sense is to find out what we can produce with it. Man is indeed the creator of the reality, which is, without him, absolutely formless. Man is therefore also the creator of truth, because that is only true which influences reality. The influence of Schiller and the American pragmatists is still strongly felt in contemporary *neo-positivism and English *neo-realism.

SCHILLER, Friedrich v.

Born in Marbach 1759, died in Weimar 1805. German poet and playwright, in philosophy influenced by the critical idealism of Kant.

SCHLEGEL, Friedrich v.

Born in Hannover 1772, died in Dresden 1829. German linguist and poet, one of the leaders of the German *Romantic School; was converted to catholicism.

SCHLEIERMACHER, Friedrich.

Born in Breslau 1768, died in Berlin 1834. German protestant theologian and philosopher, idealist, had connections with the *Romantic School, professor in Halle, minister in Berlin.

Schleiermacher considers the identity of thought and existence as the starting point and end of all philosophy. This end can however never completely be reached by us, because in our thought the real factor (nature) or the ideal factor (spirit) always dominate. In man also are nature and spirit connected. Nature gives us through observation the matter of knowledge, the spirit gives through thought the form. The form of thought are also the forms of existence. The real is known in physics, the ideal in ethics. The latter teaches that all moral activity and will must be directed towards the unity of reason and nature.

Schleiermacher agrees with *Jacobi that the great merit of Kant is that he, by removing knowledge, paved the way for faith, but he blames Kant for having limited religion to the fulfillment of the ethical obligation. In order to keep religion in its own essence, he finds its origin in the emotion and limits it to that. This emotion has been described by Schleiermacher in the beginning as an experience of the Infinite, later as a feeling of dependence on the Infinite. Religion does not inquire about the objective reality of the Infinite. It is purely immanent. It is not its duty to make a set of moral rules or express the feeling of the Infinite in concepts. The most it can do is leave it to the different positive religions to express its content in dogmas, which have no more than a symbolic value and can not be considered the expression of an absolute truth. It is not because we give the name God to the Infinite, that we can define more accurately the concept of God. Such a definition has for the religion, indeed, no importance. There is therefore, in the religion of Schleiermacher no personal concept of God.   F.S.

SCHLICK, Moritz, 1882-1936.
German natural philosopher, professor in Kiel 1921-22 and in Vienna 1922-36. Moderate neo-positivist and head of the *Wiener Kreis.

SCHOLASTICISM.
1. THE TERM. In Roman Antiquity the term scholasticus (of the Greek scholastikos) was used as an adjective and as a noun (scholar; sometimes pejorative: pedant). For Hieronymus it means learned man, grammaticus. This meaning was kept during the Middle Ages; originally scholasticus was used for the teacher who taught in the schools of liberal arts; the term has later been generalized to indicate an educated man, who had studied in the scholae. Since the Renaissance and the Reformation are called scholastici the magistri who taught philosophy (philosophia scholastica) and theology (theologia scholastica) in the schools and universities of the Middle Ages; the term got in this period generally a pejorative meaning; one used to allude to the vain speculations of the dark ages, when the human mind was the slave of Aristotle and the papacy. This pejorative meaning can also be found in the writings of the rationalistic historians of the 19th and 20th centuries, who saw in the scholasticism a philosophic-religious syncretism, which barely deserves to be mentioned in the history of philosophy. The term "the School" is usually more neutral or even in praise of the doctrine taught by the great philosophers of the Middle Ages. Neoscholasticism, definitely begun by Pope Leo XIII (*Aeterni Patris*, 1879), wants to continue the great tradition of the School.

2. NATURE OF SCHOLASTICISM. Especially during the first third of the 20th century strong controversies have been carried on about the nature of scholasticism. Some tried to define it by the *schools* where it had been taught, others by its scientific and pedagogical *methods*, its main sources (Aristotle, Plotinus), its relation to the *christian religion* or its dependence on dogma and theology. (Some historians have even wanted to enlarge the term scholasticism, and use it for every attempt to reconcile the philosophy with a positive religious system: there would therefore exist a Jewish, Islamic and even Hindu and Buddhistic scholasticism). Others again wanted to define scholasticism by its *content*: Hauréau was inclined to identify scholasticism with the *dispute about the problem of the *universalia; according* to De Wulf (at least before 1930) is scholasticism *a specific philosophical system,* which is a typical product of the medieval civilization, this system

developed gradually from the 9th to the 12th century, had its highest point in the 13th century, and had its decline in the 14th century; the scholastic synthesis is proper to all "great masters" of the 13th cent.; those who did not accept it were anti-scholastics or independents.—These disagreements are now outdated. Most of these opinions had some truth but were incomplete and often exaggerated. One should agree with them as a whole, by completing them mutually. Scholasticism is indeed the philosophy which was developed in the medieval *schools,* and had therefore a "scholastic" and technical appearance; it had its own *method* (study of the ancient sources, predilection for contemplation, aristotelian views on science, etc. . . .) and its own *expression* (use of Latin, two forms of instruction: the "lectio" or commentaries of a text, and the "disputation" or discussion of a problem; the process of the "quaestio," etc. . . .); it retained much from the antiquity, especially from *Aristotle* and *neoplatonism; scholasticism was taught in the fold of christianity,* and therefore in close connection with theology and under the surveillance of the Church. All these characteristics have had their influence in the formation of its *content,* and we do not have to reject therefore completely the ideas of Hauréau and de Wulf. From the narrow interpretation of Hauréau we should retain that logic and the problems originated in the conceptual character of the human thought have had a major role in the formation and development of scholasticism; with De Wulf we acknowledge, without rejecting the diversity of the schools and the tendencies, that several converging factors (Aristotle, neoplatonism, the Church, christianity, Latin) have given a unity to the scholasticism, which has not been achieved in any other period, and which enables use not to speak of a "Scholastic synthesis," but of a "scholastic patrimonium" (sententia communis, Gemeingut). F.V.S.

SCHOOL OF MARBURG

One of the schools in which, by the end of the 19th century the philosophy of Kant is revived in Germany under the name of *neo Kantianism. (See School of Baden). This school got its name from the fact that the most prominent representatives were teaching at the university of Marburg. They were 'Cohen and *Natrop. The followers of this school continue the development of the Kantian philosophy in the pure logic. Their thought, which has therefore many relations to the philosophy of Hegel, is sometimes also called panlogism. The Marburgers see the philosophy as a logical analysis of the conditions for knowing and willing. The ideal knowledge is, according to them, in the exact sciences. Knowledge is, under no circumstance, an image of a reality outside of knowledge, but it is the reality itself. Only one's own construction of the intellect determines the coming into being of knowledge. Reality is a whole of logical relations and nothing else. The intellect works according to categories. They are immanent to the intellect, so that all thought is a priori determined by them. Truth is agreement of the thought with these categories; untruth is the contrary. How this lack of agreement is possible, since the categories are absolutely a priori, is an unsolved problem. The willing, as for Kant, is completely formal, i.e., only determined by duty. The school of Marburg has however more interest in the social aspect of the ethics, than did Kant in the development of his doctrine. They continuously try to bring Kantian and marxian ethics together: *Cassirer, Gorland, Kelsen, Liebert, Stammler, Vorlander, Bauch. B.D.

SCHOPENHAUER, Arthur

Born in Danzig 1788, died in Frankfurt a.M. 1860. German idealist, the philosopher of pessimism.

Schopenhauer rejects the Kantian *Ding an sich* and reduces, in a positive appeal to Berkeley, the entire world to a representation of the subject. This representation is determined by the organisation of the faculty of cognition and specifically through the intuitive forms a priori of space and time, in which the possibility of an outerworld is given, and through the activity of the intellect, which, with the help of the principle of causality, connects the sensory impressions with the causes from outside and represents them graphically. The intellect can never reach the absolute.

By reflecting on himself man learns however to know himself in his deepest ground as a being, gifted with impulse, needs and desires, in one word: with *will*. Man is a willing being; the intellect has in relation to the will only a secondary and serving role. That what makes itself known to the introspection as will, makes itself known to the sensory knowledge as corporeity or matter. Corporeity is nothing else than will in an exterior appearance. The human body and the will, which can be called its soul, are therefore not two sides or aspects of a same reality, but only the will is real, the body is only appearance.

Analogically with the ground of our own being we also contemplate the other beings as objectification of a will, which differs more from ours in proportion to their differences in external appearances with our body. The absolute Worldground, from which the multiplicity of things proceeds, is the unconscious, blind will to exist. In the process of realisation, the primitive Will goes through a number of levels, which, in a platonic sense, find their exemple in the unchangeable ideas and of which man with his intellect is the highest. To man the world-as-will presents itself as an in space and time experienceable reality.

The judgment, made by man's intellect about the world and its value for man and life, can, according to Schopenhauer, only be a negative judgment. The existence of the world is already an evil: it is even, as opposed to the optimistic conceptions of *Leibniz, the worst possible. The primitive will is indeed a blind and aimless impulse, which never rests in satisfaction, but consumes itself constantly in further striving. Disillusionment will therefore always follow every seeming achievement.

This philosophical pessimism is, according to Schopenhauer, affirmed by the individual experience and by the perception of the misery in the world. This misery is indeed necessarily connected with the existence; it can never be removed or even diminished. Even civilization can not make man better or happier; on the contrary, the more knowledge develops, the stronger our knowledge develops, the stronger we feel this misery. Suffering is therefore highest in the genial man.

The only way to escape the misery of the world, is the liberation from the existence. This can be prepared by the aesthetic contemplation and the disinterested scientific research, a lasting liberation can only be reached by the "Verneigung des Willens zum Leben", a victory over the primitive Will, which is indeed will to live. If this "Verneigung" is reached (not by suicide, because only a specific form of life is destroyed in the suicide, but by a total negation of life in all its forms) then remains for us the Nirvana or the Nothingness, in which finally the final and absolute rest is imparted to us.

Schopenhauer's ethics follow this pessimism. The will which tries to keep life and affirms it, is essentially bad; the basis of the ethical good action is in the compassion, in which one takes the suffering of others on himself and therefore multiplies his own suffering.

The Primitive Will can, because of its freedom, change its impulse to existence into negation of existence, which provokes the disappearance of the world of phenomena, so that only Nothingness remains. The philosophy of Schopenhauer has therefore its crowning in the Nothingness.—F.S.

SCHROEDER, Ernst Friedrich Wilhelm Karl, 1841-1920.

German mathematician and logician. He completed the algebraic trend in the mathematical logic begun by *Boole and *Peirce. The works of Russell and Hilbert have attracted the interest of the logicians, during a few decennia, to other fields, but a series of publications by *Tarski and others have, since about 1940, underlined the validity of the use of the algebraic methods.

SCHWEITZER, Albert

Born 1875 in Alsace, theologian, physician, musician and philosopher of culture. Died 1965.

SCHWENCKFELD, Caspar (von)

German mystical thinker (1489-1561), headed since 1522 the reformation in Silesia, but separated from Luther in 1527. The invisible church and "Christ in us" mean more to him than the historic Redemptor and the church as institution.

SCIENCE

In the *antiquity*: certain knowledge of causes (*explicative knowledge). Aristotle distinguished four questions about the things which we experience about us: do they really exist? What is their essence? How are they? Why are they such? The last question is preeminently the scientific question. Because an answer to these questions requires a demonstration or proof of certitude, is science sometimes also defined as the demonstratively acquired knowledge. A knowledge acquired in this way will naturally form a system of connected truths and in *more modern times* has this systematic connection been considered as the most essential characteristic of science, which received therefore the definition: systematic whole of critically justified knowledge about similar things, seen under a specific respect and ordered according to a specific plan (*systematics, *architectonics). Not only the systematically ordered knowledge itself is called science, but also its rendering in textbooks and professional works.

The different sciences are, since old, distinguished according to the *object of study*. One speaks of a *material* object, which several sciences have in common, as e.g. man in physiology, psychology, sociology etc. and a *formal object* which is proper to a specific science and consists in the specific respect in which the material object in this

389

specific science is considered, as e.g. there exists in man organic, psychic and social life, etc. On the grounds of the *pursued aim* we can distinguish the 1)theoretical or *speculative* science, which as "pure" science strives towards cognition for cognition's sake and 2) the practical or *normative* science, which tries to reach a knowledge which will help us to act decently, inasmuch as it teaches us the exact norms through which we can achieve it. On the *method followed* is based the distinction between 1) positive or *inductive science*, limited to the study of positive facts and using the inductive methods to determine the more or less regular happenings and connections of these facts, and 2) rational or *deductive* science, which tries to *explain the perceived facts and things rationally, going out from other facts or only rationally knowable causes and principles. Since *Dilthey a distinction is made between *spiritual* and *natural* sciences: the latter is concerned with the progress of nature, which is the object of our external experience; the former with the spiritual life of man, the therefrom proceeding cultural phenomena and its historical evolution, which is all object of inner experience, through which we again live it: as opposed to the natural science is the spiritual science not susceptible of real repetition.—I.v.d.B.

SCIENCE OF ART.
See theory of art.

SCIENCE OF KNOWLEDGE
Wissenschaftslehre, term invented by Fichte for the science which studies the logical and epistemological questions: if and to what extent is science possible. The entire logic, being the theory through which we know that we know, can be considered as a science of knowledge (Wissenschaftslehre); more especially the part which deals with the proof through which we have "certain knowledge of the causes" (*science). In later years has the science of knowledge been added to logic as a more or less independent methodology, often under the name of "logic of sciences" or "applied logic".

SCIENTISM
Way of thought dominated by the idea that the positive sciences (experimental)—at least when they come to full unfolding—are able to satisfy completely the human desire for knowledge. These sciences would themselves determine what problems are justly posed: they are furthermore not dependent on philosophy and metaphysics as to the way their problems are stated, because both philosophy and metaphysics do pose only seeming problems. See *positivism.

SCOTTISH SCHOOL, ca. 1750-ca. 1850.
A philosophical school, with Thomas *Reid, Dugald *Stewart and James *Beattie as main representatives. Was especially opposed to the sceptic conclusions of David Hume, the theories of French materialism of the 18th cent. It appealed to the principles of the "common sense", which give us intuitive and evident knowledge of the reality. Sir William Hamilton (1788-1856) is usually mentioned as its latest representative.

SCOTUS
See Joannes Duns Scotus.

SCRIPTURAL PHILOSOPHY
Name given by the Calvinistic

professors D.H.Th. Vollenhoven, H. Dooyeweerdt, H. G. Stoker and others for their philosophy, on the grounds of their thesis that philosophy can only be built on the Scriptures, because only Scriptures can give it a solid basis. They reject therefore all efforts to bring about a synthesis between God's revelation and the profane or "apostate" philosophy. Philosophy should be reformed, i.e. should reject all not-scriptural motives and follow the pure calvinistic line. This does however not mean a stiffening of philosophy to a purely scriptural content. It means only that the Scriptures, as some put it, have to give the archimedic point, on which reason can lean to build its philosophical system. There is also a possible variation within this framework. Dooyeweerdt, for instance, chooses the scriptural idea of law as archimedic point, Stoker the idea of creation.—K.L.B.

SECRETAN, Charles

Born in Lausanne 1815, died there 1895. Swiss philosopher of religion, professor in Lausanne. Considers his "philosophy of freedom" as a christian philosophy, which will try to justify the foundations of the christian religion for the reason and therefore will keep the middle road between rationalism and fideism. The proof of the truth of christianity is in the fact that the dogmata of this religion satisfy the needs of the normal religious consciousness (immanent method).

SELECTION, NATURAL

Concept in the theory of *evolution. Given a certain instability in the nature and the struggle for the existence, often remain the most able individuals; this choice is called the natural selection. The value of the natural selection can not be denied, but it is often presented in an exaggerated manner.

SELF-CONSCIOUS

*Consciousness of oneself, reflection on one's own existence, the experience of the Ego as really existing and differentiated from the other (*outer-world). Kant says that the self-consciousness contains at the same time the consciousness of the outer-world. In the popular language also the consciousness of one's own value.

SELF-DETERMINATION

The principal independent choosing of one's own form of life. The reflexive activity of the intellect creates the possibility for self-determination, *self-consciousness and *self-knowledge. The animal lives irreflexively, i.e. lacks the possibility to be conscious of the separation between subject and object, oneself and the experienced world. The reflexion, necessary for every reflexive act, is the product of an higher spiritual maturity. It is less given to the infant, the untalented and the primitive man.

SELFISHNESS

*Interest which is directly and solely determined by one's own profit, more particulary considered as pleasure; leads necessarily to egoism.

SELF-KNOWLEDGE

The *reflexive knowledge which one has of oneself, of the ability and possibilities of the Ego, but especially of one's weakness and limitation. For many philosophers is the self-knowledge the cornerstone of virtue and wisdom (a.o. Socrates and Kant).

SELF-LOVE

Love of one's own being. It is not necessarily egoistic and does not necessarily require that one think himself superior to others.

SELF-MOTION

Is called in scholasticism the proper characteristic of all *life. Better is *self-industry*, because motion or activity is also proper to the dead matter, while only the organism is actively industrious for its own preservation and the preservation of the species. Typical is the continuous reaction and influence on the environment, from which matter is picked up and stimuli received, while all this becomes again useful for the own continuing existence. One can therefore also define the activity of the living beings as "self-motion through the action of stimuli".

SELLARS, Roy Wood, born 1880.

American critical realist.

SEMANTICS

Has different meanings. The philologists (since Bréal) use this term to indicate the doctrine about the meaning of the expressions of language; in an analogical way we can use the same term for the study of the interpretation of the symbols (in formal systems). These last years the term semantics has been used in more narrow sense indicating the doctrine of the relations between formal symbols and their logical meaning, mostly in contrast with the syntax which studies the rules of formalism in themselves. The doctrine of the truth, of the meaning in its different forms, ("Sinn" and "Bedeutung", as distinguished by Frege) are considered in the semantics, also the rules of the semantic paradoxes, where expressly is alluded to the expression and the truth. Is also considered as semantics, every theory or definition which starts expressly from

concepts as truth or meaning. In spite of the masterly written contribution of Tarski and Carnap, the domain of the semantics is still not clearly defined.—R.F.

SEMIOTICS (or semeiotics)

The general doctrine of the *symbolisms. Its subdivisions are the *syntax, *semantics, and *pragmaticism. The formal logic is not a part of semiotics. Semiotics does however contain all the parts of the *metalogic.

SENECA

Born in Cordoba (Spain), died 65 A.D., educator of Nero and executed by him. Main works: *Naturalium Quaestionum libri VII*, *Dailogorum libri XII* and the *Epistolae morales* composed for Lucilius. Seneca is especially interested in ethical questions, not especially trying to discover the essence of virtue, but exhorting to the real practice of it. Philosophy has for Seneca a practical aim, it must bring man to accept a specific attitude in life. This however does not exclude his interest in physical and metaphysical problems: in these he is however not very original and seems very much leaning on Posidonius. In the psychology he follows Plato, because he accepts in the hegemonikon of the soul a reasonable and reasonless part. He also emphasizes the distance between soul and body and considers the body as the jail of the soul. In ethics he emphasizes the human fragility and accepts the relation of men among themselves as the basis for the practice of charity, also for the slaves; the divinity is indeed present in all men.—G.V.

SENSATION

The old psychology looked for the basic element of the psyche in sensation. However, the analysis of the sensory experience leads to descriptive final terms which have no real existence. In any case, its characteristics are: intensity (strength), extensity (extent) and protensity (duration). One can also call the sensation the prephase of knowledge, which awaits a fulfillment. In a philosophical sense, sensation is exclusively the act of the external sense organ, free from memory, aptitude or intellect. The cooperation of these factors leads to *perception.

SENSATIONALISM (sensatio=feeling)

Doctrine which asserts that man does not know anything except that what he perceives with his senses (see experience). All activities of thought are considered as psychic events, in which sensory representations are changed and combined but still remain more or less complex sensory representations, which can again be reduced to sensory perceptions, according to the laws of this psychic event. The experience being the only thing man can know, we must classify sensationalism as one of the forms of *empiricism, but it remains different from empiricism because it limits the experience to the purely sensory. In ethics sensationalism teaches that the satisfaction of the sensory sphere is motive and aim of activity (see hedonism). Sensationalism was already defended in ancient philosophy, by the school of Cyrenaica (Aristippus) and epicurianism. The English empiricism of Bacon and Hobbes develops into the sensationalism of Hume. The sensationalism of the French Enlightenment (see Condillac, who was initially influenced by Locke) had for a long time influence on psychology.

SENSE

Sensory faculty of cognition, can be distinguished in inner and external senses; a tendency towards and an appreciation of something. Taken logically: meaning and aim of something (significant against *senseless); logical or reasonably justified connection of concepts and words (opposite of *absurd); a connection, based on human understanding, of meaningful words or terms as understandable exterior expressions of what one thinks and feels on the inside (Lat. oratio): more definitely: as enunciation (lat: enunciatio) of an inner *judgment.

SENSELESS

Something is senseless when it has no meaning for the subject, or seems to be aimless. The senseless is no essential characteristic of the object, but is applied to the object by the subject. What is senseless for me, can therefore make sense to somebody else.

SENSE-ORGAN

Organ of perception, through which man and animal can acquire impressions from the outer and inner-world. In more narrow sense only in relation to sensory perceptions, for which the sense-organ is the physiological organ. For the inner senses mostly used exclusively in the philosophical terminology as sense or sensory faculty (e.g. sensus communis).

SENSUALITY

The faculty of sensory perception. The sensory experience is then opposed to the spiritual experience. In ethics: unordered desire for physical delight (*hedonism); often in the sense of sexual desire.

SENTENTIAE

Theses and argumentations, compiled for the first time by *Petrus

393

Lombardus to serve as a basis for the instruction.

SEQUENCE

Is used in some works as the common name for *dyads, triads, tetrads etc. . . . Gentzen uses this term for an *assertion of deductibility.

SERIES

See function.

SEXTUS EMPIRICUS, 3rd cent.

Belongs to sceptical school. The *Outlines of Pyrrhonism* give a summary of the sceptic doctrine. In the *Adversus Mathematicos* (Against the Mathematicians) he attacks the theses of the stoics.

SHAFTESBURY, Anthony Ashley Cooper, third count of,

Born in London 1671, died in Naples 1713. English moralist and philosopher. Lived for some time in the Netherlands and for many years in Italy. Knew and admired the philosophy of Plato, Epictetus and Marcus Aurelius. His works were published in 1711 under the title: *Characteristics of Men, Manners, Opinions, Times.* In man are certainly passions which drive him to self-interest and happiness, but they can be subordinated to altruistic feelings, which promote the well-being of the society. Man has an innate feeling and discernment for good and evil, which Shaftesbury calls the "moral sense". He also develops an aesthetic view on world and life, in which he emphasizes the harmony in the universe and the harmony of the possibilities with the cosmic order. Shaftesbury has been numbered among the deists, he blamed the positive christianity of having taken away the purity of the human virtues, by promising rewards in the hereafter. He remained how-ever, during his entire life, loyal to the church.—F.B.

SHAME

Is the feeling of petrifaction in a being which knows that it is "uncovered" in what it is—limited, weak or malicious. The other, who finds out, can be God, the neighbor or, in a separation of the consciousness, the Ego. Shame is for Sartre the proof of the existence of the *other (autrui); for Scheler physical shame diverts a person's attention from the purely sexual in order to make possible a spiritual and personal association.

SHINE

The appearance a thing has because of the light it radiates. Heidegger thinks that being means to appear, and shine would then be identical with being. However, the sight which something shows us from nature, can be received by us from different sides, so that the representation which we form in ourselves does not show any more the being but does rather conceal it. Shine becomes then pure shine or seeming or deceit.

SIDGWICK, Henry, 1838-1900.

English philosopher who tried to unite *idealism and *utilitarianism.

SIGER OF BRABANT

Born in Brabant ca. 1240, died in Orvieto between 1281-84. Magister artium in Paris ca. 1265, taught there from the beginning a rather dangerous aristotelianism, against which Bonaventura reacted (1267, 1268), later Thomas (*De unitate intellectus,* 1270), finally the Bishop of Paris, who condemned in 1270 13 propositions, extracted from the doctrine of Siger and his followers. After a new intervention of Bonaventura (1273) and a period of confusion, Pope John XXI asked the Bishop of Paris to make a report about the errors taught at the university. The Bishop, Etienne Tempier, who was himself a very conservative theologian, overdid his work and condemned in 1277 219 propositions about the aristotelian and all pagan philosophy in general. Siger fled France and went to Rome to defend his position at the curia. He was acquitted of heresy but had to stay at the Roman curia. He died there, killed by his secretary (clericus) who had become insane. The only works of Siger are notes taken by his disciples. They cover all fields of philosophy. E. Gilson and B. Nardi doubt the authenticity of a series of commentaries on Aristotle.

The philosophical point of view of Siger is the logical and more or less fatal end of the evolution through which the faculty of liberal arts in Paris went: the study of the pagan philosophical literature and of Aristotle especially, had transformed the school of "liberal arts" into a school of philosophy, where the cult of Aristotle and the autonomy of philosophy grew more and more. There came therefore a naturalistic and rationalistic attitude into existence, which would finish into a serious crisis, as soon as it became clear that the thought of some of the philosophical thinkers was in opposition with the christian thinkers. This happened with Siger around 1270. He taught a fundamental aristotelian philosophy, completed with the metaphysics of Proclus and Avicenna, and the psychology of Averroes. This *neoplatonistic aristotelianism* was under many respects *heterodox*: the world is from eternity and necessarily created by God, who can only pro-

duce immediately one effect, namely the first heavenly Intelligence; There is only one intellectual soul for the entire humanity, and therefore only one immortal soul common to all men; there is therefore only one will for the entire humanity, namely the will of the unique intellectual soul. The freedom of this will was very much endangered because of the intellectualistic interpretation of the act of will, which Siger borrowed from Aristotle. These conceptions endangered also the moral and religious order:

1° because God, according to the system of Siger, reigns over the sublunary world through other creatures; as He also creates with the help of other creatures. 2° because the mono-psychism kills all responsibility and immortality in the human individuals. After the condemnation of 1270 Siger was well aware of the contradiction between his philosophy and his faith, all historians recognize now that he stayed a true christian. In later years he tried to lessen the tension and to explain the oppositions between his philosophy and his faith, but he did not succeed. —Dante placed Siger in the 4th heaven of the *Divina Commedia*, the heaven of light; He is a part of a crown of 12 famous thinkers, with Thomas Aquinas as coryphaeus; Siger is the personification of wisdom and Dante praises him for having remained faithful to his vocation, in spite of the enmity of the theologians.—F.V.S.

SIGN
    See symbolism.

SIGNIFICA
    Aims at the psychological and sociological investigation of the human means of understanding in

general and especially of the relativity of the meaning of the language expression. See Mannoury.

SIGWART, Christoph von, 1830-1904.
German philosopher, specialist in Logic.

SILESIUS
See Angelus Silesius.

SIMILARITY
is a *reflexive and *symmetric relation. The similarity is, in addition, *equivalent if it is *transitive. Such a similarity can be considered as an identity under a specific view-point.

SIMMEL, Georg 1858-1918.
German vitalistic philosopher, professor in Strassburg. Much under influence of *Dilthey, can be considered as a precursor of the *existence-philosophy, although his thought is closer to *pragmatism. Every man belongs to a specific type, which determines, via the physical structure, the mind. Life let only come up those thoughts which are useful for self-preservation. Knowledge is therefore in the service of life. Truth and profit for life are therefore identical. Simmel reaches here a pragmatic conception of the knowledge.

SIMPLICIUS, 6th cent. A.D.
Belongs to the neo-platonic school of Athens, accepts the complete conformity of Plato and Aristotle. Especially known for his commentaries on Aristotle's *Categories, Physics, De coelo et mundo De anima;* of importance are a.o. the many historical data he uses.

SIMPLE
Not complex. Reality can be relatively (or seen from a specific point) simple. Every structure consists eventually of simple principles; the Thomists assert that a pure spiritual being has a simple nature. Only God, according to the scholastics, is completely simple: pure act of being. In the Platonic view the appreciation of the simple ranked very high. The scholastics further worked out the doctrine of simplicity in relation to that of *perfection. See also concept, term.

SIMULTANEITY
The concept of simultaneity, which is in itself very clear, has occasioned, since the rise of the theory of *relativity, very important philosophical discussions. The theory of relativity demonstrates that it is not possible to establish without any doubt the simultaneity of events which happen at a certain distance from each other. Many philosophers have therefore concluded that to the concept simultaneity no objective sense can be connected unless the events happen at the same place. This philosophical consequence, however, is not included in the theory of relativity; it proceeds from a combination of this physical theory and a specific and very positivistic view. Even if we cannot establish the homogeneity objectively, it does not necessarily mean that homogeneity cannot exist.

SIN
Morally evil action seen in religious perspective, as a resistance against the personal God or His commandments.

SINGULAR or individual,
See concept; proposition.

SIRACH, Jesus, son of c. 200 B.C.
Author of the *Wisdom of Jesus the Son of Sirach* (Latin title: *Ecclesiasticus*), not accepted into the Protestant canon but included

396

among the books of the Apocrypha; a work of proverbial wisdom and personal confession.

SITUATION

One of the ten *categories; the further definition of the manner in which something is in a specific place, e.g. sitting, standing, kneeling, etc.

Condition in which an independent reality, as for instance man, is actually found.

SIZE

The different sorts of *numbers form ordered classes, in which the following elements are usually *greater* than the previous ones. This makes the numbers suitable for characterizing the number of a quantity and the length of an object. The number of a quantity is determined by a count, for which always a unity of length should be chosen beforehand. The measuring of other greatnesses is always reduced to the count of numbers and/or of lengths.

SKEPTICISM

The view that man never can be sure that the conviction that he has knowledge, is justified. This doubt can be limited to one domain of knowledge, e.g. metaphysics, but it can also be universal: a doubt which denies to all human knowledge, certitude and even probability (*probabilism). The reasons given for scepticism are: the insoluble differences of opinions among men (*sophists), the relativity of sensual knowledge and the lack of a satisfying criterion for truth (*Sextus Empiricus) or, for *Pyrrho, the fact that there are as many reasons for as against a proposition. This scepticism, as a doctrine of doubtfulness of all knowledge should be distinguished from the doubt as a method (even

universal), in which the truth value of human knowledge is questioned as long as it does not present itself to us with inevitable certitude.—J.P.

—In the Greek philosophy three schools belong to this attitude of mind:

1. *The Older School,* in Alexander's times; main representatives: *Pyrrho of Elis,* whose doctrine came to us through Sextus Empiricus, and *Timon of Phleius,* the syllogiser. Among the causes for the origin of scepticism we should mention in the first place, the great variety and opposition of philosophical systems. In addition: the ordinances of Alexander which had opened the world, so that the ideas and ways of life of other people were known; the events following the death of Alexander, the mutual quarrels and the tyranny have also brought a severe blow to the traditional Greek philosophy; the deep corruption in Athens during this period, had to lead to doubt about truth and virtue. The sceptics can therefore not be put on the same level as the *sophists: they are much closer to the *stoics and have a certain affinity with Democritus and Socrates.

2. *The later Academy:* belongs also to the sceptical trend, but scepticism is here less radical: it is directly directed against the dogmatism of the Stoics, so that not all knowledge of truth is abandoned. The main representatives are: *Arcesilaus and *Carneades. Arcesilaus fought as much as he could against the stoic doctrine of the cataleptic representation as criterion of truth and he accepts that the only true attitude in life for the wise man is doubt and suspension of the judgment. The wise man will not follow the rules of tradition and habit, but appeal to his own insight and

discernment. Carneades followed the same ideas but gave in to necessities of practical life. He is therefore satisfied with the probability. He opposes the Stoic doctrine of the Providence, manticism, universal sympathy astrology.

3. *Later Scepticism*, associated with the older tradition of the sceptic School, developed since the first and second century B.C. The most important representatives are *Aenesidemus, Agrippa* and *Sextus Empiricus*. These younger sceptics have summed up their criticism against dogmatism in a few main arguments which they call *tropoi*: the main idea in these basic arguments is the relativity of the observation and of every judgment; they do however prescribe certain norms in relation to practice: namely subjective observations, ideas and tendencies on the one side and on the other side law provisions, habits and scientific findings.—G.V.

SLAVE MORALITY

According to Nietzsche the morality which, as do the slaves, positively appreciates that what is weak, and calls evil that what is strong, hard and horrible. This morality would originate in the *resentment of the weak against the strong (e.g. the christian morality).

SMITH, Adam, 1723-1790.

English economist and philosopher, defended free competition and free trade as the main source of economic wealth. His main work *The Wealth of Nations* (1776) had much influence on the later development of economic theories. In ethics he followed mostly the theories of his friend *Hume; the feeling of sympathy for the fellow-man is the central phenomenon and the driving-force in ethics.

Through sympathy man recognizes and estimates virtue, it is also the basis for virtuous living.

SOCIAL (socius, companion)

In connection with the relations of men mutually, in connection with the life in *society. Aristotle says that man is from nature a social being, so that he not only strives towards a life in society but also he can not reach complete satisfaction without this life.

SOCIALISM

This term has been used first in France around 1830, indicating a social ordering which would consider the general good and not the profit of particular people, classes, parties etc. . . . (*utopians). It is only under the influence of *Marxism that a strong enmity against the existing individualistic-capitalistic regime was introduced.

SOCIETY

In a broad sense, all groups of human individuals. The problems which arise in this connection are solved, since Comte, by the *sociology.

In a narrower sense, this human group, which stays together in as much as its members work purposefully together. This co-operation can be determined contractually (see Rousseau). The unity of the society is then more based on convention than on natural or organic union, as the community. The individual is then also less affected.

SOCIOLOGISM

Theory according to which the civilisation as well in its physical as in its spiritual aspects can only be explained by social situations. The *sociology seems therefore to be the basis for all cultural sciences.

SOCIOLOGY

The science which studies the

essence of the *society and *community, their origin and forms, the relations between individuals and the community. This science has become an independent subject since *Comte (XIXth cent.), although these problems were already studied in the antiquity. The main representatives of sociology were in England: *Spencer and J. St. Mill, who followed the positivistic leanings of Comte; in Germany important contributions were made by *Hegel's philosophy of law and philosophy of history, which had influence on the historic *materialism of *Marx; also by *Dilthey who considered society and community as phenomena of the objective *spirit; *Simmel studied especially the forms of relation among individuals; *Tönnies pointed out the fundamental difference between *community and *society; *Spann was the most important representative of the universalistic school. In recent years the U.S.A. have taken in this field a very important place, however the border between sociology and social psychology is not clearly drawn.

SOCRATES, 469-399 B.C.

Son of an Athenian Sculptor Sophroniscus and a midwife Phainarete. Some claim that he was the disciple of *Anaxagoras and of Archelaus. As citizen he distinguished himself in the siege of Potides (432-429), by saving the life of the young Alcibiades, and in the battles of Delium (424) and Amphipolis (422). In 406, at the age of 63, he was named "prytanus" of the generals and participated in the sea battle near the Arginusac. In 399 he was condemned to death in Athens where he drank the poisoned cup.

The influence of Socrates on the history of Greek philosophy is ex-

treme. With him finishes the period of the old natural philosophy and turns the philosophical contemplation to the enigma, which man is for himself. It is however very difficult to evaluate the exact contribution of Socrates to philosophy since he left no writings. The oldest witnesses are, if not contradictory, at least very different from each other. According to the *Apology* and the *Memorabilia* of Xenophon, was Socrates a nobel but somewhat banal moral teacher. Aristophanes describes him in his comedy *Clouds* as a dangerous sophist. Aristotle in his *Metaphysics* characterizes him as the philosopher who studied the inductive and definition-loving method, applied to ethical concepts as justice, bravery, truth etc. . . . Plato, Socrates' genial disciple, spoke extensively about his master. In most of his dialogues is Socrates one of the parties. In the so called Socratic dialogues, of which the *Apology, Phaed. Crito* are the best known, Plato gave a very clear image of the manner in which Socrates influenced people. But often he ascribes to him ideas which are his own, so that it is not always clear to know what ideas are his and which ones are his master's.

Socrates however appears for us as a somewhat unusual citizen, who gave himself in absolute disinterest to the intellectual education of his fellow citizens. Not that he wants to give something positive, on the contrary, he is convinced that he does not know anything; but the conscience of this ignorance is for him the real wisdom. He wants to convey this wisdom to others and he verifies to see if people who claim to know something really do know. He interrogates well known authorities in several fields about their specialty, but, by continuing constantly his questions he comes eventually to the point that the man who claimed to know something has to agree that he does not know anything. This art of interrogation was compared by Socrates to the midwifery (maieutic), this method got them an "ironic" character, because it always leads to the confusion of the adversary. Socrates asked a general, one day, what bravoury was, but the general became very soon entangled in his explanations. A priest could not tell what exactly piety was, and a poet could not explain what real poetic inspiration was etc. Most of these dialogues finish in disillusionment; no definition is found which can resist the scrutinizing questioning of Socrates. The only positive result he seems to contribute is that only one thing gives value to life: to learn, as well as possible, to know oneself, by analysing accurately and intellectually what seems at first to be simple, and in this way to look for the rational meaning of life, and sometimes to find it. Socrates wanted to convince his fellow-man of this truth. He had, said he, a "demon" in himself, a warning voice which prevented him to leave even for one moment, his vocation. It could have seemed, through these questionings, that the established moral and religious values were based on loose grounds. Young people especially liked to destroy the values in which more serious people had faith, but they lacked the intellectual strength and the moral honesty which was characteristic of the thought and life of Socrates, so that Socrates was accused of sapping the traditional religion and turning the head of the younger generation.

Socrates has probably followed a too rationalistic method when he tried to lay the foundations of his ethics. He thought indeed that someone who had a clear and rational insight in the action he should pose, would necessarily act well. The conclusion of this would be that virtue can be taught as any other theoretical subject. The role of the free will is too much underestimated. Socrates had much influence through his disciple Plato and through the many socratic schools: the *Megara, the *Elic-Eretric school, the school of the *Cynici and of the *Cyrenaica.— F.D.R.

SOLIPSISM

Theoretical attitude of the one who says: only I exist, I do at least not know of any other being that it is. The basis of this idea is that everything I experience to exist, has no other existence than mine and that of my subjective situations. The other ego's are my images.

This isolation of the individual is only possible as a logical effect of *idealism, and even of the empirical idealism, which teaches that the individual ego (and not the *transcendental ego) produces the existence of the thought. Husserl tries to avoid the solipsism in his *Cartesian Meditations*. Also *subjectivism, *conscientialism.

In practical sense the term solipsism is sometimes used to indicate the attitude of people who care only for themselves (egoîsm).

SOLOVIEV, Vladimir, 1853-1900.

Russian philosopher and theologian. The divine Soleness of all the existence is the center of his thought. This Soleness can however not be seen in a pantheistic sense: the beings do not come into being through emanation but through the creation by God. From here on Soloviev conceives a philosophy

THE SISTER FRIDIAN READING ROOM

This room was the Bass Family's formal
houses many of our current periodicals
index, INFOTRAC, that will help you fi
articles you need. The INFOTRAC progi
SFC library indexes approximately 400
as diverse as Sports Illustrated and
Public Health.

18. Use INFOTRAC to identify a biogr
     H. Norman Schwarzkopf.

     title:_____

which is at the same time a philosophy of religion and a history of philosophy.

SOMA (Greek: body).
Opposed to psyche or to principle of life. Also in compound words as: somapsyche or the vegetative "Ego" (Wernicke). For Weismann, the individual body as opposed to the germplasma.

SOMBART, Werner, 1863-1941.
German economist, sociologist and philosopher.

SOPHISM
A *paralogism intentionally made with the intention to bring somebody else to error. Example: a part exists only for the whole, man is part of the state, therefore man exists only for the state.

SOPHISTS
Greek authors of the 5th-4th cent. B.C. They represent a crisis in Greek thought and form the transition between the *natural philosophy of the presocratic philosophers and the classical, towards man oriented Greek philosophy. They were strolling professors and lecturers, who wanted to teach more knowledge through instruction, and also taught the young people who wanted to become politicians, the art to convince through the use of words. They were mostly relativists, so that they tried to defend opposing ideas with the same power of persuasion. *Plato was their strongest antagonist. He reproached them to have abandoned the love of truth. In his dialogues he made fine parodies and fun of them. He perhaps did injustice to them. Aristotle does not consider them as real philosophers.

They were extremely well read, had an encyclopedic knowledge of all sciences of their time, but all this served only to furnish their speeches. The main goal was to find arguments for their art of discussion. The sophists have through this, invented the rethorical technique and have it developed. They held their own, often paradoxical ideas about the state, law and the diverse cultural problems. The most important sophists are: *Protagoras, *Gorgias, *Prodicus, *Hippias, *Antiphon, *Callicles, Lycophron, Trasymachus. See also Anonymus Iamblichi.—F.D.R.

SOREL, Georges 1847-1922
French socialist, a leader in the "syndicalist" movement around the turn of the last century. Works: *The Decomposition of Marxism* (1908), *Reflections on Violence* (1908), *Illusions of Progress* (1911).

SORITES
A shortened *polysyllogism, in which the middle conclusions are omitted. E.g. All acts of cognition have spiritual objects of cognition; spiritual objects of cognition presuppose spiritual forms of cognition; a spiritual form of cognition presupposes a spiritual independence; therefore acts of cognition presuppose a spiritual independence. The *regressive* sorites, in which in the conclusion, the first *premise is connected with the P of the last one, is also called aristotelian sorites; the *progressive* sorites, in which in the conclusion the last premise is connected with the P of the first, also called the goclenic sorites (Rud. Goclenius, 1547-1648). It is more than clear that false propositions can easily creep into a sorites.

SORROW
Spiritual affliction. Sorrow is an

emotion which strikes the entire personality. The problem of sorrow has become in the modern psychology, especially under influence of the existentialistic thought, a central anthropological problem. This means that one does not consider sorrow as a psychic attitude in itself, but that one is interested in the original experience of the sorrow as a personally experienced condition.—P.S.

SOUL (Greek: Psyche, Lat: anima)

Principle of life. When one accepts that the living beings are constituted according to the *hylemorphistic (matter-form) principle, then is the soul the substantial form of the body. The form acts according to an aim (teleologically) upon the matter (entelechy), actualizes the potency of the prime matter (materia prima). Aristotle distinguishes three forms: the vegetative soul (for plants), the sensitive soul (for animals) and the rational (human) soul. The activities of the anima intellectiva include the activities of the anima vegetativa and sensitiva. Vegetative and sensitive souls do not surpass the domain of the body, they are inseparably connected with the matter and perish with the matter. The human soul is not intrinsically bound to the matter and continues to exist independently after the disintegration of the body.

The faculties of the vegetative souls are feeding, growth and reproduction; the faculties of the sensitive soul are in addition motion, sensation and appetite. The faculties of the human soul are in addition thought and striving. Materialism, positivism and scientism teach that the activities of plants can be reduced simply to physical actions and chemical reactions. The organicism (Descartes) teaches that the plant is a machine, without an inner principle of its connected parts and without aiming. Vitalism teaches however that an higher principle should be agreed on, either as an accidental characteristic or as a complete substance. The aristotelic-thomistic view teaches on the contrary the incomplete substance, which does not exist in itself.

According to the theory of the evolution no separation exists between the different levels of life, but all proceed from one or more primitive forms. The higher forms of life came into being through milieu, heredity and point of time (Lamarck), or through natural selection (Darwin) or through abrupt mutations (De Vries).

The human soul, as principle of spiritual life, is simple and spiritual. The trichotomy, which considers the soul, the vegetative and sensitive principles of life as being really separated principia, contradicts the reality and can not explain the unity of man's life. The spiritual soul can therefore not proceed from the animal soul, neither from the soul of the parents (*generationism, traducianism). The human soul owes its existence to a creative act of God. Once created it can not be annihilated or dissolved in parts by created forces. It can however be hindered in its expressions. The survival of the soul depends therefore immediately on God, the Creator (*immortality of the soul).

Opposed to the aristotelian-thomistic conception that the soul is a substance, bearer of the qualities, materialism teaches that only physical, physico-chemical activities exist (Büchener, Pavlov, Bechterew). The philosophy of actuality rejects also the concept of substance: the being coincides with the becoming. The soul is therefore the continuously changing complex of psychic actions and experiences (Heraclitus, Bergson). The psychology of actuality (Wundt, Bergson) teaches the only existence of acts, not of things. The act-psychology thinks in the same sense. Positivism rejects the existence of the substance, starting from the postulate that science can not be reduced to metaphysics. Kant also excludes in his *Kritik der reinen Vernunft* the concept of substance.

One distinguishes the faculties of the soul according to their formal object (truth, goodness etc.) and to the nature of experience of the acts (memory, intellect, feeling, will etc.). The faculties of the soul are no parts of the soul, which is simple. The soul works through its faculties. One distinguishes the spiritual from the sensory faculties. The former are of an higher order. The precedence of intellect (intellectualism) or will (voluntarism) has not definitely been settled.

A very special conception about the soul is found by *Klages, who opposes soul and spirit to each other ("Geist der als Widersacher der Seele"). Soul is here, in vitalistic sense, the natural principle of life, that in its spontaneous, irreflexive unfolding and activity is hindered by the "Geist", which is of a rational, reflexive nature.

The problems about the soul gave rise to an age-old dispute still going on today.—P.S.

SPACE

There are three conceptions about space. The first one says that space is a reality in itself, a kind of general receptacle, in which the objects can be put and can move. In this opinion space has only mathematical qualities, it is purely extensive, empty and without physical qualities. Well known defenders of this theory are: Democritus and Clarke, a contemporary of Newton.

According to the opinion defended by Kant, space is only a form through which our senses view: we can not see things otherwise than in space and spatially because of the structure of our senses. This is the space seen as: "Anschauungsform a priori".

The third opinion considers space as an "ens rationis". It admits the reality of spatial measurements but does not consider them realities in themselves, but as abstract considerations of the measurements of the objects. This opinion is shared by Aristotle, Thomas Aquinas and many philosophers today. It is implicitly the basis of the modern sciences.

For space-time continuum see theory of *relativity.—C.J.M.v.M.-B.

SPAULDING, Edward Gleason, 1873-1940.

American philosopher, first neo-realist and later idealist.

SPECIES

A *universal concept (*predicable), which can be applied to several things (of the same sort) and indicates of them the common essence. To the species corresponds the logical essential definition (*definition) a compound concept, consisting of the nearest *genus and the *distinction of species: e.g. the plant (species) is a living (distinction of species) body (genus).

—If one accepts that several individuals (e.g. men) belong to a same species (in this sense that their essential definiteness can be expressed with the same terms and that therefore their definition is the same) the question arises if the ontological *reason of the *individuation has not really to differ from the reason of the specific perfection, so that both, correlatively united, form a structured (e.g.; hyleformically composed) *substance.

—The higher, more general species can, as classes, contain several lower species; the lowest most strict species contain only individual concepts. In logic for instance (*tree of Porphyry); in the living *nature* however is the species the most clear distinction one can make: all plants and animals consist of species, man forms one species. Every species exists in *races; the difference between species and race is not always clear. It is generally accepted that the deciding characteristic of a species is that there is an ability of mutual procreation. Crossings between different species happen, but are sterile. Although one has to agree that one species can pass into another, especially when one accepts the *evolution theory, one never has actually witnessed the creation of a new species.

In psychology, image of cognition, through which and in which something is known. The scholastic philosophy distinguishes sensory and intellectual species. The former are only sensory impressions, which determine the sensory cognition to the cognition of specific objects, while the latter are divided into *species impressae*, which determine the intellectual cognition to a specific object, and the *species expressae*, namely the *concepts in which and through which this object is known intellectually.

SPECIES-INDIVIDUAL-STRUCTURE

Everything and every event in matter is at the same time something individual and concrete and something which has some facets in common with other things and events. A specific motion of the falling of a specific stone is unique as this concrete fall, while it also belongs to the categories: "motion of falling", "stone" etc. . . . All what is physical is then holding a duality, so that it shows as well something individual as something specific.

It is therefore possible that the natural sciences conclude from experiments with concrete pieces of copper to general qualities of copper and the contrary, apply the data obtained previously to individual copper. Without species-individual-structure no induction or deduction would be possible.

SPECIFIC

Determining a *species. Opposed to generic, determining a genus.

SPECULATIVE

See science.

SPEECH

Use of language as opposed to system of language. Unity of speech is the sentence. The one who uses language combines elements of the language system and applies it to a particular situation. He has for this a certain freedom. On this is based the possibility of a particular style.

SPENCER, Herbert

Born in Derby 1820, died in London 1903. English sociologist, positivist and evolutionist.

Spencer is convinced that cognition does not reach farther than the world of the becoming, the domain of the phenomena. He therefore holds that the "synthetic philosophy", which he teaches, will bring the knowledge of the phenomena completely to a unity, by deducing them from a few a priori certain tenets: the indestructibility of matter, the continuity of motion, the continued existence of the energy. The fundamental law of all happenings in the world is the continuous re-division of matter and motion. This process is divided in origin or development and the opposite: decay. Development contains always increase in concentration and also a change from smaller to greater definiteness, and an increasing differentiation of the parts. From the simple comes the complex, from the nebula the solar system, from the first primitive form of life the most complex phenomena in man and society. This process happens purely mechanically, without any purpose.

In applying the concept of evolution in the organic and psychic, ethic and social life, Spencer uses the idea of the "struggle for existence" and of the importance of the role of the external causes and the surroundings in this life, which were explained by *Darwin.

Cognition and morality are also products of evolution. The individual has in his brainstructure the heritage of his ancestors. He is then in possession of a few truths which can not be deduced from his personal experience, in theoretical and in practical domain, and which form the basis for his knowledge and which are for him a priori while they are for the human species a posteriori. Morality has always a relation to attitudes which need always to be considered in their social aspect. Morally good is the act which is adapted to the social surroundings i.e. contributes to the well being of the acting subject, his descendants and his fellow men. Because of the evolution of the social environment, the determination of morally good and morally evil is also subject of changes. Through the inherited experience of the ancestors can man indicate the content of the morally good and judge the moral character of the actions.

The order of what can be known, which seems in its appearance to be led by the law of evolution, requires however a causal explanation, which can eventually only be found in a first cause, highest reality, infinite and absolute, which is however, because of its absoludity, unknowable. Spencer borrows here the arguments of *Hamilton for the unknowableness of the unconditioned. No attribute can be applied to the Absolute or denied. At the edge of the phenomena we stand before the inscrutable enigma: "the great Unknowable". We only see the "veil of the phenomena" and know that behind it something else must exist, but *what* it is remains forever concealed. In this *agnosticism, which in opposition of that of *Comte has a positive character, sees Spencer a good means to reconcile faith and cognition. It will be the religion of the future and its only dogma will be the recognition of the Unknowable as that through which all things exist.—F.S.

SPENGLER, Oswald, 1880-1936.

German philosopher of culture, whose *Untergang des Abendslandes*, 1918-22 had a great influence. In this work Spengler develops a relativistic philosophy of history. Every man is absolutely determined by the culture of his time. Every culture has a specific duration, after which it is inevitably doomed. This period of doom has come for the European civilization.

SPEUSIPPUS

Plato's successor as head of the Academy. First principles are Oneness and Multiplicity from which he deduces the mathematical numbers, which take in his opinion the place of the ideas of Plato. He does not, as Plato did, identify the Oneness with the Good and could therefore avoid the consequence that Multiplicity is identical with Evil. The Good, he teaches, is not in the beginning but is the result of a process of evolution. Speusippus was interested in empirical research: he wrote a work about the classification of animals and plants. He also wrote several works on ethics, which left some traces in the works of later writers.

SPINOZA, Benedictus de (Baruch d'Espinoza)

Born in Amsterdam 1632, died in The Hague 1677. Born from Portuguese-Jewish parents, mostly self-taught. Expelled from the synagogue of Amsterdam because of unorthodox ideas; in his last years for many an example of serene philosophizing.

Spinoza entered philosophy through the works of Descartes and he has in many fields developed Cartesian conceptions, but he borrowed method and content more from the Jewish philosophy and mysticism, from the Arabic philosophy and the platonism of the Renaissance. As for Descartes, Spinoza holds that clear and distinct concepts are the criterion of truth and certitude; he also uses the geometrical method in philosophy, this method starts from a few sharply composed definitions

and axioms and deduces from them theses. He uses this method because it gives man the most evident insight in the connection of the conclusions. The philosophy of Spinoza wants however to give a religiously oriented rational insight in the world, to serve as a basis for man's relation to the infinite being. Spinoza has in common with other great thinkers that his system has been interpreted in many different ways. His system and doctrine is most completely found in his posthumous work *Ethica, more geometrico demonstrata*. All fields of philosophy have their place in this work and are all related to the highest good; philosophy satisfies the urge for happiness, because it makes clear the unity of man and the all and because it connects man in intellectual love (*amor intellectualis Dei*, borrowed from Leone *Ebreo) with the infinite.

Since the order of being is identical to the order of cognition, the knowledge of the whole reality can be deduced from the ideas. The infinite plenitude of being, cause of itself, whose essence contains the existence (ontological proof of God's existence), which is in itself and is understood by itself, is the substance. Attribute is that what the intellect understands as composing the essence of the substance, while modus (way of existing) is that what is in the other and is understood by it. Only one substance can exist, God, because the substance is necessarily infinite. This substance is composed of an indefinite number of attributes, and each of them expresses the eternal and infinite essence.

God is immanent; all transcendency of God is negated; he does no more have a personality (see pantheism, monism). From the nature of God, which is considered necessary, come forth in an infinite number of ways an infinite number of things, there is however no freely choosing causality or finality. God is considered the cause of things, in the same way as a geometrical figure is considered as the cause of the resulting qualities. It is a causality in the order of cognition of logical foundation, with which the real order is identical.

It remains unclear how Spinoza saw the origin of finite things in the infinite. The one divine substance becomes conscious, in the infinite multiplicity of attributes, to be *natura naturans*: i.e. the (logical) moment, when God is going to produce a *natura naturata*. Man knows only two of the many attributes, in which God becomes conscious of himself: thought and extension. Both kinds of finite individual things, bodies and spirits, have to be understood in the corresponding attributes as in their logical ground. In addition to the multitude of attributes there will also be found a multiplicity within the attributes to explain the many separate things. This infinite number of finite ways of existence determine each other to mutual laws and order, which is borrowed either from the infinite modus of extension, or from the modus of thought. The latter is the infinite intellect as principle of thinking an unlimited number of things in an unlimited number of ways, while the former (motion and rest) is the principle producing an infinite number of details of extension.

The task of the philosopher is to reach the third level of knowledge, in which we understand the essence of the things in God as in their necessary ground. This knowledge unites us, with pleas-

ure, with the known object; this moment still is absent from the second sort, which gives the *notiones communes* or general principles of the things, while the first sort, the opinion or imagination is formed through the observation and the resulting representation, which is still subject to errors.

Affects are called by Spinoza emotions of the human body, which improve or hinder the skill in actions; the same term is used for the ideas of these emotions. The value of the affects, as well for the body as for the mind, must be measured by their ability to help us to be active in the existence, i.e. in making something happen outside of us, of which we are the adequate cause. This is so because everything tries, from nature, to continue to exist in its own existence. We must underline the fact that the body can not determine the spirit to thought and that the spirit can not determine the body to motion, rest or anything else.

The moral order coincides with the deepest order of being, which is no more for anything else, and good and evil can therefore not be determined by an aim. Virtue or strength lies in the as conscious as possible striving towards continuous existence. Beatitude is not a reward for virtue but it is virtue itself. The highest unchangable beatitude is in the *amor intellectualis Dei*. A purification of the inadequate ideas is required or a victory of reason over imagination. As long as the spirit undergoes some things, it has inadequate ideas, when it is active it has adequate ideas. The complete adequacy is reached by applying the ideas to the idea of God, and therefore seeing everything in connection and unity with God or in the light of the eternity (*sub quadam specie aeterni*). This intellectual love for God is eternal and is a participation in the eternal love, which God has for himself. As idea we are immortal, but not as an individual, working with imagination and memory. Who loves God can not desire that God loves him (as an individual) God's love for himself is however also love for man; so becomes our love social; therein lies our salvation, our happiness and our freedom of mind.

The Bible has only religious meaning and does not want to communicate knowledge. Faith and cognition are totally separate. Spinoza is a defender of freedom of conscience. He accepts a natural right which goes as far as man's power goes. In the state the human relations are regulated according to reason; men congregate in society, although they are from nature hostile to each other, because of the necessities of life and the fear of solitude. Spinoza defended first the democracy but preferred later a more aristocratic form of government.—H.R.

SPIR, African, 1837-90.

Russian philosopher, living in Switzerland, spiritualistic positivist.

SPIRIT

Originally the immaterial being which is the principle of life (*see* pneuma): Descartes still speaks of world spirits. Spirit is furthermore limited as the principle of consciousness. As such the spirit is called by °Klages the *"Widersacher"* of the soul or of the source of the vital energies, and the source of the sufferings which are created through culture. The spirit is defined in a still more narrow sense when it is considered the principle not so much of the consciousness as of the activities of consciousness (*see* Nous). Spirit is thus that which is indivisible, simple and active, be it being or force, because the spirit can be personal or impersonal. In the first case there are the pure spirits, substantial beings who possess and determine themselves completely in thinking and willing. God is such a spirit, the perfect Spirit; also those spirits whom the Christians call angels. Man, however, may be considered an incarnated spirit. The question arises then how the interaction between body and soul operates. Since Descartes the soul has no longer been considered a general principle of motion, but has been conceived as pure spirit. Even when one speaks of the spirit as of a force, this force certainly differs from matter yet is always involved with matter. Bergson believes that the spirit has to break through the resistance of matter, and the idealists think that the spirit realizes itself in and through matter. Schelling says that the Absolute Indifferent unfolds itself in spirit and nature, which opposition will eventually be lifted in an equilibrium. According to Hegel, all reality is a development of the Absolute, and spirit recognizes itself as spirit in consciousness only after being opposed to itself in Nature. A further dialectic process is then developed in the *philosophy of the Spirit*. With Hegel we can distinguish between subjective, objective and absolute spirit. The *subjective spirit* is the spiritual in the individual, the specific way in which he grasps, expresses and forms the objective and general. The *objective spirit* is the spirit of a group, existing in the consciousness of the members of this group. It is especially expressed in the life of law, state and nations. The *absolute spirit* is the divine spirit, free of subjective and objective spirits. He reveals Himself, however, in the synthesis of subjective and objective spirit, in art, religion and philosophy.—J.Gr.

SPIRITUAL

That which, being immaterial, transcends the laws of time and space and belongs therefore to an other than the material order.

Every pure spiritual being (e.g., an angel) is immaterial. Immaterial also is the being which is in one respect material but which also has immaterial qualities and structural elements (e.g., man, physical in his body, spiritual in his consciousness, thoughts and will, therefore also in his soul).

Of spiritual as well as of material reality we form a positive and a negative concept. Because we feel that we are living and are conscious of our basically one but structured activity, our acts appear to have at the same time positively organic and positively spiritual qualities, which cannot be reduced to each other. These qualities we observe immediately; the organic ones are essentially connected with matter, i.e., with movement in time and space; all the spiritual qualities point toward concentration in self-possession, such as consciousness, reflection and personal insight, freedom and autonomy. But organic and spiritual qualities, irreducible to each other, appear in the same human behavior and elucidate each other, through their opposition, in a negative way. Spiritual means immaterial, not extended in space and not divisible (but united in an indivisible, conscious and free-deciding ego); material is not-spiritual, not ego-conscious, not free (but cosmically united and governed by physical determinism).

Man, insofar as he is not physical, is free from the determinism and evolution of physical reality. This is of essential importance when one questions his origin and end; because the naturally spiritual, in its origin as in its survival, remains spiritual in its end.—L.D.R.

SPIRITUALISM

In more broad sense, is the philosophical theory which ascribes to the immaterial or spiritual in the order of existence and in particular in man, its own reality, which makes it different as well from the inorganic matter with its mechanical definiteness as from the living with its spontaneous immanent activity and makes it also independent from them. In this sense spiritualism can go together with *dualism.

In a more narrow sense spiritualism means the conception that the whole reality is, in its deepest grounds, of a spiritual nature, so that the inorganic matter as well as the organic life should be considered as phenomena of the spiritual.

As an historical movement is spiritualism born in France, as a reaction against the *ideologues. Independent thinkers tried, each in his own way, to find the foundation for a spiritualistic view of the world. The most important of those thinkers are: *Maine de Biran and *Cousin. The strongly eclectic philosophy of the latter became the official philosophy during the monarchy of July, and it still had followers by the end of the 19th century. Less eclectic is the spiritualism of *Vacherot, which seems to be very close to the German idealism; *Ravaisson-Mollien comes even to spiritualism through his attacks on eclecticism. Based on the idea of the spiritualism that life, activity and freedom have a meaning for the explanation of the things, christian thinkers are searching for a further connection between philosophy and christianity: protestant thinkers as *Secrétan; catholic thinkers as *Bordas-Demoulin, *Gratry and *Ollé-Laprune. The latter do not think that the world of the suprasensual can be reached through the ways of the intellect, but let man strive to it through will and action, and through the needs of the mind. A similar spiritualism is taught in Germany by *Eucken?—F.S.

SPIRITUALITY OF THE SOUL
The immaterial, simple and *spiritual nature of the soul, as the basis of life in man. Descartes thinks that this principle is also substantial. According to Thomistic views, it constitutes, together with matter, the human being. The soul is, however, not necessarily bound to matter: it transcends matter in its activities.

SPIRITUS (Latin: breath, spirit)
The spiritual principle in man (*soul).

SPONTANEITY
The activity because of own inner impulse. There is spontaneity in human thought in as much as it exceeds with its own force its dependence on the immediate contact with the physical experience through insight in the nature of what he experienced as being and through *abstraction, also in some degree as being-such; in *Kant's philosophy however in as much as it by means of the concept brings the multiplicity of the sensory perceived (angeschaute) in the unity of the object. The "natural" orientation of thought as opposed to the expressive *reflection. In psychology is spontaneity a trait of character, very close to the so called primary function; opposed to reactivity (secondary function).

SPONTANEOUS
That what happens, without previous initiating motion or exterior stimulus.

SPRANGER, E.
Born in Berlin 1882, later professor in Leipzig, Berlin, Tübingen. Developed the ideas of *Dilthey into a "Verstehende Psychologie", which, not as the experimental more physically oriented psychology, emphasises the understanding of senseful relations and structures. He combined Hegelian conceptions about subjective and objective spirit with the neo-kantian philosophy of values of Rickert.

He came in this way to his important work *Lebensformen*: these Ideal Types of the human attitude of the mind, which originate because "jeweils eine gestimmte Sinn- und Wertrichtung in der individuellen Struktur als herrschend gesetzt wird". He distinguishes six types: the theoretical, the aesthetical, the religious, the economic, the social and the man of power.

His "verstehende Psychologie" especially developed in his work: *Psychologie des Jugendalters*: puberty is the time when the young man becomes a personality, because he learns independently to choose a positoin in respect to the different domains of value and can bring the (physical) sexuality and the (spiritual) eroticism to an harmonic integration.—A.M.J.C.

SQUARE, LOGICAL
The schematic representation of the *opposition of the propositions. The A, E, I and O-propositions are placed in the four corners of

the square; immediate *reasoning.

STAMMLER, Rudolf, 1856-1938.

German neo-Kantian philosopher of law of the School of Marburg, professor in Berlin. Main works: *Die Lehre vom richtigen Recht,* 1902; *Theorie der Rechtswissenschaft,* 1911; *Lehrbuch der Rechtsphilosophie,* 1926; *Rechtsphilosophische Grundfragen,* 1928. Stammler applies the kantian concepts, form and matter, to the jurisprudence. The form is the right, which judges everything a priori in connection with the final goal of the community. Matter is the cooperation in the social life. Positive right is right in the real sense, only when it is directed towards the welfare of the community. Right belongs with ethics to the final order: it is a form of willing. The rights concept points in its unlimitedness to the idea of right of a universal rights appreciation. The validity of the right is connected with its ability to be carried out. This will be dependent in general from the organisation of the state. State and right are however not correlative: no state can exist without right, but right can exist without a state.—B.D.

STANDING

Social group which is not only characterized by the same economic situation and interests (*class) but also by a distinct group consciousness. This comes from the practice of a same profession or the same social function and is expressed in similar habits, morals and conception. Several philosophers tried to make the more or less natural ordering of the human society in standings, the principle of the organic extension of the state.

STATE

A *community or *society of men, based on rights, which is sovereign i.e. not dependent on other states or societies. The aim of the state is to promote the prosperity of all the subjects (persons or groups) and the protection of their rights against the subjects of the same state or against other states. The subjects of a state do not necessarily form a *people. One people can be distributed over several states and in one state could live several peoples.

STEINER, Rudolf 1861-1925.

Founder of the anthroposophy.

STEWART, Dugald, 1753-1828.

One of the most distinguished thinkers of the so called *Scottish School, who developed, through his great academic work and eloquence, the theories of this school and especially those of *Reid. He abandoned the term *common sense,* which was characteristic for this school and teaches that the fundamental laws of human belief, or the primary element of human reason are the basis for our knowledge of the reality.

STILPO

Born in Megara, taught in Athens ±320 B.C. Disciple of *Antisthenes and belonged therefore to the school of *Megara. He taught as did his colleagues, that the wise man has in himself the autonomous rule of life, and his goal is the complete rest of mind or apathy.

STIRNER, Max

(Ps. of Johann Kaspar Schmidt), born in Bayreuth 1806, died in Berlin 1856. German individualist and anarchist, follower of *Feuerbach; The individual in his ownness and privateness is the only reality and the ethical actions are only determined by the interest of the individual, with exclusion of

411

all altruistic motives and all social duties.

STOIC SCHOOL

Philosophical school who dominated during the entire hellenistic period, no less than 5 centuries (from ca. 300 B.C. to ca. 200 A.D.) the philosophical thought of antiquity. The name comes from the place where the doctrine had its origin, namely the colonnade in Athens. One distinguishes in the history of the stoic school generally three periods:

a) The older stoicism, with their main representatives: *Zeno of Citium*, the founder of the school, *Cleanthes of Assos,* disciple of Zeno and his successor as head of the school, *Chrysippus,* successor of Cleanthes, sometimes called the second founder of the school.

b) The moderate stoicism, characterized by the mingling of stoic doctrines with aristotelian and platonic elements, which was true, in certain measure, for Cleanthes; *Boetheus of Sidon, Panaetius of Rhodes* and *Posidonius of Apamea.*

c) The neo-stoicism is a return to the strict conception of the older school and an interest, about exclusively, for ethical questions. *Seneca Epictetus,* and emperor *Marcus Aurelius* are the main representatives. In what follows we explain mostly the doctrine of the older stoics.

The importance of the stoic school for the history of formal *logic* is that it was the first to be interested in a logic based on the mutual connection of propositions with each other, and not on the qualities of the concepts: so was the *proposition-logic prepared. Distinction is made between simple and complex propositions. In regard to the hypothetical reasoning (the major is a conditional judg-ment) Chrysippus distinguishes five tropes, i.e. five figures based on the arrangement of the terms and the propositions in the reasoning; about the truth value of the hypothetical judgments, the implication is considered valid if no true antecedens appears with a false consequens.

The *epistemology* of the stoic school has to be called a sensualistic materialism: all knowledge has its origin and remains at the level of the sensual: the sensory perception leaves an image; many of these images or memories constitute the experience: several similar images and experiences form a general representation (ennoia). Truth exists in the correspondence of knowledge and reality; it is not immediately in the representation, but in the following agreement; the wise man will only give this agreement to representations which are clear enough to warrant an agreement; he will therefore really catch the object of cognition with his representation, i.e. he will come to a cataleptic representation.

As origin of the existing reality the stoics accept in physics two principles: matter (as passive principle) and the creating pneuma, also called logos. This active principle penetrates the matter and produces from the formless matter the diversity of the cosmic reality. It is considered as a kind of creating fire, penetrating everywhere and which is principle of order and law in the cosmic evolution. The entire world is determined indeed by the pneumatic logos, which is working as a kind of forming germinal force (*logos spermatikos*) in every individual being and forms one being with the formless matter. So originate the different levels of perfection in the world and the distinction between plants, animals

412

and men. The world itself forms one organic whole, a perfect living being in which everything is regulated by the immanent logos. The existence of the world shows however a periodic character, in this sense that everything regularly originates from the first principles and regularly returns to these principles. The divinity is immanent, while it is in a certain way also transcendent: it is indeed the worldsoul, but mostly the highest part of it, the hegemonikon. The living beings have their own pneuma, which originates, through a process of partition, from the parents; the highest part of the human soul is the hegemonikon, seated in the heart and which is the seat of the life of cognition and striving. Man is free in the acceptance or rejection of the cosmic happenings, although this acceptance or rejection does not influence the evolution of the happenings in the world. After death the human soul continues to exist for some time.

The greatest influence of the stoics was in the domain of *ethics*, because their ideal of life did correspond very closely to the cosmopolitan and individualistic desires of this period. All men have to be considered as citizens of one and the same polis, which covers the universe so that the higher beings belong to it: the difference between Greek and barbarians has to be put aside and the slaves should be treated as human beings. The highest norm of action is to live in accordance with one's own nature, and bring one's innerness in accordance with the logos which dominates the cosmic evolution. Man therefore must avoid to be misled by passions, which would befog his judgment; the wise man strives towards a complete apathy, as a guarantee for the

moral life. The wise man will on the other hand pursue unconditionally the good; the stoics do however point out that the object of the action is indifferent; only the disposition is of importance. There are however some things for which one rather strives than some others, which one wants to avoid; if one strives to the first one then is this action, in normal circumstances, proper, but to be a completely good action one has to have the necessary disposition. Other actions which are in normal circumstances bad, can be good under certain circumstances. There is thus a very important place in morality for the inner disposition of the acting subject.—G.V.

STRATO OF LAMPSACUS
Ca. 287 head of the Lyceum for 18 years. No fragments of his metaphysics have been saved; his psychology is close to the materialistic doctrine of the pneuma of the Stoics; especially interested in physics.

STRAUSZ, David Friedrich
Born in Ludwigsburg 1808, died there 1874. German theologian and popular philosopher, follower of the leftwing of the Hegelianism, later materialist. In his much discussed *Leben Jesu* (1835) he presents the person Jesus, as he appears in the Gospels, as a myth.

STRIVING
One of the classical triad know-feel-strive, the great trio of the human faculties. In modern psychology is the power of striving (vis appetitivus) or the faculty of striving (facultas conativus) dealt under the name function of will (see will) in connection with philosophy is the faculty of striving (appetitus) generally the inclination towards an object, which is

413

suitable. One can distinguish the *sensual* appetite from the *spiritual* appetite (for the latter see will). One can also distinguish between the *natural* appetite and the *rational* appetite. The former is connected to the essence of each thing or the nature itself of the thing in as much as this is pointed towards its end (does therefore not necessarily to be sensory); the latter, also called conscious appetite follows the known form or the knowledge. The sensual rational appetite is treated in modern psychology under the *feelings and *passions. P.S.

STRUCTURAL FIGURE

is in the logical systems of the natural deduction a rule of deduction a rule of deduction which is not concerned with the logical operations (in whose formulation therefore no other signs are used than the sign of deductibility and the comma).

STRUCTURE

the ordering of parts through which a whole originates. Speaks therefore of a social structure, atomstructure. The term is often used in a narrower sense for an ordered unity whose elements, because they belong to a whole, are completely defined and can therefore not appear, at least without serious changes, outside of this whole. This is true for logical and for real totalities.

In philosophy this same image is used: Thomas Aquinas for instance considers the connection between *potency and *act as a pure correlation, and he considers the reality of every finite being as a structure, which is more or less complex according to the fact that it is a physical or spiritual being, but whose elements are in correlation to each other, in varying ways but always according to the model of the relation between potency and act. The Hegelian "Begriff" is also a structure, and it is through the moments of this totality that the dialectic thought can clear a way. L.D.R.

—In the psychology the terms structure and *Gestalt are often used one for the other. Structure is however in this sense, more than Gestalt, pointing to values, and the term is often reserved for the entire soul (Spranger). Krueger limited the meaning of the term structure—as opposed to Gestalt—to the conditions of the experience; structure has then no relation with the actual content of consciousness (e.g. a perception) but the dispositions to it. The term was also used elsewhere (L a z a r u s, Steinthal, Titchener) in another meaning.

Spranger's psychology, which teaches that man acts according to a privileged domain of value (religion, economy, etc.) is a *structural psychology*, in which man is not seen as a collection of elements, but as a totality, which is finally determined. Characteristic of this concept of structure is the dependence of the elements on a whole (Gestalt) and the insertion of this whole in a greater domain of values. P. S.

Two *aggregates* have the same structure when between their elements exists a univocal relation so that in the first function a specific relation exists between elements if in the other function a specific relation exists between the corresponding elements; identity of structure for aggregates is therefore the same as ordinal *homogeneity.

The concept structure can be adapted to deductive *systems*, if we consider the systems as a collection of objects of thought and *assertions, which are in relation to the deductive relations ordinal homogeneous.

The same concept can be adapted to the relation of a system to a symbolism (*formalism); the *symbolism* becomes then a structural symbolism.—R.F.

STUMPF, Carl, 1848-1936.
German philosopher and psychologist, professor in Berlin. Stumpf had much influence on *Husserl.

STYLE
The formal and expressive unity of the art form, in as much as this unity is the absolute graphic and aesthetic stature of the personality of the artist. The artist will, because of his connection with the spirit of the society and the period in which he lives, express the typical elements of this spirit. In this sense we can for instance speak of the baroque style, the style of the early-gothic sculpture etc., depending if the accent is put on the general typical or the individual characteristics. In neither of these cases can we consider the style as a kind of fixed shema, on the contrary, it is very dynamic and the borderlines are very difficult to draw, at the same time is its unity only revealed and realized in a living and still continued evolution. In short, style is the spiritual originality, which reveals itself in general and in a everything penetrating way in the aesthetical form of the specific artwork, the whole oeuvre of an artist or the art of a period or a social group. L.V.K.

SUAREZ, Frencesco
Born in Grenada 1548, died in Lisbon 1617. Spanish Jesuit philosopher and especially theologian, very prolific writer (28 vol.), named *Doctor eximius* by Benedict XIV. Important for philosophy are: *Disputationes metaphysicae* and *De*

legibus. The difference between philosophy and theology is for Suarez much clearer than in the philosophy of the Middle Ages, although Suarez also exposed his philosophy as a basis of his theology. He had a sharp knowledge of the philosophy of antiquity and of the Middle Ages, he gave commentaries on Thomas Aquinas whose arguments he studies very carefully and several times he does not agree with him. Sometimes he is closer to Scotus or the nominalists, whom he however attacks. Often the accusation of ecleticism has been made against him, pointing out that the systematic unity becomes weaker. He seems to be more modern because of his many quotations and the fact that he named his sources and also because he gave an historical view of the origin of the problems.

Essence and existence are, for Suarez, in the real existing things not distinguished in potency and act; he however distinguishes the essentia actualis from the essentia potentialis as ens and non-ens. He places the well known problem on another level than the one in which the thomists used to see it. The most proper to a creature, in which it differs from the Creator, is found in the existential dependence. God and creature are analogous in the "esse", but he gives a certain priority in the unity of the "esse" above the differences.

As Thomas was, so is Suarez in the question of the universalia a mitigated realist; but the intellect has a certain intuition of the individual, while Thomas thinks that it is only intellectually knowable because of the imagination. The doctrine of the abstraction has therefore in Suarez's philosophy another nuance.

Suarez attributes to the materia

prima more actuality than did Thomas. The principle of individuation is not in the materia, but in the intrinsic principles, because of which a thing exists as a being, i.e. in the physical things: in the materia, forma and the union of both.

Suarez goes always out from the individual existing thing and makes a very sharp distinction between the real and logical order.

He rejects, in the discussion about molinism, the explanations of Banez, and he himself proposes a congruism.

Hugo de Groot and other jurists acknowledge the importance of his philosophy for the natural rights, the law of nations and the constitutional law. He tries to find the just middle between the individualism and absolutism of the monarchs. He defends, in the problems of the origin, carrying and transfer of the power of the state, a sovereignty of the people as a natural right, coming from God's Will. The carrier of the power is indicated by direct intervention of God (in the Old Testament) or by the decision of the people. This doctrine of the sovereignty of the people was especially attacked in England where the King thought that he was directly called by God's grace.

The controversies, begun already during Suarez's lifetime, continue today. His influence on the scholasticism of the 17th and 18th cent. was great, also in the protestant scholasticism of the German and Dutch universities. Suarez is an important link between mediaeval and modern times.—H.R.

SUBALTERNATION

The purely quantitative opposition between two propositions, which is not a real opposition, because the general proposition presupposes the particular; e.g. all things are changeable and some things are changeable. *Subalternation of the sciences,* means their subordination on the grounds of aim, object of study and applied principles.

SUBCONSCIOUS

(Under the consciousness.) The words subconscious, *unconscious and preconscious are often used one for the other, but subconscious really means: that what in principle can not become conscious and still belongs to the psychic life (Morgan). In Freudian sense the term subconscious is used for that what can not become again conscious, except through an analysis.

SUBCONTRARY

Or seemingly contrasting, the qualitative opposition between two particular propositions, which is not a real opposition, because both can go together; e.g. some things are changeable and some things are not changeable. Both can however never be false at the same time.

SUBJECT (literally: that what is placed under, what carries, what is the basis of).

In *logic*: that of which something is said, affirmed or denied. Subject is therefore the term of a proposition which is as the bearer of the judgment, because the comprehension of the predicate is applied to its extension; mostly indicated by the symbol S. In *ontology* that what is the bearer of a determining or specifying form. So is the independent being, bearer of the "esse" according to a specific manner, the subject or suppositum, more definite the independent being, bearer of accidental definitions (as quality and quantity) and namely bearer of the activities, which also proceed from it. The subject, as origin of the activities, is opposed to the object, which is that toward which the activity is directed and is specified by it. In psychology is the subject the independent bearer of consciousness and freedom, or the person responsible for his activities. Subject is then opposed to the only sensual and vegetatively living beings or things. In a more narrow sense and in the epistemology is Subject: the bearer of the acts of cognition, either actual acts of cognition or acts of cognition as such, directed towards that which is from nature the object of human knowledge. In this latter case it is the human subject (or consciousness) in general. If one asserts that the knowing subject never can be recognized, as such, in the manner of an object, then we have a transcendental subject, in the sense the different idealistic schools attach to it (a.o. Kant, neo-kantianism, Husserl).—J.P.

SUBJECTIVE

Related to a subject, belonging to a subject and even dependent on a subject. It said of the human knowledge to indicate that this knowledge, as the activity of a subject, is determined by the way the subject exists (which is the knowing man). Because he is a physical-spiritual being, man can come to a more explicit cognition of the beings according to their existence (objective) in and from the physical experience situation, in which this existence is given him implicitly.

Subjective is often used in a pejorative sense, indicating then the knowledge which is so much determined by man that it can not reach an objective knowledge, valid in itself, or because, for instance, inclinations or emotions influence the knowledge, or because one thinks that man as man is unable to penetrate the truth. This exists in the phenomenalism.—J.P.

SUBJECTIVISM

Tendency to relate everything to the subject, so that the latter, in no way, can go outside itself. More definitely: the human knowledge is reduced to a pure condition of the knowing subject, completely explained by the subject. Knowledge has therefore no conformity with the reality as this latter is in itself independent from the subject, it is only valid for the individual subject or at least for the human subject (transcendental) as such. In ethics subjectivism denies the objectivity of the values, they are in last instance only the expression of that what the subject desires or strives for. The subjectivism finds in the relativity of the morality an indication that its thesis is valid.

SUBJECTIVITY

The quality of having a relation to the subject, to belong to the subject, to be subjective.

Subjectivity of the sensory qualities: is the term used by those who accept, on the grounds of the limitation of the senses as physical organs, that the qualities, experienced by the senses, are not something of the physical beings (interpretationism). One can however oppose to it that immediately perceived things are in fact a (objective) reality, conditioned in its being, as well through the presence of that what can be perceived as through the influence of the sensory organs by that perceivable.

The subject, as organism, is itself therefore involved in the object of the perception, but the perception does not have, for that reason, less relation to a situation which exists (and in this sense is objective)—J.P.

SUBLIMATION (Lat. sublimare, life up).

Plato called already sublimation the evolution of the (homosexual) love for the spirit, art, politics, science, the absolute truth and beauty, the Idea. The psychological use of this word begins with Nietzsche: "Sublimierter Geschlechtstrieb", the sex urge diverted from its original aim and directed towards a higher good. Psychoanalysis used the term with the restriction that the sublimation happens unconsciously. It also thought to be able to prove that the substituted higher aim is always related to the original object of the primary passion. The same term is now used to indicate the realisation of a passion or tendency in a higher form.—P.S.

SUBLIME

Aesthetical category, in which the spiritual meaning reveals itself in a graphic way as transcendent over the form—but in this form itself. The sublime has therefore at the same time something formlike and something formless. This formless can appear more implicitely as extreme widening of the form (e.g. in the Moses of Michelangelo) or as positive violation of the form (e.g. the sight of a desolate mountain range).

SUBREPTION

The unnoticed error crept in an inference.

SUBSTANCE

Has sometimes the meaning of independent reality or suppositum. One calls then *first* substance the suppositum in its concrete reality: so is the human being Peter a substance. The *second* substance is the same suppositum but in its quiddity, or considered abstractly: this can, in a proposition, be said as a predicate of a subject. E.g. Peter is a human being or has a human substance. In this sense it is the first of the ten aristotelian categories. Also the tree of Porphyry.

The meaning of the term is then further extended to all quiddity, as well to those of logical as of real contents of cognition, as well to those of accidental as of independent realities: e.g. de substance of a conception, the substance in a quality, in an attitude.

The term substance gets a metaphysical meaning when it points to the real but not perceivable ground of what an independent being is in itself and of what it remains when it changes (i.e. becomes otherwise without becoming another). It is here not an abstract aspect of a logical part, but a real principle of structure, a metaphysical part of the suppositum. This principle appears as a real subject in which accidental changes are received, as the substratum on which these accidental changes are based. The question is now: how can one prove and how has one to conceive this distinction between substance and accident.

Many reject vehemently a largely spread but untenable theory of the substance: as an unchangeable basis it would be spared of all change. There is however a saner theory: substance and accident contain nothing outside of their correlation and can therefore not be not participating in each other. Real change contains implicitly indeed a specific relation of identity and diversity: the structure of substance and accident is nothing else than the necessary following ontological basis in every finite and active reality.—L.D.R.

SUBSTANTIA

Was first used in the sense of existence and substance, for Boethius:

person. Officially accepted in the philosophy of the Middle Ages. Once it had, as a neutral plural, a physical meaning.

SUBSTITUTION

Replacement e.g. of a changeable logic symbol by a concept, so that the contentless symbol receives a specific content. For the symbol SaP, I can substitute: all whales are mammals.

SUBSTITUTION (in formal logic)

Is distinguished in universal (necessarily universal) and not necessarily universal substitution. In a *universal* substitution a variable is everywhere, where it appears in a specific whole (e.g. in a thesis), substituted by the same expression. No necessity exists for a *not-necessary universal* substitution to be substituted in all places; not necessary substitutions are generally related to complex, exchangeable expressions.

Two expressions are *exchangeable* if one can be used arbitrarily in place of the other. This is among others the case in the simple logic for equivalent propositions, in the combinatory logic for convertible expressions.

SUBSTITUTION (RULE OF)

In virtue of a rule of substitution, a specific assertion remains valid, if its variables under certain conditions, are replaced by symbols of a specific sort.

SUBSTRATUM

Underground, under-carriage, support, in indefinite sense. So is the substance in a sense the substratum of the active evolution of a being, but also more than that.

SUBSUMPTION (Lat sub-sumere)

Placing of a concept under a more embracing concept. For instance place a concept of series under a concept of genus. According to the subsumption theory, the judgment is in fact placing a subject (minor) under the extension of the predicate (major).

SUCCESSION

The fact that the parts of an extensum have a fixed order of before and after, so that one part only can be completed after the other. There is therefore succession in motion and in time. Also in the series of the natural numbers.

SUFFICIENT GROUND (or reason), principle of ——.

"All that is has a reason (ground) that it is and that it is what it is." The principle, formulated by Leibniz, is enclosed in the intelligibility of the being as being. All what is lays in a way open for the intellectual cognition. The being, as being is true (with ontological truth). Only what is absolutely not, is absolutely incomprehensible. But when the intellect grasps something as being, it does not necessarily grasp in what way

Taken logically, the principle of sufficient reason states that every proposition is logically based. The immediate ground of a proposition (at least of a deduced proposition) can be found in other propositions, but the final ground of every proposition is always the existential ground of the being.

The principle of causality proceeds logically from the principle of sufficient reason, when one asks for the sufficient ground of the being, which it does not have in itself.—J.P.

SUM (logical)

Is usually identified with the alternation.

SUMMA

Collection or compendium.

419

SUPERNATURAL

In a strict sense, everything which surpasses created nature; thus everything God grants man, not on the grounds of his nature or resulting from the psychical and moral necessities which are required by his nature, but through grace and God's goodness. Such are: the vocation of man to participate in the divine life of the Trinity and the means to reach this end: revelation, grace.

SUPERSENSUAL

What cannot be reached through the senses because it belongs, naturally, to a higher (i.e., transcending all sensory data) order.

SUPPOSE

To expect, foresee with some certitude. Also applied to something unfavorable. In both cases is the entire person involved.

SUPPOSITION

Or substitution, the sense in which a term, according to the logical requirement of the applied predicate, has to represent S and P in a proposition. There is no supposition in a proposition as: "Napoleon flees (should be: fled) from Elba". If there is a supposition, then it can be a *material* supposition, i.e. use of a term for the grammatical word itself, e.g. man is a word of three letters; or a *formal* supposition, i.e. the use of it for what the term means. This can again be taken in the real or in the metaphorical sense, e.g. the scape-goat is sent into the desert. There is also a universal and particular supposition: e.g. Dutchmen are good sailors. The term can have to be taken in broader sense: e.g. all life "proceeds" from life; or in a more narrow sense, e.g. Eve is the mother of all "living". The terms have to keep the same supposition.

SUPPOSITUM (literally: as substance, substratum, hypostase: what is under)

Received the meaning of subsisting reality: one being, as such complete, therefore uncommunicable; it is in itself and acts in itself (actiones sunt suppositorum: acts are done by the suppositum, i.e. by the whole and not by one or another part). If the suppositum is gifted with reason it is called person; otherwise it is called thing. The scholastics studied the question about the formal constituting principle of the suppositality.

SURVIVAL

Of the soul after death, is deduced by the philosophical psychology from the transcendental actions of man and the not-intrinsic tie between soul and body.

SUSO

See Henricus Suso.

SWEDENBORG, Emanuel 1688-1772

Swedish scientist, philosopher and religious mystic who, without intending to, became the founder of a religious sect which spread throughout Europe and America. Major theological works: *Arcana Coelestia* (1749-56), *Heaven and Hell, Divine Love and Wisdom*.

SYLLOGISM (Greek: syllogismos a reckoning all together).

Aristotle's term for a logically constructed *deductive *reasoning. It is a construction of thought, consisting of at least three theses, mutually connected in such a way that, if two are set up (*premises) the third (*conclusion) has necessarily to be accepted by our intellect (*consequence) e.g. what is simple can not perish, the soul is simple, the soul can therefore not perish.

There are simple or categorical syllogisms and complex or hypothetical syllogisms. A *simple* syllogism is generally composed of simple or categorical *propositions. In its usual form both *extreme terms in the premises (*major and *minor) are successively compared with a *middle term; e.g. all metals are elements, copper is a metal, copper is therefore an element. More or less diverging forms are for instance: the shorter syllogism (*enthymeme), in which one of the premises is omitted and is considered to be known; the extended syllogism (*epicheirema) in which a short proof is added for one or both premises; the chain syllogism (*pollysyllogism) and the stacked syllogism (*sorites) in which several syllogisms, complete or shortened, are connected.

A *complex* syllogism has as first proposition a complex or hypothetical *judgment, consisting not of two *terms (*S and *P) connected or separated by a *copula, but of two other propositions, connected or separated by a conjunction. This is however not sufficient, because even if a syllogism is constructed with only hypothetical propositions, it can still be in reality a simple syllogism although it seems to be a complex one, when the place of the term is occupied by subordinate propositions e.g. when a being has intellect, it is a man, if an ape can laugh then it has intellect, therefore when an ape can laugh is it a man. A real complex syllogism requires, in addition, that the second premise (assumption) be a proposition, in which one of the two parts of the first premise be affirmed or denied. According to the nature of the complex proposition, which is the first

premise, we distinguish *conjunctive* syllogisms, e.g. one can not be and a bad citizen and a good christian, we want to be good christians, we want therefore not to be bad citizens (modus ponendo tollens); *conditional* syllogisms, e.g. *if* the premises of a correct reasoning are true, then the conclusion is true—the premises are true, therefore the conclusion also (*modus ponendo ponens), or the premises are not true, therefore also the conclusion is not true (modus tollendo tollens); *distinctive* syllogism e.g. you have to pay the fine or be jailed—you pay the fine, therefore no jail (modus ponendo tollens), or you do not pay the fine, therefore jail (modus tollendo ponens). This disjunction can naturally be composed of more members, we affirm or negate then one member by affirming or negating respectively the other members. A special complex form of disjunctive syllogism is the *dilemma (tri- and polylemma).

Principles and Rules. According to the extensivists, who emphasize the logical meaning of the *extension of the concepts, the basic principle of the syllogism is the *"dictum de omni et nullo". According to the comprehensivists, who base logic on their comprehension, it is the *"nota notae est nota rei ipsius."

The classical logic teaches eight *rules or laws* of the syllogism: Four about the *terms (1. there be only three terms, two *extremes and a *middle term; 2; they can not have in the conclusion a greater extension than in the premises. 3. The *middle term; 2. they can not have clusion; 4. this middle term has to be taken, at least once, in an *universal meaning, i.e. in its complete extent) and four about the *theses (1. from two negative premises no conclusion can be drawn 2. from two affirmative premises an affirmative conclusion will be drawn 3. If one premiss is particular or negative, then the conclusion will also be negative 4. If both are particular propositions then one conclusion can be drawn.)—I.v.d.B.

SYMBIOSIS

The living together of two organisms, in which both have their advantage. A well known example: the hermit-crab, which carries a sea-anemone on its shell. This anemone defends the crab but gets also food. When the crab goes into a new shell it transplants the anemone on the new shell.

SYMBOL

In general sense a representation, which means something different, mostly something higher and more spiritual, than its material sense and content, but still in such a way that a certain analogy between both meanings justifies the new meaning. In this manner the first meaning of the representation is understood as a directive to the hidden meaning. E.g. a white flag can mean the surrender. The symbol becomes aesthetic, when this directive condenses itself into an immediate and directly graphic presence of the intended meaning. In this general sense is, indeed, all art symbolic. In a more narrow sense one speaks of symbolic art when in the general aestheic symbolism the structure of the normal symbol emerges. So e.g. in Dürer's *Melancholy* or in his *Knight, Death and devil*.

SYMBOLISM

Is an aggregate of symbols or of signs used according to common prescriptions. These prescriptions determine which symbols are to be distinguished in the symbolism. So

form in the methesis the letter „*a*" and the sign „ '" one symbol „*a*"', in the case that in this particular part of the methesis no separate rules exist for the construction of „*a*" . „*a*"' is then an *indivisible* symbol. On the other hand is „*a + b*" a *compound* symbol. It is a symbol because there exist rules for the construction of „a + b" and it is a compound symbol because it is built with several symbols according to specific rules.

A symbolism becomes means of expression when a meaning is attached to the symbols. The symbolism is *not-conventional*, when a certain resemblance exists between the symbol and that what is conveyed by the symbol; it is *conventional* if it is based on a pure convention. A not-conventional symbolism is always in a certain way natural, while a conventional symbolism is artificial.

In formal logic is the logic expressed by means of a symbolism with specific rules; in metalogic is the colloquial language usually used.—R.F.

SYMMETRIC

Is a relation which is not different from its inverse. Equilibrium is a symmetric relation, because if x is balanced with y then y is balanced with x.

SYMMETRY

The proper form, which the aesthetic rhythm acquires when it realizes itself mainly spatial-objectively. As the temporal rhythm so rises the symmetry above the purely mathematical proportion of the measure.

SYMPATHY

Presupposes in the first place the understanding of the happiness or sorrow which another experiences. The sympathy is therefore different from the *Ein(s)fühlung, in which only an identification with the other takes place. But the feeling, although necessary, is not sufficient. Sympathy also requires that we participate in the happiness and sorrow of the other. It is this participation which makes it different from the feeling with another. When both parents are at the bedside of an ailing child they both feel the same sorrow. Participating in the same sorrow, they do however not participate in each others sorrow. There is therefore feeling together but not feeling with each other. In the contagious feeling we do not participate in another's feeling but take it unconsciously over. This is therefore also different from the sympathy. The SYMPATHY-MORALITY (A. *Smith and others) finds in the sympathy the highest moral value, and deduces from the sympathy all moral actions. Its principle is: act in such a way that an impartial bystander can agree with your actions. The question is however if the morality really proceeds from the sympathy and is not presumed by the sympathy. Is it indeed not because an action is morally good that I can agree with it? If this is true, a new question arises about the necessity of the sympathy for the morality. There are indeed moral phenomena as remorse, repentance etc.; which come into being, independently from any foreign judgment.—J.Gr.

SYNCATATHESIS (Greek)
An agreeing acceptance by the intellect of that what is perceived; a term of stoicism, used by Cicero, who brought it into the Latin language.

SYNCATEGOREMATIC
Is a term which does not mean anything in itself, as do the categorematic nouns and verbs, e.g. man, philosopher, walk, but which has only a meaning when related to such a categorical term. E.g. "all", "some", and the adverbs "slowly", "rapid".

SYNCRETISM
The mingling of ideas of different origins into a whole which lacks inner unity. Especially used to indicate the mixing of the religions in Hellenism. *Eclecticism.

SYNDERESIS
Should be synteresis or spark of the soul, indicates in scholasticism the moral consciousness as the basis for the *conscience. There is however no unanimity as to the way in which the synderesis forms the basis of conscience. *Bonaventura and the tradition which he represents think that the synderesis also incites to the good, which the conscience grasps, or restrains from evil. *Thomas Aquinas, on the contrary, thinks that the conscience must apply the principles of the moral order to our concrete acts, as they are rendered spontaneously by the synderesis. The synderesis is indeed nothing else than the habitual knowledge of the moral law in its formal definition ("do what is good") and in its most general physical prescriptions: Do the good in connection with the instinct of self-preservation ("Thou shalt not kill"), with the sexual instinct ("Thou shalt not commit adultery"), with the social instinct ("Honor thy father and thy mother"), with the spiritual aspiration for truth ("Thou shalt not lie").—J.Gr.

SYNERGY (Greek: synergein=to work with)
Concept of the protestant theology meaning, the collaboration of the fallen man towards his conversion. *Synergism* is the doctrine which teaches this cooperation, op-

posed to Luther who emphasizes the only operation of God's grace and excludes all collaboration of man for his salvation. This gave rise to a violent discussion between the Lutheran theologians and the synergists, followers of Melanchthon. The synergy remained basic for the protestant theology of the 18th and 19th century. The efforts of K. Barth to remove the synergy do not seem to have much success.

SYNESIUS OF CYRENE

Born shortly after 370 A.D., in 411 bishop of Ptolemais, belongs to the school of Alexandria. Not an original thinker, close to the theories of Plotinus with some influence of Jamblichus, most important for the meeting of neoplatonism and christianity.

SYNTACTIC APPELLATION

Is a symbol used in the expression of a (syntactic) rule, as abbreviation for: all expressions of these or that form.

SYNTAX

Is in modern logic, since the basic work of Carnap *Die logische Syntax der Sprache*, understood in a sense which can be compared to the sense used in grammar. The syntax, in grammar, studies the composition of sentences with words, as opposed to the morphology, or the study of the wordforms (especially of declensions and conjugations). Applying the word syntax to a formal language, one should remember that a formal language is not only a means of expression, but also (and in a certain sense exclusively) a means to justify formal proofs. We should therefore distinguish in the logical syntax two aspects. We have on the one hand a doctrine of the structural forms or of the logical categories. On the other hand we

can, thanks to the syntactical concepts, express with strict accuracy the rules of the formal logic. It is possible to study the entire formal logic from the point of view of the syntax. (i.e. as a doctrine of a use of symbols according to specific rules). We should, in addition, be aware that from its origin, the formal logic and also the formal descriptive languages have been studied from the point of view of the syntax.—R.F.

SYNTHESIS (Greek)

Union, connection and junction of a multiplicity into a unity; opposed to *analysis. We speak of synthetically constructed concepts (*definition); of synthetic propositions, in which something is applied to the subject which is not contained in its notion; of a synthetic *method, in which the particular is seen in the light of the general concepts and principles; of a synthetic world view, as the world view of Thomas Aquinas, in which everything is seen through God as the primitive principle of all things. Kant thinks that all formation of concepts is a synthetisation: a combining of different things under specific points of view or *categories, which one again wants to bring under greater unities. The method of thought of the natural sciences, in which a series of *observations and *experimentations are connected in a natural law, several natural laws under a more general law, and these more general laws under a general theory as for instance the atom theory, seems to be for Kant the usual manner of thinking.—I.v.d.B.

For Hegel is the synthesis the result of a dialectical process, in which the *thesis, negated in the *anti-thesis and estranged from itself, is seen, because of this medi-

424

ation, from a higher plan and returns more completely and less abstractly.—J.P.

SYNTHETIC

See proposition.

SYRIANUS

Head of the Athenian School from 431-32 A.D. Wrote several commentaries on Aristotle and Plato. He does not try to reconcile both but considers the study of Aristotle as the preparation for the study of Plato; in his commentary on the *Metaphysics* he defends the doctrine of the Ideas against the attacks of Aristotle.

SYSTEM

Can be put on the same level as a (deductive) *theory. Curry gives a very broad and at the same time very accurate definition of a formal system: a formal system concerns indefinite objects of thought. The system must naturally be expressed by means of a language; if one chooses as objects of thought the symbols of the language, then the system becomes a play with symbols; this is however usually not so.

Three rules are determined in relation to the objects of thought: 1° *rules of structure, according to which other objects can be built from primitive objects of thought; 2° rules of structure, according to which assertions can be built from objects of thought; 3° rules of deduction according to which from specific assertions, characterized as valid, other valid assertions can be inferred. The rules have a certain recursive form; on the foundations of original specific primitive ob-

jects, assertions, valid assertions, others are built; on these others are again built, and so, mostly, ad infinitum.

It should be clear that a formal system does not necessarily have a pure logic as sub-division.—R.F.

SYSTEM, connection.

A system of human knowledge is the ordering of the multiplicity of the contents of thought into a (not contradicting itself but cohesive) whole. The principle of the ordering can be more subjective or objective, depending if it is found in the subjective thought process which leads to knowledge, or in the nature and requirements of that what is known. A synthesis can be more essential or more accidental, depending if the cohesion is found in a more or less fundamental aspect of thought or being.

Every science strives towards systematisation, especially metaphysics. Some thinkers, as Plotinus and Spinoza bring the whole reality into one system. The strongest system is undoubtedly the system of *Hegel, which sees the entire reality in a unique and continuous deduction a priori? Not only are all the sciences but also the entire history integrated into it.—J.P.

SYSTEMATIC

An orderly classification of a multiplicity of things and contents of knowledge, following a specific plan, into a cohesive whole. Some think that scientific knowledge is nothing else than systematically ordered knowledge. See also architectonic.

T

TABLE OF VALUES

Term which indicates a classification of the values in higher and lower values. These values, if they are many, are indeed necessarily ordered by man into a whole. This table of values can either be only actual or only render the classification which man actually made. For Michelangelo for instance would the aesthetical value have been the highest, higher than the religious, the vital or the useful value. But the real question is which value obtrudes itself objectively, which value or group of values has rightfully the primate.

TABULA RASA (blank tablet)

Image used to indicate that the human mind is on the one hand open to know all what is, and on the other hand dependent on the experience. There are no innate concepts, as opposed to the doctrine of *inneism.

TAGORE, Rabindranath 1861-1941

Hindu poet, novelist and philosopher who wished both to revive the ideals of ancient India and promote a better understanding between East and West. Awarded Nobel Prize for Literature in 1913. Among his works: *Gitanjali* (1912), *Songs of Kabir* (1915), *Nationalism* (1917), *Creative Unity* (1922).

TAINE, Hippolyte

Born in Vouziers 1828, died in Paris 1893. French critic, psychologist historian and philosopher. Uses the basic ideas and method of *positivism in the entire domain of his science and arrives thus to his "théorie du milieu": every historical fact, every personality is the product of a coincidence of preceding and contemporary circumstances, which are in fact nothing else than historical phenomena. The Infinite Substance, which is for Taine as for *Spinoza the basis of all phenomena, is only the eternal necessary legality, which dominates all happenings in the world and in man. The world however is nothing more than a system of imaginations of the human cognition, whose truth exists only in its constant and lasting cohesion; the laws of the happenings outside of us are therefore only the psychological laws of ourselves. Moral activity is a happening as any other and is dominated by the same general legality. F.S.

TAOISM

The presentation of the Way, i.e. the "natural process of growth" considered as a metaphysical ordering principle (*Tao) active in the unstable world of forms. Oldest phases: *Tao Tê Ching* (*Lao Tzu) and *Chuang tzu. *Tao* is great Unity, without attribute and name, producing everything without acting (consciously), invisible and omnipresent. The ideal: complete adaptation to the happenings in nature, no intervention, to be "dead-less".

TARSKI, Alfred

1902, Polish-American mathematician and Logician, since 1942 professor at the University of California in Berkeley. Founder of the *semantics*, which aims at the logical analysis of terms as *truth, meaning, definition*.

TASTE

The habitual aesthetic attitude as well of the artist as of the one who enjoys the art, by which they either creatively or receptively distinguish the aesthetic valuable from the aesthetic inferior and enjoy without difficulty the valuable. In the decorative arts the taste has a still more objective meaning and points to the quality of the decorative arrangement, in which it manifestates the subjective taste.

TAUTOLOGY

Unnecessary repetition of what has already been said in other words; the fault in a *definition, in which the defined is present, e.g. philosophy is the love for wisdom.

Analogous with Kant's conception of the analytical propositions, one understands in the logistics by "tautological theses" those theses which do not assert anything which is not already implicitly expressed in the principles.

TAYLOR, Alfred Edward, 1869-1945.

English theistic philosopher and historian of the philosophy, professor in Edinburgh.

TECHNICS

Uses physical tools to produce works according to specific prescriptions. A *calculus, a *formalism are technics, because they use a symbolism to infer conclusions.

TECHNIQUE

In arts, indicates the process of the material, through which the artistic form is brought in the matter to a real appearance. In the general industrial technique is the form characterized by a certain universal repetition (e.g. the form of a knife, a bridge, a bicycle), the aesthetical technique however points essentially to a formal unicity. This does however not exclude specific rules and methods for the artistic technique. These are determined first of all by the similar nature of the used material (e.g. wood, human voice, etc.) but also partially by the relative universality of the style (e.g. the technique in painting of Jan van Eyck, the poetic technique of Paul Valery, etc.) The artistic technique comes however to its highest point where it bears the stamp of the personality of the artist.—L.V.K.

TECHNOLOGY

The manufacture of tools or the use of manufactured tools as a means to reach a goal proposed by man.

There is a double contrast between the old and the new technology. The old technology uses essentially the hand and is based only on knowledge through experience. The modern technology is based on the natural and mathematical sciences, whose most important role is to manufacture machines (which, once manufactured, will produce, more or less automatically, other things). The technology is considered now as the whole of processes which, with the application of the natural sciences, permit man to dominate nature and make it subservient. The question arises now if and to what degree this application determines already the natural sciences in its relation to the reality. Bergson answers in the affirmative. There are however more important questions about the technology, because it is a fact that the technology tries to absorb man who invented it and to reduce him to a thing among things. It is, during this last year very clear that technology can lead as well to good as to evil.—J. Gr.

TEGEN, K. Einar
Born 1884, Swedish philosopher.

TELEOLOGY
See Finality.

TELESIO, Bernardino
Born in Cosenza 1508, died there 1588, Italian philosopher of nature. He requires a basis of experience for all scientific research, becomes precursor of the empiricism, but still composes aprioristic system-points. The physical things have three principles: heat, cold and matter, and they can also perceive sensually. Man has an immortal soul. Influenced by stoicism in his sensualistic epistemology and ethics.

TEMPERAMENT
Concept which is not very clearly defined: inner nature, liveliness of character; or the psychic constitution on the grounds of the physical constitution. Hippocrates drew up the theory of the four main temperaments, who would proceed from one of the "body-fluids" (humores): choleric (yellow bile), sanguine (blood), phlegmatic (phlegm), melancholic (black bile). The dimensions of the temperament are the dispositions to react fast and superficially, as opposed to slowly and more thoroughly. Sometimes one defines the temperament in function of the reactions, which definition can be exact if the restriction is made that it has to be seen as a quality of the person in connection with the physical constitution as a more or less vital basis for the behaviour.—P.S.

TEMPLE, William, 1881-1944.
English philosopher and theo-logian, Anglican archbishop of Canterbury. His writings are important for the philosophy of religion, especially his: *Nature, Man and God* (Gifford-Lectures), 1932-34.

TERENTIUS VARRO M., 116-27 B.C.
Man with great erudition, also in philosophy dependent from Posidonius. His work *Saturae Menippeae* is important for the history of philosophy. He is eclectic: his theory about the soul being a pneuma and his doctrine about god who, as a world soul, penetrates the cosmos, is of stoic origin.

TERMINISM
Indicates the logic of the *supposition, developed a.o. by *Petrus Hispanus and considered by *William of Ockham in the epistemology. His *nominalism does not only attack the existence of the *universalia in reality (extreme *realism), but denies also that they are the rendition of an essence which is due to the individuals (moderate *realism). The words are conventional, the concepts natural universalia; they have in the soul a "being thought" (*Berkeley) and have universality because they are "termini", which appear as signs (supponunt pro) for a multiplicity of individual beings.
Also *conceptualism.

TERMS, (Lat. terminare, determine or end).
First the spoken words, which as articulated soundsigns, because of human agreement, indicate and determine an idea or concept. They are divided in *categorematic* nouns and verbs and *syncategorematic* terms. Also in *simple* terms, consisting of one categorematic term (e.g. man, philosopher), and *complex* terms, made of several (e.g.

428

"rational sensual being", "somebody who studies philosophy"). Finally in univocal terms, which can be said of different things in exactly the same sense and to which answer in general the categorical *concepts (univocity); *equivocal* terms which are said of different things in an entirely different sense and to which answer not one but several concepts (*equivocity); *analogical* terms, who are said of different things in partly the same sense and to which correspond the transcendental concepts (analogy).—Terms are also the words and concepts as last elements in which a reasoning can be analysed; in other words in as much as they are used as basic element of a *reasoning (two extreme terms and a *middle term) or a judgement (*S or *major term and *P or *minor term). I.v.d.B.

TERTIUM QUID

A third possibility, which can be present in *contrary but never in *contradictory oppositions (*trichotomy). Sometimes also used to indicate the so called "tertium comparationis" of an *analogy-reasoning.

TERTULLIANUS, Quintus Septimus Florens

Born in Carthage 160, died between 220-245. After his conversion to christianity (190) and his ordination, he became an ardent defender of the christians and the main Latin apologist. In 213 he turned to montanism, and founded later a new sect. As apologist he opposed pagan philosophy and rationalism.

TETENS, Johann Nikolaus

Born in Tetenbull 1736, died in Copenhagen 1807. Wants to give an analysis of the soul based on experience, and he distinguishes for the first time three basic functions: to represent, to will and to feel. He criticizes Wolff and had influence on Kant.

TETRACTYS

The aggregate of the four first numbers which explain together the number ten, and therefore for Pythagoras also the entire reality.

TETRAD

See Triad.

THALES OF MILETE, ca. 625-545 B.C.

One of the "Seven Wise Men" and the first representative of the Greek philosophy. With him begins the older philosophy of *nature and the search for a first, lasting principle, from which the universe proceeds and develops further. This principle is water; "Everything is water": this is the first enunciation of the Greek philosopher. Thales was also interested in geometry, geography and astronomy. He taught that the world rests in the middle of the universe on water. His successors in the so called School of Milete were *Anaximander and *Anaximenes.

THEAETETUS OF ATHENS, ca. 414-369 B.C.

Mathematician, friend and disciple of Plato. With Theodorus of Cyrene the founder of the theory of the irrational numbers. Theodorus was his teacher of mathematics. This theory of the irrational numbers is found in the 10th book of Euclid. He is also the inventor of the scientific construction of the five regular bodies (Eucl. book XIII). To honor him, Plato wrote after Theaetetus' death in 369, the dialogue *Theaetetus*.

THEISM

The doctrine that God (theos)

429

is a personal being, transcendent, who created the world in a free chosen wills act. The term theism is only used for the opinion which accepts the existence of one God (monotheism). *Polytheism* posits several gods, while *pantheism* does not distinguish between god and world.

THEODICY

Term used by Leibniz (1710) in the book in which he wants to justify God against these who accuse Him because of the evil in the world. Leibniz thought indeed that this world is the best possible (radical optimism); evil is the limitation of the finite beings. *Dualism (manicheism) on the contrary, tried to find the solution of evil in two separate last principles, a good and an evil god, independent from each other. Augustine and the scholastics, who see the evil as a lack of good which should be there, explain the physical evil (suffering) as not wanted per se by God, because it is nothing positive, but wanted because of the positive good, which it is made dependent. Moral evil (sin) is permitted by God and this also has in the entire world-order a dependent place for the salvation of the good and the glory of God.

In the 19th century the word Theodicy indicated often the treatise of the natural theology or the philosophical study of God. This usage is more and more abandoned.—H.R.

THEODORUS ATHEUS

4th cent. B.C., philosopher of the School of *Cyrenaica, disciple of *Aristippus. Opposed to the absolute *hedonism. Teaches that the end of life is pleasure which man reaches through insight. He opposed the existence of the gods, and was therefore banned from Athens.

THEOLOGY

In the antiquity, mythical story of philosophical doctrine about God and the gods. The stoics distinguished between mythical or popular theology, physical or philosophical theology and political theology, or the official ordinances about the worship. The Greek Fathers of the Church used the term as well for pagan as for the christian doctrine. Tertullianus and Augustine however used it almost exclusively for the pagan doctrine about the gods. In the Latin of the Middle Ages often exclusively used for the doctrine about God, but in the big Summas it indicates the entire christian dogmatic and moral doctrine. The name *Sacra doctrina*, or sometimes *Sacra pagina, Sacra scriptura* is more often used.

Catholic theologians make a distinction between natural theology, as knowledge about God, reached through reason from the creation, and the supernatural theology, the science of the supernatural revelation. The latter was already divided in the Middle Ages in biblical-exegetic theology and systematic-speculative theology.

Theology is today the entire system of subjects dealing with God and the divine things, on the ground of supernatural revelation, namely the revealed religion, christianity, the Church. The theological subjects, dealing primarily with the establishment of the data of the tradition and their evolution with the help of the historical method, are distinct from the speculative theology and called positive theology, often not without a kind of disdain for the former. The so called new theology thinks to find

430

in the Fathers new ways to make the content of the revelation more lively for the contemporary man, than in the scholastic philosophy.— K.L.B.

THEOPHANY (literally: the appearance of the divinity in perceptible form)

The belief in such forms is found in most religions. In the Old and New Testament such appearances are also told: the most complete is found in the baptism of Christ when the three persons of the Trinity manifest their presence. A very special theophany is the incarnation of the second Person of the Trinity.

THEOPHRASTUS

Born ca. 372-71 B.C., disciple of Plato and Aristotle, close collaborator of the latter for 32 years; head of the Lyceum from 322 until his death ca. 287. Had a big audience in the lyceum and played also a political role. Wrote two long works on logic and saw logic in another light than did Aristotle (extension of a series of modi, theory of the judgment and of the hypothetic syllogism); wrote a *Metaphysica*, of which one fragment (enumeration of the difficulties against the *prima philosophia* of Aristotle) has been saved; wrote several works on physics, but few have been saved. The main work is about botany and Zoology; other writings about the history of the sciences and ethics.—G.V.

THEOREM

Is, in general, a theoretical proposition, specifically a proposition (thesis) which has to be proved from already accepted propositions, especially from principles which have not to be proved any more (*axioms). Opposed to: problem.

THEORY (Greek: viewing; Lat. speculatio: speculation)

A pure knowledge of *abstract generalities, opposed to *practice*, an applied knowledge of *concrete individual things (*science); *a-priori considerations as opposed to *aposteriori experiences. A complete and satisfactory knowledge is only had when theory and practice go together: "Theory without practice is as a wagon without axle, practice without theory as a blind man on the road." More specifically: theory is an experiment of scientific explanation of a group of phenomena from a specific cause or a principle (*hypothesis): it is more probable when it explains more facts or predicts them. According to the nature of these phenomena we distinguish a.o. a scientific theory (e.g. theory of relativity), a socio-economic theory (Marx's theory of collapse), a philosophical theory (Aristotle's theory of matter and form). The entire philosophy is such essentially theoretical because it is the universal science of concepts. It is however divided, on the grounds of the strived for aim, into a theoretical and practical part: the theoretical philosophy wants to know for the knowledge itself and contains the so called ontological sciences (natural philosophy, philosophical psychology, philosophical mathematics, metaphysics); the practical philosophy contains a knowledge to act properly: it is normative and contains the so called deontological sciences (logic, poetics, ethics). Opposed to the philosophy as a purely theoretical knowledge of necessary generalities (principles) is the applied science, as a theoretico-practical knowledge of non-concrete actual cases (facts and individuals) —I.V.D.B.

THEORY (formal)

Can be identified with a formal deductive °system. Such a system contains a deductive science or a part of a deductive science, inferred from axioms, by means of rules (and definitions); The rules have to be such that through them —and through them alone, without the help of additional intuitive representations — the theses can be deduced. The theory (or the thesis) contains all axioms, definitions, rules which are necessary for the deduction. Usually is the theory divided in two parts: on the one hand the logic, on the other hand what is proper to the studied theory (e.g. the arithmetics, the biology). The demarcation line between these two parts is still arbitrary.

We can identify the logical part of the theory with its *general-deductive* part; this can be defined as the part in which no axioms appear which affirm the reality of specific things, or which infer qualities from them.–R.F.

THEORY OF ART

All systematic explanation or effort to explain art, the work of art and the artistic creation. The artistic feeling is on the contrary more a form of aesthetic experience and belongs therefore more to the aesthetics proper. In it's more broad sense aesthetics includes the theory of art and aesthetics in the more narrow sense, i.e. the aesthetics which are interested in the explanation of the subjective experience of the esthetical in nature and in the immediate reality of life as well as in art.—The theory of art is simple SCIENCE OF ART when it tries to explain following the inductive method of the positive sciences. The last meaning of art can not be reached by the science of art, either because it limits itself to the discovery of purely physical and aesthetic laws, or because it broadens it's vision to experimental and psychological or social laws. PHILOSOPHY OF ART, on the contrary wants to give of the arts, a definite explanation, i.e. it wants to discover the deepest human and spiritual meaning. This it tried in different ways: a more a-priori way, especially used by the idealistic aesthetics and the philosophy of art; a phenomenological-descriptive way, by which the method of the phenomenology was applied to the artistic phenomena. One can easily blame the former for an unsatisfactory consideration of the actual phenomena, while we can reproach the phenomenological philosophy of art, that it very often has been unable to penetrate the last and philosophical meaning or at least of not being able to give this meaning a satisfactory basis. However necessary be the phenomenological method for the discovery of the essence of the art, however necessary it be that the philosophy of art bases it's investigation on the phenomenological method, it is still necessary for the last explanation of art to orient itself towards a transcendental metaphysics and to evoluate in the light of metaphysical principles and of an authentic ontology.–L.V.K.

THEORY OF RELATIVITY

Distinction should be made between a special and general theory of relativity.

The *special* theory of relativity has been invented by Einstein. It is an extension of the principle of relativity, known in the regular mechanics. This principle states that the mechanical phenomena appear in a system with uniform motion in the same way as they appear in a system at rest. The passengers of a moving train, when they do not look outside, can not see anything about the motion of the train. All phenomena are, for the passengers in the moving train, as if the train were not moving. Only changes in the motion can be detected inside the train.

The special theory of relativity extends this principle to electromagnetic and light-phenomena. The speed of light, within systems which move with uniform speed in regard to each other, would be the same. This theory explains why the speed of light on earth is independent from the motion of the earth.

One of the consequences of the special theory of relativity which is of special philosophical interest, is that the time duration between two events, measured by two observers who move in regard to each other with uniform motion, will be measured differently. See °simultaneity. This is connected to the classical principle of relativity which says: *mechanical* events in the train are judged differently by the passengers in the train and by observers outside of the train. An object which, in the train, falls vertically to the floor, falls, according to the observers outside, in a slanted line. The application of the principle of relativity to light, has as consequence the above described consequences for the measuring of time, because we need light signals for the determination of time at a distance. Since nobody has the means to determine if his system is really at rest or in uniform motion (all phenomena remain the same in both conditions) nobody has the means to determine who, of both observers, is right in the different conclusion of the

measurement of the time. In other words, measurements of time differ according to the motion. The same is true for special measurements of distance. It is however possible to judge absolutely, i.e., independently from the motion of the observer, the distance in time and space taken together. This leads the scientists to speak of a space-time continuum, which would exist objectively, as opposed to the subjective separated time and space continua. The *general* theory of relativity does not limit the principle of relativity to uniform motion but extends it to all motion.
A.G.M.v.M.

THEORY OF SPACE

Geometry, as a section of pure mathematics, has become a multiplicity of very different—although in many ways connected—deductive and therefore also abstract theories, which are only indirectly in contact with visual and empirical data. On the other hand we can only establish the structure of the space of our observation and the spatial qualities of the physical objects through the visual and empirical data and only describe them in geometrical terms. The need therefore arises for a branch of science which studies the problems which arise from this new and curious situation. It is the theory of space, which can be considered more or less philosophically, which will fulfill this need. This theory must consider the development of geometry as well as the data of visual and empirical nature, belonging to very different sciences: psychology, physiology, physics, astronomy, history of art and theory of art, linguistics etc. It seems necessary to distinguish the *perceptual space* and *physical space* from the *abstract spaces*, which are studied in the geometry, as a branch of pure mathematics. These abstract spaces can however help us in the description of the perceptual and physical spaces. Investigating the perceptual space, we can ask the question: what is the contribution of our different senses to the origin of our spatial representations. When we investigate the physical space the the question arises: what structural elements correspond to the qualities of the solid bodies, which ones to those of the light rays. If one is interested in the former one goes into the study of the "Körpergeometrie," if one takes interest in the latter one studies the "Lichtgeometrie" (see Reichenbach) E.W.B.

THEORY OF VALUES
See axiology.

THEORY OF VIRTUE
Description of the different virtues and their mutual order, with possible indication of their realization. Sometimes the same as *ethics.

THEOSIS
More used is *apotheosis*, deification of people during their lifetime or after their death.

THEOSOPHY (literally: wisdom of God)
Compound name for all the efforts to penetrate the real sense of life and the essence of the things, on the grounds of deeper insights, unreachable by the intellect not enlightened by God, or of truths handed down by previous wise men. The modern *Theosophic Society*, founded by the Russian Blavatsky, holds a certain syncretism of all religions. It is taught with the help of some Indian conceptions and is reserved for a few selected souls. The *anthroposophy* of R. Steiner is one of its branches.

THESIS
Is a valid *proposition. If a proof is written in the form of a genealogical tree, then in the beginning of every ramification, is an *initial* thesis (an *axiom or a proposition proceeding from an axiom by *substitution), and on the end (at the bottom) a *final thesis*. The other valid propositions, which represent degrees of the proof, are *medial* theses. Some medial theses are unexpressed, because of conciseness.

THESIS
The first of two opposite concepts. For Hegel, the starting point of a dialectical process, in which a concept, that after its negation and estrangement in the *antithesis and after the negation of the negation in the *synthesis, will be more completely known, is only known less completely and more abstractly.

THIERRY OF CHARTRES
Ca. 1100–before 1155, younger brother of *Bernard of Chartres, professor in Chartres and later in Paris, Chancellor of the School of Chartres in 1141; humanist and mathematician, author of the *Heptateuchon* (compendium of the seven liberal arts) and the *De sex dierum operibus*, inspired by Plato's *Timaeus*. Taught *ultra-realism, and inclined sometimes strongly to pantheism.

THING
In a broad sense, everything, insofar as it possesses an inner cohesion, whether it exists in thought only or exists also in reality. In the latter case the question is how a thing possesses such inner cohesion. Realism says from itself. Criticism, however, maintains that thought provides a thing with the unity which makes it a thing. In a narrow

sense, a thing is only that which is the product of human creation or action, such as a chair but not a tree.

THINK

(Latin: *cogitare;* French: *penser*). The advancing formation of thoughts by which imperfect knowledge is perfected. In opposition to some philosophical tendencies, for instance idealism, which sees in thought the highest form of spiritual activity, we have to see in the necessity of thinking an effect of the imperfection of the intellect. In the possibility of thinking, however, are the means of partly removing this imperfection.

Since man, however imperfect his observation of beings may be, already has a pregrasp of the idea of *being, through which he somewhat understands everything that is — which knowledge he expresses in the first principles—continuing thought should not only be considered as a widening of experience, but as an explanation (which is carried out through it) of what is implicitly present in the data of experience. From an everything-embracing but confused insight, thought leads to apprehending the particular ways in which diverse beings are related to each other, and leads to the final ground of the connected whole.

Thought is therefore in its evolution connected with what is, as it is. It is not, as is the case with sensual observation, regulated only by subjective necessity (like the laws of *association), but especially by the objective necessities which are included in the essential cohesion of beings. Insight into these laws is expressed in the first principles (of *identity, of *contradiction, of *excluded thirds, of *causality, of *finality). Since these laws regulate everything that is (also, therefore, the thought which is directed toward being), they are primarily laws of being and only secondarily *laws of thought*. The concepts in which we think of beings are not only *forms of thought* (Kant's view of the categories), but first of all forms of being, although we have to make a distinction between their content and the way our thinking digests this content (*see* universalia).

We had therefore better reserve the term "laws of thought" to the *laws of logic*. Logic does not occupy itself with beings in themselves (*see ontology*), nor with the way we can know beings (*epistemology*), but considers concepts and judgments as things of reason (*entia rationis*) which are useful preeminently for exact *reasoning, which makes explicit that which is implicitly accepted in judgments. An error of thought is thus a *logical error*, an infraction of the rules of logic. Not every error is due to an *error of thought; it can also be due to an error in observation or a supposed view. J.P.

THOMAS AQUINAS

Born in Rocca Secca near Naples 1224-25, descendant from the Dukes of Aquino; first education in the Benedictine Monastery of Monte Cassino, studied later at the university of Naples (1239-44), where he followed the courses of Magister Martinus and Petrus de Hibernia; became Dominican in 1244 against the opposition of his family, who kept him for several months confined. In 1245 went to Paris, followed the lessons of Albertus Magnus and followed him to Cologne in 1248, where he remained until 1252 (some think that he lived in Cologne from 1245 until 1252). He returned to Paris in

1252 as baccalaureus and started teaching. He obtained his licentia docendi only in 1256. Because of the difficulties between regular and secular professors in the school, it was only in 1257 that Thomas received his admission as magister in the theological school. From 1259 to 1265 he taught at the papal court at Orvieto, from 1265 to 1267 in charge of the studium generale of the Dominicans in Rome; from 1267-68 he taught in Viterbo at the court of Clemens IV; by the end of 1268 he returns to Paris and was involved in the discussions about averroism. In 1272 returned to Italy to head the studium generale in Naples; died March 7, 1274 in the abbey of Fossa-Nuova, on his way to the Council of Lyon.

It is generally impossible, to separate the purely philosophical works from the theological ones: the latter have in general many considerations of philosophical nature, and the purely philosophical writings deal also with theological problems. We can make a distinction between: a) commentaries. Philosophical commentaries on many works of Aristotle and on the *Liber de causis,* also commentaries on theological treatises, which are not without importance for the knowledge about the ideas of Thomas: especially should be mentioned the commentaries on the *Sententiae Petri Lombardi, In Dionysium de divini nominibus, In Boethium de Trinitate, In Boethium de hebdomadibus;* of much less importance are in this respect the commentaries on the Scriptures. —b) Synthetical works with mainly theological content, but also of philosophical importance: *Summa contra gentiles* (also called *Summa philosophica*), *Summa Theologiae,* (was not finished, there is a sup-

plement written by Reginald of Piperno) and *Compendium Theologiae.*—c) The disputationes in immediate relation to the teaching of Thomas, as well the disputationes ordinariae as quodlibetas; belong to the first group: *De veritate, De potentia, De spiritualibus creaturis, De anima, De malo, De virtutibus.* (d) the opuscula or small philosophical writings, related to many different questions: a.o. *De principiis naturae, De ente et essentia, De aeternitate mundi, De unitate intellectus, De substantiis separatis, De propositionibus modalibus.*

—EVOLUTION OF HIS THOUGHT: Through the study of the chronological classification of his works one has come in these last years to a more historical view of the philosophical thought of Thomas. One has been able to conclude that the several writings of Thomas do not form a systematic whole, free of any time element, but that the philosophical thought of the master had gone through a progressive evolution, whose traces can be found in the successive works. This evolution is sometimes only found in the formulation of specific tenets, in this sense that Thomas at one moment used regularly a fixed formula to express his ideas, whereas an other expression will be as regularly used to express the same ideas in a later period. In other cases is this evolution in the doctrine itself, as the idea of the "esse," the doctrine about the self-cognition, the doctrine about the mutual relation between intellect and will, his conception about truth; in all those cases, and probably in many more, we can find a real evolution, which is of utmost importance if we want to understand Thomas' philosophy.

—THE HISTORICAL BACKGROUND, has also been investigated these last years. We knew that Thomas had undergone the influence of Aristotle and of neo-platonism: it is however important to see how these influences came to him; more precisely to find out how the neo-platonic commentaries on Aristotle, together with the works of some Arabic writers, have brought the above mentioned synthesis into being; in this respect is the study of Thomas' commmentaries on Aristotle of most importance. A more and more serious study is also made of the relation of the philosophy of Thomas to the immediate precursors and contemporaries.

—HIS IDEA OF PHILOSOPHY. Thomas asserts in principle the independence of philosophy from revelation, and therefore from theology, as a science with its own object, principles and methods. This does however not mean that Thomas, outside of the commentaries on Aristotle, wrote many works in which he treated the subject from a purely philosophical point of view; many philosophical argumentations and considerations can be found in works written with a theological aim in mind. When one studies further the philosophical arguments used by Thomas, one finds that the proof of a specific thesis is generally limited to the search for one or more middle terms, with which a syllogism is made; these middle terms are borrowed from or can be retraced to the fundamental principles of his philosophy. A subject and a predicate are so connected with each other or separated from each other because of a middle term, borrowed from the fundamental intuitions of the thomist philosophy.

—THE EPISTEMOLOGY can generally be characterized as an intellectualistic realism, leaning mostly upon the philosophy of Aristotle and rejecting the illumination theory of Augustine. The intellectual faculty of knowledge is potentially in proportion to its objects, this means that it does not know from itself, actually, any object, not even itself. The contact with the world through the senses is the necessary medium for the intellectual cognition; this sensory knowledge presents us an object which is spatial and temporarily determined, so that it is not at the level of the intellectual knowledge and therefore not able to actuate our intellectual faculty; to do that it has to be made intelligible through the intellectus agens. Our intellectual knowledge is therefore always rare by the sensory contact with things; it is therefore also that our knowledge has a fragmentary and progressive character; we grasp gradually the different aspects of the things and reach thus an ever richer insight in the reality. Therefore also the necessity of the activity of judgment, which has to connect the separate fragments of our knowledge; All this happens in the background of the idea of being, considered by Thomas as a primum intelligibile, an initial datum, present in a virtual way in our faculty of knowledge and which is actualized through the contact with the things; the entire growth of our knowledge is therefore seen as the immanent specifying of this transcendental datum. Truth is found in the judgment; it exists in the correspondence of the act of judgment and the reality. Thomas also speaks of a truth in things; it means that the things are knowable and therefore open to the intellect. Error is possible because of the potentiality of the human cognition, which always progresses in the world of the unknown:

it will however be avoided when one does not transgress the limits of his cognition.

—Thomas has especially been a pioneer in the domain of *metaphysics;* the possibility to study metaphysics is given in the plan we have given above of his epistemology: every proposition is an affirmation of being and means the replacement of a datum of the experience in the absolute being. The horizon of every judgment is therefore the absolute being, so that the metaphysician will do nothing else than place the background in the foreground. Thomas knew how to give the "esse" its full value, because he considers it as the most fundamental act, as the perfection of all perfection; if he therefore, in the finite beings, accepts a real difference between the essence and the act of being, then he will consider these two principles as a relation of potency to act, because the being is the ultimate act of everything. And, because God has all perfection in Himself, He will be considered as the independent act of being or the fullness of being. Everything else is dependent from God in being, and therefore in everything which makes its whole perfection, so that all created things participate in the fullness of God's being, in such a way however that the participating thing, because of its participation, is constituted as participating subject. On the grounds of the analogy of being, Thomas accepts that God is not identical with the finite or in other words, that God is not the essential form of the finite. This analogy of being is itself based on the concrete experience of existence. God is thus considered as different from the world and as creating source of all the finite.

—NATURAL PHILOSOPHY AND PSYCHOLOGY. Thomas applied the hylemorphism on the entire domain of the physical world, man included. This hylemorphism itself is, in the physical world, an application of the theory of potency and act; the essence of every physical reality is seen as a compositum of indefinite matter and essential form. So is also seen the human soul as the essential form of the prime matter and as principle of all specific perfection in man, from the corporeality to the intellectual knowledge. It should however, be noted that the human soul is considered as a subsisting essential form, because the activity of the intellect is innerly and subjectively independent from the matter; the soul is therefore immortal, although it keeps after man's death, the essential tendency towards matter. Thomas distinguishes in the soul several faculties, which proceed according to a hierarchic process of emanation from the essence of the soul: he makes a distinction between intellect and will, which work however closely together and influence each other, the intellect in the order of the formal causality, the will in the order of the efficient and final causality. Next to this he distinguishes the different sensory faculties.

—Thomas' ETHICS is based on the one hand on his considerations about the final end of man's existence, and on the other hand on the knowledge of the fundamental principles of morality. The ultimate destination of man is in the knowledge and love of God, which will only be reached, in a perfect and lasting manner, after death, and this on the grounds of the human existence on earth. The moral prescriptions are concentrated by Thomas in a few fundamental insights of the human intellect, which are virtually present in the nature of this faculty, and contain all other specifications of the morality; in such a way that all concrete prescriptions, derived from the study of the human nature, will return to the fundamental principles of the moral actions.–G.V.

THOMAS BRADWARDINE

Born in England ca. 1290, died in Canterbury 1349, professor in Oxford ca. 1325, chaplain of Edward III, archbishop of Canterbury in 1349. *Doctor Profundus.* Main work: *De causa Dei contra Pelagium* (before 1325). As a mathematician he treated the philosophy "more geometrico" and taught in the natural theology a divine determinism that was very close to fatalism.

THOMASIUS, Christian

Born in Leipzig 1655, died in Halle 1728. Jurist, precursor of the *Enlightenment. Follows Pufendorf in his theory about the natural right, but does not accept an absolute positive divine right, only natural and human positive right.

THOREAU, Henry David
1817-1862

New England philosopher who associated with the Concord group of transcendentalists but remained an eccentric individualist, world-famous for his *Walden, or Life in the Woods* (1854), and certain of his essays, such as that on civil disobedience.

THORNDIKE, Edward Lee, 1874-1950.

American pragmatic philosopher, psychologist and pedagogue.

THOUGHT

Product of the activity of the intellect. In Bühler's view, it is the not further reducible unity of the process of thinking. The latter can be considered as a concatenation of representations in a logical connection (associationism), or as the conceptual presentation, judging, concluding, understanding and ordering of relations (Selz). According to Külpe, accompanying representations are not necessary. *See also* concept, idea, representation.

THRASYMACHUS

Born in Chalcedon 4th cent. B.C., disciple of *Gorgias, especially interested in rhetoric, precursor of the classical Attic rhetorics. In the *Politeia* of Plato he defends the sophist thesis that is right what brings profit to the stronger.

TILLICH, Paul

Born 1886, died 1965. German theologian and philosopher of religion, in the U.S.A. since 1933.

TIME

Presents itself as a continuum that from the past, via the present flows towards the future. The main question about time is related to its manner of existence. Does time exist in itself as an independent frame in which the events take place (Newton, Clarke) or does time only have an ideal existence, with or without foundation in reality? Those who reject time as existing in itself but do not give it a purely ideal existence (as Kant did), point out the aspect of successivity, proper to all motion, as the real foundation of time. Time is then considered as an abstraction, but an abstraction based on the successive, which is found in every motion. And, since motion and changeability are basic qualities of matter, the being-in-the-time is also such a basic quality. Time can therefore be defined with Aristotle as the possible numbering of the motion according to the before and after.

When one speaks of *the* time, one does not think especially of the succession of a specific motion (e.g. the celestial motion, which is used as a measure for time) but of the fact, that the before and after of every motion, unequivocally fixes an universal before and after. °Simultaneity, theory of °relativity.

In the time we can distinguish a *metric* and a *topological* structure. The latter has only relation to the order of before and after (A took place before B), while the metric structure has relation to the distance in time (A took place one year before B).

One chooses as ideal measure of time a motion which is continuous and uniform, and shows periodicity. A few celestial motions are very close to this ideal, as for instance the rotation of the earth and its revolution around the sun. This is therefore taken as a measure of time.—A.G.M.v.M.

TIMON OF PHLEIUS, ca. 320-ca. 230 B.C.

Belonged to the sceptic school, wrote satires against the philosophers except Xenophanes and Pyrrho. Denies the possibility to reach truth through sensory knowledge or through the intellect; judgment has therefore been suspended, which gives us at the same time rest of mind (ataraxia).

TINDAL, Matthew, 1656-1733.

One of the most prominent deists, who turned in his *Christianity as old as creation* (1730) against the positive christian religion and opposed to it a religion of reason. God gave man intellect to distinguish truth from untruth. The correspondance of our moral actions with this intellectual con-

viction is our well-being and happiness.

TOLAND, John

Born 1670, died in London 1722, British philosopher and theologian. Studied in Glasgow, Edinburgh and Leiden, published his main work *Christianity not mysterious*. The term free-thinker was first used for him. Strong opposition was brought against him for his strong criticism of revealed and miraculous religion. He lived for a long time on the continent of Europe where he had, a.o. the protection of Queen Sophy Charlotte of Prussia.

TOLSTOY, Leo 1828-1910

Great Russian novelist (*War and Peace*—1869; *Anna Karenina*—1877), who, in his later years, renounced the Russian Orthodox Church and evolved his own type of Christianity based on nonresistance to evil, social repentance, and radical opposition to the institutions of this world.

TOTALITY

Concept introduced by biologists (e.g. H. Jordan) to indicate that every being forms a natural unity, with a special connection of parts and functions. The causal factors, which we find through research, seem to be related to each other in a special way; one finds also in the living totality a richness of potencies or abilities which can become active.

TOTEMISM

Belief in a certain relationship with primitive beings, mostly seen under the form of animals. These primitive beings would continue to exist in specific species of animals and plants. The term comes from totem, a word of Ojibway Indians. Also the theory of Durkheim, who claims that the totems are the symbols of the societies and the worship of the totems the origin of religion.

TRADITIONALISM

The philosophical theory about knowledge which teaches that the individual human reason can not, on its own, reach certitude, at least not in religious and ethical domains. This certitude can only be reached by leaning on the authority of the *tradition,* which expresses itself in the testimony of the society.

Historically we find traditionalism mostly in France. With *Bonald and *Bautain it is connected with *fideism: origin of all knowledge and certitude is found in the divine revelation, which is kept and communicated in the tradition. De *Lammenais' traditionalism is free of fideism but finds the origin of knowledge in the general conviction of the human species, the universal human thought or the collective reason, which is expressed in language and tradition. —F.S.

TRADUCIANISM

The doctrine "that the child is produced in body and soul by the parents". The human soul has however an existence which is independent from matter: is therefore not produced by matter (against *physical* traducianism) and the human soul can not, being indivisible, produce another soul (against *spiritual* traducianism). Also *generationism and *creationism.

TRAGIC

The aesthetic category, in which the form—raised to the figure of an individual human consciousness—in its ruin, brought about by enemy forces, reveals a transcendent strength but also the greatness of the human existence. The tragic

has more intensity when the subject whose ruin is sought, shows more strength and fortitude. The tragic is essentially a form of representation, so that it can only be applied to the painful or terrifying happenings in real life, in an unreal sense.

TRANSCEND

Transcend something or transcend towards something. In the first case we mean to exceed or surpass something, rise above something, so that there is not only a difference in level between the transcending and the surpassed term, but that they belong to different orders, which are not connected with each other by a continuous line of evolution. This has its application in the domain of logic (for which the term *transcendental is used) and in reality (for which the term *transcendent is used). The idea of being transcends, on the one hand, because of its unlimited extent, all categories, the spirit transcends on the other hand the matter, or the cause the effect.—L.D.R.

—In the second case we mean surpass oneself from oneself to something else, or be essentially directed to something else (mostly something embracing). This transcending towards can be immanent to the subject and therefore belong to its structure. In this sense transcends man, in the existential philosophy, towards the world, towards the fellow-man, towards the "being", towards God. That to what one transcends can be called the transcendent in as much as it exists prior to it as a condition of the transcending motion.—J.P.

TRANSCENDENCE

Faculty of being *transcendent or the transcendent itself. In the latter case is mostly meant God and the divine, who transcend the entire created world. The term *transcendance* is here used as opposed to *transdescendence,* the demoniac.

Finally and especially in the existential philosophy the term transcendence indicates the act of transcending to. For Jaspers it is the openness of the human existence for the embracing absolute, of which nothing is known; for Heidegger it is the freedom of all bounds to reach for that other which is higher than what one is here and now; Sartre explains it as a continuous effort to transcend oneself transcend what one is, an effort without aim, only with a direction.—H.R.

TRANSCENDENT

What rises above a specific domain or order, is independent from it or is not completely explained by it. In the first place is transcendent the idea of being, which transgresses all categories. One uses however today the term *transcendental for this transcendence, while transcendent is opposed to *immanent. In the *order of knowledge* is transcendent the object, in as far as it is not considered as a constitutive element of the subject, but is independent from the knowledge of it (or from the striving towards it). In more limited sense is transcendent the object of the sensory experience, in as much as it goes farther than the sensory experience, or that what in principle transcends all possible sensory experience (although not all knowledge) (The unknowable in *agnosticism). In the *order of being* is transcendent what goes beyond the world as the whole of the (time-spatial) being in which man lives and with which he shares

the destiny, or even what goes beyond all beings: the "esse" itself, the "infinite", the "absolute", the "eternal". This transcendent, even if it is seen as completely independent from what is immanent (to the world as a whole) or as creative cause of it (God), can nevertheless reveal itself in the immanent. In a more narrow sense indicates the word transcendent that what goes beyond a given sphere or order. So is the living called transcendent in relation to the physical, the spiritual in relation to the corporeal.—J.P.

TRANSCENDENTAL

What is related to the *transcendent. In scholasticism one speaks of transcendental *concepts which, opposed to the categorical, transgress all categories. It is actually the idea of being and its so so called qualities as something, this, one, true, good (beautiful?). They have an unlimited extent and are, in this respect, interchangeable: *res, ens, aliquid, unum, verum, bonum, (pulchrum?) convertuntur.* In contemporary scholasticism one speaks also of transcendental *relations,* as of *relations which are related to every category of being and therefore transcend the predicamental category. They are realities which are integrally relations to something else. So is the creature integrally dependent on its creator; so is a structural principle (as potency and act) integrally connected with another principle in the same structure.—L.D.R.

In Kant's philosophy this meaning changes. To investigate the possibility of metaphysics (a knowledge of what is transcendent to the experience) Kant studies the faculty of knowledge as it exists before all experience (a priori). Transcendental means then in the first place this investigation itself, as it is not directed to the objects of knowledge but to the apriori in our knowledge of objects, as the basis itself of this knowledge. Are also called transcendental the apriori conditions in the subject, which make objective knowledge possible: the forms of time and space, the categories of thought, finally the transcendental unity of the apperception (the consciousness). There is therefore an opposition between transcendent and transcendental (what goes beyond the experience from the part of the object): We can think the transcendent, but not know (theoretically); it is however affirmed by the practical reason as a postulate. In last instance is called transcendental the application or use of immanent (to the experience) principles outside the limits of possible experience, actually something else than phenomena.—J.P.

Transcendental deduction, however, is justification of the fact that the a priori categories of the intellect are applied to the objects of experience.

TRANSCENDENTALIA
The most general concepts, which themselves transcend the highest class concepts and therefore are not univocal (see univocity), but analogical concepts (see analogy). The classical logical distinguishes six: "being", "thing", "something", the "One" or undivided, the "True", the "Good"; the "beautiful" is not an original *transcendental concept.

TRANSFINITE
See induction.

TRANSFORMATION
See function.

TRANSFORMISM
Or evolutionism, biological theory which asserts that the species in the living beings proceed from other forms, and again will change into other forms. Is practically the same as the theory of *evolution.

TRANSLATION
A formal *system is *verbally translated* if an interpretation for the expressions in this system is given in the colloquial language. A formal system can however also be *translated* through another system. One system is the translation of another if all theses of the first pass into theses of the other, by changing the symbols of the first into specific symbols of the other. Two systems are *equivalent* translations of each other, if the one is the translation of the other.

TRANSPOSITION
Formal *systems give rise to transposition, because one can go from a thesis of a system to a corresponding thesis of an *isomorph system.

TREE OF PORPHYRY
Systematic classification of the *categories of substances into *genera, *species and individuals, on the grounds of the elements which determine the essence and individual *characteristics (*see* distinction). This classification was first used by *Porphyry and in the philosophical books of the Middle Ages. It was represented as a tree (like a genealogical tree) and it became the model for all scientific methodical classifications.

TRENDELENBURG, Friedrich Adolf
Born in Eutin 1802, died in Berlin 1872, German realistic thinker; constructs on aristotelian ground ideas a system of "organic worldviews", in which the idea of appropriateness dominates and which is crowned with a concept

of God, very close to the theistic concept of God. Trendelenburg has also renewed the interest for Aristotle in the Germanic countries through his philological works.

TRIAD

Is for Kemp and others an expression with the form $ab \cdot c$, which is translated: c is between a and b. If u is the total class, then is the degenerate triad $ub \cdot c$ equivalent to: all a's are b's. According to the same principle one can construct tetrads and pentads etc., with related meanings.

TRICHOTOMY (threefold cut)

Opposed to *dichotomy. A usual logical fault in reasoning (*paralogism) is the confusion between contrast and contradiction (*opposition) by making a dichotomy, where a trichotomy should be made, and by using a *dilemma where a *trilemma is necessary.

TRILEMMA AND POLYLEMMA

Compound disjunctive *syllogisms, whose first premiss is composed of a threefold and morefold disjunctive *proposition. See also dilemma.

TROELTSCH, Ernst, 1865-1923.

German theologian and philosopher, professor in Berlin. Influenced by *Dilthey, tries however to avoid his relativism.

TRUE

Opposite of false. 1) said of the cognition; namely of the judgment; inasmuch as the judgment "says to be what it is, and not to be what it is not" (*Aristotle). *Truth. A concept can also be true, when it is not only considered in its own content, but as the rendering of something which is; then it includes however a judgment. 2) said of the beings, inasmuch as they are, by being, ground of true judgments, in other words, inasmuch as they reveal themselves to us in their being. 3) therefore in particular: that what is in itself, as it presents itself to us and is not a false seeming or imitation; = genuine, real. Especially for persons; who present themselves in their attitude and conduct as they really are and think: veracity. 4) also; that what is what is said of it, although the seeming could confuse us = genuine, pure. 5) what really took place or exists 6) said of works of art: what corresponds to that what the artist wanted to express or represent or with the deeper reality of nature and life. —J.P.

TRUTH

1) *Logical* truth is the quality of the knowledge, to coincide with what is as it is. This concurrence (*adaequatio) has to be considered as the known concurrence between the being which is thought and the thought which the knower has of the being. Opposite of *falseness.

2) *Metaphysical* truth is called the reality itself inasmuch as it is possible to be thought, i.e. ready to be known. The being is true and the truth belongs to the "being", in other words untrue knowledge can not agree with reality, and no being contains something which principally excludes the knowledge of it. Opposed to *seeming.

Truth poses some problems. How does truth originate in our cognition and what is in this respect the role of the emotive factors? Suppose that man always remains within the limits of a specific situation, how could he know that, without freeing himself in some way from this situation? How can we explain that he knows truth which is valid for everybody, absolute truth? One can also wonder

444

if the intelligibility is indeed transcendental and if the metaphysical truth does not rest eventually on an intellect?

3) *Ethical* truth is the quality of a person, that his words concur with his thoughts, insights and convictions (opposite of *lie) or that he in his conduct and actions shows himself as he is in reality; see also *veracity, *sincerity.—J.P., L.D.R.

TRUTHFUNCTION

Of a specific *proposition is a proposition whose *truthvalue is determined when the truthvalue of the intended propositions is determined. "Not-*p*" is (in the bivalent logic) a truthfunction, because not-*p* is true if *p* is untrue, and untrue if *p* is true.

TRUTHVALUES

It is accepted that every *proposition can have different truthvalues. In the (usual) bivalent logic are two truthvalues: true and untrue. They are indicated in formalisation by two specific symbols: e.g. the true by 1 the untrue by 0. One can construct systems with a specific finite number, or with an infinite number of truthvalues.

TSCHIRNHAUS(en), Ehrenfried Walther von, 1651-1708.

German philosopher, mathematician and physicist from the school of Descartes and Spinoza.

TUFTS, James Hayden, 1862-1942.

American pragmatic philosopher.

TUISM

See altruism

TUTIORISM

Principle in casuistics according to which man, in a doubt about the moral value of an action, can only follow the meaning which has moral certitude.

TYNDALL, John 1820-1983

British popularizer of science who made important contributions to molecular physics, theory of heat, optics and acoustics, and who was equally concerned with the metaphysical or religious consequences of science's inquiries. Works: *On Sound* (1867), *Contributions to Molecular Physics* (1872), *Lessons in Electricity* (1876).

TYPE (Greek: groundform, model)

Term used in psychology for what can be considered the model and exemple of the members of a group of people (race, people, status, profession etc. . . .) characterized by specific physical and mental qualities, attitudes to life and conduct. *Species and *genus are found completely and in the exact same way in the individuals of a same group, the type on the contrary will be only approximated in more or less and different measure.

B. Russell introduced this term in the *logistics.*

TYPES (in formal logic)

To avoid *paradoxes, concepts (classes, relations, individuals) are divided in *types*. In the *not-ramified theory of types*, is the type of a concept only dependent on that to which the concept can be applied. Let us conceive individuals as types *O*; we mean by this what can not be applied to anything else (in the system). One distinguishes then different types of classes. The lowest type consists of classes which are applicable to individuals: "red" is applicable to individuals, but red is not applicable to colour or form; type 2 consists of that what is applicable to classes of type 1, to qualities of qualities. So is "colour" applicable to "red" etc. For relations one should take in account the type of the antecedents and of the consequences.

The classification in the *ramified theory of types* has to do with concepts expressed by means of a paraphrase. Concepts of the same not-ramified type can be divided in several ramified types, as in the paraphrase is alluded to concepts of a more or less high type. The concepts "general" and "he who has all the qualities of a good general" are of the same not-ramified type, because both can e.g. be applied to Napoleon. The second concept however alludes to a totality of qualities, and it is not-predicatively expressed, it is therefore of an higher ramified type than the first one. The classification in ramified types is, today, mostly avoided, because the semantic paradoxes, which made this classification necessary, have been resolved by means of *snytax and *semantics.—R.F.

TZU SSU c. 335-288 B.C.

Grandson of Confucius, he wrote on the relativity of human knowledge of the universe and analyzed as many types of human action as possible.

U

UEBERMENSCH

Is for Nietzsche the new man who will surpass in the same way the ordinary man as the latter surpasses the ape. He gives sense to the world by living it up and by making everything dependent upon him.

UGLY, THE

Aesthetical category, by which a disharmony which structures itself in an aesthetical harmony becomes the immediately graphic manifestation of a value of life and a sense of existence. The ugly brings into the aesthetical the extreme tension it can support, without however breaking the aesthetical stand. The authentic ugly can appear more or less in itself. It can also be an element of other esthetic categories, as to some extent, in the tragic and the comical.

ULRICH ENGELBERTI OF STRASSBURG

Born probably ca.1230, died in Paris, 1277, Dominican, studied in Cologne with Albert the Great 1248-1256, lector in Strassburg, later provincial of the order. At his death he was working for a magister title in theology in Paris. Main work: *Summa de bono*, an incomplete theological summa. As philosopher he taught a neo-platonism, inspired by Proclus (*Liber de causis*) Avicenna and Pseudo-Dionysius.

ULTRA-REALISM

One of the extreme solutions of the problems of the *universalia:

they would be things existing in reality outside our thought. See realism.

UNAMUNO, Miguel de, 1864-1936.

Spanish antirationalistic philosopher of culture.

UNCONSCIOUS

Which belongs to the consciousness but is not actually conscious. Under the influence of the psychology of consciousness and the degrees of consciousness, one has called unconscious everything which remained beneath the "threshold" of the conscious. Already in Leibniz. In the empirical psychology, under the influence of the use of metaphors, the concept received mostly an empiristic status. The unconscious is represented as the lowest level of consciousness. (G.E. Müller, Freud). For Müller this becomes a dynamic basis for psychic life. Freud thinks that this dynamics has a libidinous character.

The concept unconscious holds a certain contradiction when brought in connection with experience. Unconscious means not conscious i.e. what can not be experienced and therefore not known. There is therefore a danger for a mythology of the unconscious. See also subconscious.—P.S.

UNDERSTAND

Know in such a way that something is apprehended by the intellect in its being or in its real cohesion and relations. In empirical psychology it is considered thinking, inasmuch as the latter—more under the influence of the Würzburg school—can be described as the apprehension of relations. This does not always have to be in representative images. In an entirely specific sense one can speak of understanding when the knowledge of human action is not only reasonable and founded upon causes, but when it finds an echo in the mind (verstehen). Understanding is, then apprehension in a larger sense. This form of thinking is typical in the mental sciences (Dilthey). see Intellect.

UNIFORM

Are two expressions when one changes over from one expression to the other by changing its arguments into arguments of the same type.

UNITY

Something considered as a whole, or negatively expressed, as undivided (indivisum in se) and distinguished from any other whole (divisum ab al io). Unities can exist in the order of knowledge (e.g., the one thought-of essence with its analogical universalities) and in the order of reality (e.g., one humanity, one human person).

Unity is the first explication of *being and has the same all-embracing extent. Unity means to be one, every being is a unity, so that unity and being are interchangeable as attributes. Unity gives occasion to many distinctions. It may be absolute unity or relative unity. Absolute unity averts all multiplicity: thus divine unity is simple (not structured and unique, related to nothing). Relative unity is relatively many, i.e., multiplicity united to a unity, one multiplicity, one order. As regards internal harmony (indivisum in se), relative unity can be of different kinds: the higher a being, the simpler its structure and the stronger its unity (so is the mind simple in its nature, not extended in space, not only undivided, but indivisible). Structure itself can be considered in its substantial core, which, according to different cases, is more or less complex, and in its evolution (e.g., the activity of knowledge and striving in man) which can be many-sided. Also in its relation to other beings (divisum ab aliis) relative unity is of many kinds; the higher a being, the more independent and free of others it is. Material things are completely dependent upon each each other; animals move with a certain spontaneity; men, who cannot be detached from the cosmic order of the world either, remain connected to each other as individuals of the same unity, but in a community of free persons, i.e., of beings who act independently.

The problems which arise in the study of unity are found in the internal structure and order of thoughts, in the internal structure and order of beings, so that philosophical investigation will be concerned principally with the one and the multiple.—L.D.R.

UNITY

That which is characteristic of the unit, and which excludes multiplicity as such.

UNITY OF GOD

Divine attribute, meaning that there is only one God (see monotheism) and that the essence of God is undivided and indivisible, and is distinguished by this attribute from all that is not God.

UNIVERSAL

Can be used in logical sense as common or proper to different things (opposite is individual); in the sense of abstract-universal (opposite of less universal and concrete); and of distributive universal (opposite of particular). Only the universal can be used in a proposition as predicate. A universal term is an abstract-general concept which is used in the proposition in its complete extent.

UNIVERSALIA

Plural of *universale*, the universal, i.e. the one in its relation to the many. It has sometimes relation to the many taken collectively and extends into the whole; sometimes to the many also not separately taken (distributive) and extends to each—to each in a specific aspect (universale abstractum). Sometimes it characterizes especially the concept, i.e. the content of thought, in as much as this can be said in the proposition as the same of several individual beings or groups of beings (*singular, *particular).

In the Middle Ages a *dispute about the universalia* arose in connection with the meaning of this universal contents of thought. *Ultra-realism affirms the existence in itself of the universalia (William of Champeaux) and the moderate *realism denies it (Abelard, Thomas Aquinas). The universale, it is true, is realised in the individual beings according to its content, but not in the *abstract way which is proper to the thought, but in concrete connection with other characteristics, especially with the individuating conditions of the here and now. One can indeed consider the universale purely in connection to its content (universale metaphysicum or directum) or as general i.e. in connection with its predicability of many. This latter happens through the *reflexion of logic (universale logicum or re-

flexum). The first one is something of the real being, the latter is a product of thought (ens rationis, *intentio secunda).

The value of reality of the universalia is limited or attacked by *terminalism and *conceptualism, the existence itself of universal concepts by strict *nominalism.— J.P.

UNIVERSALISM

Considers the universe, i.e. all the existing beings, as a unity and tries to explain from there the separate beings.—Universalism in sociology, see Spann.

UNIVERSE

The totality of all that exists in space and time. There have been various conceptions of the universe in history. Aristotle thought that the earth was its center, around which revolved four concentric spheres consisting of the elements: water, air, fire and the *quinta essentia,* which formed the sphere of the celestial bodies. The image was abandoned when Copernicus discovered that the earth was not the center of the universe. Today we know that there are many solar systems in the universe, which are again parts of galaxies. In opposition with the old conception that the matter of the celestial sphere was essentially different from that of other spheres, we now believe that there is no essential difference and that for the entire universe the same mechanical, physical and chemical laws apply.

UNIVOCITY (Lat. una-vox, one compound name)

The applicability of terms and concepts on different things in only one specific sense, so that always exactly the same thing answers to it. All categorical *concepts are univocal as for instance the concept "man", which can be said in exactly the same way of every human individual. Opposite of *equivocity, *analogy.

UNKNOWABLE

What can not be reached by the human knowledge, in absolute or in relative sense. If one recognizes the essential relation between esse and *knowing, one can only speak of unknowable if this means not to know completely. Because that what can not be known fundamentally in no respect, can also not be known as unknowable.—J.P.

UNREST

Agitation, *anguish. A general condition of the organism, as well spiritual as physical, on the grounds of anguish, which can have or not have a specific object. Some authors have considered rest and unrest as elementary dimensions of the sense of personality.

UPANISHADS

Newer parts of the *Veda, most important for the Indian thought after ± 500 B.C. They are discussions between teachers and disciples or between more and less advanced students, in which mostly temporary solutions are given to problems about the world, soul, primitive basis and background of the phenomena and their mutual relations. They are given in apodictic form, mostly without logical argumentation, but with many parallels, images, comparisons in intuitive combinations. They have mainly the desire to find the unity in, behind and before the world of phenomena, to find the "one" principle from which all that exists can be reached as a unity. The name of that "One", the formulation of it and the point of view about the One are not the same for everybody, although later writers try to show that this difference is only superficial. The most accepted idea was that the One is brahman, and among the many identifications of powers, phenomena and concepts, that the individual center of the personality is brahman, especially because of the great importance the later vedānta attributed to it. The foundations were also laid for the doctrines of *karman, transmigration and salvation. The most important upanishads are: Brhadāranyaka, Chāndogya, Katha Svertāsvatara.—J.G.

URGE

*Impulse to action, lying between emotion and intellect. It differs from passion because it is less intensive and less emotional. Cause or end of the urge can be either of a physical or spiritual nature. The cause can be conscious or unconscious. We can distinguish the *involuntary* urge (action created by habit or instinct) from the *voluntary* urge (action created by the will).

UR-MONOTHEISM

Is often used to indicate the School of Vienna, although this School itself does not use this term. Opposed to *animism and *dynamism. Its leader W. Schmidt, basing his studies on the history of culture, shows that in the oldest known cultures there was a belief in a Highest Being. Schmidt thinks that it had a purely monotheistic character and that he can prove that it is based on a primitive divine revelation.

UTILITARIANISM

Doctrine according to which the determining principle of morality would be the profit. Is good what is profitable, i.e. what promotes the happiness of man. *Bentham, Stuart Mill and others defended this doctrine, which is actually very close to *epicureanism. Epicurism remains individualistic; whereas utilitarianism is more social. Man does indeed have to choose that what guarantees the greatest sum of happiness, keeping in mind the nature, duration, intensity and effects of the satisfaction an action provides. He has especially to keep in mind that man is a social being who can only find in society his highest satisfaction, so that he has to respect the interests of the community. These interests are actually best served by the harmony of the individual interests. The principle of the utilitarianism is therefore: is good, what promotes the greatest happiness of the greatest number. —J.Gr.

UTILITY

Is as if it were the lowest form of goodness. Traditionally it was the bonum utile opposed to the bonum jucundum (pleasure) and bonum honestum (good). While pleasure and good are strived at for themselves, utility is only strived at because of the good to which it leads. Goodness exists here then only in the relation to what is good in itself.

In other words. There are two kinds of values. The first have relation to the goal, the other to the means. The latter receive their value from the end which they serve and are therefore utility values. In ethics the question arises how utility values can be strived at as if it were values based on the goal, as happens for instance for the miser who makes a goal from the possession of money.

UTOPIA

Attractive political or social ideal, which can be thought but not realized, because it does not consider the real nature of man and his actual living conditions. Such an ideal was proposed by Plato in "The State", by Thomas More in "Utopia", from which it actually got its name.

V

VAIHINGER, Hans, 1852-1933

German philosopher, professor in Halle. Founder of the "Als-ob-Philosophie", which tries to unite *pragmatism and *idealism. Main work: *Die Philosophie des Als-ob*, 1911. Knowledge is a biological function: it is as such directed to preservation and development of life. In thought have also religious and metaphysical elements their importance. Religion and philosophy are however fictions, but still useful fictions, so that we always act as if they were truths instead of fictions.

VALID

That which has the characteristic of applying to, said especially of truths.

VALID PROPOSITION

Is, in a deductive system, an axiom or a proposition which can be deduced, according to the rules of the system, from the axioms.

VALIDITYFUNCTION

Is a *proposition whose *validityvalue is determined if the validityvalues of the arguments of all functions of the *proposition-logic, which appear in this proposition, are determined. In classical logic there are only two such values: true and untrue. The negation not-p is a validityfunction, because it is true if p is untrue and untrue if p is true.

VALIDITYVALUES

In a deductive system the *propositions can usually undergo a *valuation. The values which are, in such a way, attached to the propositions, are called validityvalues. In classical logic all propositions are *true* or *untrue;* in the logic with more than two values there is place for more than two validityvalues.

VALUATION

*Truthfunction, is actually the fact that one indicates its *value-functor. The valuation of a truth-function can always be determined by a series of substitutions. This produces a so-called decision-method, because a truthfunction forms then and then only a valid proposition, when its abbreviated truthfunctor exists only of valid values (in the bivalent logic of values: true).

In the doctrine of the foundations of the mathematics methods are often used with valuation, in this sense that specific values are attached to expressions.

VALUE

Term in the contemporary philosophy, borrowed from economics, to indicate what traditionally was indicated by "bonum" (the good). That reality is also and especially exposed as good or valuable points to a change of view which started with Leibniz and was completely formed by Nietzsche.

Opposed to the *good is value the reason why the good is strived at. The apple, for instance, is not desired as such, but because of the value which it embodies. The question however is what this value is and at the same time what the essence is of the value. Is the value of the apple in the sensations of lust which it can provoke? Is the value therefore something purely subjective (von Ehrenfels)? Or is on the contrary the value a quality of the reality, totally objective, completely unreducible and sui generis—as the colours and tones (Scheler)? The value contains, for us, necessarily, a relation to striving. Speaking of the apple again: the value is not in the appeasing of the hunger as such, in the objective satisfaction of the hungry being (Stapledon), but in the objective — nutritive — quality through which the apple can appease the hunger. So is the value neither a pure quality of the reality nor a pure relation to the striving, but an objective quality of the reality in connection with the striving subject. Be only added that it is here a quality of the reality, posed in general, facing a striving subject in his essence. The value appears in several realities (the nutritive in fruit, but also in bread) and is related to a human subject in his essence as physical being.

Reality however has several qualities as the striving can also evolute in different directions: it is therefore necessary that the value differentiates itself in values or that there be multiple values. They remain however a priori, because completely independent from all actual experience. Before any experience, for instance, is the nutritive a value for man or it follows from the essence of man that he is open to the nutritive. It is at the same time clear that the values, because they are multiple and have every time a specific content, do have a general and necessary meaning. They have this meaning not therefore as pure form or through

the way they appear. They appear in the consciousness, and with an attractive and urging character. They *apply. Therefore the difficulty to determine their reality.— J.Gr.

VALUEFUNCTOR

Of a *truthfunction indicates the truthvalues of the function, which correspond to the different truthvalues of the argument or the arguments.

In a *not-abbreviated* truthfunctor the values of the arguments are expressed; if one accepts for all valuefunctors a normal order of the values, one can use *abbreviated* valuefunctors, in which only the values of the function (in the normal order) are indicated.

VANINI, Lucilio

Born in Taurisano ± 1585, died in Toulouse 1619 (burned as heretic). Influenced by Pomponatius and Caesalpinus, called nature God and matter eternal. His philosophy is somewhat pantheistic.

VARIABLES

Of different sorts should be distinguished in formal expressions. In rules and *metalogical observations are used the so called *intuitive* variables; they do however not belong to the formal theory. If usual variables are used without a substitution rule, one has *indefinite* variables. With a substitute rule one has, in an *abstractum, *bound* variables (the same variables as those of the abstractum) or *free* (this is: not-bound) variables.

One uses different series of variables, for *propositions, for *classes, for *relations, for individuals. Except in special cases, no specific variable is used for each type. In the combinatory logic only variables are used without distinction of type.—R.F.

453

VEBLEN, Thorstein 1857-1929

American social theorist who mercilessly criticized established economic and social institutions. His major work, *Theory of the Leisure Class* (1899), had a broad and fermenting influence on American social thought.

VECTOR

A magnitude which has a *direction. Force and speed for instance are vector magnitudes.

Change of a vector can therefore happen in two ways, through the enlargement or diminution of its quantitative value or by a change in direction.

VEDA

The oldest literature of India on religion and worldview (probably ± 500 B.C. with later additions). It contains systematic primitive efforts to explain the world, a very strong and consequently developed ritualism through which man should come in contact with, influence and know the not-phenomenal, and some ecstatic elements. The oral traditions in the rituals, the "knowing" (Veda), was supposed to be of supernatural origin, to express eternal truth which was contemplated by inspired men in the prehistoric times. The authority of the Veda has long been unassailable and the Veda, especially the later parts, the *Upanishads, became the basis of the Indian thought.—J.G.

VEDANTA

The school of the tratitional brahmanism in India in the last 1500 years. On the ground of the *Upanishads and the later texts which lean on the Upanishads, teaches the Vedānta that only *brahman is, that it has no definite form, that it is omniscient and omnipotent but not active, although it recreates constantly the world which is identical with brahman. Many followers of the Vedanta represented it so that the brahman emanates the universe from itself, of itself, as milk "of itself" flows. The brahman remains one and indivisible although it emanates. The product is a real transformation of its cause: the universe is related to the brahman as a fabric to the treads from which it is composed. The individual soul is an integrated component of the brahman, that is however not soiled by the karman, because it is not, as the souls, connected to a body. The Vedānta is, in fact, a doctrine of salvation and culminates in a discussion of the method to experience the salvation: it is useful to fulfill the duties which life imposes and to do the activities prescribed by the Veda, but only the knowledge of brahman, which is reached in a *yoga-course, leads to the goal. To be saved means that one is conscious of the real nature of one's own existence, it is of his being brahman, without having other experiences of consciousness. —J.G.

VERACITY

Exists in the love for truth and the horror of lies. It is for many the essence itself of morality. In the philosophy of Descartes: the veracity of God justifies the validity of the human knowledge.

VERBUM MENTIS (word of the mind)

The concept, so called because it is the spiritual expression of that what the intellect has understood or thought. Opposed to: *verbum oris*, the word spoken through the mouth.

VERIFICATION (Lat. verum facere, to make true)

Proving or establishing the truth of a thesis or *hypothesis, by supplying specific facts (inductive *method); control, further investigation, examination.

VERNIAS, Nicoletto
Died in 1499, taught in Padua the averroistic doctrine of the unity of the intellect. He accepts that the same thesis can be true for reason and false for the faith. He will later accept the immortality of the individual human soul.

VIA ANTIQUA, MODERNA
The philosophy of *William of Ockham was in the 14th century a breach with the past, more particularly with the great tradition of the moderate *realism, which went from Petrus Abealard to Thomas Aquinas and Joannes Duns Scotus; Ockham rejected the classical realism and defended *nominalism. His successors were very much aware of the revolution they introduced. They called therefore their philosophical views the *via moderna*, opposed to the philosophy of their predecessors, the *via antiqua;* they called themselves also *nominales* against *reales*.

VICE
Individual habit which leads to ethical improper acting as it proceeds from such acting. Aristotle pointed out that there exists for each *virtue two opposite vices.

VICIOUS CIRCLE or diallelon (Greek: dia-allelon)
A *paralogism, in which two theses are proved from each other, e.g., the immateriality of the soul from its immortality and its immortality from its immateriality. It is a double *petitio principii* (see hysteron proteron).

VICTOR, St., School of
Theological school with mystical character; flowering in the 12th century in Paris (abbey of St. Victor), founded by the regular canons of St. Augustine. They were especially inspired by their founder St. Augustine. They studied many philosophical problems. *Richard and *Hugo of St. Victor.

VIENNA CIRCLE
See Wiener Kreis

VINCENT OF BEAUVAIS
Died in 1264 Dominican, author of *Speculum doctrinale, historiale, naturale, morale*: encyclopedia of the profane sciences, impersonal collection.

VINCI, Leonardo da
Born in Vinci 1452, died in Cloux 1519. Famous painter, also mathematician, physicist and philosopher: he sees the natural events proceed with mathematical necessity. The motion, ground of this natural happening, is explained by a spiritual *impetus*.

VIOLENCE
Energetic superior power. A term without recognized psychological status.

VIRTUAL
What is in the power (virtus) of the cause. The effect is therefore virtually in the cause. *Virtual distinction* is called a logical distinction which is not only *formal but also based on reality: exists between aspects of the same being to which in each case different forces respond; so that this one being has, as it were, the virtuality of many or is virtually the equal of many. In man for instance exists a virtual distinction between life, animal, reason.

VIRTUE
In a broad sense, a disposition, acquired by habit, to pose a spe-

cific kind of act. Applied to theoretical or practical life, Aristotle distinguishes between *intellectual* or *dianoetical* virtues and virtues of the *will* or *moral* virtues. In a narrower or moral sense, virtue means the continuing disposition, acquired by habit, to act well (morally). This action, always and in every domain, holds to a middle course between too much and too little. There are therefore different virtues which keep to the middle between two opposite *vices; courage between cowardice and recklessness, liberality between thrift and extravagance, etc. In Christianity there are *theological* virtues, continuing dispositions toward supernatural action: faith, hope and charity.—J.Gr.

VIRTUES, CARDINAL

The principal virtues which, on the one hand, possess all the requirements of general virtues, and, on the other hand, compose moral perfection. Plato says there are four: wisdom, courage, temperance and justice. The first three correspond to the three parts of the soul, the last to the mutual relation of the parts.

VISION

Immediate apprehension, either of objects through the senses or of a significant content. In the latter sense we call it *intuition. *See also* philosophy of *mathematics.

VITALISM

Under this name are grouped a series of theories which recognize the entirely proper nature of the organic life, as opposed to the lifeless. Many of these theories have their origin in the studies of biologists who saw that their exact methods could approximate "that what is proper to *life", but could not define it. In the 18th century some opponents of the materialistic ideas accepted a mysterious "vis vitalis". Even later vitalists accepted a principle of life which was never clearly defined. They sometimes placed it more or less above matter and went therefore in a dualistic direction. Well known vitalists of this century, also called neo-vitalists are Reinke (theory of the "dominants") and Driesch ("entelechy", "psychoid").

We can also put under the vitalists the aristotelian-thomistic doctrine of the organic *life (a.o. Maritain, Sertillanges). This doctrine avoids the dualistic conception of the neo-vitalists and emphasizes the ordering of parts and functions towards an end, which is now also studied by biologists (Cuénot). Several biologists turn against vitalism, which would, in their opinion, introduce an uncontrollable factor in the thought.—M.B.

VIVEKANANDA, 1862-1902

Indian mystic, leader of an ascetic order with strong social activity, founder of the "Rāmakrsna-mission"; tried to bring an agreement between hinduism and the results of the modern scientific research.

VOLKELT, Johannes

Born in Lipnik (Galicia) 1848, died in Leipzig 1930. German critical realist; considers metaphysics possible and necessary; it contains the affirmation of the existence of psychic subjects outside of the Ego, the existence of transsubjective existences and of the identity of the world, which answers to the perception of the different subjects. The "philosophy of life" surpasses however the "scientific philosophy". The philosophy of life can penetrate the world-ground in the Absolute Spirit.

VOLTAIRE, real name Francois Marie Arouet

Born in Paris 1694, died there 1778. One of the main leaders of the Enlightenment. Through his literary style, his acid mockery and strong criticism of the Church, authorities and revealed religion, he became sometimes the celebrated intellectual leader and sometimes the expatriate. Voltaire has no philosophical system and is no deep thinker. He is a deist, rationalist when he accepts a morality and religion based on the natural reason. He thinks that the proof of God's existence can be found (we are machines produced by the eternal geometer). God gave the general laws to nature; but God's power can not avoid the evil. We do not know anything about his omniscience and absolute goodness. Religion is limited to a vague respect of man in a community to a God who, if he did not exist, should be invented. He retains the belief in personal immortality and the retribution of good and evil, but later he becomes determinist and denies the free will. The government of Louis XIV was his ideal, but without the influence of the religion; the litterateurs should take over the role of the Church, as he expected that Frederick II of Prussia would do. He collaborated for a while with the Encyclopedists.—H.R.

VOLUNTARISM

Doctrine which affirms the precedence of will above the intellect (*intellectualism): either in God, with as consequence for instance that truth and goodness are what they are, only because God wanted it that way, or in man, as defended by Franciscans (in the Middle Ages) Alexander Hales, Bonaventura and Duns Scotus, the great opponent of the thomistic intellectualism. The voluntarism of Schopenhauer is still more radical, because the world is the representation of the Will, which is nothing than will, aimless and reasonless will. In a less strict sense is voluntarism the doctrine which emphasizes the activity (which traditionally proceeds from the will): as in the Stoicism, Kant (through the primate of the practical reason), Fichte, Blondel. We can even consider existentialism as a newer form of voluntarism, is existence not considered an activity, a being busy, a taking action in the world? —J.Gr.

VORGES

See Domet de Vorges.

VORLANDER, Karl, 1860-1928

German neo-kantian of the School of *Marburg, professor in Münster.

VULGAR (Lat. vulgaris from vulgus, the people, the simple man)

Popular, plain, simple. Vulgar *knowledge,* the knowledge of the simple man (as opposed to the scientific knowledge of the expert). Vulgar *definition,* the way in which a term is usually understood (opposed to etymological definition). Vulgar *way of thinking,* the natural way of thinking in which one from a complex of probabilities or even, without thinking of grounds of proof (*premises) or means of proof (*middle terms) from one or another thing or fact concludes to a *concrete conclusion (opposed to the classical or formal and more *abstract way of thought; *reasoning).

W

WAHL, Jean
Born 1888, French existential philosopher and historian of the philosophy. Professor at the Sorbonne.

WAHLE, Richard 1857-1935
Onetime professor of philosophy at the University of Vienna who maintained that critiques of knowledge, logic and psychology had nothing to do with philosophy and who wrote devastating criticism of most philosophers, with the exception of a few such as Spinoza, Hume and Herbert. Works: *Tragicomedy of Wisdom* (1925), *Formation of Character* (1928).

WALLACE, William, 1844-97
English neo-Hegelian.

WALTER BURLEIGH (Burlaeus)
Born 1275 in England, died after 1343, taught in Oxford, Paris and Toulouse; prolific author, opponent of the *°via moderna*. Wrote a.o. *De vitis et moribus philosophorum,* history of the philosophy in essay form, which had much success.

WANG YANG-MING, 1472-1528
Most important neo-confucianist thinker after °Chu-Hsi. Identification of the spirit with the transcendent "principles" (*li*); through this is produced "sudden enlightment" (according to *Zen*).

WARD, Lester Frank, 1841-1913
American philosophical sociologist, founder of the sociology in the U.S.A., professor at Brown Univ.

WATSON, John Broadus
Born 1878, American philosopher and psychologist, founder of the "behaviorism", professor in Baltimore. Psychology, says Watson, can only study the conduct of man, but not his inner life, because all introspection is valueless for science. Died 1958.

WAVE MECHANICS
In classical physics a sharp distinction was made between phenomena (namely, of light) which could be explained with the theory of waves and phenomena (namely, of matter particles) which could be explained by the laws of mechanics. The development of the theory of atoms, however, made this distinction less absolute, which in 1924 gave L. de Broglie the idea that a wave phenomenon was connected in one way or another with every motion of material particles in the same way as waves in light.

This led to the development of a theory of wave mechanics by Schrödinger in 1926. This must be understood as an expansion of classical mechanics, indeed, to the extent that wave mechanics are capable of describing all phenomena, even atomic ones, which seem to lie outside the possibilities of classical mechanics. Classical mechanics are, in fact, a simplification of wave mechanics, usable for specific problems, in the same way as geometric optics are a simplification of the wave theory of light. Physicists agree as to the value of the wave theories as a mathematical aid in the description of physical phenomena. They don't, however, agree as to the interpretation of waves in physics. Most physicists agree that the wave function of material particles lets us know whether specific particles are present in a specific place. Here also an analogy with the waves of light is enlightening. The square of the amplitude of a light wave is a measurement for the intensity of light. So also is the square of the amplitude of a matter wave in a specific place a measurement of the probability of finding particles there.—A.G.M.v.M.

WEBER, Max, 1864-1920
German sociologist and philosopher, professor in München, brother of Alfred.

WEIGEL, Valentin
Born in Naundorf 1533, died in Zschopau 1594. Protestant minister, theosophical and mystical follower of Paracelsus. Founded his own sect. Man is a microcosm; all wisdom is based on the knowledge of man's innerness.

WEISZ, Ulrich, O.S.B.
Born in Ulm?, died 1763, author of a *Liber de emendatione intellectus* (1747), which defends the mathematical scientific method in philosophy and tries to follow Descartes, Locke and Wolff.

WELTANSCHAUUNG
Term used since Dilthey to indicate the view on life, on the world, which recognizes more or less explicitly and more or less spontaneously a group limited in time and space. *Historicism reduces philosophy to such a Weltanschauung, or at least to the study of several Weltanschauungen, which are naturally more psycho-

logical testimonies than well justified explanations of the reality.

WENZL, Alphons, O.S.B.
Born in Salzburg 1660, died in Mallersdorf 1743, very conservative post-scholastic thinker, follower of thomism.

WERTHEIMER, Max 1880-1943
An early exponent of Gestalt theory, which had at first been formulated psychologically, then enlarged into a philosophical conception of biological and social facts. Work: *Productive Thinking* (published posthumously in 1945).

WHITEHEAD, Alfred North, 1861-1947
English mathematician and philosopher, professor in London, 1914-24, and at Harvard since 1924. Published a few works on mathematical axiomatics and later, with *Russell, the gigantic *Principia Mathematica*. He later turned to the natural sciences and made finally a speculative metaphysics, which on the one hand is harmonically connected with his previous work and on the other hand shows some relationship to the ideas of Spinoza, *Bergson, S. *Alexander and C. Lloyd Morgan. He had much influence especially in the anglo-saxon world.

WHITMAN, Walt 1819-1892
American p o e t, celebrated throughout the Western world as the prophet of the age of democracy. *Leaves of Grass* (1855, first publication; later enlarged), his poetic masterpiece; *Democratic Vistas* (1871), his prose essays.

WIENER KREIS
Philosophical circle in Vienna between 1923-38, very active and defending a radical neo-positivism. Other philosophers were certainly working in the same sense (e.g.

459

*Reichenbach and the "Berliner Gruppe", J. Jorgensen in Copenhagen, E. Kaila in Helsinki, K. Ajdukiewicz in Lwow, A. I. Ayer in London) but the Wiener Kreis had very soon a greater prestige, because its many sections represented different sciences (*Schlick was a natural philosopher, H. Hahn a mathematician, *Carnap a logician, V. Kraft an historian) and several Viennese scholars, as H. Kelsen, K. Gödel, K. Popper, F. Kaufmann and L. von Bertalanffy, had close relations with the circle without agreeing completely with its neo-positivism. The sociologist of the Wiener Kreis became also the organizer of the "Unity of Science Movement" (O. Neurath), which brought together all the defenders of neo-positivism and has very much encouraged through publications and congresses the study of the exact sciences, also outside of the circle of neo-positivists. The assassination of Schlick (1936), the "Anschluss" (1938), the second WW and the death of O. Neurath (1945) made further activities of the Wiener Kreis impossible, but the neo-positivism has, although in less radical form, been more and more accepted.— E.W.B.

WILL

The spiritual faculty to pursue the intellectually-recognized good. 1) As principle of the intellectual activity knows the will the aim, the means and the effects. 2) The will is the principle of the free activity (*freedom of the will) and is as such able to determine itself and even by itself, through the choice namely between the different things, which are presented as good by the intellect. 3) the will is finally the principle of an ordered activity towards the good. Only the good is object of the will and abolishes the freedom of the will.

The willsact has three phases: 1) deliberation (I inquire), 2) decision (I will), 3) execution (I execute). The will, as pure faculty, works through deliberation in favor of the intellect as opposed to the instinctive strivings. The will works in the decision as a positive, reflexve act, to overcome as such the usual psychological automatism. In the execution the will acts to make the executive faculties work and to have them stay in working and if necessary to renew the decision.

The will is therefore, in regard to the sensual faculty of striving for a higher faculty, not found in the animal (against the sensists and evolutionists) Duns Scotus thinks that it is even higher than the intellect (*voluntarism; also Descartes and Kant): Thomas Aquinas however teaches that the primacy is on the intellect, through which the will is necessarily determined (*intellectualism)

The ground act of the will is not the striving, but the recognition of a value or love.

The empirical p s y c h o l o g y studied introspectively the process of will (N.Ach). Lindsworsky, more in respect to the willsact as a personal action, pointed out the dependence of the will on the motives, which move the will. The will itself has, according to these ideas, not to be trained; only a culture of the motives is possible (connection with pedagogics).

The modern views on the will coincide with the new anthropological data: man, entangled in his world, is determined by it, but he himself determines it also in a dialectic relation.

The will is rarely defined in the

empirical psychology as more than a faculty.—P.S.

WILL OF GOD

In theism, which defends the existence of a personal God, is the will one of the divine attributes. This divine will does not contain a desire for the possession of something which is still missed, but only love and pleasure of the possession of the infinite good, which He is himself, for which reason He wills the creation in a free choice. Although God's will is dominated by nothing above Him, his own essence is for God's will no object of a divine choice; the creatures however are the object of a divine free will choice. In strict sense does the will of God not have motives: He is indeed the Unmoved Mover of everything. God's will is therefore not moved or attracted by the already (independent from that will) existing attractiveness of the creatures: God's will makes them loveable. God's willing is autonomous.

We should distinguish from this intrinsic willing, the signs by which God's will is known to us and which we sometimes call in a metaphorical sense His will: e.g. his commandments or prohibitions, the natural law, etc.

Since the human knowledge can only proceed in separate concepts, we make a difference between the absolute Will of God and that what He wills as dependent from all kinds of circumstances. God wants the eternal well-being of man, but dependently from their own co-operation. This considered, we can say that God's will always reaches the desired effect.—H.R.

WILLIAM OF AUXERRE

Born 12th century, probably in Auxerre, died in Rome 1231, secular magister at the theological school of Paris ca. 1218-28, author of a *Summa aurea* (1215-20), a commentary on the *Sententiae* of *Petrus Lombardus. Was charged by Gregorius IX with the expurgation of the writings of Aristotle (1231) but died before finishing this task.

WILLIAM OF CHAMPEAUX, ca. 1070-1121

Disciple of *Anselm of Laon and *Roscellinus, professor in Paris in 1103, where his disciple, *Petrus Abaelard made life for him impossible with his criticism. William retired at St. Victor where he continued to teach. In 1113 he became bishop of Châlons-sur-Marne. In the discussion about the *universalia he defended several forms of *ultra-realism, but Abaelard's criticism brought him more and more to the moderate realism.

WILLIAM OF CONCHES, 1080-1145

Disciple of Bernard of Chartres, author of a *Philosophia mundi* (later rewritten under the title *Dragmaticon philosophiae*), and of a commentary on Plato's *Timaeus*, in which he defends the atomism of Democritus.

WILLIAM OF MARE

Born before 1250 in England, died in Oxford ca. 1285, Franciscan, magister regens in Paris at least from 1274-1275, disciple of Bonaventura, author of the famous *Correctiorum fratris Thomae* (ca. 1277-79).

WILLIAM OF OCKHAM

Born in Surrey, ca. 1290, died in Germany 1349/50. Became Franciscan in Oxford, ca. 1215 baccalaureus in the theology, and remained his entire life candidate for the magisterium (*inceptor*). In 1325 the pope received a complaint about Ockham's new theological ideas, and in 1327 Ockham joined the opponents of John XXII, he joined Ludwig of Baiern in Pisa and followed him to München. We do not know if Ockham was reconciled with the Church before his death. *Venerabilis inceptor.* He wrote a commentary on the *sententiae* and *7 Quodlibeta,* also a series of works on logic and physics, theological treatises and several pamphlets against the papacy, in which he stated his political views.

The founder of the *via moderna* had an unusual knowledge of the philosophical and theological tradition, especially of Aristotle, the great Arabic thinkers, Thomas Aquinas and Joannes Duns Scotus, his main opponent. He knew therefore the past, with which he broke, while he constructed a new philosophy. Some of the elements of this new philosophy were prepared by original thinkers as Durandus of St Pourçain and Petrus Aureoli. William of Ockham had a vivid sense of the concrete and the individual, and reacted energetically against all confusion or danger of confusion of the individual with the general, the concrete with the abstract, the real with the logical; he abhorred the metaphysical entities, which were so dear to the defenders of the *via antiqua,* but which he considered only as realisations of concepts. The moderate realism of Abaelard and Thomas Aquinas found no favour by Ockham, not more than the formalism of Duns Scotus (*formalitates*), because both systems gave a certain degree of objective reality to absolute concepts. Concepts are only symbols, which take in the discursive reasoning the place of a category of the real objects (*nominalism*). The individual is grasped by intuition or experience which is therefore the fundamental way of knowledge in man. This does however not mean that the abstract or conceptual knowledge has no value at all; on the contrary it is necessary and Ockham sees a great value in logic which he handles with extreme skill either to criticize the metaphysical constructions of his predecessors or to determine the limits of the possible, the not-contradictory, and all what answers to the *potentia Dei absoluta.*

This empirical and nominalistic point of view was necessarily the cause of the empoverishment of metaphysics and a more or less avowed agnosticism the spirituality and immortality of the soul, the existence and the qualities of God can not be the object of strict demonstration; the moral values are not absolute, because they depend on the divine pleasure (voluntarism); this agnosticism gives cause to fideism, which must guarantee the certitude in the question of faith and places philosophy and theology at the same level. The same fundamental position provoked in the physics a real revolution. The speculative methods of Aristotle were replaced by the experimental; as did metaphysics and psychology, so did also physics lend itself perfectly to the hunt for "entities", thanks to this notorious principle of economy (the so called "raser of Ockham"): "one can not multiply the beings without necessity".

The political philosophy of Ockham, inspired by Aristotle, attacks all forms of Cesaro-papism in the name of the essential independence of the State and the purely spiritual character of the ecclesiastical power.

The philosophy of Ockham gained interest today and the interpretations given of it are not always the same. Some think that one exaggerated the negative and destructive character of this philosophy, and that it was primarily a sane reaction against the unbridled rationalism of scholasticism and especially of scotism. The ecceptional success of the *via moderna* and its fast diffusion in the universities seem to corroborate this.—F.V.S.

WILSON, Woodrow 1856-1924

World War I President who failed to achieve his Fourteen Points and other goals at the Peace Conference, but who has since been recognized as one of the major American Presidents a n d spokesmen for the democratic process. Works: *A History of the American People* (1902), *Constitutional Government in the United States* (1908).

WINDELBAND, Wilhelm

Born in Potsdam 1848, died in Heidelberg 1915. German philosopher, leader of the School of *Baden of *neo-criticism, professor in Zürich, Freiburg i.B., Strasbourg, Heidelberg.

Windelband divides the experimental sciences into nomothetic or natural sciences and idiografic or historical sciences. The latter judges the facts according to their value, but this judgment requires a system of absolute valid values, which are given as principles of the "Normalbewustsein" purely a priori. The human activity in science, morality and art should submit to the values of truth, good and beauty. Religion contains these three classes of values, inasmuch as they are brought in relation with a transcendental reality. Later, under the influence of Hegel, did Windelband identify this reality with the "Normalbewustsein", which received at the same time a metaphysical meaning.—F.S.

WISDOM

Insight in the essence of things, their final and exact place in the classification of values. Wisdom does not necessarily contain scientific knowledge, but concordance between action and knowledge. Many consider *self-knowledge the beginning of wisdom.

WISH

Desire for something. The wish has always a specific content. *Wish-dream,* in which one satisfies specific wishes, in sleep or awake (daydream). *Wishful t h i n k i n g* concerns the creation of illusions. If the wish brings man too far from the reality, then we speak of idée fixe and in abnormal forms of wish-delirium (the insane man who lives as if his wish were realized).

WIT

A form of the *comical, in which a real or invented comical relation is expressed by means of words, generally by bringing together representations, images or expressions which are naturally strange to each other. Forms of wit are: punning, comparison, anecdote, allusion, irony, etc.

WITTGENSTEIN, Ludwig 1889-1951

German-English philosophy professor whose *Tractatus Logico-Philosophicus* (1922) had great influence on the development of logical positivism, or scientific empiricism, and inspired such thinkers as Bertrand Russell and Alfred Whitehead.

WOLFF, Christian

Christian, born in Breslau 1679, died in Halle 1754. Rationalistic philosopher of the Enlightenment in Germany inasmuch as he, confiding in the power of the intellect, wants to deduce the laws of being by thinking. He transformed, with his clarity and method, the opinions of Leibniz according to his own view, using elements of scholasticism and of Descartes. He did not take over the monadology of Leibniz, but did agree with the by God preestablished (praestabilita) harmony between body and soul, which can not affect each other. Wolff created a German philosophical terminology. Philosophy is for him the science of everything which is possible, therefore of the essences of everything. Mathematical analysis and philosophical deductive method are equal. The speculative philosophy is divided by Wolff in: 1) general or ontology, 2) special, a) cosmology, about the world, b) rational psychology, about the souls, c) natural theology, about God. This division has been too often taken over in scholastic circles, although it departs from Aristotle and Thomas Aquinas. Belong to the practical philosophy: 1) the general theory of morality with the natural right, 2) the special theory of morality, comprising a) ethics b) economics, and c) politics, about man as individual being, as member of a family and as citizen. He wants to test the concepts, deduced from the absolute, with the experience, but gives no basis why experimental knowledge and the concepts acquired by analysis should coincide. —H.R.

WOODBRIDGE, Frederick J. E. 1867-1940

American realistic philosopher.

WORD

As element of the language: a unity of an articulated (consisting of phonemes) sound and a meaning. A word can be used in different ways. Many therefore think its meaning is vague and ambiguous, and think that a logical reasoning in language is not possible. They also criticize the word as a means of understanding, because everybody represents with a specific word something else. They react against the general tendency to conclude from the existence of a word to the existence of that at which it aims; often also man thinks to know something and to understand it when he has a word for it. In "it is only a word" is word not more than: sound without meaning. Some give for the philosophy the preference to the word rather than the "concept"; according to them can the reality not be apprehended in strictly defined and therefore rigid concepts. —C.S.

WORK

The use of the intellectual faculties or physical strength in order to achieve a goal which is considered serious (compare with *play). This goal can be externally perceptible (e.g., production) or not (e.g., study).

WORK OF ART

An original form, discovered by man and realized by him in matter, by which a deeply felt experience of value is brought to immediate aesthetic clearness. The concept "work of art" is therefore not only limited to a pure beauty, but includes all the aesthetic categories, even the ugly, as long as it keeps its aesthetic character. An unsuccessful work of art is also ugly, but in an unaesthetical sense.

The *content* of the work of art is the specific value, which appears in the *form*. Since this value is illustrated not as an abstract entity but as the concrete object of a most personal experience, this content is also a (sensibly perceptible) totality of human feelings, images, representations and insights. The form however is the sensory perceptible shape in which the content finds it's immediate expression. Since in the work of art the content does not exist outside of the form and the form not outside the content, one would have a wrong idea of both by considering the content as a preexisting and purely spiritual conception, and the form as a kind of added and purely physical shape.—In the form we can distinguish a formal and an expressive aspect. The *formal* one is the value of the form as form, i.e. as an ordering, seen in itself, of the different sensible factors, which come together as a whole in the perceptible shape. *Expressive* is the form inasmuch as it is an aesthetic immediate echo and representation of the dynamic-active attitude, with which the artist personally experiences the value, which as content fills the work of art.—L.V.K.

WORLD

Is used in different meanings. Means first the whole of earth, sun, moon and stars. Sometimes we speak of "our" world, meaning our solar system. In contrast with the term "universe," can the term "world" be used in the plural. In more narrow sense used in expressions as: the old world, the new world. With the term world is also indicated a whole of similar things, as for instance the world of the sensual, the physical world, the world of the ideas, the world of thought, the world of poets, the world of the language. For the world image of the Greeks see *universe.

WORLDSOUL

A supposed, forming, animating and unity providing principle of the world. Mostly seen in analogy with the soul-body relation in man. The worldsoul takes sometimes the place of God, as in the pantheistic system of the stoics; it is sometimes more or less made subtantial and seen as an intermediary between God and the visible being, a.o. by *Plotinus.

WORLD VIEW

Explanation of the world or the all, more suggested by feeling than rationally justified, and which contains, still undifferentiated, religious faith and rational affirmation, scientific insight and magic motives. Its object is that of the philosophy, which proceeds through differentiation from the worldview.

WUNDT, Wilhelm

Born in Neckarau (Mannheim) 1832, died in Liepzig 1920. German physiologist, empirical psychologist and philosopher, psychomonist. Wundt wanted to apply the methods of the natural sciences to psychology. He abandoned the idea of the soul, carrier of the psychic phenomena and defended the theory of the psycho-physical parallelism.

The task of philosophy is, according to Wundt, to condense the results of the professional sciences into a world-view and philosophy of life, which will satisfy as well the requirements of the reason as the needs of the mind. It has therefore to transgress the limits of the experience, but can not contradict the data of the experience. The psychic is the only reality; the nature of it is the activity and the will. The religious ideas teach man to look up to the worldwill as to an infinitely perfect being, that unfolds itself in the evolution of the world, to which also corroborates the will of the individual people. —F.S.

X

XENOCRATES OF CHALCEDON

Disciple of Plato, after Speusippus head of the *Academy (339-314). Identified the mathematical numbers with the Ideas (against Plato, who accepted Idea-numbers which differ in nature from the mathematical numbers), and deduced them from two "first principles," the Unity and the duality (Plato's determining and undetermining principle). To the numbers follow in Xenocrates' hierarchy of being, the geometric bodies; finally the physical bodies. He taught that the soul is immortal and penetrates the universe, so that not only the celestial bodies are animated beings (what Plato also taught) but that also in the physical elements a divine power resides. A similar view is later defended by the stoics. Xenocrates wrote much about ethics, and was in Antiquity known as a very strict moralist.

XENOPHANES OF COLOPHON

Born ca. 570, died in Elea ca. 480 B.C., traveling poet (elegies and "siloi" or satirical poems) and author of a book *On nature,* in which he considers the divine as a thinking and all dominating principle. Considered as the precursor of *Parmenides.

XIRAU, Joaquin, 1905-46

Catalonian philosopher, professor in Barcelona, since 1939 in Mexico.

Y

YOGA

In India, methodical effort to free oneself from the necessity to be regenerated, to realize the unity with the One (*brahman) or to be united with God. The yogins (those who strive towards that end) try to reach through physical and spiritual methods of concentration and mortification applied in a systematical way, higher states of consciousness and, through that, to acquire the liberation of the reincarnation. The eight stages of a yoga "course" are: abstain from any bad or evil action; complete self-control; get used to a specific restful sitting posture; regulation of breath; detract the senses from the objects; spiritual concentration; meditation in homogeneous concentration; complete absorption, unio mystica, identification with the aim of the striving.

YOU

The other with whom I have a personal relation.

YU-LAN FUNG 1895-

Chinese professor of philosophy who attempted to purify Neo-Confucianism of its Buddhist elements, he is the author of such standard works as *History of Chinese Philosophy* (1930-33) and *The New Rational Philosophy* (1939).

Z

ZABARELLA, Giacomo

Born in Padua 1533, died there 1589, wants to bring together the explanations on Aristotle given by Averroes and Alexander of Aphrodisias: God is the only *intellectus agens* matter is eternal.

ZELLER, Eduard, 1814-1908

German philosopher and historian of Greek philosophy, professor in Berlin.

ZEN, (Jap.: Chin. *Ch'an*, Sanskrit: *Dhyana*: "meditation").

Chinese-Buddhistic philosophical system, probably proceding from the Mahayana-conception of *Sûnyatâ*, "the Emptiness" as highest reality, with specific neotaloitic representations. We can not reach Reality with our intellect, only by sudden enlightment, it can be "found" with the help of paradoxes as exercises of meditation.

ZENO OF CITIUM

Founder of the Stoic School, was its head from 262-61 B.C. Gave to the cosmopolitism of the Hellenic period its metaphysical basis, through his doctrine about the unity of the universe, the creating pneuma that animates the world, the homonoia which unites all men as brothers of a community, the ideal of wisdom according to which man must bring his innerness in correspondence with the cosmic evolution.

ZENO OF ELEA, ± 490-± 430 B.C.

Disciple of °Parmenides, defended the theory of his master in a series of famous arguments through the absurd. He attacks the rationality of multiplicity and of space, but especially of motion. Achilles can actually catch up with a tortoise, but we can not understand it, because he must always cover half of the distance, and this ad infinitum; the flying arrow must actually be at rest because at any given moment is it at a certain place. How can the ear catch really the falling of grains, because no one separate grain makes a noise? Aristotle has refuted these arguments.

ZERO

As number of an empty class, is often considered as a natural number. But also is the class of the whole, of the rational numbers is an o-element, characterized by the peculiarity, that $o + x = x + o = x$ and $o.x = x.o = o$